THE CLEAR
QURAN®
Series
A THEMATIC ENGLISH TRANSLATION
ENGLISH ONLY

Translator
Dr. Mustafa Khattab

Chief Editors
Abu-Isa Webb
Aaron Wannamaker
Hisham Sharif

Translation Approval
This Thematic English Translation of the Message of the Quran
has been approved by
AL-AZHAR, ISLAMIC RESEARCH ACADEMY
GENERAL DEPARTMENT FOR RESEARCH, WRITING & TRANSLATION
Cairo, Egypt
A copy of the certificate of approval is available upon request

Translated by Dr. Mustafa Khattab

For more information about this translation visit: TheClearQuran.org

Paperback ISBN: 978-1-967112-00-5

HardCover ISBN: 978-1-967112-01-2

Published by
The Clear Publishing
444 E. Roosevelt Rd, Suite 173, Lombard, IL 60148, USA
Tel: Tel: +1 (888-273-2754)
Email: ClearQuran@TheClearPublishing.com - Web: TheClearPublishing.com
For additional information, questions, comments or to request additional literature on
the Quran, Islam and Muslims please contact us.

SI HABLAS ESPAÑOL y quieres una copia del Corán en Español o pedir in-
formación y literatura sobre El Corán, El Islam, o Los Musulmanes o quieres
respuestas a tus preguntas contáctenos al ClearQuran@librodesignos.org

1-877-722-7185 - www.librodesignos.org

Publisher's Notes

Please Note: The Quran, sometimes written as "Koran," is the sacred book of Muslims, who believe that God has revealed His word and message to humanity throughout the ages. For example, we believe that Moses was given the Torah, David was given the Psalms, and Jesus was given the Gospel. In the same way, we believe that Muhammad was given the Quran. Muslims therefore treat the holy books of other faiths with great care and respect. For instance, we do not read these books in the bathroom or place them on the floor. It is our request that you treat this book with the same respect and handle it as you would your own scripture. If you do not want this copy, please do not throw it away. You may give it to any Muslim you know or your nearest Islamic center. You may also call us at 1-888-273-2754, and we will arrange to pick it up.

❊❊❊

The Clear Publishing seeks to bring the Quran's message to you free of the political agendas and Islamophobic polemics that have dominated the airwaves and print media. Our goal is to provide a direct-to-you source of authentic information that brings to light the Quranic message so that you may judge for yourself the source of guidance for around 2 billion fellow human beings.

Sources portraying themselves as honest brokers of information, like the news media, often take liberties when presenting verses from the Quran without providing the relevant context. Now that you have this translation, we humbly request that when you hear someone quoting the Quran:
1) Ask for an exact reference in the form of the *sûrah* (chapter) and verse number.
2) Read verses that are grouped together along with their headings and related headings to understand the verses in their proper context.
3) When reading the Quran, don't rely only on the so-called "expert" opinions you may have heard; rather, form your own opinion.

If you would like more information or are not sure of the meaning of one or more verses, we will be glad to answer any questions. Just as you would go to a Christian to ask questions about Christianity or a Pundit to ask about Hinduism, why not do the same when it comes to the Quran, Islam, or Muslims? Call or e-mail us at: 1-888-273-2754 or ClearQuran@TheClearPublishing.com. Our web page is TheClearPublishing.com.

What you have here in your possession is the translation of the message of the Quran. It is the best effort of an individual to explain, as closely as possible, the meaning from the original Arabic language. However, it is NOT THE QURAN, which can only be in ARABIC. To truly understand its meaning, one must master Arabic, for no other language can duplicate the power and impact carried by the original verses. This translation is an attempt to bring the glory of the message to those who speak and know only English.

We hope that, whether you believe this to be a revealed book or not, you will find important guidance in this divine book and remove previously conceived biases against the Quran, Islam, and Muslims. We pray that God Almighty will guide us all to His straight path and ultimate salvation.

❊❊❊

Translator's Notes

It was a summer day in Toronto and I had just finished leading the Friday congregation at a downtown mosque. On the way home I had an unlikely encounter, since all my cab-drivers in Toronto had been Muslims so far. That day my driver was non-Muslim, so he was able to identify me as Muslim simply because of my traditional Arab garb. Out of nowhere, he commented, "I think Muslims are good, but Islam is evil!" Taken aback by this Fox News style rhetoric, I responded, "Well, first of all thanks for the compliment about Muslims, but why do you think Islam is bad?" He replied, "Because your holy book calls me an animal." In astonishment, I answered, "I know the whole Quran by heart and I don't think it says that anywhere!" He cited 8:55, and I responded by telling him that the word *dâbbah* in Arabic does not mean an animal but a living being (*see* 24:45). He persisted, saying that his translation says so. I later checked many popular translations by Muslims and non-Muslims and realized that the man was right. This fateful encounter opened my eyes to the rampant mistranslations and misrepresentations of the Quran.

The Quran was revealed to Prophet Muḥammad in the 7th century and was not translated into English by a Muslim until the 20th century. Many Muslims had long believed that the Quran should only be read in Arabic, the original language of revelation. This led to many inaccurate, ill-willed translations by missionaries and orientalists—which explains why we still see some words like 'holy war' and 'infidels' as well as many theological inaccuracies in some existing translations. All this leads to endless false assumptions about Islam and Muslims. Some Muslim translators are no better off than their non-Muslim counterparts because they are not well-versed in Arabic, or English, or Islamic studies, or translation, or all of the above. Looking up words in an Arabic-English dictionary or copying earlier translations when frustrated does not always guarantee accuracy in translation. There are some noteworthy modern translations like that of Dr. Ahmad Zaki Hammad (2007) and Dr. M.A.S. Abdel Haleem (2004), but many are either overtranslated, making it difficult for laypeople to understand, or undertranslated, doing a great disservice to the Quran. This is why I saw a need for an accurate, smooth, and accessible translation.

To achieve accuracy, I have made use of the greatest and most celebrated works of old and modern *tafsîr* (Quran commentaries), and shared the work with several Imams in North America for feedback and insight. For clarity, every effort has been made to select easy to understand words and phrases that reflect the beauty and power of the original text. Along with informative footnotes, verses have been grouped and titled based on their themes for a better understanding of the chapters, their main concepts, and internal coherence.

Thanks to our editing and proofreading teams led by Abu-Isa Webb, I believe that what you are holding in your hands now is the most accurate and eloquent translation of the Final Revelation: *The Clear Quran*®.

Mustafa Khattab

STYLISTIC FEATURES OF THE QURAN

The Quran was revealed in 7th century Arabia, where people took so much pride in their mastery of Arabic that literary fairs were commonly held and prized poems were inscribed in gold for all to see. The Quran, which is believed to be God's inimitable Word, is a literary miracle, unmatched by any other work of Arabic literature. While Arabic has served as the medium for communicating the Quranic message, the Quran has forever changed the landscape of Arabic literary tradition, promoting Arabic to a leading world language and influencing other languages including Farsi, Urdu, Swahili, Turkish, Spanish, and many others. Several sciences have emerged to serve the Quran such as *tafsîr* (Quranic commentary), *tawḥîd* (theology), *fiqh* (jurisprudence), *tajwîd* (phonetic rules of recitation), *qirâ'ât* (styles of recitation), *naḥw* and *ṣarf* (grammar and morphology), *balâghah* (rhetoric), and *khaṭṭ* (calligraphy). Algebra was also developed in part to solve issues related to the distribution of inheritance shares laid out in Chapter 4. Together with the *Sunnah* or the example of the Prophet, the Quran is the bedrock of Muslim civilization and the main source of Islamic law and practice. The following are some of the distinctive stylistic features of the Quran in its original Arabic form.

STRUCTURE

The body of the Quran is made up of 6236 verses (or *âyât*, plural of *âyah*, which literally means sign, proof, or miracle), composed of 114 chapters in more than 600 pages. A chapter (or *sûrah*) usually takes its name from the main theme, a story, or a distinctive word within it. With the exception of Chapter 9, all chapters begin with the *basmalah*: "In the Name of God—the Most Compassionate, Most Merciful." Depending on their respective chapter, verses typically rhyme and vary in length—some are long (2:282 is the longest at fifteen lines long), while others are short (20:1 is the shortest at only two Arabic letters). The Quran is divided into 30 parts (or *ajzâ'*, plural of *juz'*), each with 8 subparts (or *arbâ'*, plural of *rub'*), making it convenient for reading and memorization.

Of the Quran's 114 chapters, eighty-six are classified as Meccan because they were revealed before the Prophet's emigration to Medina. These chapters focus mainly on restoring the belief in One God. The other twenty-eight chapters are categorized as Medinian since they were revealed after the Prophet's emigration from Mecca with an emphasis on the commandments regarding a Muslim's relationship with their Lord, their fellow humans, and the rest of God's creation. Some Meccan chapters may have Medinian verses and vice versa. Chapters and passages were revealed over a period of twenty-three years to address issues facing the Muslim community. As instructed by God through the angel Gabriel, the Prophet ordered his scribes to arrange chapters mostly according to their lengths, with the longest chapters first, not chronologically.

Although the Quran is not arranged chronologically, the chapters are perfectly interrelated. Some of the stories or themes that are touched on passingly in one chapter are explained in detail in the next chapter (*see* 12:105 and 13:1-17). In some cases, both the end of a chapter and the beginning of the next chapter cover the same subject (*see* 53:57-62 and 54:1-5). One chapter might give some stories and the next will continue the narrative by adding more stories (*see* chapters 37 and 38). Additionally, two consecutive chapters might cover the exact same themes, but in a different order (*see* chapters 55 and 56).

Quranic chapters have diverse themes, with main overarching subjects (e.g., verses 2:221-242), interjected by secondary subjects (e.g., verses 2:238-239). In essence, all themes have a common denominator: one's relationship with their Creator and the rest of His creation. Assuming that not everyone will read the Quran in its entirety, readers will run into this common denominator at any given chapter.

STYLE

With the word 'Quran' (lit., recitation) repeated about seventy times, the Quran is unique in that it actually speaks about itself, its Revealer, its purpose, its devotees, and its detractors. The author of this profound book is nowhere to be found on the cover; rather He reveals Himself on every page, speaking with authority, offering compelling proofs, giving commandments to prophets, believers, and all of humanity.

Perhaps one of the most visible stylistic features of the Quran is repetition, which comes in three different forms:

1) **Repetitive phrases** such as "Then which of your Lord's favours will you both deny?" which appears a total of thirty-one times in Chapter 55 and "Woe on that Day to the deniers!" which appears ten times in Chapter 77. Far from redundancy, the purpose of repetition in these two instances is to create an impact by reinforcing the point being made—to acknowledge God's many blessings in the former and deter people from denying God in the latter. This rhetorical device is still employed by many modern orators. One of the most notable examples is the repetition of "I have a dream" and "Let freedom ring" in Martin Luther King's 1963 famous speech.

2) **Repetitive themes** such as the arguments for God's oneness, uniqueness, and power in chapters 16, 35, and 112; the comparison between Paradise and Hell in chapters 37, 39, 40, and 41; and the horrors of Judgment Day in chapters 77, 78, 79, 80, and 81. The purpose is to emphasize a recurring theme (e.g., the reward of the believers and disbelievers) or present more details (e.g., the testimony of bodily organs in 41:19-24 and the fruit of the *Zaqqûm* tree in 37:62-68).

3) **Repetitive stories** such as the story of Moses in chapters 7, 18, 26, and 28 and Abraham in chapters 2, 6, 19, and 37. The purpose is to reassure the Prophet and focus on a different aspect of the life of these prophets. For example, the highlights of the story of Moses in Chapter 7 are the arrogance of Pharaoh, the defeat of the magicians, and the suffering of the Children of Israel. In Chapter 26, the focus shifts to Moses' childhood, his unintentional killing of an Egyptian man, as well as his escape to Midian and his marriage.

The fact that these repetitive themes and stories are perfectly consistent, despite having been revealed over the course of two decades to an unlettered prophet, is yet another proof of the divine source of the Quran.

Sarcasm is another common feature of the Quran, especially when it talks about the fate of those who ridicule the truth (*see* 24:53 and 44:49). So readers can expect to see a warning such as: "Give them good news of a painful punishment." This style aims at paying the ridiculers back in kind as well as adding more intensity to the warning.

Many passages in the Quran utilize a preferential style called *tafḍīl*—that is to say, two things share a certain quality but one of them supersedes the other. For example, the Quran says repeatedly that the people of Pharaoh were more powerful and resourceful than the people of Mecca. However, some structures look like *tafḍīl* but do not actually signify a comparison in quality. The assumption that both sides share the same quality but one is greater than the other is what causes confusion in most translations of the Quran. For example, when 12:33 suggests that going to prison is dearer to Joseph than committing adultery, this does not mean that either option is dear to him. Similarly, 17:84 suggests that the believers' Way is better in guidance than that of the pagans, but in truth the latter is not guided at all. Furthermore, 11:78 suggests that Lot instructs men that the single women of his nation are purer for marriage than other men, when other men are not pure for marriage in the first place.

EMPHASIS

Emphasis is commonplace in the Quran, especially where a concept is likely to be challenged by the skeptics. Sometimes one or more emphasis words are used, such as 'surely,' 'indeed,' and 'certainly' (*see* 15:9). The repetition of a sentence two consecutive times is also used as emphasis, such as 102:3-4: "But no! You will soon come to know. Again, no! You will soon come to know." The repetition of a verb in its noun form can also be used to similar effect. If translated literally, 56:4 will read, "When the earth will be shaken with a shaking," whereas the meaning is: "When the earth will be violently shaken." Lastly, an oath is one of the most common forms of emphasis. God has the right to swear by any of His creation, such as the sun and the moon, the day and night, the heavens and earth (91:1-6). However, a Muslim can only swear by God.

PERSONS, TIME, AND PLACE

To prove its divine nature, the Quran often refers to past events that were not known to anyone at the time of the revelation (*see* 12:25-42 and 27:17-28), constantly reminding the Prophet that, since he was not an eyewitness to these events, it was through divine revelation that he came to know about them (*see* 12:102). The Quran also foretells future events that were later proven true (*see* 30:1-6 and 48:27).

Unlike English, the Arabic language has only three tenses: past, present, and future. The Quran is unique in using the past tense to refer to future events, particularly when it describes the Day of Judgment (*see* 39:68-75). In addition to reminding us that God is not bound by the limits of time, the aim is to give the impression that these events are so certain to happen that it is as if they have already happened. However, when these sentences are translated into English (or any other language for that matter), the future tense is used.

Generalizations are also common in the Quran, where "the people," or "the Jews," etc., actually refers to a small group that said or did something that was not challenged by the larger group (*see* 5:64).

With some exceptions, the Quran does not dwell on the names of persons, places, or times (*see* for example 2:259 and 18:9-26). Rather, attention is usually focused on the moral of the story, making it valid for every people, time, and place.

To express the greatness and magnitude of a definite noun (such as *the* Straight Path, *the* Merciful Lord, etc.), the Quran often uses that name in an indefinite form (*a* Straight Path, *a* Merciful Lord, etc.), but this translation uses the definite form in these instances in order to maintain the true meaning in English.

The Quran states that the pleasures which God has prepared for the believers in Paradise are beyond human comprehension (*see* 32:17). Hence, generic terms (e.g., rivers, gardens, fruits, garments of silk, bracelets of gold, etc.) are often used to describe these pleasures in an appealing way, bringing it down to our level of understanding, whereas the realities of Paradise are far beyond these descriptions. These terms are no different than those one would have used in 1876 C.E. to describe a cutting-edge smartphone to Alexander Graham Bell, the inventor of the telephone.

LETTERS AND PRONOUNS

Of the twenty-nine letters of the Arabic alphabet, only fourteen appear in various combinations at the beginning of twenty-nine chapters of the Quran. These letters are: *Nūn, Ṣād, Ḥa, Kāf, Ya, Mīm, Qāf, Alif, Ṭa, 'Aīn, Lām, Ha, Sīn,* and *Ra.* According to Ibn Kathîr, a renowned Quran commentator, in his explanation of 2:1, these letters can be arranged into an Arabic sentence that reads نَصٌّ حَكِيمٌ قَاطِعٌ لَهُ سِرّ which roughly translates to: "A wise, decisive text, full of wonders." Although several theories have been suggested by scholars regarding the meaning of these letters, it is commonly believed that these letters are among the miracles of the Quran and, as such, no one knows their actual meaning except God.

Unlike other conjunctions like *fa* ف (then/right after) and *thumma* ثم (then/later), *wa* و (and) does not signify an order of events. The subjects of 'and' clauses have sometimes been rearranged for better flow in English, such as 'day and night' instead of 'night and day,' 'seen and unseen' instead of 'unseen and seen,' etc. (*see* 35:19-22).

One of the first things that strikes novice readers of the Quran is that the word 'We' is frequently used when God speaks (*see* 15:9-23). This plural form, known as the royal we, is employed to indicate reverence and not number. Almost always, 'God,' 'I,' or 'He' is mentioned either before or after to emphasize God's oneness.

Another visible stylistic feature is the 'rotation of pronouns' (*iltifât*) found throughout the Quran, alternating between first person, second person, and third person (*see* 17:1). If rendered verbatim into English this rhetorical device becomes entirely meaningless, as it is rarely found in any Indo-European language at all, and almost never in English.

A similar feature is found in the referential nature of pronouns in either language. In Classical Arabic, especially in the Quran, the repeated use of a single pronoun (such as 'he') rotates in reference, which is to say it first speaks of the first speaker, then the next use speaks of the second speaker, then back to the first, all using the same pronoun (*see* 26:24-31). In this way, repeatedly using "he said" would indicate a dialogue, whereas a direct translation of the conversation would be rendered as a monologue in English. The same can be said of other pronouns such as 'they.'

THE QURANIC CHALLENGE

Unlike any other scripture, the Quran poses a falsification test to those who challenge its authenticity which, over time, was made easier and easier. The first challenge was to produce a similar book in Arabic (17:88). Next, the challenge was reduced to only ten chapters (11:13). Finally, the challenge was to only produce one chapter similar to it (10:38), and despite the shortest chapter being only ten words (Chapter 108), none have been able to match it. The Quran also challenges readers to find contradictions (4:82). Some have attempted these challenges, only to prove their inability to match the elegance and eloquence of the divine revelation or their ignorance of the nuances of Arabic syntax and grammar.

⬳⳿⁓⳾⬳

NOTES ON TRANSLATION

God's names and attributes are capitalized as well as pronouns used to reference Him.

Proper nouns referring to events and cosmology are also capitalized, such as the Day of Judgment, the Day, the Hour, the Hereafter, Paradise, and Hell.

In some cases, the use of a pronoun would be confusing or misleading, so it has been replaced with the corresponding noun for clarity. Similarly, in some places where the 'rotation of pronouns' (*iltifât*) is found in the Arabic, pronouns have been altered in English to maintain pronoun agreement.

Gendered pronouns have been replaced with 'they' where the meaning is neutral, except in the case of God, Who is referred to as 'He' despite being gender-neutral in order to preserve the use of a singular pronoun, while avoiding the use of 'it.'

Unless otherwise indicated, Biblical quotations are from *The Holy Bible: International Standard Version*, copyright © the ISV Foundation, 1996-2012.

Half brackets ⸢ ⸣ indicate words inserted into the English which do not directly correspond to Arabic words in the original text.

Words that have entered regular use in English such as "Quran" are spelled in English rather than transcribed.

The most frequently used speech verb in the Quran is "said," especially in conversation. To enrich conversations in English, several speech verbs are used in this translation (such as replied, cried, protested, pleaded, and threatened), depending on the meaning (*see* 18:71-73).

The name "Muḥammad" appears only four times in the Quran. In some cases, words such as "Prophet" and "Messenger" are used to address him. But most of the time, the Prophet is addressed in the second person "you," this is when "O Prophet" will be used between half brackets ⸢ ⸣ to indicate that "you" is referring to Prophet Muḥammad and not to the believers or anyone else.

"The Day of Judgment" and "Judgment Day" are equivalent and used interchangably depending on the flow in English.

Abbreviations used in this translation:
A.H. After *Hijrah*
B.C.E. Before Common Era
C.E. Common Era
e.g., exempli gratia, 'for example'
i.e., id est, 'that is to say'
lit., literally

GOD'S BEAUTIFUL NAMES & ATTRIBUTES

Following the stance of *Ahl As-Sunnah wal-Jamâ'ah*, **this translation confirms God's Attributes such as His Face, Hands, and Eyes, as well as the fact that He is established above the Throne—in a manner that befits His Majesty and Honour.** These attributes can be found in 11:37, 13:2, and 48:10. In some places, the word "Face" in relation to God is sometimes understood to mean "He Alone." This understanding can be found in verse 28:88, which reads, "Everything is bound to perish except He Alone" and verse 55:27 which reads, "Only your Lord Himself, full of Majesty and Honour, will remain forever." This is based on commentary from scholars, such as Ibn Taimiyah, Ibn Kathîr, Al-Qurṭubi, Aṭ-Ṭabari, Al-Baghawi, As-Sa'di, Ibn 'Ashûr, and many others. In the words of Imam Ibn Taimiyah in his *Fatâwa* (collection of religious rulings), "The fact that God's Face, full of Majesty and Honour, will remain forever means in essence: He Himself." In the same way, if a verse states that something good is done "seeking God's Face," this style is understood in Arabic rhetoric (*balâghah*) to mean "it is done sincerely for God, seeking to please Him Alone." Footnotes include the literal translation to emphasize that God does have a Face, but not like ours.

❦❧✿❦❧

TRANSLITERATION TABLE

Arabic	IPA	Trans.	Example	Arabic	IPA	Trans.	Example
ا	aː	*â*	*Fâtiḥah*	ظ	ðˤ	*ẓ*	*Ẓihâr*
ء	ʔ	*'*	*Nisâ'*	ع	ʕ	*'*	*An'âm*
ب	b	*b*	*Baqarah*	غ	ɣ	*gh*	*Ghâfir*
ت	t	*t*	*Tîn*	ف	f	*f*	*Furqân*
ث	θ	*th*	*Kawthar*	ق	q	*q*	*Qalam*
ج	dʒ	*j*	*Fajr*	ك	k	*k*	*Kahf*
ح	ħ	*ḥ*	*Ḥajj*	ل	l	*l*	*'Alaq*
خ	x	*kh*	*Ikhlâṣ*	م	m	*m*	*Mariam*
د	d	*d*	*Balad*	ن	n	*n*	*Nûḥ*
ذ	ð	*ẓ*	*Ẓâriyât*	هـ	h	*h*	*Humazah*
ر	r	*r*	*A'râf*	و	w	*w*	*Wâqi'ah*
ز	z	*z*	*Nâzi'ât*	ـُو	uː	*û*	*Burûj*
س	s	*s*	*Isrâ'*	ى	j	*y*	*Yâ-Sîn*
ش	ʃ	*sh*	*Hashr*	ـِى	iː	*î*	*Ibrâhîm*
ص	sˤ	*ṣ*	*'Aṣr*	ـَ	a	*a*	*Shams*
ض	dˤ	*ḍ*	*Ḍuḥa*	ـِ	ɪ	*i*	*Jinn*
ط	tˤ	*ṭ*	*Ṭâ-Hâ*	ـُ	ʊ	*u*	*Mulk*

MAP OF ARABIA AND AREA IN THE 7ᵀᴴ CENTURY C.E.

COMMON QUESTIONS

WHAT IS ISLAM?

Islam did not start with Prophet Muḥammad in the 7th century. Technically, Islam is the message that was delivered by all the prophets of God from Adam to Muḥammad. Islam is neither named after a person or a tribe nor does it end with an –ism. Though each prophet had a relatively different law, the essence of the message of Islam was always the same: have faith in one God and do good. In the Bible, the first four of the Ten Commandments enjoin the worship of one God; the rest urge believers to avoid what is wrong and to do what is good. All prophets and their followers (including Jesus and his disciples) are simply called "Muslims" in the Quran. Hence, anyone who submits to God and strives to be a good person can be called a 'muslim' (with a small 'm') from a linguistic perspective.

Every human being is born with the innate will (*fiṭrah*) to submit to God, but parents and society change this nature, and in order to relate to the Almighty, many have put a face on God (mostly human or animal) throughout history. The process of restoring the *fiṭrah* is called reversion.

Islam is not only a religion, but a comprehensive way of life. Based on common sense and clear-cut teachings, Islam defines the rights and responsibilities of every individual in regards to their relationship with God and His creation. It balances the spiritual and material needs of its followers and helps them gain happiness in this life and salvation in the next.

WHO IS A MUSLIM?

A 'Muslim' (with a capital 'M') is someone who practices Islam. Muslims follow the five pillars of Islam:

-*Shahâdah*, testifying that there is only One God and Muḥammad is His last Prophet
-*Ṣalâh*, praying five times a day
-*Ṣawm*, fasting from dawn to sunset during the month of Ramaḍân
-*Zakâh,* paying alms-tax on savings worth 85 g of gold or more, if the amount is kept for a year
-*Ḥajj*, performing pilgrimage to Mecca, if physically and financially able to.

Muslims also believe in the six articles of faith:

-Almighty God	-His scriptures
-His angels	-Free choice, fate, and destiny
-His prophets	-The Day of Judgment

Islam is the fastest growing religion in the world. Totalling about 2 billion, Muslims make up one-quarter of the world's population. Muslims come from different ethnic, cultural, and social backgrounds. Contrary to the common belief, not all Muslims are Arab; not all Arabs are Muslim. Arabs make up less than 18% of the world's Muslim population. Indonesia (a single non-Arab Muslim country in Southeast Asia) has more Muslims than all Arab countries combined.

Islam should not be judged by what any Muslim does, but Muslims should be judged based on what Islam teaches. Islam is perfect; Muslims are not.

WHO IS PROPHET MUḤAMMAD?

The Prophet was born in Mecca in the year 570 C.E. His father died before his birth and his mother died when he was six years old. As he grew up, he acquired the epithet 'the trustworthy.' Muḥammad had long detested the idolatry, social injustice, and corruption found in society. At the age of forty, he received the first revelation of the Quran from God through the angel Gabriel. Since the Prophet could not read or write, he had scribes write down passages over the course of their revelation. The Quran was also memorized word for word by the Prophet and many of his companions. Although the Prophet performed many miracles, such as the splitting of the moon (*see* 54:1), water gushing out from between his fingers, multiplying food, still the Quran is his greatest miracle.

Just like many previous prophets, Muḥammad and his early followers were persecuted—and some were even killed—for advocating revolutionary ideas such as social justice and women's rights. As the persecution grew fierce, the Prophet and many of his companions emigrated to the city of Medina, 260 miles to the north of Mecca. This emigration (*Hijrah*) marks the beginning of the Muslim calendar. After several years, Mecca ultimately surrendered peacefully to Muḥammad who issued a universal amnesty.

Before the Prophet passed away at the age of sixty-three, the greater part of the Arabian Peninsula had become Muslim, and within a century of his death, Islam had spread to Spain in the west and as far east as China. The rapid spread of Islam (especially to territories previously occupied by the Byzantine and Persian empires) was mostly because of its simple teachings and social justice.

WHY DO MUSLIMS CALL GOD 'ALLAH'?

Arab Muslims, Christians, and Jews call God 'Allah.' The word 'Allah' is unique in the sense that it has no plural or gender. It literally means in Arabic "the One, True God." Allah has many attributes and beautiful names such as the Most Compassionate, the Most Merciful, the All-Loving, the Judge, the Creator, and the Provider. In his native tongue of Aramaic, Jesus used *Alaha* to refer to God. Moses used, among other things, *Eloh* in Hebrew. *Allah*, *Alaha*, and *Eloh* come from three Semitic languages: Arabic, Aramaic, and Hebrew, respectively.

The proper name 'Allah' can be translated as God. Even though this is an imperfect translation, it leaves readers unfamiliar with Arabic with a better understanding and connection to the translation.

WHAT IS THE QURAN?

The Quran is the holy book of Islam. It is a collection of revelations that were received by the Prophet Muhammad over the course of twenty-three years in the 7th century C.E. There is only one version of the Quran, perfectly preserved in written and oral records around the world for nearly 1400 years.

The Quran is the only book in history that has been memorized verbatim by millions of people. Chapters were written down separately during the life of the Prophet and were collected in one volume within two years of his death. Exact copies were later duplicated from the original collection during the reign of the 3rd Caliph, 'Uthmân ibn 'Affân, and sent to major Muslim cities. Today, all copies of the Quran (called *maṣâḥif*, plural of *muṣḥaf*) are perfect duplicates of the original.

The Quran emphasizes universal ethics such as honesty, sincerity, generosity, mercy, and standing up for what is right. It aims at humanizing humanity and deifying God and therefore condemns those who personify God and idolize their fellow created beings.

WAS THE QURAN COPIED FROM THE BIBLE?

It is worth mentioning that the first Arabic translation of the Bible was done centuries after the Prophet's death. From an Islamic point of view, similarities between the Quran and the Bible (especially historical stories such as that of Joseph, Moses, and Jesus) stem from the fact that both scriptures came originally from the same source—divine revelation.

Because of differences in transmission and interpretation of different versions of the Bible, over time the stories changed. The Quranic narratives now appear considerably different. For example, unlike the Quran (20:120-122), in the book of Genesis, Eve was tempted to eat from the tree and therefore she is to blame for the Fall. Also, according to the Quran (Chapter 19), prophets are infallible of sin. But in the Bible, some prophets are guilty of shameful and even criminal acts. For example, David impregnated his neighbour's wife (Bathsheba) before conspiring to get her husband (Uriah) killed (II Samuel 11:1-27), Lot had sex with his two daughters (Genesis 19:30-38), and Noah got drunk and naked (Genesis 9:20-21).

Some Biblical stories are not in the Quran and vice versa. For example, the Biblical story of Isaiah is not in the Quran, while the story of Moses and Al-Khaḍir mentioned in Chapter 18 of the Quran is not in the Bible. Also, there are three miracles of Jesus in the Quran that are not in the Bible (*see* 5:110-115).

Although both scriptures emphasize global ethics (such as dignity, kindness, and charity), each revolves around a different theology. Both have contrasting views on the perception of God, Jesus, salvation, crucifixion, and the original sin.

IS ISLAM COMPATIBLE WITH SCIENCE?

Although the Quran is a book of signs, not a book of science, there are many scientific references in the Quran such as the formation and developmental phases of an embryo in the uterus (23:12–14 and 22:5), the Big Bang (21:30), the constant expansion of the universe (51:47–8), spherical shape of the earth (39:5 and 79:30), the earth's rotation (27:88), and many others that have become known only in the last two centuries.

According to an Arab proverb, "The ink of a scholar is holier than the blood of a martyr." Islam's emphasis on education galvanized learning and science in the Muslim world culminating in what is known as the Islamic Golden Age. For centuries, Muslims pioneered medicine, anatomy, mathematics, geography, astronomy, architecture, and many other sciences. Algebra, alchemy, and alcohol are all Arabic words. *The Canon of Medicine* by Avicenna (Ibn Sina, 980-1037 C.E.) was a primary medical text in medieval Europe for more than 700 years. Many surgical tools that are in use today were invented by Albucasis (Alzahrâwi, 936-1013 C.E.). Mariam Al-Astrolabiya, a female Muslim scholar who lived in the 10th century in Syria, was famous for designing and constructing astrolabes. Arabic numerals (0, 1, 2, 3, etc.) are used worldwide.

Muslims invented numerous sciences and developed many others (which they had inherited from the Romans, Greeks, Persians, Indians, and others) and laid the foundations to the European industrial revolution. The invention of cameras, computers, and navigation systems could not have been possible without the contributions of Muslim scholars.

WHAT IS SHARIA LAW?
Linguistically, Sharia means a pathway. Technically, it is the Muslim law, derived mainly from the Quran and the teachings of Prophet Muḥammad, governing every aspect of a Muslim's life. Sharia is made up of thousands of teachings and rulings covering theology, acts of worship, manners, human interactions, business transactions, family relations (marriage, divorce, inheritance, etc.), war and peace, belief in the unseen (God, angels, and the Hereafter), and criminal law.

Sharia mainly aims at protecting 5 things: 1) Life 2) Honour 3) Freedom to practice one's faith 4) Intellect 5) Property. Therefore, there are punishments in Islamic Law for violating any of these rights. Every country has punishments for offences—even though the penalty for the same crime may vary from one country to another. To say that Sharia is all about chopping people's hands off is like saying that the American law is all about killing people with the electric chair! Non-Muslims living in predominantly Muslim countries are free to follow the personal laws of their own faith. Of the fifty-seven Muslim countries in the world, the great majority are mainly secular, not Sharia-based.

Muslims living in the West follow the law of the land and maintain Sharia mainly in personal matters (such as prayers, marriage, and inheritance). Sharia also forbids the consumption of pork, alcohol, and drugs. Smoking is frowned upon.

IS ISLAM COMPATIBLE WITH MODERN DEMOCRACY?
We have to make the distinction between what Islam teaches and how countries in the Muslim world are run. As pointed out earlier, many Muslim countries are secular-based, not fully subscribing to Islamic morals or western democratic values. Islam and modern democracies have many things in common. For example, many of the fundamental principles in the Universal Declaration of Human Rights

are acceptable Islamically. What makes Islamic values unique is that they do not change over time, what is right in the sight of God is always right and what is wrong is always wrong. On the other hand, many secular freedoms (which have been mostly adopted in the last few decades) are still subject to debate in western societies. For example, marijuana, same-sex marriage, abortion, incest, and prostitution are legal in some democracies and illegal in some others. The same applies to euthanasia and the death penalty. Moreover, in a secular society, the majority's opinion prevails. In the Islamic concept of *shûra*, the truth prevails even if it is held by a minority. For example, the segregation of blacks and whites under the Jim Crow Laws and abuses against Indigenous Peoples would be prohibited under Sharia, since discrimination based on colour or race goes against Islamic beliefs.

WHY ARE THERE VIOLENT PASSAGES IN THE QURAN?
Life is sacred in Islam. The Quran (5:32) states, "Whoever takes a life ..., it will be as if they killed all of humanity; and whoever saves a life, it will be as if they saved all of humanity." Those who manipulate verses from the Quran by taking them out of context to justify violence against innocents contradict the Quran's call for tolerance and peaceful co-existence. Islam is unequivocally against terrorism (*see* 5:33). At the same time, Islam teaches that Muslims should stand up for the truth and fight for justice.

We have to keep in mind that all violent passages in the Quran (including verses in chapters 2, 8, 9, 47, and 48) were revealed in relation to conflicts between early Muslims and the pagans of Mecca over 1400 years ago. As such, all passages should be understood in their historical context. In Islam, fighting is allowed against aggressors regardless of their faith. Fighting against innocents is prohibited regardless of their faith. Overall, violent passages in the Quran talk about one of three things:
-Fighting back in self-defence.
-Making peace if attackers cease.
-Or resuming the fight if a truce is violated.

The Prophet set the etiquettes of fighting as follows: "Do not ask God to meet your enemies in battle" and "Do not start a war. If you must fight, then strike only at those ´combatants` who attacked you. Do not attack women, children, the elderly, or those retreating in their places of worship. Do not cut down trees or kill animals."

WHAT IS THE ORIGIN OF RELIGIOUS VIOLENCE?
No religion condones the killing of innocents, but some people manipulate religion to justify acts of violence. So, even if Islam and other faiths have never existed, humans would have come up with other excuses to fight for domination. We have seen notorious anti-religion, secularist ideologies, like those championed by Mao and Stalin (two of the top mass murderers in modern history), which were responsible for over seventy million deaths in the 20th century.

Most victims of violence in the Muslim world are Muslims, who are either killed by unjustified wars, suicide bombs, or drone attacks. Over the last few decades, hundreds of thousands have been killed—most of them civilians—and many others wounded or displaced. Justice, dignity, and education, some of the most fundamental aspects of human rights, are the key to peace and prosperity anywhere in the world.

ARE WOMEN ABUSED IN ISLAM?

The Quran makes it clear that men and women are equal before God and the Law (16:97 and 33:35). Abuses against some Muslim women (e.g., honour killings and forced marriages) are cultural practices in some Muslim countries that contradict Islamic teachings.

There are many prominent Muslim women in every field: education, science, business, etc. Even though scholars disagree on whether women can become heads of state, several Muslim women have been elected president and prime minister in Muslim-majority countries like Indonesia, Pakistan, Bangladesh, and Türkiye. The high status of women in Islam explains why 75% of reverts to Islam are female.

WHY DO MUSLIM WOMEN WEAR THE ḤIJAB?

The veil is deeply rooted in all Abrahamic traditions. Christian icons such as Mary and Mother Teresa are always depicted with veils. In the Quran and the teachings of the Prophet, both men and women are urged to be modest in their dress and behaviour. Ḥijab is worn by adult Muslim women in the presence of adult males outside of their immediate family.

WHAT ARE THE RIGHTS OF NON-MUSLIMS IN ISLAM?

Islam guarantees the freedom of non-Muslims to practice their faith and protection for their places of worship. The Prophet said, "Whoever harms a non-Muslim under the protection of Islam, I shall be their opponent on Judgment Day and they will not even smell Paradise." The Quran teaches that there are three types of brotherhood: brotherhood in humanity (this includes all human beings), biological brotherhood (one's siblings), and brotherhood in faith (fellow Muslims).

Islam allows giving charity to non-Muslims and exchanging gifts and visits with them. The Quran (60:8-9) exhorts Muslims to be kind and generous to non-Muslims. It forbids forcing non-Muslims to convert to Islam (2:256). For centuries, non-Muslim communities thrived under Muslim rule. Many Christians and Jews occupied prominent positions in the courts of some Muslim caliphs, serving as translators, physicians, and architects.

DO MUSLIMS BELIEVE IN OTHER PROPHETS?

As listed on the next page, the Quran mentions twenty-five prophets by name—of whom five are given the honorary title of 'the Messengers of Firm Resolve,' namely Abraham, Noah, Moses, Jesus, and Muḥammad. The Quran (12:111) says, "In their stories there is truly a lesson for people of reason." Some of the most common names in the Muslim world include 'Îsa (Jesus in Arabic), Mûsa

(Moses), Mariam (Mary), Yûsuf (Joseph), and Ibrâhîm (Abraham). Jesus is mentioned by name in the Quran twenty-five times, Mary thirty-one times (compared to eighteen times in the Bible), whereas Prophet Muḥammad is mentioned by name only four times. Chapter 19 of the Quran is named after Mary. Muslims believe that Jesus is the Christ and the Messiah. They also believe in his virgin birth, ascension, and second coming.

⛧⛧⛧

PROPHETS MENTIONED IN THE QURAN

ENGLISH	TRANSLITERATION OF ARABIC	ENGLISH	TRANSLITERATION OF ARABIC
Aaron	Hârûn	John the Baptist	Yaḥya
Abraham	Ibrâhîm		
Adam	Âdam	Jonah	Yûnus
David	Dâwûd	Joseph	Yûsuf
Elias	Ilyâs	Lot	Lûṭ
Elisha	Al-Yasa'	Moses	Mûsa
Enoch	Idrîs	Muḥammad	Muḥammad
Hûd	Hûd	Noah	Nûḥ
Isaac	Isḥâq	Ṣâliḥ	Ṣâliḥ
Ishmael	Ismâ'îl	Shu'aib	Shu'aib
Jacob	Ya'qûb	Solomon	Sulaimân
Jesus	'Îsa	Zachariah	Zakariya
Job	Aiyûb	Ẕul-Kifl	Ẕul-Kifl

As the Quran teaches Muslims not to exalt one prophet over others (2:285), it is customary to say "peace be upon him" when the name of any of the prophets is mentioned.

Selected Teachings of the Prophet Muḥammad

On the Environment and Animal Rights

"If Judgment Day arrives and you have a seedling in your hand, plant it regardless" and "Don't waste water even if you live by a river." The Prophet prohibited polluting water sources and promised a heavenly reward for planting trees to feed animals, birds, and humans. He taught that a good deed done to an animal is like a good deed done to a human being, while an act of cruelty to an animal is as bad as cruelty to a human being. He prohibited the use of live birds and animals as a target for arrows, the killing of animals for sport, slaughtering an animal in front of other animals, and forbade overburdening animals and underfeeding them.

On the Treatment of Others

The Prophet said that smiling is a charity and taught: "They are not of us, those who do not show respect to our seniors or show mercy to our youngsters." He gave women the right to inheritance, education, to own property, and have a say in marriage and said, "The best among the believers are those who are best to their wives," and that Paradise lies under the feet of the mother.

He received Christians in his mosque and allowed them to pray there when the time for their prayers came. He also commemorated the day Moses and the Children of Israel were saved from Pharaoh and his army by fasting and ordering Muslims to fast—a practice that has continued until today.

He said, "O humanity! Your Lord is one and your ancestry [i.e., Adam and Eve] is one. No Arab is superior to a non-Arab and no non-Arab is superior to an Arab, nor is any white superior to any black or any black superior to any white except on account of their piety," and "None of you truly believes until they love for others what they love for themselves."

On the Best Way of Life

The Prophet set out a way of life through his own example, but he also had the following to say on living a fulfilling life. "The ʿtrueʾ Muslim is the one who does not harm people with their hands or tongue." "Seeking knowledge is an obligation on every Muslim." "Don't respond to evil by evil, but by doing what is good." "Show mercy to those on earth and God will show mercy to you."

"Take advantage of five matters before the coming of five things: your health before you fall sick, your wealth before you become poor, your free time before you become busy, your youth before you become old, and your life before your death."

"Be mindful of God and He will always be with you. Remember God in times of prosperity and He will remember you in times of adversity. And know that what has passed you by [and you have failed to attain] was not going to befall you, and what has befallen you was not going to pass you by. And know that victory comes with perseverance, relief with affliction, and ease with hardship."

THE CLEAR QURAN®

Series

ENGLISH ONLY

A THEMATIC ENGLISH TRANSLATION

CHAPTERS BY THEMES

The Quran has three main themes:

C⋆ **Doctrine** (e.g., acts of worship, human interactions, family relations, and business transactions), which focuses mainly on a Muslim's relationship with God, other people, and the rest of God's creation.

⧖ **Stories** (e.g., the story of Moses, Noah, and Ṣâliḥ), which served two purposes: to reassure the Prophet's heart, as he was met with rejection in Mecca, and as cautionary tales for the pagans (*see* 11:120-123). Other stories (e.g., Joseph and Job) focus on moral lessons.

☼ **The Unseen** (e.g., the belief in God and His qualities, as well as angels, resurrection, judgment, etc.), which reaffirms one's faith in the divine through one's heart, not eyes.

Some chapters contain more than one theme, and some individual verses may touch on a theme not presented here, but the following table represents the general themes covered in the body of the text.

1. The Opening *(Al-Fâtiḥah)*

This Meccan chapter, which is recited a total of seventeen times in the five daily prayers, serves as the cornerstone of the Quran, and it is customary to say "Âmîn" or "Amen" at the end. It sums up the relationship between the Creator and His creation, God's undisputed authority in this world and the Hereafter, and humanity's constant dependence on Him for guidance and assistance. It identifies God as the Lord of all worlds, i.e. everything from animals and plants to humans and even angels. The underlying theme is to acknowledge that He is the only god worthy of worship—a simple truth which the disbelievers fail to grasp. All fundamental principles encapsulated in this chapter are spelled out in the rest of the Quran.

❉ ❉ ❉

> Based on the instruction in 16:98, it is recommended to
> say the following before reading the Quran:
> "I seek refuge with God from Satan, the accursed."

Prayer for Guidance

1. In the Name of God—
the Most Compassionate, Most Merciful.
2. All praise is for God—Lord of all worlds,
3. the Most Compassionate, Most Merciful,
4. Master of the Day of Judgment.
5. You ˹alone˺ we worship
and You ˹alone˺ we ask for help.
6. Guide us along the Straight Path,
7. the Path of those You have blessed—
not those You are displeased with,
or those who are astray.

2. The Cow (Al-Baqarah)

This Medinian chapter, which takes its name from the story of the cow in verses 67–73, details the main concepts of the previous chapter, with emphasis on the qualities of the believers, disbelievers, and hypocrites; God's power to create and resurrect; the enmity of Satan towards Adam and his descendants; as well as God's covenant with Moses and the Children of Israel. Several rulings are given in regards to marital relationships, bequest, jihad, fasting, pilgrimage, donations, debts, and interest. Unlike the next chapter, which focuses on the Christian perception of Jesus, this chapter dedicates a sizable portion to Jewish attitudes and practices.

In the Name of God—the Most Compassionate, Most Merciful

Qualities of the Believers

1. *Alif-Lãm-Mĩm.*[1] 2. This is the Book! There is no doubt about it[2]—a guide for those mindful ˹of God˺,[3] 3. who believe in the unseen,[4] establish prayer, and donate from what We have provided for them, 4. and who believe in what has been revealed to you ˹O Prophet˺[5] and what was revealed before you, and have sure faith in the Hereafter. 5. It is they who are ˹truly˺ guided by their Lord, and it is they who will be successful.

Qualities of the Disbelievers

6. As for those who persist in disbelief, it is the same whether you warn them or not—they will never believe. 7. God has sealed their hearts and their hearing, and their sight is covered. They will suffer a tremendous punishment.

Qualities of the Hypocrites

8. And there are some who say, "We believe in God and the Last Day," yet they are not ˹true˺ believers. 9. They seek to deceive God and the believers, yet they only deceive themselves, but they fail to perceive it. 10. There is sickness in their hearts, and God ˹only˺ lets their sickness increase. They will suffer a painful punishment for their lies. 11. When they are told, "Do not spread corruption in the land," they reply, "We are only peace-makers!"[6] 12. Indeed, it is they who are the corruptors, but they fail to perceive it. 13. And when they are told, "Believe as others believe," they reply, "Will we believe as the fools believe?" Indeed, it is they who are fools, but they do not know. 14. When they meet the believers they say, "We believe." But when alone with their evil associates they say, "We are definitely with you; we were only mocking." 15. God will throw their mockery back at them, leaving them to continue wandering blindly in their defiance. 16. They are the ones who trade guidance for misguidance. But this trade is profitless, and they are not ˹rightly˺ guided.

Hypocrites' Example

17. Their example is that of someone who kindles a fire, but when it lights up

---

1   *See* Stylistic Features for information about these letters.
2   i.e., there is no doubt regarding its authenticity or consistency.
3   The word *muttaqi* (plural *muttaqûn*) can be translated as one who is mindful ˹of God˺, devout, pious, God-fearing, righteous, or God-conscious.
4   i.e., the belief in God, the angels, and the Day of Judgment.
5   *See* Notes on Translation for information about the use of ˹O Prophet˺.
6   When they were criticized for their close association with the pagans who were hostile to Muslims, they would argue that they only wanted to make peace between Muslims and their enemies.

...ound them, God takes away their light, leaving them in complete darkness—unable to see. **18.** They are ˹wilfully˺ deaf, dumb, and blind, so they will never return ˹to the Right Path˺.

Another Example

19. Or ˹those caught in˺ a rainstorm from the sky with darkness, thunder, and lightning. They press their fingers into their ears at the sound of every thunder-clap for fear of death. And God encompasses the disbelievers ˹by His might˺. **20.** It is as if the lightning were about to snatch away their sight. Whenever lightning strikes, they walk in its light, but when darkness covers them, they stand still. Had God willed, He could have taken away their hearing and sight. Surely God is Most Capable of everything.

Order to Worship God Alone

21. O humanity! Worship your Lord, Who created you and those before you, so that you may become mindful ˹of Him˺. **22.** ˹He is the One˺ Who has made the earth a place of settlement for you and the sky a canopy; and sends down rain from the sky, causing fruits to grow as a provision for you. So do not knowingly set up equals to God ˹in worship˺.

The Challenge of the Quran

23. And if you are in doubt about what We have revealed to Our servant,[7] then produce a chapter like it and call your helpers other than God, if what you say is true. **24.** But if you are unable to do so—and you will never be able to do so—then fear the Fire fuelled with people and stones, which is prepared for the disbelievers.

Reward of the Believers

25. Give good news ˹O Prophet˺ to those who believe and do good that they will have Gardens under which rivers flow. Whenever provided with fruit, they will say, "This is what we were given before," for they will be served fruit that looks similar ˹but tastes different˺. They will have pure spouses,[8] and they will be there forever.

Wisdom Behind Parables

26. Surely God does not shy away from using the parable of a mosquito or what is even smaller. As for the believers, they know that it is the truth from their Lord. And as for the disbelievers, they argue, "What does God mean by such a parable?" Through this ˹test˺, He leaves many to stray, and guides many. And He leaves none to stray except the rebellious— **27.** those who violate God's covenant after it has been affirmed, break whatever ˹ties˺ God has ordered to be maintained, and spread corruption in the land. It is they who are the ˹true˺ losers.

God's Creation

28. How can you deny God? You were lifeless and He gave you life, then He will cause you to die and again bring you to life, and then to Him you will ˹all˺ be returned. **29.** He is the One Who created everything in the earth for you. Then He turned towards the heaven, forming it into seven heavens. And He has ˹perfect˺ knowledge of all things.

Honouring Adam

30. ˹Remember˺ when your Lord said to the angels, "I am going to place a successive ˹human˺ authority on earth." They asked ˹God˺, "Will You place in it someone who will spread corruption there and shed

---

7 Prophet Muḥammad.
8 Residents of Paradise will be in a perfect condition. There will be neither physical impurities such as illness, urination, defecation, or menstruation; nor spiritual blemishes such as jealousy, envy, or hatred.

blood while we glorify Your praises and proclaim Your holiness?" God responded, "I know what you do not know."[9] **31.** He taught Adam the names of all things, then He presented them to the angels and said, "Tell Me the names of these, if what you say is true?" **32.** They replied, "Glory be to You! We have no knowledge except what You have taught us. You are truly the All-Knowing, All-Wise." **33.** God said, "O Adam! Inform them of their names." Then when Adam did, God said, "Did I not tell you that I know the secrets of the heavens and the earth, and I know what you reveal and what you conceal?" **34.** And ʿrememberʾ when We said to the angels, "Prostrate before Adam,"[10] so they all did—but not *Iblîs*,[11] who refused and acted arrogantly,[12] becoming unfaithful.

Temptation and Fall

35. We cautioned, "O Adam! Live with your wife in Paradise and eat as freely as you please, but do not approach this tree, or else you will be wrongdoers." **36.** But Satan deceived them—leading to their fall from the ʿblissfulʾ state they were in,[13] and We said, "Descend from the heavens ʿto the earthʾ as enemies to each other.[14] You will find in the earth a residence and provision for your appointed stay." **37.** Then

Adam was inspired with words ʿof prayerʾ by his Lord,[15] so He accepted his repentance. Surely He is the Accepter of Repentance, Most Merciful. **38.** We said, "Descend all of you! Then when guidance comes to you from Me, whoever follows it, there will be no fear for them, nor will they grieve. **39.** But those who disbelieve and deny Our signs will be the residents of the Fire. They will be there forever."

Advice to the Israelites

40. O children of Israel![16] Remember My favours upon you. Fulfil your covenant and I will fulfil Mine, and stand in awe of Me ʿaloneʾ. **41.** Believe in My revelations which confirm your Scriptures. Do not be the first to deny them or trade them for a fleeting gain.[17] And be mindful of Me. **42.** Do not mix truth with falsehood or hide the truth knowingly. **43.** Establish prayer, pay alms-tax,[18] and bow down with those who bow down.

More Advice

44. Do you preach righteousness and fail to practice it yourselves, although you read the Scripture? Do you not understand? **45.** And seek help through patience and prayer. Indeed, it is a burden except

9   God knew that there would be many righteous people who would do good, make peace, and stand up for justice. Since humans have free choice, whoever chooses to believe and do good is better in the sight of God than all other beings, and whoever chooses to disbelieve and do evil is worse than all other beings. *See* 98:6-8.
10 Prostration in this verse does not mean worship, but an act of respect. A similar occurrence can be found in Chapter 12, where Jacob, his wife, and his eleven children knelt down before Joseph.
11 *Iblîs* was the name of Satan before his fall from grace. *Iblîs* was not an angel, but one of the jinn (*see* 18:50). Jinn is another creation of God, similar to humans in that they—unlike angels—have free will, but are made of smokeless fire and live in another plane of existence.
12 The command to prostrate was a test of obedience. Satan arrogantly refused to comply because he believed he was superior to Adam—arguing that Adam was made of mud while Satan was made of fire (*see* 7:12).
13 Both Adam and Eve were deceived, both sinned, and both were later forgiven. There is no concept of original sin in Islam.
14 i.e., humans and Satan.
15 The prayer that Adam and Eve were inspired to say is mentioned in 7:23, "Our Lord! We have wronged ourselves. If You do not forgive us and have mercy on us, we will certainly be losers."
16 Israel is another name for Prophet Jacob.
17 Trading God's revelations for a fleeting gain is a recurring theme in the first few chapters of the Quran. This refers to the practice of some Jewish authorities in Medina who contradicted certain rulings in the Torah by giving people lenient opinions only to please them in exchange for money.
18 The alms-tax (*zakâh*) is the payment of 2.5% of someone's savings only if the amount is equivalent to or greater than 85 g of gold, if that amount remains untouched for a whole Islamic year—around 355 days.

for the humble— **46.** those who are certain that they will meet their Lord and to Him they will return.

God's Favours upon the Israelites
1) Honour

47. O Children of Israel! Remember ˈallˈ the favours I granted you and how I honoured you above the others.[19] **48.** Guard yourselves against the Day on which no soul will be of help to another. No intercession[20] will be accepted, no ransom taken, and no help will be given.

Favour 2) Ending Persecution

49. ˈRememberˈ how We delivered you from the people of Pharaoh, who afflicted you with dreadful torment, slaughtering your sons and keeping your women. That was a severe test from your Lord.

Favour 3) Parting the Sea

50. And ˈrememberˈ when We parted the sea, rescued you, and drowned Pharaoh's people before your very eyes.

Favour 4) Forgiving Calf-Worship

51. And ˈrememberˈ when We appointed forty nights for Moses, then you worshipped the calf in his absence, acting wrongfully. **52.** Even then We ˈstillˈ forgave you so perhaps you would be grateful.

Favour 5) Revealing the Torah

53. And ˈrememberˈ when We gave Moses the Scripture—the Decisive Authority that perhaps you would be ˈrightlyˈ guided.

Favour 6) The Way to Forgiveness

54. And ˈrememberˈ when Moses said to his people, "O my people! Surely you have wronged yourselves by worshipping the calf, so turn in repentance to your Creator and execute ˈthe calf-worshippers among ˈyourselves. That is best for you in the sight of your Creator." Then He accepted your repentance. Surely He is the Accepter of Repentance, Most Merciful.

Favour 7) Forgiving the Demand to See God

55. And ˈrememberˈ when you said, "O Moses! We will never believe you until we see God with our own eyes," so a thunderbolt struck you while you were looking on. **56.** Then We brought you back to life after your death, so that perhaps you would be grateful.

Favour 8) Food and Shade

57. And ˈrememberˈ when ˈ We shaded you with clouds and sent down to you manna and quails,[21] ˈsayingˈ, "Eat from the good things We have provided for you." The evildoers ˈcertainlyˈ did not wrong Us, but wronged themselves.

Favour 9) Permission to Enter Jerusalem

58. And ˈrememberˈ when We said, "Enter this city and eat freely from wherever you please; enter the gate with humility, saying, 'Absolve us.' We will forgive your sins and multiply the reward for the good-doers." **59.** But the wrongdoers changed the words they were commanded to say. So We sent down a punishment from the heavens upon them for their rebelliousness.

---

19 Meaning, I chose you above all peoples of your time.
20 "Intercession" is the act of pleading with God on behalf of another person on the Day of Judgment.
21 Manna (heavenly bread) and quails (chicken-like birds) sustained the children of Israel in the wilderness after they left Egypt.

Favour 10) Water for All

60. And ˹remember˺ when Moses prayed for water for his people, We said, "Strike the rock with your staff." Then twelve springs gushed out, ˹and˺ each tribe knew its drinking place. ˹We then said,˺ "Eat and drink of God's provisions, and do not go about spreading corruption in the land."

Punishment for Defiance

61. And ˹remember˺ when you said, "O Moses! We cannot endure the same meal ˹every day˺. So ˹just˺ call upon your Lord on our behalf, He will bring forth for us some of what the earth produces of herbs, cucumbers, garlic, lentils, and onions." Moses scolded ˹them˺, "Do you exchange what is better for what is worse? ˹You can˺ go down to any village and you will find what you have asked for." They were stricken with disgrace and misery, and they invited the displeasure of God for rejecting God's signs and unjustly killing the prophets. This is ˹a fair reward˺ for their disobedience and violations.

Reward of the Believers

62. Indeed, the believers, Jews, Christians, and Sabians[22]—whoever ˹truly˺ believes in God and the Last Day and does good will have their reward with their Lord. And there will be no fear for them, nor will they grieve.[23]

God's Covenant with the Israelites

63. And ˹remember˺ when We took a covenant from you and raised the mountain above you ˹saying˺, "Hold firmly to that ˹Scripture˺ which We have given you and observe its teachings so perhaps you will become mindful ˹of God˺." 64. Yet you turned away afterwards. Had it not been for God's grace and mercy upon you, you would have certainly been of the losers.

Punishment for the Sabbath-Breakers

65. You are already aware of those of you who broke the Sabbath. We said to them, "Be disgraced apes!"[24] 66. So We made their fate an example to present and future generations, and a lesson to the God-fearing.

Story of the Cow

67. And ˹remember˺ when Moses said to his people, "God commands you to sacrifice a cow."[25] They replied, "Are you mocking us?" Moses responded, "I seek refuge in God from acting foolishly!" 68. They said, "Call upon your Lord to clarify for us what type ˹of cow˺ it should be!" He replied, "God says, 'The cow should neither be old nor young but in between. So do as you are commanded!'" 69. They said, "Call upon your Lord to specify for us its colour." He replied, "God says, 'It should be a bright yellow cow—pleasant to see.'" 70. Again they said, "Call upon your Lord so that He may make clear to us which cow, for all cows look the same to us. Then, God willing, we will be guided ˹to the right one˺." 71. He replied, "God says, 'It should have been used neither to till the soil nor water the fields; wholesome and without blemish.'" They said, "Now you have come with the truth." Yet they still slaughtered it hesi-

---

22　The Sabians are an indigenous group that believes in a supreme being and lives mostly in Iraq.
23　This verse should be understood in light of 3:19 and 3:85. For more details, see the Introduction.
24　The chosen opinion among scholars is that those who broke the Sabbath were turned into real apes. Imam Mujâhid, however, maintained that they just behaved like apes.
25　This chapter is named after the cow in this story, which happened at the time of Moses. A rich man was killed by his nephew, his only heir, and the body was thrown at the door of an innocent man. After a long investigation, no one was identified as the killer. Moses prayed for guidance and was told that the only way to find the killer was to sacrifice a cow and strike the victim with a piece of it. When this was done, the victim spoke miraculously and said who the killer was.

tantly! **72.** ˈThis isˈ when a man was killed and you disputed who the killer was, but God revealed what you concealed. **73.** So We instructed, "Strike the dead body with a piece of the cow." This is how ˈeasilyˈ God brings the dead to life, showing you His signs so that you may understand. **74.** Even then your hearts became hardened like a rock or even harder, for some rocks gush rivers; others split, spilling water; while others are humbled in awe of God. And God is never unaware of what you do.

Disobedient Israelites

75. Do you ˈbelievers stillˈ expect them to be true to you, though a group of them would hear the word of God then knowingly corrupt it after understanding it? **76.** When they meet the believers they say, "We believe." But in private they say ˈto each otherˈ, "Will you disclose to the believers the knowledge God has revealed to you,[26] so that they may use it against you before your Lord? Do you not understand?" **77.** Do they not know that God is aware of what they conceal and what they reveal? **78.** And among them are the illiterate who know nothing about the Scripture except lies, and ˈsoˈ they ˈwishfullyˈ speculate. **79.** So woe[27] to those who distort the Scripture with their own hands then say, "This is from God"—seeking a fleeting gain! So woe to them for what their hands have written, and woe to them for what they have earned.

Argument and Refutation

80. ˈSome ofˈ the Jews claim, "The Fire will not touch us except for a number of days." Say, ˈO Prophet,ˈ "Have you taken a pledge from God—for God never breaks His word—or are you ˈjustˈ saying about God what you do not know?" **81.** But no! Those who commit evil and are engrossed in sin will be the residents of the Fire. They will be there forever. **82.** And those who believe and do good will be the residents of Paradise. They will be there forever.

The Israelites' Failure to Keep Covenants

83. And ˈrememberˈ when We took a covenant from the children of Israel ˈstatingˈ, "Worship none but God; be kind to parents, relatives, orphans and the needy; speak kindly to people; establish prayer; and pay alms-tax." But you ˈIsraelitesˈ turned away—except for a few of you—and were indifferent. **84.** And ˈrememberˈ when We took your covenant that you would neither shed each other's blood nor expel each other from their homes, you gave your pledge and bore witness. **85.** But here you are, killing each other and expelling some of your people from their homes, aiding one another in sin and aggression; and when those ˈexpelledˈ come to you as captives, you still ransom them—though expelling them was unlawful for you.[28] Do you believe in some of the Scripture and reject the rest? Is there any reward for those who do so among you other than disgrace in this worldly life and being subjected to the harshest punishment on the Day of Judgment? For God is never unaware of what you do. **86.** These are the ones who trade the Hereafter for the life of this world. So their punishment will not be reduced, nor will they be helped.

Denying God's Prophets

87. Indeed, We gave Moses the Book and sent after him successive messengers. And We gave Jesus, son of Mary, clear proofs

---

26 i.e., verses prophesizing the coming of the Prophet in the Torah (including Deuteronomy 18:15-18 and 33:2).
27 i.e., warning of a curse or punishment.
28 The indigenous people of Medina were divided into two warring groups: *Al-Aws* and *Al-Khazraj*. Some Jewish tribes were allied with the former and others with the latter, which meant that in times of war each of these Jewish tribes had to fight along with their allies against their enemies, including other Jews. When the Prophet migrated to Medina, he brought about a lasting peace in the city.

and supported him with the holy spirit.[29] Why is it that every time a messenger comes to you ˈIsraelitesˈ with something you do not like, you become arrogant, rejecting some and killing others? **88.** They say, "Our hearts are unreceptive!"[30] In fact, God has condemned them for their disbelief. They have but little faith.

Rejecting the Quran

89. Although they used to pray for victory ˈby means of the Prophetˈ over the polytheists,[31] when there came to them a Book from God which they recognized,[32] confirming the Scripture they had ˈin their handsˈ, they rejected it. So may God's condemnation be upon the disbelievers. **90.** Miserable is the price they have sold their souls for—denying God's revelation and resenting God for granting His grace to whoever He wills of His servants! They have earned wrath upon wrath. And such disbelievers will suffer a humiliating punishment.

Excuse for Rejecting the Quran

91. When it is said to them: "Believe in what God has revealed," they reply, "We only believe in what was sent down to us," and they deny what came afterwards, though it is the truth confirming their own Scriptures! Ask ˈthem, O Prophetˈ, "Why then did you kill God's prophets before, if you are ˈtrulyˈ believers?"

Moses Was Defied Too

92. Indeed, Moses came to you with clear proofs, then you worshipped the calf in his absence, acting wrongfully. **93.** And when We took your covenant and raised the mountain above you ˈsayingˈ, "Hold

firmly to that ˈScriptureˈ which We have given you and obey," they answered, "We hear and disobey." The love of the calf was rooted in their hearts because of their disbelief. Say, ˈO Prophetˈ, "How evil is what your ˈso-calledˈ belief prompts you to do, if you ˈactuallyˈ believe ˈin the Torahˈ!"

Clinging to Life

94. Say, ˈO Prophetˈ, "If the ˈeternalˈ Home of the Hereafter with God is exclusively for you ˈIsraelitesˈ out of all humanity, then wish for death if what you say is true!" **95.** But they will never wish for that because of what their hands have done.[33] And God has ˈperfectˈ knowledge of the wrongdoers. **96.** You will surely find them clinging to life more eagerly than any other people, even more than polytheists. Each one of them wishes to live a thousand years. But even if they were to live that long, it would not save them from the punishment. And God is All-Seeing of what they do.

Rejecting the Truth

97. Say, ˈO Prophetˈ, "Whoever is an enemy of Gabriel should know that he revealed this ˈQuranˈ to your heart by God's Will, confirming what came before it—a guide and good news for the believers." **98.** Whoever is an enemy of God, His angels, His messengers, Gabriel, and Michael, then ˈlet them know thatˈ God is certainly the enemy of the disbelievers. **99.** Indeed, We have sent down to you ˈO Prophetˈ clear revelations. ˈButˈ none will deny them except the rebellious. **100.** Why is it that every time they make a covenant, a group of them casts it aside? In fact, most of them do not believe. **101.** Now, when a messenger from God has come to

---

29 The holy spirit is Gabriel, a mighty angel created from light, whose main duty is to communicate God's messages to prophets.
30 Their hearts are unreceptive because they claim they have enough knowledge already.
31 lit., the disbelievers.
32 i.e., the Quran.
33 i.e., disobeying God, killing some of the prophets (including Zachariah and John the Baptist), claiming to have killed Jesus, accusing Mary of adultery, and dealing with usury. See 4:153-158.

them—confirming their own Scriptures—some of the People of the Book cast the Book of God behind their backs as if they did not know.

Attachment to Magic

102. They ˹instead˺ followed the magic promoted by the devils during the reign of Solomon. Never did Solomon disbelieve, rather the devils disbelieved. They taught magic to the people, along with what had been revealed to the two angels, Hârût and Mârût, in Babylon.[34] The two angels never taught anyone without saying, "We are only a test ˹for you˺, so do not abandon ˹your˺ faith." Yet people learned ˹magic˺ that caused a rift ˹even˺ between husband and wife; although their magic could not harm anyone except by God's Will. They learned what harmed them and did not benefit them—although they already knew that whoever buys into magic would have no share in the Hereafter. Miserable indeed was the price for which they sold their souls, if only they knew! **103.** If only they were faithful and mindful ˹of God˺, there would have been a better reward from God, if only they knew!

Advice for the Believers

104. O believers! Do not say, "*Râ'ina.*" [Herd us!] But say, "*Unẓurna,*" [Tend to us!] and listen ˹attentively˺.[35] And the disbelievers will suffer a painful punishment. **105.** The disbelievers from the People of the Book and the polytheists would not

want you to receive any blessing from your Lord, but God selects whoever He wills for His mercy. And God is the Lord of infinite bounty.

Obeying the Messenger

106. If We ever abrogate[36] a verse or cause it to be forgotten, We replace it with a better or similar one. Do you not know that God is Most Capable of everything? **107.** Do you not know that the kingdom of the heavens and the earth belongs ˹only˺ to God, and you have no guardian or helper besides God? **108.** Or do you ˹believers˺ intend to ask of your Messenger as Moses was asked before?[37] But whoever trades belief for disbelief has truly strayed from the Right Way.

Adhering to the Straight Path

109. Many among the People of the Book wish they could turn you ˹believers˺ back to disbelief because of their envy, after the truth has been made clear to them. Pardon and bear with them until God delivers His decision. Surely God is Most Capable of everything. **110.** Establish prayer, and pay alms-tax. Whatever good you send forth for yourselves, you will ˹certainly˺ find ˹its reward˺ with God. Surely God is All-Seeing of what you do.

Claims and Refutations

111. The Jews and Christians each claim that none will enter Paradise except those

---

34 The two angels, Hârût and Mârût, were sent to enlighten the people in Babylon so they would not confuse magic tricks with miracles. Still some people abused this knowledge, causing mischief in the land. These practices persisted until the time of Solomon, who himself was falsely accused of utilizing magic to run his kingdom, subdue the jinn, and control the wind.

35 Some of the disbelievers used to play with words when they addressed the Prophet in order to ridicule him. So instead of saying, *râ'ina* "listen to us," they would say, *râ'îna* "our shepherd" or "the foolish among us." They would say loudly, "We listen," then whisper, "but we disobey!" and say, "Hear us," then, "may you never hear!" They used to say to each other, "If he had truly been a prophet of God, he would have known that we are mocking him." Therefore, this verse (along with 4:46) was revealed commanding the believers to avoid such words altogether. Better words are recommended.

36 The Quran was revealed over a period of twenty-three years. New rules were introduced when the believers were ready to accept and apply them. Replacing a ruling with another is called abrogation (*naskh*). For example, alcohol consumption was forbidden over three stages (*see* 2:219, 4:43, and 5:90, respectively). Some of the Prophet's companions said, "If drinking had been forbidden from day one, no one would have accepted Islam!"

37 i.e., asking to make God visible to them and make the angels talk to them.

of their own faith. These are their desires. Reply, ʿO Prophet,ʾ "Show ʿmeʾ your proof if what you say is true." **112.** But no! Whoever submits themselves to God and does good will have their reward with their Lord. And there will be no fear for them, nor will they grieve. **113.** The Jews say, "The Christians have nothing to stand on" and the Christians say, "The Jews have nothing to stand on," although both recite the Scriptures. And those ʿpagansʾ who have no knowledge say the same ʿabout people of faithʾ. Surely God will judge between them on the Day of Judgment regarding their dispute.

Condemning Attacks on Places of Worship

114. Who does more wrong than those who prevent God's Name from being mentioned in His places of worship and strive to destroy them? Such people have no right to enter these places except with fear.[38] For them there is disgrace in this world and they will suffer a tremendous punishment in the Hereafter. **115.** To God belong the east and the west, so wherever you turn you are facing ʿtowardsʾ God.[39] Surely God is All-Encompassing,[40] All-Knowing.

God is in No Need of Children

116. They say, "God has offspring."[41] Glory be to Him! In fact, to Him belongs whatever is in the heavens and the earth—all are subject to His Will. **117.** ʿHe isʾ the Originator of the heavens and the earth! When He decrees a matter, He simply tells it, "Be!" And it is!

True Guidance

118. Those who have no knowledge say, "If only God would speak to us or a sign would come to us!" The same was said by those who came before. Their hearts are all alike. Indeed, We have made the signs clear for people of sure faith. **119.** We have surely sent you with the truth ʿO Prophetʾ as a deliverer of good news and a warner. And you will not be accountable for the residents of the Hellfire. **120.** Never will the Jews or Christians be pleased with you, until you follow their faith. Say, "God's guidance is the only ʿtrueʾ guidance." And if you were to follow their desires after ʿallʾ the knowledge that has come to you, there would be none to protect or help you against God. **121.** Those We have given the Book follow it as it should be followed. It is they who ʿtrulyʾ believe in it. As for those who reject it, it is they who are the losers.

Reminder of Favours upon the Israelites

122. O Children of Israel! Remember My favours upon you and how I honoured you above the others. **123.** And guard yourselves against the Day when no soul will be of any help to another. No ransom will be taken, no intercession accepted, and no help will be given.

Abraham in Mecca

124. ʿRememberʾ when Abraham was tested by his Lord with ʿcertainʾ commandments, which he fulfilled. God said, "I will certainly make you into a role model for the people." Abraham asked, "What about my offspring?" God replied, "My covenant is not extended to the wrongdoers." **125.** And ʿrememberʾ when We made the Sacred House[42] a centre and a sanctuary

---

38 Or, "Such people should have never even entered these places with reverence."
39 lit., wherever you turn, there is the Face of God.
40 His mercy and knowledge covers all.
41 Jesus in Christianity, the angels in pagan Arab mythology, etc.
42 "The Sacred House" (*Ka'bah*) is a cube-shaped building in Mecca, Islam's holiest sanctuary, which Muslims face when they pray five times a day.

for the people 'saying', "'You may' take the standing-place of Abraham[43] as a site of prayer." And We entrusted Abraham and Ishmael to purify My House for those who circle it, who meditate in it, and who bow and prostrate themselves 'in prayer'.

Abraham's Prayers

126. And 'remember' when Abraham said, "My Lord, make this city 'of Mecca' secure and provide fruits to its people— those among them who believe in God and the Last Day." He answered, "As for those who disbelieve, I will let them enjoy themselves for a little while, then I will condemn them to the torment of the Fire. What an evil destination!"

Raising the Foundation of the Sacred House

127. And 'remember' when Abraham raised the foundation of the House with Ishmael, 'both praying,' "Our Lord! Accept 'this' from us. You are indeed the All-Hearing, All-Knowing. 128. Our Lord! Make us both 'fully' submit to You[44] and from our descendants a nation that will submit to You. Show us our rituals, and turn to us in grace. You are truly the Accepter of Repentance, Most Merciful. 129. Our Lord! Raise from among them a messenger who will recite to them Your revelations, teach them the Book and wisdom, and purify them. Indeed, You 'alone' are the Almighty, All-Wise."

One God

130. And who would reject the faith of Abraham except a fool! We certainly chose him in this life, and in the Hereafter he will surely be among the righteous. 131. When his Lord ordered him, "Submit 'to My Will'," he responded, "I submit to the Lord of all worlds." 132. This was the advice of Abraham—as well as Jacob—to his children, 'saying', "Indeed, God has chosen for you this faith; so do not die except in 'a state of full' submission." 133. Or did you witness when death came to Jacob? He asked his children, "Who will you worship after my passing?" They replied, "We will 'continue to' worship your God, the God of your forefathers—Abraham, Ishmael, and Isaac—the One God. And to Him we 'all' submit." 134. That was a community that had already gone before. For them is what they earned and for you is what you have earned. And you will not be accountable for what they have done.

Prophets of Islam

135. The Jews and Christians each say, "Follow our faith to be 'rightly' guided." Say, 'O Prophet,' "No! We follow the faith of Abraham, the upright—who was not a polytheist." 136. Say, 'O believers,' "We believe in God and what has been revealed to us; and what was revealed to Abraham, Ishmael, Isaac, Jacob, and his descendants; and what was given to Moses, Jesus, and other prophets from their Lord. We make no distinction between any of them. And to God we all submit." 137. So if they believe in what you believe, then they will indeed be 'rightly' guided. But if they turn away, they are simply opposed 'to the truth'. But God will spare you their evil. For He is the All-Hearing, All-Knowing.

Many Messengers; One Message

138. This is the 'natural' Way of God. And who is better than God in ordaining a way? And we worship 'none but' Him. 139. Say, "Would you dispute with us about God, while He is our Lord and your Lord? We are accountable for our deeds and you for yours. And we are devoted to Him 'alone'. 140. Or do you claim that

---

43 "The standing-place of Abraham" is the stone on which Abraham stood while he was building the Ka'bah.
44 lit., make both of us Muslims. The word "Muslim" means "one who submits to God." All of the prophets submitted to God and were, therefore, Muslims.

Abraham, Ishmael, Isaac, Jacob, and his descendants were all Jews or Christians?" Say, "Who is more knowledgeable: you or God?" Who does more wrong than those who hide the testimony they received from God? And God is never unaware of what you do. **141.** That was a community that had already gone before. For them is what they earned and for you is what you have earned. And you will not be accountable for what they have done.

New Direction of Prayer

142. The foolish among the people will ask, "Why did they turn away from the direction of prayer they used to face?"[45] Say, ˹O Prophet,˺ "The east and west belong ˹only˺ to God. He guides whoever He wills to the Straight Path." **143.** And so We have made you ˹believers˺ an upright[46] community so that you may be witnesses over humanity and that the Messenger may be a witness over you. We assigned your former direction of prayer only to distinguish those who would remain faithful to the Messenger from those who would lose faith. It was certainly a difficult test except for those ˹rightly˺ guided by God. And God would never discount your ˹previous acts of˺ faith. Surely God is Ever Gracious and Most Merciful to humanity.

Order to Face Mecca in Prayer

144. Indeed, We see you ˹O Prophet˺ turning your face towards the sky. Now We will make you turn towards a direction ˹of prayer˺ that will please you. So turn your face towards the Sacred Mosque ˹in Mecca˺—wherever you are, turn your faces towards it. Those who were given the Scripture certainly know this to be the truth from their Lord. And God is never unaware of what they do. **145.** Even if you were to bring every proof to the People of the Book, they would not accept your di-

rection ˹of prayer˺, nor would you accept theirs; nor would any of them accept the direction ˹of prayer˺ of another. And if you were to follow their desires after ˹all˺ the knowledge that has come to you, then you would certainly be one of the wrongdoers.

The Truth About the Prophet

146. Those We have given the Scripture recognize this ˹Prophet˺ as they recognize their own children. Yet a group of them hides the truth knowingly. **147.** ˹This is˺ the truth from your Lord, so do not ever be one of those who doubt. **148.** Everyone turns to their own direction ˹of prayer˺. So compete with one another in doing good. Wherever you are, God will bring you all together ˹for judgment˺. Surely God is Most Capable of everything.

Order to Face the Sacred Mosque

149. Wherever you are ˹O Prophet˺, turn your face towards the Sacred Mosque. This is certainly the truth from your Lord. And God is never unaware of what you ˹all˺ do. **150.** Wherever you are ˹O Prophet˺, turn your face towards the Sacred Mosque. And wherever you ˹believers˺ are, face towards it, so that people will have no argument against you, except the wrongdoers among them. Do not fear them; fear Me, so that I may ˹continue to˺ perfect My favour upon you and so you may be ˹rightly˺ guided.

God's Favour upon the Believers

151. Since We have sent you a messenger from among yourselves—reciting to you Our revelations, purifying you, teaching you the Book and wisdom, and teaching you what you never knew— **152.** remember Me; I will remember you. And thank Me, and never be ungrateful.

---

45 For about sixteen months after daily prayers became obligatory, Muslims used to face towards Jerusalem before the order came to face a new *qiblah* (direction of prayer)—the Sacred Mosque in Mecca.
46 i.e., moderate, balanced, and outstanding.

Patience in Difficult Times

153. O believers! Seek comfort in patience and prayer. God is truly with those who are patient. 154. Never say that those martyred in the cause of God are dead—in fact, they are alive! But you do not perceive it. 155. We will certainly test you with a touch of fear and famine and loss of property, life, and crops. Give good news to those who patiently endure— 156. who say, when struck by a disaster, "Surely to God we belong and to Him we will ˹all˺ return." 157. They are the ones who will receive God's blessings and mercy. And it is they who are ˹rightly˺ guided.

A Pilgrimage Ritual

158. Indeed, ˹the hills of˺ Ṣafa and Marwah[47] are among the symbols of God. So whoever makes the major or minor pilgrimage to the ˹Sacred˺ House,[48] let them walk between ˹the two hills˺. And whoever does good willingly, God is truly Appreciative, All-Knowing.

Warning to the Disbelievers

159. Those who hide the clear proofs and guidance that We have revealed—after We made it clear for humanity in the Book—will be condemned by God and ˹all˺ those who condemn. 160. As for those who repent, mend their ways, and let the truth be known, they are the ones to whom I will turn ˹in forgiveness˺, for I am the Accepter of Repentance, Most Merciful. 161. Surely those who disbelieve and die as disbelievers are condemned by God, the angels, and all of humanity. 162. They will be in Hell forever. Their punishment will not be lightened, nor will they be delayed ˹from it˺.

God's Great Signs

163. Your God is ˹only˺ One God. There is no god ˹worthy of worship˺ except Him— the Most Compassionate, Most Merciful. 164. Indeed, in the creation of the heavens and the earth; the alternation of the day and the night; the ships that sail the sea for the benefit of humanity; the rain sent down by God from the skies, reviving the earth after its death; the scattering of all kinds of creatures throughout; the shifting of the winds; and the clouds drifting between the heavens and the earth—in all of this˺ are surely signs for people of understanding.

Associating Others with God

165. Still there are some who take others as God's equal—they love them as they should love God—but the ˹true˺ believers love God even more. If only the wrongdoers could see the ˹horrible˺ punishment ˹awaiting them˺, they would certainly realize that all power belongs to God and that God is indeed severe in punishment.

Losers Disowning Each Other

166. ˹Consider the Day˺ when those who misled others will disown their followers—when they face the torment—and the bonds that united them will be cut off. 167. The ˹misled˺ followers will cry, "If only we could have a second chance, we would disown them as they disowned us." And so God will make them remorseful of their misdeeds. And they will never ˹be able to˺ leave the Fire.

Warning Against Satan

168. O humanity! Eat from what is lawful and good on the earth and do not follow Satan's footsteps. He is truly your sworn enemy. 169. He only incites you to commit evil and indecency, and to claim against God what you do not know.

---

47 Ṣafa and Marwah are two hills near the Ka'bah in Mecca.
48 Known as ḥajj and 'umrah respectively, pilgrimage to the Sacred Mosque in Mecca.

Blind Following

170. When it is said to them, "Follow what God has revealed," they reply, "No! We ˈonlyˈ follow what we found our forefathers practicing." ˈWould they still do so,ˈ even if their forefathers had ˈabsolutelyˈ no understanding or guidance?

Example of the Disbelievers

171. The example of the disbelievers ˈnot responding to the Messenger's warningˈ is like a flock not comprehending the calls and cries of the shepherd. ˈThey are wilfullyˈ deaf, dumb and blind so they have no understanding.

Forbidden Foods

172. O believers! Eat from the good things We have provided for you. And give thanks to God if you ˈtrulyˈ worship Him ˈaloneˈ. 173. He has only forbidden you ˈto eatˈ carrion, blood, swine,[49] and what is slaughtered in the name of any other than God. But if someone is compelled by necessity—neither driven by desire nor exceeding immediate need—they will not be sinful. Surely God is All-Forgiving, Most Merciful.

Hiding the Truth

174. Indeed, those who hide God's revelations, trading them for a fleeting gain consume nothing but fire into their bellies. God will neither speak to them on the Day of Judgment, nor will He purify them. And they will suffer a painful punishment. 175. They are the ones who trade guidance for misguidance and forgiveness for punishment. How persistent are they in pursuit of the Fire! 176. That is because God has revealed the Book in truth. And surely those who differ regarding it are totally engrossed in opposition.

True Righteousness

177. Righteousness is not in turning your faces towards the east or the west. Rather, the righteous are those who believe in God, the Last Day, the angels, the Books, and the prophets; who give charity out of their cherished wealth to relatives, orphans, the poor, ˈneedyˈ travellers, beggars, and for freeing captives; who establish prayer, pay alms-tax, and keep the pledges they make; and who are patient in times of suffering, adversity, and in ˈthe heat ofˈ battle. It is they who are true ˈin faithˈ, and it is they who are mindful ˈof Godˈ.

Law of Retaliation[50]

178. O believers! ˈThe law ofˈ retaliation is set for you in cases of murder—a free man for a free man, a slave for a slave, and a female for a female.[51] But if the offender is pardoned by the victim's guardian,[52] then blood-money should be decided fairly[53] and payment should be made courteously. This is a concession and a mercy from your Lord. But whoever transgresses after that will suffer a painful punishment. 179. There is ˈsecurity ofˈ life for you in ˈthe law ofˈ retaliation, O people of reason, so that you may become mindful ˈof Godˈ.

Last Will and Bequests

180. It is prescribed that when death approaches any of you—if they leave something of value—a will should be made in favour of parents and immediate family

---

49 Eating pork is forbidden in the Old Testament in Leviticus 11:7-8 and Deuteronomy 14:8.
50 The closest heirs of the victim of an intentional killing have the right to demand the execution of the killer through legal channels. They also have the right to waive the punishment as an act of charity.
51 No one else should be executed in place of the killer. This verse was revealed regarding a particular incident. Nevertheless, the killer is killed regardless of the difference in gender or status, unless the victim's family opts for blood money.
52 The guardian is the victim's closest heir—male or female.
53 Or according to common law.

with fairness.[54] ʿThis isʾ an obligation on those who are mindful ʿof Godʾ. **181.** But whoever changes the will after hearing it,[55] the blame will only be on those who made the change. Indeed, God is All-Hearing, All-Knowing. **182.** Whoever suspects an error or an injustice in the will and brings about a ʿfairʾ settlement among the parties will not be sinful. Surely God is All-Forgiving, Most Merciful.

Rules of Fasting

183. O believers! Fasting is prescribed for you—as it was for those before you[56]—so perhaps you will become mindful ʿof Godʾ. **184.** ʿFast aʾ prescribed number of days.[57] But whoever of you is ill or on a journey, then ʿlet them fastʾ an equal number of days ʿafter Ramaḍânʾ. For those who can only fast with extreme difficulty,[58] compensation can be made by feeding a needy person ʿfor every day not fastedʾ. But whoever volunteers to give more, it is better for them. And to fast is better for you, if only you knew.

Excellence of Ramaḍân

185. Ramaḍân is the month in which the Quran was revealed as a guide for humanity with clear proofs of guidance and the Decisive Authority. So whoever is present this month, let them fast. But whoever is ill or on a journey, then ʿlet them fastʾ an equal number of days ʿafter Ramaḍânʾ. God intends ease for you, not hardship, so that you may complete the prescribed period and proclaim the greatness of God for guiding you, and perhaps you will be grateful.

God Is Always Near

186. When My servants ask you ʿO Prophetʾ about Me: I am truly near. I respond to one's prayer when they call upon Me. So let them respond ʿwith obedienceʾ to Me and believe in Me, perhaps they will be guided ʿto the Right Wayʾ.

Intimacy During the Nights of Ramaḍân

187. It has been made permissible for you to be intimate with your wives during the nights preceding the fast. Your spouses are a garment[59] for you as you are for them. God knows that you were deceiving yourselves.[60] So He has accepted your repentance and pardoned you. So now you may be intimate with them and seek what God has prescribed for you.[61] ʿYou mayʾ eat and drink until you see the light of dawn breaking the darkness of night, then complete the fast until nightfall. Do not be intimate with your spouses while you are meditating in the mosques. These are the limits set by God, so do not exceed them. This is how God makes His revelations clear to people, so they may become mindful ʿof Himʾ.

Warning Against Injustice

188. Do not consume one another's wealth unjustly, nor deliberately bribe authorities in order to devour a portion of others' property, knowing that it is a sin.

True Righteousness

189. They ask you ʿO Prophetʾ about the phases of the moon. Say, "They are a means for people to determine time and

---

54 This ruling should be understood in light of the inheritance laws in 4:11-12, which give specific shares to parents and close relatives. Relatives who do not have a share may get a bequest up to one third of the estate.
55 After the death of the one who made the will.
56 i.e., the followers of previous prophets.
57 i.e., the month of Ramaḍân, the 9th month in the Islamic calendar.
58 In the case of old age or chronic disease.
59 "Garment" (libâs) is a metaphor for comfort, chastity, and protection.
60 Initially, intimate relations during the night of Ramaḍân were not permissible. Since some Muslims could not resist not having intercourse with their spouses, this verse was revealed allowing intimacy during the nights preceding the fast.
61 This implies offspring.

pilgrimage." Righteousness is not in entering your houses from the back doors.[62] Rather, righteousness is to be mindful ʿof God'. So enter your homes through their ʿproper' doors, and be mindful of God so you may be successful.

Etiquette of Fighting Enemy Combatants

190. Fight in the cause of God ʿonly' against those who wage war against you, but do not exceed the limits.[63] God does not like transgressors. **191.** Kill them wherever you come upon them[64] and drive them out of the places from which they have driven you out. For persecution[65] is far worse than killing. And do not fight them at the Sacred Mosque unless they attack you there. If they do so, then fight them—that is the reward of the disbelievers. **192.** But if they cease, then surely God is All-Forgiving, Most Merciful.

Resisting Oppression

193. Fight against them ʿif they persecute you' until there is no more persecution, and ʿyour' devotion will be to God ʿalone'. If they stop ʿpersecuting you', let there be no hostility except against the aggressors. **194.** ʿThere will be retaliation in' a sacred month for ʿan offence in' a sacred month,[66] and all violations will bring about retaliation. So, if anyone attacks

you, retaliate in the same manner. ʿBut' be mindful of God, and know that God is with those mindful ʿof Him'. **195.** Spend in the cause of God and do not let your own hands throw you into destruction ʿby withholding'. And do good, for God certainly loves the good-doers.

Some Pilgrimage Rituals

196. Complete the pilgrimage and minor pilgrimage for God.[67] But if prevented ʿfrom proceeding', then ʿoffer' whatever sacrificial animals you can afford. And do not shave your heads until the sacrificial animal reaches its destination. But if any of you is ill or has a scalp ailment ʿrequiring shaving', then compensate either by fasting, charity, or a sacrificial offering. In times of peace, you may combine the pilgrimage and minor pilgrimage then make the sacrificial offering you can afford. Whoever cannot afford that ʿoffering', let them fast three days during pilgrimage and seven after returning ʿhome'—completing ten. These offerings are for those who do not live near the Sacred House. And be mindful of God, and know that God is severe in punishment.

---

62   Before Islam, there was a superstitious practice for pilgrims to enter their homes through the back door upon returning from the pilgrimage. The verse suggests that being devoted to God wholeheartedly is more important than blindly following old traditions.

63   "Do not exceed the limits" refers to Islamic warfare guidelines set by the Prophet. In an authentic saying collected by Abu Dawûd, he is reported to have instructed the Muslim army, "Depart in the Name of God and with His help—following the way of the Messenger of God. Do not kill an old man, a child, or a woman. Do not mutilate dead bodies of the enemy. Be gracious and courteous, for God loves those who act with grace." The Prophet also says, "Do not wish to meet your enemy in battle but always pray for well-being. If fighting is a must, then be steadfast."

64   This is probably the most misquoted verse from the Quran. To properly understand the verse, we need to put it into context. Misquoting verses and taking them out of context can be applied to any scripture. For example, in the Bible, Jesus says, "Do not think that I came to bring peace on earth. I did not come to bring peace but a sword!" (Matthew 10:34). He also says, "But as for these enemies of mine who did not want me to be their king—bring them here and slaughter them in my presence!" (Luke 19:27). And Moses says, "The Lord is a man of war, the Lord is his name." (Exodus 15:3). For more details, *see* the Introduction.

65   Persecuting Muslims to abandon their faith.

66   The sacred months are the 1st, 7th, 11th, and 12th months of the Islamic calendar.

67   *Hajj*, the pilgrimage to Mecca, is required at least once in a Muslim's lifetime if they are physically and financially able to. *'Umrah*, which is a short version of *ḥajj*, is recommended, but not obligatory.

More Pilgrimage Rituals

197. ˹Commitment to˺ pilgrimage is made in appointed months.[68] Whoever commits to ˹performing˺ pilgrimage, let them stay away from intimate relations, foul language, and arguments during pilgrimage. Whatever good you do, God ˹fully˺ knows of it. Take ˹necessary˺ provisions ˹for the journey˺—surely the best provision is righteousness. And be mindful of Me, O people of reason! **198.** There is no blame on you for seeking the bounty of your Lord ˹during this journey˺.[69] When you return from 'Arafât,[70] praise God near the sacred place[71] and praise Him for having guided you, for surely before this ˹guidance˺ you were astray. **199.** Then go forth with the rest of the pilgrims. And seek God's forgiveness. Surely God is All-Forgiving, Most Merciful.

Praying for the Best of Both Worlds

200. When you have fulfilled your sacred rites, praise God as you used to praise your forefathers ˹before Islam˺, or even more passionately. There are some who say, "Our Lord! Grant us ˹Your bounties˺ in this world," but they will have no share in the Hereafter. **201.** Yet there are others who say, "Our Lord! Grant us the good of this world and the Hereafter, and protect us from the torment of the Fire." **202.** It is they who will receive a ˹heavenly˺ reward for the good they have done. And God is swift in reckoning.[72]

More Pilgrimage Rituals

203. And remember God during ˹these˺ appointed days.[73] Whoever departs swiftly on the second day is not sinful, neither

are those who stay behind ˹till the third—seeking additional reward˺, so long as they are mindful ˹of their Lord˺. And be mindful of God, and know that to Him you will ˹all˺ be gathered.

Those Who Spread Mischief

204. There are some ˹hypocrites˺ who impress you with their views regarding worldly affairs and openly call upon God to witness what is in their hearts, yet they are your worst adversaries. **205.** And when they leave ˹you˺,[74] they strive throughout the land to spread mischief in it and destroy crops and cattle. God does not like mischief. **206.** When it is said to them, "Fear God," pride carries them off to sin. Hell will be their proper place. What an evil place to rest! **207.** And there are those who would dedicate their lives to God's pleasure. And God is Ever Gracious to ˹His˺ servants.

Warning Against the Devil

208. O believers! Enter into Islam wholeheartedly and do not follow Satan's footsteps. Surely he is your sworn enemy. **209.** If you falter after receiving the clear proofs, then know that God is indeed Almighty, All-Wise.

Waiting for Judgment?

210. Are they waiting for God ˹Himself˺ to come to them in the shade of clouds, along with the angels? ˹If He did˺, then the matter would be settled ˹at once˺. And to God ˹all˺ matters will be returned ˹for judgment˺. **211.** Ask the Children of Israel how many clear signs We have given them. And whoever trades God's favour—after receiving

---

68   Although pilgrimage is performed over the course of a few days in the 12th month of the Islamic calendar, the intention to perform pilgrimage can be made during the 10th, 11th, and the first half of the 12th months.
69   By trading during *ḥajj* season.
70   'Arafât is a hill in Saudi Arabia, near Mecca, which is visited during pilgrimage.
71   A sacred place called *Muzdalifah*.
72   Swift in reckoning (*sarî'ul-ḥisâb*) means "He is quick in recording the deeds and judging them."
73   The 11th-13th of *Ẓul-Ḥijjah*, the 12th month of the Islamic calendar. These days are part of pilgrimage rituals.
74   Another possible translation: "And when they assume authority, they strive ..."

it—'for disbelief' should know that God is indeed severe in punishment.

Life as a Test

212. The life of this world has been made appealing to the disbelievers, and they mock the believers. Those who are mindful 'of God' will rank above them on the Day of Judgment. And God provides for whoever He wills without limit.

Why Prophets Were Sent

213. Humanity had once been one community 'of believers before they lost faith'. Then God raised prophets as deliverers of good news and as warners, and revealed to them the Scriptures in truth to judge among people regarding their disputes. And no one disputed the Scriptures except the very people who received them after clear proofs had come to them—out of jealousy. Then God, by His grace, has guided the believers to the truth regarding those disputes. And God guides whoever He wills to the Straight Path.

Faith Reinforced by Affliction

214. Do you think you will be admitted into Paradise without being tested like those before you? They were afflicted with suffering and adversity and were so 'violently' shaken that 'even' the Messenger and the believers with him cried out, "When will God's help come?" Indeed, God's help is 'always' near.

Charity Begins at Home

215. They ask you 'O Prophet in' what 'way' they should donate. Say, "Whatever donations you give are for parents, relatives, orphans, the poor, and 'needy' travellers. Whatever good you do is certainly well known to God."

Fighting in Self-Defence

216. Fighting has been made obligatory upon you 'believers', though you dislike it. Perhaps you dislike something which is good for you and like something which is bad for you. God knows and you do not know.

Fighting in the Sacred Months

217. They[75] ask you 'O Prophet' about fighting in the sacred months.[76] Say, "Fighting during these months is a great sin. But hindering 'others' from the Path of God, rejecting Him, and expelling the worshippers from the Sacred Mosque is 'a' greater 'sin' in the sight of God. For persecution[77] is far worse than killing. And they will not stop fighting you until they turn you away from your faith—if they can. And whoever among you renounces their own faith and dies a disbeliever, their deeds will become void in this life and in the Hereafter. It is they who will be the residents of the Fire. They will be there forever."

Reward of the Devout

218. Surely those who have believed, emigrated, and struggled in the Way of God—they can hope for God's mercy. And God is All-Forgiving, Most Merciful.

Questions to the Prophet

219. They ask you 'O Prophet' about intoxicants and gambling. Say, "There is great evil in both, as well as some benefit for people—but the evil outweighs the benefit."[78] They 'also' ask you 'O Prophet' what they should donate. Say, "Whatever you can spare." This is how God makes His revelations clear to you 'believers', so perhaps you may reflect 220. upon this world and the Hereafter. And they ask

---

75 The pagans of Mecca.
76 *See* footnote for 2:194.
77 Persecuting Muslims to abandon their faith.
78 See footnote for 4:43.

you ˓O Prophet˒ concerning orphans. Say, "Improving their condition is best. And if you partner with them, they are bonded with you ˓in faith˒.[79] And God knows who intends harm and who intends good. Had God willed, He could have made it difficult for you.[80] Surely God is Almighty, All-Wise."

Marrying Believers

221. Do not marry polytheistic women until they believe; for a believing slave-woman is better than a free polytheist, even though she may look pleasant to you. And do not marry your women to polytheistic men until they believe, for a believing slave-man is better than a free polytheist, even though he may look pleasant to you. They invite ˓you˒ to the Fire while God invites ˓you˒ to Paradise and forgiveness by His grace.[81] He makes His revelations clear to the people so perhaps they will be mindful.

Intercourse During Menstruation

222. They ask you ˓O Prophet˒ about menstruation. Say, "Beware of its harm! So keep away, and do not have intercourse with your wives during their monthly cycles until they are purified.[82] When they purify themselves, then you may approach them in the manner specified by God. Surely God loves those who always turn to Him in repentance and those who purify themselves." 223. Your

wives are like farmland for you,[83] so approach them ˓consensually˒ as you please.[84] And send forth something good for yourselves.[85] Be mindful of God, and know that you will meet Him. And give good news to the believers.

Rules Regarding Oaths

224. Do not use God's Name in your oaths as an excuse for not doing good, not guarding against evil, or not making peace between people. And God is All-Hearing, All-Knowing. 225. God will not hold you accountable for unintentional oaths, but for what you intended in your hearts. And God is All-Forgiving, Most Forbearing.

Vowing Not to Touch One's Own Wife

226. Those who swear not to have intercourse with their wives must wait for four months.[86] If they change their mind, then God is certainly All-Forgiving, Most Merciful. 227. But if they settle on divorce, then God is indeed All-Hearing, All-Knowing.

Waiting Period After Divorce

228. Divorced women must wait three monthly cycles ˓before they can re-marry˒. It is not lawful for them to conceal what God has created in their wombs,[87] if they ˓truly˒ believe in God and the Last Day. And their husbands reserve the right

---

79   Literal translation, "They are your brothers."
80   By not allowing partnership between you and orphans.
81   lit., "by His permission."
82   Do not have intercourse with them until their menstruation is over and they have taken a full bath.
83   Ḥarth means "farmland"—the husband being like a farmer, the wife like productive land, and children like seeds—a metaphor for fertility and growth.
84   It is permissible to have intimate relations in any position. However, vaginal penetration during monthly cycles, or while bleeding persists after childbirth up to forty days, is not permitted.
85   This can either imply "sending forth good deeds that will be rewarded in the next life" or—according to some interpretations—"engaging in foreplay with one's spouse before intercourse."
86   This ruling is called īlâ'. Īlâ' means that a husband vows not to be intimate with his wife because of a dispute or any other legitimate reason. The verse here says if it is four months or less and the husband keeps his vow, then he does not have to make up for breaking his vow (by feeding ten poor people, or fasting three days), otherwise he will need to make up for breaking his vow. If the vow is made for over four months, the wife has the right to seek divorce after four months. Īlâ' should be avoided altogether since it deprives the wife of her right to sexual satisfaction. Instead, counselling is a better alternative at the time of dispute.
87   This could mean "pregnancy" or "accurate information about monthly cycles."

to take them back within that period if they desire reconciliation. Women have rights similar to those of men equitably, although men have a degree ´of responsibility` above them. And God is Almighty, All-Wise.

Proper Way to Divorce

229. Divorce may be retracted twice, then the husband must retain ´his wife` with honour or separate ´from her` with grace.[88] It is not lawful for husbands to take back anything of the dowry given to their wives, unless the couple fears not being able to keep within the limits of God.[89] So if you fear they will not be able to keep within the limits of God, there is no blame if the wife compensates the husband to obtain divorce.[90] These are the limits set by God, so do not transgress them. And whoever transgresses the limits of God, they are the ´true` wrongdoers.

Husband Remarrying His Ex-Wife

230. So if a husband divorces his wife ´three times`, then it is not lawful for him to remarry her until after she has married another man and then is divorced. Then it is permissible for them to reunite, as long as they feel they are able to maintain the limits of God. These are the limits set by God, which He makes clear for people of knowledge.

Etiquette of Divorce

231. When you divorce women and they have ´almost` reached the end of their waiting period, either retain them honourably or let them go honourably. But do not retain them ´only` to harm them ´or` to take advantage ´of them`. Whoever does that surely wrongs his own soul. Do not take God's revelations lightly. Remember God's favours upon you as well as the Book and wisdom[91] He has sent down for your guidance. Be mindful of God, and know that God has ´perfect` knowledge of all things.

Remarrying One's Ex-Spouse

232. When you have divorced women and they have reached the end of their waiting period, do not prevent them from re-marrying their ex-husbands if they come to an honourable agreement. This is enjoined on whoever has faith in God and the Last Day. This is purer and more dignifying for you. God knows and you do not know.

Nursing Children After Divorce

233. ´Divorced` mothers will breastfeed their offspring for two whole years, for those who wish to complete the nursing ´of their child`. The child's father will provide reasonable maintenance and clothing for the mother ´during that period`. No one will be charged with more than they can bear. No mother or father should be made to suffer for their child. The ´father's` heirs are under the same obligation. But if both sides decide—after mutual consultation and consent—to wean a child, then there is no blame on them. If you decide to have your children nursed by a wet-nurse, it is permissible as long as you pay fairly. Be mindful of God, and know that God is All-Seeing of what you do.

---

88 A husband may separate from his wife after each of the first two counts of divorce or at the end of her waiting period (see 65:1-5) with dignity. If he chooses to stay with her after the first two counts of divorce then divorces her a third time, the marriage is terminated at the end of her third waiting period. The wife will have to marry and divorce another man before she can be remarried to her ex-husband (see 2:230). However, a woman marrying someone with the intention of getting divorced, in order to return to her first husband, is forbidden.

89 The "limits of God" implies fidelity to one's spouse according to God's commands.

90 If the wife does not want to continue in the marriage for legitimate reasons, then she can return the dowry (mahr) to the husband in compensation for divorce. This ruling is called khul'.

91 "Wisdom" means the "sunnah" or the tradition of the Prophet when it is mentioned along with the Book (i.e., the Quran).

Widows' Waiting Period

234. As for those of you who die and leave widows behind, let them observe a waiting period of four months and ten days. When they have reached the end of this period, then you[92] are not accountable for what they decide for themselves in a reasonable manner. And God is All-Aware of what you do.

Proposing to Widowed or Divorced Women

235. There is no blame on you for subtly showing interest in ˹divorced or widowed˺ women[93] or for hiding ˹the intention˺ in your hearts. God knows that you are considering them ˹for marriage˺. But do not make a secret commitment with them—you can only show interest in them appropriately. Do not commit to the bond of marriage until the waiting period expires. Know that God is aware of what is in your hearts, so beware of Him. And know that God is All-Forgiving, Most Forbearing.

Divorce Before Consummation

236. There is no blame if you divorce women before the marriage is consummated or the dowry is settled. But give them a ˹suitable˺ compensation—the rich according to his means and the poor according to his. A reasonable compensation is an obligation on the good-doers. **237.** And if you divorce them before consummating the marriage but after deciding on a dowry, pay half of the dowry, unless the wife graciously waives it or the husband graciously pays in full. Graciousness is closer to righteousness. And

do not forget kindness among yourselves. Surely God is All-Seeing of what you do.

Observing Prayers[94]

238. Observe the ˹five obligatory˺ prayers—especially the middle prayer[95]—and stand in true devotion to God. **239.** If you are in danger, pray on foot or while riding. But when you are safe, ˹take time to˺ remember God for teaching you what you did not know.

Widows' Original Waiting Period

240. Those of you who die leaving widows should bequeath for them a year's maintenance without forcing them out.[96] But if they choose to leave, you are not accountable for what they reasonably decide for themselves. And God is Almighty, All-Wise.

Care for Divorced Women

241. Reasonable provisions must be made for divorced women—a duty on those mindful ˹of God˺. **242.** This is how God makes His revelations clear to you, so perhaps you will understand.

Sacrifices in God's Cause

243. Have you ˹O Prophet˺ not seen those who fled their homes in the thousands for fear of death?[97] God said to them, "Die!" then He gave them life. Surely God is ever Bountiful to humanity, but most people are ungrateful. **244.** Fight in the cause of God, and know that God is All-Hearing, All-Knowing. **245.** Who will lend to God a good loan which God will multiply many times over? It is God ˹alone˺ who

---

92 i.e., the guardians.
93 During their waiting periods.
94 The passage that discusses prayer falls between the passages that discuss divorce and women's rights after divorce because it serves as a reminder that prayers should motivate spouses to always be mindful of their Lord during their marriage and also after divorce so no one will be wronged in anyway.
95 As mentioned in several authentic sayings of Prophet Muḥammad, the middle prayer is the afternoon prayer, 'Aṣr.
96 This ruling was later replaced by the ruling in 2:234.
97 They fled in the wake of a plague or an enemy attack.

decreases and increases ˹wealth˺. And to Him you will ˹all˺ be returned.

Prophet Samuel

246. Have you not seen those chiefs of the Children of Israel after Moses? They said to one of their prophets, "Appoint for us a king, ˹and˺ we will fight in the cause of God." He said, "Are you not going to cower if ordered to fight?" They replied, "How could we refuse to fight in the cause of God, while we were driven out of our homes and ˹separated from˺ our children?" But when they were ordered to fight, they fled, except for a few of them. And God has ˹perfect˺ knowledge of the wrongdoers.

King Saul

247. Their prophet told them, "God has appointed Saul[98] to be your king." They protested, "How can he be our king when some of us are more deserving of kingship than he, and he has not been blessed with vast riches?" He replied, "God has chosen him over you and blessed him with knowledge and stature. God grants kingship to whoever He wills. And God is All-Bountiful, All-Knowing." **248.** Their prophet further told them, "The sign of Saul's kingship is that the Ark will come to you—containing reassurance[99] from your Lord and relics of the family of Moses and the family of Aaron,[100] which will be carried by the angels. Surely in this is a sign for you, if you ˹truly˺ believe."

Saul's Victory

249. When Saul marched forth with his army, he cautioned: "God will test you with a river. So whoever drinks ˹his fill˺ from it is not with me, and whoever does not taste it—except a sip from the hollow of his hands—is definitely with me." They all drank ˹their fill˺ except for a few! When he and the ˹remaining˺ faithful with him crossed the river, they said, "Now we are no match for Goliath and his warriors." But those ˹believers˺ who were certain they would meet God reasoned, "How many times has a small force vanquished a mighty army by the Will of God! And God is ˹always˺ with the steadfast."

David Kills Goliath

250. When they advanced to face Goliath and his warriors, they prayed, "Our Lord! Shower us with perseverance, make our steps firm, and give us victory over the disbelieving people." **251.** So they defeated them by God's Will, and David killed Goliath. And God blessed David with kingship and wisdom and taught him what He willed. Had God not repelled a group of people by ˹the might of˺ another, corruption would have dominated the earth, but God is Gracious to all. **252.** These are God's revelations which We recite to you ˹O Prophet˺ in truth. And you are truly one of the messengers.

Some Messengers Raised in Rank

253. We have chosen some of those messengers above others.[101] God spoke directly to some, and raised some high in rank. To Jesus, son of Mary, We gave clear proofs and supported him with the holy spirit.[102] If God had willed, succeeding generations would not have fought ˹among themselves˺ after receiving the clear proofs. But they differed—some believed while others disbelieved. Yet if God had willed, they would not have fought one another. But God does what He wills.

---

98 Ṭalût.
99 Reassurance refers to the Torah.
100 i.e., the staff of Moses and fragments of the Tablets.
101 Those messengers mentioned earlier in this chapter (see verse 136).
102 i.e., Gabriel.

Spending in God's Way

254. O believers! Donate from what We have provided for you before the arrival of a Day when there will be no bargaining,[103] friendship,[104] or intercession. Those who disbelieve are 'truly' the wrongdoers.

One True God

255. God! There is no god 'worthy of worship' except Him, the Ever-Living, All-Sustaining. Neither drowsiness nor sleep overtakes Him. To Him belongs whatever is in the heavens and whatever is on the earth. Who could possibly intercede with Him without His permission? He 'fully' knows what is ahead of them and what is behind them, but no one can grasp any of His knowledge—except what He wills 'to reveal'. His Seat[105] encompasses the heavens and the earth, and the preservation of both does not tire Him. For He is the Most High, the Greatest.[106]

Free Will in Accepting Islam

256. Let there be no compulsion in religion, for the truth stands out clearly from falsehood.[107] So whoever renounces false gods and believes in God has certainly grasped the firmest, unfailing hand-hold. And God is All-Hearing, All-Knowing.
257. God is the Guardian of the believers—He brings them out of darkness and into light. As for the disbelievers, their guardians are false gods who lead them out of light and into darkness. It is they who will be the residents of the Fire. They will be there forever.

Abraham and the Arrogant King

258. Are you 'O Prophet' not aware of the one who argued with Abraham about his Lord because God had granted him kingship? 'Remember' when Abraham said, "My Lord is the One Who has power to give life and cause death." He argued, "I too have the power to give life and cause death." Abraham challenged 'him', "God causes the sun to rise from the east. So make it rise from the west." And so the disbeliever was dumbstruck. And God does not guide the wrongdoing people.

Story of Ezra

259. Or 'are you not aware of' the one who passed by a city which was in ruins. He wondered, "How could God bring this back to life after its destruction?" So God caused him to die for a hundred years then brought him back to life. God asked, "How long have you remained 'in this state'?" He replied, "Perhaps a day or part of a day." God said, "No! You have remained here for a hundred years! Just look at your food and drink—they have not spoiled. 'But now' look at 'the remains of' your donkey! And 'so' We have made you into a sign for humanity. And look at the bones 'of the donkey', how We bring them together then clothe them with flesh!"[108] When this was made clear to him, he declared, "'Now' I know that God is Most Capable of everything."

Abraham Inquiring About Resurrection

260. And 'remember' when Abraham said, "My Lord! Show me how you give life to the dead." God responded, "Do you

---

not believe?" Abraham replied, "Yes I do, but just so my heart can be reassured." God said, "Then bring four birds, train them to come to you, 'then cut them into pieces,' and scatter them on different hilltops. Then call them back, they will fly to you in haste. And 'so you will' know that God is Almighty, All-Wise."

Multiplied Rewards for Charity

261. The example of those who spend their wealth in the cause of God is that of a grain that sprouts into seven ears, each bearing one hundred grains. And God multiplies 'the reward even more' to whoever He wills. For God is All-Bountiful, All-Knowing.

Sincere Charity

262. Those who spend their wealth in the cause of God and do not follow their charity with reminders of their generosity or hurtful words—they will get their reward from their Lord, and there will be no fear for them, nor will they grieve. 263. Kind words and forgiveness are better than charity followed by injury. And God is Self-Sufficient, Most Forbearing.

Parable for Wasted Charity

264. O believers! Do not waste your charity with reminders 'of your generosity' or hurtful words, like those who donate their wealth just to show off and do not believe in God or the Last Day. Their example is that of a hard barren rock covered with a thin layer of soil hit by a strong rain—leaving it just a bare stone. Such people are unable to preserve the reward of their charity. God does not guide 'such' disbelieving people.

Parable for Accepted Charity

265. And the example of those who donate their wealth, seeking God's pleasure and believing the reward is certain,[109] is that of a garden on a fertile hill: when heavy rain falls, it yields up twice its normal produce. If no heavy rain falls, a drizzle is sufficient. And God is All-Seeing of what you do.

Wasted Reward

266. Would any of you wish to have a garden with palm trees, grapevines, and all kinds of fruits with rivers flowing underneath and as they grow very old with dependent children, a fiery whirlwind hits the garden, burning it all up? This is how God makes His revelations clear to you, so perhaps you will reflect.

Quality Charity

267. O believers! Donate from the best of what you have earned and of what We have produced for you from the earth. Do not pick out worthless things for donation, which you yourselves would only accept with closed eyes. And know that God is Self-Sufficient, Praiseworthy.

Devil Discouraging Charity

268. The Devil threatens you with 'the prospect of' poverty and bids you to the shameful deed 'of stinginess', while God promises you forgiveness and 'great' bounties from Him. And God is All-Bountiful, All-Knowing.

Wisdom as a Privilege, Not a Right

269. He grants wisdom to whoever He wills. And whoever is granted wisdom is certainly blessed with a great privilege. But none will be mindful 'of this' except people of reason.

Donating Openly and Secretly

270. Whatever charities you give or vows you make are surely known to God. And the wrongdoers will have no helpers. 271. To give charity publicly is good, but

---

109   It could also mean "... seeking God's pleasure and proving their sincerity."

to give to the poor privately is better for you, and will absolve you of your sins. And God is All-Aware of what you do.[110] **272.** You are not responsible for people's guidance ˹O Prophet˺—it is God Who guides whoever He wills. Whatever you ˹believers˺ spend in charity, it is for your own good—as long as you do so seeking the pleasure of God.[111] Whatever you donate will be paid back to you in full, and you will not be wronged.

Caring for the Needy

273. ˹Charity is˺ for the needy who are too engaged in the cause of God to move about in the land ˹for work˺. Those unfamiliar with their situation will think they are not in need ˹of charity˺ because they do not beg. You can recognize them by their appearance. They do not beg people persistently. Whatever you give in charity is certainly well known to God. **274.** Those who spend their wealth in charity day and night, secretly and openly—their reward is with their Lord, and there will be no fear for them, nor will they grieve.

Interest Prohibited

275. Those who consume interest will stand ˹on Judgment Day˺ like those driven to madness by Satan's touch. That is because they say, "Trade is no different than interest." But God has permitted trading and forbidden interest. Whoever refrains—after having received warning from their Lord—may keep their previous gains, and their case is left to God. As for those who persist, it is they who will be the residents of the Fire. They will be there forever. **276.** God has made interest fruitless and charity fruitful. And God does not like any ungrateful evildoer.

True Believers

277. Indeed, those who believe, do good, establish prayer, and pay alms-tax will receive their reward from their Lord, and there will be no fear for them, nor will they grieve.

Warning Against Interest

278. O believers! Fear God, and give up outstanding interest if you are ˹true˺ believers. **279.** If you do not, then beware of a war with God and His Messenger! But if you repent, you may retain your principal—neither inflicting nor suffering harm.

Kindness in Collecting Debts

280. If it is difficult for someone to repay a debt, postpone it until a time of ease. And if you waive it as an act of charity, it will be better for you, if only you knew.

Reminder of Judgment Day

281. Be mindful of the Day when you will ˹all˺ be returned to God, then every soul will be paid in full for what it has done, and none will be wronged.[112]

Writing and Witnessing a Debt Contract

282. O believers! When you contract a loan for a fixed period of time, commit it to writing. Let the scribe maintain justice between the parties. The scribe should not refuse to write as God has taught them to write. They will write what the debtor dictates, bearing God in mind and not defrauding the debt. If the debtor is incompetent, weak, or unable to dictate, let their guardian dictate for them with justice. Call upon two of your men to witness. If two men cannot be found, then one man and two women of your choice will witness—so if one of the women forgets the other

---

110 Donations for a public cause may be done openly to encourage others to donate, whereas it is recommended to give charity to the poor secretly.
111 lit., seeking the Face of God.
112 Verse 281 is believed by many scholars to be the last verse revealed of the Quran.

may remind her.[113] The witnesses must not refuse when they are summoned. You must not be against writing ʿcontractsʾ for a fixed period—whether the sum is small or great. This is more just ʿfor youʾ in the sight of God, and more convenient to establish evidence and remove doubts. However, if you conduct an immediate transaction among yourselves, then there is no need for you to record it, but call upon witnesses when a deal is finalized. Let no harm come to the scribe or witnesses. If you do, then you have gravely exceeded ʿyour limitsʾ. Be mindful of God, for God ʿis the One Whoʾ teaches you. And God has ʿperfectʾ knowledge of all things.

Taking Collateral

283. If you are on a journey and a scribe cannot be found, then a security can be taken. If you trust one another, then ʿthere is no need for a security, butʾ the debtor should honour this trust ʿby repaying the debtʾ—and let them fear God, their Lord. And do not conceal the testimony, for whoever conceals it, their hearts are indeed sinful. And God ʿfullyʾ knows what you do.

God's Might

284. To God ʿaloneʾ belongs whatever is in the heavens and whatever is on the earth. Whether you reveal what is in your hearts or conceal it, God will call you to account for it. He forgives whoever He wills, and punishes whoever He wills. And God is Most Capable of everything.

Articles of Faith

285. The Messenger ʿfirmlyʾ believes in what has been revealed to him from his Lord, and so do the believers. They ʿallʾ believe in God, His angels, His Books, and His messengers. ʿThey proclaim,ʾ "We make no distinction between any of His messengers." And they say, "We hear and obey. ʿWe seekʾ Your forgiveness, our Lord! And to you ʿaloneʾ is the final return."

Prayer for Grace

286. God does not require of any soul more than what it can afford. All good will be for its own benefit, and all evil will be to its own loss. ʿThe believers pray,ʾ "Our Lord! Do not punish us if we forget or make a mistake. Our Lord! Do not place a burden on us like the one you placed on those before us. Our Lord! Do not burden us with what we cannot bear. Pardon us, forgive us, and have mercy on us. You are our ʿonlyʾ Guardian. So grant us victory over the disbelieving people."[114]

---

113 2:282 (the longest verse in the Quran) instructs the believers to record loans in all fairness and to have witnesses. Based on the wording of this verse, two reliable and experienced men should witness the loan agreement, not just any two men. If two qualified men can't be found, then one man and two women will witness. Generally, in Islamic law, the word of reliable Muslim men and women is equally accepted and valued. For example, a *ḥadīth* reported by a woman (like 'Aishah, may God be please with her) is as important as a *ḥadīth* reported by a man (like Abu Hurairah, may God be please with him). Also, if someone saw the new moon of Ramaḍān, some scholars say that people should fast, whether it was sighted by a reliable man or woman.

114 Those who persecute us because of our faith.

3. The Family of 'Imrân (Âli-'Imrân)

This Medinian chapter takes its name from the Family of 'Imrân mentioned in verse 33. Like the previous chapter, it reiterates the fact that God is the source of divine revelation and affirms the belief in God as the only Lord and Islam as His only accepted religion. The story of the birth of Mary, John the Baptist, and Jesus is mentioned, along with a challenge to the Christian perception of Jesus. The chapter also touches on early battles against the Meccan pagans with emphasis on the lessons to be drawn from the Muslims' defeat at the Battle of Uḥud, which took place in 3 A.H./625 C.E. The virtue of being mindful of God is highlighted at the end of this chapter and the beginning of the next one.

In the Name of God—the Most Compassionate, Most Merciful

Scriptures as a Source of Guidance

1. *Alif-Lãm-Mĩm.* 2. God! There is no god 'worthy of worship' except Him—the Ever-Living, All-Sustaining. 3. He has revealed to you 'O Prophet' the Book in truth, confirming what came before it, as He revealed the Torah and the Gospel 4. previously, as a guide for people, and 'also' revealed the Decisive Authority.[115] Surely those who reject God's revelations will suffer a severe torment. For God is Almighty, capable of punishment.

God Almighty

5. Surely nothing on earth or in the heavens is hidden from God. 6. He is the One Who shapes you in the wombs of your mothers as He wills. There is no god 'worthy of worship' except Him—the Almighty, All-Wise.

Precise and Elusive Verses

7. He is the One Who has revealed to you 'O Prophet' the Book, of which some verses are precise—they are the foundation of the Book—while others are elusive.[116] Those with deviant hearts follow the elusive verses seeking 'to spread' doubt through their 'false' interpretations—but none grasps their 'full' meaning except God. As for those well-grounded in knowledge, they say, "We believe in this 'Quran'—it is all from our Lord." But none will be mindful 'of this' except people of reason. 8. 'They say,' "Our Lord! Do not let our hearts deviate after you have guided us. Grant us Your mercy. You are indeed the Giver 'of all bounties'. 9. Our Lord! You will certainly gather all humanity for the 'promised' Day—about which there is no doubt. Surely God does not break His promise."

Punishment of the Disbelievers

10. Indeed, neither the wealth nor children[117] of the disbelievers will be of any benefit to them against God—and they will be the fuel for the Fire. 11. Their fate will be like that of the people of Pharaoh and those before them—they all rejected Our signs, so God seized them for their sins. And God is severe in punishment. 12. 'O Prophet!' Tell the disbelievers, "Soon you will be overpowered and driven to Hell—what an evil place to rest!"

---

115 The one distinguishing between right and wrong (*Al-Furqãn*) is one of the names of the Quran.
116 The precise verses are easy to understand and deal mostly with matters of belief and practice, such as the belief in one God (Chapter 112), forbidden foods (*see* 5:3), and the commandments in 6:151-152 and 17:23-39. As for the elusive verses, their full meaning is known only to God, such as the meaning of letter combinations at the beginning of some chapters, such as *Alif-Lãm-Mĩm* (*see* Stylistic Features), and how God is established above the Throne.
117 Wealth and children were considered the most important things in pre-Islamic Arabia, and so the frequent mention of these things in the Quran is meant to represent all worldly gains.

God's Help at the Battle of Badr[118]

13. Indeed, there was a sign for you in the two armies that met in battle—one fighting for the cause of God and the other in denial. The believers saw their enemy twice their number.[119] But God supports with His victory whoever He wills. Surely in this is a lesson for people of insight.

Temporary Pleasures

14. The enjoyment of ʿworldlyʾ desires—women, children,[120] treasures of gold and silver, fine horses, cattle, and fertile land—has been made appealing to people. These are the pleasures of this worldly life, but with God is the finest destination.

Everlasting Delight

15. Say, ʿO Prophet,ʾ "Shall I inform you of what is better than ʿall ofʾ this? Those mindful ʿof Godʾ will have Gardens with their Lord under which rivers flow, to stay there forever, and pure spouses,[121] along with God's pleasure." And God is All-Seeing of ʿHisʾ servants, **16.** who pray, "Our Lord! We have believed, so forgive our sins and protect us from the torment of the Fire." **17.** ʿIt is theyʾ who are patient, sincere, obedient, and charitable, and who pray for forgiveness before dawn.[122]

One God

18. God ʿHimselfʾ is a Witness that there is no god ʿworthy of worshipʾ except Him—and so are the angels and people of knowledge. He is the Maintainer of jus-

tice. There is no god ʿworthy of worshipʾ except Him—the Almighty, All-Wise.

One Way

19. Certainly, God's only Way is Islam.[123] Those who were given the Scripture did not dispute ʿamong themselvesʾ out of mutual envy until knowledge came to them.[124] Whoever denies God's signs, then surely God is swift in reckoning. **20.** So if they argue with you ʿO Prophetʾ, say, "I have submitted myself to God, and so have my followers." And ask those who were given the Scripture and the illiterate ʿpeopleʾ,[125] "Have you submitted yourselves ʿto Godʾ?" If they submit, they will be ʿrightlyʾ guided. But if they turn away, then your duty is only to deliver ʿthe messageʾ. And God is All-Seeing of ʿHisʾ servants.

Reward of the Rebellious

21. Indeed, those who deny God's signs, kill the prophets unjustly, and kill people who stand up for justice—give them good news of a painful punishment. **22.** They are the ones whose deeds are wasted in this world and the Hereafter. And they will have no helpers.

Rejecting God's Judgment

23. Have you not seen those who were given a portion of the Scriptures?[126] Yet when they are invited to the Book of God to settle their disputes, some of them turn away heedlessly. **24.** This is because they say, "The Fire will not touch us except for a few days." They

---

118 Badr is the name of the location where the Muslim army and the pagan army of Mecca fought in 2 A.H./624 C.E. The Muslim army was made up of over 300 soldiers whereas the pagan army was over 1000.
119 It can also be understood that the disbelievers were made to think there were twice as many believers in the battlefield.
120 *Banîn* means sons. In the ancient Arab culture, sons were a source of pride for their parents and tribes. This is because they provided for their families and took up arms in defence of their tribes.
121 *See* footnote for 2:25.
122 Optional prayers before dawn are recommended and are more likely to be accepted.
123 i.e., full submission to the Will of God.
124 No community split into believers and disbelievers until they received the knowledge given by their prophet.
125 This refers to the pagans of Arabia before Islam.
126 i.e., the Torah.

have been deceived in their faith by their wishful lying. **25.** But how ʿhorribleʾ will it be when We gather them together on the Day about which there is no doubt—when every soul will be paid in full for what it has done, and none will be wronged!

God's Infinite Power

26. Say, ʿO Prophet,ʾ "O God! Lord over all authorities! You give authority to whoever You please and remove it from who You please; You honour whoever You please and disgrace who You please—all good is in Your Hands. Surely You ʿaloneʾ are Most Capable of everything. **27.** You cause the night to pass into the day and the day into the night. You bring forth the living from the dead and the dead from the living. And You provide for whoever You will without limit."

Taking Disbelievers as Guardians[127]

28. Believers should not take disbelievers as guardians instead of the believers—and whoever does so will have nothing to hope for from God—unless it is a precaution against their tyranny. And God warns you about Himself. And to God is the final return.

God's Infinite Knowledge

29. Say, ʿO Prophet,ʾ "Whether you conceal what is in your hearts or reveal it, it is known to God. For He knows whatever is in the heavens and whatever is on the earth. And God is Most Capable of everything."

Accountability for Good and Evil

30. ʿWatch forʾ the Day when every soul will be presented with whatever good it has done. And it will wish that its misdeeds were far off. And God warns you about Himself. And God is Ever Gracious to ʿHisʾ servants.

Obeying God and His Messenger

31. Say, ʿO Prophet,ʾ "If you ʿsincerelyʾ love God, then follow me; God will love you and forgive your sins. For God is All-Forgiving, Most Merciful." **32.** Say, ʿO Prophet,ʾ "Obey God and His Messenger." If they still turn away, then truly God does not like the disbelievers.

Blessed People

33. Indeed, God chose Adam, Noah, the family of Abraham, and the family of 'Imrân above all people ʿof their timeʾ. **34.** They are descendants of one another. And God is All-Hearing, All-Knowing.

Birth of Mary

35. ʿRememberʾ when the wife of 'Imrân said, "My Lord! I dedicate what is in my womb entirely to Your service,[128] so accept it from me. You ʿaloneʾ are truly the All-Hearing, All-Knowing." **36.** When she delivered, she said, "My Lord! I have given birth to a girl,"—and God fully knew what she had delivered—"and the male is not like the female.[129] I have named her Mary, and I seek Your protection for her and her offspring from Satan, the accursed."[130] **37.** So her Lord accepted her graciously and blessed her with a pleasant upbringing—entrusting her to the care of Zachariah. Whenever Zachariah visited her in the sanctuary, he found her supplied with provisions. He exclaimed, "O Mary! Where did this come from?" She replied, "It is from God. Surely God provides for whoever He wills without limit."

Birth of John the Baptist

38. Then and there Zachariah prayed to his Lord, saying, "My Lord! Grant me—by your grace—righteous offspring. You are

---

127 Like 4:139 and 4:144, this verse forbids the believers from taking the disbelievers who were at war with Muslims as strategic allies.
128 i.e., dedicating the child to service in the temple.
129 Service at the temple was hosted by males only.
130 The prayers of Mary's mother were answered. In a *ḥadîth* collected by Bukhâri and Muslim, the Prophet says, "Every child is touched by Satan when they are born—and they cry because of this contact—except Jesus and his mother."

certainly the Hearer of ˹all˺ prayers." **39.** So the angels called out to him while he stood praying in the sanctuary, "God gives you good news of ˹the birth of˺ John who will confirm the Word of God and will be a great leader, chaste, and a prophet among the righteous." **40.** Zachariah exclaimed, "My Lord! How can I have a son when I am very old and my wife is barren?" He replied, "So will it be. God does what He wills." **41.** Zachariah said, "My Lord! Grant me a sign." He said, "Your sign is that you will not ˹be able to˺ speak to people for three days except through gestures. Remember your Lord often and glorify ˹Him˺ morning and evening."

Mary Chosen over All Women

42. And ˹remember˺ when the angels said, "O Mary! Surely God has selected you, purified you, and chosen you over all women of the world. **43.** O Mary! Be devout to your Lord, prostrate yourself ˹in prayer˺ and bow along with those who bow down." **44.** This is news of the unseen that We reveal to you ˹O Prophet˺. You were not with them when they cast lots to decide who would be Mary's guardian, nor were you there when they argued ˹about it˺.

Birth of Jesus Christ

45. ˹Remember˺ when the angels proclaimed, "O Mary! God gives you good news of a Word[131] from Him, his name will be the Messiah,[132] Jesus, son of Mary; honoured in this world and the Hereafter, and he will be one of those nearest ˹to God˺. **46.** And he will speak to people in ˹his˺ infancy and adulthood and will be one of the righteous." **47.** Mary wondered, "My Lord! How can I have a child when no man has ever touched me?" An angel replied, "So will it be. God creates what He wills. When

He decrees a matter, He simply tells it, 'Be!' And it is!

The Mission and Miracles of Jesus

48. "And God will teach him writing and wisdom, the Torah and the Gospel, **49.** and ˹make him˺ a messenger to the Children of Israel ˹to proclaim,˺ 'I have come to you with a sign from your Lord: I will make for you a bird from clay, breathe into it, and it will become a ˹real˺ bird—by God's Will. I will heal the blind and the leper and raise the dead to life—by God's Will. And I will prophesize what you eat and store in your houses. Surely in this is a sign for you if you ˹truly˺ believe. **50.** And I will confirm the Torah revealed before me and legalize some of what had been forbidden to you. I have come to you with a sign from your Lord, so be mindful of God and obey me. **51.** Surely God is my Lord and your Lord. So worship Him ˹alone˺. This is the Straight Path.'"

The Disciples

52. When Jesus sensed disbelief from his people, he asked, "Who will stand up with me for God?" The disciples replied, "We will stand up for God. We believe in God, so bear witness that we have submitted." **53.** ˹They prayed to God,˺ "Our Lord! We believe in Your revelations and follow the messenger, so count us among those who bear witness."

Conspiracy Against Jesus

54. And the disbelievers made a plan ˹against Jesus˺, but God also planned—and God is the best of planners. **55.** ˹Remember˺ when God said, "O Jesus! I will take you[133] and raise you up to Myself. I will deliver you from those who disbelieve, and elevate your followers above the disbelievers until

---

131 In the Quran, Jesus is called the "Word" of God since he was created with the word "Be!"
132 Messiah (*Masîḥ*) means the "anointed one." It is used in the Quran exclusively as a title for Jesus Christ.
133 *'Mutawaffika'* means literally: "I will make you reach the end of your worldly term." The popular Muslim belief is that a conspiracy was made to kill Jesus. God made the main culprit who betrayed Jesus look exactly like Jesus, while the culprit was crucified. Similar to Christians, Muslims believe in the second coming of Jesus.

the Day of Judgment. Then to Me you will ˹all˺ return, and I will settle all your disputes.

Fair Reward

56. "As for those who disbelieve, I will subject them to a severe punishment in this life and the Hereafter, and they will have no helpers. **57.** And as for those who believe and do good, they will be rewarded in full. And God does not like the wrongdoers." **58.** We recite ˹all˺ this to you ˹O Prophet˺ as one of the signs[134] and ˹as˺ a wise reminder.

Jesus and Adam

59. Indeed, the example of Jesus in the sight of God is like that of Adam. He created him from dust, then said to him, "Be!" And he was! **60.** This is the truth from your Lord, so do not be one of those who doubt.

Disputes over Jesus

61. Now, whoever disputes with you ˹O Prophet˺ concerning Jesus after full knowledge has come to you, say, "Come! Let us gather our children and your children, our women and your women, ourselves and yourselves—then let us sincerely invoke God's curse upon the liars." **62.** Certainly, this is the true narrative, and there is no god ˹worthy of worship˺ except God. And indeed, God ˹alone˺ is the Almighty, All-Wise. **63.** If they turn away, then surely God has ˹perfect˺ knowledge of the corruptors.

Devotion to God Alone

64. Say, ˹O Prophet,˺ "O People of the Book! Let us come to common terms: that we will worship none but God, associate none with Him, nor take one another as lords instead of God." But if they turn away, then say, "Bear witness that we have submitted ˹to God alone˺.'"

The Truth About Abraham

65. O People of the Book! Why do you argue about Abraham, while the Torah and the Gospel were not revealed until long after him? Do you not understand? **66.** Here you are! You disputed about what you have ˹little˺ knowledge of,[135] but why do you now argue about what you have no knowledge of?[136] God knows and you do not know. **67.** Abraham was neither a Jew nor a Christian; he submitted in all uprightness[137] and was not a polytheist. **68.** Indeed, those who have the best claim to Abraham are his followers, this Prophet,[138] and the believers. And God is the Guardian of those who believe.

Distorting the Truth

69. Some of the People of the Book wish to mislead you ˹believers˺. They mislead none but themselves, yet they fail to perceive it. **70.** O People of the Book! Why do you reject the signs of God while you bear witness ˹to their truth˺? **71.** O People of the Book! Why do you mix the truth with falsehood and hide the truth knowingly?

Deception Exposed

72. A group among the People of the Book said ˹to one another˺, "Believe in what has been revealed to the believers in the morning and reject it in the evening, so they may abandon their faith. **73.** And only believe those who follow your religion." Say, ˹O Prophet,˺ "Surely, ˹the only˺ true guidance is God's guidance." ˹They also said,˺ "Do not believe that someone will receive ˹revealed˺ knowledge similar to yours or argue against you before your Lord." Say, ˹O Prophet,˺ "Indeed, all bounty is in the Hands of God— He grants it to whoever He wills. And God is All-Bountiful, All-Knowing." **74.** He chooses whoever He wills to receive His mercy. And God is the Lord of infinite bounty.

---

134 As a testament to your prophethood.
135 The perception of Jesus.
136 Abraham being Jewish or Christian.
137 Linguistically, "Muslim" means "someone who has submitted themselves to God."
138 Muḥammad.

Honouring Trusts

75. There are some among the People of the Book who, if entrusted with a stack of gold, will readily return it. Yet there are others who, if entrusted with a single coin, will not repay it unless you constantly demand it. This is because they say, "We are not accountable for ˹exploiting˺ the Gentiles."[139] And ˹so˺ they attribute lies to God knowingly. **76.** Absolutely! Those who honour their trusts and shun evil—surely God loves those who are mindful ˹of Him˺.

Breaking God's Covenant

77. Indeed, those who trade God's covenant and their oaths for a fleeting gain will have no share in the Hereafter. God will neither speak to them, nor look at them, nor purify them on the Day of Judgment. And they will suffer a painful punishment.

Distorting the Scripture

78. There are some among them who distort the Book with their tongues to make you think this ˹distortion˺ is from the Book—but it is not what the Book says. They say, "It is from God"—but it is not from God. And ˹so˺ they attribute lies to God knowingly.

Prophets Never Claim Divinity

79. It is not appropriate for someone who God has blessed with the Scripture, wisdom, and prophethood to say to people, "Worship me instead of God." Rather, he would say, "Be devoted to the worship of your Lord ˹alone˺, by virtue of what you read in the Scripture and what you teach." **80.** And he would never ask you to take angels and prophets as lords. Would he ask you to disbelieve after you have submitted?

God's Covenant with Prophets

81. ˹Remember˺ when God made a covenant with the prophets, ˹saying,˺ "Now that I have given you the Book and wisdom, if there comes to you a messenger[140] confirming what you have, you must believe in him and support him." He added, "Do you affirm this covenant and accept this commitment?" They said, "Yes, we do." God said, "Then bear witness, and I too am a Witness." **82.** Whoever turns back after this, they will be the rebellious.

Full Submission

83. Do they desire a way other than God's—knowing that all those in the heavens and the earth submit to His Will, willingly or unwillingly, and to Him they will ˹all˺ be returned?

Prophets of Islam

84. Say, ˹O Prophet,˺ "We believe in God and what has been revealed to us and what was revealed to Abraham, Ishmael, Isaac, Jacob, and his descendants; and what was given to Moses, Jesus, and other prophets from their Lord—we make no distinction between any of them, and to Him we ˹fully˺ submit."

The Only Way

85. Whoever seeks a way other than Islam,[141] it will never be accepted from them, and in the Hereafter they will be among the losers.

Deviating from the Right Path

86. How will God guide a people who chose to disbelieve after they had believed, acknowledged the Messenger to be true, and received clear proofs? For God does not guide the wrongdoing people. **87.** Their reward is that they will be condemned by God, the angels, and all of humanity. **88.** They will be in Hell forever. Their punishment will not be lightened, nor will they be delayed ˹from it˺. **89.** As for those who repent afterwards and mend their ways, then surely God is All-Forgiving, Most Merciful.

---

139 "Gentiles" here refers to the pagans of Arabia.
140 Muḥammad.
141 i.e., full submission to the Will of God.

Dying in a State of Disbelief

90. Indeed, those who disbelieve after having believed then increase in disbelief, their repentance will never be accepted.[142] It is they who are astray. **91.** Indeed, if each of those who disbelieve then die as disbelievers were to offer a ransom of enough gold to fill the whole world, it would never be accepted from them. It is they who will suffer a painful punishment, and they will have no helpers.

Righteous Giving

92. You will never achieve righteousness until you donate some of what you cherish. And whatever you give is certainly well known to God.

Jacob's Dietary Restriction

93. All food was lawful for the children of Israel, except what Israel[143] made unlawful for himself before the Torah was revealed.[144] Say, 'O Prophet,' "Bring the Torah and read it, if your claims are true." **94.** Then whoever still fabricates lies about God, they will be the 'true' wrongdoers. **95.** Say, 'O Prophet,' "God has declared the truth. So follow the Way of Abraham, the upright—who was not a polytheist."

Pilgrimage to the Sacred House in Mecca

96. Surely the first House 'of worship' established for humanity is the one at Bakkah—a blessed sanctuary and a guide for 'all' people. **97.** In it are clear signs and the standing-place of Abraham. Whoever enters it should be safe. Pilgrimage to this House is an obligation by God upon whoever is able among the people.[145] And whoever disbelieves, then surely God is not in need of 'any of His' creation.

Rejecting the Truth

98. Say, 'O Prophet,' "O People of the Book! Why do you deny the revelations of God, when God is a Witness to what you do?" **99.** Say, "O People of the Book! Why do you turn the believers away from the Way of God—striving to make it 'appear' crooked, while you are witnesses 'to its truth'? And God is never unaware of what you do."

Warning Against Evil Influence

100. O believers! If you were to yield to a group of those who were given the Scripture, they would turn you back from belief to disbelief. **101.** How can you disbelieve when God's revelations are recited to you and His Messenger is in your midst? Whoever holds firmly to God is surely guided to the Straight Path.

Warning Against Disunity

102. O believers! Be mindful of God in the way He deserves,[146] and do not die except in 'a state of full' submission 'to Him'.[147] **103.** And hold firmly together to the rope of God[148] and do not be divided. Remember God's favour upon you when you were enemies, then He united your hearts, so you—by His grace—became brothers. And you were at the brink of a fiery pit and He saved you from it. This is how God makes His revelations clear to you, so that you may be 'rightly' guided. **104.** Let there be a group among you who call 'others' to goodness, encourage what is good, and forbid what is evil—it is they who will be successful. **105.** And do not be like those who split 'into sects' and differed after clear proofs

---

142   Their repentance will not be accepted if they die as disbelievers.
143   Jacob.
144   When Jacob fell sick, he made camel meat unlawful for himself, but not for the rest of his people.
145   Pilgrimage is obligatory on every Muslim at least once in their lifetime if the person is physically and financially able.
146   Meaning, always be conscious of Him; obedient and grateful to Him.
147   lit., except as Muslims.
148   i.e., God's covenant.

had come to them. It is they who will suffer a tremendous punishment.

The Joyful and the Miserable

106. On that Day some faces will be bright while others gloomy. To the gloomy-faced it will be said, "Did you disbelieve after having believed? So taste the punishment for your disbelief." 107. As for the bright-faced, they will be in God's mercy, where they will remain forever. 108. These are God's revelations We recite to you ˹O Prophet˺ in truth. And God desires no injustice to ˹His˺ creation. 109. To God ˹alone˺ belongs whatever is in the heavens and whatever is on the earth. And to God ˹all˺ matters will be returned ˹for judgment˺.

Excellence of the Muslim Nation

110. You are the best community ever raised for humanity—you encourage good, forbid evil, and believe in God. Had the People of the Book believed, it would have been better for them. Some of them are faithful, but most are rebellious.

Reward of the Rebellious

111. They can never inflict harm on you, except a little annoyance.[149] But if they meet you in battle, they will flee and they will have no helpers. 112. They will be stricken with disgrace wherever they go, unless they are protected by a covenant with God or a treaty with the people. They have invited the displeasure of God and have been branded with misery for rejecting God's revelations and murdering ˹His˺ prophets unjustly. This is ˹a fair reward˺ for their disobedience and violations.

Upright People of the Book

113. Yet they are not all alike: there are some among the People of the Book who are up-right, who recite God's revelations throughout the night, prostrating ˹in prayer˺. 114. They believe in God and the Last Day, encourage good and forbid evil, and race with one another in doing good. They are ˹truly˺ among the righteous. 115. They will never be denied the reward for any good they have done. And God has ˹perfect˺ knowledge of those mindful ˹of Him˺.

Warning Against Hypocrites

116. Indeed, neither the wealth nor children of the disbelievers will be of any benefit to them against God. It is they who will be the residents of the Fire. They will be there forever. 117. The good they do in this worldly life is like the harvest of an evil people struck by a bitter wind, destroying it ˹completely˺. God never wronged them, but they wronged themselves.

Association with Hypocrites

118. O believers! Do not associate closely with others who would not miss a chance to harm you. Their only desire is to see you suffer. Their prejudice has become evident from what they say—and what their hearts hide is far worse. We have made Our revelations clear to you, if only you understood. 119. Here you are! You love them but they do not love you, and you believe in all Scriptures. When they meet you they say, "We believe." But when alone, they bite their fingertips in rage. Say, ˹O Prophet,˺ "˹May you˺ die of your rage!" Surely God knows best what is ˹hidden˺ in the heart. 120. When you ˹believers˺ are touched with good, they grieve; but when you are afflicted with evil, they rejoice. ˹Yet,˺ if you are patient and mindful ˹of God˺, their schemes will not harm you in the least. Surely God is Fully Aware of what they do.

---

149   i.e., they can only annoy you with their words.

The Battle of Uḥud[150]

121. ˹Remember, O Prophet,˺ when you left your home in the early morning to position the believers in the battlefield. And God is All-Hearing, All-Knowing. **122.** ˹Remember˺ when two groups among you ˹believers˺ were about to cower, then God reassured them. So in God let the believers put their trust.

The Battle of Badr

123. Indeed, God made you victorious at Badr when you were ˹vastly˺ outnumbered. So be mindful of God, perhaps you will be grateful. **124.** ˹Remember, O Prophet,˺ when you said to the believers, "Is it not enough that your Lord will send down a reinforcement of three thousand angels for your aid?" **125.** Most certainly, if you ˹believers˺ are firm and mindful ˹of God˺ and the enemy launches a sudden attack on you, God will reinforce you with five thousand angels designated ˹for battle˺. **126.** God ordained this ˹reinforcement˺ only as good news for you and reassurance for your hearts. And victory comes only from God—the Almighty, All-Wise— **127.** to destroy a group of the disbelievers and humble the rest, causing them to withdraw in disappointment.

God Is the Judge

128. You ˹O Prophet˺ have no say in the matter.[151] It is up to God to turn to them in mercy or punish them, for indeed they are wrongdoers. **129.** To God ˹alone˺ belongs whatever is in the heavens and whatever is on the earth. He forgives whoever He wills, and punishes whoever He wills. And God is All-Forgiving, Most Merciful.

Warning Against Interest

130. O believers! Do not consume interest, multiplying it many times over. And be mindful of God, so you may prosper. **131.** Guard yourselves against the Fire prepared for the disbelievers. **132.** Obey God and the Messenger, so you may be shown mercy.

Reward of the Righteous

133. And hasten towards forgiveness from your Lord and a Paradise as vast as the heavens and the earth, prepared for those mindful ˹of God˺. **134.** ˹They are˺ those who donate in prosperity and adversity, control their anger, and pardon others. And God loves the good-doers. **135.** ˹They are˺ those who, upon committing an evil deed or wronging themselves, remember God and seek forgiveness for their sins—and who forgives sins except God?—and they do not knowingly persist in wrongdoing. **136.** Their reward is forgiveness from their Lord and Gardens under which rivers flow, staying there forever. How excellent is the reward for those who work ˹righteousness˺!

Battle Between Good and Evil

137. Similar situations came to pass before you, so travel throughout the land and see the fate of the deniers. **138.** This[152] is an insight to humanity—a guide and a lesson to the God-fearing.

---

150   Uḥud is the name of the location where a battle took place in 3 A.H./625 C.E. between 750 Muslims and 3700 Meccans. This battle came only a year after the Meccan army was defeated at the Battle of Badr by the vastly outnumbered Muslim army. Initially, Muslims were winning the second battle. However, events took a different turn when the archers, who had been positioned by the Prophet on the mount of Uḥud, left their strategic position in pursuit of spoils of war—allowing a surprise attack by the Meccan cavalry. Many Muslims were martyred and Prophet Muḥammad himself was injured.

151   When the Prophet was injured at the Battle of Uḥud, some of his companions suggested that he should pray against the pagans of Mecca. He responded, "I have not come to condemn people, but as a mercy to pray for their guidance." The verse here says that it is not up to the Prophet whether they believe or disbelieve. A prophet's only duty is to convey the message. Eventually, almost all Meccans accepted Islam before the death of the Prophet.

152   "This" either refers to how the forces of evil are ultimately destroyed, or that the Quran is a reminder of the destruction of evildoers.

Reassuring the Believers

139. Do not falter or grieve, for you will have the upper hand, if you are ʿtrueʾ believers. **140.** If you have suffered injuries ʿat Uḥudʾ, they suffered similarly ʿat Badrʾ. We alternate these days ʿof victory and defeatʾ among people so that God may reveal the ʿtrueʾ believers, choose martyrs from among you—and God does not like the wrongdoers— **141.** and distinguish the ʿtrueʾ believers and destroy the disbelievers.

Believers Tested

142. Do you think you will enter Paradise without God proving which of you ʿtrulyʾ struggled ʿfor His causeʾ and patiently endured? **143.** You certainly wished ʿfor the opportunityʾ for martyrdom before encountering it, now you have seen it with your own eyes.

Believers Disheartened[153]

144. Muḥammad is no more than a messenger; other messengers have gone before him. If he were to die or to be killed, would you regress into disbelief? Those who do so will not harm God whatsoever. And God will reward those who are grateful. **145.** No soul can ever die without God's Will at the destined time. Those who desire worldly gain, We will let them have it, and those who desire heavenly reward, We will grant it to them. And We will reward those who are grateful.

Reward of the Steadfast

146. ʿImagineʾ how many devotees fought along with their prophets and never faltered despite whatever ʿlossesʾ they suffered in the cause of God, nor did they weaken or give in! God loves those who persevere. **147.** And all they said was, "Our Lord! Forgive our sins and excesses, make our steps firm, and give us victory over the disbelieving people." **148.** So God gave them the reward of this world and the excellent reward of the Hereafter. For God loves the good-doers.

Yielding to the Disbelievers

149. O believers! If you yield to the disbelievers, they will drag you back to disbelief—and you will become losers. **150.** But no! God is your Guardian, and He is the best Helper. **151.** We will cast horror into the hearts of the disbelievers for associating ʿfalse godsʾ with God—a practice He has never authorized. The Fire will be their home—what an evil place for the wrongdoers to stay!

Victory Denied at Uḥud

152. Indeed, God fulfilled His promise to you when you ʿinitiallyʾ swept them away by His Will, then your courage weakened and you disputed about the command and disobeyed,[154] after God had brought victory within your reach. Some of you were after worldly gain while others desired a heavenly reward. He denied you victory over them as a test, yet He has pardoned you. And God is Gracious to the believers.

The Army Retreats

153. ʿRememberʾ when you were running far away ʿin panicʾ—not looking at anyone—while the Messenger was calling to you from behind! So God rewarded your disobedience with distress upon distress. Now, do not grieve over the victory you were denied or the injury you suffered. And God is All-Aware of what you do. **154.** Then after distress, He sent down serenity in the form of drowsiness overcoming some of you, while others were disturbed by evil thoughts about God—the thoughts of ʿpre-Islamicʾ ignorance. They ask, "Do we

---

153 The faith of many Muslims was shaken when the pagan army spread rumours that Muḥammad was killed in the Battle of Uḥud.
154 The archers disputed whether to keep their positions after the initial victory. Eventually, most of them decided to go in pursuit of the spoils of war, disobeying the Prophet's direct orders not to leave their position no matter what happened. Defeat became inevitable.

have a say in the matter?" Say, ˈO Prophet,ˈ "All matters are destined by God." They conceal in their hearts what they do not reveal to you. They say ˈto themselvesˈ, "If we had any say in the matter, none of us would have come to die here." Say, ˈO Prophet,ˈ "Even if you were to remain in your homes, those among you who were destined to be killed would have met the same fate." Through this, God tests what is within you and purifies what is in your hearts. And God knows best what is ˈhiddenˈ in the heart.

The Deserters

155. Indeed, those ˈbelieversˈ who fled on the day when the two armies met were made to slip by Satan because of their misdeeds. But God has pardoned them. Surely God is All-Forgiving, Most Forbearing.

It Is All Destined

156. O believers! Do not be like the unfaithful[155] who say about their brothers who travel throughout the land or engage in battle, "If they had stayed with us, they would not have died or been killed." God makes such thinking a cause of agony in their hearts. It is God who gives life and causes death. And God is All-Seeing of what you do. **157.** Should you be martyred or die in the cause of God, then His forgiveness and mercy are far better than whatever ˈwealthˈ those ˈwho stay behindˈ accumulate. **158.** Whether you die or are martyred—all of you will be gathered before God.

Prophet's Kindness to the Believers

159. It is out of God's mercy that you ˈO Prophetˈ have been lenient with them. Had you been cruel or hard-hearted, they would have certainly abandoned you. So pardon them, ask God's forgiveness for them, and consult with them in ˈconductingˈ matters. Once you make a decision, put your trust in God. Surely God loves those who trust in Him.

Victory Is from God

160. If God helps you, none can defeat you. But if He denies you help, then who else can help you? So in God let the believers put their trust.

Spoils of War

161. It is not appropriate for a prophet to illegally withhold spoils of war. And whoever does so, it will be held against them on the Day of Judgment. Then every soul will be paid in full for what it has done, and none will be wronged.

Good-Doers and Wrongdoers

162. Are those who seek God's pleasure like those who deserve God's wrath? Hell is their home. What an evil destination! **163.** They ˈeachˈ have varying degrees in the sight of God. And God is All-Seeing of what they do.

The Prophet as a Blessing

164. Indeed, God has done the believers a ˈgreatˈ favour by raising a messenger from among them—reciting to them His revelations, purifying them, and teaching them the Book and wisdom. For indeed they had previously been clearly astray.

Lessons from the Battle of Uḥud

165. Why is it when you suffered casualities ˈat Uḥudˈ—although you had made your enemy suffer twice as much ˈat Badrˈ—you protested, "How could this be?"? Say, ˈO Prophet,ˈ "It is because of your disobedience." Surely God is Most Capable of everything. **166.** So what you suffered on the day the two armies met was by God's Will, so that He might distinguish the ˈtrueˈ believers **167.** and expose the hypocrites. When it was said to them, "Come fight in the cause of God or ˈat leastˈ defend yourselves," they replied, "If we had known there was fighting, we would have definitely gone with you." They were closer to disbelief than to belief on that day—for saying with their mouths what was

---

155 i.e., the hypocrites.

not in their hearts. God is All-Knowing of what they hide. **168.** Those who sat at home, saying about their brothers, "Had they listened to us, they would not have been killed." Say, ˹O Prophet,˼ "Try not to die[156] if what you say is true!"

Martyrs Honoured

169. Never think of those martyred in the cause of God as dead. In fact, they are alive with their Lord, well provided for— **170.** rejoicing in God's bounties and being delighted for those yet to join them. There will be no fear for them, nor will they grieve. **171.** They are joyful for receiving God's grace and bounty, and that God does not deny the reward of the believers.

Reward of the Steadfast

172. ˹As for˼ those who responded to the call of God and His Messenger after their injury,[157] those of them who did good and were mindful ˹of God˼ will have a great reward. **173.** Those who were warned, "Your enemies have mobilized their forces against you, so fear them," the warning only made them grow stronger in faith and they replied, "God ˹alone˼ is sufficient ˹as an aid˼ for us and ˹He˼ is the best Protector." **174.** So they returned with God's favours and grace, suffering no harm. For they sought to please God. And surely God is ˹the˼ Lord of infinite bounty. **175.** That ˹warning˼ was only ˹from˼ Satan, trying to prompt you to fear his followers.[158] So do not fear them; fear Me if you are ˹true˼ believers.

Disbelievers' Delusion

176. ˹O Prophet!˼ Do not grieve for those who race to disbelieve—surely they will not harm God in the least. It is God's Will to disallow them a share in the Hereafter, and they will suffer a tremendous punishment. **177.** Those who trade belief for disbelief will never harm God in the least, and they will suffer a painful punishment. **178.** Those who disbelieve should not think that living longer is good for them. They are only given more time to increase in sin, and they will suffer a humiliating punishment.

Sincerity Test

179. God would not leave the believers in the condition you were in, until He distinguished the good from the evil ˹among you˼. Nor would God ˹directly˼ reveal to you the unseen,[159] but He chooses whoever He Wills as a messenger. So believe in God and His messengers. And if you are faithful and mindful ˹of God˼, you will receive a great reward.

Reward of the Stingy

180. And do not let those who ˹greedily˼ withhold God's bounties think it is good for them—in fact, it is bad for them! They will be leashed ˹by their necks˼ on the Day of Judgment with whatever ˹wealth˼ they used to withhold. And God is the ˹sole˼ inheritor of the heavens and the earth. And God is All-Aware of what you do.

Blasphemy Exposed

181. Indeed, God has heard those ˹among the Jews˼ who said, "God is poor; we are rich!" We have certainly recorded their slurs

---

156 i.e., try not to die when your time comes.
157 The Prophet realized that the city of Medina became vulnerable after the Muslim loss at Uḥud. So on the next day of the battle he decided to lead a small force of his companions—many of whom had been wounded at Uḥud—to chase away the Meccan army which was camping at a place called Ḥamrâ' Al-Asad—not far from Medina. Abu Sufyân, commander of the Meccan army, sent a man to discourage the Muslims from following the Meccans. Although the man falsely claimed that the Meccans were mobilizing to launch a decisive attack on Medina, the Prophet became more determined to chase them away. Eventually, the Meccans decided to flee and not waste their victory after the Prophet sent a revert to Islam—who was friends with Abu Sufyân—to convince him to withdraw; otherwise Muslims were going to avenge their loss at Uḥud.
158 This refers to the warning mentioned in 3:173.
159 i.e., the distinction between the true believers and hypocrites.

and their killing of prophets unjustly. Then We will say, "Taste the torment of burning! **182.** This is ˹the reward˺ for what your hands have done. And God is never unjust to ˹His˺ creation."

Rejecting God's Messengers

183. Those ˹are the same people˺ who say, "God has commanded us not to believe in any messenger unless he brings us an offering to be consumed by fire ˹from the sky˺." Say, ˹O Prophet,˺ "Other prophets did in fact come to you[160] before me with clear proofs and ˹even˺ what you demanded—why then did you kill them, if what you say is true?" **184.** If you are rejected by them, so too were messengers before you who came with clear proofs, divine Books, and enlightening Scriptures.[161]

Death Is Inevitable

185. Every soul will taste death. And you will only receive your full reward on the Day of Judgment. Whoever is spared from the Fire and is admitted into Paradise will ˹indeed˺ triumph, whereas the life of this world is no more than the delusion of enjoyment.

Patience Tested

186. You ˹believers˺ will surely be tested in your wealth and yourselves,[162] and you will certainly hear many hurtful words from those who were given the Scripture before you and ˹from˺ the polytheists. But if you are patient and mindful ˹of God˺—surely this is a resolve to aspire to.

Breaking God's Covenant

187. ˹Remember, O Prophet,˺ when God took the covenant of those who were given the Scripture to make it known to people and not hide it, yet they cast it behind their backs and traded it for a fleeting gain. What a miserable profit! **188.** Do not let those who

rejoice in their misdeeds and love to take credit for what they have not done think they will escape torment. They will suffer a painful punishment.

God's Signs

189. To God ˹alone˺ belongs the kingdom of the heavens and the earth. And God is Most Capable of everything. **190.** Indeed, in the creation of the heavens and the earth and the alternation of the day and night there are signs for people of reason.

A Prayer of the Righteous

191. ˹They are˺ those who remember God while standing, sitting, and lying on their sides, and reflect on the creation of the heavens and the earth ˹and pray˺, "Our Lord! You have not created ˹all of˺ this without purpose. Glory be to You! Protect us from the torment of the Fire. **192.** Our Lord! Indeed, those You commit to the Fire will be ˹completely˺ disgraced! And the wrongdoers will have no helpers. **193.** Our Lord! We have heard the caller[163] to ˹true˺ belief, ˹proclaiming,˺ 'Believe in your Lord ˹alone˺,' so we believed. Our Lord! Forgive our sins, absolve us of our misdeeds, and join us with the virtuous when we die. **194.** Our Lord! Grant us what You have promised us through Your messengers and do not put us to shame on Judgment Day—for certainly You never fail in Your promise."

Prayers Answered

195. So their Lord responded to them: "I will never deny any of you—male or female—the reward of your deeds. Both are equal in reward. Those who migrated or were expelled from their homes, and were persecuted for My sake and fought and ˹some˺ were martyred—I will certainly forgive their sins and admit them into Gardens under which rivers

---

160 i.e., your forefathers.
161 i.e., the original Torah of Moses and the Gospel of Jesus.
162 Meaning, a believer is always tested through the loss of wealth as well as sickness, injuries, and the loss of life.
163 The caller is Muḥammad.

flow, as a reward from God. And with God is the finest reward!"

Disbelievers' Brief Enjoyment

196. Do not be deceived by the prosperity of the disbelievers throughout the land. **197.** It is only a brief enjoyment. Then Hell will be their home—what an evil place to rest!

Believers' Everlasting Delight

198. But those who are mindful of their Lord will be in Gardens under which rivers flow, to stay there forever—as an accommodation from God. And what is with God is best for the virtuous.

Believers Among People of the Book

199. Indeed, there are some among the People of the Book who truly believe in God and what has been revealed to you 'believers' and what was revealed to them. They humble themselves before God—never trading God's revelations for a fleeting gain. Their reward is with their Lord. Surely God is swift in reckoning.

Advice for Success

200. O believers! Patiently endure, persevere, stand on guard,[164] and be mindful of God, so you may be successful.

4. Women (An-Nisâ')

This chapter focuses on the rights of women (hence the chapter's name), the law of inheritance, care for orphans, lawful and unlawful women to marry, and standing for justice (see the remarkable example of justice to a Jew in verses 105-112). As the chapter progresses, the focus shifts to the etiquette of striving in the cause of God and the relationship between Muslims and the People of the Book, culminating in a rebuttal to the claims about the crucifixion and divinity of Jesus. Like the previous and the next chapters, this chapter also deals with the issue of hypocrisy—a common theme in many other Medinian chapters.

In the Name of God—the Most Compassionate, Most Merciful

Commitment to God and Kinship Ties

1. O humanity! Be mindful of your Lord Who created you from a single soul, and from it He created its mate,[165] and through both He spread countless men and women. And be mindful of God—in Whose Name you appeal to one another—and 'honour' family ties. Surely God is ever Watchful over you.

Orphans Given back Their Wealth

2. Give orphans their wealth 'when they reach maturity', and do not exchange your worthless possessions for their valuables, nor cheat them by mixing their wealth with your own. For this would indeed be a great sin.

Bridal Gifts

3. If you fear you might fail to give orphan women their 'due' rights 'if you were to marry them', then marry other women of

---

164   Râbiṭo refers to watching over the borders of one's homeland. It can also mean keeping up one's prayers.
165   i.e., Adam and Eve.

your choice—two, three, or four. But if you are afraid you will fail to maintain justice, then ´content yourselves with´ one[166] or those ´bondwomen´ in your possession.[167] This way you are less likely to commit injustice. 4. Give women ´you wed´ their due dowries graciously. But if they waive some of it willingly, then you may enjoy it freely with a clear conscience.

Managing Wealth Responsibly

5. Do not entrust the incapable ´among your dependants´ with your wealth which God has made a means of support for you—but feed and clothe them from it, and speak to them kindly.

Orphans' Wealth

6. Test ´the competence of´ the orphans until they reach a marriageable age. Then if you feel they are capable of sound judgment, return their wealth to them. And do not consume it wastefully and hastily before they grow up ´to demand it´. If the guardian is well-off, they should not take compensation; but if the guardian is poor, let them take a reasonable provision. When you give orphans back their property, call in witnesses. And sufficient is God as a ´vigilant´ Reckoner.

Inheritance Law[168] 1) Males & Females

7. For men there is a share in what their parents and close relatives leave, and for women there is a share in what their parents and close relatives leave—whether it is little or much. ´These are´ obligatory shares.

Acts of Kindness

8. If ´non-inheriting´ relatives, orphans,[169] or the needy are present at the time of distribution, offer them a ´small´ provision from it and speak to them kindly.

Caring for Orphans

9. Let the guardians be as concerned ´for the orphans´ as they would if they were to ´die and´ leave ´their own´ helpless children behind. So let them be mindful of God and speak equitably. 10. Indeed, those who unjustly consume orphans' wealth ´in fact´ consume nothing but fire into their bellies. And they will be burned in a blazing Hell!

Inheritance Law 2) Offspring & Parents

11. God commands you regarding your children: the share of the male will be

---

166 The Quran is the only scripture that says marry only one. Unlike any previous faith, Islam puts a limit on the number of wives a man can have. Under certain circumstances, a Muslim man may marry up to four wives as long as he is able to provide for them and maintain justice among them—otherwise it is unlawful. With the exception of Jesus Christ and John the Baptist (neither of whom were married), almost all religious figures in the Bible had more than one wife. According to the Bible, Solomon had 700 wives and 300 concubines (1 Kings 11:3) and his father, David, had many wives and concubines (2 Samuel 5:13).

167 A bondwoman is a female slave that a man owned either through purchase or taking her captive in war—a common ancient practice in many parts of the world. Islam opened the door for ending slavery by making it an act of charity to free slaves. Many sins (such as breaking one's oath, unintentional killing, and intercourse with one's wife during the day of fasting in Ramaḍân) can be atoned by freeing a slave. According to Islamic teachings, no free person can be enslaved. Islam also improved the condition of slaves. It was unlawful to separate a mother from her child. Children born to a slave-master were deemed free, and their mother would gain her freedom upon the death of her master. With regards to slaves, Prophet Muḥammad says, "Feed them from what you eat, clothe them from what you wear, and do not overwhelm them with work unless you assist them." He also says, "Whoever kills his slave will be killed and whoever injures his slave will be injured." In recent times, slavery has been outlawed in all countries—including the Muslim world.

168 Inheritance entitlements of immediate family members (children, parents, full- and half-brothers and sisters, and spouses) are given in the following verses: 7, 11-13, 32-33, and 176. Shares are determined mainly according to the closeness of the heir to the deceased (i.e., close relatives get more than distant relatives), age (i.e., those who are young get more than those who are old), and—to a lesser degree—gender.

169 For example, in the case of orphaned children whose grandfather then dies, leaving behind other children, some scholars rule that an obligatory bequest should be made to them despite not having a share in inheritance.

twice that of the female.[170] If you leave only two 'or more' females, their share is two-thirds of the estate. But if there is only one female, her share will be one-half. Each parent is entitled to one-sixth if you leave offspring.[171] But if you are childless and your parents are the only heirs, then your mother will receive one-third.[172] But if you leave siblings, then your mother will receive one-sixth[173] —after the fulfilment of bequests and debts.[174] 'Be fair to' your parents and children, as you do not 'fully' know who is more beneficial to you.[175] 'This is' an obligation from God. Surely God is All-Knowing, All-Wise.

Inheritance Law 3) Spouses, 4) Maternal Siblings

12. You will inherit half of what your wives leave if they are childless. But if they have children, then 'your share is' one-fourth of the estate—after the fulfilment of bequests and debts. And your wives will inherit one-fourth of what you leave if you are childless. But if you have children, then your wives will receive one-eighth of your estate—after the fulfilment of bequests and debts. And if a man or a woman leaves neither parents nor children but only a brother or a sister

'from their mother's side', they will each inherit one-sixth, but if they are more than one, they 'all' will share one-third of the estate[176]—after the fulfilment of bequests and debts without harm 'to the heirs'.[177] 'This is' a commandment from God. And God is All-Knowing, Most Forbearing.

Compliance with Inheritance Laws

13. These 'entitlements' are the limits set by God. Whoever obeys God and His Messenger will be admitted into Gardens under which rivers flow, to stay there forever. That is the ultimate triumph! 14. But whoever disobeys God and His Messenger and exceeds their limits will be cast into Hell, to stay there forever. And they will suffer a humiliating punishment.

Illegal Sexual Relationships[178]

15. 'As for' those of your women who commit illegal intercourse—call four witnesses from among yourselves. If they testify, confine the offenders to their homes until they die or God ordains a 'different' way for them. 16. And the two among you who commit this sin—discipline them. If they repent and mend their ways, relieve them. Surely God is ever Accepting of Repentance, Most Merciful.

---

170 According to Islamic law of inheritance, a female—whether she is a mother, a wife, a sister, a daughter, etc.—gets one of three shares, depending on her closeness to the deceased:
- *Less than a male's share.* If she is a daughter, she will get half of the share of her brother, since he—unlike his sister—has to provide for the family and pay a dowry at the time of his marriage.
- *More than a male's share.* For example, if a man leaves $24 000 and six sons, two brothers, a wife, and a mother. The wife will get one-eighth ($3000), the mother one-sixth ($4000), each of the sons will receive about $2 833 and the two brothers will not get anything.
- *An equal share.* This is in the case of siblings from the mother's side (mentioned in verse 12 of this chapter).
171 "Offspring" here means any number of children—male or female.
172 And the father will take the rest of the estate.
173 Although the existence of siblings reduces the mother's share from one-third to one-sixth, siblings themselves do not receive a share of inheritance and the rest of the estate goes to the father.
174 Debts as well as any other financial obligations (such as funeral expenses, unfulfilled vows, or unpaid dowry) have to be repaid before the fulfilment of bequests, then the estate can be distributed among the heirs. A person can bequest up to one-third of their estate for charities as well as individuals who are not entitled to a share in inheritance.
175 You do not know who will benefit you by looking after you during your life or doing good deeds on your behalf after your death.
176 If there are two or more brothers and sisters from the mother's side, they share one-third equally—the female will receive the same share of the male.
177 Harming the heirs includes giving away more than one-third of the estate as a bequest.
178 This ruling was later replaced by the punishment mentioned in 24:2.

Accepted and Rejected Repentance

17. God only accepts the repentance of those who commit evil ignorantly ˈor recklesslyˈ then repent soon after[179]—God will pardon them. And God is All-Knowing, All-Wise. **18.** However, repentance is not accepted from those who knowingly persist in sin until they start dying, and then cry, "Now I repent!" nor those who die as disbelievers. For them We have prepared a painful punishment.

Abusing Women Financially

19. O believers! It is not permissible for you to inherit women against their will[180] or mistreat them to make them return some of the dowry ˈas a ransom for divorceˈ—unless they are found guilty of adultery.[181] Treat them fairly. If you happen to dislike them, you may hate something which God turns into a great blessing. **20.** If you desire to replace a wife with another and you have given the former ˈevenˈ a stack of gold ˈas a dowryˈ, do not take any of it back. Would you ˈstillˈ take it unjustly and very sinfully? **21.** And how could you take it back after having enjoyed each other intimately and she has taken from you a firm commitment?[182]

Lawful and Unlawful Women to Marry[183]

22. Do not marry former wives of your fathers—except what was done previously. It was indeed a shameful, despicable, and evil practice. **23.** ˈAlsoˈ forbidden to you for marriage are your mothers, your daughters, your sisters, your paternal and maternal aunts, your brother's daughters, your sister's daughters, your foster-mothers, your foster-sisters, your mothers-in-law, your stepdaughters under your guardianship if you have consummated marriage with their mothers—but if you have not, then you can marry them—nor the wives of your own sons, nor two sisters together at the same time—except what was done previously. Surely God is All-Forgiving, Most Merciful. **24.** Also ˈforbidden areˈ married women—except ˈfemaleˈ captives in your possession.[184] This is God's commandment to you. Lawful to you are all beyond these—as long as you seek them with your wealth in a legal marriage, not in fornication. Give those you have consummated marriage with their due dowries. It is permissible to be mutually gracious regarding the set dowry. Surely God is All-Knowing, All-Wise.

Marrying Bondwomen

25. But if any of you cannot afford to marry a free believing woman, then ˈlet him marryˈ a believing bondwoman possessed by one of you. God knows best ˈthe state ofˈ your faith ˈand theirsˈ. You are from one another.[185] So marry them with the permission of their owners,[186] giving them their dowry in fairness, if they are chaste, neither promiscuous nor having secret affairs. If they commit indecency after marriage, they receive half the punishment of free women.[187] This is for those of you who fear falling into sin. But if you are patient, it is better for you. And God is All-Forgiving, Most Merciful.

---

179 A person's repentance will be accepted as long as they repent any time before their death. But one should not procrastinate because they do not know when they will die.
180 For example, a man would prevent a female relative (such as his sister or mother) from getting married so he can secure her estate for himself.
181 lit., blatant misconduct. If someone's wife has been found guilty of adultery, he has the right to ask for his dowry back.
182 i.e., the promise to live with her in kindness or divorce her with dignity.
183 Marriage to any of the listed women became null and void with the revelation of these verses.
184 A man was not allowed to have a relationship with a bondwoman who he had taken captive in war unless he made sure she was not pregnant. This was verified by her having at least one monthly cycle. See footnote for 4:3.
185 Do not be ashamed to marry a bondwoman since you are all part of the same human family and God knows you are doing so to avoid illegal relationships.
186 A married slave-woman is forbidden from having a relationship with her master.
187 i.e., fifty lashes.

God's Grace

26. It is God's Will to make things clear to you, guide you to the 'noble' ways of those before you, and turn to you in mercy. For God is All-Knowing, All-Wise. **27.** And it is God's Will to turn to you in grace, but those who follow their desires wish to see you deviate entirely 'from God's Way'. **28.** And it is God's Will to lighten your burdens, for humankind was created weak.

Prohibition of Abuse

29. O believers! Do not devour one another's wealth illegally, but rather trade by mutual consent. And do not kill 'each other or' yourselves. Surely God is ever Merciful to you. **30.** And whoever does this sinfully and unjustly, We will burn them in the Fire. That is easy for God.

Avoiding Major Sins

31. If you avoid the major sins forbidden to you, We will absolve you of your 'lesser' misdeeds and admit you into a place of honour.[188]

Inheritance Law 5) Contentment

32. And do not crave what God has given some of you over others. Men will be rewarded according to their deeds and women 'equally' according to theirs. Rather, ask God for His bounties. Surely God has 'perfect' knowledge of all things. **33.** And We have appointed heirs to what has been left by parents and next of kin. As for those you have made a pledge to, give them their share.[189] Surely God is a Witness over all things.

Husbands as Providers and Guardians

34. Men are the caretakers of women, as men have been provisioned by God over women and tasked with supporting them financially. And righteous women are devoutly obedient and, when alone, protective of what God has entrusted them with.[190] And if you sense ill-conduct from your women, advise them 'first', 'if they persist,' do not share their beds, 'but if they still persist,' then discipline them.[191] But if they change their ways, do not be unjust to them. Surely God is Most High, All-Great.

Reconciling Married Couples

35. If you anticipate a split between them, appoint a mediator from his family and another from hers. If they desire reconciliation, God will restore harmony between them. Surely God is All-Knowing, All-Aware.

The Kind, the Stingy, and the Insincere

36. Worship God 'alone' and associate none with Him. And be kind to parents, relatives, orphans, the poor, near and distant neighbours, close friends, 'needy' travellers, and those 'bondspeople' in your possession. Surely God does not like whoever is arrogant, boastful— **37.** those who are stingy, promote stinginess among people, and withhold God's bounties. We have prepared for the disbelievers a humiliating punishment. **38.** Likewise for those who spend their wealth to show off and do not believe in God or the Last Day. And whoever takes Satan as an associate—what an evil associate they have!

---

188 i.e., Paradise.
189 This pledge was a common practice before Islam between friends and allies—taking oaths to inherit each other. This practice came to an end with the revelation of verse 8:75 of the Quran. Although friends and allies do not have a share in inheritance anymore, they still can get some of the estate through bequest.
190 i.e., their husbands' honour and wealth.
191 Disciplining one's wife is the final resort. The earliest commentators understood that this was to be light enough not to leave a mark, should be done with nothing bigger than a tooth stick, and should not be on the face. Prophet Muhammad said to his companions "Do not beat the female servants of God." He said that honourable husbands do not beat their wives, and he himself never hit a woman or a servant. If a woman feels her husband is ill-behaved, then she can get help from her guardian or seek divorce.

Divine Justice

39. What harm could have come to them if they had believed in God and the Last Day and donated from what God has provided for them? And God has ˹perfect˺ knowledge of them. **40.** Indeed, God never wrongs ˹anyone˺—even by an atom's weight.[192] And if it is a good deed, He will multiply it many times over and will give a great reward out of His grace.

Witnesses on Judgment Day

41. So how will it be when We bring a witness from every faith-community and bring you ˹O Prophet˺ as a witness against yours? **42.** On that Day, those who denied ˹God˺ and disobeyed the Messenger will wish they were reduced to dust. And they will never be able to hide anything from God.[193]

Purification Before Prayers

43. O believers! Do not approach prayer while intoxicated[194] until you are aware of what you say, nor in a state of ˹full˺ impurity[195]—unless you merely pass through ˹the mosque˺—until you have bathed. But if you are ill, on a journey, or have relieved yourselves, or been intimate with your wives and cannot find water, then purify yourselves with clean earth, wiping your faces and hands.[196] And God is Ever-Pardoning, All-Forgiving.

Warning Against Deviance

44. Have you ˹O Prophet˺ not seen those who were given a portion of the Scriptures yet trade it for misguidance and wish to see you deviate from the ˹Right˺ Path? **45.** God knows best who your enemies are! And God is sufficient as a Guardian, and He is sufficient as a Helper.

Humility with the Prophet[197]

46. Some Jews take words out of context and say, "We listen and we disobey," "Hear! May you never hear," and "Râ'ina!"—playing with words and discrediting the faith. Had they said ˹courteously˺, "We hear and obey," "Listen to us," and "Unẓurna," it would have been better for them and more proper. God has condemned them for their disbelief, so they do not believe except for a few.

Reward for Rejecting the Truth

47. O you who were given the Book! Believe in what We have revealed—confirming your own Scriptures—before We wipe out ˹your˺ faces, turning them backwards, or We condemn the defiant as We did to the Sabbath-breakers.[198] And God's command is always executed!

The Only Unforgivable Sin

48. Indeed, God does not forgive associating others with Him ˹in worship˺,[199] but forgives anything else of whoever He wills. And whoever associates others with God has indeed committed a grave sin.

---

192 lit., the smallest particle of dust (ẓarrah).
193 Prophet Muḥammad asked one of his companions, 'Abdullah ibn Mas'ûd, to recite some verses of the Quran for him because he loved to hear it from someone other than himself. 'Abdullah recited from the beginning of this chapter until he reached verse 42. When he was told he may stop, 'Abdullah said he looked at the face of Prophet and saw tears rolling down his cheeks.
194 Intoxicants were prohibited in the Quran in three stages: 2:219, 4:43, and finally 5:90-91.
195 i.e., after sexual intercourse or a wet dream.
196 This ruling is called tayammum or 'dry ablution.' If someone cannot find water or is unable to use it because of illness or cold weather, then they are allowed to touch clean earth, sand, etc. with the palms of their hands once then blow in their hands and wipe over their face and hands.
197 See footnote for 2:104.
198 See 7:163-165.
199 A person will never be forgiven if they die as a disbeliever. But if they repent before their death and mend their ways, then their repentance will be accepted (see 25:68-70).

Self-Righteousness

49. Have you ˹O Prophet˺ not seen those who ˹falsely˺ elevate themselves? It is God who elevates whoever He wills. And none will be wronged ˹even by the width of˺ the thread of a date stone. **50.** See how they fabricate lies against God—this alone is a blatant sin.

False Reassurance

51. Have you ˹O Prophet˺ not seen those who were given a portion of the Scriptures yet believe in idols and false gods and re-assure the disbelievers[200] that they are better guided than the believers? **52.** It is they who have been condemned by God. And whoever is condemned by God will have no helper.

Envy Breeds Disbelief

53. Do they have control over shares of the kingdom? If so, they would not have given anyone so much as the speck on a date stone. **54.** Or do they envy the people for God's bounties? Indeed, We have given the descendants of Abraham the Book and wisdom, along with great authority. **55.** Yet some believed in him while others turned away from him.[201] Hell is sufficient as a torment!

Punishment of the Disbelievers

56. Surely those who reject Our signs, We will cast them into the Fire. Whenever their skin is burnt completely, We will replace it so they will ˹constantly˺ taste the punishment. Indeed, God is Almighty, All-Wise.

Reward of the Believers

57. As for those who believe and do good, We will admit them into Gardens under which rivers flow, to stay there for ever and ever. There they will have pure spouses,[202] and We will place them under a vast shade.

Maintaining Justice

58. Indeed, God commands you to return trusts to their rightful owners;[203] and when you judge between people, judge with fairness. What a noble commandment from God to you! Surely God is All-Hearing, All-Seeing.

Divine Judgment

59. O believers! Obey God and obey the Messenger and those in authority among you. Should you disagree on anything, then refer it to God and His Messenger, if you ˹truly˺ believe in God and the Last Day. This is the best and fairest resolution.

Hypocrites Rejecting Divine Judgment

60. Have you ˹O Prophet˺ not seen those who claim they believe in what has been revealed to you and what was revealed before you? They seek the judgment of false judges, which they were commanded to reject. And Satan ˹only˺ desires to lead them farther away. **61.** When it is said to them, "Come to God's revelations and to the Messenger," you see the hypocrites turn away from you stubbornly. **62.** How ˹horrible˺ will it be if a disaster strikes them because of what their hands have done, then they come to you swearing by God, "We intended nothing but goodwill and reconciliation." **63.** ˹Only˺ God knows what is in their hearts. So turn away from them, caution them, and give them advice that will shake their very souls.

Obeying the Messenger

64. We only sent messengers to be obeyed by God's Will. If only those ˹hypocrites˺

---

200 i.e., the polytheists.
201 i.e., Abraham or Muḥammad.
202 *See* footnote for 2:25.
203 This verse was revealed right after Mecca had peacefully surrendered to the Muslims. 'Ali ibn Abi Ṭâlib, the Prophet's cousin and son-in-law, took the Ka'bah's key by force from Othmân ibn Ṭalḥa, the non-Muslim keeper of the Ka'bah. The verse was revealed to the Prophet inside the Ka'bah with the order to give the key back to its rightful owner. He ordered Ali to return the key to the keeper immediately along with an apology. Othmân was also promised that his family would keep the key forever. The keeper was so touched by the Quranic sense of justice that he decided to accept Islam.

came to you ˻O Prophet˼—after wronging themselves—seeking God's forgiveness and the Messenger prayed for their forgiveness, they would have certainly found God ever Accepting of Repentance, Most Merciful.

Unconditional Obedience

65. But no! By your Lord, they will never be ˻true˼ believers until they accept you ˻O Prophet˼ as the judge in their disputes, and find no resistance within themselves against your decision and submit wholeheartedly. 66. If We had commanded them to sacrifice themselves or abandon their homes, none would have obeyed except for a few. Had they done what they were advised to do,[204] it would have certainly been far better for them and more reassuring, 67. and We would have granted them a great reward by Our grace 68. and guided them to the Straight Path.

Reward for Obedience

69. And whoever obeys God and the Messenger will be in the company of those blessed by God: the prophets, the people of truth, the martyrs, and the righteous—what honourable company! 70. This is God's favour, and God fully knows ˻who deserves it˼.

Advice to the Army

71. O believers! Take your precautions and go forth either in groups or together. 72. There will be some among you who will lag behind so that if you face a disaster, they will say, "God has blessed us for not being there among them." 73. But if you return with God's bounties, they will say—as if there had been no bond between you—"We wish we had been there with them to share the great gain!"

Fighting Against Oppression

74. Let those who would sacrifice this life for the Hereafter fight in the cause of God. And whoever fights in God's cause—whether they achieve martyrdom or victory—We will honour them with a great reward. 75. And what is it with you? You do not fight in the cause of God and for oppressed men, women, and children who cry out, "Our Lord! Deliver us from this land of oppressors! Appoint for us a saviour; appoint for us a helper—all by Your grace."

Fighting Satan's Allies

76. Believers fight for the cause of God, whereas disbelievers fight for the cause of the Devil. So fight against Satan's ˻evil˼ forces. Indeed, Satan's schemes are ever weak.

Those Who Cower

77. Have you ˻O Prophet˼ not seen those who had been told, "Do not fight! Rather, establish prayer and pay alms-tax."? Then once the order came to fight, a group of them feared those ˻hostile˼ people as God should be feared—or even more. They said, "Our Lord! Why have You ordered us to fight? If only You had delayed ˻the order for˼ us for a little while!" Say, ˻O Prophet,˼ "The enjoyment of this world is so little, whereas the Hereafter is far better for those mindful ˻of God˼. And none of you will be wronged ˻even by the width of˼ the thread of a date stone.

Divine Destiny

78. "Wherever you may be, death will overcome you—even if you were in fortified towers." When something good befalls them, they say, "This is from God," but when something evil befalls them, they say, "This is from you." Say, ˻O Prophet,˼ "Both have been destined by God." So what is the matter with these people? They can hardly comprehend anything! 79. Whatever good

---

204 i.e., obeying God and His Messenger.

befalls you is from God and whatever evil befalls you is from yourself.[205] We have sent you ˹O Prophet˺ as a messenger to ˹all˺ people. And God is sufficient as a Witness.

Obeying the Messenger

80. Whoever obeys the Messenger has truly obeyed God. But whoever turns away, then ˹know that˺ We have not sent you ˹O Prophet˺ as a keeper over them. 81. And they say, "We obey," but when they leave you, a group of them would spend the night contradicting what they said. God records all their schemes. So turn away from them, and put your trust in God. And God is sufficient as a Trustee of Affairs.

Reflecting on the Quran

82. Do they not then reflect on the Quran? Had it been from anyone other than God, they would have certainly found in it many inconsistencies.

Spreading Rumours

83. And when they hear news of security or fear,[206] they publicize it. Had they referred it to the Messenger or their authorities, those with sound judgment among them would have validated it. Had it not been for God's grace and mercy, you would have followed Satan—except for a few.

Show of Strength

84. So fight in the cause of God ˹O Prophet˺. You are accountable for none but yourself. And motivate the believers ˹to fight˺, so perhaps God will curb the disbelievers' might. And God is far superior in might and in punishment.

Good and Evil Intercession

85. Whoever intercedes for a good cause will have a share in the reward, and whoever intercedes for an evil cause will have a share in the burden. And God is Watchful over all things.

Responding to Greetings

86. And when you are greeted, respond with a better greeting or at least similarly. Surely God is a ˹vigilant˺ Reckoner of all things.

Assembly for Judgment Day

87. God, there is no god ˹worthy of worship˺ except Him. He will certainly gather ˹all of˺ you together on the Day of Judgment—about which there is no doubt. And whose word is more truthful than God's?

Stance on Hypocrites

88. Why are you ˹believers˺ divided into two groups regarding the hypocrites while God allowed them to regress ˹to disbelief˺ because of their misdeeds? Do you wish to guide those left by God to stray? And whoever God leaves to stray, you will never find for them a way. 89. They wish you would disbelieve as they have disbelieved, so you may all be alike. So do not take them as allies unless they emigrate in the cause of God. But if they turn away, then seize them and kill them wherever you find them, and do not take any of them as allies or helpers,[207] 90. except those who are allies of a people you are bound with in a treaty or those wholeheartedly opposed to fighting either you or their own people. If God had willed, He would have empowered them to fight you. So if they refrain from fighting you and offer you peace, then God does not permit you to harm them. 91. You will find others who wish to be safe from you and their own people. Yet they cannot resist the temptation ˹of disbelief or hostility˺. If they

---

205 Both good and evil are destined by God. The good comes as God's reward for good deeds, whereas the bad comes as God's punishment for evil deeds. In some cases, bad things happen to good people to test their faith, or as an atonement for their sins, or as part of a process of replacing something with what is better (e.g., a job or a spouse).
206 i.e., when they get the news of victory or a threat.
207 The verse discusses a group of people who nominally became Muslims and secretly supported the enemies of Muslims. For those hypocrites to prove their loyalty, they were commanded to emigrate and join the ranks of the believers, or they would be considered enemies.

do not keep away, offer you peace, or refrain from attacking you, then seize them and kill them wherever you find them. We have given you full permission over such people.

Killing a Believer Unintentionally

92. It is not lawful for a believer to kill another except by mistake. And whoever kills a believer unintentionally must free a believing slave and pay blood-money to the victim's family—unless they waive it charitably. But if the victim is a believer from a hostile people, then a believing slave must be freed. And if the victim is from a people bound with you in a treaty, then blood-money must be paid to the family along with freeing a believing slave. Those who are unable, let them fast two consecutive months—as a means of repentance to God. And God is All-Knowing, All-Wise.

Killing a Believer Intentionally

93. And whoever kills a believer intentionally, their reward will be Hell—where they will stay indefinitely.[208] God will be displeased with them, condemn them, and will prepare for them a tremendous punishment.

Random Fighting

94. O believers! When you struggle in the cause of God, be sure of who you fight. And do not say to those who offer you ʿgreetings ofʾ peace, "You are no believer!"—seeking a fleeting worldly gain.[209] Instead, God has infinite bounties ʿin storeʾ. You were initially like them then God blessed you ʿwith Islamʾ. So be sure! Indeed, God is All-Aware of what you do.

Struggling in God's Cause

95. Those believers who stay at home—except the ones with valid excuses[210]—are not equal to those who strive in the cause of God with their wealth and their lives. God has elevated in rank those who strive with their wealth and their lives above those who stay behind ʿwith valid excusesʾ. God has promised each a fine reward, but those who strive will receive a far better reward than others— **96.** far superior ranks, forgiveness, and mercy from Him. And God is All-Forgiving, Most Merciful.

Yielding to Oppression

97. When the angels seize the souls of those who have wronged themselves[211]— scolding them, "What was the matter with you?" they will reply, "We were oppressed in the land." The angels will respond, "Was God's earth not spacious enough for you to emigrate?" It is they who will have Hell as their home—what an evil destination! **98.** Except helpless men, women, and children who cannot afford a way out— **99.** it is right to hope that God will pardon them. For God is Ever-Pardoning, All-Forgiving.

Migrating in God's Cause

100. Whoever emigrates in the cause of God will find many safe havens and bountiful resources throughout the earth. Those who leave their homes and die while emigrating to God and His Messenger—their reward has already been secured with God. And God is All-Forgiving, Most Merciful.

Shortening Prayers

101. When you travel through the land, it is permissible for you to shorten the

---

208 If a Muslim commits a major sin (such as intentional killing or adultery) and dies without repenting, they will be punished in Hell according to the severity or magnitude of the sin, then eventually be taken out of Hell. No Muslim will stay in Hell forever.
209 i.e., spoils of war.
210 This includes women, the elderly, the sick, etc.
211 This verse refers to some of those who had accepted Islam secretly in Mecca but refused to emigrate to Medina along with the rest of the believers. Some of them were killed in the Battle of Badr when they were rallied by the Meccans to fight against the Muslims. The verse also applies to any Muslim who accepts abuse and refuses to move to another place where they can live with dignity and practice their faith freely.

prayer[212]—'especially' if you fear an attack by the disbelievers. Indeed, the disbelievers are your sworn enemies.

Praying in a State of Fear

102. When you 'O Prophet' are 'campaigning' with them and you lead them in prayer, let one group of them pray with you—while armed. When they prostrate themselves, let the other group stand guard behind them. Then the group that has not yet prayed will then join you in prayer—and let them be vigilant and armed.[213] The disbelievers would wish to see you neglect your weapons and belongings, so they could launch a sweeping assault on you. But there is no blame if you lay aside your weapons when overcome by heavy rain or illness—but take precaution. Indeed, God has prepared a humiliating punishment for the disbelievers. 103. When the prayers are over, remember God—whether you are standing, sitting, or lying down. But when you are secure, establish regular prayers. Indeed, performing prayers is a duty on the believers at the appointed times.

Diligence Against the Enemy

104. Do not falter in pursuit of the enemy— if you are suffering, they too are suffering. But you can hope to receive from God what they can never hope for. And God is All-Knowing, All-Wise.

Justice to a Jew[214]

105. Indeed, We have sent down the Book to you 'O Prophet' in truth to judge between people by means of what God has shown you. So do not be an advocate for the deceitful. 106. And seek God's forgiveness—indeed, God is All-Forgiving, Most Merciful.

107. Do not advocate for those who wrong themselves.[215] Surely God does not like those who are deceitful, sinful. 108. They try to hide 'their deception' from people, but they can never hide it from God—in Whose presence they plot by night what is displeasing to Him. And God is Fully Aware of what they do. 109. Here you are! You 'believers' are advocating for them in this life, but who will 'dare to' advocate for them before God on the Day of Judgment? Or who will come to their defence?

After Sin

110. Whoever commits evil or wrongs themselves then seeks God's forgiveness will certainly find God All-Forgiving, Most Merciful. 111. And whoever commits a sin—it is only to their own loss. God is All-Knowing, All-Wise. 112. And whoever commits an evil or sinful deed then blames it on an innocent person, they will definitely bear the guilt of slander and blatant sin.

God's Grace to the Prophet

113. Had it not been for God's grace and mercy, a group of them would have sought to deceive you 'O Prophet'. Yet they would deceive none but themselves, nor can they harm you in the least. God has revealed to you the Book and wisdom and taught you what you never knew. Great 'indeed' is God's favour upon you!

Secret Talks

114. There is no good in most of their secret talks—except those encouraging charity, kindness, or reconciliation between people. And whoever does this seeking God's pleasure, We will grant them a great reward.

---

212 Generally, it is permissible for Muslims who are travelling a distance of 85 km or more to shorten their prayers. A four-unit prayer is reduced to two.
213 When the first group prays, the second group stands guard behind them, then the first group withdraws to the back when they finish their prayers and stand guard when the second group moves up to pray.
214 Verses 105-112 were revealed in defence of Zaid ibn As-Samîn, a Jewish man, who was falsely accused of theft. A shield was stolen by a Muslim named Ṭu'mah ibn Obairaq and entrusted to Zaid. Ṭu'mah's family rushed to his defence and accused Zaid of the crime. They also tried to influence Prophet Muḥammad to make a decision in favour of Ṭu'mah and punish the Jew, but the verses were soon revealed declaring Zaid's innocence.
215 lit., deceive themselves.

Opposing the Messenger

115. And whoever defies the Messenger after guidance has become clear to them and follows a path other than that of the believers, We will let them pursue what they have chosen, then burn them in Hell—what an evil end!

Unforgivable Sin

116. Surely God does not forgive associating ˹others˺ with Him ˹in worship˺,[216] but forgives anything else of whoever He wills. Indeed, whoever associates ˹others˺ with God has clearly gone far astray.

Satan's Allies

117. Instead of God, they only invoke female gods[217] and they ˹actually˺ invoke none but a rebellious Satan— 118. cursed by God—who said, "I will surely take hold of a certain number of Your servants. 119. I will certainly mislead them and delude them with empty hopes. Also, I will order them and they will slit the ears of cattle[218] and alter God's creation." And whoever takes Satan as a guardian instead of God has certainly suffered a tremendous loss. 120. Satan only makes them ˹false˺ promises and deludes them with ˹empty˺ hopes. Truly Satan promises them nothing but delusion. 121. It is they who will have Hell as their home, and they will find no escape from it!

Reward of the Believers

122. And those who believe and do good, We will soon admit them into Gardens under which rivers flow, to stay there for ever and ever. God's promise is ˹always˺ true. And whose word is more truthful than God's?

Doing, Not Wishing

123. ˹Divine grace is˺ neither by your wishes nor those of the People of the Book! Whoever commits evil will be rewarded accordingly, and they will find no protector or helper besides God. 124. But those who do good—whether male or female—and have faith will enter Paradise and will never be wronged ˹even as much as˺ the speck on a date stone.

Abraham's Way

125. And who is better in faith than those who ˹fully˺ submit themselves to God, do good, and follow the Way of Abraham, the upright? God chose Abraham as a close friend. 126. To God ˹alone˺ belongs whatever is in the heavens and whatever is on the earth. And God is Fully Aware of everything.

Caring for Female Orphans

127. They ask you ˹O Prophet˺ regarding women. Say, "It is God Who instructs you regarding them. Instruction has ˹already˺ been revealed in the Book[219] concerning the orphan women you deprive of their due rights[220] but still wish to marry, also helpless children, as well as standing up for orphans' rights. And whatever good you do is certainly well known to God."

Reconciling Married Couples

128. If a woman fears indifference or neglect from her husband, there is no blame on either of them if they seek ˹fair˺ settlement, which is best. Humans are ever inclined to selfishness.[221] But if you are gracious and mindful

---

216 This applies to those who die in a state of disbelief in God. But those who repent before their death and mend their ways, their repentance will be accepted (see 25:68-70).
217 The pagans of Arabia used to shape their idols as females and give them feminine names such as Al-Lât, Al-'Uzza, and Manât.
218 Slitting the ears of cattle dedicated to idols was a superstitious practice before Islam.
219 This refers to verses 2-11 of this chapter.
220 i.e., their inheritance and dowries.
221 This implies that many husbands and wives are unwilling to give the other their rights.

'of God', surely God is All-Aware of what you do.

Maintaining Justice Among Wives

129. You will never be able to maintain 'emotional' justice between your wives—no matter how keen you are. So do not totally incline towards one leaving the other in suspense.[222] And if you do what is right and are mindful 'of God', surely God is All-Forgiving, Most Merciful. **130.** But if they choose to separate, God will enrich both of them from His bounties. And God is Ever-Bountiful, All-Wise.

God's Might and Grace

131. To God 'alone' belongs whatever is in the heavens and whatever is on the earth. Indeed, We have commanded those given the Scripture before you, as well as you, to be mindful of God. But if you disobey, then 'know that' to God belongs whatever is in the heavens and the earth. And God is Self-Sufficient, Praiseworthy. **132.** To God 'alone' belongs whatever is in the heavens and whatever is on the earth. And God is sufficient as a Trustee of Affairs. **133.** If it is His Will, He can remove you altogether, O humanity, and replace you with others. And God is Most Capable to do so. **134.** Whoever desires the reward of this world, then 'let them know that' with God are the rewards of this world and the Hereafter. And God is All-Hearing, All-Seeing.

Standing up for Justice

135. O believers! Stand firm for justice as witnesses for God even if it is against yourselves, your parents, or close relatives. Be they rich or poor, God is best to ensure their interests. So do not let your desires cause you to deviate 'from justice'. If you distort the testimony or refuse to give it, then 'know that' God is certainly All-Aware of what you do.

True Belief

136. O believers! Have faith in God, His Messenger, the Book He has revealed to His Messenger, and the Scriptures He revealed before. Indeed, whoever denies God, His angels, His Books, His messengers, and the Last Day has clearly gone far astray.

Warning Against Hypocrites

137. Indeed, those who believed then disbelieved, then believed and again disbelieved—'only' increasing in disbelief—God will neither forgive them nor guide them to the 'Right' Way. **138.** Give good news of a painful punishment to hypocrites, **139.** who choose disbelievers as allies instead of the believers. Do they seek honour and power through that company? Surely all honour and power belongs to God.

Shunning Ridiculers

140. He has already revealed to you in the Book that when you hear God's revelations being denied or ridiculed, then do not sit in that company unless they engage in a different topic, or else you will be like them.[223] Surely God will gather the hypocrites and disbelievers all together in Hell.

Hypocritical Stance

141. 'The hypocrites are' those who wait to see what happens to you. So if God grants you victory, they say 'to you', "Were we not on your side?" But if the disbelievers have a share 'of victory', they say 'to them', "Did we not have the advantage over you, yet we protected you from the believers?" God will judge between 'all of' you on the Day of Judgment. And God will never grant the disbelievers a way over the believers.

Qualities of the Hypocrites

142. Surely the hypocrites seek to deceive God, but He outwits them. When they

---

222 Do not leave one hanging—not fully enjoying the rights of a married woman and not fully divorced.
223 This refers to 6:68.

stand up for prayer, they do it half-heart-edly only to be seen by people—hardly re-membering God at all. **143.** Torn between belief and disbelief—belonging neither to these ʹbelieversʹ nor those ʹdisbelieversʹ. And whoever God leaves to stray, you will never find for them a way.

Unacceptable Guardianship

144. O believers! Do not take disbelievers as allies instead of the believers. Would you like to give God solid proof against yourselves?

Reward of Hypocrites

145. Surely the hypocrites will be in the lowest depths of the Fire—and you will never find for them any helper— **146.** except those who repent, mend their ways, hold fast to God, and are sincere in their devotion to God; they will be with the be-lievers. And God will grant the believers a great reward. **147.** Why should God punish you if you are grateful and faithful? God is ever Appreciative, All-Knowing.

Negativity in Public

148. God does not like negative thoughts to be voiced—except by those who have been wronged.[224] God is All-Hearing, All-Knowing. **149.** Whether you reveal or conceal a good or pardon an evil—surely God is Ever-Pardoning, Most Capable.

Faith in All Prophets

150. Surely those who deny God and His messengers and wish to make a distinction between God and His messengers,[225] say-

ing, "We believe in some and disbelieve in others," desiring to forge a compromise, **151.** they are indeed the true disbelievers. And We have prepared for the disbelievers a humiliating punishment. **152.** As for those who believe in God and His messengers—accepting all; rejecting none—He will surely give them their rewards. And God is All-Forgiving, Most Merciful.

Moses and the Children of Israel

153. The People of the Book demand that you ʹO Prophetʹ bring down for them a rev-elation in writing from heaven.[226] They de-manded what is even greater than this from Moses, saying, "Make God visible to us!" So a thunderbolt struck them for their wrongdo-ing. Then they took the calf for worship after receiving clear signs. Still We forgave them for that ʹafter their repentanceʹ and gave Moses compelling proof. **154.** We raised the Mount over them ʹas a warningʹ for ʹbreak-ingʹ their covenant and said, "Enter the gate ʹof Jerusalemʹ with humility." We also warned them, "Do not break the Sabbath," and took from them a firm covenant.

Falsehood About Mary and Jesus

155. ʹThey were condemnedʹ for breaking their covenant, rejecting God's signs, killing the prophets unjustly, and for saying, "Our hearts are unreceptive!"[227]—it is God Who has sealed their hearts for their disbelief, so they do not believe except for a few— **156.** and for their denial and outrageous accusation against Mary,[228] **157.** and for boasting, "We killed the Messiah, Jesus, son of Mary, the messenger of God." But they neither killed nor crucified him—it was only

---

224 i.e., God does not like talking about people behind their backs—except when someone who has been wronged seeks counselling or assistance from authorities.
225 By their claim that they believe in God but still reject some of His messengers.
226 i.e., they demanded the Quran to be revealed all at once in writing similar to the Tablets of Moses. This demand is refuted in 25:32.
227 Their hearts are unreceptive because they claim they have enough knowledge already.
228 i.e., they slandered Mary by claiming that she conceived Jesus through an illegal relationship.

made to appear so.[229] Even those who argue for this ´crucifixion` are in doubt. They have no knowledge whatsoever—only making assumptions. They certainly did not kill him. **158.** Rather, God raised him up to Himself. And God is Almighty, All-Wise. **159.** Every one of the People of the Book will definitely believe in him before his death.[230] And on the Day of Judgment Jesus will be a witness against them.

Consequences of Disobedience

160. We forbade the Jews certain foods that had been lawful to them for their wrongdoing, and for hindering many from the Way of God, **161.** taking interest despite its prohibition, and consuming people's wealth unjustly. We have prepared for the disbelievers among them a painful punishment. **162.** But those with firm knowledge among them and those with true faith believe in what has been revealed to you ´O Prophet` and what was revealed before you—´especially` those who establish prayer—and those who pay alms-tax and believe in God and the Last Day, to these ´people` We will grant a great reward.

Messengers of Islam

163. Indeed, We have sent revelation to you ´O Prophet` as We sent revelation to Noah and the prophets after him. We also sent revelation to Abraham, Ishmael, Isaac, Jacob, and his descendants, ´as well as` Jesus, Job, Jonah, Aaron, and Solomon. And to David We gave the Psalms. **164.** There are messengers whose stories We have told you already and others We have not. And to Moses God spoke directly. **165.** ´All were` messengers delivering good news and warnings so humanity

should have no excuse before God after ´the coming of` the messengers. And God is Almighty, All-Wise.

Muḥammad's Messengership

166. Yet ´if you are denied, O Prophet,` God bears witness to what He has sent down to you—He has sent it with His knowledge. The angels too bear witness. And God ´alone` is sufficient as a Witness.

Punishment for Rejecting the Truth

167. Those who disbelieve and hinder ´others` from the Way of God have certainly strayed far away. **168.** Those who disbelieve and wrong themselves—surely God will neither forgive them nor guide them to any path **169.** except that of Hell, to stay there for ever and ever. And that is easy for God.

Universality of Islam

170. O humanity! The Messenger has certainly come to you with the truth from your Lord, so believe for your own good. But if you disbelieve, then ´know that` to God belongs whatever is in the heavens and the earth. And God is All-Knowing, All-Wise.

Wake-up Call

171. O People of the Book! Do not go to extremes regarding your faith; say nothing about God except the truth.[231] The Messiah, Jesus, son of Mary, was no more than a messenger of God and the fulfillment of His Word through Mary and a spirit ´created by a command` from Him.[232] So believe in God and His messengers and do not say, "Trinity." Stop!—for your own

---

229 The popular belief among Muslims is that a conspiracy was made to kill Jesus, God made the main culprit who betrayed Jesus look exactly like Jesus, then he was crucified in Jesus' place. Jesus was raised safe and sound to the heavens. Muslims also believe in the second coming of Jesus.

230 Scholars disagree whether Jews and Christians will come to realize that Jesus is a prophet of God at the time of their death or before the death of Jesus after his second coming.

231 The Jews are warned against denying Jesus as the Messiah, while Christians are warned against calling Jesus God.

232 i.e., Jesus was created by God's Word "Be!" and he was, and life was breathed into Jesus by the holy spirit (the angel Gabriel) at the command of God.

good. God is only One God. Glory be to Him! He is far above having a son! To Him belongs whatever is in the heavens and whatever is on the earth. And God is sufficient as a Trustee of Affairs. 172. The Messiah would never be too proud to be a servant of God, nor would the angels nearest to God. Those who are too proud and arrogant to worship Him will be brought before Him all together.

The Reward

173. As for those who believe and do good, He will reward them in full and increase them out of His grace. But those who are too proud and arrogant, He will subject them to a painful punishment. And besides God they will find no protector or helper.

Universal Call to Islam

174. O humanity! There has come to you conclusive evidence from your Lord. And We have sent down to you a brilliant light. 175. As for those who believe in God and

hold fast to Him, He will admit them into His mercy and grace and guide them to Himself through the Straight Path.

Inheritance Law 6)   Full Siblings[233]

176. They ask you 'for a ruling, O Prophet'. Say, "God gives you a ruling regarding those who die without children or parents." If a man dies childless and leaves behind a sister, she will inherit one-half of his estate, whereas her brother will inherit all of her estate if she dies childless. If this person leaves behind two sisters, they together will inherit two-thirds of the estate. But if the deceased leaves male and female siblings, a male's share will be equal to that of two females. God makes 'this' clear to you so you do not go astray. And God has 'perfect' knowledge of all things.[234]

5. The Spread Table (Al-Mâ'idah)

This Medinian chapter takes its name from the story of the table mentioned in verses 112-115. Several rulings are laid out, including permissible and prohibited foods, hunting while on pilgrimage, and making a bequest while travelling. A reference is made to God's covenants with the Jews and Christians and how those covenants were repeatedly violated. The believers are urged to comply with God's judgment as communicated by the Prophet. Some topics that have been touched on in the previous chapters are detailed here, including making up for a broken oath, the sanctity of the human life, and the humanity of Jesus.

In the Name of God—the Most Compassionate, Most Merciful

---

233   This ruling also applies to brothers and sisters from the father's side—if they are the only heirs.
234   This verse is placed at the end of the chapter and not with similar verses at the beginning to connect the end of this chapter with the next one or, according to Al-Fakhr Ar-Râzi, either to tie the end of the chapter with its beginning for emphasis, as found in 20:2 and 124 as well as 23:1 and 117, or to emphasize God's knowledge, just like the first verse emphasizes His power.

Honouring Obligations

1. O believers! Honour your obligations. All grazing livestock has been made lawful to you—except what is hereby announced to you and hunting while on pilgrimage. Indeed, God commands what He wills.

God's Sanctities

2. O believers! Do not violate God's rituals ˹of pilgrimage˺, the sacred months, the sacrificial animals, the ˹offerings decorated with˺ garlands, nor those ˹pilgrims˺ on their way to the Sacred House seeking their Lord's bounty and pleasure. When pilgrimage has ended, you are allowed to hunt. Do not let the hatred of a people who once barred you from the Sacred Mosque provoke you to transgress. Cooperate with one another in goodness and righteousness, and do not cooperate in sin and transgression. And be mindful of God. Surely God is severe in punishment.

Forbidden Foods

3. Forbidden to you are carrion, blood, and swine; what is slaughtered in the name of any other than God; what is killed by strangling, beating, a fall, or by being gored to death; what is partly eaten by a predator unless you slaughter it; and what is sacrificed on altars. You are also forbidden to draw lots for decisions.[235] This is all evil. Today the disbelievers have given up all hope of ˹undermining˺ your faith. So do not fear them; fear Me! Today I have perfected your faith for you, completed My favour upon you, and chosen Islam as your way. But whoever is compelled by extreme hunger—not intending to sin—then surely God is All-Forgiving, Most Merciful.

Lawful Foods

4. They ask you, ˹O Prophet,˺ what is permissible for them ˹to eat˺. Say, "What is good and lawful. Also what is caught by your hunting animals and birds of prey which you have trained as instructed by God. So eat what they catch for you, but mention the Name of God over it ˹first˺." And be mindful of God. Surely God is swift in reckoning.

What to Eat and Who to Marry

5. Today all good, pure foods have been made lawful for you. Similarly, the food of the People of the Book[236] is permissible for you and yours is permissible for them. And ˹permissible for you in marriage˺ are chaste believing women as well as chaste women of those given the Scripture before you—as long as you pay them their dowries in wedlock, neither fornicating nor taking them as mistresses. And whoever rejects the faith, all their good deeds will be void ˹in this life˺ and in the Hereafter they will be among the losers.

Purification Before Prayer

6. O believers! When you rise up for prayer, wash your faces and your hands up to the elbows, wipe your heads, and wash your feet to the ankles. And if you are in a state of ˹full˺ impurity,[237] then take a full bath. But if you are ill, on a journey, or have relieved yourselves, or have been intimate with your wives and cannot find water, then purify yourselves with clean earth by wiping your faces and hands.[238] It is not God's Will to burden you, but to purify you and complete His favour upon you, so perhaps you will be grateful.

God's Favour to the Believers

7. Remember God's favour upon you and the covenant He made with you when you said, "We hear and obey." And be mindful

---

235 To make a decision in pre-Islamic Arabia, a person would draw one of three straws: one saying "Do it," the other "Do not do it," and the third was left blank, whereas in Islam there is a special prayer (called *istikhârah*) for guidance when making a decision.
236 "The food of the People of the Book" here means the meat of the animals slaughtered by the Jews and Christians.
237 For example, following sexual intercourse or a wet dream.
238 This ruling is called *tayammum* or 'dry ablution.' *See* footnote for 4:43.

of God. Surely God knows best what is ˈhiddenˈ in the heart.

Be Just

8. O believers! Stand firm for God and bear true testimony. Do not let the hatred of a people lead you to injustice. Be just! That is closer to righteousness. And be mindful of God. Surely God is All-Aware of what you do.

Reward of Belief and Disbelief

9. God has promised those who believe and do good ˈHisˈ forgiveness and a great reward. **10.** As for those who disbelieve and deny Our signs, they are the residents of the Hellfire.

Believers Saved from Harm

11. O believers! Remember God's favour upon you: when a people sought to harm you, but He held their hands back from you. Be mindful of God. And in God let the believers put their trust.

God's Covenant with the Israelites

12. God made a covenant with the Children of Israel and appointed twelve leaders from among them and ˈthenˈ said, "I am truly with you. If you establish prayer, pay alms-tax, believe in My messengers, support them, and lend to God a good loan, I will certainly forgive your sins and admit you into Gardens under which rivers flow. And whoever among you disbelieves afterwards has truly strayed from the Right Way."

The Covenant Is Broken

13. But for breaking their covenant, We condemned them and hardened their hearts. They distorted the words of the Scripture and neglected a portion of what they had been commanded to uphold. You ˈO Prophetˈ will always find deceit on their part, except for a few. But pardon them and bear with them. Indeed, God loves the good-doers.

Covenant with Christians Broken Too

14. And from those who say, "We are Christians," We took their covenant, but they neglected a portion of what they had been commanded to uphold. So We let hostility and enmity arise between them until the Day of Judgment, and soon God will inform them of all they have done.

The Prophet's Mission

15. O People of the Book! Now Our Messenger has come to you, revealing much of what you have hidden of the Scriptures and disregarding much. There certainly has come to you from God a light and a clear Book **16.** through which God guides those who seek His pleasure to the ways of peace, brings them out of darkness and into light by His Will, and guides them to the Straight Path.

Jesus Is Not God

17. Indeed, those who say, "God is the Messiah, son of Mary," have fallen into disbelief. Say, ˈO Prophet,ˈ "Who has the power to prevent God if He chose to destroy the Messiah, son of Mary, his mother, and everyone in the world all together?" To God ˈaloneˈ belongs the kingdom of the heavens and the earth and everything in between. He creates whatever He wills. And God is Most Capable of everything.

Children of God?

18. The Jews and the Christians each say, "We are the children of God and His most beloved!" Say, ˈO Prophet,ˈ "Why then does He punish you for your sins? No! You are only humans like others of His Own making. He forgives whoever He wills and punishes whoever He wills. To God ˈaloneˈ belongs the kingdom of the heavens and the earth and everything in between. And to Him is the final return."

No Excuse

19. O People of the Book! Our Messenger has indeed come to you, making things clear to you after an interval between the messengers so you do not say, "There has never come to us a deliverer of good news or a warner." Now there has come to you a deliverer of good news and a warner. And God is Most Capable of everything.

The Israelites Ordered to Enter the Holy Land

20. And 'remember' when Moses said to his people, "O my people! Remember God's favours upon you when He raised prophets from among you, made you sovereign,[239] and gave you what He had never given anyone in the world.[240] **21.** O my people! Enter the Holy Land which God has destined for you 'to enter'. And do not turn back or else you will become losers." **22.** They replied, "O Moses! There is an enormously powerful people there, so we will never 'be able to' enter it until they leave. If they do, then we will enter!" **23.** Two God-fearing men—who had been blessed by God—said, "Surprise them through the gate. If you do, you will certainly prevail. Put your trust in God if you are 'truly' believers." **24.** 'Yet' they said, "O Moses! 'Still' we will never enter as long as they remain there. So go—both you and your Lord—and fight; we are staying right here!"

Forty Years in the Wilderness

25. Moses pleaded, "My Lord! I have no control over anyone except myself and my brother. So set us apart from the rebellious people." **26.** God replied, "Then this land is forbidden to them for forty years, during which they will wander through the land. So do not grieve for the rebellious people."

Abel Killed by Cain[241]

27. Relate to them in truth 'O Prophet' the story of Adam's two sons—how each offered a sacrifice: one's offering was accepted while the other's was not, so he threatened 'his brother', "I will kill you!" His brother replied, "God only accepts 'the offering' of the sincerely devout. **28.** If you raise your hand to kill me, I will not raise mine to kill you, because I fear God—the Lord of all worlds. **29.** I want to let you bear your sin against me along with your other sins, then you will be one of those destined to the Fire. And that is the reward of the wrongdoers." **30.** Still the other convinced himself to kill his own brother, so he killed him—becoming a loser. **31.** Then God sent a crow digging 'a grave' in the ground 'for a dead crow', in order to show him how to bury the corpse of his brother. He cried, "Alas! Have I 'even' failed to be like this crow and bury the corpse of my brother?" So he became regretful.[242]

Value of Human Life

32. That is why We ordained for the Children of Israel that whoever takes a life—unless as a punishment for murder or mischief in the land—it will be as if they killed all of humanity; and whoever saves a life, it will be as if they saved all of humanity.[243] 'Although' Our messengers already came to them with clear proofs, many of them still transgressed afterwards through the land.

---

239 He rescued you from Egypt where the Pharaoh treated you like slaves and blessed you with freedom so you can manage your own affairs.
240 i.e., the miracles of splitting the sea, water coming out of the rock, manna and quails, and clouds shading them.
241 Hâbîl and Qâbîl, respectively.
242 In Islam, regret for doing something wrong is essential for repentance. But in the case of Cain, his regret was not for killing his brother, but for failing to bury his corpse to hide the evidence of his crime. Therefore, his regret was not intended as a step towards repentance.
243 Although this is addressed to the Children of Israel, it is applicable to everyone at all times.

Anti-Terrorism Law

33. Indeed, the penalty for those who wage war against God and His Messenger and spread mischief in the land is death, crucifixion, cutting off their hands and feet on opposite sides, or exile from the land. This ˹penalty˺ is a disgrace for them in this world, and they will suffer a tremendous punishment in the Hereafter.[244] **34.** As for those who repent before you seize them, then know that God is All-Forgiving, Most Merciful.

Closer to God

35. O believers! Be mindful of God and seek what brings you closer to Him and struggle in His Way, so you may be successful.

Reward of the Disbelievers

36. As for the disbelievers, even if they were to possess everything in the world twice over ˹and offer it all˺ to ransom themselves from the punishment of the Day of Judgment, it would never be accepted from them. And they will suffer a painful punishment. **37.** They will be desperate to get out of the Fire but they will never be able to. And they will suffer an everlasting punishment.

Punishment of Theft

38. As for male and female thieves, cut off their hands for what they have done—a deterrent from God. And God is Almighty, All-Wise.[245] **39.** But whoever repents after their wrongdoing and mends their ways, God will surely turn to them in forgiveness. Indeed, God is All-Forgiving, Most Merciful.

God's Might and Grace

40. Do you not know that the kingdom of the heavens and the earth belongs to God ˹alone˺? He punishes whoever He wills and forgives whoever He wills. And God is Most Capable of everything.

Do Not Be Disheartened

41. O Messenger! Do not grieve for those who race to disbelieve—those who say, "We believe" with their tongues, but their hearts are in disbelief. Nor those among the Jews who eagerly listen to lies, attentive to those who are too arrogant to come to you. They distort the Scripture, taking rulings out of context, then say, "If this is the ruling you get ˹from Muḥammad˺, accept it. If not, beware!" Whoever God allows to be deluded, you can never be of any help to them against God. It is not God's Will to purify their hearts. For them is disgrace in this world and they will suffer a tremendous punishment in the Hereafter.

Fair Judgment

42. They eagerly listen to falsehood and consume forbidden gain.[246] So if they come to you ˹O Prophet˺, either judge between them or turn away from them. If you turn away from them, they cannot harm you whatsoever. But if you judge between them, then do so with justice. Surely God loves those who are just. **43.** But why do they come to you for judgment when they ˹already˺ have the Torah containing God's judgment, then they turn away after all? They are not ˹true˺ believers.

Judging by the Torah

44. Indeed, We revealed the Torah, containing guidance and light, by which the prophets, who submitted themselves to God, made judgments for Jews. So too did the rabbis and scholars judge according to God's Book, with which they were entrusted and of which they were made keepers. So do not fear the people; fear Me! Nor trade my revelations for a fleeting gain. And those who do not judge by what God has revealed are ˹truly˺ the disbelievers.

---

244 The goal of this ruling is to protect all members of the society—Muslims and non-Muslims—against crimes committed by individuals who have no regard for the law or human rights.
245 Strict conditions and requirements must be met, making it almost impossible for this punishment to be carried out.
246 i.e., bribes and interest.

Justice System

45. We ordained for them in the Torah, "A life for a life, an eye for an eye, a nose for a nose, an ear for an ear, a tooth for a tooth—and for wounds equal retaliation." But whoever waives it charitably, it will be atonement for them. And those who do not judge by what God has revealed are ˹truly˺ the wrongdoers.

Judging by the Gospel

46. Then in the footsteps of the prophets, We sent Jesus, son of Mary, confirming the Torah revealed before him. And We gave him the Gospel containing guidance and light and confirming what was revealed in the Torah—a guide and a lesson to the God-fearing. **47.** So let the people of the Gospel judge by what God has revealed in it. And those who do not judge by what God has revealed are ˹truly˺ the rebellious.

Judging by the Quran

48. We have revealed to you ˹O Prophet˺ this Book with the truth, as a confirmation of previous Scriptures and a supreme authority on them. So judge between them by what God has revealed, and do not follow their desires over the truth that has come to you. To each of you We have ordained a code of law and a way of life. If God had willed, He would have made you one community, but His Will is to test you with what He has given ˹each of˺ you. So compete with one another in doing good. To God you will all return, then He will inform you ˹of the truth˺ regarding your differences.

God's Judgment

49. And judge between them ˹O Prophet˺ by what God has revealed, and do not follow their desires. And beware, so they do not lure you away from some of what God has revealed to you. If they turn away ˹from God's judgment˺, then know that it is God's Will to repay them for some of their sins, and that many people are indeed rebellious. **50.** Is it the judgment of ˹pre-Islamic˺ ignorance they seek? Who could be a better judge than God for people of sure faith?

Hypocrites' Guardians

51. O believers! Take neither Jews nor Christians as guardians—they are guardians of each other.[247] Whoever does so will be counted as one of them. Surely God does not guide the wrongdoing people. **52.** You see those with sickness in their hearts racing for their guardianship, saying ˹in justification˺, "We fear a turn of fortune will strike us." But perhaps God will bring about ˹your˺ victory or another favour by His command, and they will regret what they have hidden in their hearts. **53.** ˹Only then,˺ the believers will ask ˹one another˺, "Are these the ones who swore solemn oaths by God that they were with you?" Their deeds have been in vain, so they have become losers.

True Believers

54. O believers! Whoever among you abandons their faith, God will replace them with others who love Him and are loved by Him. They will be humble with the believers but firm towards the disbelievers, struggling in the Way of God; fearing no blame from anyone. This is the favour of God. He grants it to whoever He wills. And God is All-Bountiful, All-Knowing.

True Guardianship

55. Your only guardians are God, His Messenger, and fellow believers—who establish prayer and pay alms-tax with humility. **56.** Whoever allies themselves with God,

---

247 *Wali* means guardian, caretaker, protector, provider, ally, etc. The Prophet for example says, "A woman should not get married without a *wali*."—that is a guardian such as her father to represent her in the marriage and make sure she receives her full rights. The verse forbids Muslims from allying with the Jews and Christians (or anyone else) conspiring to persecute Muslims. On the other hand, as long as non-Muslims are not at war with Muslims or persecuting them, the Quran (60:8) commands Muslims to be kind and gracious to them.

His Messenger, and fellow believers, then it is certainly God's party that will prevail.

Unacceptable Guardianship

57. O believers! Do not seek the guardianship of those given the Scripture before you and the disbelievers who have made your faith a mockery and amusement. And be mindful of God if you are 'truly' believers. **58.** When you call to prayer, they mock it in amusement. This is because they are a people without understanding.

Who Deserves Resentment?

59. Say, 'O Prophet,' "O People of the Book! Do you resent us only because we believe in God and what has been revealed to us and what was revealed before—while most of you are rebellious?" **60.** Say, 'O Prophet,' "Shall I inform you of those who deserve a worse punishment from God 'than the rebellious'? It is those who earned God's condemnation and displeasure—some being reduced to apes and pigs[248] and worshippers of false gods. These are far worse in rank and farther astray from the Right Way."

Hypocrites Among Jews

61. When they come to you 'believers' they say, "We believe." But they are committed to disbelief when they enter and when they leave. And God knows what they hide. **62.** You see many of them racing towards sin, transgression, and consumption of forbidden gain. Evil indeed are their actions! **63.** Why do their rabbis and scholars not forbid them from saying what is sinful and consuming what is unlawful? Evil indeed is their inaction!

God Is Ever Generous

64. 'Some among' the Jews said, "God is tight-fisted."[249] May their fists be tied and they be condemned for what they said. Rather, He is open-handed,[250] giving freely as He pleases. That which has been revealed to you 'O Prophet' from your Lord will only cause many of them to increase in wickedness and disbelief. We have stirred among them hostility and hatred until the Day of Judgment. Whenever they kindle the fire of war, God puts it out. And they strive to spread corruption in the land. And God does not like corruptors.

Worst of Both Worlds

65. Had the People of the Book only been faithful and mindful 'of God', We would have certainly absolved them of their sins and admitted them into the Gardens of Bliss. **66.** And had they observed the Torah, the Gospel, and what has been revealed to them from their Lord, they would have been overwhelmed with provisions from above and below. Some among them are upright, yet many do nothing but evil.

A Messenger's Duty Is to Convey

67. O Messenger! Convey everything revealed to you from your Lord. If you do not, then you have not delivered His message. God will 'certainly' protect you from the people. Indeed, God does not guide the people who disbelieve.

Adherence to Scriptures

68. Say, 'O Prophet,' "O People of the Book! You have nothing to stand on unless you observe the Torah, the Gospel, and what has been revealed to you from your Lord." And your Lord's revelation to you 'O Prophet' will only cause many of them to increase in wickedness and disbelief. So do not grieve for the people who disbelieve.

---

248 Literally or metaphorically. See footnote for 2:65.
249 lit., God's Hand is tied up 'with greed'.
250 We believe that God has Hands, but not like ours. *See* the Introduction for details.

True Belief in God

69. Indeed, the believers, Jews, Sabians[251] and Christians—whoever ʿtrulyʾ believes in God and the Last Day and does good, there will be no fear for them, nor will they grieve.

The Israelites Rejecting Messengers

70. Indeed, We took a covenant from the Children of Israel and sent them messengers. Whenever a messenger came to them with what they did not desire, they denied some and killed others. 71. They thought there would be no consequences, so they turned a blind eye and a deaf ear. Yet God turned to them in forgiveness ʿafter their repentanceʾ, but again many became blind and deaf. And God is All-Seeing of what they do.

One God, Not Three

72. Those who say, "God is the Messiah, son of Mary," have certainly fallen into disbelief. The Messiah ʿhimselfʾ said, "O Children of Israel! Worship God—my Lord and your Lord." Whoever associates others with God ʿin worshipʾ will surely be forbidden Paradise by God. Their home will be the Fire. And the wrongdoers will have no helpers. 73. Those who say, "God is one in a Trinity," have certainly fallen into disbelief. There is only One God. If they do not stop saying this, those who disbelieve among them will be afflicted with a painful punishment.

Still Not Too Late

74. Will they not turn to God in repentance and seek His forgiveness? And God is All-Forgiving, Most Merciful.

Jesus Was Human, Not Divine

75. The Messiah, son of Mary, was no more than a messenger. ʿManyʾ messengers had ʿcome andʾ gone before him. His mother was a woman of truth. They both ate food.[252] See how We make the signs clear to them, yet see how they are deluded ʿfrom the truthʾ!

Follow the Truth

76. Say, ʿO Prophet,ʾ "How can you worship besides God those who can neither harm nor benefit you? And God ʿaloneʾ is the All-Hearing, All-Knowing." 77. Say, "O People of the Book! Do not go to extremes in your faith beyond the truth, nor follow the vain desires of those who went astray before ʿyouʾ. They misled many and strayed from the Right Way."

Evildoers Among the Israelites

78. The disbelievers among the Children of Israel were condemned in the revelations of David and Jesus, son of Mary. That was for their disobedience and violations. 79. They did not forbid one another from doing evil. Evil indeed was what they did! 80. You see many of them taking the disbelievers[253] as allies. Truly wicked are their misdeeds, which have earned them God's wrath. And they will be in everlasting torment. 81. Had they believed in God, the Prophet, and what has been revealed to him, they would have never taken those ʿpagansʾ as allies. But most of them are rebellious.

Those Most Gracious Towards Believers

82. You will surely find the most bitter towards the believers to be the Jews and polytheists and the most gracious to be those who call themselves Christian. That is because there are priests and monks among them and because they are not arrogant. 83. When they

---

251 *See* footnote for 2:62.
252 i.e., they were in need of food for nourishment. According to some scholars, this implies that Jesus and his mother had to relieve themselves after the food had been digested. Almighty God is far above depending on food or having to go to the restroom.
253 i.e., the pagans.

listen to what has been revealed to the Messenger, you see their eyes overflowing with tears for recognizing the truth. They say, "Our Lord! We believe, so count us among the witnesses. **84.** Why should we not believe in God and the truth that has come to us? And we long for our Lord to include us in the company of the righteous." **85.** So God will reward them for what they said with Gardens under which rivers flow, to stay there forever. And that is the reward of the good-doers. **86.** As for those who disbelieve and reject Our signs, they will be the residents of the Hellfire.

Be Moderate

87. O believers! Do not forbid the good things which God has made lawful for you, and do not transgress. Indeed, God does not like transgressors. **88.** Eat of the good, lawful things provided to you by God. And be mindful of God in Whom you believe.

Broken Oaths

89. God will not call you to account for your thoughtless oaths, but He will hold you accountable for deliberate oaths. The penalty for a broken oath is to feed ten poor people from what you normally feed your own family, or to clothe them, or to free a bondsperson. But if none of this is affordable, then you must fast three days. This is the penalty for breaking your oaths. So be mindful of your oaths. This is how God makes things clear to you, so perhaps you will be grateful.

Forbidden Items

90. O believers! Intoxicants, gambling, idols, and drawing lots for decisions[254] are all evil of Satan's handiwork. So shun them so you may be successful. **91.** Satan's plan is to stir up hostility and hatred between you with intoxicants and gambling and to prevent you from remembering God and praying. Will you not then abstain? **92.** Obey God and obey the Messenger and beware! But if you

turn away, then know that Our Messenger's duty is only to deliver ʿthe messageʾ clearly.

The Past Is Forgiven

93. There is no blame on those who believe and do good for what they had consumed before ʿthe prohibitionʾ, as long as they fear God, have faith, and do what is good; then they believe and act virtuously, then become fully mindful ʿof Godʾ and do righteous deeds. For God loves the good-doers.

Hunting While on Pilgrimage

94. O believers! God will surely test you with game within the reach of your hands and spears to distinguish those who fear Him in secret. Whoever transgresses from now on will suffer a painful punishment. **95.** O believers! Do not kill game while on pilgrimage. Whoever kills game intentionally must compensate by offering its equivalence—as judged by two just men among you—to be offered at the Sacred House, or by feeding the needy, or by fasting so that they may taste the consequences of their violations. God has forgiven what has been done. But those who persist will be punished by God. And God is Almighty, capable of punishment.

Seafood Is Lawful

96. It is lawful for you to hunt and eat seafood, as a provision for you and for travellers. But hunting on land is forbidden to you while on pilgrimage. Be mindful of God to Whom you all will be gathered.

Pilgrimage Symbols

97. God has made the Ka'bah—the Sacred House—a sanctuary of well-being for all people, along with the sacred months, the sacrificial animals, and the ʿofferings decorated withʾ garlands. All this so you may know that God knows whatever is in the heavens and whatever is on the earth, and that He has ʿperfectʾ knowledge

---

254　See footnote for 5:3.

of everything. **98.** Know that God is severe in punishment and that He is All-Forgiving, Most Merciful. **99.** The Messenger's duty is only to deliver ˹the message˺. And God ˹fully˺ knows what you reveal and what you conceal.

Good and Evil Not Equal

100. Say, ˹O Prophet,˺ "Good and evil are not equal, though you may be dazzled by the abundance of evil. So be mindful of God, O people of reason, so you may be successful."

Unnecessary Questions[255]

101. O believers! Do not ask about any matter which, if made clear to you, may disturb you. But if you inquire about what is being revealed in the Quran, it will be made clear to you. God has forgiven what was done ˹in the past˺.[256] And God is All-Forgiving, Most Forbearing. **102.** Some people before you asked such questions then denied their answers.

Camels Dedicated to Idols

103. God has never ordained the ˹so-called˺ *baḥîrah*, *sâ'ibah*, *waṣîlah*, and *ḥâm* camels.[257] But the disbelievers[258] just fabricate lies about God, and most of them lack understanding. **104.** When it is said to them, "Come to God's revelations and to the Messenger," they reply, "What we found our forefathers practicing is good enough for us." ˹Would they still do so,˺ even if their forefathers had absolutely no knowledge or guidance?

Everyone Accountable for Themselves

105. O believers! You are accountable only for yourselves.[259] It will not harm you if someone chooses to deviate—as long as you are ˹rightly˺ guided. To God you will all return, and He will inform you of what you used to do.

Verifying Bequests

106. O believers! When death approaches any of you, call upon two just Muslim men to witness as you make a bequest; otherwise, two non-Muslims if you are afflicted with death while on a journey.[260] If you doubt ˹their testimony˺, keep them after prayer and let them testify under oath ˹saying˺, "By God! We would never sell our testimony for any price, even in favour of a close relative, nor withhold the testimony of God. Otherwise, we would surely be sinful." **107.** If they are found guilty ˹of false testimony˺, let the deceased's two closest heirs affected by the bequest replace the witnesses and testify under oath ˹saying˺, "By God! Our testimony is truer than theirs. We have not transgressed. Otherwise, we would surely be wrongdoers." **108.** In this way it is more likely that witnesses will give true testimony or else fear that their oaths could be refuted by those of the heirs. Be mindful of God and obey. For God does not guide the rebellious people.

God Asking the Messengers

109. ˹Consider˺ the Day God will gather the messengers and say, "What response did you receive?" They will reply, "We have no knowledge ˹compared to You˺! You ˹alone˺ are indeed the Knower of all unseen."

---

255 Some Muslims would ask the Prophet unnecessary and sometimes meaningless questions. For example: who their fathers were, where their lost animals were, what they had in their pockets, etc. Some would even demand new rulings that would probably make things difficult for some Muslims or even themselves.

256 This implies that either these minor details have been overlooked by God out of His mercy or that God has forgiven them for these unnecessary questions.

257 These camels were allowed by pagan Arabs to pasture freely and were not to be used for labour or transportation after fathering or giving birth to a certain number of male or female camels.

258 i.e., the pagans.

259 After fulfilling their obligation of delivering the truth, enjoining what is good, and forbidding what is evil.

260 If no Muslim witnesses can be found.

5. The Spread Table (Al-Mâ'idah)

God's Favours upon Jesus

110. And ʾon Judgment Dayʾ God will say, "O Jesus, son of Mary! Remember My favour upon you and your mother: how I supported you with the holy spirit[261] so you spoke to people in ʾyourʾ infancy and adulthood. How I taught you writing, wisdom, the Torah, and the Gospel. How you moulded a bird from clay—by My Will—and breathed into it and it became a ʾrealʾ bird—by My Will. How you healed the blind and the lepers—by My Will. How you brought the dead to life—by My Will. How I prevented the Children of Israel from harming you when you came to them with clear proofs and the disbelievers among them said, "This is nothing but pure magic." 111. And how I inspired the disciples, "Believe in Me and My messenger!" They declared, "We believe and bear witness that we fully submit ʾto Godʾ."[262]

Miracle of the Table

112. ʾRememberʾ when the disciples asked, "O Jesus, son of Mary! Would your Lord be willing to send down to us a table spread with food from heaven?" Jesus answered, "Fear God if you are ʾtrulyʾ believers." 113. They said, "We ʾonlyʾ wish to eat from it to reassure our hearts, to verify you are indeed truthful to us, and to become its witnesses." 114. Jesus, son of Mary, prayed, "O God, our Lord! Send us from heaven a table spread with food as a feast for us—the first and last of us—and as a sign from You. Provide for us! You are indeed the Best Provider." 115. God answered, "I am sending it down to you. But whoever among you denies afterwards will be subjected to a torment I have never inflicted on anyone of My creation."

Jesus Denying Claim to Divinity

116. And ʾon Judgment Dayʾ God will say, "O Jesus, son of Mary! Did you ever ask the people to worship you and your mother as gods besides God?" He will answer, "Glory be to You! How could I ever say what I had no right to say? If I had said such a thing, you would have certainly known it. You know what is ʾhiddenʾ within me, but I do not know what is within You. Indeed, You ʾaloneʾ are the Knower of all unseen. 117. I never told them anything except what You ordered me to say: "Worship God—my Lord and your Lord!" And I was witness over them as long as I remained among them. But when You took me,[263] You were the Witness over them—and You are a Witness over all things. 118. If You punish them, they belong to You after all.[264] But if You forgive them, You are surely the Almighty, All-Wise." 119. God will declare, "This is the Day when ʾonlyʾ the faithful will benefit from their faithfulness. Theirs are Gardens under which rivers flow, to stay there for ever and ever. God is pleased with them and they are pleased with Him. That is the ultimate triumph." 120. To God ʾaloneʾ belongs the kingdom of the heavens and the earth and everything within. And He is Most Capable of everything.

---

261 i.e., the angel Gabriel.
262 lit., Muslims.
263 This refers to the ascension of Jesus Christ. *See* footnote for 3:54.
264 i.e., as Your creation, they cannot escape the punishment.

6. Cattle (Al-An'âm)

Like the previous chapter, this Meccan chapter masterfully demonstrates God's power and knowledge, and thoroughly refutes pagan beliefs and unfounded practices, including animal offerings to the idols. Permissible and prohibited foods are explained in more detail than in the previous chapter. The nature of prophethood is defined, making it clear that messengers cannot do anything without the Will of God. This chapter begins by highlighting God's authority, just like the ending of the previous chapter, and concludes by emphasizing accountability for one's deeds, just like the beginning of the next chapter.

In the Name of God—the Most Compassionate, Most Merciful

Rejecting the Almighty

1. All praise is for God Who created the heavens and the earth and made darkness and light.[265] Yet the disbelievers set up equals to their Lord ʿin worshipʾ. 2. He is the One Who created you from clay,[266] then appointed a term ʿfor your deathʾ and another known only to Him ʿfor your resurrectionʾ—yet you continue to doubt! 3. He is the Only True God in the heavens and the earth. He knows whatever you conceal and whatever you reveal, and knows whatever you do.

Taking God's Signs Lightly

4. Whenever a sign comes to them from their Lord, they turn away from it. 5. They have indeed rejected the truth when it came to them, so they will soon face the consequences of their ridicule.

Fate of the Deniers

6. Have they not seen how many ʿdisbelievingʾ peoples We destroyed before them? We had made them more established in the land than you. We sent down abundant rain for them and made rivers flow at their feet. Then We destroyed them for their sins and replaced them with other peoples.

Demanding Written Scripture[267]

7. Had We sent down to you ʿO Prophetʾ a revelation in writing and they were to touch it with their own hands, the disbelievers would still have said, "This is nothing but pure magic!"

Demanding to See an Angel

8. They say, "Why has no ʿvisibleʾ angel come with him?" Had We sent down an angel, the matter would have certainly been settled ʿat onceʾ,[268] and they would have never been given more time ʿto repentʾ. 9. And if We had sent an angel, We would have certainly made it ʿassume the form ofʾ a man—leaving them more confused than they already are.

Fate of the Ridiculers

10. ʿOtherʾ messengers had already been ridiculed before you ʿO Prophetʾ, but those who mocked them were overtaken by what they used to ridicule. 11. Say, "Travel throughout the land and see the fate of the deniers."

---

265 "Light" is always used in the Quran in the singular (*nûr*), whereas "darkness" is used in the plural (*ẓulumât*). *Nûr* is usually used in a metaphorical sense to refer to true guidance, whereas *ẓulumât* refers to different forms of misguidance.

266 i.e., created your father, Adam, from clay. Some scholars suggest that if we examine all the minerals found in the earth (potassium, nitrogen, and carbon), we find that these are the same minerals that make up our body. Furthermore when we die, our bodies are absorbed back into the ground. And when we are resurrected, we will be resurrected from the ground (*see* 20:55).

267 Similar to the Tablets of Moses.

268 i.e., they would have been destroyed immediately upon denying the angel.

God Almighty

12. Ask ˹them, O Prophet˺, "To whom belongs everything in the heavens and the earth?" Say, "To God!" He has taken upon Himself to be Merciful. He will certainly gather ˹all of˺ you together for the Day of Judgment—about which there is no doubt. But those who have ruined themselves will never believe. 13. To Him belongs whatever exists in the day and night. And He is the All-Hearing, All-Knowing.

God Is the Guardian

14. Say, ˹O Prophet,˺ "Will I take any guardian other than God, the Originator of the heavens and the earth, Who provides for all and is not in need of provision?" Say, "I have been commanded to be the first to submit and not be one of the polytheists." 15. Say, "I truly fear—if I were to disobey my Lord—the torment of a tremendous Day." 16. Whoever is spared the torment of that Day will have certainly been shown God's mercy. And that is the absolute triumph.

God Reigns Supreme

17. If God touches you with harm, none can undo it except Him. And if He touches you with a blessing, He is Most Capable of everything. 18. He reigns supreme over His creation. And He is the All-Wise, All-Aware.

God Is the Best Witness

19. Ask ˹them, O Prophet˺, "Who is the best witness?" Say, "God is! He is a Witness between me and you. And this Quran has been revealed to me so that, with it, I may warn you and whoever it reaches. Do you ˹pagans˺ testify that there are other gods besides God?" ˹Then˺ say, "I will never testify ˹to this˺!" ˹And˺ say, "There is only One God. And I totally reject whatever ˹idols˺ you associate with Him."

Recognizing the Prophet

20. Those to whom We gave the Scripture recognize him ˹to be a true prophet˺ as they recognize their own children. Those who have ruined themselves will never believe. 21. Who does more wrong than those who fabricate lies against God or deny His signs? Indeed, the wrongdoers will never succeed.

The Polytheists

22. ˹Consider˺ the Day We will gather them all together then ask those who associated others ˹with God in worship˺, "Where are those gods you used to claim?" 23. Their only argument will be: "By God, our Lord! We were never polytheists." 24. See how they will lie about themselves and how those ˹gods˺ they fabricated will fail them!

Disbelievers Turning Away

25. There are some of them who ˹pretend to˺ listen to your recitation ˹of the Quran˺, but We have cast veils over their hearts—leaving them unable to comprehend it—and deafness in their ears. Even if they were to see every sign, they still would not believe in them. The disbelievers would ˹even˺ come to argue with you, saying, "This ˹Quran˺ is nothing but ancient fables!" 26. They turn others away from the Prophet and distance themselves as well. They ruin none but themselves, yet they fail to perceive it.

Horrified by the Fire

27. If only you could see when they will be detained before the Fire! They will cry, "Oh! If only we could be sent back, we would never deny the signs of our Lord and we would ˹surely˺ be of the believers." 28. But no! ˹They only say this˺ because the truth they used to hide will become all too clear to them. Even if they were to be sent back, they would certainly revert to what they were forbidden. Indeed they are liars!

Deniers of the Hereafter

29. They insisted, "There is nothing beyond this worldly life and we will never be resurrected." 30. But if only you could see when

they will be detained before their Lord! He will ask 'them', "Is this 'Hereafter' not the truth?" They will cry, "Absolutely, by our Lord!" He will say, "Then taste the punishment for your disbelief." **31.** Losers indeed are those who deny the meeting with God until the Hour takes them by surprise, then they will cry, "Woe to us for having ignored this!" They will bear 'the burden of' their sins on their backs. Evil indeed is their burden!

Fleeting Enjoyment

32. This worldly life is no more than play and amusement, but far better is the 'eternal' Home of the Hereafter for those mindful 'of God'. Will you not then understand?

Not the First Rejected Prophet

33. We certainly know that what they say grieves you 'O Prophet'. It is not your honesty they question—it is God's signs that the wrongdoers deny. **34.** Indeed, messengers before you were rejected but patiently endured rejection and persecution until Our help came to them. And God's promise 'to help' is never broken. And you have already received some of the narratives of these messengers.

Disbelievers, No Matter What

35. If you find their denial unbearable, then build—if you can—a tunnel through the earth or stairs to the sky to bring them a 'more compelling' sign. Had God so willed, He could have guided them all. So do not be one of those ignorant 'of this fact'.

Deaf to the Truth

36. Only the attentive will respond 'to your call'. As for the dead, God will raise them up, then to Him they will 'all' be returned. **37.** They ask, "Why has no 'other' sign been sent down to him from his Lord?" Say, 'O

Prophet,' "God certainly has the power to send down a sign"—though most of them do not know.

The Animal Kingdom

38. All living beings roaming the earth and winged birds soaring in the sky are communities like yourselves.[269] We have left nothing out of the Record.[270] Then to their Lord they will be gathered all together.

Guidance Is from God Only

39. Those who deny Our signs are 'wilfully' deaf and dumb—lost in darkness. God leaves whoever He wills to stray and guides whoever He wills to the Straight Way.

God Alone Removes Hardships

40. Ask 'them, O Prophet', "Imagine if you were overwhelmed by God's torment or the Hour—would you call upon any other than God 'for help'? 'Answer me' if your claims are true! **41.** No! He is the only One you would call. And if He willed, He could remove the affliction that made you invoke Him. Only then will you forget whatever you associate with Him 'in worship'."

Deniers' Gradual Destruction

42. Indeed, We have sent messengers before you 'O Prophet' to other people who We put through suffering and adversity 'for their denial', so perhaps they would be humbled. **43.** Why did they not humble themselves when We made them suffer? Instead, their hearts were hardened, and Satan made their misdeeds appealing to them. **44.** When they became oblivious to warnings, We showered them with everything they desired. But just as they became prideful of what they were given, We seized them by surprise, then they instantly fell into despair! **45.** So the wrong-

---

269 God has created living beings (like animals, birds, and fish) just like He created human beings. He provides for all and is merciful to all. They all belong to communities and have their own systems of living.
270 The Record refers to the Preserved Tablet (*Al-Lawḥ Al-Maḥfûẓ*) in which God has written the destiny of His entire creation.

doers were utterly uprooted. And all praise is for God—Lord of all worlds.

Only God Can Relieve Affliction

46. Ask ˹them, O Prophet˺, "Imagine if God were to take away your hearing or sight, or seal your hearts—who else other than God could restore it?" See ˹O Prophet˺ how We vary the signs, yet they still turn away. **47.** Ask, "Imagine if God's punishment were to overwhelm you with or without warning—who would be destroyed other than the wrongdoers?"

The Messengers' Duty

48. We have sent messengers only as deliverers of good news and as warners. Whoever believes and does good, there will be no fear for them, nor will they grieve. **49.** But those who deny Our signs will be afflicted with punishment for their rebelliousness.

No More than a Prophet

50. Say, ˹O Prophet,˺ "I do not say to you that I possess God's treasuries or know the unseen, nor do I claim to be an angel. I only follow what is revealed to me." Say, "Are those blind ˹to the truth˺ equal to those who can see? Will you not then reflect?"

The Quran as a Warning

51. Warn with this ˹Quran˺ those who are awed by the prospect of being gathered before their Lord—when they will have no protector or intercessor besides Him—so perhaps they will be mindful ˹of Him˺.

Influential Meccans vs. Poor Believers[271]

52. ˹O Prophet!˺ Do not dismiss those ˹poor believers˺ who invoke their Lord morning and evening, seeking His pleasure.[272] You are not accountable for them whatsoever, nor are they accountable for you. So do not dismiss them, or you will be one of the wrongdoers. **53.** In this way We have tested some by means of others, so those ˹disbelievers˺ may say, "Has God favoured these ˹poor believers˺ out of all of us?" Does God not best recognize the grateful? **54.** When the believers in Our revelations come to you, say, "Peace be upon you! Your Lord has taken upon Himself to be Merciful. Whoever among you commits evil ignorantly ˹or recklessly˺ then repents afterwards and mends their ways, then God is truly All-Forgiving, Most Merciful." **55.** This is how We make Our signs clear, so the way of the wicked may become distinct.

Only One God

56. Say, ˹O Prophet,˺ "I have been forbidden to worship those you invoke besides God." Say, "I will not follow your desires, for I then would certainly be astray and not one of those ˹rightly˺ guided."

Desperate to Be Destroyed

57. Say, ˹O Prophet,˺ "Indeed, I stand on a clear proof from my Lord—yet you have denied it. That ˹torment˺ you seek to hasten is not within my power. It is only God Who decides ˹its time˺. He declares the truth. And He is the Best of Judges." **58.** Say ˹also˺, "If what you seek to hasten were within my power, the matter between us would have already been settled. But God knows the wrongdoers best."

God's Infinite Knowledge

59. With Him are the keys of the unseen—no one knows them except Him.[273] And He knows what is in the land and sea. Not even a leaf falls without His knowledge, nor a grain in the darkness of the earth or any-

---

271 Some of the influential leaders of Mecca asked the Prophet to send poor Muslims away if he ever wanted these elites to sit and listen to his message. These verses were revealed commanding the Prophet to keep the company of the poor and not alienate them.
272 lit., seeking His Face.
273 The five keys of the unseen are mentioned in 31:34.

thing—green or dry—but is 'written' in a perfect Record.[274]

Sleep: The Twin Brother of Death

60. He is the One Who calls back your souls by night and knows what you do by day, then revives you daily to complete your appointed term. To Him is your 'ultimate' return, then He will inform you of what you used to do. **61.** He reigns supreme over all of His creation, and sends recording-angels, watching over you. When death comes to any of you, Our angels take their soul, never neglecting this duty. **62.** Then they are 'all' returned to God—their True Master. Judgment is His 'alone'. And He is the Swiftest Reckoner.

God's Power

63. Say, 'O Prophet,' "Who rescues you from the darkest times on land and at sea? He 'alone' you call upon with humility, openly and secretly: "If You rescue us from this, we will be ever grateful." **64.** Say, "'Only' God rescues you from this and any other distress, yet you associate others with Him 'in worship'". **65.** Say, "He 'alone' has the power to unleash upon you a torment from above or below you or split you into 'conflicting' factions and make you taste the violence of one another." See how We vary the signs, so perhaps they will comprehend.

Deniers of the Truth

66. Still your people 'O Prophet' have rejected this 'Quran', although it is the truth. Say, "I am not a keeper over you." **67.** Every 'destined' matter has a 'set' time to transpire. And you will soon come to know.

Mockers of the Quran

68. And when you come across those who ridicule Our revelations, do not sit with them unless they engage in a different topic. Should Satan make you forget, then once you remember, do not 'continue to' sit with the wrongdoing people. **69.** Those mindful 'of God' will not be accountable for those 'who ridicule it' whatsoever—their duty is to advise, so perhaps the ridiculers will abstain.

Way to Salvation

70. And leave those who take this[275] faith 'of Islam' as mere play and amusement and are deluded by 'their' worldly life. Yet remind them by this 'Quran', so no one should be ruined for their misdeeds. They will have no protector or intercessor other than God. Even if they were to offer every 'possible' ransom, none will be accepted from them. Those are the ones who will be ruined for their misdeeds. They will have a boiling drink and painful punishment for their disbelief.

Almighty God

71. Ask 'them, O Prophet', "Should we invoke, other than God, those 'idols' which cannot benefit or harm us, and turn back to disbelief after God has guided us? 'If we do so, we will be' like those disoriented by devils in the wilderness, while their companions call them to guidance, 'saying', 'Come to us!' Say, 'O Prophet,' "God's guidance is the 'only' true guidance. And we are commanded to submit to the Lord of all worlds, **72.** establish prayer, and be mindful of Him. To Him you will all be gathered together. **73.** He is the One Who created the heavens and the earth in truth. On the Day 'of Judgment' He will say, 'Be!' And there will be! His command is truth. All authority is His 'alone'[276] on the Day the Trumpet will be blown.[277] He is the Knower of all—seen or unseen. And He is the All-Wise, All-Aware."

---

274 See footnote for 6:38.
275 lit., their faith (which they are supposed to follow).
276 God grants authority to some of His servants in this world, but none will have authority on Judgment Day except Him. See 3:26.
277 On the Day of Judgment, the Trumpet will be blown by an angel—causing all to die. When it is blown a second time, everyone will be raised from the dead for judgment (see 39:68).

Abraham Corrects His Father

74. And ˹remember˺ when Abraham said to his father, Âzar, "Do you take idols as gods? It is clear to me that you and your people are entirely misguided."

Abraham Refutes Celestial Worship

75. We also showed Abraham the wonders of the heavens and the earth, so he would be sure in faith. 76. When the night grew dark upon him, he saw a star and said, "This is my Lord!" But when it set, he said, "I do not love things that set." 77. Then when he saw the moon rising, he said, "This one is my Lord!" But when it disappeared, he said, "If my Lord does not guide me, I will certainly be one of the misguided people." 78. Then when he saw the sun shining, he said, "This must be my Lord—it is the greatest!" But again when it set, he declared, "O my people! I totally reject whatever you associate ˹with God in worship˺. 79. I have turned my face towards the One Who has originated the heavens and the earth—being upright—and I am not one of the polytheists."

Abraham Debates His People

80. And his people argued with him. He responded, "Are you arguing with me about God, while He has guided me? I am not afraid of whatever ˹idols˺ you associate with Him—˹none can harm me,˺ unless my Lord so wills. My Lord encompasses everything in ˹His˺ knowledge. Will you not be mindful? 81. And how should I fear your associate-gods, while you have no fear in associating ˹others˺ with God—a practice He has never authorized? Which side has more right to security? ˹Tell me˺ if you really know!" 82. It is ˹only˺ those who are faithful and do not tarnish their faith with falsehood[278] who are guaranteed security and are ˹rightly˺ guided. 83. This was the argument We gave Abraham against his people. We elevate in rank whoever We please. Surely your Lord is All-Wise, All-Knowing.

Abraham and Other Noble Prophets

84. And We blessed him with Isaac and Jacob. We guided them all as We previously guided Noah and those among his descendants: David, Solomon, Job, Joseph, Moses, and Aaron. This is how We reward the good-doers. 85. Likewise, ˹We guided˺ Zachariah, John, Jesus, and Elias, who were all of the righteous. 86. ˹We also guided˺ Ishmael, Elisha, Jonah, and Lot, favouring each over other people ˹of their time˺. 87. And ˹We favoured˺ some of their forefathers, their descendants, and their brothers. We chose them and guided them to the Straight Path.

Prophetic Guidance

88. This is God's guidance with which He guides whoever He wills of His servants. Had they associated others with Him ˹in worship˺, their ˹good˺ deeds would have been wasted. 89. Those were the ones to whom We gave the Scripture, wisdom, and prophethood. But if these ˹pagans˺ disbelieve in this ˹message˺, then We have already entrusted it to a people who will never disbelieve in it.[279] 90. These ˹prophets˺ were ˹rightly˺ guided by God, so follow their guidance. Say, "I ask no reward of you for this ˹Quran˺—it is a reminder to the whole world."

Scriptures Denied

91. And they[280] have not shown God His proper reverence when they said, "God has revealed nothing to any human being." Say, ˹O Prophet,˺ "Who then revealed the Book brought forth by Moses as a light and guidance for people, which you split into separate sheets—revealing some and hiding much? You have been taught ˹through this

---

278   i.e., associating false gods in worship with the Almighty.
279   i.e., the companions of the Prophet.
280   Some Jews.

Quran' what neither you nor your forefathers knew." Say, 'O Prophet,' "God 'revealed it'!" Then leave them to amuse themselves with falsehood.

Quran for All

92. This is a blessed Book which We have revealed—confirming what came before it—so you may warn the Mother of Cities[281] and everyone around it. Those who believe in the Hereafter 'truly' believe in it and guard their prayers.

Fate of the Wicked

93. Who does more wrong than the one who fabricates lies against God or claims, "I have received revelations!"—although nothing was revealed to them—or the one who says, "I can reveal the like of God's revelations!"? If you 'O Prophet' could only see the wrongdoers in the throes of death while the angels are stretching out their hands 'saying', "Give up your souls! Today you will be rewarded with the torment of disgrace for telling lies about God and for being arrogant towards His revelations!" 94. 'Today' you have come back to Us all alone as We created you the first time—leaving behind everything We have provided you with. We do not see your intercessors with you—those you claimed were God's partners 'in worship'. All your ties have been broken and all your claims have let you down.

God's Power of Creation

95. Indeed, God is the One Who causes seeds and fruit stones to sprout. He brings forth the living from the dead and the dead from the living. That is God! How can you then be deluded 'from the truth'? 96. He causes the dawn to break, and has made the night for rest and 'made' the sun and the moon 'to travel' with precision. That is the design of the Almighty, All-Knowing. 97. And He is the One Who has made the stars as your guide through the darkness of land and sea. We have already made the signs clear for people who know. 98. And He is the One Who originated you all from a single soul,[282] then assigned you a place to live and another to 'be laid to' rest. We have already made the signs clear for people who comprehend. 99. And He is the One Who sends down rain from the sky—causing all kinds of plants to grow—producing green stalks from which We bring forth clustered grain. And from palm trees come clusters of dates hanging within reach. 'There are' also gardens of grapevines, olives, and pomegranates, similar 'in shape' but dissimilar 'in taste'. Look at their fruit as it yields and ripens! Indeed, in these are signs for people who believe.

God Has No Children

100. Yet they associate the jinn[283] with God 'in worship', even though He created them, and they falsely attribute to Him sons[284] and daughters[285] out of ignorance. Glorified and Exalted is He above what they claim! 101. 'He is' the Originator of the heavens and earth. How could He have children when He has no mate? He created all things and has 'perfect' knowledge of everything.

Worship God Alone

102. That is God—your Lord! There is no god 'worthy of worship' except Him. 'He is' the Creator of all things, so worship Him 'alone'. And He is the Maintainer of everything. 103. No vision can encompass Him,

---

281 "The Mother of Cities" is an honorary title given to the City of Mecca because of its great religious significance as the home of God's first house of worship ever built on earth, and perhaps because of its central location as well.
282 i.e., Adam.
283 Jinn are another creation of God, made of "smokeless fire," and inhabit a realm parallel to our own. Like us, they have free will and can choose guidance or disobedience.
284 i.e., "Jesus" in Christian belief.
285 i.e., "the angels" in pre-Islamic Arab tradition.

6. Cattle (Al-An'âm)

but He encompasses all vision. For He is the Most Subtle, All-Aware.[286]

Call to Humanity

104. Indeed, there have come to you insights from your Lord. So whoever chooses to see, it is for their own good. But whoever chooses to be blind, it is to their own loss. And I am not a keeper over you. **105.** And so We vary our signs to the extent that they will say, "You have studied ˹previous scriptures˺,"[287] and We make this ˹Quran˺ clear for people who know.

Guidance Is from God Alone

106. ˹O Prophet!˺ Follow what is revealed to you from your Lord—there is no god ˹worthy of worship˺ except Him—and turn away from the polytheists. **107.** Had God willed, they would not have been polytheists. We have not appointed you as their keeper, nor are you their maintainer.

God Is the Judge

108. ˹O believers!˺ Do not insult what they invoke besides God or they will insult God spitefully out of ignorance. This is how We have made each people's deeds appealing to them. Then to their Lord is their return, and He will inform them of what they used to do.

Signs of No Use

109. They swear by God their most solemn oaths that if a sign were to come to them, they would certainly believe in it. Say, ˹O Prophet,˺ "Signs are only with God." What will make you ˹believers˺ realize that even if a sign were to come to them, they still would not believe? **110.** We turn their hearts and eyes away ˹from the truth˺ as they refused to believe at first, leaving them to wander blindly in their defiance. **111.** Even if We had sent them the angels, made the dead speak to them, and assembled before their own eyes every sign ˹they demanded˺, they still would not have believed—unless God so willed. But most of them are ignorant ˹of this˺.

The Deception

112. And so We have made for every prophet enemies—devilish humans and jinn—whispering to one another with elegant words of deception. Had it been your Lord's Will, they would not have done such a thing. So leave them and their deceit, **113.** so that the hearts of those who disbelieve in the Hereafter may be receptive to it, be pleased with it, and be persistent in their evil pursuits.

The Perfect Book

114. ˹Say, O Prophet,˺ "Should I seek a judge other than God while He is the One Who has revealed for you the Book ˹with the truth˺ perfectly explained?" Those who were given the Scripture know that it has been revealed ˹to you˺ from your Lord in truth. So do not be one of those who doubt. **115.** The Word of your Lord has been perfected in truth and justice. None can change His Words. And He is the All-Hearing, All-Knowing.

Most Are Deviant

116. ˹O Prophet!˺ If you were to obey most of those on earth, they would lead you away from God's Way. They follow nothing but assumptions and do nothing but lie. **117.** Indeed, your Lord knows best who has strayed from His Way and who is ˹rightly˺ guided.

---

286 No one is able to see God in this world, but there is extensive evidence in the Quran and the teachings of the Prophet that the believers will be able to see their Lord on the Day of Judgment.

287 Allegations have always been made that the Prophet copied the Quran from the Bible, mostly because of similar narratives in both Scriptures (such as the stories of Adam, Joseph, Moses, and others). Historically, the Bible was not translated into Arabic until centuries after the Prophet. Even if an Arabic translation of the Bible existed at his time, he could not have copied it because he could not read or write. From an Islamic point of view, similarities stem from the fact that both scriptures came originally from the same source—divine revelation. For more details, *see* the Introduction.

74 of 392

Lawful and Unlawful Meat

118. So eat only of what is slaughtered in God's Name if you truly believe in His revelations. **119.** Why should you not eat of what is slaughtered in God's Name when He has already explained to you what He has forbidden to you—except when compelled by necessity? Many ˹deviants˺ certainly mislead others by their whims out of ignorance. Surely your Lord knows the transgressors best. **120.** Shun all sin—open and secret. Indeed, those who commit sin will be punished for what they earn. **121.** Do not eat of what is not slaughtered in God's Name. For that would certainly be ˹an act of˺ disobedience. Surely the devils whisper to their ˹human˺ associates to argue with you.[288] If you were to obey them, then you ˹too˺ would be polytheists.

Metaphor for Believers and Disbelievers

122. Can those who had been dead, to whom We gave life and a light with which they can walk among people, be compared to those in complete darkness from which they can never emerge?[289] That is how the misdeeds of the disbelievers have been made appealing to them. **123.** And so We have placed in every society the most wicked to conspire in it. Yet they plot only against themselves, but they fail to perceive it.

Craving Prophethood

124. Whenever a sign comes to them, they say, "We will never believe until we receive what God's messengers received." God knows best where to place His message. The wicked will soon be overwhelmed by humiliation from God and a severe punishment for their evil plots.

Open and Restricted Hearts

125. Whoever God wills to guide, He opens their heart to Islam.[290] But whoever He wills to leave astray, He makes their chest tight and constricted as if they were climbing up into the sky. This is how God dooms those who disbelieve. **126.** That is your Lord's Path—perfectly straight. We have already made the signs clear to those who are mindful. **127.** They will have the Home of Peace with their Lord, Who will be their Guardian because of what they used to do.

Humans and Jinn on Judgment Day

128. ˹Consider˺ the Day He will gather them ˹all˺ together and say, "O assembly of jinn! You misled humans in great numbers." And their human associates will say, "Our Lord! We benefited from each other's company,[291] but now we have reached the term which You appointed for us." ˹Then˺ He will say, "The Fire is your home, yours to stay in forever, except whoever God wills to spare."[292] Surely your Lord is All-Wise, All-Knowing. **129.** This is how We make the wrongdoers ˹destructive˺ allies of one another because of their misdeeds.

Confession of Evil Humans and Jinn

130. ˹God will ask,˺ "O assembly of jinn and humans! Did messengers not come from among you, proclaiming My revelations and warning you of the coming of this Day of yours?" They will say, "We confess against ourselves!" For they have been deluded by ˹their˺ worldly life. And they will testify against themselves that they were disbelievers. **131.** This ˹sending of the messengers˺ is because your Lord would never destroy a society for their wrongdoing while its people are unaware ˹of the truth˺.

---

288 Because Muslims are allowed to eat the meat of animals slaughtered properly and not carrion, the pagans of Mecca used to argue, "Why are you only allowed to eat what you yourselves kill but not what God causes to die?"
289 The Quran often compares disbelief to death and blindness whereas belief is compared to life and the ability to see.
290 Islam literally means 'submission to the Will of God.'
291 For example, the jinn helped humans with magic, while the jinn had a feeling of importance when they had a human following.
292 i.e., disobedient Muslims. They will be punished according to the severity of their sins, but eventually no Muslim will stay in Hell forever.

The Good and the Evil

132. They will each be assigned ranks according to their deeds. And your Lord is not unaware of what they do.

God Is Not in Need of His Creation

133. Your Lord is the Self-Sufficient, Full of Mercy. If He wills, He can do away with you and replace you with whoever He wills, just as He produced you from the offspring of other people. **134.** Indeed, what you have been promised will certainly come to pass. And you will have no escape.

Warning to Meccan Pagans

135. Say, ˹O Prophet,˺ "O my people! Persist in your ways, for I ˹too˺ will persist in mine. You will soon know who will fare best in the end. Indeed, the wrongdoers will never succeed."

Unfair Giving²⁹³

136. The pagans set aside for God a share of the crops and cattle He created, saying, "This ˹portion˺ is for God," so they claim, "and this ˹one˺ for our associate-gods." Yet the portion of their associate-gods is not shared with God while God's portion is shared with their associate-gods. What unfair judgment!

Self-Destruction²⁹⁴

137. Likewise, the pagans' evil associates have made it appealing to them to kill their own children—only leading to their destruction as well as confusion in their faith. Had it been God's Will, they would not have done such a thing. So leave them and their falsehood.

Idols' Share in Cattle and Crops

138. They say, "These cattle and crops are reserved—none may eat them except those we permit," so they claim. Some other cattle are exempted from labour and others are not slaughtered in God's Name—falsely attributing lies to Him. He will repay them for their lies. **139.** They ˹also˺ say, "The offspring of this cattle is reserved for our males and forbidden to our females; but if it is stillborn, they may all share it." He will repay them for their falsehood. Surely He is All-Wise, All-Knowing.

Lost in Ignorance

140. Lost indeed are those who have murdered their own children foolishly out of ignorance and have forbidden what God has provided for them—falsely attributing lies to God. They have certainly strayed and are not ˹rightly˺ guided.

God's Bounties

141. He is the One Who produces gardens—both cultivated and wild²⁹⁵—and palm trees, crops of different flavours, olives, and pomegranates—similar ˹in shape˺, but dissimilar ˹in taste˺. Eat of the fruit they bear and pay the dues at harvest, but do not waste. Surely He does not like the wasteful.

Four Pairs of Cattle, Male and Female²⁹⁶

142. Some cattle are fit for labour, others are too small.²⁹⁷ Eat of what God has provided for you and do not follow Satan's footsteps. Certainly, he is your sworn enemy. **143.** ˹God has created˺ four pairs: a pair of sheep and a pair of goats—ask ˹them, O Prophet˺, "Has He forbidden ˹to you˺ the

---

293 The pagans used to assign God a share of their property (as a charity to the poor) and another to their idols (as a fee to idol keepers). However, God's share always ended up in the pockets of the keepers, whereas the share of false gods was never donated to the poor.

294 Some pagan Arabs used to kill their own children (especially females) for fear of poverty. Others would vow to sacrifice a son if blessed with a certain number of sons.

295 Or trellised and untrellised.

296 These four pairs were the main domesticated cattle in Arabia at the time of revelation.

297 Strong cattle like camels and oxen can be used for labour, whereas smaller ones like goats and sheep are not suitable for labour but are good for their meat, milk, hide, etc.

two males or the two females or what is in the wombs of the two females? Tell me with knowledge, if what you say is true."— **144.** and a pair of camels and a pair of oxen. Ask ˹them˺, "Has He forbidden ˹to you˺ the two males or the two females or what is in the wombs of the two females? Or were you present when God gave you this commandment?" Who does more wrong than those who fabricate lies against God to mislead others without ˹any˺ knowledge? Surely God does not guide the wrongdoing people.

Meat Forbidden to Muslims

145. Say, ˹O Prophet,˺ "I do not find in what has been revealed to me anything forbidden to eat except carrion, running blood, swine—which is impure—or a sinful offering in the name of any other than God. But if someone is compelled by necessity—neither driven by desire nor exceeding immediate need—then surely your Lord is All-Forgiving, Most Merciful."

Meat Forbidden to Jews

146. For those who are Jewish, We forbade every animal with undivided hoofs and the fat of oxen and sheep except what is joined to their backs or intestines or mixed with bone. In this way We rewarded them for their violations. And We are certainly truthful. **147.** But if they deny you ˹O Prophet˺, say, "Your Lord is infinite in mercy, yet His punishment will not be averted from the wicked people."

Free Choice

148. The polytheists will argue, "Had it been God's Will, neither we nor our forefathers would have associated others with Him ˹in worship˺ or made anything unlawful." Likewise, those before them rejected the truth until they tasted Our punishment. Ask ˹them, O Prophet˺, "Do you have any knowledge that you can produce for us? Surely you follow

nothing but ˹false˺ assumptions and you do nothing but lie." **149.** Say, "God has the most conclusive argument. Had it been His Will, He would have imposed guidance upon all of you." **150.** Say, ˹O Prophet,˺ "Bring your witnesses who can testify that God has forbidden this." If they ˹falsely˺ testify, do not testify with them. And do not follow the desires of those who deny Our proofs, disbelieve in the Hereafter, and set up equals with their Lord.

God's Commandments

151. Say, ˹O Prophet,˺ "Come! Let me recite to you what your Lord has forbidden to you: do not associate others with Him ˹in worship˺. ˹Do not fail to˺ honour your parents. Do not kill your children for fear of poverty. We provide for you and for them. Do not come near indecencies, openly or secretly. Do not take a ˹human˺ life—made sacred by God—except with ˹legal˺ right.[298] This is what He has commanded you, so perhaps you will understand. **152.** And do not come near the wealth of the orphan—unless intending to enhance it—until they attain maturity. Give full measure and weigh with justice. We never require of any soul more than what it can afford. Whenever you speak,[299] maintain justice—even regarding a close relative. And fulfil your covenant with God. This is what He has commanded you, so perhaps you will be mindful. **153.** Indeed, that is My Path—perfectly straight. So follow it and do not follow other ways, for they will lead you away from His Way. This is what He has commanded you, so perhaps you will be conscious ˹of God˺."

The Torah

154. Additionally, We gave Moses the Scripture, completing the favour upon those who do good, detailing everything, and as a guide and a mercy, so perhaps they would be certain of the meeting with their Lord.

---

298 For example, in retaliation for intentional killing through legal channels.
299 i.e., when you testify or judge.

The Quran

155. This is a blessed Book We have revealed. So follow it and be mindful ˹of God˺, so you may be shown mercy. **156.** You ˹pagans˺ can no longer say, "Scriptures were only revealed to two groups before us and we were unaware of their teachings." **157.** Nor can you say, "If only the Scriptures had been revealed to us, we would have been better guided than they." Now there has come to you from your Lord a clear proof[300]—a guide and mercy. Who then does more wrong than those who deny God's revelations and turn away from them? We will reward those who turn away from Our revelations with a dreadful punishment for turning away.

Waiting for the Apocalypse?

158. Are they awaiting the coming of the angels, or your Lord ˹Himself˺, or some of your Lord's ˹major˺ signs? On the Day your Lord's signs arrive, belief will not benefit those who did not believe earlier or those who did no good through their faith.[301] Say, "Keep waiting! We too are waiting."

Not Responsible

159. Indeed, you ˹O Prophet˺ are not responsible whatsoever for those who have divided their faith and split into sects. Their judgment rests only with God. And He will inform them of what they used to do.

Reward for Good and Evil Deeds

160. Whoever comes with a good deed will be rewarded tenfold. But whoever comes with a bad deed will be punished for only one. None will be wronged.

Way of Life

161. Say, ˹O Prophet,˺ "Surely my Lord has guided me to the Straight Path, a perfect way, the faith of Abraham, the upright, who was not one of the polytheists." **162.** Say, "Surely my prayer, my sacrifice, my life, and my death are all for God—Lord of all worlds. **163.** He has no partner. So I am commanded, and so I am the first to submit."

Divine Justice

164. Say, ˹O Prophet,˺ "Should I seek a lord other than God while He is the Lord of everything?" No one will reap except what they sow. No soul burdened with sin will bear the burden of another. Then to your Lord is your return, and He will inform you of your differences.

Test of Life

165. He is the One Who has placed you as successors on earth and elevated some of you in rank over others, so He may test you with what He has given you. Surely your Lord is swift in punishment, but He is certainly All-Forgiving, Most Merciful.

7. The Heights (Al-A'râf)

This chapter takes its name from the heights mentioned in verse 46. Like many other Meccan chapters, it recounts the stories of earlier prophets who were denied by their own people and how the deniers were eventually destroyed. As mentioned in the previous chapter (6:10-11), these stories are meant to reassure the Prophet and warn his people of God's

---

300 i.e., the Quran.
301 This refers to disobedient believers who neither did any good nor repented before the time of their death or the arrival of the Day of Judgment. This is supported by authentic narrations from the Prophet.

torment. The story of Satan's arrogance and Adam's temptation and fall are detailed, along with lessons for the believers to beware of Satan's whispers. Details about Paradise and Hell (verses 36-53) here are unmatched by any previous chapter. The powerlessness of idols is further emphasized. Full obedience to God and His prophets is stressed in this chapter and the next.

In the Name of God—the Most Compassionate, Most Merciful

Advice to the Prophet

1. *Alif-Lãm-Mĩm-Şãd.* 2. 'This is' a Book sent down to you 'O Prophet'—do not let anxiety into your heart regarding it—so with it you may warn 'the disbelievers', and as a reminder to the believers.

Advice to Humanity

3. Follow what has been sent down to you from your Lord, and do not take others as guardians besides Him. How seldom are you mindful! 4. 'Imagine' how many societies We have destroyed! Our torment took them by surprise 'while sleeping' at night or midday. 5. Their only cry—when overwhelmed by Our torment—was, "We have indeed been wrongdoers."

Response to Messengers

6. We will surely question those who received messengers and We will question the messengers 'themselves'. 7. Then We will give them a full account with sure knowledge—for We were never absent.

Weighing Deeds on Judgment Day

8. The weighing on that Day will be just. As for those whose scale will be heavy 'with good deeds', 'only' they will be successful. 9. But those whose scale is light, they have doomed themselves for wrongfully denying Our signs.

Satan's Arrogance

10. We have indeed established you on earth and provided you with a means of livelihood. 'Yet' you seldom give any thanks. 11. Surely We created you,[302] then shaped you, then said to the angels, "Prostrate before Adam," so they all did—but not *Iblîs*,[303] who refused to prostrate with the others. 12. God asked, "What prevented you from prostrating when I commanded you?" He replied, "I am better than he is: You created me from fire and him from clay." 13. God said, "Then get down from Paradise! It is not for you to be arrogant here. So get out! You are truly one of the disgraced." 14. He appealed, "Then delay my end until the Day of their resurrection." 15. God said, "You are delayed 'until the appointed Day'."[304] 16. He said, "For leaving me to stray I will lie in ambush for them on Your Straight Path. 17. I will approach them from their front, their back, their right, their left, and then You will find most of them ungrateful." 18. God said, "Get out of Paradise! You are disgraced and rejected! I will certainly fill up Hell with you and your followers all together."

Adam and Eve: Temptation and Fall

19. 'God said,' "O Adam! Live with your wife in Paradise and eat from wherever you please, but do not approach this tree, or else you will be wrongdoers." 20. Then Satan tempted them in order to expose what was hidden of their nakedness. He said, "Your Lord has forbidden this tree to you only to

---

302   i.e., your father, Adam.
303   See footnote for 2:34.
304   Satan asked to be allowed to live until humans are resurrected in order to escape death at the end of time. He was told he was going to live only until the time appointed by God Almighty.

prevent you from becoming angels or immortals." **21.** And he swore to them, "I am truly your sincere advisor." **22.** So he brought about their fall through deception. And when they tasted of the tree, their nakedness was exposed to them, prompting them to cover themselves with leaves from Paradise. Then their Lord called out to them, "Did I not forbid you from that tree and ˹did I not˺ tell you that Satan is your sworn enemy?" **23.** They replied, "Our Lord! We have wronged ourselves. If You do not forgive us and have mercy on us, we will certainly be losers." **24.** God said, "Descend as enemies to each other.[305] You will find in the earth a residence and provision for your appointed stay." **25.** He added, "There you will live, there you will die, and from there you will be resurrected."

Best Clothing

26. O children of Adam! We have provided for you clothing to cover your nakedness and as an adornment. However, the best clothing is righteousness. This is one of God's bounties, so perhaps you will be mindful.

Warning Against Satan

27. O children of Adam! Do not let Satan deceive you as he tempted your parents out of Paradise and caused their cover to be removed in order to expose their nakedness. Surely he and his soldiers watch you from where you cannot see them. We have made the devils allies of those who disbelieve. **28.** Whenever they commit a shameful deed,[306] they say, "We found our forefathers doing it and God has commanded us to do it." Say, "No! God never commands what is shameful. How can you attribute to God what you do not know?" **29.** Say, ˹O Prophet,˺ "My Lord has commanded uprightness and dedication ˹to Him alone˺ in worship, calling upon Him with

sincere devotion. Just as He first brought you into being, you will be brought to life again." **30.** He has guided some, while others are destined to stray. They have taken devils as their masters instead of God—thinking they are ˹rightly˺ guided.

The Lawful and the Forbidden

31. O Children of Adam! Dress properly whenever you are at worship. Eat and drink, but do not waste. Surely He does not like the wasteful. **32.** Ask, ˹O Prophet,˺ "Who has forbidden the adornments and lawful provisions God has brought forth for His servants?" Say, "They are for the enjoyment of the believers in this worldly life, but they will be exclusively theirs on the Day of Judgment."[307] This is how We make Our revelations clear for people of knowledge. **33.** Say, "My Lord has only forbidden open and secret indecencies, sinfulness, unjust aggression, associating ˹others˺ with God ˹in worship˺—a practice He has never authorized—and attributing to God what you do not know." **34.** For each community there is an appointed term. When their time arrives, they can neither delay it for a moment, nor could they advance it.

Receiving the Truth

35. O children of Adam! When messengers from among yourselves come to you reciting My revelations—whoever shuns evil and mends their ways, there will be no fear for them, nor will they grieve. **36.** But those who receive Our revelations with denial and arrogance will be the residents of the Fire. They will be there forever.

Evil Leaders and Their Followers

37. Who does more wrong than those who fabricate lies against God or deny His revelations? They will receive what is destined for

---

305 There will be enmity between humans and Satan.
306 It was customary for the pagans of Mecca to circle the Ka'bah while naked. So verses 26-31 of this chapter were revealed commanding the believers to cover themselves properly when praying to their Lord.
307 The pleasures of this worldly life are shared by believers and disbelievers, whereas the pleasures of the Hereafter will be enjoyed exclusively by the believers.

them,[308] until Our messenger-angels arrive to take their souls, asking them, "Where are those 'false gods' you used to invoke besides God?" They will cry, "They have failed us," and they will confess against themselves that they were indeed disbelievers. **38.** God will say, "Enter the Fire along with the 'evil' groups of jinn and humans that preceded you." Whenever a group enters Hell, it will curse the preceding one until they are all gathered inside, the followers will say about their leaders, "Our Lord! They have misled us, so multiply their torment in the Fire." He will answer, "It has already been multiplied for all, but you do not know." **39.** Then the leaders will say to their followers, "You were no better than us! So taste the torment for what you used to commit."

Punishment of the Disbelievers

40. Surely those who receive our revelations with denial and arrogance, the gates of heaven will not be opened for them, nor will they enter Paradise until a camel passes through the eye of a needle. This is how We reward the wicked. **41.** Hell will be their bed; flames will be their cover. This is how We reward the wrongdoers.

Reward of the Believers

42. As for those who believe and do good— We never require of any soul more than what it can afford—it is they who will be the residents of Paradise. They will be there forever. **43.** We will remove whatever bitterness they had in their hearts.[309] Rivers will flow under their feet. And they will say, "Praise be to God for guiding us to this. We would have never been guided if God had not guided us. The messengers of our Lord had certainly come with the truth." It will

be announced to them, "This is Paradise awarded to you for what you used to do."

The Lord's Promise

44. The residents of Paradise will call out to the residents of the Fire, "We have certainly found our Lord's promise to be true. Have you too found your Lord's promise to be true?" They will reply, "Yes, we have!" Then a caller will announce to both, "May God's condemnation be upon the wrongdoers, **45.** those who hindered 'others' from God's Way, strived to make it 'appear' crooked, and disbelieved in the Hereafter."

People on the Heights[310]

46. There will be a barrier between Paradise and Hell. And on the heights 'of that barrier' will be people[311] who will recognize 'the residents of' both by their appearance.[312] They will call out to the residents of Paradise, "Peace be upon you!" They will have not yet entered Paradise, but eagerly hope to. **47.** When their eyes will turn towards the residents of Hell, they will pray, "Our Lord! Do not join us with the wrongdoing people." **48.** Those on the heights will call out to some 'tyrants in the Fire', who they will recognize by their appearance, saying, "Your large numbers and arrogance are of no use 'today'! **49.** Are these 'humble believers' the ones you swore would never be shown God's mercy?" 'Finally, those on the heights will be told:' "Enter Paradise! There will be no fear for you, nor will you grieve."

Disbelievers Begging Believers

50. The residents of the Fire will then cry out to the residents of Paradise, "Aid us with some water or any provision God

308 i.e., they will receive all provisions and bounties destined for them by their Lord.
309 i.e., the bitterness they had in their hearts towards other believers who wronged them in the worldly life.
310 This is a group of people whose good deeds equal their bad deeds, so they will be held on the heights separating Paradise and Hellfire until their judgment is settled.
311 Although the word "rijâl" generally means "men," some Quran commentators believe that the word "rijâl" here can also mean "people," but they are called men since men make up the majority in the group. In some Arabic dialects, "rijâl" is the plural of "rajul" (man) and "rajulah" (woman).
312 The faces of the residents of Paradise will be bright, whereas those of the residents of Hell will be gloomy.

has granted you." They will reply, "God has forbidden both to the disbelievers,
51. those who took this[313] faith ˺of Islam˼ as mere amusement and play and were deluded by ˹their˺ worldly life." ˹God will say,˺ "Today We will ignore them just as they ignored the coming of this Day of theirs and for rejecting Our revelations."

Too Late

52. We have certainly brought them a Book which We explained with knowledge—a guide and mercy for those who believe.
53. Do they only await the fulfilment ˹of its warning˺? The Day it will be fulfilled, those who ignored it before will say, "The messengers of our Lord certainly came with the truth. Are there any intercessors who can plead on our behalf? Or can we be sent back so we may do ˹good,˺ unlike what we used to do?" They will have certainly ruined themselves, and whatever ˹gods˺ they fabricated will fail them.

The Almighty Creator

54. Indeed your Lord is God Who created the heavens and the earth in six Days,[314] then established Himself above the Throne. He makes the day and night overlap in rapid succession. He created the sun, the moon, and the stars—all subjected by His command. The creation and the command belong to Him ˹alone˺. Blessed is God—Lord of all worlds! **55.** Call upon your Lord humbly and secretly. Surely He does not like the transgressors. **56.** Do not spread corruption in the land after it has been set in order. And call upon Him with hope and fear. Indeed, God's mercy is always close to the good-doers.

Parable of Resurrection

57. He is the One Who sends the winds ushering in His mercy. When they bear heavy clouds, We drive them to a lifeless land and then cause rain to fall, producing every type of fruit. Similarly, We will bring the dead to life, so perhaps you will be mindful.

Parable of Believers and Disbelievers

58. The fertile land produces abundantly by the Will of its Lord, whereas the infertile land hardly produces anything. This is how We vary ˹Our˺ lessons to those who are thankful.

Prophet Noah

59. Indeed, We sent Noah to his people. He said, "O my people! Worship God—you have no other god except Him. I truly fear for you the torment of a tremendous Day."

His People's Response

60. But the chiefs of his people said, "We surely see that you are clearly misguided."
61. He replied, "O my people! I am not misguided! But I am a messenger from the Lord of all worlds, **62.** conveying to you my Lord's messages and giving you ˹sincere˺ advice. And I know from God what you do not know. **63.** Do you find it astonishing that a reminder should come to you from your Lord through one of your own, warning you, so you may beware and perhaps be shown mercy?"

The Fate of His People

64. But they rejected him, so We saved him and those with him in the Ark, and drowned those who rejected Our signs. They were certainly a blind people.

Prophet Hûd

65. And to the people of 'Âd We sent their brother Hûd. He said, "O my people! Worship God—you have no other god except Him. Will you not then fear Him?"

---

313 lit., their faith (which they are supposed to follow).
314 The word day is not always used in the Quran to mean a 24-hour period. According to 22:47, a heavenly Day is 1000 years of our time. The Day of Judgment will be 50 000 years of our time (see 70:4). Hence, the six Days of creation refer to six eons of time, known only by God.

7. The Heights (Al-A'râf)

His People's Response

66. The disbelieving chiefs of his people responded, "We surely see you as a fool, and we certainly think you are a liar." **67.** Hûd replied, "O my people! I am no fool! But I am a messenger from the Lord of all worlds, **68.** conveying to you my Lord's messages. And I am your sincere advisor. **69.** Do you find it astonishing that a reminder should come to you from your Lord through one of your own so he may warn you? Remember that He made you successors after the people of Noah and increased you greatly in stature. So remember God's favours, so you may be successful." **70.** They said, "Have you come to us so that we would worship God alone and abandon what our forefathers used to worship? Then bring us what you threaten us with, if what you say is true!" **71.** He said, "You will certainly be subjected to your Lord's torment and wrath. Do you dispute with me regarding the so-called gods which you and your forefathers have made up—a practice God has never authorized? Then wait! I too am waiting with you."

The Fate of His People

72. So We saved him and those with him by Our mercy and uprooted those who denied Our signs. They were not believers.

Prophet Ṣâliḥ

73. And to the people of Thamûd We sent their brother Ṣâliḥ. He said, "O my people! Worship God—you have no other god except Him. A clear proof has come to you from your Lord: this is God's she-camel as a sign to you. So leave her to graze ˹freely˺ on God's land and do not harm her, or else you will be overcome by a painful punishment. **74.** Remember when He made you successors after 'Âd and established you in the land—˹and˺ you built palaces on its plains and carved homes into mountains. So remember God's favours, and do not go about spreading corruption in the land."

His People's Response

75. The arrogant chiefs of his people asked the lowly who believed among them, "Are you certain that Ṣâliḥ has been sent by his Lord?" They replied, "We certainly believe in what he has been sent with." **76.** The arrogant said, "We surely reject what you believe in." **77.** Then they killed the she-camel—defying their Lord's command—and challenged ˹Ṣâliḥ˺, "Bring us what you threaten us with, if you are ˹truly˺ one of the messengers."

The Fate of His People

78. Then an ˹overwhelming˺ earthquake struck them, and they fell lifeless in their homes. **79.** So he turned away from them, saying, "O my people! Surely I conveyed to you my Lord's message and gave you ˹sincere˺ advice, but you do not like ˹sincere˺ advisors."

Prophet Lot

80. And ˹remember˺ when Lot scolded ˹the men of˺ his people, ˹saying,˺ "Do you commit a shameful deed that no man has ever done before? **81.** You lust after men instead of women! You are certainly transgressors."

His People's Response

82. But his people's only response was to say, "Expel them from your land! They are a people who wish to remain chaste!"

The Fate of His People

83. So We saved him and his family except his wife, who was one of the doomed. **84.** We poured upon them a rain ˹of brimstone˺. See what was the end of the wicked!

Prophet Shu'aib

85. And to the people of Midian We sent their brother Shu'aib. He said, "O my people! Worship God—you have no other god except Him. A clear proof has already come to you from your Lord. So give just measure and weight, do not defraud people of their property, nor spread corruption in the land after it has been set in order. This is for your own good, if you are ˹truly˺ believers. **86.** And do not lie in ambush on every road—threatening and hindering those who believe in God from His Path and striving to make it ˹appear˺ crooked. Remember when you were few, then He increased you in number. And consider the fate of the corruptors! **87.** If some of you do believe in what I have been sent with while others do not, then be patient until God judges between us. He is the Best of Judges."

His People's Response

88. The arrogant chiefs of his people threatened, "O Shu'aib! We will certainly expel you and your fellow believers from our land, unless you return to our faith." He replied, "Even if we hate it? **89.** We would surely be fabricating a lie against God if we were to return to your faith after God has saved us from it. It does not befit us to return to it unless it is the Will of God, our Lord. Our Lord has encompassed everything in ˹His˺ knowledge. In God we trust. Our Lord! Judge between us and our people with truth. You are the best of those who judge."

The Fate of His People

90. The disbelieving chiefs of his people threatened, "If you follow Shu'aib, you will surely be losers!" **91.** Then an ˹overwhelming˺ earthquake struck them and they fell lifeless in their homes. **92.** Those who rejected Shu'aib were ˹wiped out˺ as if they had never lived there. Those who rejected Shu'aib were the true losers. **93.** He turned away from them, saying, "O my people! Indeed, I have delivered to you the messages of my Lord and gave you ˹sincere˺ advice. How can I then grieve for those who chose to disbelieve?"

Destroyed Peoples

94. Whenever We sent a prophet to a society, We afflicted its ˹disbelieving˺ people with suffering and adversity, so perhaps they would be humbled. **95.** Then We changed their adversity to prosperity until they flourished and argued ˹falsely˺, "Our forefathers ˹too˺ had been visited by adversity and prosperity."[315] So We seized them by surprise, while they were unaware.

Learn from History

96. Had the people of those societies been faithful and mindful ˹of God˺, We would have overwhelmed them with blessings from heaven and earth. But they disbelieved, so We seized them for what they used to commit. **97.** Did the people of those societies feel secure that Our punishment would not come upon them by night while they were asleep? **98.** Or did they feel secure that Our punishment would not come upon them by day while they were at play? **99.** Did they feel secure against God's planning? None would feel secure from God's planning except the losers. **100.** Is it not clear to those who take over the land after ˹the destruction of˺ its former residents that—if We will—We can punish them ˹too˺ for their sins and seal their hearts so they will not hear ˹the truth˺?

Sealed Hearts

101. We have narrated to you ˹O Prophet˺ some of the stories of those societies. Surely, their messengers came to them with clear proofs, but still they would not believe in what they had already denied. This is how God seals the hearts of the disbelievers. **102.** We did not find most of them true to their covenant. Rather, We found most of them truly rebellious.

Prophet Moses

103. Then after them We sent Moses with Our signs to Pharaoh and his chiefs, but they

---

315 They argued that life has its ups and downs and, therefore, they did not perceive adversity as a punishment or prosperity as a test—arguing that the same thing happened to their ancestors.

wrongfully rejected them. See what was the end of the corruptors! 104. And Moses said, "O Pharaoh! I am truly a messenger from the Lord of all worlds, 105. obliged to say nothing about God except the truth. Indeed, I have come to you with clear proof from your Lord, so let the children of Israel go with me." 106. Pharaoh said, "If you have come with a sign, then bring it if what you say is true." 107. So Moses threw down his staff and—behold!—it became a real snake. 108. Then he drew his hand ˹out of his collar˺ and it was ˹shining˺ white for all to see.

Moses vs. Pharaoh's Magicians

109. The chiefs of Pharaoh's people said, "He is indeed a skilled magician, 110. who seeks to drive you from your land." ˹So Pharaoh asked,˺ "What do you propose?" 111. They replied, "Let him and his brother wait and send mobilizers to all cities 112. to bring you every clever magician." 113. The magicians came to Pharaoh, saying, "Shall we receive a ˹suitable˺ reward if we prevail?" 114. He replied, "Yes, and you will certainly be among those closest to me." 115. They asked, "O Moses! Will you cast, or shall we be the first to cast?" 116. Moses said, "You first." So when they did, they deceived the eyes of the people, stunned them, and made a great display of magic. 117. Then We inspired Moses, "Throw down your staff," and—behold!—it devoured the objects of their illusion! 118. So the truth prevailed and their illusions failed.

Magicians Become Believers

119. So Pharaoh and his people were defeated right there and put to shame. 120. And the magicians fell down, prostrating. 121. They declared, "We ˹now˺ believe in the Lord of all worlds— 122. the Lord of Moses and Aaron." 123. Pharaoh threatened, "How dare you believe in him before I give you permission? This must be a conspiracy you devised

in the city to drive out its people, but soon you will see. 124. I will certainly cut off your hands and feet on opposite sides, then crucify you all." 125. They responded, "Surely to our Lord we will ˹all˺ return. 126. Your rage towards us is only because we believed in the signs of our Lord when they came to us. Our Lord! Shower us with perseverance, and let us die while submitting ˹to You˺."[316]

Pharaoh's Persecution of the Israelites

127. The chiefs of Pharaoh's people protested, "Are you going to leave Moses and his people free to spread corruption in the land and abandon you and your gods?" He responded, "We will kill their sons and keep their women.[317] We will completely dominate them."

Moses Reassures His People

128. Moses reassured his people, "Seek God's help and be patient. Indeed, the earth belongs to God ˹alone˺. He grants it to whoever He chooses of His servants. The ultimate outcome belongs ˹only˺ to the righteous." 129. They complained, "We have always been oppressed—before and after you came to us ˹with the message˺." He replied, "Perhaps your Lord will destroy your enemy and make you successors in the land to see what you will do."

Egypt Plagued

130. Indeed, We afflicted Pharaoh's people with famine and shortage of crops so they might come back ˹to their senses˺. 131. In times of prosperity, they said, "This is what we deserve," but in adversity, they blamed it on Moses and those with him.[318] Surely all is destined by God. Yet most of them did not know.

---

316 lit., as Muslims.
317 As we did before the birth of Moses.
318 In psychology, this is called self-serving bias and scapegoating.

Pharaoh's People in Denial

132. They said, "No matter what sign you may bring to deceive us, we will never believe in you." **133.** So We plagued them with floods, locusts, lice, frogs, and blood—all as clear signs, but they persisted in arrogance and were a wicked people. **134.** When tormented, they pleaded, "O Moses! Pray to your Lord on our behalf, by virtue of the covenant He made with you. If you help remove this torment from us, we will certainly believe in you and let the Children of Israel go with you." **135.** But as soon as We removed the torment from them—until they met their inevitable fate[319]—they broke their promise. **136.** So We inflicted punishment upon them, drowning them in the sea for denying Our signs and being heedless of them. **137.** And 'so' We made the oppressed people successors of the eastern and western lands, which We had showered with blessings. 'In this way' the noble Word of your Lord was fulfilled for the Children of Israel for what they had endured. And We destroyed what Pharaoh and his people constructed and what they established.

The Israelites Demanding an Idol

138. We brought the Children of Israel across the sea and they came upon a people devoted to idols. They demanded, "O Moses! Make for us a god like their gods." He replied, "Indeed, you are a people acting ignorantly! **139.** What they follow is certainly doomed to destruction and their deeds are in vain." **140.** He added, "Shall I seek for you a god other than God, while He has honoured you above the others?" **141.** And 'remember' when We rescued you from the people of Pharaoh, who afflicted you with dreadful torment—killing your sons and keeping your women. That was a severe test from your Lord.

Moses' Appointment with God

142. We appointed for Moses thirty nights then added another ten—completing his Lord's term of forty nights. Moses commanded his brother Aaron, "Take my place among my people, do what is right, and do not follow the way of the corruptors." **143.** When Moses came at the appointed time and his Lord spoke to him, he asked, "My Lord! Reveal Yourself to me so I may see You." God answered, "You cannot see Me! But look at the mountain. If it remains firm in its place, only then will you see Me." When his Lord appeared to the mountain, He levelled it to dust and Moses collapsed unconscious. When he recovered, he cried, "Glory be to You! I turn to You in repentance and I am the first of the believers." **144.** God said, "O Moses! I have 'already' elevated you above all others by My messages and speech.[320] So hold firmly to what I have given you and be grateful."

The Tablets

145. We wrote for him on the Tablets 'the fundamentals' of everything; commandments and explanations of all things. 'We commanded,' "Hold to this firmly and ask your people to take the best of it.[321] I will soon show 'all of' you the home of the rebellious.[322] **146.** I will turn away from My signs those who act unjustly with arrogance in the land. And even if they were to see every sign, they still would not believe in them. If they see the Right Path, they will not take it. But if they see a crooked path, they will follow it. This is because they denied Our signs and were heedless of them. **147.** The deeds of those who deny Our signs and the meeting 'with God' in the Hereafter will be in vain. Will they be rewarded except for what they have done?"

319 i.e., their drowning in the sea.
320 God reminds Moses that even though his request to see God was denied, he has already been favoured by God over the people of his time through prophethood and direct communication with the Almighty.
321 To follow the commandments that generate more rewards than others, to put grace before justice, etc.
322 This could either mean the ruins of destroyed nations or the Hellfire which is the home of the wicked.

The Golden Calf

148. In the absence of Moses, his people made from their ˹golden˺ jewellery an idol of a calf that made a lowing sound. Did they not see that it could neither speak to them nor guide them to the ˹Right˺ Path? Still they took it as a god and were wrongdoers. **149.** Later, when they were filled with remorse and realized they had gone astray, they cried, "If our Lord does not have mercy on us and forgive us, we will certainly be losers." **150.** When Moses returned to his people, ˹totally˺ furious and sorrowful, he said, "What an evil thing you committed in my absence! Did you want to hasten your Lord's torment?" Then he threw down the Tablets and grabbed his brother by the hair, dragging him closer. Aaron pleaded, "O son of my mother! The people overpowered me and were about to kill me. So do not ˹humiliate me and˺ make my enemies rejoice, nor count me among the wrongdoing people."

Moses Prays for Forgiveness

151. Moses prayed, "My Lord! Forgive me and my brother! And admit us into Your mercy. You are the Most Merciful of the merciful." **152.** Those who worshipped the calf will certainly be afflicted with wrath from their Lord as well as disgrace in the life of this world. This is how We reward those who invent falsehood. **153.** But those who commit evil, then repent and become ˹true˺ believers, your Lord will certainly be All-Forgiving, Most-Merciful. **154.** When Moses' anger subsided, he took up the Tablets whose text contained guidance and mercy for those who stand in awe of their Lord.

Begging for God's Mercy

155. Moses chose seventy men from among his people for Our appointment and, when they were seized by an earthquake,[323] he cried,

"My Lord! Had You willed, You could have destroyed them long ago, and me as well. Will You destroy us for what the foolish among us have done? This is only a test from You—by which You allow whoever you will to stray and guide whoever You will. You are our Guardian. So forgive us and have mercy on us. You are the best forgiver. **156.** Ordain for us what is good in this life and the next. Indeed, we have turned to You ˹in repentance˺." God replied, "I will inflict My torment on whoever I will. But My mercy encompasses everything. I will ordain mercy for those who shun evil, pay alms-tax, and believe in Our revelations.

Prophet Muḥammad in the Bible

157. "˹They are˺ the ones who follow the Messenger, the unlettered Prophet, whose description they find in their Torah and the Gospel.[324] He commands them to do good and forbids them from evil, permits for them what is lawful and forbids to them what is impure, and relieves them from their burdens and the shackles that bound them. ˹Only˺ those who believe in him, honour and support him, and follow the light sent down to him will be successful."

Universality of Islam

158. Say, ˹O Prophet,˺ "O humanity! I am God's Messenger to you all. To Him ˹alone˺ belongs the kingdom of the heavens and the earth. There is no god ˹worthy of worship˺ except Him. He gives life and causes death." So believe in God and His Messenger, the unlettered Prophet, who believes in God and His revelations. And follow him, so you may be ˹rightly˺ guided.

The Israelites Tested

159. There are some among the people of Moses who guide with the truth and establish justice accordingly. **160.** We divided

---

323 For asking Moses to make God visible to them.
324 Some Muslim scholars cite Deuteronomy 18:15-18 and 33:2, Isaiah 42, and John 14:16 as examples of the description of Prophet Muḥammad in the Bible. However, Bible scholars interpret these verses differently. The name of Prophet Muḥammad appears several times in the Gospel of Barnabas, which is deemed apocryphal by Christian authorities.

them into twelve tribes—each as a community. And We revealed to Moses, when his people asked for water, "Strike the rock with your staff." Then twelve springs gushed out. Each tribe knew its drinking place. We shaded them with clouds and sent down to them manna and quails,[325] ˹saying˺, "Eat from the good things We have provided for you." They ˹certainly˺ did not wrong Us, but wronged themselves. **161.** And ˹remember˺ when it was said to them, "Enter this city ˹of Jerusalem˺ and eat from wherever you please. Say, 'Absolve us,' and enter the gate with humility. We will forgive your sins, ˹and˺ We will multiply the reward for the good-doers." **162.** But the wrongdoers among them changed the words they were commanded to say. So We sent down a punishment from the heavens upon them for their wrongdoing.

The Sabbath-Breakers

163. Ask them ˹O Prophet˺ about ˹the people of˺ the town which was by the sea, who broke the Sabbath.[326] During the Sabbath, ˹abundant˺ fish would come to them clearly visible, but on other days the fish were never seen. In this way We tested them for their rebelliousness. **164.** When some of ˹the righteous among˺ them questioned ˹their fellow Sabbath-keepers˺, "Why do you ˹bother to˺ warn those ˹Sabbath-breakers˺ who will either be destroyed or severely punished by God?" They replied, "Just to be free from your Lord's blame, and so perhaps they may abstain." **165.** When they ignored the warning they were given, We rescued those who used to warn against evil and overtook the wrongdoers with a dreadful punishment for their rebelliousness. **166.** But

when they stubbornly persisted in violation, We said to them, "Be disgraced apes!"[327]

The Israelites Tested Again

167. And ˹remember, O Prophet,˺ when your Lord declared that He would send against them others who would make them suffer terribly until the Day of Judgment. Indeed, your Lord is swift in punishment, but He is certainly All-Forgiving, Most Merciful. **168.** We dispersed them through the land in groups—some were righteous, others were less so. We tested them with prosperity and adversity, so perhaps they would return ˹to the Right Path˺.

Their Successors

169. Then they were succeeded by other generations who inherited the Scripture. They indulged in unlawful gains, claiming, "We will be forgiven ˹after all˺." And if similar gain came their way, they would seize it. Was a covenant not taken from them in the Scripture that they would not say anything about God except the truth? And they were already well-versed in its teachings. But the ˹eternal˺ Home of the Hereafter is far better for those mindful ˹of God˺. Will you not then understand? **170.** As for those who firmly abide by the Scripture and establish prayer—surely We never discount the reward of those acting righteously.

Covenant with the Israelites

171. And ˹remember˺ when We raised the mountain over them as if it were a cloud and they thought it would fall on them.[328] ˹We said,˺ "Hold firmly to that ˹Scripture˺ which

---

325   Manna (heavenly bread) and quails (chicken-like birds) sustained the children of Israel in the wilderness after they left Egypt.

326   The people of Aylah, an ancient town by the Red Sea, were forbidden to catch fish on the Sabbath. However, on Saturdays fish were everywhere, whereas on weekdays no fish were seen. To get around the prohibition, some decided to lay their nets on Fridays and collect the fish caught in their nets on Sundays. Those opposed to this practice were divided into two groups: one group tried to convince the offenders to honour the Sabbath, but soon gave up when their advice was not taken seriously. The second group was persistent in giving advice to the Sabbath-breakers. Eventually, the Sabbath-breakers were punished whereas the other two groups were saved.

327   Literally or metaphorically. *See* footnote for 2:65.

328   The mountain was raised over their heads when Moses came to them with the teachings of the Torah and was met with defiance. So the mountain was raised as a miracle and a display of God's infinite power over them.

We have given you and observe its teachings so perhaps you will become mindful ˹of God˺."

Covenant with Humanity

172. And ˹remember˺ when your Lord brought forth from the loins of the children of Adam their descendants and had them testify regarding themselves. ˹God asked,˺ "Am I not your Lord?" They replied, "Yes, You are! We testify." ˹He cautioned,˺ "Now you have no right to say on Judgment Day, 'We were not aware of this.' 173. Nor say, 'It was our forefathers who had associated others ˹with God in worship˺ and we, as their descendants, followed in their footsteps. Will you then destroy us for the falsehood they invented?'" 174. This is how We make our signs clear, so perhaps they will return ˹to the Right Path˺.

The Deviant Scholar[329]

175. And relate to them ˹O Prophet˺ the story of the one to whom We gave Our signs, but he abandoned them, so Satan took hold of him, and he became a deviant. 176. If We had willed, We would have elevated him with Our signs, but he clung to this life—following his evil desires. His example is that of a dog: if you chase it away, it pants, and if you leave it, it ˹still˺ pants. This is the example of the people who deny Our signs.[330] So narrate ˹to them˺ stories ˹of the past˺, so perhaps they will reflect. 177. What an evil example of those who denied Our signs! They ˹only˺ wronged their own souls.

Guidance from God Only

178. Whoever God guides is truly guided. And whoever He leaves to stray, they are the ˹true˺ losers. 179. Indeed, We have destined many jinn and humans for Hell. They have hearts they do not understand with, eyes they

do not see with, and ears they do not hear with. They are like cattle. In fact, they are even less guided! Such ˹people˺ are ˹entirely˺ heedless.

God's Beautiful Names

180. God has the Most Beautiful Names. So call upon Him by them, and keep away from those who abuse His Names.[331] They will be punished for what they used to do.

The Guided and the Misguided

181. And among those We created is a group that guides with the truth and establishes justice accordingly. 182. As for those who deny Our signs, We will gradually draw them to destruction in ways they cannot comprehend. 183. I ˹only˺ delay their end for a while, but My planning is flawless.

Rejecting the Prophet

184. Have they not ever given it a thought? Their fellow man[332] is not insane. He is only sent with a clear warning. 185. Have they ever reflected on the wonders of the heavens and the earth, and everything God has created, and that perhaps their end is near? So what message after this ˹Quran˺ would they believe in? 186. Whoever God allows to stray, none can guide, leaving them to wander blindly in their defiance.

Time of the Final Hour

187. They ask you ˹O Prophet˺ regarding the Hour, "When will it be?" Say, "That knowledge is only with my Lord. He alone will reveal it when the time comes. It is too tremendous for the heavens and the earth and will only take you by surprise." They ask you as if you had full knowledge of it. Say, "That knowledge is only with God, but most people do not know." 188. Say, "I have no power to benefit or protect myself, except by the

---

329 Bal'am ibn Ba'ûrâ' was a scholar who lived at the time of Moses but later deviated from the truth.
330 Regardless of whether they are warned or not, still they will not believe.
331 Those who twist God's Names then use them to call false Gods. For example, *Allât*, a name of one of the idols was derived from *God* (the One God), *Al-'Uzza* was derived from *Al-'Azîz* (the Almighty), and *Manât* was derived from *Al-Mannân* (the Bestower).
332 i.e., Muḥammad.

Will of God. If I had known the unknown, I would have benefited myself enormously, and no harm would have ever touched me. I am only a warner and deliverer of good news for those who believe."

Going Astray

189. He is the One Who created you from a single soul, then from it made its spouse so he may find comfort in her. After he had been united with her, she carried a light burden that developed gradually. When it grew heavy, they prayed to God, their Lord, "If you grant us good offspring, we will certainly be grateful." **190.** But when He granted their descendants good offspring, they associated false gods in what He has given them. Exalted is God above what they associate ˹with Him˺!

Helpless Gods

191. Do they associate ˹with God˺ those ˹idols˺ which cannot create anything, but are in fact created; **192.** which cannot help them, or even help themselves? **193.** And if you ˹idolaters˺ call upon them for guidance, they cannot respond to you. It is all the same whether you call them or remain silent. **194.** Those ˹idols˺ you invoke besides God are created beings like yourselves. So call upon them and see if they will answer you, if your claims are true! **195.** Do they have feet to walk with? Or hands to hold with? Or eyes to see with? Or ears to hear with? Say, ˹O Prophet,˺ "Call upon your associate-gods and conspire against me without delay!

God Is the Protector

196. "Indeed, my Protector is God Who has revealed this Book. For He ˹alone˺ protects the righteous. **197.** But those ˹false gods˺ you call besides Him can neither help you nor even themselves." **198.** If you ˹idolaters˺ call them to guidance, they cannot hear. And you ˹O Prophet˺ may see them facing towards you, but they cannot see.

Grace and Tolerance

199. Be gracious, enjoin what is right, and turn away from those who act ignorantly.

Evil Impulses

200. If you are tempted by Satan, then seek refuge with God. Surely He is All-Hearing, All-Knowing. **201.** Indeed, when Satan whispers to those mindful ˹of God˺, they remember ˹their Lord˺ then they start to see ˹things˺ clearly. **202.** But the devils persistently plunge their ˹human˺ associates[333] deeper into wickedness, sparing no effort.

Only a Messenger

203. If you ˹O Prophet˺ do not bring them a sign ˹which they demanded˺, they ask, "Why do you not make it yourself?" Say, "I only follow what is revealed to me from my Lord. This ˹Quran˺ is an insight from your Lord—a guide and a mercy for those who believe."

Honouring the Quran

204. When the Quran is recited, listen to it attentively and be silent, so you may be shown mercy.

Being in Awe of God

205. Remember your Lord inwardly with humility and reverence and in a moderate tone of voice, both morning and evening. And do not be one of the heedless. **206.** Surely those ˹angels˺ nearest to your Lord are not too proud to worship Him. They glorify Him. And to Him they prostrate.

---

333   lit., their brothers.

8. The Spoils of War *(Al-Anfâl)*

This chapter was revealed in Medina to explain how the spoils of war should be distributed following the believers' victory over the Meccan pagans at Badr in 2 A.H./624 C.E. The chapter urges the believers to be true to God and His Messenger, reminding them of how they were outnumbered but God sent down angels for their aid. It is made clear that although victory comes only from God, the believers should always be ready to defend themselves and be open for peace. The pagans are warned that their plots to hinder others from God's Way and oppose the truth will only end in failure—a theme emphasized in both the previous and the following chapters.

In the Name of God—the Most Compassionate, Most Merciful

Distribution of Spoils of War[334]

1. They ask you ˹O Prophet˺ regarding the spoils of war. Say, "Their distribution is decided by God and His Messenger. So be mindful of God, settle your affairs, and obey God and His Messenger if you are ˹true˺ believers."

Qualities of True Believers

2. The ˹true˺ believers are only those whose hearts tremble at the remembrance of God, whose faith increases when His revelations are recited to them, and who put their trust in their Lord. 3. ˹They are˺ those who establish prayer and donate from what We have provided for them. 4. It is they who are the true believers. They will have elevated ranks, forgiveness, and an honourable provision from their Lord.

Opposition to Fighting

5. Similarly, when your Lord brought you ˹O Prophet˺ out of your home for a just cause, a group of believers was totally against it. 6. They disputed with you about the truth af-

ter it had been made clear, as if they were being driven to death with their eyes wide open.

Establishing the Truth

7. ˹Remember, O believers,˺ when God promised ˹to give˺ you the upper hand over either target, you wished to capture the unarmed party.[335] But it was God's Will to establish the truth by His Words and uproot the disbelievers; 8. to firmly establish the truth and wipe out falsehood—even to the dismay of the wicked.

Divine Reinforcement

9. ˹Remember˺ when you cried out to your Lord for help, He answered, "I will reinforce you with a thousand angels—followed by many others."[336] 10. And God made this a sign of victory and reassurance to your hearts. Victory comes only from God. Surely God is Almighty, All-Wise.

Sense of Serenity

11. ˹Remember˺ when He caused drowsiness to overcome you, giving you sereni-

---

334   Following the victory of the Muslims over the Meccan army at Badr, some Muslims disagreed on the way the spoils of war should be distributed, so these verses were revealed.

335   After many years of persecution in Mecca, the Prophet and many of his early followers decided to emigrate secretly to Medina, about 250 miles to the north, leaving behind their homes and valuables, which were soon taken over by the pagans of Mecca. To avenge this financial loss, the Prophet decided to capture an unarmed Meccan trade caravan headed by Abu Sufyân, a Meccan chief. Eventually, the caravan escaped, but the Meccans mobilized an army of over 1000 well-armed soldiers, more than three times the size of the Muslim force. Many Muslims had hoped to capture the caravan without having to meet the Meccan army in battle. Although the Muslims were vastly outnumbered and lightly-armed, they still won this decisive battle.

336   Five thousand angels in total, as mentioned in 3:125.

ty.[337] And He sent down rain from the sky to purify you, free you from Satan's whispers, strengthen your hearts, and make ˹your˺ steps firm.

Warning to Meccan Pagans

12. ˹Remember, O Prophet,˺ when your Lord revealed to the angels, "I am with you. So make the believers stand firm. I will cast horror into the hearts of the disbelievers. So strike their necks and strike their fingertips." 13. This is because they defied God and His Messenger. And whoever defies God and His Messenger, then ˹know that˺ God is surely severe in punishment. 14. That ˹worldly punishment˺ is yours, so taste it! Then the disbelievers will suffer the torment of the Fire.

Do Not Flee

15. O believers! When you face the disbelievers in battle, never turn your backs to them. 16. And whoever does so on such an occasion—unless it is a manoeuvre or to join their own troops—will earn the displeasure of God, and their home will be Hell. What an evil destination!

Victory from God

17. It was not you ˹believers˺ who killed them, but it was God Who did so. Nor was it you ˹O Prophet˺ who threw ˹a handful of sand at the disbelievers˺,[338] but it was God Who did so, rendering the believers a great favour. Surely God is All-Hearing, All-Knowing. 18. As such, God frustrates the evil plans of the disbelievers.

Reasoning with Pagans

19. If you ˹Meccans˺ sought judgment, now it has come to you. And if you cease, it will be for your own good. But if you persist, We will persist. And your forces—no matter how numerous they might be—will not

benefit you whatsoever. For God is certainly with the believers.

Hearing and Obeying

20. O believers! Obey God and His Messenger and do not turn away from him while you hear ˹his call˺. 21. Do not be like those who say, "We hear," but in fact they are not listening. 22. Indeed, the worst of all beings in the sight of God are the ˹wilfully˺ deaf and dumb, who do not understand.[339] 23. Had God found any goodness in them, He would have certainly made them hear. ˹But˺ even if He had made them hear, they would have surely turned away heedlessly.

Reminder to the Believers

24. O believers! Respond to God and His Messenger when he calls you to that which gives you life. And know that God stands between a person and their heart, and that to Him you will all be gathered. 25. Beware of a trial that will not only affect the wrongdoers among you. And know that God is severe in punishment.

God's Help

26. Remember when you had been vastly outnumbered and oppressed in the land,[340] constantly in fear of attacks by your enemy, then He sheltered you, strengthened you with His help, and provided you with good things so perhaps you would be thankful.

Warning to the Believers

27. O believers! Do not betray God and the Messenger, nor betray your trusts knowingly. 28. And know that your wealth and your children are only a test and that with God is a great reward.

Reward of the Believers

29. O believers! If you are mindful of God, He will grant you a decisive authority, ab-

337 This happened the night before the battle.
338 Before the battle, the Prophet threw a handful of sand at the disbelievers and prayed for their defeat.
339 This refers metaphorically to the disbelievers who fail to see and hear the truth.
340 i.e., Mecca.

solve you of your sins, and forgive you. And God is the Lord of infinite bounty.

Pagan Conspiracy

30. And ˹remember, O Prophet,˺ when the disbelievers conspired to capture, kill, or exile you. They planned, but God also planned. And God is the best of planners.

Pagan Challenge

31. Whenever Our revelations are recited to them, they challenge ˹you˺, "We have already heard ˹the recitation˺. If we wanted, we could have easily produced something similar. This ˹Quran˺ is nothing but ancient fables!"

Pagan Denial

32. And ˹remember˺ when they prayed, "O God! If this is indeed the truth from You, then rain down stones upon us from the sky or overcome us with a painful punishment." **33.** But God would never punish them while you ˹O Prophet˺ were in their midst. Nor would He ever punish them if they prayed for forgiveness.

Punishment Deserved

34. And why should God not punish them while they hinder pilgrims from the Sacred Mosque, claiming to be its rightful guardians? None has the right to guardianship except those mindful ˹of God˺, but most pagans do not know. **35.** Their prayer at the Sacred House was nothing but whistling and clapping. So taste the punishment for your disbelief.

Pagans' Wasted Efforts

36. Surely the disbelievers spend their wealth to hinder others from the Path of God. They will continue to spend to the point of regret. Then they will be defeated and the disbelievers will be driven into Hell,

37. so God may separate the evil from the good. He will pile up the evil ones all together and then cast them into Hell. They are the ˹true˺ losers.

Peace Offer

38. Tell the disbelievers that if they desist, their past will be forgiven. But if they persist, then they have an example in those destroyed before them. **39.** Fight against them until there is no more persecution—and ˹your˺ devotion will be entirely to God. But if they desist, then surely God is All-Seeing of what they do. **40.** And if they do not comply, then know that God is your Protector. What an excellent Protector, and what an excellent Helper!

Distribution of Spoils of War

41. Know that whatever spoils you take, one-fifth is for God and the Messenger, his close relatives, orphans, the poor, and ˹needy˺ travellers, if you ˹truly˺ believe in God and what We revealed to Our servant on that decisive day when the two armies met ˹at Badr˺. And God is Most Capable of everything. **42.** ˹Remember˺ when you were on the near side of the valley, your enemy on the far side, and the caravan was below you. Even if the two armies had made an appointment ˹to meet˺, both would have certainly missed it.[341] Still it transpired so God may establish what He had destined—that those who were to perish and those who were to survive might do so after the truth had been made clear to both. Surely God is All-Hearing, All-Knowing.

Vision of Enemy Force

43. ˹Remember, O Prophet,˺ when God showed them in your dream as few in number. Had He shown them to you as many, you ˹believers˺ would have certainly faltered and disputed in the matter. But God spared you ˹from that˺. Surely He knows

---

341 The battle was not planned since the Muslim force was after the caravan. Had the two armies made plans to meet in battle at that time and place, they both probably would have missed each other.

---

best what is ˹hidden˺ in the heart. **44.** Then when your armies met, God made them appear as few in your eyes, and made you appear as few in theirs, so God may establish what He had destined. And to God ˹all˺ matters will be returned ˹for judgment˺.

Word of Advice

45. O believers! When you face an enemy, stand firm and remember God often so you may triumph. **46.** Obey God and His Messenger and do not dispute with one another, or you would be discouraged and weakened. Persevere! Surely God is with those who persevere. **47.** Do not be like those ˹pagans˺ who left their homes arrogantly, only to be seen by people and to hinder others from God's Path. And God is Fully Aware of what they do.

Satan Tempts the Meccan Pagans

48. And ˹remember˺ when Satan made their ˹evil˺ deeds appealing to them, and said, "No one can overcome you today. I am surely by your side." But when the two forces faced off, he cowered and said, "I have absolutely nothing to do with you. I certainly see what you do not see. I truly fear God, for God is severe in punishment."

Trust in God

49. ˹Remember˺ when the hypocrites and those with sickness in their hearts said, "These ˹believers˺ are deluded by their faith." But whoever puts their trust in God, surely God is Almighty, All-Wise.

Evil Ending

50. If only you could see when the angels take the souls of the disbelievers, beating their faces and backs, ˹saying,˺ "Taste the torment of burning! **51.** This is ˹the reward˺ for what your hands have done. And God is never unjust to ˹His˺ creation."

Fate of the Wicked

52. Their fate is that of the people of Pharaoh and those before them—they all disbelieved in God's signs, so God seized them for their sins. Indeed, God is All-Powerful, severe in punishment. **53.** This is because God would never discontinue His favour to a people until they discontinue their faith. Surely God is All-Hearing, All-Knowing. **54.** That was the case with Pharaoh's people and those before them—they all rejected the signs of their Lord, so We destroyed them for their sins and drowned Pharaoh's people. They were all wrongdoers.

Those Who Violate Peace Treaties

55. Indeed, the worst of all beings in the sight of God are those who persist in disbelief, never to have faith— **56.** ˹namely˺ those with whom you ˹O Prophet˺ have entered into treaties, but they violate them every time, not fearing the consequences. **57.** If you ever encounter them in battle, make a fearsome example of them, so perhaps those who would follow them may be deterred.

No Betrayal in Treaties

58. And if you ˹O Prophet˺ see signs of betrayal by a people, respond by openly terminating your treaty with them. Surely God does not like those who betray.

Military Deterrence

59. Do not let those disbelievers[342] think they are not within reach. They will have no escape. **60.** Prepare against them what you ˹believers˺ can of ˹military˺ power and cavalry to deter God's enemies and your enemies as well as other enemies unknown to you but known to God. Whatever you spend in the cause of God will be paid to you in full and you will not be wronged.

Advice to the Prophet: Opt for Peace

61. If the enemy is inclined towards peace, make peace with them. And put your trust in God. Indeed, He ʿaloneʾ is the All-Hearing, All-Knowing. **62.** But if their intention is only to deceive you, then God is certainly sufficient for you. He is the One Who has supported you with His help and with the believers. **63.** He brought their hearts together. Had you spent all the riches in the earth, you could not have united their hearts. But God has united them. Indeed, He is Almighty, All-Wise. **64.** O Prophet! God is sufficient for you and for the believers who follow you.

Readiness to Fight

65. O Prophet! Motivate the believers to fight. If there are twenty steadfast among you, they will overcome two hundred. And if there are one hundred of you, they will overcome one thousand of the disbelievers, for they are a people who do not comprehend. **66.** Now God has lightened your burden, for He knows that there is weakness in you. So if there are a hundred steadfast among you, they will overcome two hundred. And if there be one thousand, they will overcome two thousand, by God's Will. And God is with the steadfast.

Decision on Captives

67. It is not fit for a prophet that he should take captives until he has thoroughly subdued the land. You ʿbelieversʾ settled with the fleeting gains of this world,[343] while God's aim ʿfor youʾ is the Hereafter. God is Almighty, All-Wise. **68.** Had it not been for a prior decree from God,[344] you would have certainly been disciplined with a tremendous punishment for whatever ʿransomʾ you have taken. **69.** Now enjoy what you have taken, for it is lawful and good. And be mindful of God. Surely God is All-Forgiving, Most Merciful.

Ransomed Captives

70. O Prophet! Tell the captives in your custody, "If God finds goodness in your hearts, He will give you better than what has been taken

from you, and forgive you. For God is All-Forgiving, Most Merciful." **71.** But if their intention is only to betray you ʿO Prophetʾ, they sought to betray God before. But He gave you power over them. And God is All-Knowing, All-Wise.

Guardianship Among Believers

72. Those who believed, emigrated, and strived with their wealth and lives in the cause of God, as well as those who gave them shelter and help—they are truly guardians of one another. As for those who believed but did not emigrate, you have no obligations to them until they emigrate. But if they seek your help ʿagainst persecutionʾ in faith, it is your obligation to help them, except against people bound with you in a treaty. God is All-Seeing of what you do.

Guardianship Among Disbelievers

73. As for the disbelievers, they are guardians of one another. And unless you ʿbelieversʾ act likewise, there will be great oppression and corruption in the land.

True Believers

74. Those who believed, migrated, and struggled in the cause of God, and those who gave ʿthemʾ shelter and help, they are the true believers. They will have forgiveness and an honourable provision.

Relatives Inherit One Another

75. And those who later believed, migrated, and struggled alongside you, they are also with you. But only blood relatives are now entitled to inherit from one another, as ordained by God. Surely God has ʿfullʾ knowledge of everything.[345]

---

343 i.e., ransom.
344 The decree that ransoming captives will be allowed.
345 This verse ended a previous ruling that allowed inheritance between Muslims from Mecca (Al-Muhâjirûn, the Emigrants) and Muslims from Medina (Al-Anṣâr, the Helpers). Now, only relatives can inherit from one another, whereas non-heirs can receive a share through bequest, up to one third of the estate. See 4:7, 11-13, 32-33, and 176.

9. Repentance *(At-Tawbah)*

This chapter, which is perceived as a continuation of the previous chapter, begins by openly terminating the peace treaties constantly violated by the pagans. The believers are urged to march forth with the Prophet for the Battle of Tabûk in the summer of 9 A.H./631 C.E. Hypocrites are exposed and their false excuses are refuted. Muslims are reminded of how God turned the believers' initial defeat into sweeping victory at the Battle of Ḥunain and how God saved His Messenger from the pagans during his migration to Medina. God's acceptance of repentance is echoed throughout the chapter, hence its title.

Declaration to the Polytheists[346]

1. 'This is' a discharge from all obligations, by God and His Messenger, to the polytheists you 'believers' have entered into treaties with: 2. "You 'polytheists' may travel freely through the land for four months, but know that you will have no escape from God, and that God will disgrace the disbelievers." 3. A declaration from God and His Messenger 'is made' to all people on the day of the greater pilgrimage[347] that God and His Messenger are free of the polytheists. So if you 'pagans' repent, it will be better for you. But if you turn away, then know that you will have no escape from God. And give good news 'O Prophet' to the disbelievers of a painful punishment.

Exception to the Declaration

4. As for the polytheists who have honoured every term of their treaty with you and have not supported an enemy against you, honour your treaty with them until the end of its term. Surely God loves those who are mindful 'of Him'.

After the Grace Period

5. But once the Sacred Months have passed, kill the polytheists 'who violated their treaties' wherever you find them,[348] capture them, besiege them, and lie in wait for them on every way. But if they repent, perform prayers, and pay alms-tax, then set them free. Indeed, God is All-Forgiving, Most Merciful.

Pagans Seeking Protection

6. And if anyone from the polytheists asks for your protection 'O Prophet', grant it to them so they may hear the Word of God, then escort them to a place of safety, for they are a people who have no knowledge.

Treacherous Polytheists

7. How can such polytheists have a treaty with God and His Messenger, except those you have made a treaty with at the Sacred Mosque?[349] So, as long as they are true to you, be true to them. Indeed God loves those who are mindful 'of Him'. 8. How 'can they have a treaty'? If they were to have the upper hand over you, they would have no respect for kinship or treaty. They only flatter you with their tongues, but their hearts are in denial, and most of them are rebellious.

---

346 This is the only chapter in the Quran that does not begin with: "In the Name of God—the Most Compassionate, Most Merciful." The reason is that this chapter is considered to be a continuation of the previous one, and that it begins with an open termination of treaties not fully respected by the polytheists. Since this constitutes a declaration of war, it would not be fitting to open with the mention of God's compassion and mercy.

347 The 10ᵗʰ of Ẓul-Ḥijjah, a significant day in the greater pilgrimage *(hajj)*. The lesser pilgrimage is known as *'umrah*.

348 i.e., inside or outside the sanctuary of the Sacred House in Mecca.

349 This is known as the Treaty of Ḥudaibiyah, which was signed by the Prophet and the pagans of Mecca in 6 A.H./628 C.E., diffusing the tension between Muslims and the Meccans and affirming a 10-year peace truce. The treaty was violated by the Meccans in 8 A.H/630 C.E.

Arab Pagans

9. They chose a fleeting gain over God's revelations, hindering ˹others˺ from His Way. Evil indeed is what they have done! **10.** They do not honour the bonds of kinship or treaties with the believers. It is they who are the transgressors. **11.** But if they repent, perform prayer, and pay alms-tax, then they are your brothers in faith. This is how We make the revelations clear for people of knowledge. **12.** But if they break their oaths after making a pledge and attack your faith, then fight the champions of disbelief—who never honour their oaths—so perhaps they will desist.

Order to Fight

13. Will you not fight those who have broken their oaths, conspired to expel the Messenger ˹from Mecca˺, and attacked you first? Do you fear them? God is more deserving of your fear, if you are ˹true˺ believers. **14.** ˹So˺ fight them and God will punish them at your hands, put them to shame, help you overcome them, and soothe the feelings of the believers— **15.** removing rage from their hearts. And God pardons whoever He wills. For God is All-Knowing, All-Wise.

Wisdom Behind Fighting

16. Do you ˹believers˺ think that you will be left without God proving who among you ˹truly˺ struggles ˹in His cause˺ and never takes trusted allies other than God, His Messenger, or the believers? And God is All-Aware of what you do.

Maintenance of Mosques

17. It is not for the polytheists to maintain the mosques of God while they openly profess disbelief. Their deeds are void, and they will be in the Fire forever. **18.** The mosques of God should only be maintained by those who believe in God and the Last Day, establish prayer, pay alms-tax, and fear none but God. It is right to hope that they will be among the ˹truly˺ guided.

Not Equal

19. Do you ˹pagans˺ consider providing the pilgrims with water and maintaining the Sacred Mosque as equal to believing in God and the Last Day and struggling in the cause of God? They are not equal in God's sight. And God does not guide the wrongdoing people.

Reward of the Believers

20. Those who have believed, emigrated, and strived in the cause of God with their wealth and their lives are greater in rank in the sight of God. It is they who will triumph. **21.** Their Lord gives them good news of His mercy, pleasure, and Gardens with everlasting bliss, **22.** to stay there for ever and ever. Surely with God is a great reward.

Warning to the Believers

23. O believers! Do not take your parents and siblings as trusted allies if they choose disbelief over belief. And whoever of you does so, they are the ˹true˺ wrongdoers. **24.** Say, ˹O Prophet,˺ "If your parents and children and siblings and spouses and extended family and the wealth you have acquired and the trade you fear will decline and the homes you cherish—˹if all these˺ are more beloved to you than God and His Messenger and struggling in His Way, then wait until God brings about His Will. God does not guide the rebellious people."

Victory Is from God Alone

25. Indeed God has given you ˹believers˺ victory on many battlefields, even at the Battle of Ḥunain[350] when you took pride in your great numbers, but they proved of no advantage to you. The earth, despite its vastness, seemed to close in on you, then you turned back in retreat. 26. Then God sent down His re-assurance[351] upon His Messenger and the believers, and sent down forces[352] you could not see, and punished those who disbelieved. Such was the reward of the disbelievers. 27. Then afterwards God will turn in grace to whoever He wills.[353] And God is All-Forgiving, Most Merciful.

No More Idolatry at the Ka'bah

28. O believers! Indeed, the polytheists are ˹spiritually˺ impure,[354] so they should not approach the Sacred Mosque after this year.[355] If you fear poverty, God will enrich you out of His bounty, if He wills. Surely, God is All-Knowing, All-Wise.

Command to Fight

29. Fight those who do not believe in God and the Last Day, nor comply with what God and His Messenger have forbidden, nor embrace the religion of truth from among those who were given the Scripture,[356] until they pay the tax,[357] willingly submitting, fully humbled.

Blind Following

30. The Jews say, "Ezra is the son of God," while the Christians say, "The Messiah is the son of God." Such are their baseless assertions, only parroting the words of earlier disbelievers. May God condemn them! How can they be deluded ˹from the truth˺? 31. They have taken their rabbis and monks as well as the Messiah, son of Mary, as lords besides God,[358] even though they were commanded to worship none but One God. There is no god ˹worthy of worship˺ except Him. Glorified is He above what they associate ˹with Him˺!

---

350 After the Muslims' victory in Mecca in 8 A.H/630 C.E., almost all Arab tribes pledged allegiance to the Prophet except some tribes such as Hawâzin and Thaqîf. Both tribes decided to attack the Muslims, so the Prophet led an army of 12 000 soldiers to attack the two tribes. Since that was the largest Muslim army ever mobilized, some Muslims expressed their conviction that such an army could not be defeated. However, on the way to battle, the Muslim army was ambushed and most soldiers fled, except for the Prophet and a few loyalists. Eventually, the Muslims were re-organized and won a decisive battle.

351 lit., tranquility.

352 i.e., angels.

353 i.e., God will accept those who embrace Islam. Almost all of Arabia became Muslim before the death of Prophet Muḥammad in 11 A.H./632 C.E.

354 i.e., impure spiritually because of idolatry, not physically.

355 The 9ᵗʰ year of the Prophet's migration from Mecca to Medina.

356 To fully understand this verse we need to bear in mind that Quranic verses are of two types. General verses talk about belief in God, good manners, and acts of worship. Specific verses, such as this verse, were revealed in regards to particular situations. This chapter came at a time when the pagans of Arabia (and their allies) repeatedly violated treaties they had signed with the Prophet. Muslims had to fight for the survival of their newly established state in Medina. So this verse discusses dealing with those who violated their agreements and attacked the Muslims. Offenders were fought, unless they stopped their aggression. If they chose not to accept Islam, they were obligated to pay Jizya-tax.

357 Taxation systems have existed since ancient times. There are several references in the Old Testament (e.g., Ezra 4:20). In the New Testament, Jesus allows paying taxes to Caesar (Luke 20:25). Under Islamic rule, all individuals had financial obligations—Muslims paid zakâh (2.5% of their savings) and non-Muslims (ẓimmîs) were required to pay jizyah (tax for protection from foreign enemies). The jizyah was an average of one dinar (4.25 g of gold) annually. Women, children, the elderly, the clergy, the poor, and those who were unable to work were exempt. Those who opted to join the army were also exempt. Poor ẓimmîs were supported financially by the state. Muslim rulers refunded the jizyah if they failed to protect their non-Muslim subjects.

358 When 'Adi ibn Ḥâtim, a companion of the Prophet, heard this verse, he said, "But the Jews and Christians do not worship their rabbis and monks!" The Prophet replied, "Do the rabbis and monks not forbid the permissible and permit the forbidden, and they obey them?" 'Adi answered, "Yes, they do." The Prophet concluded, "This is how they worship them." Collected by At-Tirmiẓi.

9. Repentance (At-Tawbah)

The True Faith

32. They wish to extinguish God's light[359] with their mouths, but God will only allow His light to be perfected, even to the dismay of the disbelievers. **33.** He is the One Who has sent His Messenger with 'true' guidance and the religion of truth, making it prevail over all others, even to the dismay of the polytheists.

Unlawful Gains

34. O believers! Indeed, many rabbis and monks consume people's wealth wrongfully and hinder 'others' from the Way of God. Give good news of a painful torment to those who hoard gold and silver and do not spend it in God's cause. **35.** The Day 'will come' when their treasure will be heated up in the Fire of Hell, and their foreheads, sides, and backs branded with it. 'It will be said to them,' "This is the treasure you hoarded for yourselves. Now taste what you hoarded!"

Honouring the Sacred Months

36. Indeed, the number of months ordained by God is twelve—in God's Record[360] since the day He created the heavens and the earth—of which four are sacred. That is the Right Way. So do not wrong one another during these months. And fight the polytheists together as they fight together against you. And know that God is with those mindful 'of Him'. **37.** Reallocating the sanctity of 'these' months[361] is an increase in disbelief, by which

the disbelievers are led 'far' astray. They adjust the sanctity one year and uphold it in another, only to maintain the number of months sanctified by God, violating the very months God has made sacred. Their evil deeds have been made appealing to them. And God does not guide the disbelieving people.

Clinging to This Life

38. O believers! What is the matter with you that when you are asked to march forth in the cause of God, you cling firmly to 'your' land?[362] Do you prefer the life of this world over the Hereafter? The enjoyment of this worldly life is insignificant compared to that of the Hereafter. **39.** If you do not march forth, He will afflict you with a painful torment and replace you with other people. You are not harming Him in the least. And God is Most Capable of everything.

Supporting the Prophet

40. 'It does not matter' if you 'believers' do not support him, for God did in fact support him when the disbelievers drove him out 'of Mecca' and he was only one of two. While they both were in the cave, he reassured his companion,[363] "Do not worry; God is certainly with us." So God sent down His serenity upon the Prophet, supported him with forces you 'believers' did not see, and made the word of the disbelievers lowest, while the Word of God is supreme. And God is Almighty, All-Wise. **41.** 'O believers!' March forth whether it

---

359 i.e., religion of truth.

360 i.e., the Preserved Tablet in which everything is written.

361 The sacred months are the 11th, 12th, 1st, and 7th of the Islamic calendar. Since the polytheists knew that it was forbidden to fight in the sacred months, they used to transfer the sanctity to other months, say for example, the 3rd, 4th, 8th, and 10th as long as they maintained the sanctity of any four months throughout the year.

362 The fast pace of the spread of Islam in Arabia in the 7th century was intimidating to the world's two superpowers of that time: the Romans and Persians. The Prophet received the news that a Roman army was being mobilized to launch an attack on the newly established Muslim state in Medina, so he announced that he was going to march to Tabûk, located over 700 miles to the north, to meet the Romans in the summer of 9 A.H./631 C.E. It was a time of hardship because of the scorching heat, the long distance, and the financial situation of the Muslims. Although the Prophet was able to mobilize over 30 000 Muslims for battle, many others did not join the army with or without valid excuses. Eventually, the Roman forces were discouraged from fighting and fled to Damascus and other cities under Roman rule. Therefore, the Prophet returned to Medina with a feeling of triumph. With a new power now emerging in Arabia, many tribes started to switch their alliances from Caesar to the Prophet.

363 Abu Bakr Aṣ-Ṣiddîq, Islam's first Caliph and a prominent figure in Islamic history. He accompanied the Prophet during his emigration from Mecca to Medina after years of persecution at the hands of the Meccan pagans.

is easy or difficult for you, and strive with your wealth and your lives in the cause of God. That is best for you, if only you knew.

False Excuse 1) Inability

42. Had the gain been within reach and the journey shorter, they would have followed you, but the distance seemed too long for them. And they will swear by God, "Had we been able, we would have certainly joined you." They are ruining themselves. And God knows that they are surely lying. **43.** May God pardon you ʿO Prophetʾ! Why did you give them permission ʿto stay behindʾ before those who told the truth were distinguished from those who were lying?

Exemption from Fighting

44. Those who believe in God and the Last Day do not ask for exemption from striving with their wealth and their lives. And God has perfect knowledge of those who are mindful ʿof Himʾ. **45.** No one would ask for exemption except those who have no faith in God or the Last Day, and whose hearts are in doubt, so they are torn by their doubts.

The Trouble-Makers

46. Had they ʿreallyʾ intended to march forth, they would have made preparations for it. But God disliked that they should go, so He let them lag behind, and it was said ʿto themʾ, "Stay with those ʿhelplessʾ who remain behind." **47.** Had they gone forth with you ʿbelieversʾ, they would have been nothing but trouble for you, and would have scrambled around, seeking to spread discord in your midst. And some of you would have eagerly listened to them. And God has ʿperfectʾ knowledge of the wrongdoers. **48.** They had already sought to spread discord before[364] and devised every ʿpossibleʾ plot against you

ʿO Prophetʾ, until the truth came and God's Will prevailed—much to their dismay.

False Excuse 2) Temptation

49. There are some of them who say, "Exempt me and do not expose me to temptation."[365] They have already fallen into temptation. And Hell will surely engulf the disbelievers.

Those Who Stayed Behind

50. If a blessing befalls you ʿO Prophetʾ, they grieve, but if a disaster befalls you, they say, "We took our precaution in advance," and turn away, rejoicing. **51.** Say, "Nothing will ever befall us except what God has destined for us. He is our Protector." So in God let the believers put their trust. **52.** Say, "Are you awaiting anything to befall us except one of the two best things: ʿvictory or martyrdomʾ? But we are awaiting God to afflict you with torment either from Him or at our hands. So keep waiting! We too are waiting with you."

Unaccepted Contributions

53. Say, ʿO Prophet,ʾ "ʿWhether youʾ donate willingly or unwillingly, it will never be accepted from you, for you have been a rebellious people." **54.** And what prevented their donations from being accepted is that they have lost faith in God and His Messenger, they never come to prayer except half-heartedly, and they never donate except resentfully. **55.** So let neither their wealth nor children impress you ʿO Prophetʾ. God only intends to torment them through these things in this worldly life, then their souls will depart while they are disbelievers.

False Oaths

56. They swear by God that they are part of you, but they are not. They only say so out of

---

364 For example, 'Abdullâh ibn Ubai ibn Salûl, a chief hypocrite, marched with the Prophet for the Battle of Uḥud in the outskirts of Medina, then decided not to join the fight and returned to Medina with his followers who made up around one third of the Muslim army.

365 Another hypocrite by the name of Jadd ibn Qais came to the Prophet asking to be exempt from joining the army because he had a weakness for women and he was afraid that he would be tempted by Roman women.

fear. **57.** If only they could find a refuge, or a cave, or any hiding-place, they would rush headlong towards it.

Discontent with Charity

58. There are some of them who are critical of your distribution of alms ˹O Prophet˺. If they are given some of it they are pleased, but if not they are enraged. **59.** If only they had been content with what God and His Messenger had given them and said, "God is sufficient for us! God will grant us out of His bounty, and so will His Messenger. To God ˹alone˺ we turn with hope."

Alms-Tax Recipients

60. Alms-tax is only for the poor and the needy, for those employed to administer it, for those whose hearts are attracted ˹to the faith˺, for ˹freeing˺ slaves, for those in debt, for God's cause, and for ˹needy˺ travellers. ˹This is˺ an obligation from God. And God is All-Knowing, All-Wise.

Criticizing the Prophet

61. And there are others who hurt the Prophet by saying, "He listens to anyone." Say, ˹O Prophet,˺ "He listens to what is best for you. He believes in God, has faith in the believers, and is a mercy for those who believe among you." Those who hurt God's Messenger will suffer a painful punishment.

The Disgrace

62. They swear by God to you ˹believers˺ in order to please you, while it is the pleasure of God and His Messenger they should seek, if they are ˹true˺ believers. **63.** Do they not know that whoever opposes God and His Messenger will be in the Fire of Hell forever? That is the ultimate disgrace.

Blasphemy Exposed

64. The hypocrites fear that a chapter should be revealed about them, exposing what is in their hearts. Say, ˹O Prophet,˺ "Keep mocking! God will definitely bring to light what you fear." **65.** If you question them, they will certainly say, "We were only talking idly and joking around." Say, "Was it God, His revelations, and His Messenger that you ridiculed?" **66.** Make no excuses! You have lost faith after your belief. If We pardon a group of you,[366] We will punish others for their wickedness.

Punishment of the Hypocrites

67. The hypocrites, both men and women, are all alike: they encourage what is evil, forbid what is good, and withhold ˹what is in˺ their hands. They neglected God, so He neglected them. Surely the hypocrites are the rebellious. **68.** God has promised the hypocrites, both men and women, and the disbelievers an everlasting stay in the Fire of Hell—it is sufficient for them. God has condemned them, and they will suffer a never-ending punishment.

Fate of the Disbelievers

69. ˹You hypocrites are˺ like those ˹disbelievers˺ before you. They were far superior to you in might and more abundant in wealth and children. They enjoyed their share in this life. You have enjoyed your share, just as they did. And you have engaged in idle talk, just as they did. Their deeds have become void in this world and the Hereafter. And it is they who are the ˹true˺ losers. **70.** Have they not received the stories of those ˹destroyed˺ before them: the people of Noah, 'Âd, and Thamûd, the people of Abraham, the residents of Midian, and the overturned cities ˹of Lot˺?[367] Their messengers came to them with clear proofs. God would have never wronged them, but it was they who wronged themselves.

---

366 i.e., those who will repent.
367 The overturned cities of Sodom and Gomorrah.

Reward of the Believers

71. The believers, both men and women, are guardians of one another. They encourage good and forbid evil, establish prayer and pay alms-tax, and obey God and His Messenger. It is they who will be shown God's mercy. Surely God is Almighty, All-Wise. **72.** God has promised the believers, both men and women, Gardens under which rivers flow, to stay there forever, and splendid homes in the Gardens of Eternity, and—above all—the pleasure of God. That is ˹truly˺ the ultimate triumph.

Returning Favour with Ingratitude

73. O Prophet! Struggle against the disbelievers and the hypocrites, and be firm with them. Hell will be their home. What an evil destination! **74.** They swear by God that they never said anything ˹blasphemous˺, while they did in fact utter a blasphemy, lost faith after accepting Islam, and plotted what they could not carry out.[368] It is only through resentment that they pay God and His Messenger back for enriching them out of His bounty! If they repent, it will be better for them. But if they turn away, God will torment them with a painful punishment in this world and the Hereafter, and they will have no one on earth to protect or help them.

The Ungrateful

75. And there are some who had made a vow to God: "If He gives us from His bounty, we will surely spend in charity and be of the righteous." **76.** But when He gave them out of His bounty, they withheld it and turned away indifferently. **77.** So He caused hypocrisy to plague their hearts until the Day they will meet Him, for breaking their promise to God and for their lies. **78.** Do they not know that God ˹fully˺

knows their ˹evil˺ thoughts and secret talks, and that God is the Knower of all unseen?

Donations Criticized[369]

79. ˹There are˺ those who slander ˹some of˺ the believers for donating liberally and mock others for giving only the little they can afford. God will throw their mockery back at them, and they will suffer a painful punishment. **80.** ˹It does not matter˺ whether you ˹O Prophet˺ pray for them to be forgiven or not. Even if you pray for their forgiveness seventy times, God will never forgive them. That is because they have lost faith in God and His Messenger. And God does not guide the rebellious people.

False Excuse 3) Heat

81. Those ˹hypocrites˺ who remained behind rejoiced for doing so in defiance of the Messenger of God and hated ˹the prospect of˺ striving with their wealth and their lives in the cause of God. They said ˹to one another˺, "Do not march forth in the heat." Say, ˹O Prophet,˺ "The Fire of Hell is far hotter!" If only they could comprehend! **82.** So let them laugh a little—they will weep much as a reward for what they have committed.

Instructions to the Prophet

83. If God returns you ˹O Prophet˺ to a group of them and they ask to go forth with you, say, "You will not ever go forth or fight an enemy along with me. You preferred to stay behind the first time, so stay with those ˹helpless˺ who remain behind." **84.** And do not ever offer ˹funeral˺ prayers for any of their dead, nor stand by their grave ˹at burial˺, for they have lost faith in God and His Messenger and died rebellious. **85.** And let neither their wealth nor children impress you ˹O Prophet˺. God only intends to torment them through these things in this world, and

---

368 i.e., some of them tried to assassinate the Prophet on the way back from Tabûk.
369 Not only did the hypocrites withhold their wealth, but they were also critical of those who donated. If a rich believer gave generously, the hypocrites would say, "He is showing off," and if a poor believer gave what they could afford, they would say, "This is not good enough."

'then' their souls will depart while they are disbelievers.

The Unfaithful

86. Whenever a chapter is revealed stating, "Believe in God and struggle along with His Messenger," the rich among them would ask to be exempt, saying, "Leave us with those who remain behind." **87.** They preferred to stay behind with the helpless, and their hearts have been sealed so they do not comprehend.

The Faithful

88. But the Messenger and the believers with him strived with their wealth and their lives. They will have all the best, and it is they who will be successful. **89.** God has prepared for them Gardens under which rivers flow, to stay there forever. That is the ultimate triumph.

Unfaithful Nomads

90. Some nomadic Arabs 'also' came with excuses, seeking exemption. And those who were untrue to God and His Messenger remained behind 'with no excuse'. The unfaithful among them will be afflicted with a painful punishment.

Valid Excuses

91. There is no blame on the weak, the sick, or those lacking the means 'if they stay behind', as long as they are true to God and His Messenger. There is no blame on the good-doers. And God is All-Forgiving, Most Merciful. **92.** Nor 'is there any blame on' those who came to you 'O Prophet' for mounts, then when you said, "I can find no mounts for you," they left with eyes overflowing with tears out of grief that they had nothing to contribute.

Invalid Excuses

93. Blame is only on those who seek exemption from you although they have the means. They preferred to stay behind with the help-

less, and God has sealed their hearts so they do not realize 'the consequences'. **94.** They will make excuses to you 'believers' when you return to them. Say, "Make no excuses, 'for' we will not believe you. God has already informed us about your 'true' state 'of faith'. Your 'future' deeds will be observed by God and His Messenger as well. And you will be returned to the Knower of the seen and unseen, then He will inform you of what you used to do." **95.** When you return, they will swear to you by God so that you may leave them alone. So leave them alone—they are truly evil. Hell will be their home as a reward for what they have committed. **96.** They will swear to you in order to please you. And even if you are pleased with them, God will never be pleased with the rebellious people.

Unfaithful Nomads

97. The nomadic Arabs 'around Medina' are far worse in disbelief and hypocrisy, and less likely to know the laws revealed by God to His Messenger. And God is All-Knowing, All-Wise. **98.** And among the nomads are those who consider what they donate to be a loss and await your misfortune. May ill-fortune befall them! And God is All-Hearing, All-Knowing.

Faithful Nomads

99. However, among the nomadic Arabs are those who believe in God and the Last Day, and consider what they donate as a means of coming closer to God and 'receiving' the prayers of the Messenger. It will certainly bring them closer. God will admit them into His mercy. Surely God is All-Forgiving, Most Merciful.

The Foremost

100. As for the foremost—the first of the Emigrants[370] and the Helpers[371]—and those who follow them in goodness, God

---

370 i.e., the early Muslims who emigrated from Mecca to Medina, known as *Al-Muhâjirûn*.
371 i.e., those from Medina, known as *Al-Anşâr*, who accepted Islam and sheltered Muslim emigrants from Mecca.

is pleased with them and they are pleased with Him. And He has prepared for them Gardens under which rivers flow, to stay there for ever and ever. That is the ultimate triumph.

Master Hypocrites

101. Some of the nomads around you 'believers' are hypocrites, as are some of the people of Medina. They have mastered hypocrisy. They are not known to you 'O Prophet'; they are known to Us. We will punish them twice 'in this world',[372] then they will be brought back 'to their Lord' for a tremendous punishment.

Those Who Are Forgiven

102. Some others have confessed their wrongdoing: they have mixed goodness with evil.[373] It is right to hope that God will turn to them in mercy. Surely God is All-Forgiving, Most Merciful. 103. Take from their wealth 'O Prophet' charity to purify and bless them, and pray for them—surely your prayer is a source of comfort for them. And God is All-Hearing, All-Knowing. 104. Do they not know that God alone accepts the repentance of His servants and receives 'their' charity, and that God alone is the Accepter of Repentance, Most Merciful?

A Second Chance

105. Tell 'them, O Prophet', "Do as you will. Your deeds will be observed by God, His Messenger, and the believers. And you will be returned to the Knower of the seen and unseen, then He will inform you of what you used to do."

The Three Who Remained Behind[374]

106. And some others are left for God's decision, either to punish them or turn to them in mercy. And God is All-Knowing, All-Wise.

The Mosque of Harm

107. There are also those 'hypocrites' who set up a mosque 'only' to cause harm, promote disbelief, divide the believers, and as a base for those who had previously fought against God and His Messenger.[375] They will definitely swear, "We intended nothing but good," but God bears witness that they are surely liars. 108. Do not 'O Prophet' ever pray in it. Certainly, a mosque founded on righteousness from the first day is more worthy of your prayers. In it are men who love to be purified.[376] And God loves those who purify themselves. 109. Which is better: those who laid the foundation of their building on the fear and pleasure of God, or those who did so on the edge of a crumbling cliff that tumbled down with them into the Fire of Hell? And God does not guide the wrongdoing people. 110. The building which they erected will never cease to fuel hypocrisy in their hearts until their hearts are torn apart. And God is All-Knowing, All-Wise.

The Finest Bargain

111. God has indeed purchased from the believers their lives and wealth in exchange for Paradise. They fight in the cause of God and

---

372 Through disgrace in this world and bad ending of their lives.
373 They have mixed their adherence to Islam with their disobedience to march forth with the Prophet to Tabûk.
374 This verse refers to Ka'b ibn Mâlik, Murarah ibn Rabi', and Hilâl ibn Umaiyah, the three companions who remained in Medina with no excuse, but were honest about what they did. They were boycotted by the Muslims for about fifty days until verses 118-119 of this chapter were revealed declaring the acceptance of their repentance.
375 Abu 'Âmer Ar-Râhib was a monk who fought against the Muslims at the Battle of Badr. He ordered a group of twelve hypocrites to build a mosque near the Mosque of Qubâ', the first mosque built by Muslims and also where the Prophet and his companions would pray. The new mosque, commonly referred to as Masjid Ad-Dirâr (Mosque of Harm), was intended to attract other hypocrites and reduce the number of Muslims who prayed at Qubâ'. The hypocrites who built the mosque also anticipated the arrival of Abu 'Âmer with Roman forces to expel the Prophet and Muslims out of Medina. Upon a request from these hypocrites, the Prophet had planned to visit the new mosque once he returned from Tabûk, but verses 107-110 of this chapter were revealed, warning the Prophet against that mosque. According to some narrations, the Prophet ordered this mosque to be burned down.
376 See footnote for 7:46.

kill or are killed. This is a true promise binding on Him in the Torah, the Gospel, and the Quran. And whose promise is truer than God's? So rejoice in the exchange you have made with Him. That is 'truly' the ultimate triumph. 112. 'It is the believers' who repent, who are devoted to worship, who praise 'their Lord', who fast, who bow down and prostrate themselves, who encourage good and forbid evil, and who observe the limits set by God. And give good news to the believers.

Praying for the Polytheists

113. It is not 'proper' for the Prophet and the believers to seek forgiveness for the polytheists, even if they were close relatives, after it has become clear to the believers that they are bound for the Hellfire. 114. As for Abraham's prayer for his father's forgiveness, it was only in fulfilment of a promise he had made to him. But when it became clear to Abraham that his father was an enemy of God, he broke ties with him.[377] Abraham was truly tender-hearted, forbearing. 115. God would never consider a people deviant after He has guided them, until He makes clear to them what they must avoid. Surely God has 'full' knowledge of everything.

God's Might

116. Indeed, to God 'alone' belongs the kingdom of the heavens and the earth. He gives life and causes death. And besides God you have no guardian or helper.

God's Mercy

117. God has certainly turned in mercy to the Prophet[378] as well as the Emigrants and the Helpers who stood by him in the time of hardship, after the hearts of a group of them had almost faltered. He then ac-cepted their repentance. Surely He is Ever Gracious and Most Merciful to them.

The Three[379]

118. And 'God has also turned in mercy to' the three who had remained behind, 'whose guilt distressed them' until the earth, despite its vastness, seemed to close in on them, and their souls were torn in anguish. They knew there was no refuge from God except in Him. Then He turned to them in mercy so that they might repent. Surely God 'alone' is the Accepter of Repentance, Most Merciful. 119. O believers! Be mindful of God and be with the truthful.

A Fine Reward

120. It was not 'proper' for the people of Medina and the nomadic Arabs around them to avoid marching with the Messenger of God or to prefer their own lives above his. That is because whenever they suffer from thirst, fatigue, or hunger in the cause of God; or tread on a territory, unnerving the disbelievers; or inflict any loss on an enemy—it is written to their credit as a good deed. Surely God never discounts the reward of the good-doers. 121. And whenever they make a donation, small or large, or cross a valley 'in God's cause'—it is written to their credit, so that God may grant them the best reward for what they used to do.

Gaining Knowledge

122. 'However,' it is not necessary for the believers to march forth all at once. Only a party from each group should march forth, leaving the rest to gain religious knowledge then enlighten their people when they return to them, so that they 'too' may beware 'of evil'.

---

377 Abraham promised to pray for his father's forgiveness in 19:47 and 60:4, but when his father died as a disbeliever he discontinued praying for him.

378 The Prophet is forgiven for exempting all those who came to him with excuses regardless of their honesty, or for seeking forgiveness for the polytheists.

379 See footnote for verse 106 of this chapter.

Firmness with the Disbelievers[380]

123. O believers! Fight the disbelievers around you and let them find firmness in you. And know that God is with those mindful 'of Him'.

Hypocrites Reacting to Revelation

124. Whenever a chapter is revealed, some of them ask 'mockingly', "Which of you has this increased in faith?" As for the believers, it has increased them in faith and they rejoice. **125.** But as for those with sickness in their hearts,[381] it has increased them only in wickedness upon their wickedness, and they die as disbelievers. **126.** Do they not see that they are tried once or twice every year?[382] Yet they neither repent nor do they learn a lesson. **127.** Whenever a chapter is revealed, they look at one another, 'saying,' "Is anyone watching you?" Then they slip away. 'It is' God 'Who' has turned their hearts away because they are a people who do not comprehend.

Invitation to All

128. There certainly has come to you a messenger from among yourselves. He is concerned by your suffering, anxious for your well-being, and gracious and merciful to the believers. **129.** But if they turn away, then say, 'O Prophet,' "God is sufficient for me. There is no god 'worthy of worship' except Him. In Him I put my trust. And He is the Lord of the Mighty Throne."

❦

10. Jonah *(Yûnus)*

Similar to the previous chapter, this Meccan chapter emphasizes God's acceptance of repentance, most notably in the case of the people of Jonah (verse 98). The pagan claims against the Quran are refuted both in this chapter and the next. The short span of this worldly life and people's ingratitude to their Creator are elaborated upon. The Prophet is urged to exercise patience in the face of denial. The stories of Noah's people and Pharaoh's people are citied as cautionary tales to the Meccan deniers, setting the stage for more elaborate warnings in the next chapter.

In the Name of God—the Most Compassionate, Most Merciful

Universal Messenger

1. *Alif-Lām-Ra.* These are the verses of the Book, rich in wisdom. **2.** Is it astonishing to people that We have sent revelation to a man from among themselves, 'instructing him,' "Warn humanity and give good news to the believers that they will have an honourable status with their Lord."? Yet the disbelievers said, "Indeed, this 'man' is clearly a magician!"

Origin of Creation

3. Surely your Lord is God Who created the heavens and the earth in six Days,[383] then established Himself above the Throne, conducting every affair. None can intercede except by His permission. That is God—your Lord, so worship Him 'alone'. Will you not then be mindful? **4.** To Him is your return all together. God's promise is 'always' true.

---

380 This verse talks exclusively about the disbelievers at war with Muslims. *See* 2:190-193 and 60:8-9.
381 i.e., hypocrites.
382 Their hypocrisy is exposed over and over again.
383 *See* footnote for 7:54.

Indeed, He originates the creation then resurrects it so that He may justly reward those who believe and do good. But those who disbelieve will have a boiling drink and a painful punishment for their disbelief.

Signs in God's Creation

5. He is the One Who made the sun a radiant source and the moon a reflected light, with precisely ordained phases, so that you may know the number of years and calculation ʿof timeʾ. God did not create all this except for a purpose. He makes the signs clear for people of knowledge. **6.** Surely in the alternation of the day and the night, and in all that God has created in the heavens and the earth, there are truly signs for those mindful ʿof Himʾ.

Deniers of Resurrection

7. Indeed, those who do not expect to meet Us, being pleased and content with this worldly life, and who are heedless of Our signs, **8.** they will have the Fire as a home because of what they have committed.

Guided by Faith

9. Surely those who believe and do good, their Lord will guide them ʿto Paradiseʾ through their faith, rivers will flow under their feet in the Gardens of Bliss, **10.** in which their prayer will be, "Glory be to You, O God!" and their greeting will be, "Peace!" and their closing prayer will be, "All praise is for God—Lord of all worlds!"

No Rush for Evil

11. If God were to hasten evil for people[384] as they wish to hasten good, they would have certainly been doomed. But We leave those who do not expect to meet Us to wander blindly in their defiance.

The Ungrateful

12. Whenever someone is touched by hardship, they cry out to Us, whether lying on their side, sitting, or standing. But when We relieve their hardship, they return to their old ways as if they had never cried to Us to remove any hardship! This is how the misdeeds of the transgressors have been made appealing to them.

Warning to the Meccan Pagans

13. We surely destroyed ʿotherʾ peoples before you when they did wrong, and their messengers came to them with clear proofs but they would not believe! This is how We reward the wicked people. **14.** Then We made you their successors in the land to see how you would act.

The Pagans Demand a New Quran

15. When Our clear revelations are recited to them, those who do not expect to meet Us say ʿto the Prophetʾ, "Bring us a different Quran or make some changes in it." Say ʿto themʾ, "It is not for me to change it on my own. I only follow what is revealed to me. I fear, if I were to disobey my Lord, the punishment of a tremendous Day." **16.** Say, "Had God willed, I would not have recited it to you, nor would He have made it known to you. I had lived my whole life among you before this ʿrevelationʾ. Do you not understand?" **17.** Who does more wrong than those who fabricate lies against God or deny His revelations? Indeed, the wicked will never succeed.

False Gods

18. They worship besides God others who can neither harm nor benefit them, and say, "These are our intercessors with God." Ask ʿthem, O Prophetʾ, "Are you informing God of something He does not know in the heavens or the earth? Glorified and Exalted is He above what they associate ʿwith Himʾ!"

---

384 When they pray against themselves or their children, or when they demand to be destroyed.

106

No Longer United by Faith

19. Humanity was once nothing but a single community ʿof believersʾ, but then they differed.[385] Had it not been for a prior decree from your Lord,[386] their differences would have been settled ʿat onceʾ.

Demanding a New Miracle[387]

20. They ask, "Why has no ʿotherʾ sign been sent down to him from his Lord?" Say, ʿO Prophet,ʾ "ʿʾThe knowledge ofʾ the unseen is with God alone. So wait! I too am waiting with you."

Returning Favour with Denial

21. When We give people a taste of mercy after being afflicted with a hardship, they swiftly devise plots against Our revelations! Say, ʿO Prophet,ʾ "God is swifter in devising ʿpunishmentʾ. Surely Our messenger-angels record whatever you devise."

Metaphor for Human Ingratitude

22. He is the One Who enables you to travel through land and sea. And it so happens that you are on ships, sailing with a favourable wind, to the passengers' delight. Suddenly, the ships are overcome by a gale wind and those on board are overwhelmed by waves from every side, and they assume they are doomed. They cry out to God ʿaloneʾ in sincere devotion, "If You save us from this, we will certainly be grateful." **23.** But as soon as He rescues them, they transgress in the land unjustly. O humanity! Your transgression is only against your own souls. ʿThere is onlyʾ brief enjoyment in this worldly life, then to Us is your return, and then We will inform you of what you used to do.

This Fleeting Life

24. The life of this world is just like rain We send down from the sky, producing a mixture of plants which humans and animals consume. Then just as the earth looks its best, perfectly beautified, and its people think they have full control over it, there comes to it Our command by night or by day, so We mow it down as if it never flourished yesterday! This is how We make the signs clear for people who reflect.

Invitation to Paradise

25. And God invites ʿallʾ to the Home of Peace and guides whoever He wills to the Straight Path. **26.** Those who do good will have the finest reward[388] and ʿevenʾ more.[389] Neither gloom nor disgrace will cover their faces. It is they who will be the residents of Paradise. They will be there forever.

Warning Against Hell

27. As for those who commit evil, the reward of an evil deed is its equivalent. Humiliation will cover them—with no one to protect them from God—as if their faces were covered with patches of the night's deep darkness. It is they who will be the residents of the Fire. They will be there forever.

False Gods and Their Followers

28. ʿConsiderʾ the Day We will gather them all together then say to those who associated others ʿwith God in worshipʾ, "Stay in your places—you and your associate-gods." We will separate them from each other, and their associate-gods will say, "It was not us that you worshipped! **29.** God is sufficient as a Witness between each of us that we were totally unaware of your worship." **30.** Then and there every soul will face ʿthe consequences ofʾ what it had done. They all will

---

385 i.e., they split into believers and disbelievers.
386 That He will delay their judgment until the Hereafter.
387 The pagans of Mecca were not satisfied with the literary miracle of the Quran, so they demanded a tangible miracle such as the staff of Moses.
388 Paradise.
389 Seeing Almighty God in the Hereafter.

be returned to God—their True Master. And whatever ʿgodsʾ they fabricated will fail them.

Questions to Pagans: 1) Who Provides?

31. Ask ʿthem, O Prophetʾ, "Who provides for you from heaven and earth? Who owns ʿyourʾ hearing and sight? Who brings forth the living from the dead and the dead from the living? And who conducts every affair?" They will ʿsurelyʾ say, "God." Say, "Will you not then fear ʿHimʾ? **32.** That is God—your True Lord. So what is beyond the truth except falsehood? How can you then be turned away?" **33.** And so your Lord's decree has been proven true against the rebellious—that they will never believe.

2) Who Creates?

34. Ask ʿthem, O Prophetʾ, "Can any of your associate-gods originate creation and then resurrect it?" Say, "ʿOnlyʾ God originates creation and then resurrects it. How can you then be deluded ʿfrom the truthʾ?"

3) Who Guides?

35. Ask ʿthem, O Prophetʾ, "Can any of your associate-gods guide to the truth?" Say, "ʿOnlyʾ God guides to the truth." Who then is more worthy to be followed: the One Who guides to the truth or those who cannot find the way unless guided? What is the matter with you? How do you judge? **36.** Most of them follow nothing but ʿinheritedʾ assumptions. ʿAndʾ surely assumptions can in no way replace the truth. God is indeed All-Knowing of what they do.

The Challenge of the Quran

37. It is not ʿpossibleʾ for this Quran to have been produced by anyone other than God. In fact, it is a confirmation of what came before, and an explanation of the Scripture. It is, without a doubt, from the Lord of all worlds. **38.** Or do they claim, "He[390] made it up!"? Tell them ʿO Prophetʾ, "Produce one chapter like it then, and seek help from whoever you can—other than God—if what you say is true!" **39.** In fact, they ʿhastilyʾ rejected the Book without comprehending it and before the fulfilment of its warnings. Similarly, those before them were in denial. See then what was the end of the wrongdoers!

It Is God Who Guides

40. Some of them will ʿeventuallyʾ believe in it; others will not. And your Lord knows best the corruptors. **41.** If they deny you, then say, "My deeds are mine and your deeds are yours. You are free of what I do and I am free of what you do!" **42.** Some of them listen to what you say, but can you make the deaf hear even though they do not understand? **43.** And some of them look at you, but can you guide the blind even though they cannot see?[391] **44.** Indeed, God does not wrong people in the least, but it is people who wrong themselves.

Short Life

45. On the Day He will gather them, it will be as if they had not stayed ʿin the worldʾ except for an hour of a day,[392] ʿas though they were onlyʾ getting to know one another. Lost indeed will be those who denied the meeting with God, and were not ʿrightlyʾ guided!

Warning Before Judgment

46. Whether We show you ʿO Prophetʾ some of what We threaten them with, or cause you to die ʿbefore thatʾ, to Us is their return and God is a Witness over what they do. **47.** And for every community there is a messenger. After their messenger

---

390 The Prophet.
391 This refers metaphorically to the pagans who fail to see and hear the truth.
392 i.e., only for a short period of time.

has come,[393] judgment is passed on them in all fairness, and they are not wronged.

When the Time Comes ...

48. They ask ˈthe believersˈ, "When will this threat come to pass if what you say is true?" 49. Say, ˈO Prophet,ˈ "I have no power to benefit or protect myself, except by the Will of God." For each community there is an appointed term. When their time arrives, they cannot delay it for a moment, nor could they advance it.

God's Torment

50. Tell them ˈO Prophetˈ, "Imagine if His torment were to overcome you by night or day—do the wicked realize what they are ˈreallyˈ asking Him to hasten? 51. Will you believe in it only after it has overtaken you? Now? But you always wanted to hasten it!" 52. Then the wrongdoers will be told, "Taste the torment of eternity! Are you not rewarded except for what you used to commit?"

God's Promise

53. They ask you ˈO Prophetˈ, "Is this true?" Say, "Yes, by my Lord! Most certainly it is true! And you will have no escape." 54. If every wrongdoer were to possess everything in the world, they would surely ransom themselves with it. They will hide ˈtheirˈ remorse when they see the torment. And they will be judged in all fairness, and none will be wronged. 55. Surely to God belongs whatever is in the heavens and the earth. Surely God's promise is ˈalwaysˈ true, but most of them do not know. 56. He ˈis the One Whoˈ gives life and causes death, and to Him you will ˈallˈ be returned.

Excellence of the Quran

57. O humanity! Indeed, there has come to you a warning from your Lord, a cure for what is in the hearts, a guide, and a mercy for the believers. 58. Say, ˈO Prophet,ˈ "In God's grace and mercy let them rejoice. That is far better than whatever ˈwealthˈ they amass."

God's Provisions

59. Ask ˈthe pagans, O Prophetˈ, "Have you seen that which God has sent down for you as a provision, of which you have made some lawful and some unlawful?"[394] Say, "Has God given you authorization, or are you fabricating lies against God?" 60. What do those who fabricate lies against God expect on Judgment Day? Surely God is ever Bountiful to humanity,[395] but most of them are ungrateful.

God's Knowledge

61. There is no activity you may be engaged in ˈO Prophetˈ or portion of the Quran you may be reciting, nor any deed you ˈallˈ may be doing except that We are a Witness over you while doing it. Not ˈevenˈ an atom's weight is hidden from your Lord on earth or in heaven; nor anything smaller or larger than that, but is ˈwrittenˈ in a perfect Record.[396]

God's Close Servants

62. There will certainly be no fear for the close servants of God, nor will they grieve. 63. ˈThey areˈ those who are faithful and are mindful ˈof Himˈ. 64. For them is good news in this worldly life and the Hereafter. There is no change in the promise of God. That is ˈtrulyˈ the ultimate triumph.

---

393 Either in this life to deliver the message or on the Day of Judgment to testify for or against them.
394 This refers to 6:138-139.
395 By delaying their punishment and allowing them time to repent.
396 The Record refers to the Preserved Tablet (Al-Lawḥ Al-Maḥfûẓ) in which God has written the destiny of His entire creation.

The Almighty

65. Do not let their words grieve you ˹O Prophet˺. Surely all honour and power belongs to God. He is the All-Hearing, All-Knowing. **66.** Certainly to God ˹alone˺ belong all those in the heavens and all those on the earth. And what do those who associate others with God really follow? They follow nothing but assumptions and do nothing but lie. **67.** He is the One Who has made the night for you to rest in and the day bright. Surely in this are signs for people who listen.

God Has No Children

68. They[397] say, "God has offspring."[398] Glory be to Him! He is the Self-Sufficient. To Him belongs whatever is in the heavens and whatever is on the earth. You have no proof of this! Do you say about God what you do not know? **69.** Say, ˹O Prophet,˺ "Indeed, those who fabricate lies against God will never succeed." **70.** ˹It is only˺ a brief enjoyment in this world, then to Us is their return, then We will make them taste the severe punishment for their disbelief.

Noah and His People

71. Relate to them ˹O Prophet˺ the story of Noah when he said to his people, "O my People! If my presence and my reminders to you of God's signs are unbearable to you, then ˹know that˺ I have put my trust in God. So devise a plot along with your associate-gods—and you do not have to be secretive about your plot—then carry it out against me without delay! **72.** And if you turn away, ˹remember˺ I have never demanded a reward from you ˹for delivering the message˺. My reward is only from God. And I have been commanded to be one of those who submit ˹to God˺." **73.** But they still rejected him, so We saved him and those with him in the Ark and made them successors, and drowned those who rejected Our

signs. See then what was the end of those who had been warned!

Messengers After Noah

74. Then after him We sent ˹other˺ messengers to their ˹own˺ people and they came to them with clear proofs. But they would not believe in what they had rejected before. This is how We seal the hearts of the transgressors.

Moses and Aaron

75. Then after these ˹messengers˺ We sent Moses and Aaron to Pharaoh and his chiefs with Our signs. But they behaved arrogantly and were a wicked people. **76.** When the truth came to them from Us, they said, "This is certainly pure magic!" **77.** Moses responded, "Is this what you say about the truth when it has come to you? Is this magic? Magicians will never succeed." **78.** They argued, "Have you come to turn us away from the faith of our forefathers so that the two of you may become supreme in the land? We will never believe in you!" **79.** Pharaoh demanded, "Bring me every skilled magician." **80.** When the magicians came, Moses said to them, "Cast whatever you wish to cast!" **81.** When they did, Moses said, "What you have produced is mere magic, God will surely make it useless, for God certainly does not set right the work of the corruptors. **82.** And God establishes the truth by His Words—even to the dismay of the wicked."

A Few Believers

83. But no one believed in Moses except a few youths of his people, while fearing that Pharaoh and their own chiefs might persecute them. And certainly Pharaoh was a tyrant in the land, and he was truly a transgressor. **84.** Moses said, "O my people! If you do believe in God and submit ˹to His Will˺, then put your trust in Him." **85.** They replied, "In God we trust. Our Lord! Do not subject us to the persecution of the

---

397 The Christians, pagans, etc.
398 Jesus in Christianity, the angels in pagan Arab mythology, etc.

oppressive people, **86.** and deliver us by Your mercy from the disbelieving people."

Power of Prayer

87. We revealed to Moses and his brother, "Appoint houses for your people in Egypt. Turn these houses into places of worship, establish prayer, and give good news to the believers!" **88.** Moses prayed, "Our Lord! You have granted Pharaoh and his chiefs luxuries and riches in this worldly life, ˹which they abused˺ to lead people astray from Your Way! Our Lord, destroy their riches and harden their hearts so that they will not believe until they see the painful punishment." **89.** God responded ˹to Moses and Aaron˺,³⁹⁹ "Your prayer is answered! So be steadfast and do not follow the way of those who do not know."

End of Pharaoh

90. We brought the Children of Israel across the sea. Then Pharaoh and his soldiers pursued them unjustly and oppressively. But as Pharaoh was drowning, he cried out, "I believe that there is no god except that in whom the Children of Israel believe, and I am ˹now˺ one of those who submit." **91.** ˹He was told,˺ "Now ˹you believe˺? But you always disobeyed and were one of the corruptors. **92.** Today We will preserve your corpse so that you may become an example⁴⁰⁰ for those who come after you. And surely most people are heedless of Our examples!"

God's Grace to the Israelites

93. Indeed, We settled the Children of Israel in a blessed land,⁴⁰¹ and granted them good, lawful provisions. They did not differ until knowledge came to them.⁴⁰² Surely your Lord will judge between them on the Day of Judgment regarding their differences.

Confirming the Truth

94. If you ˹O Prophet˺ are in doubt about ˹these stories˺ that We have revealed to you, then ask those who read the Scripture before you. The truth has certainly come to you from your Lord, so do not be one of those who doubt, **95.** and do not be one of those who deny God's signs or you will be one of the losers.⁴⁰³

Jonah's People Spared from Torment

96. Indeed, those against whom your Lord's decree ˹of torment˺ is justified will not believe— **97.** even if every sign were to come to them—until they see the painful punishment. **98.** If only there had been a society which believed ˹before seeing the torment˺ and, therefore, benefited from its belief, like the people of Jonah.⁴⁰⁴ When they believed, We lifted from them the torment of disgrace in this world and allowed them enjoyment for a while.⁴⁰⁵

Conviction, Not Compulsion

99. Had your Lord so willed ˹O Prophet˺, all ˹people˺ on earth would have certainly believed, every single one of them! Would you then force people to become believers?

---

399   Moses prayed while Aaron said, "Amen." So it is as if both of them prayed.
400   lit., sign.
401   In Egypt, Jerusalem, and other places.
402   They did not split into believers and disbelievers until they received the knowledge given to their prophets.
403   When these verses were revealed, the Prophet responded, "I am not in doubt and I will not ask ˹anyone˺."
404   Initially, the people of Jonah rejected his message. When he was told they would be punished after three days for their defiance, he left his city without God's permission before its destruction. Jonah's people became convinced that they were going to be destroyed when he left them and they saw signs of the imminent torment, so they felt remorseful and cried out for forgiveness before the coming of the punishment. Therefore, God accepted their repentance and the torment was retracted.
405   i.e., until the end of their term.

100. It is not for any soul to believe except by God's leave, and He will bring His wrath upon those who are unmindful.

Invitation to Think

101. Say, ʿO Prophet,ʾ "Consider all that is in the heavens and the earth!" Yet neither signs nor warners are of any benefit to those who refuse to believe. **102.** Are they waiting for ʿanythingʾ except the same torments that befell those before them? Say, "Keep waiting then! I too am waiting with you." **103.** Then We saved Our messengers and those who believed. For it is Our duty to save the believers.

True Faith

104. Say, ʿO Prophet,ʾ "O humanity! If you are in doubt of my faith, then ʿknow thatʾ I do not worship those ʿidolsʾ you worship instead of God. But I worship God, Who has the power to cause your death. And I have been commanded, 'Be one of the believers,' **105.** and, 'Be steadfast in faith in all uprightness, and do not be one of the polytheists,' **106.** and 'Do not invoke. instead of God.

what can neither benefit nor harm you—for if you do, then you will certainly be one of the wrongdoers,' **107.** and 'If God touches you with harm, none can undo it except Him. And if He intends good for you, none can withhold His bounty. He grants it to whoever He wills of His servants. And He is the All-Forgiving, Most Merciful.'"

Call to Humanity

108. Say, ʿO Prophet,ʾ "O humanity! The truth has surely come to you from your Lord. So whoever chooses to be guided, it is only for their own good. And whoever chooses to stray, it is only to their own loss. And I am not a keeper over you."

Advice to the Prophet

109. And follow what is revealed to you, and be patient until God passes His judgment. For He is the Best of Judges.

11. Hûd *(Hûd)*

This Meccan chapter is named after Prophet Hûd, whose story is mentioned in verses 50-60. More details are given about Noah in this chapter than the previous chapter and Chapter 7. Just like the previous chapter, the stories of destroyed disbelievers are meant to deter the Arab pagans and reassure the Prophet of his ultimate triumph, and a reference is made to the reward of the believers and the punishment of the disbelievers in the Hereafter.

In the Name of God—the Most Compassionate, Most Merciful

Message of the Quran

1. *Alif-Lãm-Ra.* ʿThis isʾ a Book whose verses are well perfected and then fully explained. ʿIt isʾ from the One ʿWho isʾ All-Wise, All-Aware. **2.** ʿTell them, O Prophet,ʾ "Worship none but God. Surely I am a warner and deliverer of good news to you from Him. **3.** And seek your Lord's forgiveness and turn to Him in repentance. He will grant you a good provision for an appointed term and graciously reward the doers of good. But if you turn away, then I truly fear for you the torment of a formidable Day. **4.** To God is your return. And He is Most Capable of everything."

Hiding Disbelief

5. Indeed, they[406] enfold ˹what is in˺ their hearts, ˹trying˺ to hide it from Him! But even when they cover themselves with their clothes, He knows what they conceal and what they reveal. Surely He knows best what is ˹hidden˺ in the heart.

God's Might

6. There is no moving creature on earth whose provision is not guaranteed by God. And He knows where it lives and where it is laid to rest. All is ˹written˺ in a perfect Record.[407] **7.** He is the One Who created the heavens and the earth in six Days[408]—and His Throne was upon the waters—in order to test which of you is best in deeds. And if you ˹O Prophet˺ say, "Surely you will ˹all˺ be raised up after death," the disbelievers will certainly say, "That is nothing but pure magic!" **8.** And if We delay their punishment until an appointed time, they will definitely say, "What is holding it back?" Indeed, on the Day it overtakes them, it will not be averted from them, and they will be overwhelmed by what they used to ridicule.

Adversity and Prosperity

9. If We give people a taste of Our mercy then take it away from them, they become utterly desperate, ungrateful. **10.** But if We give them a taste of prosperity after being touched with adversity, they say, "My ills are gone," and become totally prideful and boastful, **11.** except those who patiently endure and do good. It is they who will have forgiveness and a mighty reward.

Pagan Annoyances

12. Perhaps you ˹O Prophet˺ may wish to give up some of what is revealed to you and may be distressed by it because they say, "If only a treasure had been sent down to him, or an angel had come with him!" You are only a warner, and God is the Trustee of All Affairs.

Challenging the Pagans

13. Or do they say, "He[409] has fabricated this ˹Quran˺!"? Say, ˹O Prophet,˺ "Produce ten fabricated chapters like it and seek help from whoever you can—other than God—if what you say is true!" **14.** But if your helpers fail you, then know that it has been revealed with the knowledge of God, and that there is no god ˹worthy of worship˺ except Him! Will you ˹not˺ then submit ˹to God˺?

Fleeting Gain

15. Whoever desires ˹only˺ this worldly life and its luxuries, We will pay them in full for their deeds in this life—nothing will be left out. **16.** It is they who will have nothing in the Hereafter except the Fire. Their efforts in this life will be fruitless and their deeds will be useless.

Everlasting Gain

17. ˹Can these people be compared to˺ those ˹believers˺ who stand on clear proof from their Lord, backed by ˹the Quran as˺ a witness from Him, and preceded by the Book of Moses ˹which was revealed˺ as a guide and mercy? It is those ˹believers˺ who have faith in it. But whoever from the ˹disbelieving˺ groups rejects it, the Fire will be their destiny. So do not be in doubt of it. It is certainly the truth from your Lord, but most people do not believe.

---

406   The hypocrites or the disbelievers.
407   *See* footnote for 10:61.
408   See footnote for 7:54.
409   The Prophet.

The Losers

18. Who does more wrong than those who fabricate lies against God? They will be brought before their Lord, and the witnesses[410] will say, "These are the ones who lied against their Lord." Surely God's condemnation is upon the wrongdoers, **19.** who hinder ˹others˺ from God's Path, striving to make it ˹appear˺ crooked, and disbelieve in the Hereafter. **20.** They will never frustrate God on earth, and they will have no protector besides God. Their punishment will be multiplied, for they failed to hear or see ˹the truth˺. **21.** It is they who have ruined themselves, and whatever ˹gods˺ they fabricated will fail them. **22.** Without a doubt, they will be the worst losers in the Hereafter.

The Winners

23. Surely those who believe, do good, and humble themselves before their Lord will be the residents of Paradise. They will be there forever.

The Disbelievers and the Believers

24. The example of these two parties is that of the blind and the deaf, compared to the seeing and the hearing. Can the two be equal? Will you not then be mindful?

Prophet Noah

25. Surely We sent Noah to his people. ˹He said,˺ "Indeed, I am sent to you with a clear warning **26.** that you should worship none but God. I truly fear for you the torment of a painful Day." **27.** The disbelieving chiefs of his people said, "We see you only as a human being like ourselves, and we see that no one follows you except the lowliest among us, who do so ˹hastily˺ without thinking.[411] We do not see anything that makes ˹all of˺

you any better than us. In fact, we think you are liars."

Noah's Argument

28. He said, "O my people! Consider if I stand on a clear proof from my Lord and He has blessed me with a mercy from Himself,[412] which you fail to see. Should we ˹then˺ force it on you against your will? **29.** O my people! I do not ask you for a payment for this ˹message˺. My reward is only from God. And I will never dismiss the believers, for they will surely meet their Lord. But I can see that you are a people acting ignorantly. **30.** O my people! Who would protect me from God if I were to dismiss them? Will you not then be mindful? **31.** I do not say to you that I possess God's treasuries or know the unseen, nor do I claim to be an angel, nor do I say that God will never grant goodness to those you look down upon. God knows best what is ˹hidden˺ within them. ˹If I did,˺ then I would truly be one of the wrongdoers."

His People's Response

32. They protested, "O Noah! You have argued with us far too much, so bring upon us what you threaten us with, if what you say is true." **33.** He responded, "It is God Who can bring it upon you if He wills, and then you will have no escape! **34.** My advice will not benefit you—no matter how hard I try—if God wills ˹for˺ you to stray. He is your Lord, and to Him you will ˹all˺ be returned."

The Pagans Discredit the Quran

35. Or do they say, "He[413] has fabricated this ˹Quran˺!"? Say, ˹O Prophet,˺ "If I have done so, then I bear the burden of that sin! But I am free from your sinful accusation."

---

410   i.e., the angels and the prophets.
411   Typically, the poor and the helpless are the first to believe in prophets, taking them as saviours, whereas the rich and powerful are hesitant to believe, perceiving the new faith as a threat to their influence.
412   Mercy here means prophethood.
413   The Prophet Muḥammad.

The Ark

36. And it was revealed to Noah, "None of your people will believe except those who already have. So do not be distressed by what they have been doing. **37.** And build the Ark under Our ˹watchful˺ Eyes and directions, and do not plead with Me for those who have done wrong, for they will surely be drowned." **38.** So he began to build the Ark, and whenever some of the chiefs of his people passed by, they mocked him. He said, "If you laugh at us, we will ˹soon˺ laugh at you similarly. **39.** You will soon come to know who will be visited by a humiliating torment ˹in this life˺ and overwhelmed by an everlasting punishment ˹in the next˺."

The Flood

40. And when Our command came and the oven burst ˹with water˺,[414] We said ˹to Noah˺, "Take into the Ark a pair from every species along with your family—except those against whom the decree ˹to drown˺ has already been passed—and those who believe." But none believed with him except for a few. **41.** And he said, "Board it! In the Name of God it will sail and cast anchor. Surely my Lord is All-Forgiving, Most Merciful."

Noah's Son

42. And ˹so˺ the Ark sailed with them through waves like mountains. Noah called out to his son, who stood apart, "O my dear son! Come aboard with us and do not be with the disbelievers." **43.** He replied, "I will take refuge on a mountain, which will protect me from the water." Noah cried, "Today no one is protected from God's decree except those to whom He shows mercy!" And the waves came between them, and his son was among the drowned. **44.** And it was said, "O earth! Swallow up your water. And O sky! Withhold ˹your rain˺." The floodwater receded and the decree was carried out. The Ark rested on Mount Judi, and it was said, "Away with the wrongdoing people!"

Noah Pleading for His Son

45. Noah called out to his Lord, saying, "My Lord! Certainly my son is ˹also˺ of my family, Your promise is surely true, and You are the most just of all judges!" **46.** God replied, "O Noah! He is certainly not of your family—he was entirely of unrighteous conduct. So do not ask Me about what you have no knowledge of! I warn you so you do not fall into ignorance." **47.** Noah pleaded, "My Lord, I seek refuge in You from asking You about what I have no knowledge of, and unless You forgive me and have mercy on me, I will be one of the losers." **48.** It was said, "O Noah! Disembark with Our peace and blessings on you and some of the descendants of those with you. As for the others, We will allow them ˹a brief˺ enjoyment, then they will be touched with a painful punishment from Us."

Stories of the Past

49. This is one of the stories of the unseen, which we reveal to you ˹O Prophet˺. Neither you nor your people knew it before this. So be patient! Surely the ultimate outcome belongs ˹only˺ to the righteous.

Prophet Hûd

50. And to the people of 'Âd We sent their brother Hûd. He said, "O my people! Worship God. You have no god other than Him. You do nothing but fabricate lies ˹against God˺. **51.** O my people! I do not ask you for any reward for this ˹message˺. My reward is only from the One Who created me. Will you not then understand? **52.** And O my people! Seek your Lord's forgiveness and turn to Him in repentance. He will shower you with rain in abundance, and add strength to your strength. So do not turn away, persisting in wickedness."

---

414 Noah was given a signal that once the water gushes out of a particular oven then the Flood is about to begin. It can also be translated as: "The fountains of the earth gushed forth."

His People's Response and His Argument

53. They argued, "O Hûd! You have not given us any clear proof, and we will never abandon our gods upon your word, nor will we believe in you. **54.** All we can say is that some of our gods have possessed you with evil." He said, "I call God to witness, and you too bear witness, that I 'totally' reject whatever you associate **55.** with Him 'in worship'. So let all of you plot against me without delay! **56.** I have put my trust in God—my Lord and your Lord. There is no living creature that is not completely under His control.[415] Surely my Lord's Way is perfect justice.[416] **57.** But if you turn away, I have already delivered to you what I have been sent with. My Lord will replace you with others. You are not harming Him in the least. Indeed, my Lord is a 'vigilant' Keeper over all things."

The Torment

58. When Our command came, We rescued Hûd and those who believed with him by a mercy from Us, saving them from a harsh torment. **59.** That was 'Âd. They denied the signs of their Lord, disobeyed His messengers, and followed the command of every stubborn tyrant. **60.** They were followed by a curse in this world, as they will be on the Day of Judgment. Surely 'Âd denied their Lord. So away with 'Âd, the people of Hûd.

Prophet Ṣâliḥ

61. And to the people of Thamûd We sent their brother Ṣâliḥ. He said, "O my people! Worship God. You have no god other than Him. He 'is the One Who' produced you from the earth and settled you on it. So seek His forgiveness and turn to Him in repentance. Surely my Lord is Ever Near, All-Responsive 'to prayers'."

His People's Argument

62. They argued, "O Ṣâliḥ! We truly had high hopes in you before this.[417] How dare you forbid us to worship what our forefathers had worshipped? We are certainly in alarming doubt about what you are inviting us to."

His Response

63. He responded, "O my people! Consider if I stand on a clear proof from my Lord and He has blessed me with a mercy from Him. Who could help me against God if I were to disobey Him? You would only contribute to my doom. **64.** And O my people! This she-camel of God is a sign for you.[418] So leave her to graze 'freely' on God's earth and do her no harm, or a swift punishment will overtake you!" **65.** But they killed her, so he warned 'them', "You have 'only' three 'more' days to enjoy life in your homes—this is an unfailing promise!"

The Torment

66. When Our command came, We saved Ṣâliḥ and those who believed with him by a mercy from Us and spared them the disgrace of that Day. Surely your Lord 'alone' is the All-Powerful, Almighty. **67.** And the 'mighty' blast overtook the wrongdoers, so they fell lifeless in their homes, **68.** as if they had never lived there. Surely Thamûd denied their Lord, so away with Thamûd!

Abraham Visited by Angels

69. And surely Our messenger-angels came to Abraham with good news 'of a son'. They greeted 'him with', "Peace!" And he replied, "Peace 'be upon you'!" Then it was not long before he brought 'them' a 'fat,' roasted calf. **70.** And when he saw that their hands did not reach for the food, he became suspi-

---

415 lit., there is no moving creature that He does not hold by its forelock.
416 lit., my Lord is on the Straight Path.
417 They believed that Ṣâliḥ had the potential to be their future leader.
418 The she-camel came out of a mountain as a sign for them.

cious and fearful of them.[419] They reassured 'him', "Do not be afraid! We are 'angels' sent 'only' against the people of Lot."

Good News to Sarah

71. And his wife was standing by, so she laughed,[420] then We gave her good news of 'the birth of' Isaac, and, after him, Jacob. **72.** She wondered, "Oh, my! How can I have a child in this old age, and my husband here is an old man? This is truly an astonishing thing!" **73.** They responded, "Are you astonished by God's decree? May God's mercy and blessings be upon you, O people of this house. Indeed, He is Praiseworthy, All-Glorious."

Abraham Pleading for Lot's People

74. Then after the fear had left Abraham, and the good news had reached him, he began to plead with Us for the people of Lot. **75.** Truly, Abraham was forbearing, tender-hearted, and ever turning 'to his Lord'. **76.** 'The angels said,' "O Abraham! Plead no more! Your Lord's decree has already come, and they will certainly be afflicted with a punishment that cannot be averted!"

Lot's Handsome Guests

77. When Our messenger-angels came to Lot, he was distressed and worried by their arrival.[421] He said, "This is a terrible day." **78.** And 'the men of' his people—who were used to shameful deeds—came to him rushing. He pleaded, "O my people! Here are my daughters[422] 'for marriage'—they are pure for you. So fear God, and do not humiliate me by disrespecting my guests. Is there not 'even' a single right-minded man among you?" **79.** They argued, "You cer-

tainly know that we have no need for your daughters. You already know what we desire!" **80.** He responded, "If only I had the strength 'to resist you' or could rely on a strong supporter."

Reassuring Lot

81. The angels said, "O Lot! We are the messengers of your Lord. They will never reach you. So travel with your family in the dark of night, and do not let any of you look back, except your wife. She will certainly suffer the fate of the others.[423] Their appointed time is the morning. Is the morning not near?"

The Torment

82. When Our command came, We turned the cities upside down and rained down on them clustered stones of baked clay, **83.** marked by your Lord 'O Prophet'. And these stones are not far from the 'pagan' wrongdoers!

Prophet Shu'aib

84. And to the people of Midian We sent their brother Shu'aib. He said, "O my people! Worship God. You have no god other than Him. And do not give short measure and weight. I do see you in prosperity now, but I truly fear for you the torment of an overwhelming Day. **85.** O my people! Give full measure and weigh with justice. Do not defraud people of their property, nor go about spreading corruption in the land. **86.** What is left 'as a lawful gain' by God is far better for you if you are 'truly' believers. And I am not a keeper over you."

His People's Response

87. They asked 'sarcastically', "O Shu'aib! Does your prayer command you that we

---

419 In ancient Middle Eastern culture, if a guest refused to eat the food provided by their host, it was a sign of ill-will.
420 She laughed after her husband was assured that the guests intended no harm or when she heard the news of the imminent destruction of the sinful people of Lot.
421 Since the angels came in the form of handsome men, Lot was worried for the dignity and safety of his guests among his people—not knowing that they were angels.
422 Single women of his community.
423 Lot's wife disbelieved in his message. It is believed that she is the one who informed the people of Lot's handsome guests.

should abandon what our forefathers worshipped or give up managing our wealth as we please? Indeed, you are such a tolerant, sensible man!"

Shu'aib's Argument

88. He said, "O my people! Consider if I stand on a clear proof from my Lord and He has blessed me with a good provision from Him. I do not want to do what I am forbidding you from. I only intend reform to the best of my ability. My success comes only through God. In Him I trust and to Him I turn. **89.** O my people! Do not let your opposition to me lead you to a fate similar to that of the people of Noah, or Hûd, or Ṣâliḥ. And the people of Lot are not far from you.[424] **90.** So seek your Lord's forgiveness and turn to Him in repentance. Surely my Lord is Most Merciful, All-Loving."

The Threat

91. They threatened, "O Shu'aib! We do not comprehend much of what you say, and surely we see you powerless among us. Were it not for your clan, we would have certainly stoned you, for you are nothing to us."

Shu'aib's Response

92. He said, "O my people! Do you have more regard for my clan than for God, turning your back on Him entirely? Surely my Lord is Fully Aware of what you do. **93.** O my people! Persist in your ways, for I ˈtooˈ will persist in mine. You will soon come to know who will be visited by a humiliating torment and is a liar! And watch! I too am watching with you!"

The Torment

94. When Our command came, We saved Shu'aib and those who believed with him by a mercy from Us. And the ˈmightyˈ blast overtook the wrongdoers, so they fell lifeless in their homes, **95.** as if they had never lived

there. So away with Midian as it was with Thamûd!

Prophet Moses

96. Indeed, We sent Moses with Our signs and compelling proof **97.** to Pharaoh and his chiefs, but they followed the command of Pharaoh, and Pharaoh's command was not well guided. **98.** He will be before his people on the Day of Judgment and will lead them into the Fire. What an evil place to be led into! **99.** They were followed by a curse in this ˈlifeˈ and ˈwill receive anotherˈ on the Day of Judgment. What an evil gift to receive!

Reward of Wickedness

100. These are accounts, We relate to you ˈO Prophetˈ, of the ˈdestroyedˈ cities. Some are still standing ˈbarrenˈ, while others have been mowed down. **101.** We did not wrong them, rather they wronged themselves. The gods they invoked beside God were of no help at all when the command of your Lord came, and only contributed to their ruin. **102.** Such is the ˈcrushingˈ grip of your Lord when He seizes the societies entrenched in wrongdoing. Indeed, His grip is ˈterriblyˈ painful and severe.

Judgment Day

103. Surely in this is a sign for those who fear the torment of the Hereafter. That is a Day for which humanity will be gathered and a Day ˈthat will beˈ witnessed ˈby allˈ. **104.** We only delay it for a fixed term. **105.** When that Day arrives, no one will dare speak except with His permission. Some of them will be miserable, others joyful.

The Miserable

106. As for those bound for misery, they will be in the Fire, where they will be sighing and gasping, **107.** staying there

---

424 Geographically and chronologically.

forever, as long as the heavens and the earth will endure, except what your Lord wills.[425] Surely your Lord does what He intends.

The Joyful

108. And as for those destined to joy, they will be in Paradise, staying there forever, as long as the heavens and the earth will endure, except what your Lord wills[426]—a 'generous' giving, without end.

Blind Following

109. So do not be in doubt 'O Prophet' about what those 'pagans' worship. They worship nothing except what their forefathers worshipped before 'them'. And We will certainly give them their share 'of punishment' in full, without any reduction.

The Torah

110. Indeed, We had given Moses the Scripture, but differences arose regarding it. Had it not been for a prior decree from your Lord,[427] their differences would have been settled 'at once'. They are truly in alarming doubt about it. **111.** And surely your Lord will fully pay all for their deeds. He is certainly All-Aware of what they do.

Advice to the Believers

112. So be steadfast as you are commanded 'O Prophet', along with those who turn 'in submission to God' with you. And do not transgress. Surely He is All-Seeing of what you 'believers' do. **113.** And do not be inclined to the wrongdoers or you will be touched by the Fire. For then you would have no protectors other than God,

nor would you be helped. **114.** Establish prayer 'O Prophet' at both ends of the day and in the early part of the night.[428] Surely good deeds wipe out evil deeds. That is a reminder for the mindful. **115.** And be patient! Certainly God does not discount the reward of the good-doers.

Speaking out Against Evil

116. If only there had been among the 'destroyed' peoples before you, 'O believers,' virtuous individuals who forbade corruption in the land—other than the few We had saved 'from the torment'. But the wrongdoers 'only' pursued their 'worldly' pleasures, becoming wicked. **117.** And your Lord 'O Prophet' would never destroy a society unjustly while its people were acting rightly.

Free Choice

118. Had your Lord so willed, He would have certainly made humanity one single community 'of believers', but they will always 'choose to' differ— **119.** except those shown mercy by your Lord—and so He created them 'to choose freely'. And so the Word of your Lord will be fulfilled: "I will surely fill up Hell with jinn and humans all together."

Moral of the Stories

120. And We relate to you 'O Prophet' the stories of the messengers to reassure your heart. And there has come to you in this 'chapter' the truth, a warning 'to the disbelievers', and a reminder to the believers. **121.** Say to those who disbelieve, "Persist in your ways; we will certainly persist in ours. **122.** And wait! Surely we 'too' are waiting."

---

425 Sinful believers will eventually be removed from Hell after receiving their punishment.
426 Except the time they spend on earth and in the grave, or except the time the sinful believers spend in Hell before being transferred to Paradise.
427 That He will delay their judgment until the Hereafter.
428 This verse talks about the five daily prayers. The prayers at the two ends of the day are the dawn prayer (*Fajr*) at one end and the afternoon prayers (* Zuhr* and '*Aṣr*) at the other. Prayers in the early part of the night include the sunset (*Maghrib*) and late evening ('*Ishâ'*) prayers.

God Almighty

123. To God ʿaloneʾ belongs the knowledge of what is hidden in the heavens and the earth. And to Him all matters are returned. So wor- ship Him and put your trust in Him. And your Lord is never unaware of what you do.

12. Joseph *(Yûsuf)*

Rightfully called 'the best of stories,' this uplifting Meccan chapter was revealed along with the two previous chapters at a critical time in the life of the Prophet following the death of his wife Khadîjah and his uncle Abu Ṭâlib, his two main supporters, shortly after a 3-year boycott by the Meccan pagans to suppress the believers. This is the story of Joseph whose half-brothers were driven by jealousy, conspiring to distance him from his father Jacob. Joseph was sold into slavery in Egypt, falsely accused, and imprisoned for several years, only to become Egypt's Chief Minister. Just like Joseph, the Prophet had to live away from his hometown, was faced with false allegations and abused by his own people, but ultimately became Arabia's undisputed leader. When the Prophet triumphed over Mecca after many years of persecution, he treated the very people who abused him with grace, recalling the words of Joseph when his brothers begged for mercy in verse 92, "There is no blame on you today. May God forgive you! He is the Most Merciful of the merciful!"

In the Name of God—the Most Compassionate, Most Merciful

The Best of Stories

1. *Alif-Lãm-Ra.* These are the verses of the clear Book. **2.** Indeed, We have sent it down as an Arabic Quran[429] so that you may understand.[430] **3.** We relate to you ʿO Prophetʾ the best of stories through Our revelation of this Quran, though before this you were totally unaware ʿof themʾ.

Joseph's Dream

4. ʿRememberʾ when Joseph said to his father, "O my dear father! Indeed I dreamt of eleven stars, and the sun, and the moon—I saw them prostrating to me!"[431] **5.** He replied, "O my dear son! Do not relate your vision to your brothers, or they will devise a plot against you. Surely Satan is a sworn enemy to humankind. **6.** And so will your Lord choose you ʿO Josephʾ, and teach you the interpretation of dreams, and per-

---

429 Quran literally means recitation.
430 The address here is to the Arabs and, by extension, all of humanity.
431 This dream came true at the end of the story (*see* 12:100).

fect His favour upon you and the descendants of Jacob—'just' as He once perfected it upon your forefathers, Abraham and Isaac. Surely your Lord is All-Knowing, All-Wise."

Conspiracy by Joseph's Brothers

7. Indeed, in the story of Joseph and his brothers there are lessons for all who ask. 8. 'Remember' when they said 'to one another', "Surely Joseph and his brother 'Benjamin' are more beloved to our father than we, even though we are a group of so many.[432] Indeed, our father is clearly mistaken. 9. Kill Joseph or cast him out to some 'distant' land so that our father's attention will be only ours, then after that you may 'repent and' become righteous people!" 10. One of them said, "Do not kill Joseph. But if you must do something, throw him into the bottom of a well so perhaps he may be picked up by some travellers."

Convincing Jacob

11. They said, "O our father! Why do you not trust us with Joseph, although we truly wish him well? 12. Send him out with us tomorrow so that he may enjoy himself and play. And we will really watch over him." 13. He responded, "It would truly sadden me if you took him away with you, and I fear that a wolf may devour him while you are negligent of him." 14. They said, "If a wolf were to devour him, despite our strong group, then we would certainly be losers!" 15. And so, when they took him away and decided to throw him into the bottom of

the well, We inspired him: "'One day' you will remind them of this deed of theirs while they are unaware 'of who you are'."

Faking Joseph's Death

16. Then they returned to their father in the evening, weeping. 17. They cried, "Our father! We went racing and left Joseph with our belongings, and a wolf devoured him! But you will not believe us, no matter how truthful we are." 18. And they brought his shirt, stained with false blood.[433] He responded, "No! Your souls must have tempted you to do something 'evil'. So 'I can only endure with' beautiful patience![434] It is God's help that I seek to bear your claims."

Joseph Sold into Slavery

19. And there came some travellers, and they sent their water-boy who let down his bucket into the well. He cried out, "Oh, what a great find! Here is a boy!" And they took him secretly 'to be sold' as merchandise, but God is All-Knowing of what they did. 20. They 'later' sold him for a cheap price, just a few silver coins—only wanting to get rid of him.[435]

Joseph in Egypt

21. The man from Egypt[436] who bought him said to his wife, "Take good care of him, perhaps he may be useful to us or we may adopt him as a son." This is how We established Joseph in the land, so that We might teach him the interpretation of dreams. God's Will always prevails, but most people do not know. 22. And when he reached

432 Unlike Joseph's other brothers, Benjamin was Joseph's full brother. They lost their mother at a young age, so their half-brothers thought that their father loved them more.
433 They stained Joseph's shirt with blood from a sheep, but forgot to tear his shirt. So Jacob became suspicious when he saw the intact shirt.
434 i.e., patience without complaining.
435 Other possible translations: 1. "... so little did they value him." 2. "... they had no interest in him." In any case, they wanted to sell him immediately before someone claimed him. According to some Quran commentators, it was Joseph's brothers who sold him to the travellers after he was picked up from the well. The verse states that Joseph was sold for a few worthless coins. Ironically, in 12:88 Joseph's brothers came to him after he became Egypt's Chief Minister, begging for supplies and saying that the only money they could afford was a few worthless coins. This is when Joseph revealed his true identity to them.
436 Potiphar, the Chief Minister of Egypt (Al-'Azîz).

maturity, We gave him wisdom and knowledge. This is how We reward the good-doers.

The Temptation

23. And the lady, in whose house he lived, tried to seduce him. She locked the doors ˹firmly˺ and said, "Come to me!" He replied, "God is my refuge! It is ˹not right to betray˺ my master, who has taken good care of me. Indeed, the wrongdoers never succeed." **24.** She advanced towards him, and he would have done likewise, had he not seen a sign from his Lord.[437] This is how We kept evil and indecency away from him, for he was truly one of Our chosen servants. **25.** They raced for the door and she tore his shirt from the back, only to find her husband at the door. She cried, "What is the penalty for someone who tried to violate your wife, except imprisonment or a painful punishment?"

The Witness

26. Joseph responded, "It was she who tried to seduce me." And a witness from her own family testified: "If his shirt is torn from the front, then she has told the truth and he is a liar. **27.** But if it is torn from the back, then she has lied and he is truthful." **28.** So when her husband saw that Joseph's shirt was torn from the back, he said ˹to her˺, "This must be ˹an example˺ of the cunning of you ˹women˺! Indeed, your cunning is so shrewd! **29.** O Joseph! Forget about this. And you ˹O wife˺! Seek forgiveness for your sin.[438] It certainly has been your fault."

The Women and Joseph's Beauty

30. Some women of the city gossiped, "The Chief Minister's wife is trying to seduce her slave-boy. Love for him has plagued her heart. Indeed, we see that she is clearly mistaken."[439] **31.** When she heard about their gossip,[440] she invited them and set a banquet for them. She gave each one a knife, then said ˹to Joseph˺, "Come out before them." When they saw him, they were so stunned ˹by his beauty˺ that they cut their hands,[441] and exclaimed, "Good God! This cannot be human; this must be a noble angel!" **32.** She said, "This is the one for whose love you criticized me! I did try to seduce him but he ˹firmly˺ refused. And if he does not do what I order him to, he will certainly be imprisoned and ˹fully˺ disgraced."[442]

The Lesser of Two Evils

33. Joseph prayed, "My Lord! I would rather be in jail than do what they invite me to. And if You do not turn their cunning away from me, I might yield to them and fall into ignorance." **34.** So his Lord responded to him, turning their cunning away from him. Surely He is the All-Hearing, All-Knowing. **35.** And so it occurred to those in charge, despite seeing all the proofs ˹of his innocence˺, that he should be imprisoned for a while.[443]

Dreams of the Two Inmates

36. And two other servants went to jail with Joseph. One of them said, "I dreamt I was pressing wine." The other said, "I dreamt I was carrying ˹some˺ bread on my head, from which birds were eating." ˹Then both said,˺

---

437 Joseph received warning against fornication either through divine inspiration or a vision of his father.
438 She was urged to seek forgiveness from her husband.
439 The women's only objection was because the wife of the Chief Minister was in love with someone raised in her house like a son.
440 lit., 'their cunning' because the women themselves were probably interested in Joseph.
441 The women were cutting fruit, and when Joseph came out they were so impressed by his beauty that they sliced through the fruit and into their hands without knowing.
442 The women tried to convince him to obey the Chief Minister's wife, so Joseph prayed to God to keep him away from them.
443 To stop women from being charmed by Joseph's beauty, or to put an end to the rumours, or to keep him away from the Minister's wife.

"Tell us their interpretation, for we surely see you as one of the good-doers."

Invitation to the Truth

37. Joseph replied, "I can even tell you what kind of meal you will be served before you receive it. This 'knowledge' is from what my Lord has taught me. I have shunned the faith of a people who disbelieve in God and deny the Hereafter. **38.** I follow the faith of my fathers: Abraham, Isaac, and Jacob. It is not 'right' for us to associate anything with God 'in worship'. This is part of God's grace upon us and humanity, but most people are not grateful. **39.** O my fellow-prisoners! Which is far better: many different lords or God—the One, the Supreme? **40.** Whatever 'idols' you worship instead of Him are mere names which you and your forefathers have made up[444]—a practice God has never authorized. It is only God Who decides. He has commanded that you worship none but Him. That is the upright faith, but most people do not know.

Interpretation of the Dreams

41. "O my fellow-prisoners! 'The first' one of you will serve wine to his master, and the other will be crucified and the birds will eat from his head. The matter about which you inquired has been decided." **42.** Then he said to the one he knew would survive, "Mention me in the presence of your master.[445]" But Satan made him forget to mention Joseph to his master, so he remained in prison for several years.

The King's Dream

43. And 'one day' the King[446] said, "I dreamt of seven fat cows eaten up by seven skinny ones; and seven green ears of grain and 'seven' others dry. O chiefs! Tell me the meaning of my dream if you can interpret dreams." **44.** They replied, "These are confused visions and we do not know the interpretation of such dreams." **45.** 'Finally,' the surviving ex-prisoner remembered 'Joseph' after a long time and said, "I will tell you its interpretation, so send me forth 'to Joseph'."

Interpretation of the King's Dream

46. 'He said,' "Joseph, O man of truth! Interpret for us 'the dream of' seven fat cows eaten up by seven skinny ones; and seven green ears of grain and 'seven' others dry, so that I may return to the people and let them know." **47.** Joseph replied, "You will plant 'grain' for seven consecutive years, leaving in the ear whatever you will harvest, except for the little you will eat. **48.** Then after that will come seven years of great hardship which will consume whatever you have saved, except the little you will store 'for seed'. **49.** Then after that will come a year in which people will receive abundant rain and they will press 'oil and wine'."

Joseph Declared Innocent

50. The King 'then' said, "Bring him to me." When the messenger came to him, Joseph said, "Go back to your master and ask him about the case of the women who cut their hands. Surely my Lord has 'full' knowledge of their cunning." **51.** The King asked 'the women', "What did you get when you tried to seduce Joseph?" They replied, "God forbid! We know nothing indecent about him." Then the Chief Minister's wife admitted, "Now the truth has come to light. It was I who tried to seduce him, and he is surely

444 Meaning, "You call them gods while in fact they are not gods."
445 The King of Egypt.
446 In the Bible (the Book of Genesis), this ruler is referred to as a pharaoh, while in the Quran he is referred to as a king. Typically, Egypt was ruled by pharaohs, but there existed a brief period in Egyptian history in which Egypt was ruled by the Hyksos invaders (1700-1550 B.C.E.). Hyksos rulers were called kings, not pharaohs. Joseph entered Egypt during the reign of the Hyksos, who used to appoint some foreigners to prominent positions in Egypt. According to *The Jewish Encyclopedia*, "Those who regard the Joseph stories as historical generally hold that the Pharaoh by whom Joseph was made the practical ruler of Egypt was one of the Hyksos kings." "Joseph," *The Jewish Encyclopedia*, Volume VII (London: Funk and Wagnalls Company, 1916), p. 252.

truthful. **52.** From this, Joseph should know that I did not speak dishonestly about him in his absence, for God certainly does not guide the scheming of the dishonest. **53.** And I do not seek to free myself from blame, for indeed the soul is ever inclined to evil, except those shown mercy by my Lord. Surely my Lord is All-Forgiving, Most Merciful."

Joseph, the Chief Minister

54. The King said, "Bring him to me. I will employ him exclusively in my service." And when Joseph spoke to him, the King said, "Today you are highly esteemed and fully trusted by us." **55.** Joseph proposed, "Put me in charge of the store-houses of the land, for I am truly reliable and adept." **56.** This is how We established Joseph in the land to settle wherever he pleased. We shower Our mercy on whoever We will, and We never discount the reward of the good-doers. **57.** And the reward of the Hereafter is far better for those who are faithful and are mindful ˹of God˺.

Joseph's Brothers Visit Egypt[447]

58. And Joseph's brothers came and entered his presence. He recognized them but they were unaware of who he really was. **59.** When he had provided them with their supplies, he demanded, "Bring me your brother on your father's side.[448] Do you not see that I give full measure and I am the best of hosts? **60.** But if you do not bring him to me ˹next time˺, I will have no grain for you, nor will you ever come close to me again." **61.** They promised, "We will try to convince his father to let him come. We will certainly do ˹our best˺." **62.** Joseph ordered his servants to put his brothers' money back into their saddlebags so that they would find it when they returned to their family and perhaps they would come back.

The Brothers Return Home

63. When Joseph's brothers returned to their father, they pleaded, "O our father! We have been denied ˹further˺ supplies. So send our brother with us so that we may receive our measure, and we will definitely watch over him." **64.** He responded, "Should I trust you with him as I once trusted you with his brother ˹Joseph˺? But ˹only˺ God is the best Protector, and He is the Most Merciful of the merciful." **65.** When they opened their bags, they discovered that their money had been returned to them. They argued, "O our father! What more can we ask for? Here is our money, fully returned to us. Now we can buy more food for our family. We will watch over our brother, and obtain an extra camel-load of grain. That load can be easily secured."

Jacob's Wisdom

66. Jacob insisted, "I will not send him with you until you give me a solemn oath by God that you will certainly bring him back to me, unless you are totally overpowered." Then after they had given him their oaths, he concluded, "God is a Witness to what we have said." **67.** He then instructed ˹them˺, "O my sons! Do not enter ˹the city˺ all through one gate, but through separate gates.[449] I cannot help you against ˹what is destined by˺ God in the least. It is only God Who decides. In Him I put my trust. And in Him let the faithful put their trust." **68.** Then when they entered as their father had instructed them, this did not help them against ˹the Will of˺ God whatsoever. It was just a desire in Jacob's heart which he satisfied. He was truly blessed with ˹great˺ knowledge because of what We had taught him, but most people have no knowledge.

---

447 Joseph's family was affected by famine, so they had to travel to Egypt to buy supplies.

448 i.e., Benjamin. When Joseph hosted his half-brothers, they told him the number of people in their household for future supplies.

449 He told them that every three or four of them should enter through a different gate. His desire was to protect them from envy and harm.

The Royal Cup[450]

69. When they entered Joseph's presence, he called his brother ˹Benjamin˺ aside, and confided ˹to him˺, "I am indeed your brother ˹Joseph˺! So do not feel distressed about what they have been doing." **70.** When Joseph had provided them with supplies, he slipped the royal cup into his brother's bag. Then a herald cried, "O people of the caravan! You must be thieves!" **71.** They asked, turning back, "What have you lost?" **72.** The herald ˹along with the guards˺ replied, "We have lost the King's measuring cup. And whoever brings it will be awarded a camel-load ˹of grain˺. I guarantee it." **73.** Joseph's brothers replied, "By God! You know well that we did not come to cause trouble in the land, nor are we thieves." **74.** Joseph's men asked, "What should be the price for theft, if you are lying?" **75.** Joseph's brothers responded, "The price will be ˹the enslavement of˺ the one in whose bag the cup is found. That is how we punish the wrongdoers."

Joseph Takes Benjamin

76. Joseph began searching their bags before that of his brother ˹Benjamin˺, then brought it out of Benjamin's bag. This is how We inspired Joseph to plan. He could not have taken his brother under the King's law, but God had so willed. We elevate in rank whoever We will. But above those ranking in knowledge is the One All-Knowing. **77.** ˹To distance themselves,˺ Joseph's brothers argued, "If he has stolen, so did his ˹full˺ brother before."[451] But Joseph suppressed his outrage—revealing nothing to them—and said ˹to himself˺, "You are in such an evil position,[452] and God knows best ˹the truth of˺ what you claim." **78.** They appealed, "O Chief Minister! He has a very

old father, so take one of us instead. We surely see you as one of the good-doers." **79.** Joseph responded, "God forbid that we should take other than the one with whom we found our property. Otherwise, we would surely be unjust."

Bad News for Jacob, Again

80. When they lost all hope in him, they spoke privately. The eldest of them said, "Do you not know that your father had taken a solemn oath by God from you, nor how you failed him regarding Joseph before? So I am not leaving this land until my father allows me to, or God decides for me. For He is the Best of Judges. **81.** Return to your father and say, 'O our father! Your son committed theft. We testify only to what we know. We could not guard against the unforeseen.[453] **82.** Ask ˹the people of˺ the land where we were and the caravan we travelled with. We are certainly telling the truth.'"

Jacob's Grief

83. He cried, "No! Your souls must have tempted you to do something ˹evil˺. So ˹I am left with nothing but˺ beautiful patience![454] I trust God will return them all to me. Surely He ˹alone˺ is the All-Knowing, All-Wise." **84.** He turned away from them, lamenting, "Alas, poor Joseph!" And his eyes turned white out of the grief he suppressed.[455] **85.** They said, "By God! You will not cease to remember Joseph until you lose your health or ˹even˺ your life." **86.** He replied, "I complain of my anguish and sorrow only to God, and I know from God what you do not know. **87.** O my sons! Go and search ˹diligently˺

---

450 The King's cup was also used as the standard measure for grain.
451 Joseph was falsely accused of theft when he was young.
452 He meant: I did not steal anything, nor did my brother ˹Benjamin˺. You are the real thieves; you stole me from my father and threw me into the well.
453 We did not know when we gave you our solemn oath that our brother was going to steal.
454 i.e., patience without complaining.
455 Jacob cried for so long that he became very weak-sighted. Some scholars suggest that he lost his sight completely. This does not contradict Jacob's beautiful patience because he did not complain to anyone, but expressed his sorrow only to God.

for Joseph and his brother. And do not lose hope in the mercy of God, for no one loses hope in God's mercy except those with no faith."

Joseph Reveals His Identity

88. When they entered Joseph's presence, they pleaded, "O Chief Minister! We and our family have been touched with hardship, and we have brought only a few worthless coins, but ˹please˺ give us our supplies in full and be charitable to us. Indeed, God rewards the charitable." **89.** He asked, "Do you remember what you did to Joseph and his brother in your ignorance?" **90.** They replied ˹in shock˺, "Are you really Joseph?" He said, "I am Joseph, and here is my brother ˹Benjamin˺! God has truly been gracious to us. Surely whoever is mindful ˹of God˺ and patient, then certainly God never discounts the reward of the good-doers."

Brothers' Apology Accepted

91. They admitted, "By God! God has truly preferred you over us, and we have surely been sinful." **92.** Joseph said, "There is no blame on you today. May God forgive you! He is the Most Merciful of the merciful! **93.** Go with this shirt of mine and cast it over my father's face, and he will regain his sight. Then come back to me with your whole family."

Jacob Regains His Sight

94. When the caravan departed ˹from Egypt˺, their father said ˹to those around him˺, "You may think I am senile, but I certainly sense the smell of Joseph." **95.** They replied, "By God! You are definitely still in your old delusion." **96.** But

when the bearer of the good news arrived, he cast the shirt over Jacob's face, so he regained his sight. Jacob then said ˹to his children˺, "Did I not tell you that I truly know from God what you do not know?" **97.** They begged, "O our father! Pray for the forgiveness of our sins. We have certainly been sinful." **98.** He said, "I will pray to my Lord for your forgiveness.[456] He ˹alone˺ is indeed the All-Forgiving, Most Merciful."

Joseph's Dream Comes True

99. When they entered Joseph's presence, he received his parents ˹graciously˺ and said, "Enter Egypt, God willing, in security." **100.** Then he raised his parents to the throne, and they all fell down in prostration to Joseph,[457] who then said, "O my dear father! This is the interpretation of my old dream. My Lord has made it come true. He was truly kind to me when He freed me from prison, and brought you all from the desert after Satan had ignited rivalry between me and my siblings.[458] Indeed my Lord is subtle in fulfilling what He wills. Surely He ˹alone˺ is the All-Knowing, All-Wise."

Joseph's Prayer

101. "My Lord! You have surely granted me authority and taught me the interpretation of dreams. ˹O˺ Originator of the heavens and the earth! You are my Guardian in this world and the Hereafter. Allow me to die as one who submits[459] and join me with the righteous."

Reminders to Prophet Muḥammad

102. That is from the stories of the unseen which We reveal to you ˹O Prophet˺.

---

456 Jacob delayed the prayer for his children to be forgiven until pre-dawn, which is a blessed time for supplication.

457 Joseph's parents and his eleven brothers prostrated before him out of respect, not as an act of worship. This was permissible in their tradition, but in Islam, Muslims prostrate only to God.

458 Joseph did not mention how God saved him from the well because he did not want to embarrass his brothers after forgiving them.

459 lit., as a Muslim.

You were not present when they 'all'⁴⁶⁰ made up their minds, and when they plotted 'against Joseph'. 103. And most people will not believe—no matter how keen you are— 104. even though you are not asking them for a reward for this 'Quran'. It is only a reminder to the whole world. 105. How many signs in the heavens and the earth do they pass by with indifference! 106. And most of them do not believe in God without associating others with Him 'in worship'. 107. Do they feel secure that an overwhelming torment from God will not overtake them, or that the Hour will not take them by surprise when they least expect 'it'?

Invitation with Knowledge and Wisdom

108. Say, 'O Prophet,' "This is my way. I invite to God with insight—I and those who follow me. Glory be to God, and I am not one of the polytheists."

God's Messengers

109. We only sent before you 'O Prophet' men inspired by Us from among the people of each society. Have the deniers not travelled through the land to see what was the end of those 'destroyed' before them? And surely the 'eternal' Home of the Hereafter is far better for those mindful 'of God'. Will you not then understand? 110. And when the messengers despaired and their people thought the messengers had been denied help, Our help came to them 'at last'. We then saved whoever We willed, and Our punishment is never averted from the wicked people.

Messengers' Stories in the Quran

111. In their stories there is truly a lesson for people of reason. This message cannot be a fabrication, rather 'it is' a confirmation of previous revelation, a detailed explanation of all things, a guide, and a mercy for people of faith.

13. Thunder *(Ar-Ra'd)*

This chapter, which takes its name from the thunder in verse 13, elaborates upon the last verses of the previous chapter (starting with 105) relating to God's magnificent signs in the heavens and earth which are met with neglect by the deniers; God's knowledge, might, and unwavering support for His prophets; the authenticity of the Quran; and warnings to the disbelievers. The chapter touches on the qualities of the believers and the disbelievers and the reward for each. All these themes are reiterated in the next two chapters.

In the Name of God—the Most Compassionate, Most Merciful

The Truth

1. *Alif-Lãm-Mĩm-Ra.* These are the verses of the Book. What has been revealed to you 'O Prophet' from your Lord is the truth, but most people do not believe.

---

460 This includes Joseph's brothers, the travellers who picked him up from the well and sold him into slavery, and the Chief Minister's wife and other women in the city.

God's Might

2. It is God Who has raised the heavens without pillars—as you can see—then established Himself above the Throne. He has subjected the sun and the moon, each orbiting for an appointed term. He conducts the whole affair. He makes the signs clear so that you may be certain of the meeting with your Lord. **3.** And He is the One Who spread out the earth and placed firm mountains and rivers upon it, and created fruits of every kind in pairs.[461] He covers the day with night. Surely in this are signs for those who reflect. **4.** And on the earth there are ˹different˺ neighbouring tracts, gardens of grapevines, ˹various˺ crops, palm trees—some stemming from the same root, others standing alone. They are all irrigated with the same water, yet We make some taste better than others. Surely in this are signs for those who understand.

Denying Resurrection

5. ˹Now,˺ if anything should amaze you ˹O Prophet˺, then it is their question: "When we are reduced to dust, will we really be raised as a new creation?" It is they who have disbelieved in their Lord. It is they who will have shackles around their necks. And it is they who will be the residents of the Fire. They will be there forever.

Hastening the Torment

6. They ask you ˹O Prophet˺ to hasten the torment rather than grace, though there have ˹already˺ been ˹many˺ torments before them. Surely your Lord is full of forgiveness for people, despite their wrongdoing, and your Lord is truly severe in punishment.

Demanding a Sign from the Prophet[462]

7. The disbelievers say, "If only a sign could be sent down to him from his Lord." You ˹O Prophet˺ are only a warner. And every people had a guide.

God's Knowledge

8. God knows what every female bears and what increases and decreases in the wombs.[463] And with Him everything is determined with precision. **9.** ˹He is the˺ Knower of the seen and the unseen—the All-Great, Most Exalted. **10.** It is the same ˹to Him˺ whether any of you speaks secretly or openly, whether one hides in the darkness of night or goes about in broad daylight.

God's Power

11. For each one there are successive angels before and behind, protecting them by God's command. Indeed, God would never change a people's state ˹of favour˺ until they change their own state ˹of faith˺. And if it is God's Will to torment a people, it can never be averted, nor can they find a protector other than Him.

Display of Divine Power

12. He is the One Who shows you lightning, inspiring ˹you with˺ hope and fear,[464] and produces heavy clouds. **13.** The thunder glorifies His praises, as do the angels in awe of Him. He sends thunderbolts, striking with them whoever He wills. Yet they dispute about God. And He is tremendous in might.

Useless Idols

14. Calling upon Him ˹alone˺ is the truth. But those ˹idols˺ the pagans invoke besides Him ˹can˺ never respond to them in any way. ˹It is˺ just like someone who stretches out their hands to water, ˹asking it˺ to reach their mouths, but it can never do so. The calls of the disbelievers are only in vain.

---

461 Males and females, sweet and bitter, etc.
462 Like the staff of Moses.
463 He knows whether the egg will be fertilized or not, whether the baby will be born before or after nine months, whether the pregnancy will end with delivery or miscarriage, and whether there will be one baby or more.
464 Hope of rain and fear of torment.

13. Thunder (Ar-Ra'd)

The True Lord

15. To God ʿaloneʾ bow down ʾin submissionʾ⁴⁶⁵ all those in the heavens and the earth—willingly or unwillingly—as do their shadows, morning and evening.

Almighty God or Powerless Gods?

16. Ask ʾthem, O Prophetʾ, "Who is the Lord of the heavens and the earth?" Say, "God!" Ask ʾthemʾ, "Why then have you taken besides Him lords who cannot even benefit or protect themselves?" Say, "Can the blind and the sighted be equal? Or can darkness and light be equal?"⁴⁶⁶ Or have they associated with God partners who ʾsupposedlyʾ produced a creation like His, leaving them confused between the two creations? Say, "God is the Creator of all things, and He is the One, the Supreme."

Parable of Truth and Falsehood

17. He sends down rain from the sky, causing the valleys to flow, each according to its capacity. The currents then carry along rising foam, similar to the slag produced from metal that people melt in the fire for ornaments or tools. This is how God compares truth to falsehood. The ʾworthlessʾ scum is then cast away, but what benefits people remains on the earth. This is how God sets forth parables.

Blindness to the Truth

18. Those who respond to ʾthe call ofʾ their Lord will have the finest reward. As for those who do not respond to Him, even if they were to possess everything in the world twice over, they would certainly offer it to ransom themselves. They will face strict judgment, and Hell will be their home. What an evil place to rest! **19.** Can the one who knows that your Lord's revelation to you ʾO

Prophetʾ is the truth be like the one who is blind? None will be mindful ʾof thisʾ except people of reason.

People of Reason

20. ʾThey areʾ those who honour God's covenant, never breaking the pledge; **21.** and those who maintain whatever ʾtiesʾ God has ordered to be maintained, stand in awe of their Lord, and fear strict judgment. **22.** And ʾthey areʾ those who endure patiently, seeking their Lord's pleasure,⁴⁶⁷ establish prayer, donate from what We have provided for them—secretly and openly—and respond to evil with good. It is they who will have the ultimate abode: **23.** the Gardens of Eternity, which they will enter along with the righteous among their parents, spouses, and descendants. And the angels will enter upon them from every gate, ʾsayingʾ **24.** "Peace be upon you for your perseverance. How excellent is the ultimate abode!"

The Wicked

25. And those who violate God's covenant after it has been affirmed, break whatever ʾtiesʾ God has ordered to be maintained, and spread corruption in the land—it is they who will be condemned and will have the worst abode.⁴⁶⁸

Worldly Delusions

26. God gives abundant or limited provisions to whoever He wills. And the disbelievers become prideful of ʾthe pleasures ofʾ this worldly life. But the life of this world, compared to the Hereafter, is nothing but a fleeting enjoyment.

Remembrance of God

27. The disbelievers say, "If only a sign could be sent down to him from

---

465 lit., prostrate. Meaning, all beings submit to His Will.
466 Blindness and darkness are commonly used as an analogy for disbelief, whereas the ability to see and light refer to true faith in God.
467 lit., seeking their Lord's Face.
468 i.e., the Hellfire.

his Lord."⁴⁶⁹ Say, ˹O Prophet,˺ "Indeed, God leaves to stray whoever He wills, and guides to Himself whoever turns to Him— **28.** those who believe and whose hearts find comfort in the remembrance of God. Surely in the remembrance of God do hearts find comfort. **29.** Those who believe and do good, for them will be bliss and an honourable destination."

Denying the Most Compassionate

30. And so We have sent you ˹O Prophet˺ to a community, like ˹We did with˺ earlier communities, so that you may recite to them what We have revealed to you. Yet they deny the Most Compassionate.⁴⁷⁰ Say, "He is my Lord! There is no god ˹worthy of worship˺ except Him. In Him I put my trust, and to Him I turn ˹in repentance˺."

Deniers Will Always Deny

31. If there were a recitation that could cause mountains to move, or the earth to split, or the dead to speak, ˹it would have been this Quran˺. But all matters are by God's Will. Have the believers not yet realized that had God willed, He could have guided all of humanity? And disasters will continue to afflict the disbelievers or strike close to their homes for their misdeeds, until God's promise comes to pass. Surely God never fails in His promise. **32.** Other messengers had already been ridiculed before you, but I delayed the disbelievers ˹for a while˺ then seized them. And how ˹horrible˺ was My punishment!

Falsehood Made Appealing

33. Is ˹there any equal to˺ the Vigilant One Who knows what every soul commits? Yet the pagans have associated others with God ˹in worship˺. Say, ˹O Prophet,˺ "Name them! Or do you ˹mean to˺ inform Him of something He does not know on the earth? Or are these ˹gods˺ just empty words?" In fact, the disbelievers' falsehood has been made so appealing to them that they have been turned away from the Path. And whoever God leaves to stray will be left with no guide. **34.** For them is punishment in this worldly life, but the punishment of the Hereafter is truly far worse. And none can shield them from God.

Paradise Described

35. The description of the Paradise promised to the righteous is that under it rivers flow; eternal is its fruit as well as its shade. That is the ˹ultimate˺ outcome for the righteous. But the outcome for the disbelievers is the Fire!

Embracing the Quran

36. ˹The believers among˺ those who were given the Scripture rejoice at what has been revealed to you ˹O Prophet˺, while some ˹disbelieving˺ factions deny a portion of it. Say, "I have only been commanded to worship God, associating none with Him ˹in worship˺. To Him I invite ˹all˺, and to Him is my return." **37.** And so We have revealed it as an authority in Arabic. And if you were to follow their desires after ˹all˺ the knowledge that has come to you, there would be none to protect or shield you from God.

The Last of Many

38. We have certainly sent messengers before you ˹O Prophet˺ and blessed them with wives and offspring. It was not for any messenger to bring a sign without God's permission. Every destined matter has a ˹set˺ time. **39.** God eliminates and confirms what He wills, and with Him is the Master Record.⁴⁷¹

---

469 The disbelievers demanded a tangible miracle such as the staff of Moses.
470 See 17:110 and 25:60.
471 This refers to the Preserved Tablet, *Al-Lawḥ Al-Maḥfûẓ*, in which God has written the destiny of His entire creation.

Deliver, Not Judge

40. Whether We show you ˹O Prophet˺ some of what We threaten them with, or cause you to die ˹before that˺, your duty is only to deliver ˹the message˺. Judgment is for Us.

Warning to the Pagans

41. Do they not see that We gradually reduce their land from its borders? God decides—none can reverse His decision. And He is swift in reckoning. 42. Those ˹disbelievers˺ before them ˹secretly˺ planned, but God has the ultimate plan. He knows what every soul commits. And the disbelievers will soon know who will have the ultimate outcome. 43. The disbelievers say, "You ˹Muḥammad˺ are no messenger." Say, ˹O Prophet,˺ "God is sufficient as a Witness between me and you, as is whoever has knowledge of the Scripture."

14. Abraham *(Ibrâhîm)*

This Meccan chapter is named after Prophet Abraham who, upon settling his wife Hagar and his son Ishmael in what later became the city of Mecca, invokes God to protect his descendants from idol-worship, a practice that Meccans were entrenched in at the time of this revelation (verses 35-41). The chapter also refers to some of God's favours, which are met with ingratitude and denial. A sizable portion reveals how the disbelievers will be let down by Satan and tormented in Hell, wishing they had believed, according to the next chapter (15:2).

In the Name of God—the Most Compassionate, Most Merciful

Warning to the Disbelievers

1. *Alif-Lãm-Ra.* ˹This is˺ a Book which We have revealed to you ˹O Prophet˺ so that you may lead people out of darkness and into light, by the Will of their Lord, to the Path of the Almighty, the Praiseworthy— 2. God, to Whom belongs whatever is in the heavens and whatever is on the earth. And woe to the disbelievers because of a severe torment! 3. ˹They are˺ the ones who favour the life of this world over the Hereafter and hinder ˹others˺ from the Way of God, striving to make it ˹appear˺ crooked. It is they who have gone far astray.

Delivering the Message

4. We have not sent a messenger except in the language of his people to clarify ˹the message˺ for them. Then God leaves whoever He wills to stray and guides whoever He wills. And He is the Almighty, All-Wise.

Prophet Moses

5. Indeed, We sent Moses with Our signs, ˹ordering him,˺ "Lead your people out of darkness and into light, and remind them of God's days ˹of favour˺." Surely in this are signs for whoever is steadfast, grateful. 6. ˹Consider˺ when Moses said to his people, "Remember God's favour upon you when He rescued you from the people of Pharaoh, who afflicted you with dreadful torment—slaughtering your sons and keeping your women. That was a severe test from your Lord. 7. And ˹remember˺ when your Lord proclaimed, 'If you are grateful, I will certainly give you more. But if you are ungrateful, surely My punishment is severe.'" 8. Moses added, "If you along with

everyone on earth were to be ungrateful, then 'know that' God is indeed Self-Sufficient, Praiseworthy."

Warning to the Pagans of Mecca

9. Have you not 'already' received the stories of those who were before you: the people of Noah, 'Âd, Thamûd, and those after them? Only God knows how many they were. Their messengers came to them with clear proofs, but they put their hands over their mouths[472] and said, "We totally reject what you have been sent with, and we are certainly in alarming doubt about what you are inviting us to."

Disbelievers' Arguments

10. Their messengers asked 'them', "Is there any doubt about God, the Originator of the heavens and the earth? He is inviting you in order to forgive your sins, and delay your end until your appointed term."[473] They argued, "You are no more than humans like us! You 'only' wish to turn us away from what our forefathers worshipped. So bring us some compelling proof." 11. Their messengers said to them, "We are 'indeed' only humans like you, but God favours whoever He chooses of His servants. It is not for us to bring you any proof without God's permission. And in God let the believers put their trust. 12. Why should we not put our trust in God, when He has truly guided us to 'the very best of' ways? Indeed, we will patiently endure whatever harm you may cause us. And in God let the faithful put their trust."

Disbelievers' Fate

13. The disbelievers then threatened their messengers, "We will certainly expel you from our land, unless you return to our faith." So their Lord revealed to them, "We will surely destroy the wrongdoers, 14. and make you reside in the land after them. This is for whoever is in awe of standing before Me and fears My warning." 15. And both sides called for judgment, so every stubborn tyrant was doomed. 16. Awaiting them is Hell, and they will be left to drink oozing pus, 17. which they will sip with difficulty, and can hardly swallow. Death will overwhelm them from every side, yet they will not 'be able to' die. Awaiting them still is harsher torment.

Wasted Deeds

18. The parable of the deeds of those who disbelieve in their Lord is that of ashes fiercely blown away by wind on a stormy day. They will gain nothing from what they have earned. That is 'truly' the farthest one can stray.

A Reminder to Humanity

19. Have you not seen that God created the heavens and the earth for a reason? If He wills, He can eliminate you and produce a new creation. 20. And that is not difficult for God 'at all'.

Disbelievers Disowning Each Other

21. They will all appear before God, and the lowly 'followers' will appeal to the arrogant 'leaders', "We were your 'dedicated' followers, so will you 'then' protect us from God's torment in any way?" They will reply, "Had God guided us, we would have guided you. 'Now' it is all the same for us whether we suffer patiently or impatiently, there is no escape for us."

Satan's Talk[474]

22. And Satan will say 'to his followers' after the judgment has been passed, "Indeed, God has made you a true promise. I

---

472 This can mean that the disbelievers bit their own hands in rage, or they covered their own mouths mockingly, or that they put their hands over their messengers' mouths to silence them.

473 It is out of God's mercy that He does not hasten your punishment but delays your death until your destined time.

474 On the Day of Judgment, when the wicked realize that they are doomed, they will blame Satan for their great loss and will plead to him to do whatever he can to rescue them from the Hellfire. Satan will then stand up and deliver the speech quoted in this verse.

too made you a promise, but I failed you. I did not have any authority over you. I only called you, and you responded to me. So do not blame me; blame yourselves. I cannot save you, nor can you save me. Indeed, I denounce your previous association of me with God ʿin loyaltyʾ. Surely the wrongdoers will suffer a painful punishment."

Reward of the Believers

23. Those who believe and do good will be admitted into Gardens, under which rivers flow—to stay there forever by the Will of their Lord—where they will be greeted with "Peace!"

Parable of Good and Evil Words

24. Do you not see how God compares a good word to a good tree? Its root is firm and its branches reach the sky, **25.** ʿalwaysʾ yielding its fruit in every season by the Will of its Lord. This is how God sets forth parables for the people, so perhaps they will be mindful. **26.** And the parable of an evil word is that of an evil tree, uprooted from the earth, having no stability.

The Firm Word

27. God makes the believers steadfast with the firm Word ʿof faithʾ[475] in this worldly life and the Hereafter. And God leaves the wrongdoers to stray. For God does what He wills.

Reward of the Ungrateful

28. Have you not seen those ʿdisbelieversʾ who meet God's favours with ingratitude and lead their own people to their doom? **29.** In Hell they will burn. What an evil place for settlement. **30.** They set up equals to God to mislead ʿothersʾ from His Way. Say, ʿO Prophet,ʾ "Enjoy yourselves! Surely your destination is the Fire."

Order to the Prophet

31. Tell My believing servants to establish prayer and donate from what We have provided for them—openly and secretly—before the arrival of a Day in which there will be no ransom or friendly connections.

God's Favours

32. It is God Who created the heavens and the earth and sends down rain from the sky, causing fruits to grow as a provision for you. He has subjected the ships for your service, sailing through the sea by His command, and has subjected the rivers for you. **33.** He has ʿalsoʾ subjected for you the sun and the moon, both constantly orbiting, and has subjected the day and night for you. **34.** And He has granted you all that you asked Him for. If you tried to count God's blessings, you would never be able to number them. Indeed humankind is truly unfair, ʿtotallyʾ ungrateful.[476]

Abraham's Prayers

35. ʿRememberʾ when Abraham prayed, "My Lord! Make this city ʿof Meccaʾ secure, and keep me and my children away from the worship of idols. **36.** My Lord! They have caused many people to go astray. So whoever follows me is with me, and whoever disobeys me—then surely You are ʿstillʾ All-Forgiving, Most Merciful. **37.** Our Lord! I have settled some of my offspring in a barren valley, near Your Sacred House, our Lord, so that they may establish prayer. So make the hearts of ʿbelievingʾ people incline towards them and provide them with fruits, so perhaps they will be thankful. **38.** Our Lord! You certainly know what we conceal and what we reveal. Nothing on earth or in heaven is hidden from God. **39.** All praise is for God who has blessed me with Ishmael and Isaac in my old age. My Lord is indeed the Hearer of ʿallʾ prayers. **40.** My Lord! Make me and those ʿbelieversʾ of my descendants keep up prayer. Our Lord!

---

475 That there is only one God worthy of worship.
476 In this context, "humankind" refers only to those who deny God's favours.

Accept my prayers. **41.** Our Lord! Forgive me, my parents, and the believers on the Day when the judgment will come to pass."

Warning to the Wicked

42. Do not think ˹O Prophet˺ that God is unaware of what the wrongdoers do. He only delays them until a Day when ˹their˺ eyes will stare in horror— **43.** rushing forth, heads raised, never blinking, hearts void. **44.** And warn the people of the Day when the punishment will overtake ˹the wicked among˺ them, and the wrongdoers will cry, "Our Lord! Delay us for a little while. We will respond to Your call and follow the messengers!" ˹It will be said,˺ "Did you not swear before that you would never be removed ˹to the next life˺?" **45.** You passed by the ruins of those ˹destroyed peoples˺ who had wronged themselves.[477] It was made clear to you how We dealt with them, and We gave you ˹many˺ examples. **46.** They devised every plot, which was fully known to God, but their plotting was not enough to ˹even˺ overpower mountains ˹let alone God˺.

Reward of the Wicked

47. So do not think ˹O Prophet˺ that God will fail to keep His promise to His messengers. God is indeed Almighty, capable of punishment. **48.** ˹Watch for˺ the Day ˹when˺ the earth will be changed into a different earth and the heavens as well, and all will appear before God—the One, the Supreme. **49.** On that Day you will see the wicked bound together in chains, **50.** with garments of tar, and their faces covered with flames. **51.** As such, God will reward every soul for what it has committed. Surely God is swift in reckoning.

A Universal Message

52. This ˹Quran˺ is a ˹sufficient˺ message for humanity so that they may take it as a warning and know that there is only One God, and so that people of reason may be mindful.

15. The Stone Valley *(Al-Ḥijr)*

This Meccan chapter takes its name from the place mentioned in 80-84, where the people of Ṣâliḥ once lived. Other destroyed peoples are mentioned as a warning to the Arab deniers, who are also warned at the beginning of the next chapter. Satan's arrogance towards God and enmity towards humanity are emphasized. The Prophet is urged to exercise patience and seek comfort in worship.

In the Name of God—the Most Compassionate, Most Merciful

Warning to the Disbelievers

1. *Alif-Lãm-Ra.* These are the verses of the Book; the clear Quran. **2.** ˹The day will come when˺ the disbelievers will certainly wish they had submitted ˹to God˺.[478] **3.** ˹So˺ let them eat and enjoy themselves and be diverted by ˹false˺ hope, for they will soon know. **4.** We have never destroyed a society without a destined term. **5.** No people can advance their doom, nor can they delay it.

---

477 Arab traders used to pass by the homes of some destroyed nations on their journeys to Syria and Yemen (such as 'Âd and Thamûd, respectively), stopping shortly for rest.
478 lit., had been Muslims.

The Pagans Mocking the Prophet

6. They say, "O you to whom the Reminder[479] is revealed! You must be insane! **7.** Why do you not bring us the angels, if what you say is true?" **8.** We do not send the angels down except for a just cause, and then ˹the end of˺ the disbelievers will not be delayed. **9.** It is certainly We Who have revealed the Reminder, and it is certainly We Who will preserve it.

Committed to Disbelief

10. Indeed, We sent messengers before you ˹O Prophet˺ among the groups of early peoples, **11.** but no messenger ever came to them without being mocked. **12.** This is how We allow disbelief ˹to seep˺ into the hearts of the wicked. **13.** They would not believe in this ˹Quran˺ despite the ˹many˺ examples of those ˹destroyed˺ before. **14.** And even if We opened for them a gate to heaven, through which they continued to ascend, **15.** still they would say, "Our eyes have truly been dazzled! In fact, we must have been bewitched."

Divine Power

16. Indeed, We have placed constellations in the sky, and adorned it for all to see. **17.** And We protected it from every accursed devil, **18.** except the one eavesdropping, who is then pursued by a visible flare.[480] **19.** As for the earth, We spread it out and placed upon it firm mountains, and caused everything to grow there in perfect balance. **20.** And We made in it means of sustenance for you and others, who you do not provide for. **21.** There is not any means ˹of sustenance˺ whose reserves We do not hold, only bringing it forth in precise measure. **22.** We send fertilizing winds, and bring down rain from the sky for you to drink. It is not you who hold its reserves. **23.** Surely it is We Who give life and cause death. And We are the ˹Eternal˺ Successor.[481] **24.** We certainly know those who have gone before you and those who will come after ˹you˺. **25.** Surely your Lord ˹alone˺ will gather them together ˹for judgment˺. He is truly All-Wise, All-Knowing.

Creation of Adam

26. Indeed, We created man from sounding clay moulded from black mud. **27.** As for the jinn, We created them earlier from smokeless fire. **28.** ˹Remember, O Prophet˺ when your Lord said to the angels, "I am going to create a human being from sounding clay moulded from black mud.[482] **29.** So when I have fashioned him and had a spirit of My Own ˹creation˺ breathed into him, fall down in prostration to him."

Satan's Defiance

30. So the angels prostrated all together— **31.** but not Iblîs,[483] who refused to prostrate with the others. **32.** God asked, "O Iblîs! What is the matter with you that you did not join others in prostration?" **33.** He replied, "It is not for me to prostrate to a human You created from sounding clay moulded from black mud." **34.** God commanded, "Then get out of Paradise, for you are truly cursed. **35.** And surely upon you is condemnation until the Day of Judgment."

Satan's Appeal

36. Satan appealed, "My Lord! Then delay my end until the Day of their resurrection." **37.** God said, "You will be delayed **38.** until the appointed Day." **39.** Satan responded, "My Lord! For allowing me to stray I will surely tempt them on earth and mislead them all together, **40.** except Your chosen servants

---

479 i.e., the Quran.
480 Some jinn used to eavesdrop on the angels in heaven so they could disclose this information to their human associates. But this practice came to an end when the Prophet was sent with the message of Islam. See 72:8-10.
481 God will remain eternally after all pass away.
482 This does not contradict other verses that say Adam was created out of dust and those that say he was made out of mud. Adam was created in stages: first from dust, which was later turned into mud, then clay. This is similar to saying: I made a loaf of bread out of grain, or flour, or dough.
483 See footnote for 2:34.

among them." **41.** God said, "This is the Way, binding on Me: **42.** you will certainly have no authority over My servants, except the deviant who follow you, **43.** and surely Hell is their destined place, all together. **44.** It has seven gates, to each a group of them is designated."

The Righteous in Paradise

45. Indeed, the righteous will be amid Gardens and springs. **46.** 'It will be said to them,' "Enter in peace and security." **47.** We will remove whatever bitterness they had in their hearts.[484] In a friendly manner, they will be on thrones, facing one another. **48.** No fatigue will touch them there, nor will they ever be asked to leave.

God's Grace and Torment

49. Inform My servants 'O Prophet' that I am truly the All-Forgiving, Most Merciful, **50.** and that My torment is indeed the most painful.

Abraham Visited by Angels

51. And inform them 'O Prophet' about Abraham's guests **52.** who entered upon him and greeted 'him with', "Peace!" He 'later' said, "Surely we are afraid of you."[485] **53.** They reassured 'him', "Do not be afraid! Surely we give you good news of a knowledgeable son." **54.** He wondered, "Do you give me good news despite my old age? What unlikely news!" **55.** They responded, "We give you good news in all truth, so do not be one of those who despair." **56.** He exclaimed, "Who would despair of the mercy of their Lord except the misguided?" **57.** He 'then' added, "What is your mission, O messenger-angels?" **58.** They replied, "We have actually been sent to a wicked people. **59.** As for the fam-ily of Lot, we will certainly deliver them all, **60.** except his wife. We have determined that she will be one of the doomed."

Lot Visited by Angels

61. So when the messengers came to the family of Lot, **62.** he said, "You must be strangers!" **63.** They responded, "We have come to you with that 'torment' which they have doubted. **64.** We come to you with the truth, and we are certainly truthful. **65.** So travel with your family in the dark of night, and follow 'closely' behind them. Do not let any of you look back, and go where you are commanded." **66.** We revealed to him this decree: "Those 'sinners' will be uprooted in the morning."

Destruction of the People of Lot

67. And there came the men of the city, rejoicing. **68.** Lot pleaded, "Indeed, these are my guests, so do not embarrass me. **69.** Fear God and do not humiliate me." **70.** They responded, "Have we not forbidden you from protecting anyone?" **71.** He said, "O my people! Here are my daughters[486] 'so marry them' if you wish to do so." **72.** By your life 'O Prophet',[487] they certainly wandered blindly, intoxicated 'by lust'. **73.** So the 'mighty' blast overtook them at sunrise. **74.** And We turned the cities 'of Sodom and Gomorrah' upside down and rained upon them stones of baked clay. **75.** Surely in this are signs for those who contemplate. **76.** Their ruins still lie along a known route. **77.** Surely in this is a sign for those who believe.

The People of Shu'aib

78. And the residents of the Forest were truly wrongdoers, **79.** so We inflicted punishment upon them. The ruins of both nations still lie on a well-known road.

---

484 i.e., the bitterness they had in their hearts towards other believers who wronged them in the worldly life.
485 As mentioned in 11:69-70, the angels came to Abraham in the form of men and when he offered them food, they did not eat. In ancient Middle Eastern culture, if a guest refused to eat the food provided by their host, it was a sign of ill-will.
486 Single women of his community.
487 This is the only time in the Quran where God swears by the life of a human being. Elsewhere God swears by the sun, the moon, the stars, and other marvels of His creation.

The People of Ṣâliḥ

80. Indeed, the residents of the Stone Valley also denied the messengers.[488] 81. We gave them Our signs, but they turned away from them. 82. They carved their homes in the mountains, feeling secure. 83. But the ʿmightyʾ blast overtook them in the morning, 84. and all they achieved was of no help to them.

Advice to the Prophet

85. We have not created the heavens and the earth and everything in between except for a purpose. And the Hour is certain to come, so forgive graciously. 86. Surely your Lord is the Master Creator, All-Knowing. 87. We have certainly granted you the seven often-repeated verses[489] and the great Quran. 88. Do not let your eyes crave the ʿfleetingʾ pleasures We have provided for some of the disbelievers, nor grieve for them. And be gracious to the believers.

More Advice to the Prophet

89. And say, "I am truly sent with a clear warning"— 90. ʿa warningʾ similar to what We sent to those who divided ʿthe Scripturesʾ, 91. who ʿnowʾ accept parts of the Quran, rejecting others. 92. So by your Lord! We will certainly question them all 93. about what they used to do. 94. So proclaim what you have been commanded, and turn away from the polytheists. 95. Surely We will be sufficient for you against the mockers, 96. who set up ʿotherʾ gods with God. They will soon come to know.

God Is the Refuge

97. We certainly know that your heart is truly distressed by what they say. 98. So glorify the praises of your Lord and be one of those who ʿalwaysʾ pray, 99. and worship your Lord until the inevitable[490] comes your way.

಄ఀఀಊఀఀ

16. Bees *(An-Naḥl)*

This Meccan chapter, also known as the Chapter of Blessings (Sûratu An-Ni'am), takes its name from the bees mentioned in verses 68-69, which are described as one of God's numerous favours to humanity. Instead of showing gratitude to God for all these blessings, the pagans wilfully set up idols, associating them with God in worship. They are also condemned for burying their daughters alive (verses 58-59). References are made to grateful believers and ungrateful disbelievers along with the ultimate reward for each group. Abraham is cited close to the end of the chapter as a grateful servant of God, whose example should be emulated by all believers. The chapter concludes by instructing the Prophet to endure patiently and invite all to the Way of God with wisdom and grace.

In the Name of God—the Most Compassionate, Most Merciful

Warning of Judgment

1. The command of God is at hand, so do not hasten it. Glorified and Exalted is He above what they associate ʿwith Him in worshipʾ!

God's Favours: 1) Divine Guidance

2. He sends down the angels with revelation by His command to whoever He wills of His servants, ʿstating:ʾ "Warn ʿhumani-

---

488 lit., messengers, because denying Ṣâliḥ was equal to denying all of God's messengers.
489 Chapter 1 of the Quran.
490 i.e., lit., what is certain—death.

ty' that there is no god 'worthy of worship'
except Me, so be mindful of Me 'alone'."

Favour 2) The Heavens and Earth

3. He created the heavens and the earth for a
purpose. Exalted is He above what they associate with Him 'in worship'!

Favour 3) Creation of Humans

4. He created humans from a sperm-drop,
then—behold!—they openly challenge
'Him'.

Favour 4) Animals

5. And He created the cattle for you as a
source of warmth, food, and 'many other'
benefits. 6. They are also pleasing to you
when you bring them home and when you
take them out to graze. 7. And they carry your
loads to 'distant' lands which you could not
otherwise reach without great hardship. Surely your Lord is Ever Gracious, Most Merciful. 8. 'He also created' horses, mules, and
donkeys for your transportation and adornment. And He creates what you do not know.

Favour 5) The Way of Islam

9. It is upon God 'alone' to 'clearly' show
the Straight Way. Other ways are deviant.
Had He willed, He would have easily imposed guidance upon all of you.

Favour 6) Water

10. He is the One Who sends down rain
from the sky, from which you drink and by
which plants grow for your cattle to graze.
11. With it He produces for you 'various'
crops, olives, palm trees, grapevines, and
every type of fruit. Surely in this is a sign
for those who reflect.

Favour 7) Celestial Events

12. And He has subjected for your benefit
the day and the night, the sun and the moon.
And the stars have been subjected by His

command. Surely in this are signs for those
who understand.

Favour 8) Other Creation

13. And 'He subjected' for you whatever
He has created on earth of varying colours.[491] Surely in this is a sign for those
who are mindful.

Favour 9) Seas

14. And He is the One Who has subjected the sea, so from it you may eat tender
seafood and extract ornaments to wear.
And you see the ships ploughing their way
through it, so you may seek His bounty
and give thanks 'to Him'.

Favour 10) Natural Marvels

15. He has placed into the earth firm
mountains, so it does not shake with you,
as well as rivers, and pathways so you may
find your way. 16. Also by landmarks and
stars do people find their way.

Almighty God or Powerless Gods?

17. Can the One Who creates be equal to
those who do not? Will you not then be
mindful? 18. If you tried to count God's
blessings, you would never be able to
number them. Surely God is All-Forgiving, Most Merciful. 19. And God knows
what you conceal and what you reveal.
20. But those 'idols' they invoke besides
God cannot create anything—they themselves are created. 21. They are dead, not
alive—not even knowing when their followers will be resurrected. 22. Your God is
'only' One God. As for those who do not
believe in the Hereafter, their hearts are in
denial, and they are too proud. 23. Without
a doubt, God knows what they conceal and
what they reveal. He certainly does not
like those who are too proud.

491   The verse refers to the diverse creatures that have been created for the service of humanity.

Reward of the Wicked

24. And when it is said to them, "What has your Lord revealed?" They say, "Ancient fables!" 25. Let them bear their burdens in full on the Day of Judgment as well as some of the burdens of those they mislead without knowledge. Evil indeed is what they will bear! 26. Indeed, those before them had plotted, but God struck at the ˹very˺ foundation of their structure, so the roof collapsed on top of them, and the torment came upon them from where they did not expect.[492] 27. Then on the Day of Judgment He will humiliate them and say, "Where are My ˹so-called˺ associate-gods for whose sake you used to oppose ˹the believers˺?" Those gifted with knowledge will say, "Surely disgrace and misery today are upon the disbelievers." 28. Those whose souls the angels seize while they wrong themselves will then offer ˹full˺ submission ˹and say falsely,˺ "We did not do any evil." ˹The angels will say,˺ "No! Surely God fully knows what you used to do. 29. So enter the gates of Hell, to stay there forever. Indeed, what an evil home for the arrogant!"

Reward of the Righteous

30. And ˹when˺ it is said to those mindful ˹of God˺, "What has your Lord revealed?" They say, "All the best!" For those who do good in this world, there is goodness. But far better is the ˹eternal˺ Home of the Hereafter. How excellent indeed is the home of the righteous: 31. the Gardens of Eternity which they will enter, under which rivers flow. In it they will have whatever they desire. This is how God rewards the righteous— 32. those whose souls the angels take while they are virtuous, saying ˹to them˺, "Peace be upon you! Enter Paradise for what you used to do."

Warning to Pagan Deniers

33. Are they only awaiting the coming of the angels or the command of your Lord ˹O Prophet˺? So were those before them.

And God never wronged them, but it was they who wronged themselves. 34. Then the evil ˹consequences˺ of their deeds overtook them, and they were overwhelmed by what they used to ridicule.

False Argument

35. The polytheists argue, "Had God willed, neither we nor our forefathers would have worshipped anything other than Him, nor prohibited anything without His command." So did those before them. Is not the messengers' duty only to deliver ˹the message˺ clearly?

Same Fate

36. We surely sent a messenger to every community, saying, "Worship God and shun false gods." But some of them were guided by God, while others were destined to stray. So travel throughout the land and see the fate of the deniers! 37. Even though you ˹O Prophet˺ are keen on their guidance, God certainly does not guide those He leaves to stray, and they will have no helpers.

The Resurrection

38. They swear by God their most solemn oaths that God will never raise the dead to life. Yes ˹He will˺! It is a true promise binding on Him, but most people do not know. 39. ˹He will do that˺ to make clear to them what they disagreed on, and for the disbelievers to know that they were liars. 40. If We ever will something ˹to exist˺, all We say is: "Be!" And it is!

Reward of the Steadfast

41. As for those who emigrated in ˹the cause of˺ God after being persecuted, We will surely bless them with a good home in this world. But the reward of the Hereafter is far better, if only they knew. 42. ˹It is˺ they who have patiently endured, and in their Lord they put their trust.

---

492   This verse refers to a tyrant king who ordered the building of a tower so he can reach the heavens and fight God and the angels. Eventually the tower collapsed, leaving the tyrant crushed.

Messengers Are Not Angels

43. We did not send ʿmessengersʾ before you ʿO Prophetʾ except mere men inspired by Us. If you ʿpolytheistsʾ do not know ʿthis already', then ask those who have knowledge ʿof the Scripturesʾ. **44.** ʿWe sent themʾ with clear proofs and divine Books. And We have sent down to you ʿO Prophetʾ the Reminder, so that you may explain to people what has been revealed for them, and perhaps they will reflect.

Warning to the Wicked

45. Do those who devise evil plots feel secure that God will not cause the earth to swallow them? Or that the torment will not come upon them in ways they cannot comprehend? **46.** Or that He will not seize them while they go about ʿtheir dayʾ, for then they will have no escape? **47.** Or that He will not destroy them gradually? But your Lord is truly Ever Gracious, Most Merciful.

Everything Submits to God

48. Have they not considered how the shadows of everything God has created incline to the right and the left ʿas the sun movesʾ, totally submitting to God in all humility? **49.** And to God ʿaloneʾ bows down ʿin submission'[493] whatever is in the heavens and whatever is on the earth of living creatures, as do the angels—who are not too proud ʿto do soʾ. **50.** They[494] fear their Lord above them, and do whatever they are commanded.

One God Alone

51. And God has said, "Do not take two gods. There is only One God. So be in awe of Me ʿaloneʾ." **52.** To Him belongs whatever is in the heavens and the earth, and to Him ʿaloneʾ is the everlasting devotion. Will you then fear any other than God?

Ingratitude to God

53. Whatever blessings you have are from God. Then whenever hardship touches you, to Him ʿaloneʾ you cry ʿfor helpʾ. **54.** Then as soon as He removes the hardship from you, a group of you associates ʿothersʾ with their Lord ʿin worshipʾ, **55.** only returning Our favours with ingratitude. So enjoy yourselves, for you will soon know.

Offerings to Idols

56. And they ʿevenʾ assign to those ʿidolsʾ—who know nothing—a share of what We have provided for them. By God! You will certainly be questioned about whatever ʿliesʾ you used to fabricate ʿagainst Godʾ.

God's Daughters?

57. And they attribute ʿangels asʾ daughters to God—glory be to Him!—the opposite of what they desire for themselves. **58.** Whenever one of them is given the good news of a baby girl, his face grows gloomy, as he suppresses his rage. **59.** He hides himself from the people because of the bad news he has received. Should he keep her in disgrace, or bury her ʿaliveʾ in the ground? Evil indeed is their judgment![495] **60.** To those who disbelieve in the Hereafter belong all evil qualities, whereas to God belong the finest attributes. And He is the Almighty, All-Wise.

Favour 11) Allowing Time for Repentance

61. If God were to punish people ʿimmediatelyʾ for their wrongdoing, He would not have left a single living being on earth. But He delays them for an appointed term. And when their time arrives, they cannot delay it for a moment, nor could they advance it.

---

493 lit., prostrates.
494 The angels.
495 Some pagan Arabs used to bury their infant daughters alive for fear of shame or poverty. This practice was condemned and abolished by Islam. *See* 6:151 and 81:8-9.

Empty Hopes

62. They attribute to God what they hate ʾfor themselvesʾ,[496] and their tongues utter the lie that they will have the finest reward. Without a doubt, for them is the Fire, where they will be abandoned.

Evil Communities

63. By God! We have surely sent messengers to communities before you ʾO Prophetʾ, but Satan made their misdeeds appealing to them. So he is their patron today, and they will suffer a painful punishment. **64.** We have revealed to you the Book only to clarify for them what they differed about, and as a guide and mercy for those who believe.

Favour 12) Rain

65. And God sends down rain from the sky, giving life to the earth after its death. Surely in this is a sign for those who listen.

Favour 13) Cattle and Milk

66. And there is certainly a lesson for you in cattle: We give you to drink of what is in their bellies, from between digested food and blood: pure milk, pleasant to drink.[497] **67.** And from the fruits of palm trees and grapevines you derive intoxicants[498] as well as wholesome provision. Surely in this is a sign for those who understand.

Favour 14) Bees and Honey

68. And your Lord inspired the bees: "Make ʾyourʾ homes in the mountains, the trees, and in what people construct, **69.** and feed from ʾthe flower ofʾ any fruit ʾyou pleaseʾ and follow the ways your Lord has made easy for you." From their bellies comes forth liquid of varying colours, in which there is healing for people. Surely in this is a sign for those who reflect.

God's Power over Humans

70. God has created you, and then causes you to die. And some of you are left to reach the most feeble stage of life so that they may know nothing after having known much. Indeed, God is All-Knowing, Most Capable.

Favour 15) Provisions

71. And God has favoured some of you over others in provision. But those who have been much favoured would not share their wealth with those ʾbondspeopleʾ in their possession, making them their equals.[499] Do they then deny God's favours?

Favour 16) Spouses and Offspring

72. And God has made for you spouses of your own kind, and given you through your spouses children and grandchildren.[500] And He has granted you good, lawful provisions. Are they then faithful to falsehood and ungrateful for God's favours?

Parables for Powerless Gods and Almighty God

73. Yet they worship besides God those ʾidolsʾ who do not afford them any provision from the heavens and the earth, nor do they have the power to. **74.** So do not set up equals to God, for God certainly knows and you do not know. **75.** God sets forth a parable: a slave who lacks all means, compared to a ʾfreeʾ man to whom We granted a good provision, of which he donates ʾfreely,ʾ openly and secretly. Are they equal? Praise be to God. In fact, most of them do not know. **76.** And God sets forth a parable of two men: one of them is dumb, incapable of anything.

---

496 They say that God has daughters (i.e., the angels), although they themselves do not like to have daughters.
497 lit., pleasant for those who drink.
498 Intoxicants were later prohibited in the Quran in three stages: 2:219, 4:43, and finally 5:90-91.
499 In other words, if the pagan slave-masters are not willing to be equal to their slaves, why would they make anyone equal to God—the Supreme Master and Creator of all things?
500 *Ḥafadah* means grandchildren, but can also mean children-in-law.

He is a burden on his master. Wherever he is sent, he brings no good. Can such a person be equal to the one who commands justice and is on the Straight Path?[501]

God's Knowledge and Might

77. To God ˹alone˺ belongs ˹the knowledge of˺ the unseen in the heavens and the earth. Bringing about the Hour would only take the blink of an eye, or even less. Surely God is Most Capable of everything.

Favour 17) Senses

78. And God brought you out of the wombs of your mothers while you knew nothing, and gave you hearing, sight, and intellect so perhaps you would be thankful.

Favour 18) Birds

79. Have they not seen the birds glide in the open sky? None holds them up except God. Surely in this are signs for those who believe.

Favour 19) Homes

80. And God has made your homes a place to rest, and has given you tents from the hide of animals, light to handle when you travel and when you camp. And out of their wool, fur, and hair He has given you furnishings and goods for a while.

Favour 20) Shelters

81. And God has provided you shade out of what He created, and has given you shelter in the mountains. He has also provided you with clothes protecting you from the heat ˹and cold˺, and armour shielding you in battle. This is how He perfects His favour upon you, so perhaps you will ˹fully˺ submit ˹to Him˺.

Denying God's Favours

82. But if they turn away, then your duty ˹O Prophet˺ is only to deliver ˹the message˺ clearly. 83. They are aware of God's favours, but still deny them. And most of them are ˹truly˺ ungrateful.

Fate of the Disbelievers

84. ˹Consider, O Prophet,˺ the Day We will call ˹a prophet as˺ a witness from every faith-community. Then the disbelievers will neither be allowed to plead nor appease ˹their Lord˺. 85. And when the wrongdoers face the punishment, it will not be lightened for them, nor will they be delayed ˹from it˺. 86. And when the polytheists see their associate-gods, they will say, "Our Lord! These are our associate-gods that we used to invoke besides You." Their gods will throw a rebuttal at them, ˹saying,˺ "You are definitely liars." 87. They will offer ˹full˺ submission to God on that Day, and whatever ˹gods˺ they fabricated will fail them. 88. For those who disbelieve and hinder ˹others˺ from the Way of God, We will add more punishment to their punishment for all the corruption they spread.

Prophets Witness Against Disbelievers

89. ˹Consider, O Prophet,˺ the Day We will call against every faith-community a witness of their own. And We will call you to be a witness against these ˹people of yours˺. We have revealed to you the Book as an explanation of all things, a guide, a mercy, and good news for those who ˹fully˺ submit.

God's Commands and Prohibitions

90. Indeed, God commands justice, grace, as well as generosity to close relatives. He forbids indecency, wickedness, and aggression. He instructs you so perhaps you will be mindful.

---

501 The two parables emphasize that Almighty God masterfully conducts the affairs of the heavens and the earth, whereas false gods are incapable of anything. If this is the case, these gods are not His equal and He is the only one worthy of worship.

Honouring Pledges

91. Honour God's covenant when you make a pledge, and do not break your oaths after confirming them, having made God your guarantor. Surely God knows all you do. **92.** Do not be like the woman who ˹foolishly˺ unravels her yarn after it is firmly spun, by taking your oaths as a means of deceiving one another in favour of a stronger group. Surely God tests you through this. And on the Day of Judgment He will certainly make your differences clear to you.

Favour 21) Free Choice

93. Had God willed, He could have easily made you one community ˹of believers˺, but He leaves to stray whoever He wills and guides whoever He wills.[502] And you will certainly be questioned about what you used to do.

Honouring Agreements

94. And do not take your oaths as a means of deceiving one another or your feet will slip after they have been firm. Then you will taste the evil ˹consequences˺ of hindering ˹others˺ from the Way of God, and you will suffer a tremendous punishment. **95.** And do not trade God's covenant for a fleeting gain. What is with God is certainly far better for you, if only you knew. **96.** Whatever you have will end, but whatever God has is everlasting. And We will certainly reward the steadfast according to the best of their deeds.

Reward of the Good-Doers

97. Whoever does good, whether male or female, and is a believer, We will surely bless them with a good life, and We will certainly reward them according to the best of their deeds.

Advice to the Believers

98. When you recite the Quran, seek refuge with God from Satan, the accursed. **99.** He certainly has no authority over those who believe and put their trust in their Lord. **100.** His authority is only over those who take him as a patron and who—under his influence—associate ˹others˺ with God ˹in worship˺.

Who Is the Fabricator?

101. When We replace a verse with another[503]—and God knows best what He reveals—they say, "You ˹Muḥammad˺ are just a fabricator." In fact, most of them do not know. **102.** Say, "The holy spirit[504] has brought it down from your Lord with the truth to reassure the believers, and as a guide and good news for those who submit ˹to God˺." **103.** And We surely know that they say, "No one is teaching him except a human." But the man they refer to speaks a foreign tongue, whereas this ˹Quran˺ is ˹in˺ eloquent Arabic.[505] **104.** Surely those who do not believe in God's revelations will never be guided by God, and they will suffer a painful punishment. **105.** No one fabricates lies except those who disbelieve in God's revelations, and it is they who are the ˹true˺ liars.

Abandoning Faith

106. Whoever disbelieves in God after their belief—not those who are forced while their hearts are firm in faith,[506] but those who embrace disbelief wholeheartedly—they will be condemned by God and suffer a tremendous punishment. **107.** This is because they prefer the life of this world over the Hereafter. Surely God never guides those who ˹choose to˺ disbelieve. **108.** They are the ones whose

---

502 He guides those who are sincere in their quest for guidance.
503 See footnote for 2:106.
504 The angel Gabriel.
505 Some Meccan pagans claimed that the Prophet received the Quran from a non-Arab slave owned by an Arab pagan.
506 This refers to 'Ammâr ibn Yâsser, an early revert to Islam, who was tortured to leave Islam. To save his life, 'Ammâr pretended to denounce Islam, but his heart was full of faith. When he told the Prophet about what happened, this verse was revealed, reassuring him that his faith was intact.

hearts, ears, and eyes are sealed by God, and it is they who are ʿtrulyʾ heedless. **109.** Without a doubt, they will be the losers in the Hereafter. **110.** As for those who emigrated after being compelled ʿto renounce Islamʾ, then struggled ʿin God's causeʾ, and persevered, your Lord ʿO Prophetʾ is truly All-Forgiving, Most Merciful after all.

Pay Day

111. ʿConsiderʾ the Day ʿwhenʾ every soul will come pleading for itself, and each will be paid in full for what it did, and none will be wronged.

The Ungrateful People

112. And God sets forth the example of a society which was safe and at ease, receiving its provision in abundance from all directions. But its people met God's favours with ingratitude, so God made them taste the clutches of hunger and fear for their misdeeds. **113.** A messenger of their own actually did come to them, but they denied him. So the torment overtook them while they persisted in wrongdoing.

Lawful and Prohibited Foods

114. So eat from the good, lawful things which God has provided for you, and be grateful for God's favours, if you ʿtrulyʾ worship Him ʿaloneʾ. **115.** He has only forbidden you ʿto eatʾ carrion, blood, swine,[507] and what is slaughtered in the name of any other than God. But if someone is compelled by necessity—neither driven by desire nor exceeding immediate need—then surely God is All-Forgiving, Most Merciful.

Warning to the Polytheists

116. Do not falsely declare with your tongues, "This is lawful, and that is unlawful," ʿonlyʾ fabricating lies against God. In-

deed, those who fabricate lies against God will never succeed. **117.** ʿIt is onlyʾ a brief enjoyment, then they will suffer a painful punishment.

Prohibited Foods for Jews

118. To the Jews, We have forbidden what We related to you before.[508] We did not wrong them, but it was they who wronged themselves.

God Accepts Repentance

119. As for those who commit evil ignorantly ʿor recklesslyʾ, then repent afterwards and mend their ways, then your Lord is surely All-Forgiving, Most Merciful.

Prophet Abraham

120. Indeed, Abraham was a model of excellence: devoted to God, ʿperfectlyʾ upright—not a polytheist— **121.** ʿutterlyʾ grateful for God's favours. ʿSoʾ He chose him and guided him to the Straight Path. **122.** We blessed him with all goodness in this world,[509] and in the Hereafter he will certainly be among the righteous. **123.** Then We revealed to you ʿO Prophet, sayingʾ: "Follow the faith of Abraham, the upright, who was not one of the polytheists." **124.** ʿHonouringʾ the Sabbath was ordained only for those who disputed about Abraham.[510] And surely your Lord will judge between them on the Day of Judgment regarding their disputes.

Inviting to Islam

125. Invite ʿallʾ to the Way of your Lord with wisdom and kind advice, and only debate with them in the best manner. Surely your Lord ʿaloneʾ knows best who has strayed from His Way and who is ʿrightlyʾ guided.

---

507 See footnote for 2:173.
508 What is mentioned in 6:146.
509 i.e., honourable mention and a righteous family.
510 This verse refers to the Jews who claimed that Abraham was Jewish. See 3:65-68.

Grace Is Best

126. If you retaliate, then let it be equivalent to what you have suffered. But if you patiently endure, it is certainly best for those who are patient. **127.** Be patient ˹O Prophet˺, for your patience is only with God's help. Do not grieve over those ˹who disbelieve˺, nor be distressed by their schemes. **128.** Surely God is with those who shun evil and who do good ˹deeds˺.

⁕

17. The Night Journey *(Al-Isrâ')*

Since Abraham is praised in the last verses of the previous chapter as a role model for the world, this Meccan chapter speaks of how the Prophet is honoured in this world through the Night Journey from Mecca to Jerusalem then to the heavens and back to Mecca—all in one night (verses 1 and 60). He will also be honoured on the Day of Judgment through the station of praise where he will make intercession (verse 79). The children of Israel are referred to passingly at the end of the previous chapter, but more insights are given about them both at the beginning and the end of this chapter. The key to success in this life and salvation in the next is encapsulated in a set of divine commandments (verses 22-39), along with a warning against Satan and his whispers (verses 61-65). The chapter is critical of the pagan arguments against resurrection and their ridiculous demands (verses 89-93). Criticism of attributing partners and children to God is carried over to the next chapter.

In the Name of God—the Most Compassionate, Most Merciful

Journey from Mecca to Jerusalem

1. Glory be to the One Who took His servant ˹Muḥammad˺ by night from the Sacred Mosque to the Farthest Mosque whose surroundings We have blessed, so that We may show him some of Our signs.[511] Indeed, He[512] alone is the All-Hearing, All-Seeing. **2.** And We gave Moses the Scripture and made it a guide for the Children of Israel, ˹stating:˺ "Do not take besides Me any other Trustee of Affairs, **3.** ˹O˺ descendants of those We carried with Noah ˹in the Ark˺! He was indeed a grateful servant."

---

511 *Al-Isrâ'* refers to the Prophet's Night Journey from Mecca to Jerusalem about a year before his emigration (or *Hijrah*) from Mecca to Medina. This journey came as a comfort for the Prophet after several years of hardship and persecution, which included a 3-year siege by Meccan pagans, who drove the Muslims out of the city and forbade anyone from trading, marrying, or feeding them. This was followed by the "Year of Sadness," which included the death of the Prophet's uncle Abu Ṭâlib, the major defender of Muḥammad despite his disbelief in his message, as well as the death of the Prophet's beloved wife Khadîjah. The Prophet was carried overnight by a noble steed (called *Burâq*) from Mecca to Jerusalem where he met some earlier prophets and led them in prayer. He was later carried to the heavens (this journey is called *Al-Mi'râj*, or the Ascension) where he received direct orders from God to observe five daily prayers. The Ascension is referred to in 53:13–18.

512 i.e., God.

The Two Corruptions

4. And We warned the Children of Israel in the Scripture, "You will certainly cause corruption in the land twice, and you will become extremely arrogant. **5.** When the first of the two warnings comes to pass, We will send against you some of Our servants of great might, who will ravage your homes. This will be a warning fulfilled. **6.** Then ˹after your repentance˺ We will give you the upper hand over them and aid you with wealth and offspring, causing you to outnumber them. **7.** If you act rightly, it is for your own good, but if you do wrong, it is to your own loss. And when the second warning comes to pass, your enemies will ˹be left to˺ totally disgrace you and enter that place of worship as they entered it the first time, and they will utterly destroy whatever falls into their hands. **8.** Perhaps your Lord will have mercy on you ˹if you repent˺, but if you return ˹to sin˺, We will return ˹to punishment˺. And We have made Hell a ˹permanent˺ confinement for the disbelievers."

The Message of the Quran

9. Surely this Quran guides to what is most upright, and gives good news to the believers—who do good—that they will have a mighty reward. **10.** And ˹it warns˺ those who do not believe in the Hereafter ˹that˺ We have prepared for them a painful punishment.

Prayers in Anger

11. And humans ˹swiftly˺ pray for evil[513] as they pray for good. For humankind is ever hasty.

The Day and Night

12. We made the day and night as two signs. So We made the sign of the night devoid of light, and We made the sign of the day ˹perfectly˺ bright, so that you may seek the bounty of your Lord and know the number of years and calculation ˹of time˺. And We have explained everything in detail.

The Record of Deeds

13. We have bound every human's destiny to their neck.[514] And on the Day of Judgment We will bring forth to each ˹person˺ a record which they will find laid open. **14.** ˹And it will be said,˺ "Read your record. You ˹alone˺ are sufficient this Day to take account of yourself." **15.** Whoever chooses to be guided, it is only for their own good. And whoever chooses to stray, it is only to their own loss. No soul burdened with sin will bear the burden of another. And We would never punish ˹a people˺ until We have sent a messenger ˹to warn them˺.

Punishment of the Wicked

16. Whenever We intend to destroy a society, We command its elite ˹to obey God˺ but they act rebelliously in it. So the decree ˹of punishment˺ is justified, and We destroy it utterly. **17.** ˹Imagine˺ how many peoples We have destroyed after Noah! And sufficient is your Lord as All-Aware and All-Seeing of the sins of His servants.

This Life or the Next?

18. Whoever desires this fleeting world ˹alone˺, We hasten in it whatever We please to whoever We will; then We destine them for Hell, where they will burn, condemned and rejected. **19.** But whoever desires the Hereafter and strives for it accordingly, and is a ˹true˺ believer, it is they whose striving will be appreciated. **20.** We provide both the former and the latter from the bounty of your Lord. And the bounty of your Lord can never be withheld. **21.** See how We have favoured some over others ˹in this life˺, but the Hereafter is certainly far greater in rank and in favour.

---

513 Some people are quick to pray against themselves or others in times of anger and frustration.

514 This refers to the deeds that one is destined to do of their own free will. Out of His infinite knowledge, God knows people's choices even before they make them. In the Hereafter, He will raise them from the dead for judgment.

Commandments: 1) Worship God Alone, 2) Honour Your Parents

22. Do not set up any other god with God, or you will end up condemned, abandoned. **23.** For your Lord has decreed that you worship none but Him. And honour your parents. If one or both of them reach old age in your care, never say to them 'even' 'ugh,' nor yell at them. Rather, address them respectfully. **24.** And be humble with them out of mercy, and pray, "My Lord! Be merciful to them as they raised me when I was young." **25.** Your Lord knows best what is within yourselves. If you are righteous, He is certainly All-Forgiving to those who 'constantly' turn to Him.

3) Give and 4) Do Not Waste

26. Give to close relatives their due, as well as the poor and 'needy' travellers. And do not spend wastefully. **27.** Surely the wasteful are 'like' brothers to the devils. And the Devil is ever ungrateful to his Lord. **28.** But if you must turn them down 'because you lack the means to give'—while hoping to receive your Lord's bounty—then 'at least' give them a kind word.

5) Spend Moderately

29. Do not be so tight-fisted, for you will be blameworthy; nor so open-handed, for you will end up in poverty. **30.** Surely your Lord gives abundant or limited provisions to whoever He wills. He is certainly All-Aware, All-Seeing of His servants.

6) Treasure Your Children

31. Do not kill your children for fear of poverty. We provide for them and for you. Surely killing them is a heinous sin.

7) Do Not Commit Adultery

32. Do not go near adultery. It is truly a shameful deed and an evil way.

8) Do Not Kill

33. Do not take a 'human' life—made sacred by God—except with 'legal' right.[515] If anyone is killed unjustly, We have given their heirs[516] the authority, but do not let them exceed limits in retaliation,[517] for they are already supported 'by law'.

9) Protect Orphans' Wealth, 10) Honour Pledges

34. Do not come near the wealth of the orphan—unless intending to enhance it—until they attain maturity. Honour 'your' pledges, for you will surely be accountable for them.

11) Maintain Fairness

35. Give in full when you measure, and weigh with an even balance. That is fairest and best in the end.

12) Be Sure

36. Do not follow what you have no 'sure' knowledge of. Indeed, all will be called to account for 'their' hearing, sight, and intellect.

13) Be Humble

37. And do not walk on the earth arrogantly. Surely you can neither crack the earth nor stretch to the height of the mountains.

Compliance with the Commandments

38. The violation of any of these 'commandments' is detestable to your Lord. **39.** This is part of the wisdom which your Lord has revealed to you 'O Prophet'. And do not set up any other god with God 'O humanity', or you will be cast into Hell, blameworthy, rejected.

Rebuttal to a Pagan Claim

40. Has your Lord favoured you 'pagans' with sons and taken angels as 'His' daugh-

---

515 For example, in retaliation for intentional killing through legal channels.
516 Here the word *wali*, "heir," actually means *awliyâ'* or "heirs," which includes the closest relatives, both men and women.
517 By killing anyone other than the killer, or killing others with the killer.

ters?[518] You are truly making an outrageous claim. **41.** We have surely varied ʼthe signsʼ in this Quran so perhaps they may be mindful, but it only drives them farther away.

Other Gods?

42. Say, ʼO Prophet,ʼ "Had there been other gods besides Him—as they claim—then they would have certainly sought a way to ʼchallengeʼ the Lord of the Throne." **43.** Glorified and Highly Exalted is He above what they claim! **44.** The seven heavens, the earth, and all those in them glorify Him. There is not a single thing that does not glorify His praises—but you ʼsimplyʼ cannot comprehend their glorification. He is indeed Most Forbearing, All-Forgiving.

The Pagans Mock the Quran

45. When you ʼO Prophetʼ recite the Quran, We put a hidden barrier between you and those who do not believe in the Hereafter. **46.** We have cast veils over their hearts—leaving them unable to comprehend it—and deafness in their ears. And when you mention your Lord alone in the Quran, they turn their backs in aversion. **47.** We know best how they listen to your recitation and what they say privately—when the wrongdoers say, "You would only be following a bewitched man." **48.** See how they call you names ʼO Prophetʼ![519] So they have gone so ʼfarʼ astray that they cannot find the ʼRightʼ Way.

The Resurrection

49. And they say ʼmockinglyʼ, "When we are reduced to bones and ashes, will we really be raised as a new creation?" **50.** Say, ʼO Prophet,ʼ "ʼYes, even ifʼ you become stones, or iron, **51.** or whatever you think is harder to bring to life!" Then they will ask ʼyouʼ, "Who will bring us back ʼto lifeʼ?"

Say, "The One Who created you the first time." They will then shake their heads at you and ask, "When will that be?" Say, "Perhaps it is soon!" **52.** On the Day He will call you, you will ʼinstantlyʼ respond by praising Him,[520] thinking you had remained ʼin the worldʼ only for a little while.

Advice to the Prophet

53. Tell My ʼbelievingʼ servants to say only what is best. Satan certainly seeks to sow discord among them. Satan is indeed a sworn enemy to humankind.

Invitation to the Disbelievers

54. Your Lord knows you best. He may have mercy on you if He wills, or punish you if He wills. We have not sent you ʼO Prophetʼ as a keeper over them. **55.** Your Lord knows best all those in the heavens and the earth. And We have surely favoured some prophets above others, and to David We gave the Psalms.[521]

Other Gods Besides God?

56. Say, ʼO Prophet,ʼ "Invoke those you claim ʼto be divineʼ[522] besides Him—they do not have the power to undo harm from you or transfer it ʼto someone elseʼ." **57.** ʼEvenʼ the closest ʼto Godʼ of those invoked would be seeking a way to their Lord, hoping for His mercy, and fearing His punishment. Indeed, your Lord's torment is fearsome.

Signs Always Denied

58. There is not a ʼwickedʼ society that We will not destroy or punish with a severe torment before the Day of Judgment. That is written in the Record. **59.** Nothing keeps Us from sending the ʼdemandedʼ signs except that they had ʼalreadyʼ been denied by earlier peoples. And We gave Thamûd the

---

518 Some pagans had the belief that the angels are the daughters of God.
519 They rejected you as a magician, a poet, a fabricator, and mad man.
520 When everyone is raised from the dead, they will all praise God, regardless of what they had believed in this life.
521 The reason David is singled out here is because some Jewish authorities at the time of the Prophet claimed that no scripture had been revealed after Moses. So this verse refutes this claim by referring to the Psalms of David.
522 i.e., Jesus, Ezra, and the angels. Idol worship is refuted in other passages such as 7:191-198 and 34:22.

she-camel as a clear sign, but they wrong-fully rejected it.[523] We only send the signs as a warning.

Signs as a Test

60. And ˈrememberˈ, O Prophetˈ when We told you, "Certainly your Lord encompass-es the people." And We have made what We brought you to see[524] as well as the cursed tree ˈmentionedˈ in the Quran[525] only as a test for the people. We keep warning them, but it only increases them greatly in defiance.

Satan's Defiance

61. And ˈrememberˈ when We said to the angels, "Prostrate before Adam," so they all did—but not *Iblîs*,[526] who protested, "Should I prostrate to the one You have created from mud?" 62. Adding, "Do you see this one you honoured above me? If you delay my end until the Day of Judgment, I will certainly take hold of his descendants, except for a few." 63. God responded, "Be gone! Who-ever of them follows you, Hell will surely be the reward for all of you—an ample reward. 64. And incite whoever you can of them with your voice, mobilize against them all your cavalry and infantry, manipulate them in their wealth and children, and make them promises." But Satan promises them noth-ing but delusion. 65. ˈGod addedˈ, "You will truly have no authority over My ˈfaithfulˈ servants." And sufficient is your Lord as a Guardian.

Human Ingratitude

66. It is your Lord Who steers the ships for you through the sea, so that you may seek His bounty. Surely He is ever Merciful to you. 67. When you are touched with hard-ship at sea, you ˈtotallyˈ forget all ˈthe godsˈ you ˈnormallyˈ invoke, except Him. But when He delivers you ˈsafelyˈ to shore, you turn away. Humankind is ever ungrateful.

False Immunity

68. Do you feel secure that He will not cause the land to swallow you up, or unleash upon you a storm of stones? Then you will find none to protect you. 69. Or do you feel se-cure that He will not send you back to sea once again, and send upon you a violent storm, drowning you for your denial? Then you will find none to avenge you against Us.

God's Favours to Humanity

70. Indeed, We have dignified the children of Adam, carried them on land and sea, granted them good and lawful provisions, and privileged them far above many of Our creatures.

The Record of Deeds

71. ˈBeware ofˈ the Day We will summon every people with their leader.[527] So who-ever will be given their record in their right hand will read it ˈhappilyˈ and will not be wronged ˈeven by the width ofˈ the thread of a date stone. 72. But whoever is blind ˈto the truthˈ in this ˈworldˈ will be blind in the Hereafter, and ˈevenˈ far more astray from the ˈRightˈ Way.

Temptation by Meccan Pagans

73. They definitely ˈthought theyˈ were about to lure you away from what We have revealed to you ˈO Prophetˈ, hoping that you would attribute something else to Us falsely—and then they would have certain-

---

523 Or they did wrong by it.
524 During the Night Journey mentioned in 17:1.
525 The tree of *Zaqqûm* which grows in the depths of Hell as mentioned in 37:62-65. The pagans of Mecca used to make fun of the Prophet and say, "How can a tree grow in Hell?"
526 See footnote for 2:34.
527 Other meanings include: with their record of deeds, or their prophet, or their scripture.

ly taken you as a close friend.[528] **74.** Had We not made you steadfast, you probably would have inclined to them a little, **75.** and then We truly would have made you taste double ˻punishment˼ both in this life and after death, and you would have found no helper against Us. **76.** They were about to intimidate you to drive you out of the land ˹of Mecca˺, but then they would not have survived after you ˹had left˺ except for a little while. **77.** ˹This has been˺ Our way with the messengers We sent before you. And you will never find any change in Our way.

Advice to the Prophet

78. Observe the prayer from the decline of the sun until the darkness of the night and the recitation at dawn, for certainly the dawn prayer is witnessed ˹by angels˺.[529] **79.** And rise at ˹the last˺ part of the night, offering additional prayers, so your Lord may raise you to a station of praise.[530] **80.** And say, "My Lord! Grant me an honourable entrance and an honourable exit[531] and give me a supporting authority from Yourself." **81.** And declare, "The truth has come and falsehood has vanished. Indeed, falsehood is bound to vanish."

The Quran as a Healing

82. We send down the Quran as a healing and mercy for the believers, but it only increases the wrongdoers in loss.

Arrogance and Ingratitude

83. When We grant people Our favours, they turn away, acting arrogantly. But when touched with evil, they lose all hope. **84.** Say, ˹O Prophet,˺ "Everyone acts in their own way. But your Lord knows best whose way is rightly guided."

Question by Pagans

85. They ask you ˹O Prophet˺ about the spirit. Say, "Its nature is known only to my Lord, and you ˹O humanity˺ have been given but little knowledge."

The Quran as a Favour

86. If We willed, We could have certainly taken away what We have revealed to you ˹O Prophet˺—then you would find none to guarantee its return from Us— **87.** had it not been for the mercy of your Lord. Indeed, His favour upon you is immense.

The Quran Challenge

88. Say, ˹O Prophet,˺ "If ˹all˺ humans and jinn were to come together to produce the equivalent of this Quran, they could not produce its equal, no matter how they supported each other."

Meaningless Demands

89. And We have truly set forth every ˹kind of˺ lesson for humanity in this Quran, yet most people persist in disbelief. **90.** They challenge ˹the Prophet˺, "We will never believe in you until you cause a spring to gush forth from the earth for us, **91.** or until you have a garden of palm trees and vineyards, and cause rivers to flow abundantly in it, **92.** or cause the sky to fall upon us in pieces, as you have claimed, or bring God and the angels before us, face to face, **93.** or until you have a house of gold, or you ascend into heaven—and even then we will not believe in your ascension until you bring down to

---

528 The pagans of Mecca tried in vain to dissuade the Prophet from preaching the message of Islam. In some instances they offered to worship his God if he agreed to bow to their idols, and some even offered him riches and positions if he just stopped preaching in the city.
529 This verse gives the times of the five daily prayers: the decline of the sun refers to the afternoon and late afternoon prayers, the darkness of night refers to sunset and late evening prayers, then the dawn prayer.
530 This refers to the time when the Prophet will make intercession (shafâ'ah) on the Day of Judgment.
531 This verse was revealed when the Prophet received the order to emigrate from Mecca to Medina. So here he is praying to leave Mecca honourably and enter Medina honourably. It can also apply to any worldly activity that a person starts and finishes.

us a book that we can read." Say, "Glory be to my Lord! Am I not only a human messenger?"

An Angelic Messenger?

94. And nothing has prevented people from believing when guidance comes to them except their protest: "Has God sent a human as a messenger?" 95. Say, ʿO Prophet,ʾ "Had there been angels walking the earth, well settled, We would have surely sent down for them an angel from heaven as a messenger." 96. Say, "Sufficient is God as a Witness between me and you. He is certainly All-Knowing, All-Seeing of His servants."

Reward of the Wicked

97. Whoever God guides is truly guided. And whoever He leaves to stray, you will find no guardians for them besides Him. And We will drag them on their faces on the Day of Judgment—deaf, dumb, and blind. Hell will be their home. Whenever it dies down, We will flare it up for them. 98. That is their reward for rejecting Our signs and asking ʿmockinglyʾ, "When we are reduced to bones and ashes, will we really be raised as a new creation?" 99. Have they not realized that God, Who created the heavens and the earth, can ʿeasilyʾ re-create them? He has ʿalreadyʾ set for them a time, about which there is no doubt. But the wrongdoers persist in denial. 100. Say ʿto them, O Prophetʾ, "Even if you were to possess the ʿinfiniteʾ treasuries of my Lord's mercy, then you would certainly withhold ʿthemʾ, fearing they would run out—for humankind is ever stingy!"

Pharaoh Challenges Moses

101. We surely gave Moses nine clear signs.[532] ʿYou, O Prophet, canʾ ask the Children of Israel. When Moses came to them, Pharaoh said to him, "I really think that you, O Moses, are bewitched." 102. Moses replied, "You know well that none has sent these ʿsignsʾ down except the Lord of the heavens and the earth as insights. And I really think that you, O Pharaoh, are doomed." 103. So Pharaoh wanted to scare the Israelites out of the land ʿof Egyptʾ, but We drowned him and all of those with him. 104. And We said to the Children of Israel after Pharaoh, "Reside in the land, but when the promise of the Hereafter comes to pass,[533] We will bring you all together."

The Noble Quran

105. We have sent down the Quran in truth, and with the truth it has come down. We have sent you ʿO Prophetʾ only as a deliverer of good news and a warner. 106. ʿIt isʾ a Quran We have revealed in stages so that you may recite it to people at a deliberate pace. And We have sent it down in successive revelations. 107. Say, ʿO Prophet,ʾ "Believe in this ʿQuranʾ, or do not. Indeed, when it is recited to those who were gifted with knowledge[534] before it ʿwas revealedʾ, they fall upon their faces in prostration, 108. and say, 'Glory be to our Lord! Surely the promise of our Lord has been fulfilled.' 109. And they fall down upon their faces weeping, and it increases them in humility."

Advice to the Prophet

110. Say, ʿO Prophet,ʾ "Call upon God or call upon the Most Compassionate—whichever you call, He has the Most Beautiful Names." Do not recite your prayers too loudly or si-

---

532 The nine signs of Moses are: the staff, the hand (both mentioned in 20:17-22), famine, shortage of crops, floods, locusts, lice, frogs, and blood (all mentioned in 7:130-133). These signs came as proofs for Pharaoh and the Egyptians. Otherwise, Moses had some other signs such water gushing out of the rock after he hit it with his staff, and splitting the sea.
533 This may also refer to the second warning in 17:7.
534 i.e., the faithful among the scholars of the Torah and the Gospel.

lently, but seek a way between. **111.** And say, "All praise is for God, Who has never had ʾanyʾ offspring;[535] nor does He have a partner in ʾgoverningʾ the kingdom;[536] nor is He pathetic, needing a protector.[537] And revere Him immensely."

❧

18. The Cave *(Al-Kahf)*

This Meccan chapter takes its name from the story of the people of the cave in verses 9-26. According to Ibn ʾAbbâs, the Prophet was asked about the youths who hid in a cave, a king who dominated large parts of the world, and about the spirit, so 18:9-26, 18:83-99, and 17:85 were revealed. The Prophet says in an authentic narration collected by At-Tirmiẓi, "No one's feet will move on Judgment Day until they are asked about four things: 1) What they did in their youth. 2) How they earned and spent their wealth. 3) What they did with their knowledge. 4) And how they spent their lives." Interestingly, these four questions correspond to the four stories mentioned in this chapter: 1) The story of the youths and the cave. 2) The story of the wealthy man with two gardens. 3) The story of Moses and the man of knowledge. 4) And finally the story of Ẓul-Qarnain and his life and travels in the service of God. The four stories are interjected by warnings to the disbelievers and good news to the believers. Like the story of the people of the cave, some miraculous stories appear in the next chapter.

In the Name of God—the Most Compassionate, Most Merciful

Message of the Quran

1. All praise is for God Who has revealed the Book to His servant,[538] allowing no crookedness in it, **2.** ʾmaking itʾ perfectly upright, to warn ʾthe disbelieversʾ of a severe torment from Him; to give good news to the believers—who do good— that they will have a fine reward, **3.** in which they will remain forever; **4.** and to warn those who claim, "God has offspring."[539] **5.** They have no knowledge of this, nor did their forefathers. What a terrible claim that comes out of their mouths! They say nothing but lies.

Be Steadfast

6. Now, perhaps you ʾO Prophetʾ will grieve yourself to death over their denial, if they ʾcontinue toʾ disbelieve in this message. **7.** We have indeed made whatever is on earth as an adornment for it, in order to test which of them is best in deeds. **8.** And

---

535   i.e., Jesus, Ezra, or the angels.
536   i.e., another God equal to Him.
537   i.e., the idols.
538   Prophet Muḥammad.
539   i.e., Jesus in Christianity and the angels in pagan Arab tradition.

We will certainly reduce whatever is on it to barren ground.

Story 1) The People of the Cave

9. Have you ˹O Prophet˺ thought that the people of the cave and the plaque were ˹the only˺ wonders of Our signs?[540] **10.** ˹Remember˺ when those youths took refuge in the cave, and said, "Our Lord! Grant us mercy from Yourself and guide us rightly through our ordeal." **11.** So We caused them to fall into a dead sleep[541] in the cave for many years, **12.** then We raised them so We may show which of the two groups would make a better estimation of the length of their stay.[542]

Standing up for the Truth

13. We relate to you ˹O Prophet˺ their story in truth. They were youths who truly believed in their Lord, and We increased them in guidance. **14.** And We strengthened their hearts when they stood up and declared, "Our Lord is the Lord of the heavens and the earth. We will never call upon any god besides Him, or we would truly be uttering an outrageous lie." **15.** ˹Then they said to one another,˺ "These people of ours have taken gods besides Him. Why do they not produce a clear proof of them? Who then does more wrong than those who fabricate lies against God? **16.** Since you have distanced yourselves from them and what they worship besides God, take refuge in the cave. Your Lord will extend His mercy to you and accommodate you in your ordeal."

In the Cave

17. And you would have seen the sun, as it rose, inclining away from their cave to the right, and as it set, declining away from them to the left, while they lay in its open space.[543] That is one of the signs of God. Whoever God guides is truly guided. But whoever He leaves to stray, you will never find for them a guiding mentor. **18.** And you would have thought they were awake,[544] though they were asleep. We turned them over, to the right and left, while their dog stretched his forelegs at the entrance. Had you looked at them, you would have certainly fled away from them, filled with horror.

The Youths Are Awakened

19. And so We awakened them so that they might question one another. One of them exclaimed, "How long have you remained ˹asleep˺?" Some replied, "Perhaps a day, or part of a day." They said ˹to one another˺, "Your Lord knows best how long you have remained. So send one of you with these silver coins of yours to the city, and let him find which food is the purest, and then bring you provisions from it. Let him be ˹exceptionally˺ cautious, and do not let him give you away. **20.** For, indeed, if they find out about you, they will stone you ˹to death˺, or force you back into their faith, and then you will never succeed."

The Hideout Is Found

21. That is how We caused them to be discovered so that their people might know that God's promise ˹of resurrection˺ is true

---

540 Ar-Raqîm is the plaque that was placed at the entrance of the cave with the names and story of the People of the Cave. This is the story of a group of Christian youths who hid inside a cave outside the city of Ephesus around 250 C.E., to escape persecution at the hands of pagans during the reign of the Roman emperor Decius. The Quran does not give an exact number of the youths, although many scholars believe there were seven in addition to a dog. The youths slept for 300 years, plus nine (300 solar years equal 309 lunar years).

541 lit., We cast a cover of ˹deep˺ sleep over their ears.

542 The People of the Cave themselves disagreed on how long they had slept in the cave. See 18:19.

543 While they slept in the open space of the cave, fresh air blew through the cave, but they were protected from the heat of the sun.

544 This is because, during their long sleep, their eyes were open, their hair grew long, and their bodies rolled over to the right and left to prevent bedsores.

and that there is no doubt about the Hour.[545] When the people disputed with each other about the case of the youth ʿafter their deathʾ,[546] some proposed, "Build a structure around them. Their Lord knows best about them." Those who prevailed in the matter said, "We will surely build a place of worship over them."

How Many Were They?

22. Some will say, "They were three, their dog was the fourth," while others will say, "They were five, their dog was the sixth," ʿonlyʾ guessing blindly. And others will say, "They were seven and their dog was the eighth." Say, ʿO Prophet,ʾ "My Lord knows best their ʿexactʾ number. Only a few people know as well." So do not argue about them except with sure knowledge,[547] nor consult any of those ʿwho debateʾ about them.

Say, "God Willing"

23. And never say of anything, "I will definitely do this tomorrow," **24.** without adding, "if God so wills!" But if you forget, then remember your Lord, and say, "I trust my Lord will guide me to what is more right than this."

Time Spent in the Cave

25. They had remained in their cave for three hundred years, adding nine.[548] **26.** Say, ʿO Prophet,ʾ "God knows best how long they stayed. With Him ʿaloneʾ is ʿtheʾ knowledge ofʿ the unseen of the heavens and the earth. How perfectly He hears and sees! They have no guardian besides Him, and He shares His command with none."

Advice to the Prophet

27. Recite what has been revealed to you from the Book of your Lord. None can change His Words, nor can you find any refuge besides Him. **28.** And patiently stick with those who call upon their Lord morning and evening, seeking His pleasure.[549] Do not let your eyes look beyond them, desiring the luxuries of this worldly life. And do not obey those whose hearts We have made heedless of Our remembrance, who follow ʿonlyʾ their desires and whose state is ʿtotalʾ loss.

Warning to the Disbelievers

29. And say, ʿO Prophet,ʾ "ʿThis isʾ the truth from your Lord. Whoever wills let them believe, and whoever wills let them disbelieve." Surely We have prepared for the wrongdoers a Fire whose walls will ʿcompletelyʾ surround them. When they cry for aid, they will be aided with water like molten metal, which will burn ʿtheirʾ faces. What a horrible drink! And what a terrible place to rest!

Reward of the Believers

30. As for those who believe and do good, We certainly never deny the reward of those who are best in deeds. **31.** It is they who will have the Gardens of Eternity, with rivers flowing under their feet. There they will be adorned with bracelets of gold, and wear green garments of fine silk and rich brocade, reclining there on ʿcanopiedʾ couches. What a marvellous reward! And what a fabulous place to rest!

Story 2) The Owner of the Two Gardens

32. Give them ʿO Prophetʾ an example of two men. To ʿthe disbelievingʾ one We gave two gardens of grapevines, which We

---

545 Their antique silver coins gave them away. People rushed to the cave to greet the youths, who finally passed away and were buried in the cave. The King decided to build a place of worship at the cave to commemorate their story.
546 Some pagans suggested that a wall should be built to seal off the cave, whereas the believers decided to build a place of worship at the cave to honour those youths.
547 Based on what has been revealed in the Quran.
548 Three hundred years in the Gregorian calendar equal three hundred and nine years in the Islamic lunar calendar.
549 lit., seeking His Face.

surrounded with palm trees and placed ʿvariousʾ crops in between. **33.** Each garden yielded ʿallʾ its produce, never falling short. And We caused a river to flow between them. **34.** And he had other resources[550] ʿas wellʾ. So he boasted to a ʿpoorʾ companion of his, while conversing with him, "I am greater than you in wealth and superior in manpower." **35.** And he entered his property, while wronging his soul, saying, "I do not think this will ever perish, **36.** nor do I think the Hour will ʿeverʾ come. And if in fact I am returned to my Lord, I will definitely get a far better outcome than ʿallʾ this."

The Rebuttal

37. His ʿbelievingʾ companion replied, while conversing with him, "Do you disbelieve in the One Who created you from dust,[551] then ʿdeveloped youʾ from a sperm-drop, then formed you into a man? **38.** But as for me: He is God, my Lord, and I will never associate anyone with my Lord ʿin worshipʾ. **39.** If only you had said, upon entering your property, 'This is what God has willed! There is no power except with God!' Even though you see me inferior to you in wealth and offspring, **40.** perhaps my Lord will grant me ʿsomethingʾ better than your garden, and send down upon your garden a thunderbolt from the sky, turning it into a barren waste. **41.** Or its water may sink ʿinto the earthʾ, and then you will never be able to seek it out."

The Punishment

42. And so all his produce was ʿtotallyʾ ruined, so he started to wring his hands for all he had spent on it, while it had collapsed on its trellises. He cried, "Alas! I wish I had never associated anyone with my Lord ʿin worshipʾ!" **43.** And he had no manpower to

help him against God, nor could he ʿevenʾ help himself. **44.** At this time, support comes ʿonlyʾ from God—the True ʿLordʾ. He is best in reward and best in outcome.

Fleeting and Everlasting Gains

45. And give them a parable of this worldly life. ʿIt isʾ like the plants of the earth, thriving when sustained by the rain We send down from the sky. Then they ʿsoonʾ turn into chaff scattered by the wind. And God is fully capable of ʿdoingʾ all things. **46.** Wealth and children are the adornment of this worldly life, but the everlasting good deeds are far better with your Lord in reward and in hope.[552]

Judgment Day

47. ʿBeware ofʾ the Day We will blow the mountains away, and you will see the earth laid bare. And We will gather all ʿhumankindʾ, leaving none behind. **48.** They will be presented before your Lord in rows, ʿand the deniers will be told,ʾ "You have surely returned to Us ʿall aloneʾ as We created you the first time, although you ʿalwaysʾ claimed that We would never appoint a time for your return." **49.** And the record ʿof deedsʾ will be laid ʿopenʾ, and you will see the wicked in fear of what is ʿwrittenʾ in it. They will cry, "Woe to us! What kind of record is this that does not leave any sin, small or large, unlisted?" They will find whatever they did present ʿbefore themʾ. And your Lord will never wrong anyone.

Satan and His Followers

50. And ʿrememberʾ when We said to the angels, "Prostrate before Adam," so they all did—but not *Iblîs*,[553] who was one of the jinn, but he rebelled against the command of his Lord. Would you then take him and

---

550 The word *"thamar"* can mean fruits, gold and silver, etc.
551 Created your father, Adam, from dust.
552 This refers to good deeds that will benefit the believer in the Hereafter such as prayers or praises of God such as saying: *'Subḥâna-Allâh'* (Glory be to God), *'Alḥamdulillâh'* (Praise be to God), *'Lâ ilâha illa-Allâh'* (There is no god ʿworthy of worshipʾ except God), and *'Allâhu akbar'* (God is the Greatest).
553 *See* footnote for 2:34.

his descendants as patrons instead of Me, although they are your enemy? What an evil alternative for the wrongdoers ˹to choose˺! **51.** I never called them to witness the creation of the heavens and the earth or ˹even˺ their own creation, nor would I take the misleaders as helpers. **52.** And ˹beware of˺ the Day He will say, "Call upon those you claimed were My associate-gods." So they will call them, but will receive no response. And We will make them ˹all˺ share in the same doom. **53.** The wicked will see the Fire and realize that they are bound to fall into it, and will find no way to avoid it.

Denying the Quran

54. We have surely set forth in this Quran every ˹kind of˺ lesson for people, but humankind is the most argumentative of all beings. **55.** And nothing prevents people from believing when guidance comes to them and from seeking their Lord's forgiveness except ˹their demand˺ to meet the same fate of earlier deniers or that the torment would confront them face to face. **56.** We do not send the messengers except as deliverers of good news and warners. But the disbelievers argue in falsehood, ˹hoping˺ to discredit the truth with it, and make a mockery of My revelations and warnings. **57.** And who does more wrong than those who, when reminded of their Lord's revelations, turn away from them and forget what their own hands have done? We have certainly cast veils over their hearts—leaving them unable to comprehend this ˹Quran˺—and deafness in their ears. And if you ˹O Prophet˺ invite them to ˹true˺ guidance, they will never be ˹rightly˺ guided.

God's Forbearance

58. Your Lord is the All-Forgiving, Full of Mercy. If He were to seize them ˹immediately˺ for what they commit, He would have certainly hastened their punishment. But they have an appointed time, from which they will find no refuge. **59.** Those ˹are the˺ societies We destroyed when they persisted in wrong,[554] and We had set a time for their destruction.

Story 3) Moses and Al-Khaḍir

60. And ˹remember˺ when Moses said to his young assistant, "I will never give up until I reach the junction of the two seas, even if I travel for ages."[555] **61.** But when they ˹finally˺ reached the point where the seas met, they forgot their ˹salted˺ fish, and it made its way into the sea, slipping away ˹wondrously˺. **62.** When they had passed further, he said to his assistant, "Bring us our meal! We have certainly been exhausted by today's journey." **63.** He replied, "Do you remember when we rested by the rock? ˹That is when˺ I forgot the fish. None made me forget to mention this except Satan. And the fish made its way into the sea miraculously."[556] **64.** Moses responded, "That is ˹exactly˺ what we were looking for."[557] So they returned, retracing their footsteps.

The Encounter

65. There they found a servant of Ours, to whom We had granted mercy from Us and enlightened with knowledge of Our Own. **66.** Moses said to him, "May I follow you, provided that you teach me some of the right guidance you have been taught?" **67.** He said, "You certainly cannot be pa-

---

554 i.e., the peoples of ʿÂd and Thamûd.
555 It is reported in an authentic narration collected by Bukhâri that a man approached Moses after he gave a talk and asked him, "Who is the most knowledgeable person on earth?" Moses responded, "That would be me!" So God revealed to Moses that he should not have said this and there was in fact someone who was more knowledgeable than him. Moses was commanded to travel to meet this man, named Al-Khaḍir, at the junction of the two seas (which could be the northern part of Sinai between the Red Sea and the Mediterranean Sea, or the Southern part of Sinai where the Red Sea splits into the Gulf of Suez and the Gulf of Aqaba).
556 Another possible translation: "The ˹salted˺ fish must have made its way into the sea. How strange!"
557 Moses was given a sign: when he and his assistant Joshua (or Yûsha' ibn Nûn) lost their food (a salted fish), this would be the place where they would find the man of knowledge.

tient ˈenoughˈ with me. **68.** And how can you be patient with what is beyond your ˈrealm ofˈ knowledge?" **69.** Moses assured ˈhimˈ, "You will find me patient, God willing, and I will not disobey any of your orders." **70.** He responded, "Then if you follow me, do not question me about anything until I ˈmyselfˈ clarify it for you."

The Ship Incident

71. So they set out, but after they had boarded a ship, the man made a hole in it. Moses protested, "Have you done this to drown its people? You have certainly done a terrible thing!" **72.** He replied, "Did I not say that you cannot have patience with me?" **73.** Moses pleaded, "Excuse me for forgetting, and do not be hard on me."

The Boy Incident

74. So they proceeded until they came across a boy, and the man killed him. Moses protested, "Have you killed an innocent soul, who killed no one? You have certainly done a horrible thing." **75.** He answered, "Did I not tell you that you cannot have patience with me?" **76.** Moses replied, "If I ever question you about anything after this, then do not keep me in your company, for by then I would have given you enough of an excuse."

The Wall Incident

77. So they moved on until they came to the people of a town. They asked them for food, but the people refused to give them hospitality. There they found a wall ready to collapse, so the man set it right. Moses protested, "If you wanted, you could have demanded a fee for this." **78.** He replied, "This is the parting of our ways. I will explain to you what you could not bear patiently.

The Ship

79. "As for the ship, it belonged to some poor people, working at sea. So I intended to damage it, for there was a ˈtyrantˈ king ahead of them who seizes every ˈgoodˈ ship by force.

The Boy

80. "And as for the boy, his parents were ˈtrueˈ believers, and we[558] feared that he would pressure them into defiance and disbelief. **81.** So we hoped that their Lord would give them another, more virtuous and caring in his place.

The Wall

82. "And as for the wall, it belonged to two orphan boys in the city, and under the wall was a treasure that belonged to them, and their father had been a righteous man. So your Lord willed that these children should come of age and retrieve their treasure, as a mercy from your Lord. I did not do it ˈallˈ on my own. This is the explanation of what you could not bear patiently."[559]

Story 4) Ƶul-Qarnain

83. They ask you ˈO Prophetˈ about Ƶul-Qarnain. Say, "I will relate to you something of his narrative."[560] **84.** Surely We established him in the land, and gave him the means to all things.

Journey to the West

85. So he travelled a course, **86.** until he reached the setting ˈpointˈ of the sun, which appeared to him to be setting in a spring of

---

558 This is the royal 'we'.

559 The Prophet commented on the story, "I wish Moses had been more patient so we can learn more from that wise man."

560 This is the story of a righteous king who travelled far and wide. He is titled Ƶul-Qarnain (lit., the man of the two horns) because of his journeys to the far east and far west (or the two horns/points of sunrise and sunset). Some believe Ƶul-Qarnain was Alexander the Great, but this is not sound since Alexander the Great was a polytheist. Many scholars believe it was Abu Kuraib Al-Ḥamiri, a righteous king from Yemen.

murky water, where he found some people. We said, "O Ẓul-Qarnain! Either punish them or treat them kindly." **87.** He responded, "Whoever does wrong will be punished by us, then will be returned to their Lord, Who will punish them with a horrible torment. **88.** As for those who believe and do good, they will have the finest reward, and we will assign them easy commands."

Journey to the East

89. Then he travelled a ˹different˺ course **90.** until he reached the rising ˹point˺ of the sun. He found it rising on a people for whom We had provided no shelter from it.[561] **91.** So it was. And We truly had full knowledge of him.

Another Journey

92. Then he travelled a ˹third˺ course **93.** until he reached ˹a pass˺ between two mountains. He found in front of them a people who could hardly understand ˹his˺ language. **94.** They pleaded, "O Ẓul-Qarnain! Surely Gog and Magog[562] are spreading corruption throughout the land. Should we pay you tribute, provided that you build a wall between us and them?" **95.** He responded, "What my Lord has provided for me is far better. But assist me with resources, and I will build a barrier between you and them. **96.** Bring me blocks of iron!" Then, when he had filled up ˹the gap˺ between the two mountains, he ordered, "Blow!" When the iron became red hot, he said, "Bring me molten copper to pour over it." **97.** And so the enemies could neither scale nor tunnel through it. **98.** He declared, "This is a mercy from my Lord. But when the promise of my Lord comes

to pass, He will level it to the ground. And my Lord's promise is ever true." **99.** On that Day, We will let them[563] surge ˹like waves˺ over one another. Later, the Trumpet will be blown,[564] and We will gather all ˹people˺ together.

The Wicked on Judgment Day

100. On that Day We will display Hell clearly for the disbelievers, **101.** those who turned a blind eye to My Reminder[565] and could not stand listening ˹to it˺. **102.** Do the disbelievers think they can ˹simply˺ take My servants[566] as lords instead of Me? We have surely prepared Hell as an accommodation for the disbelievers.

The Losers

103. Say, ˹O Prophet,˺ "Shall we inform you of who will be the biggest losers of deeds? **104.** ˹They are˺ those whose efforts are in vain in this worldly life, while they think they are doing good!" **105.** It is they who reject the signs of their Lord and their meeting with Him, rendering their deeds void, so We will not give their deeds any weight on Judgment Day. **106.** That is their reward: Hell, for their disbelief and mockery of My signs and messengers.

The Winners

107. Indeed, those who believe and do good will have the Gardens of Paradise[567] as an accommodation, **108.** where they will be forever, never desiring anywhere else.

Recording God's Knowledge

109. Say, ˹O Prophet,˺ "If the ocean were ink for ˹writing˺ the Words of my Lord, it

---

561 They either had no clothes or homes to protect them from the sun.
562 Gog and Magog are two wild peoples who were sealed off by a barrier built by Ẓul-Qarnain to stop them from raiding their peaceful neighbours. There are many speculations as to their location, but none is supported by reliable sources. Their coming out is mentioned in 21:96-97 as one of the major signs of the final Hour.
563 Gog and Magog.
564 On the Day of Judgment, the Trumpet will be blown by an angel—causing all to die. When it is blown a second time, everyone will be raised from the dead to be assembled for the Judgment (see 39:68).
565 i.e., the Quran.
566 i.e., Jesus, Ezra, and the angels.
567 Al-Firdaws, the highest place in Paradise.

would certainly run out before the Words of my Lord were finished, even if We refilled it with its equal."

Have Faith and Do Good

110. Say, 'O Prophet,' "I am only a man like you, 'but' it has been revealed to me that your God is only One God. So whoever hopes for the meeting with their Lord, let them do good deeds and associate none in the worship of their Lord."

19. Mary *(Mariam)*

This Meccan chapter recounts the miraculous stories of the birth of Jesus by the virgin Mary (after whom the chapter is named) and the birth of John the Baptist to old Zachariah and his elderly, barren wife. Other prophets are cited as recipients of God's favour and grace. Attributing children to God (verses 88-95) and denial of resurrection (verses 66-70) are rejected as outrageous and blasphemous. Both the end of this chapter and the beginning of the next one talk about the purpose of revealing the Quran.

In the Name of God—the Most Compassionate, Most Merciful

Zachariah's Prayer

1. *Kãf-Ha-Ya-'Aĩn-Ṣãd.* **2.** 'This is' a reminder of your Lord's mercy to His servant Zachariah, **3.** when he cried out to his Lord privately, **4.** saying, "My Lord! Surely my bones have become brittle, and grey hair has spread across my head, but I have never been disappointed in my prayer to You, my Lord! **5.** And I am concerned about 'the faith of' my relatives after me, since my wife is barren. So grant me, by Your grace, an heir, **6.** who will inherit 'prophethood' from me and the family of Jacob, and make him, O Lord, pleasing 'to You'!"

Prayer Answered

7. 'The angels announced,' "O Zachariah! Indeed, We give you the good news of 'the birth of' a son, whose name will be John—a name We have not given to anyone before." **8.** He wondered, "My Lord! How can I have a son when my wife is barren, and I have become extremely old?"

9. An angel replied, "So will it be! Your Lord says, 'It is easy for Me, just as I created you before, when you were nothing!'" **10.** Zachariah said, "My Lord! Grant me a sign." He responded, "Your sign is that you will not 'be able to' speak to people for three nights, despite being healthy." **11.** So he came out to his people from the sanctuary, signalling to them to glorify 'God' morning and evening.

John's Noble Qualities

12. 'It was later said,' "O John! Hold firmly to the Scriptures." And We granted him wisdom while 'he was still' a child, **13.** as well as purity and compassion from Us. And he was God-fearing, **14.** and kind to his parents. He was neither arrogant nor disobedient. **15.** Peace be upon him the day he was born, and the day of his death, and the day he will be raised back to life!

Gabriel Visits Mary

16. And mention in the Book ˹O Prophet, the story of˺ Mary when she withdrew from her family to a place in the east, **17.** screening herself off from them. Then We sent to her Our angel, ˹Gabriel,˺ appearing before her as a man, perfectly formed. **18.** She appealed, "I truly seek refuge in the Most Compassionate from you! ˹So leave me alone˺ if you are God-fearing." **19.** He responded, "I am only a messenger from your Lord, ˹sent˺ to bless you with a pure son." **20.** She wondered, "How can I have a son when no man has ever touched me, nor am I unchaste?" **21.** He replied, "So will it be! Your Lord says, 'It is easy for Me. And so will We make him a sign for humanity and a mercy from Us.' It is a matter ˹already˺ decreed."

Jesus' Virgin Birth

22. So she conceived him and withdrew with him to a remote place. **23.** Then the pains of labour drove her to the trunk of a palm tree. She cried, "Alas! I wish I had died before this, and was a thing long forgotten!" **24.** So a voice[568] reassured her from below her, "Do not grieve! Your Lord has provided a stream at your feet. **25.** And shake the trunk of this palm tree towards you, it will drop fresh, ripe dates upon you. **26.** So eat and drink, and put your heart at ease. But if you see any of the people, say, 'I have vowed silence[569] to the Most Compassionate, so I am not talking to anyone today.'"

Reaction to Baby Jesus

27. Then she returned to her people, carrying him. They said ˹in shock˺, "O Mary! You have certainly done a horrible thing! **28.** O sister of Aaron![570] Your father was not an indecent man, nor was your mother unchaste." **29.** So she pointed to the baby. They ex-claimed, "How can we talk to someone who is an infant in the cradle?"

Baby Jesus Talks

30. Jesus declared, "I am truly a servant of God. He has destined me to be given the Scripture and to be a prophet. **31.** He has made me a blessing wherever I go, and bid me to establish prayer and give alms-tax as long as I live, **32.** and to be kind to my mother. He has not made me arrogant or defiant. **33.** Peace be upon me the day I was born, the day I die, and the day I will be raised back to life!"

Christians and Jews Differ on Jesus

34. That is Jesus, son of Mary. ˹And this is˺ a word of truth, about which they dispute. **35.** It is not for God to take a son! Glory be to Him. When He decrees a matter, He simply tells it, "Be!" And it is! **36.** ˹Jesus also declared,˺ "Surely God is my Lord and your Lord, so worship Him ˹alone˺. This is the Straight Path." **37.** Yet their ˹various˺ groups have differed among themselves ˹about him˺, so woe to the disbelievers when they face a tremendous Day! **38.** How clearly will they hear and see on the Day they will come to Us! But today the wrongdoers are clearly astray.

Warning to the Disbelievers

39. And warn them ˹O Prophet˺ of the Day of Regret, when all matters will be settled, while they are ˹engrossed˺ in heedlessness and disbelief. **40.** Indeed, it is We Who will succeed the earth and whoever is on it. And to Us they will ˹all˺ be returned.

Abraham and His Father, Âzar

41. And mention in the Book ˹O Prophet, the story of˺ Abraham. He was surely a man of truth and a prophet. **42.** ˹Remember˺ when he said to his father, "O dear father! Why do

---

568 This was the voice of baby Jesus. Some say it was Gabriel.
569 lit., fast ˹from speech˺. Linguistically, *ṣawm* means to abstain from something, such as food, speaking, and playing.
570 i.e., his twin in virtue. They meant that they did not expect her to do something like that because they held her in high esteem like Aaron, Moses' brother (perhaps because she was his descendant).

you worship what can neither hear nor see, nor benefit you at all? **43.** O dear father! I have certainly received some knowledge which you have not received, so follow me and I will guide you to the Straight Path. **44.** O dear father! Do not worship Satan. Surely Satan is ever rebellious against the Most Compassionate. **45.** O dear father! I truly fear that you will be touched by a torment from the Most Compassionate, and become Satan's companion ˹in Hell˺."

Âzar's Angry Response

46. He threatened, "How dare you reject my idols, O Abraham! If you do not desist, I will certainly stone you ˹to death˺. So be gone from me for a long time!" **47.** Abraham responded, "Peace be upon you! I will pray to my Lord for your forgiveness. He has truly been Most Gracious to me. **48.** As I distance myself from ˹all of˺ you and from whatever you invoke besides God, I will ˹continue to˺ call upon my Lord ˹alone˺, trusting that I will never be disappointed in invoking my Lord." **49.** So after he had left them and what they worshipped besides God, We granted him Isaac and Jacob, and made each of them a prophet. **50.** We showered them with Our mercy, and blessed them with honourable mention.[571]

Prophet Moses

51. And mention in the Book ˹O Prophet, the story of˺ Moses. He was truly a chosen man, and was a messenger and a prophet. **52.** We called him from the right side of Mount Ṭûr, and drew him near, speaking ˹with him˺ directly. **53.** And We appointed for him—out of Our grace—his brother, Aaron, as a prophet.

Prophet Ishmael

54. And mention in the Book ˹O Prophet, the story of˺ Ishmael. He was truly a man of his word, and was a messenger and a prophet. **55.** He used to urge his people to pray and give alms-tax. And his Lord was well pleased with him.

Prophet Enoch

56. And mention in the Book ˹O Prophet, the story of˺ Enoch. He was surely a man of truth and a prophet. **57.** And We elevated him to an honourable status.[572]

Noble Prophets

58. Those were ˹some of˺ the prophets who God has blessed from among the descendants of Adam, and of those We carried with Noah ˹in the Ark˺, and of the descendants of Abraham and Israel,[573] and of those We ˹rightly˺ guided and chose. Whenever the revelations of the Most Compassionate were recited to them, they fell down, prostrating and weeping.

Evil Successors

59. But they were succeeded by generations who neglected prayer and followed their lusts and so will soon face the evil consequences.[574] **60.** As for those who repent, believe, and do good, it is they who will be admitted into Paradise, never being denied any reward. **61.** ˹They will be in˺ the Gardens of Eternity, promised in trust by the Most Compassionate to His servants. Surely His promise will be fulfilled. **62.** There they will never hear any idle talk—only ˹greetings of˺ peace. And there they will have their provisions morning and evening.[575] **63.** That is Paradise, which We will grant to whoever is devout among Our servants.

---

571 On a daily basis, Muslims invoke God's blessings upon Prophet Muḥammad and his family and Prophet Abraham and his family, in both obligatory and optional prayers.
572 Prophet Enoch (*Idrîs*) is said to be in the fourth heaven.
573 Israel is another name for Jacob.
574 The word *ghai* can either mean the evil consequences or a valley in Hell where they will be punished.
575 There is no day or night in Paradise, only light. The verse says that the residents of Paradise will either be receiving provisions around these worldly times or without failure. Words such as morning and evening are used to make it easier for the people to understand.

Gabriel's Response to the Prophet[576]

64. "We only descend by the command of your Lord. To Him belongs whatever is before us, and whatever is behind us, and everything in between. And your Lord is never forgetful. **65.** ˹He is the˺ Lord of the heavens, and the earth, and everything in between. So worship Him ˹alone˺, and be steadfast in His worship. Do you know of anyone equal to Him ˹in His attributes˺?"

The Deniers of Resurrection

66. Yet ˹some˺ people ask ˹mockingly˺, "After I die, will I really be raised to life again?" **67.** Do ˹such˺ people not remember that We created them before, when they were nothing? **68.** By your Lord ˹O Prophet˺! We will surely gather them along with the devils, and then set them around Hell on their knees. **69.** Then We will certainly begin by dragging out of every group the ones most defiant to the Most Compassionate. **70.** And We truly know best who is most deserving of burning in it. **71.** There is none of you who will not pass over it.[577] ˹This is˺ a decree your Lord must fulfil. **72.** Then We will deliver those who were devout, leaving the wrongdoers there on their knees.

Arrogant Disbelievers

73. When Our clear revelations are recited to them, the disbelievers ask the believers ˹mockingly˺, "Which of the two of us is better in status and superior in assembly?" **74.** ˹Imagine, O Prophet˺ how many peoples We have destroyed before them, who were far better in luxury and splendour! **75.** Say, ˹O Prophet,˺ "Whoever is ˹entrenched˺ in misguidance, the Most Compassionate will allow them plenty of time, until—behold!—they face what they are threatened with: either the torment or the Hour. Only then will they realize who is worse in position and inferior in manpower."

Reward of the Devout

76. And God increases in guidance those who are ˹rightly˺ guided. And the everlasting good deeds are far better with your Lord in reward and in outcome.[578]

A Denier of Resurrection

77. Have you seen ˹O Prophet˺ the one[579] who rejects Our revelations yet boasts, "I will definitely be granted ˹plenty of˺ wealth and children ˹if there is an afterlife˺."? **78.** Has he looked into the unseen or taken a pledge from the Most Compassionate? **79.** Not at all! We certainly record whatever he claims and will increase his punishment extensively. **80.** And We will inherit what he boasts of, and he will come before Us all by himself.

Believers and Disbelievers on Judgment Day

81. They have taken other gods, instead of God, seeking strength ˹and protection˺ through them. **82.** But no! Those ˹gods˺ will deny their worship and turn against them. **83.** Do you ˹O Prophet˺ not see that We have sent the devils against the disbelievers, constantly inciting them? **84.** So do not be in haste against them, for indeed We are ˹closely˺ counting down their days. **85.** ˹Watch for˺ the Day We will gather the righteous before the Most Compassionate as an honoured delegation, **86.** and drive the wicked to Hell like a thirsty herd. **87.** None will have the right to intercede, except those who have taken a covenant from the Most Compassionate.[580]

---

576 This passage is a response to the Prophet's request to be visited by Gabriel more often.
577 This refers to the bridge (known as Aṣ-Ṣirâṭ) which is extended over Hell. Both the believers and disbelievers will be made to cross that bridge. The believers will cross it safely, each at a different speed according to the strength of their faith, whereas the disbelievers and the hypocrites will plunge into the Fire.
578 See footnote for 18:46.
579 This statement was made by Al-ʿÂṣ ibn Wael, a Meccan pagan who staunchly disbelieved in resurrection.
580 No one will be allowed to intercede except those who firmly believe in Almighty God.

God's Children?

88. They[581] say, "The Most Compassionate has offspring." 89. You have certainly made an outrageous claim, 90. by which the heavens are about to burst, the earth to split apart, and the mountains to crumble to pieces 91. in protest of attributing children to the Most Compassionate. 92. It does not befit ˹the majesty of˺ the Most Compassionate to have children. 93. There is none in the heavens or the earth who will not return to the Most Compassionate in full submission. 94. Indeed, He fully knows them and has counted them precisely. 95. And each of them will return to Him on the Day of Judgment all alone.

Believers' Love for One Another

96. As for those who believe and do good, the Most Compassionate will ˹certainly˺ bless them with ˹genuine˺ love.

The Message of the Quran

97. Indeed, We have made this ˹Quran˺ easy in your own language ˹O Prophet˺ so with it you may give good news to the righteous and warn those who are contentious. 98. ˹Imagine˺ how many peoples We have destroyed before them! Do you ˹still˺ see any of them, or ˹even˺ hear from them the slightest sound?

❧

20. Ṭâ-Hâ *(Ṭâ-Hâ)*

Since Moses and Adam are mentioned passingly in the previous chapter, their stories are recounted here in great detail. This Meccan chapter reassures the Prophet that the truth always prevails even against the most tyrannical opposition (in the form of Pharaoh) and that God is able to open even the hardest of hearts (in the form of Pharaoh's magicians). Both the beginning and the end of the chapter emphasize the divine nature of the Quran as a source of guidance and eternal bliss. Those who turn away from the Quranic reminder are warned of misery in this world and horrifying punishment on the Day of Judgment. The Prophet is advised to seek comfort in patience and prayer against pagan denial, which is detailed at the beginning of the next chapter.

In the Name of God—the Most Compassionate, Most Merciful

Almighty God's Revelation

1. *Ṭâ-Hâ.* 2. We have not revealed the Quran to you ˹O Prophet˺ to cause you distress, 3. but as a reminder to those in awe ˹of God˺. 4. ˹It is˺ a revelation from the One Who created the earth and the high heavens— 5. the Most Compassionate, ˹Who is˺ established above the Throne. 6. To Him belongs whatever is in the heavens and whatever is on the earth and whatever is in between and whatever is underground. 7. Whether you speak openly ˹or not˺, He certainly knows what is secret and what is even more hidden. 8. God—there is no god ˹worthy of worship˺ except Him. He has the Most Beautiful Names.

---

581 The pagans who claimed that the angels are God's daughters, the Christians who claim that Jesus is the son of God, etc.

Moses' Great Encounter

9. Has the story of Moses reached you ˹O Prophet˺? **10.** When he saw a fire, he said to his family, "Wait here, ˹for˺ I have spotted a fire. Perhaps I can bring you a torch from it, or find some guidance at the fire."[582] **11.** But when he approached it, he was called, "O Moses! **12.** It is truly I. I am your Lord! So take off your sandals, for you are in the sacred valley of Ṭuwa. **13.** I have chosen you, so listen to what is revealed: **14.** 'It is truly I. I am God! There is no god ˹worthy of worship˺ except Me. So worship Me ˹alone˺, and establish prayer for My remembrance. **15.** The Hour is sure to come. My Will is to keep it hidden, so that every soul may be rewarded according to their efforts. **16.** So do not let those who disbelieve in it and follow their desires distract you from it, or you will be doomed.'"

Two Signs for Moses

17. ˹God added,˺ "And what is that in your right hand, O Moses?" **18.** He replied, "It is my staff! I lean on it, and with it I beat down ˹branches˺ for my sheep, and have other uses for it."[583] **19.** God said, "Throw it down, O Moses!" **20.** So he did, then—behold!—it became a serpent, slithering. **21.** God said, "Take it, and have no fear. We will return it to its former state. **22.** And put your hand under your armpit, it will come out ˹shining˺ white, unblemished,[584] as another sign, **23.** so that We may show you some of Our greatest signs. **24.** Go to Pharaoh, for he has truly transgressed ˹all bounds˺."

Moses Prays for Help

25. Moses prayed, "My Lord! Uplift my heart for me, **26.** and make my task easy, **27.** and remove the impediment from my tongue **28.** so people may understand my speech,[585] **29.** and grant me a helper from my family, **30.** Aaron, my brother. **31.** Strengthen me through him, **32.** and let him share my task, **33.** so that we may glorify You much **34.** and remember You much, **35.** for truly You have ˹always˺ been overseeing us." **36.** God responded, "All that you requested has been granted, O Moses!

God's Favours to Young Moses

37. "And surely We had shown you favour before, **38.** when We inspired your mother with this: **39.** 'Put him into a chest, then put it into the river. The river will wash it ashore, and he will be taken by ˹Pharaoh,˺ an enemy of Mine and his.' And I endeared you with love from Me[586] ˹O Moses˺ so that you would be brought up under My ˹watchful˺ Eye. **40.** ˹Remember˺ when your sister came along and proposed, 'Shall I direct you to someone who will nurse him?'[587] So We reunited you with your mother so that her heart would be put at ease, and she would not grieve. ˹Later˺ you killed a man ˹by mistake˺, but We saved you from sorrow, as well as other tests We put you through. Then you stayed for a number of years among the people of Midian. Then you came here as pre-destined, O Moses! **41.** And I have selected you for My service.

---

582 Moses and his family lost their way in the dark while they were travelling from Midian to Egypt.
583 Moses could have just said, "A staff." But he volunteered to talk about the uses of the staff, adding that there are many other uses he has not mentioned, with the hope that God would ask him about it more. The reason is that Moses wanted to prolong the conversation with God as much as he could.
584 Moses, who was dark-skinned, was asked to put his hand under his armpit. When he took it out it was shining white, but not out of a skin condition like vitiligo.
585 Moses put a brand of fire in his mouth, which hindered his speech as he grew up. In this verse, he prays to God to help him speak clearly, and his prayer is answered.
586 In other words, God made Moses a likeable person so Pharaoh and his wife would agree to keep him.
587 Moses had refused all wet-nurses that were brought for him.

Orders to Moses and Aaron

42. "Go forth, you and your brother, with My signs and never falter in remembering Me. **43.** Go, both of you, to Pharaoh, for he has truly transgressed ˹all bounds˺. **44.** Speak to him gently, so perhaps he may be mindful ˹of Me˺ or fearful ˹of My punishment˺." **45.** They both pleaded, "Our Lord! We fear that he may be quick to harm us or act tyrannically." **46.** God reassured ˹them˺, "Have no fear! I am with you, hearing and seeing. **47.** So go to him and say, 'Indeed we are both messengers from your Lord, so let the Children of Israel go with us, and do not oppress them. We have come to you with a sign from your Lord. And salvation will be for whoever follows the ˹right˺ guidance. **48.** It has indeed been revealed to us that the punishment will be upon whoever denies ˹the truth˺ and turns away.'"

Pharaoh's Arrogance

49. Pharaoh asked, "Who then is the Lord of you two, O Moses?" **50.** He answered, "Our Lord is the One Who has given everything its ˹distinctive˺ form, then guided ˹it˺." **51.** Pharaoh asked, "And what about previous peoples?" **52.** He replied, "That knowledge is with my Lord in a Record. My Lord neither falters nor forgets ˹anything˺." **53.** ˹He is the One˺ Who has laid out the earth for ˹all of˺ you, and set in it pathways for you, and sends down rain from the sky, causing various types of plants to grow, **54.** ˹so˺ eat and graze your cattle. Surely in this are signs for people of sound judgment. **55.** From the earth We created you, and into it We will return you, and from it We will bring you back again.

The Challenge

56. And We certainly showed Pharaoh all of Our signs,[588] but he denied them and refused ˹to believe˺. **57.** He said, "Have you come to drive us out of our land with your magic, O Moses? **58.** We can surely meet you with similar magic. So set for us an appointment that neither of us will fail to keep, in a central place." **59.** Moses said, "Your appointment is on the Day of the Festival, and let the people be gathered mid-morning."

Moses' Warning

60. Pharaoh then withdrew, orchestrated his scheme, then returned. **61.** Moses warned the magicians, "Woe to you! Do not fabricate a lie against God,[589] or He will wipe you out with a torment. Whoever fabricates ˹lies˺ is bound to fail." **62.** So the magicians disputed the matter among themselves, conversing privately. **63.** They concluded, "These two are only magicians who want to drive you out of your land with their magic, and do away with your most cherished traditions. **64.** So orchestrate your plan, then come forward in ˹perfect˺ ranks. And whoever prevails today will certainly be successful."

Moses Prevails

65. They said, "O Moses! Either you cast, or let us be the first to cast." **66.** Moses responded, "No, you go first." And suddenly their ropes and staffs appeared to him—by their magic—to be slithering. **67.** So Moses concealed fear within himself. **68.** We reassured ˹him˺, "Do not fear! It is certainly you who will prevail. **69.** Cast what is in your right hand, and it will swallow up what they have made, for what they have made is no more than a magic trick. And magicians can never succeed wherever they go."

Magicians Become Believers

70. So the magicians fell down in prostration, declaring, "We believe in the Lord of Aaron and Moses." **71.** Pharaoh threatened, "How dare you believe in him before I give you permission? He must be your master who taught you magic. I will certainly cut off your hands and feet on opposite sides, and crucify you on the trunks of palm trees.

---

588   *See* footnote for 17:101.
589   By saying that Moses' miracle is pure magic.

You will really see whose punishment is more severe and more lasting." 72. They responded, "By the One Who created us! We will never prefer you over the clear proofs that have come to us. So do whatever you want! Your authority only covers the ʿfleetingʾ life of this world. 73. Indeed, we have believed in our Lord so He may forgive our sins and that magic you have forced us to practice. And God is far superior ʿin rewardʾ and more lasting ʿin punishmentʾ."

Reward of Disbelievers and Believers

74. Whoever comes to their Lord as an evil-doer will certainly have Hell, where they can neither live nor die. 75. But whoever comes to Him as a believer, having done good, they will have the highest ranks: 76. the Gardens of Eternity, under which rivers flow, where they will stay forever. That is the reward of those who purify themselves.

Pharaoh's Doom

77. And We surely inspired Moses, ʿsayingʾ, "Leave with My servants ʿat nightʾ and strike a dry passage for them across the sea. Have no fear of being overtaken, nor be concerned ʿof drowningʾ." 78. Then Pharaoh pursued them with his soldiers—but how overwhelming were the waters that submerged them! 79. And ʿsoʾ Pharaoh led his people astray, and did not guide ʿthem rightlyʾ.

God's Favours to the Israelites

80. O Children of Israel! We saved you from your enemy, and made an appointment with you[590] on the right side of Mount Ṭûr, and sent down to you manna and quails,[591] 81. ʿsayingʾ, "Eat from the good things We have

provided for you, but do not transgress in them, or My wrath will befall you. And whoever My wrath befalls is certainly doomed. 82. But I am truly Most Forgiving to whoever repents, believes, and does good, then persists on ʿtrueʾ guidance."

The Golden Calf

83. ʿGod asked,ʾ "Why have you come with such haste ahead of your people, O Moses?"[592] 84. He replied, "They are close on my tracks. And I have hastened to You, my Lord, so You will be pleased." 85. God responded, "We have indeed tested your people in your absence, and the Sâmiri[593] has led them astray." 86. So Moses returned to his people, furious and sorrowful. He said, "O my people! Had your Lord not made you a good promise?[594] Has my absence been too long for you? Or have you wished for wrath from your Lord to befall you, so you broke your promise to me?"[595]

The Calf Worshippers

87. They argued, "We did not break our promise to you of our own free will, but we were made to carry the burden of the people's ʿgoldenʾ jewellery,[596] then we threw it ʿinto the fireʾ, and so did the Sâmiri." 88. Then he moulded for them an idol of a calf that made a lowing sound. They said, "This is your god and the god of Moses, but Moses forgot ʿwhere it wasʾ!" 89. Did they not see that it did not respond to them, nor could it protect or benefit them?

Aaron's Stance

90. Aaron had already warned them beforehand, "O my people! You are only being tested by this, for indeed your ʿone

---

590 i.e., your prophet to receive the Tablets for your guidance.
591 Manna (heavenly bread) and quails (chicken-like birds) sustained the children of Israel in the wilderness after they left Egypt.
592 Moses selected a delegation of seventy people from his community to go to Mount Ṭûr where it was appointed for him to receive the Tablets. On the way, he rushed for the appointment with God, arriving before the delegation.
593 The Sâmiri, or the man from Samaria, was a hypocrite who led the Children of Israel into idol-worship.
594 To reveal the Torah for their guidance.
595 To worship God alone until Moses returned with the Tablets.
596 The jewellery they borrowed from their Egyptian neighbours before they fled Egypt.

true' Lord is the Most Compassionate. So follow me and obey my orders." **91.** They replied, "We will not cease to worship it until Moses returns to us." **92.** Moses scolded 'his brother', "O Aaron! What prevented you, when you saw them going astray, **93.** from following after me? How could you disobey my orders?"[597] **94.** Aaron pleaded, "O son of my mother! Do not seize me by my beard or 'the hair of' my head. I really feared that you would say, 'You have caused division among the Children of Israel, and did not observe my word.'"

The Sâmiri's Punishment

95. Moses then asked, "What did you think you were doing, O Sâmiri?" **96.** He said, "I saw what they did not see, so I took a handful 'of dust' from the hoof-prints of 'the horse of' the messenger-angel 'Gabriel' then cast it 'on the moulded calf'. This is what my lower-self tempted me into."[598] **97.** Moses said, "Go away then! And for 'the rest of your' life you will surely be crying, 'Do not touch 'me'!'[599] Then you will certainly have a fate[600] that you cannot escape. Now look at your god to which you have been devoted: we will burn it up, then scatter it in the sea completely." **98.** 'Then Moses addressed his people,' "Your only god is God, there is no god 'worthy of worship' except Him. He encompasses everything in 'His' knowledge."

The Deniers of the Quran

99. This is how We relate to you 'O Prophet' some of the stories of the past. And We have certainly granted you a Reminder[601] from Us. **100.** Whoever turns away from it will surely bear the burden 'of sin' on the Day of Judgment, **101.** suffering its consequences forever. What an evil burden they will carry on Judgment Day! **102.** 'Beware of' the Day the Trumpet will be blown,[602] and We will gather the wicked on that Day blue-faced 'from horror and thirst'.[603] **103.** They will whisper among themselves, "You stayed no more than ten days 'on the earth'." **104.** We know best what they will say—the most reasonable of them will say, "You stayed no more than a day."

Mountains on Judgment Day

105. And 'if' they ask you 'O Prophet' about the mountains, 'then' say, "My Lord will wipe them out completely, **106.** leaving the earth level and bare, **107.** with neither depressions nor elevations to be seen."

People on Judgment Day

108. On that Day all will follow the caller 'for assembly', 'and' none will dare to deviate. All voices will be hushed before the Most Compassionate. Only whispers[604] will be heard. **109.** On that Day no intercession will be of any benefit, except by those granted permission by the Most Compassionate and whose words are agreeable to Him. **110.** He 'fully' knows what is ahead of them and what is behind them,[605] but they cannot encompass

---

597 Moses' orders are mentioned in 7:142.
598 This verse could also be translated as follows: "I had an insight which they did not have, then grasped some knowledge from the messenger 'Moses', but 'later' threw it away. This is what my lower-self tempted me to do." According to many Quran commentators, while Moses and the Children of Israel were crossing the sea to escape abuse by Pharaoh and his people, the Sâmiri saw Gabriel on a horse leading the way, and every time the horse touched the ground, it turned green. So the Sâmiri took a handful of dust from the hoof-prints of the horse, and later tossed it at the calf so it started to make a lowing sound.
599 Meaning, alienated in the dessert, away from the people.
600 lit., destined time.
601 The Quran.
602 See footnote for 18:99.
603 This can also mean "blind."
604 This can also mean "footsteps."
605 God fully knows what fate awaits them and what they did in the world.

Him in 'their' knowledge.[606] **111.** And all faces will be humbled before the Ever-Living, All-Sustaining. And those burdened with wrongdoing will be in loss. **112.** But whoever does good and is a believer will have no fear of being wronged or denied 'their reward'.

The Quran

113. And so We have sent it down as an Arabic Quran and varied the warnings in it, so perhaps they will shun evil or it may cause them to be mindful. **114.** Exalted is God, the True King! Do not rush to recite 'a revelation of' the Quran 'O Prophet' before it is 'properly' conveyed to you,[607] and pray, "My Lord! Increase me in knowledge."

Satan vs. Adam

115. And indeed, We once made a covenant with Adam, but he forgot, and 'so' We did not find determination in him. **116.** And 'remember' when We said to the angels, "Prostrate before Adam," so they all did—but not *Iblîs*,[608] who refused 'arrogantly'. **117.** So We cautioned, "O Adam! This is surely an enemy to you and to your wife. So do not let him drive you both out of Paradise, for you 'O Adam' would then suffer 'hardship'. **118.** Here it is guaranteed that you will never go hungry or unclothed, **119.** nor will you 'ever' suffer from thirst or 'the sun's' heat."[609]

The Temptation

120. But Satan whispered to him, saying, "O Adam! Shall I show you the Tree of Immortality and a kingdom that does not fade away?" **121.** So they both ate from the tree and then their nakedness was exposed to them, prompting them to cover themselves with leaves from Paradise. So Adam dis-

obeyed his Lord, and 'so' lost his way.[610] **122.** Then his Lord chose him 'for His grace', accepted his repentance, and guided him 'rightly'.

The Fall

123. God said, "Descend, both of you, from here together 'with Satan' as enemies to each other. Then when guidance comes to you from Me, whoever follows My guidance will neither go astray 'in this life' nor suffer 'in the next'. **124.** But whoever turns away from My Reminder will certainly have a miserable life,[611] then We will raise them up blind on the Day of Judgment." **125.** They will cry, "My Lord! Why have you raised me up blind, although I used to see?" **126.** God will respond, "It is so, just as Our revelations came to you and you neglected them, so Today you are neglected." **127.** This is how We reward whoever transgresses and does not believe in the revelations of their Lord. And the punishment of the Hereafter is far more severe and more lasting.

Warning to Meccan Pagans

128. Is it not yet clear to them how many peoples We destroyed before them, whose ruins they still pass by? Surely in this are signs for people of sound judgment. **129.** Had it not been for a prior decree from your Lord[612] 'O Prophet' and a term already set, their 'instant' doom would have been inevitable.

Advice to the Prophet

130. So be patient 'O Prophet' with what they say. And glorify the praises of your Lord before sunrise and before sunset, and glorify Him in the hours of the night and

---

606   Or "... they cannot encompass His knowledge."
607   The Prophet was eager to recite the Quran while it was being revealed to him through the angel Gabriel. So he was told that his memorization was guaranteed once the verses were properly delivered to him.
608   *See* footnote for 2:34.
609   There is no sun or cold weather in Paradise, only light. *See* 76:13.
610   Unlike the Bible (Genesis 3), the Quran does not blame Eve for Adam's fall from the Garden.
611   The Reminder is another name for the Quran.
612   That He will delay their judgment until the Hereafter.

at both ends of the day,[613] so that you may be pleased 'with the reward'. **131.** Do not let your eyes crave what We have allowed some of the disbelievers to enjoy; the 'fleeting' splendour of this worldly life, which We test them with. But your Lord's provision 'in the Hereafter' is far better and more lasting. **132.** Bid your people to pray, and be diligent in 'observing' it. We do not ask you to provide. It is We Who provide for you. And the ultimate outcome is 'only' for 'the people of' righteousness.

Warning to the Pagans

133. They demand, "If only he could bring us a sign from his Lord!"[614] Have they not 'already' received a confirmation of what is in earlier Scriptures?[615] **134.** Had We destroyed them with a torment before this 'Prophet came', they would have surely argued, "Our Lord! If only You had sent us a messenger, we would have followed Your revelations before being humiliated and put to shame." **135.** Say 'to them, O Prophet', "Each 'of us' is waiting, so keep waiting! You will soon know who is on the Straight Path and is 'rightly' guided."

21. The Prophets *(Al-Anbiyâ')*

Like the previous chapter, this is another Meccan chapter that aims at reassuring the Prophet by reminding him of God's grace and support to His prophets, including Abraham, Job, Jonah, Zachariah, and Jesus. The Prophet is said to be sent as a mercy to the whole world (verse 107). Warnings of the horrors of Judgment Day are dispersed throughout the chapter and are carried over to the next chapter.

In the Name of God—the Most Compassionate, Most Merciful

Indifference to the Truth

1. 'The time of' people's judgment has drawn near, yet they are heedlessly turning away. **2.** Whatever new reminder comes to them from their Lord, they only listen to it jokingly, **3.** with their hearts 'totally' distracted. The evildoers would converse secretly, 'saying,' "Is this 'one' not human like yourselves? Would you fall for 'this' witchcraft, even though you can 'clearly' see?" **4.** The Prophet responded, "My Lord 'fully' knows every word spoken in the heavens and the

earth. For He is the All-Hearing, All-Knowing." **5.** Yet they say, "This 'Quran' is a set of confused dreams! No, he has fabricated it! No, he must be a poet! So let him bring us a 'tangible' sign like those 'prophets' sent before." **6.** Not a 'single' society We destroyed before them ever believed 'after receiving the signs'. Will these 'pagans' then believe?

Human, Not Angelic Messengers

7. We did not send 'messengers' before you 'O Prophet' except mere men inspired by

---

613 This verse refers to the times of the five daily prayers.
614 The pagans of Mecca were not satisfied with a literary miracle in the form of the Quran, so they asked for a tangible miracle (*see* 17:90-91) similar to the staff of Moses.
615 This either refers to the Biblical stories confirmed by the Quran or the prophecies of Muḥammad in the Bible. Some Muslim scholars cite Deuteronomy 18:15-18 and 33:2, Isaiah 42, and John 14:16 as examples of the description of Prophet Muḥammad in the Bible. However, Bible scholars interpret these verses differently.

Us. If you ʿpolytheistsʾ do not know ʿthis already', then ask those who have knowledge ʿof the Scripturesʾ. **8.** We did not give those messengers ʿsupernaturalʾ bodies that did not need food, nor were they immortal. **9.** Then We fulfilled Our promise to them, saving them along with whoever We willed and destroying the transgressors.

Reasoning with Meccan Pagans

10. We have surely revealed to you a Book, in which there is glory for you. Will you not then understand? **11.** ʿImagineʾ how many societies of wrongdoers We have destroyed, raising up other people after them! **12.** When the wrongdoers sensed ʿthe arrival ofʾ Our torment, they started to run away from their cities. **13.** ʿThey were told,ʾ "Do not run away! Return to your luxuries and your homes, so you may be questioned ʿabout your fateʾ." **14.** They cried, "Woe to us! We have surely been wrongdoers." **15.** They kept repeating their cry until We mowed them down, ʿleaving themʾ lifeless.[616]

Divine Amusement?

16. We did not create the heavens and the earth and everything in between for sport. **17.** Had We intended to take ʿsomeʾ amusement, We could have found it in Our presence, if that had been Our Will. **18.** In fact, We hurl the truth against falsehood, leaving it crushed, and it quickly vanishes. And woe be to you for what you claim![617] **19.** To Him belong all those in the heavens and the earth. And those nearest to Him are not too proud

to worship Him, nor do they tire. **20.** They glorify ʿHimʾ day and night, never wavering.

False Gods

21. Or have they taken gods from the earth, who can raise the dead? **22.** Had there been other gods besides God in the heavens or the earth, both ʿrealmsʾ would have surely been corrupted. So Glorified is God, Lord of the Throne, far above what they claim. **23.** He cannot be questioned about what He does, but they will ʿallʾ be questioned. **24.** Or have they taken other gods besides Him? Say, ʿO Prophet,ʾ "Show ʿmeʾ your proof. Here is ʿthe Quran,ʾ the Reminder for those with me; along with ʿearlier Scriptures,ʾ the Reminder for those before me."[618] But most of them do not know the truth, so they turn away. **25.** We never sent a messenger before you ʿO Prophetʾ without revealing to him: "There is no god ʿworthy of worshipʾ except Me, so worship Me ʿaloneʾ."

A Pagan Claim

26. And they say, "The Most Compassionate has offspring!"[619] Glory be to Him! In fact, those ʿangelsʾ are only ʿHisʾ honoured servants, **27.** who do not speak until He has spoken, ʿonlyʾ acting at His command. **28.** He ʿfullyʾ knows what is ahead of them and what is behind them. They do not intercede except for whom He approves, and they tremble in awe of Him. **29.** Whoever of them were to say, "I am a god besides Him," they would be rewarded with Hell by Us. This is how We reward the wrongdoers.

Miracles in the Universe

30. Do the disbelievers not realize that the heavens and earth were ʿonceʾ one mass

---

616 lit., extinguished like ashes.
617 That God has a partner and children.
618 The Prophet is ordered to challenge the pagans to produce logical and scriptural proofs for the existence of other gods beside God. The verses then argue that if there is more than one god, the different gods would have fought among themselves for domination, and the whole universe would have been ruined. The Quran, the Torah, and the Gospel are all in agreement that there is only One God.
619 Some pagans claimed that the angels are God's daughters.

then We split them apart?[620] And We created from water every living thing. Will they not then believe? **31.** And We have placed firm mountains upon the earth so it does not shake with them, and made in it broad pathways so they may find their way. **32.** And We have made the sky a well-protected canopy, still they turn away from its signs.[621] **33.** And He is the One Who created the day and the night, the sun and the moon—each travelling in an orbit.

Fleeting World

34. We have not granted immortality to any human before you 'O Prophet': so if you die, will they live forever? **35.** Every soul will taste death. And We test you 'O humanity' with good and evil as a trial, then to Us you will 'all' be returned.

Warning to the Polytheists

36. When the disbelievers see you 'O Prophet', they only make fun of you, 'saying,' "Is this the one who speaks 'ill' of your gods?" while they disbelieve at the mention of the Most Compassionate. **37.** Humankind is made of haste. I will soon show you My signs, so do not ask Me to hasten them. **38.** They ask 'the believers', "When will this threat come to pass if what you say is true?" **39.** If only the disbelievers knew that a time will come when they will not be able to keep the Fire off their faces or backs, nor will they be helped. **40.** In fact, the Hour will take them by surprise, leaving them stunned. So they will not be able to avert it, nor will it be delayed from them. **41.** 'Other' messengers had already been ridiculed before you 'O Prophet', but those who mocked them were overtaken by what they used to ridicule.

Questions to the Pagans

42. Ask 'them, O Prophet,' "Who can defend you by day or by night against the Most Compassionate?" Still they turn away from the remembrance of their Lord. **43.** Or do they have gods—other than Us—that can protect them? They cannot 'even' protect themselves, nor will they be aided against Us. **44.** In fact, We have allowed enjoyment for these 'Meccans' and their forefathers for such a long time 'that they took it for granted'. Do they not see that We gradually reduce 'their' land from its borders? Is it they who will then prevail?

Warning of Torment

45. Say, 'O Prophet,' "I warn you only by revelation." But the deaf cannot hear the call when they are warned! **46.** If they were touched by even a breath of your Lord's torment, they would certainly cry, "Woe to us! We have really been wrongdoers."

Divine Justice

47. We will set up the scales of justice on the Day of Judgment, so no soul will be wronged in the least. And 'even' if a deed is the weight of a mustard seed, We will bring it forth. And sufficient are We as a 'vigilant' Reckoner.

The Torah

48. Indeed, We granted Moses and Aaron the Decisive Authority—a light and a reminder for the righteous, **49.** who are in awe of their Lord without seeing Him,[622] and are fearful of the Hour.

The Quran

50. And this 'Quran' is a blessed reminder which We have revealed. Will you 'pagans' then deny it?

---

620 This probably refers to the event commonly known as the Big Bang, according to some modern scholars. And God knows best.

621 The signs of the sky include the galaxies, planets, stars, etc., all of which have an orbit. Our planet orbits the sun, the sun orbits the Milky Way Galaxy, and the Milky Way Galaxy orbits the Virgo Supercluster, etc.

622 This can also mean that they are in awe of their Lord as much in private as they are in public.

Prophet Abraham

51. And indeed, We had granted Abraham sound judgment early on, for We knew him well ʿto be worthy of itʾ. **52.** ʿRememberʾ when he questioned his father and his people, "What are these statues to which you are so devoted?" **53.** They replied, "We found our forefathers worshipping them." **54.** He responded, "Indeed, you and your forefathers have been clearly astray." **55.** They asked, "Have you come to us with the truth, or is this a joke?" **56.** He replied, "In fact, your Lord is the Lord of the heavens and the earth, Who created them ʿbothʾ. And to that I bear witness." **57.** ʿThen he said to himself,ʾ "By God! I will surely plot against your idols after you have turned your backs and gone away." **58.** So he smashed them into pieces, except the biggest of them, so they might turn to it ʿfor answersʾ.

His People's Reaction

59. They protested, "Who dared do this to our gods? It must be an evildoer!" **60.** Some said, "We heard a young man, called Abraham, speaking ʿillʾ of them." **61.** They demanded, "Bring him before the eyes of the people, so that they may witness ʿhis trialʾ." **62.** They asked, "Was it you who did this to our gods, O Abraham?" **63.** He replied ʿsarcasticallyʾ, "No, this one—the biggest of them—did it! So ask them, if they can talk!" **64.** So they came back to their senses, saying ʿto one anotherʾ, "You yourselves are truly the wrongdoers!" **65.** Then they ʿquicklyʾ regressed to their ʿoriginalʾ mindset, ʿarguing,ʾ "You already know that those ʿidolsʾ cannot talk." **66.** He rebuked ʿthemʾ, "Do you then worship—instead of God—what can neither benefit nor harm you in any way? **67.** Shame on you and whatever you worship instead of God! Do you not have

any sense?" **68.** They concluded, "Burn him up to avenge your gods, if you must act."

Abraham Prevails

69. We ordered, "O fire! Be cool and safe for Abraham!"[623] **70.** They had sought to harm him, but We made them the worst losers. **71.** Then We delivered him, along with Lot, to the land We had showered with blessings for all people.[624] **72.** And We blessed him with Isaac ʿas a sonʾ and Jacob ʿas a grandsonʾ, as an additional favour—making all of them righteous. **73.** We ʿalsoʾ made them leaders, guiding by Our command, and inspired them to do good deeds, establish prayer, and pay alms-tax. And they were devoted to Our worship.

Prophet Lot

74. And to Lot We gave wisdom and knowledge, and delivered him from the society engrossed in shameful practices. They were certainly an evil, rebellious people. **75.** And We admitted him into Our mercy, ʿforʾ he was truly one of the righteous.

Prophet Noah

76. And ʿrememberʾ when Noah had cried out to Us earlier, so We responded to him and delivered him and his family[625] from the great distress. **77.** And We made him prevail over those who had rejected Our signs. They were truly an evil people, so We drowned them all.

Prophet David and Prophet Solomon

78. And ʿrememberʾ when David and Solomon passed judgment regarding the crops ruined ʿat nightʾ by someone's sheep, and We were witness to their judgments. **79.** We guided ʿyoungʾ Solomon to a fairer settle-

---

623 It is reported in a *ḥadîth* collected by Bukhâri that Abraham said, while being thrown into the fire, "God ʿaloneʾ is sufficient ʿas an aidʾ for us and ʿHeʾ is the best Protector."

624 Abraham and his nephew, Lot, migrated from Babel, Iraq to Jerusalem.

625 i.e., the believers in his family.

ment,[626] and granted each of them wisdom and knowledge. We subjected the mountains as well as the birds to hymn ˹Our praises˺ along with David. It is We Who did ˹it all˺. **80.** We taught him the art of making body armour to protect you in battle. Will you then be grateful? **81.** And to Solomon We subjected the raging winds, blowing by his command to the land We had showered with blessings. It is We Who know everything. **82.** And ˹We subjected˺ some jinn[627] that dived for him,[628] and performed other duties. It is We Who kept them in check.

Prophet Job

83. And ˹remember˺ when Job cried out to his Lord, "I have been touched with adversity,[629] and You are the Most Merciful of the merciful." **84.** So We answered his prayer and removed his adversity, and gave him back his family, twice as many, as a mercy from Us and a lesson for the ˹devoted˺ worshippers.

More Prophets

85. And ˹remember˺ Ishmael, Enoch, and Ẓul-Kifl.[630] They were all steadfast. **86.** We admitted them into Our mercy, for they were truly of the righteous.

Prophet Jonah

87. And ˹remember˺ when the Man of the Whale stormed off ˹from his city˺ in a rage, thinking We would not restrain him.[631] Then in the ˹veils of˺ darkness[632] he cried out, "There is no god ˹worthy of worship˺ except You. Glory be to You! I have certainly done wrong." **88.** So We answered his prayer and rescued him from anguish. And so do We save the ˹true˺ believers.

Prophet Zachariah

89. And ˹remember˺ when Zachariah cried out to his Lord, "My Lord! Do not leave me childless, though You are the Best of Successors."[633] **90.** So We answered his prayer, granted him John, and made his wife fertile. Indeed, they used to race in doing good, and call upon Us with hope and fear, totally humbling themselves before Us.

Prophet Jesus and His Mother

91. And ˹remember˺ the one who guarded her chastity, so We breathed into her through Our angel, ˹Gabriel,˺[634] making her and her son a sign for all peoples.

One Way

92. ˹O prophets!˺ Indeed, this religion of yours is ˹only˺ one, and I am your Lord, so worship Me ˹alone˺. **93.** Yet the people have divided it into sects. But to Us they will all

---

626 A man's flock of sheep strayed into another man's vineyard, eating and destroying all his produce. When the two men came to David for judgment, he ruled that the shepherd must give his animals to the vineyard owner in compensation for the damage. On their way out, the two men met young Solomon and the shepherd complained to him. Solomon discussed the case with his father, and suggested that the sheep should be kept with the man who lost his produce so he may benefit from their milk and wool, while the shepherd worked on the farm to restore it to its original state. Eventually the famer would take back his farm in perfect condition, and the sheep would be returned to the shepherd. David was impressed by his son's insight and approved his fair judgment immediately.

627 lit., devils.

628 The jinn dived to bring him pearls.

629 This refers to his loss of health, wealth, and children.

630 Scholars are in disagreement as to whether Ẓul-Kifl was a prophet or just a righteous man. Those who maintain that he was a prophet identify him with various Biblical prophets such as Ezekiel, Isaiah, and Obadiah.

631 Or "thinking We will let him get away with it." Jonah had been met with denial for many years. When he sensed the coming of God's torment, he abandoned his city without God's permission. Eventually, his people repented before the coming of the torment, and God accepted their repentance (see 10:98), whereas Jonah ended up in the belly of the whale (see 37:140-148).

632 The darkness of the night, the sea, and the belly of the whale.

633 Meaning, "You will be there for eternity after all pass away."

634 Gabriel breathed into the sleeves of Mary's garment so she conceived Jesus.

return. **94.** So whoever does good and is a believer will never be denied ˹the reward for˺ their striving, for We are recording it all.

The People of Hell

95. It is impossible for a society which We have destroyed to ever rise again, **96.** until ˹after˺ Gog and Magog have broken loose ˹from the barrier˺,[635] swarming down from every hill, **97.** ushering in the True Promise.[636] Then—behold!—the disbelievers will stare ˹in horror, crying,˺ "Oh, woe to us! We have truly been heedless of this. In fact, we have been wrongdoers." **98.** Certainly you ˹disbelievers˺ and whatever you worship instead of God will be the fuel of Hell.[637] You are ˹all˺ bound to enter it. **99.** Had those idols been ˹true˺ gods, they would not have entered it. And they will be there forever. **100.** In it they will groan, and will not be able to hear.

The People of Paradise

101. Surely those for whom We have destined the finest reward will be kept far away from Hell, **102.** not even hearing the slightest hissing from it. And they will delight forever in what their souls desire. **103.** The Supreme Horror ˹of that Day˺ will not disturb them, and the angels will greet them, ˹saying,˺ "This is your Day, which you have been promised." **104.** On that Day We will roll up the heavens like a scroll of writings. Just as We produced the first creation, ˹so˺ shall We reproduce it. That is a promise binding on Us. We truly uphold ˹Our promises˺! **105.** Surely, following the ˹heavenly˺ Record, We decreed in the Scriptures: "My righteous servants shall inherit the land."[638]

Advice for the Prophet

106. Surely this ˹Quran˺ is sufficient ˹as a reminder˺ for those devoted to worship. **107.** We have sent you ˹O Prophet˺ only as a mercy for the whole world. **108.** Say, "What has been revealed to me is this: 'Your God is only One God.' Will you then submit?" **109.** If they turn away, then say, "I have warned you all equally. I do not know if what you are threatened with is near or far. **110.** God surely knows what you say openly and whatever you hide. **111.** I do not know if this ˹delay˺ is possibly a test for you and an enjoyment for a while." **112.** ˹In the end,˺ the Prophet said, "My Lord! Judge ˹between us˺ in truth. And our Lord is the Most Compassionate, Whose help is sought against what you claim."[639]

22. The Pilgrimage *(Al-Ḥajj)*

This Medinian chapter takes its name from the passage that talks about pilgrimage rituals (verses 25-37), along with condemnations to the pagans for hindering the believers from reaching the Sacred House in Mecca. After fifteen years of persecution, here the believers receive the permission to fight back in self-defence (verse 39). Idolatry is condemned and the idols are rejected as pathetic, incapable of even creating a fly. In conclusion, the believers are told that they can achieve success through prayer and good deeds—a theme which extends to the beginning of the next chapter.

635   *See* 18:93-99.
636   i.e., the Final Hour.
637   *See* footnote for 43:57-58.
638   This refers to Psalm 37:29: "The righteous shall inherit the land." *See* footnote for 39:47.
639   Meaning, "We seek God's help against your claims that He has partners ˹in worship˺."

In the Name of God—the Most Compassionate, Most Merciful

The Horror of Judgment Day

1. O humanity! Fear your Lord, for the ˹violent˺ quaking at the Hour is surely a dreadful thing. 2. The Day you see it, every nursing mother will abandon what she is nursing, and every pregnant woman will deliver her burden ˹prematurely˺. And you will see people ˹as if they were˺ drunk, though they will not be drunk; but the torment of God is ˹terribly˺ severe.

Denying God's Might

3. ˹Still˺ there are some who dispute about God without knowledge, and follow every rebellious devil. 4. It has been decreed for such devils that whoever takes them as a guide will be misguided and led by them into the torment of the Blaze.

God's Power to Create

5. O humanity! If you are in doubt about the Resurrection, then ˹know that˺ We did create you[640] from dust, then from a sperm-drop,[641] then ˹developed you into˺ a clinging clot,[642] then a lump of flesh[643]—fully formed or unformed[644]—in order to demonstrate ˹Our power˺ to you. ˹Then˺ We settle whatever ˹embryo˺ We will in the womb for an appointed term, then bring you forth as infants, so that you may reach your prime. Some of you ˹may˺ die ˹young˺, while others are left to reach the most feeble stage of life so that they may know nothing after having known much. And you see the earth lifeless, but as soon as We send down rain upon it, it begins to stir ˹to life˺ and swell, producing every type of pleasant plant. 6. That is because God ˹alone˺ is the Truth, He ˹alone˺ gives life to the dead, and He ˹alone˺ is Most Capable of everything. 7. And certainly the Hour is coming, there is no doubt about it. And God will surely resurrect those in the graves.

Punishment of the Wicked

8. ˹Still˺ there are some who dispute about God without knowledge, guidance, or an enlightening scripture, 9. turning away ˹in pride˺ to lead ˹others˺ astray from God's Way. They will suffer disgrace in this world, and on the Day of Judgment We will make them taste the torment of burning. 10. ˹They will be told,˺ "This is ˹the reward˺ for what your hands have done. And God is never unjust to ˹His˺ creation."

Half-Hearted Worship

11. And there are some who worship God on the verge ˹of faith˺: if they are blessed with something good, they are content with it; but if they are afflicted with a trial, they relapse ˹into disbelief˺,[645] losing this world and the Hereafter. That is ˹truly˺ the clearest loss. 12. They call besides God what can neither harm nor benefit them. That is ˹truly˺ the farthest one can stray. 13. They invoke those whose worship leads to harm, not benefit. What an evil patron and what an evil associate!

Reward of True Believers

14. Indeed, God will admit those who believe and do good into Gardens, under which rivers flow. Surely God does what He wills.

---

640 Your father, Adam.
641 *Nutfah* refers to the union of male and female gametes (sperm and egg) which results in the zygote after fertilization.
642 *'Alaqah*, meaning the embryo resembles a leech.
643 *Muḍghah*, meaning it resembles a chewed morsel.
644 Fully formed or defected, evolving into a healthy embryo or ending in miscarriage.
645 lit., they tumble on their faces.

A Challenge to the Cynics

15. Whoever thinks that God will not help His Prophet in this world and the Hereafter, let them stretch out a rope to the ceiling and strangle themselves, then let them see if this plan will do away with ˹the cause of˺ their rage.[646]

The Sole Guide and Judge

16. And so We revealed this ˹Quran˺ as clear verses. And God certainly guides whoever He wills. **17.** Indeed, the believers, Jews, Sabians,[647] Christians, Magi,[648] and the polytheists—God will judge between them ˹all˺ on Judgment Day. Surely God is a Witness over all things.

Submission to the Almighty

18. Do you not see that to God bow down ˹in submission˺[649] all those in the heavens and all those on the earth, as well as the sun, the moon, the stars, the mountains, the trees, and ˹all˺ living beings, as well as many humans, while many are deserving of punishment. And whoever God disgraces, none can honour. Surely God does what He wills.

The Believers and Disbelievers

19. These are two opposing groups that disagree about their Lord: as for the disbelievers, garments of Fire will be cut out for them and boiling water will be poured over their heads, **20.** melting whatever is in their bel-lies, along with their skin. **21.** And awaiting them are maces of iron. **22.** Whenever they try to escape from Hell—out of anguish—they will be forced back into it, ˹and will be told,˺ "Taste the torment of burning!" **23.** ˹But˺ God will surely admit those who believe and do good into Gardens, under which rivers flow, where they will be adorned with bracelets of gold and pearls, and their clothing will be silk, **24.** for they have been guided to the best of speech, and they have been guided to the Commendable Path.[650]

Violating the Sacred Mosque[651]

25. Indeed, those who persist in disbelief and hinder ˹others˺ from the Way of God and from the Sacred Mosque[652]—which We have appointed for all people, residents and visitors alike—along with whoever intends to deviate by doing wrong in it,[653] We will cause them to taste a painful punishment.

The Pilgrimage

26. And ˹remember˺ when We assigned to Abraham the site of the House, ˹saying,˺ "Do not associate anything with Me ˹in worship˺ and purify My House for those who circle ˹the Ka'bah˺, stand ˹in prayer˺, and bow and prostrate themselves. **27.** Call ˹all˺ people to the pilgrimage.[654] They will come to you on foot and on every lean camel from every distant path, **28.** so they may obtain the benefits ˹in store˺ for them,[655] and pronounce the Name of God on appointed days

---

646 Meaning, no matter what the deniers do, God will never stop supporting His Prophet.
647 See footnote for 2:62.
648 Magi (singular: magus): Zoroastrians; fire-worshippers.
649 lit., prostrate. Meaning, all beings submit to His Will.
650 Another possible translation: "... and they have been guided to the Path of the Praiseworthy ˹God˺."
651 This was revealed after the pagans of Mecca had refused to let the Prophet and his companions proceed to the Sacred Mosque to perform the minor pilgrimage ('umrah), although they came all the way from Medina. Eventually, an agreement was made, stipulating that the Muslims return to Medina and come back the following year for 'umrah.
652 The Sacred Mosque is in Mecca.
653 Generally, intending to do wrong does not necessitate a punishment, unless the person acts upon it. But the Sacred Mosque is unique in that intending to sin in it is sufficient to bring punishment from God, unless the person repents.
654 According to Ibn Kathîr, Abraham said to God, "But my voice cannot reach all peoples." God responded, "You make the call, and We will deliver the invitation to all."
655 Spiritual benefits such as prayers, pilgrimage, and forgiveness of sins, as well as worldly benefits such as meeting Muslims from everywhere and trading.

over the sacrificial animals He has provided for them. So eat from their meat and feed the desperately poor. **29.** Then let them groom themselves,[656] fulfil their vows, and circle the Ancient House."

Total Devotion to God

30. That is so. And whoever honours the rituals of God, it is best for them in the sight of their Lord. The ʿmeat ofʾ cattle has been made lawful for you, except what has ʿalreadyʾ been recited to you.[657] So shun the impurity of idolatry, and shun words of falsehood. **31.** Be upright ʿin devotionʾ to God, associating none with Him ʿin worshipʾ. For whoever associates ʿothersʾ with God is like someone who has fallen from the sky and is either snatched away by birds or swept by the wind to a remote place. **32.** That is so. And whoever honours the symbols of God, it is certainly out of the piety of the heart. **33.** You may benefit from sacrificial animals for an appointed term,[658] then their place of sacrifice is at the Ancient House.

Good News for the Humble

34. For every community We appointed a rite of sacrifice so that they may pronounce the Name of God over the sacrificial animals He has provided for them. For your God is only One God, so submit yourselves to Him ʿaloneʾ. And give good news ʿO Prophetʾ to the humble: **35.** those whose hearts tremble at the remembrance of God, who patiently endure whatever may befall them, and who establish prayer and donate from what We have provided for them.

Purpose of Sacrificial Animals

36. We have made sacrificial camels ʿand cattleʾ among the symbols of God, in which there is ʿmuchʾ good for you. So pronounce the Name of God over them when they are lined up ʿfor sacrificeʾ. Once they have fallen ʿlifelessʾ on their sides, you may eat from their meat, and feed the needy—those who do not beg, and those who do. In this way We have subjected these ʿanimalsʾ to you so that you may be grateful. **37.** Neither their meat nor blood reaches God. Rather, it is your piety that reaches Him. This is how He has subjected them to you so that you may proclaim the greatness of God for what He has guided you to, and give good news to the good-doers.

Permission to Fight in Self-Defence

38. Indeed, God defends those who believe. Surely God does not like whoever is deceitful, ungrateful. **39.** Permission ʿto fight backʾ is ʿherebyʾ granted to those being fought, for they have been wronged.[659] And God is truly Most Capable of helping them ʿprevailʾ. **40.** ʿThey areʾ those who have been expelled from their homes for no reason other than proclaiming: "Our Lord is God." Had God not repelled ʿthe aggression ofʾ some people by means of others, destruction would have surely claimed monasteries, churches, synagogues, and mosques in which God's Name is often mentioned. God will certainly help those who stand up for Him. God is truly All-Powerful, Almighty. **41.** ʿThey areʾ those who, if established in the land by Us, would perform prayer, pay alms-tax, encourage what is good, and forbid what is evil. And with God rests the outcome of all affairs.

Warning to Meccan Pagans

42. If they deny you ʿO Prophetʾ, so did the people of Noah before them, as well as ʿthe

---

656 Shaving their hair, clipping nails, and taking a shower.
657 *See* 5:3.
658 Milking or riding them until the time for sacrifice.
659 For over thirteen years, Muslims had not been allowed to fight back against the brutality of the Meccan pagans, leading to the emigration of the Prophet and many of his companions to Medina. As the hostilities continued, this verse was later revealed allowing Muslims to fight back in self-defence.

tribes of 'Âd and Thamûd, **43.** the people of Abraham, the people of Lot, **44.** and the residents of Midian. And Moses was denied 'too'. But I delayed 'the fate of' the disbelievers 'until their appointed time' then seized them. And how severe was My response! **45.** Many are the societies We have destroyed for persisting in wrongdoing, leaving them in total ruin. 'Many are' also the abandoned wells and lofty palaces! **46.** Have they not travelled throughout the land so their hearts may reason, and their ears may listen? Indeed, it is not the eyes that are blind, but it is the hearts in the chests that grow blind. **47.** They challenge you 'O Prophet' to hasten the torment. And God will never fail in His promise. But a day with your Lord is indeed like a thousand years by your counting. **48.** Many are the societies whose end We delayed while they did wrong, then seized them. And to Me is the final return.

The Prophet's Duty

49. Say, 'O Prophet,' "O humanity! I am only sent to you with a clear warning. **50.** So those who believe and do good will have forgiveness and an honourable provision. **51.** But those who strive to discredit Our revelations, they will be the residents of the Hellfire."

Satan's Influence

52. Whenever We sent a messenger or a prophet before you 'O Prophet' and he recited 'Our revelations', Satan would influence 'people's understanding of' his recitation. But 'eventually' God would eliminate Satan's influence. Then God would 'firmly' establish His revelations. And God is All-Knowing, All-Wise. **53.** All that so He may make Satan's influence a trial for those 'hypocrites' whose hearts are sick and those 'disbelievers' whose hearts are hardened. Surely the wrongdoers are totally engrossed in opposition. **54.** 'This is' also so that those gifted with knowledge would know that this 'revelation' is the truth from your Lord, so they have faith in it, and so their hearts would submit humbly to it. And God surely guides the believers to the Straight Path. **55.** Yet the disbelievers will persist in doubt about this 'revelation' until the Hour takes them by surprise, or the torment of a terminating[660] Day comes to them.

Justice on Judgment Day

56. All authority on that Day is for God 'alone'.[661] He will judge between them. So those who believe and do good will be in the Gardens of Bliss. **57.** But those who disbelieve and deny Our revelations, it is they who will suffer a humiliating punishment. **58.** As for those who emigrate in the cause of God and then are martyred or die, God will indeed grant them a good provision. Surely God is the Best Provider. **59.** He will certainly admit them into a place they will be pleased with. For God is truly All-Knowing, Most Forbearing.

Divine Justice

60. That is so. And whoever retaliates in equivalence to the injury they have received, and then are wronged 'again', God will certainly help them. Surely God is Ever-Pardoning, All-Forgiving.

God's Power

61. That is because God causes the night to merge into the day, and the day into the night. Indeed, God is All-Hearing, All-Seeing. **62.** That is because God 'alone' is the Truth and what they invoke besides Him is falsehood, and God 'alone' is truly the Most High, All-Great. **63.** Do you not see that God sends down rain from the sky, then the earth becomes green? Surely God is Most Subtle, All-Aware. **64.** To

---

660 The Day 'of Judgment' is described as *'aqîm* (lit., barren) because it will terminate all forms of life on earth and no new day will be born.

661 God grants authority to some of His servants in this world, but none will have authority on Judgment Day except Him. *See* 3:26.

Him belongs whatever is in the heavens and whatever is on the earth. God ˈaloneˈ is truly the Self-Sufficient, Praiseworthy.

God's Grace

65. Do you not see that God has subjected to you[662] whatever is in the earth as well as the ships ˈthatˈ sail through the sea by His command? He keeps the sky from falling down on the earth except by His permission. Surely God is Ever Gracious and Most Merciful to humanity. **66.** And He is the Qne Who gave you life, then will cause you to die, and then will bring you back to life. ˈButˈ surely humankind is ever ungrateful.

One Message, Different Laws

67. For every community We appointed a code[663] of life to follow.[664] So do not let them dispute with you ˈO Prophetˈ in this matter. And invite ˈallˈ to your Lord, for you are truly on the Right Guidance. **68.** But if they argue with you, then say, "God knows best what you do." **69.** God will judge between you ˈallˈ on Judgment Day regarding your differences. **70.** Do you not know that God ˈfullyˈ knows whatever is in the heavens and the earth? Surely it is all ˈwrittenˈ in a Record. That is certainly easy for God.

Almighty God or False Gods?

71. Yet they worship besides God that for which He has sent down no authority, and of which they have no knowledge. The wrongdoers will have no helper. **72.** Whenever Our clear revelations are recited to them, you ˈO Prophetˈ recognize rage on the faces of the disbelievers, as if they are going to snap at those who recite Our revelations to them. Say, "Shall I inform you of something far more enraging than that? ˈIt isˈ the Fire with which God has threatened those who disbelieve. What an evil destination!"

The Fly Challenge

73. O humanity! A lesson is set forth, so listen to it ˈcarefullyˈ: those ˈidolsˈ you invoke besides God can never create ˈso much asˈ a fly, even if they ˈallˈ were to come together for that. And if a fly were to snatch anything away from them, they cannot ˈevenˈ retrieve it from the fly. How powerless are those who invoke and those invoked![665] **74.** They have not shown God the reverence He deserves. Surely God is All-Powerful, Almighty.

Divine Choice

75. God selects messengers from both angels and people, for God is truly All-Hearing, All-Seeing. **76.** He knows what is ahead of them and what is behind them. And to God ˈallˈ matters will be returned ˈfor judgmentˈ.

Advice to the Believers

77. O believers! Bow down, prostrate yourselves, worship your Lord, and do ˈwhat isˈ good so that you may be successful. **78.** Strive for ˈthe cause ofˈ God in the way He deserves, for ˈit isˈ He ˈWhoˈ has chosen you, and laid upon you no hardship in the religion—the way of your forefather Abraham. ˈIt is Godˈ Who named you ‘the ones who submit’[666] ˈin theˈ earlier ˈScripturesˈ and in this ˈQuranˈ, so that the Messenger may be a witness over you, and that you may be witnesses over humanity. So establish prayer, pay alms-tax, and hold fast to God. He ˈaloneˈ is your Guardian. What an excellent Guardian, and what an excellent Helper!

---

662 For your service.
663 All prophets came with the same message: have faith in one God and do good. But each faith-community had their own law.
664 The Muslim code of life is called *Sharia*, which means a "path." For more information, *see* the Introduction.
665 Another possible translation: "How weak are the seekers (i.e., the idols) and the sought (i.e., the fly)!"
666 i.e., Muslims.

23. The Believers *(Al-Mu'minûn)*

This Meccan chapter emphasizes that the believers are guaranteed success (verse 1), whereas the disbelievers are bound to fail (verse 117). Like the previous chapter, it makes the case for God's oneness as well as His power to create and resurrect. The last part is dedicated to the judgment of the believers and the disbelievers, focusing on the fate of the wicked who abuse the believers. This theme extends to the next chapter.

In the Name of God—the Most Compassionate, Most Merciful

The True Believers

1. Successful indeed are the believers: 2. those who humble themselves in prayer; 3. those who avoid idle talk; 4. those who pay alms-tax;[667] 5. those who guard their chastity[668] 6. except with their wives or those ˹bondwomen˺ in their possession,[669] for then they are free from blame, 7. but whoever seeks beyond that are the transgressors; 8. ˹the believers are also˺ those who are true to their trusts and covenants; 9. and those who are ˹properly˺ observant of their prayers. 10. These are the ones who will be awarded 11. Paradise as their own.[670] They will be there forever.

The Creation of Humans

12. And indeed, We created humankind[671] from an extract of clay, 13. then placed each ˹human˺ as a sperm-drop[672] in a secure place, 14. then We developed the drop into a clinging clot, then developed the clot into a lump ˹of flesh˺, then developed bones out of this lump, then clothed the bones with flesh, then We brought it into being as a new creation.[673] So Blessed is God, the Best of Creators. 15. After that you will surely die, 16. then on the Day of Judgment you will be resurrected.

God's Power

17. And indeed, We created above you seven levels ˹of heaven˺. We are never unmindful of ˹Our˺ creation. 18. We send down rain from the sky in perfect measure, causing it to soak into the earth. And We are surely able to take it away. 19. With it We produce for you gardens of palm trees and grapevines, in which there are abundant fruits, and from which you may eat, 20. as well as ˹olive˺ trees which grow at Mount Sinai, providing oil and a condiment to eat. 21. And there is certainly a lesson for you in cattle, from whose bellies We give you ˹milk˺ to drink, and in them are many other benefits for you, and from them you may eat. 22. And you are carried upon ˹some of˺ them and upon ships.

Prophet Noah

23. Indeed, We sent Noah to his people. He declared, "O my people! Worship God ˹alone˺. You have no god other than Him. Will you not then fear ˹Him˺?" 24. But the disbelieving chiefs of his people said ˹to the masses˺, "This is only a human like you, who wants to be superior to you. Had God willed, He could have easily sent down angels ˹instead˺. We have never heard of this in ˹the history of˺ our forefathers. 25. He is simply insane, so bear with him for a while."[674]

---

667 *Zakâh* means purification and growth. Paying alms-tax and charity are forms of purifying one's wealth.
668 lit., private parts.
669 *See* footnote for 4:3.
670 *Al-Firdaws*, the highest place in Paradise.
671 Adam.
672 *See* footnote for 22:5.
673 This happens when the spirit is breathed into the embryo.
674 So he may recover from his "madness" or die.

The Flood

26. Noah prayed, "My Lord! Help me, because they have denied ˹me˺." **27.** So We inspired him: "Build the Ark under Our ˹watchful˺ Eyes and directions. Then when Our command comes and the oven bursts ˹with water˺,[675] take on board a pair from every species along with your family—except those against whom the decree ˹to drown˺ has already been passed. And do not plead with Me for those who have done wrong, for they will surely be drowned." **28.** Then when you and those with you have settled in the Ark, say, "All praise is for God, Who saved us from the wrongdoing people." **29.** And pray, "My Lord! Allow me a blessed landing, for You are the best accommodator." **30.** Surely in this are lessons.[676] And We ˹always˺ put ˹people˺ to the test.

Prophet Hûd[677]

31. Then We raised another generation after them, **32.** and sent to them a messenger from among themselves, ˹declaring,˺ "Worship God ˹alone˺. You have no god other than Him. Will you not then fear ˹Him˺?" **33.** But the chiefs of his people—who disbelieved, denied the meeting ˹with God˺ in the Hereafter, and were spoiled by the worldly luxuries We had provided for them—said ˹to the masses˺, "This is only a human like you. He eats what you eat, and drinks what you drink. **34.** And if you ˹ever˺ obey a human like yourselves, then you would certainly be losers. **35.** Does he promise you that once you are dead and reduced to dust and bones, you will be brought forth ˹alive˺? **36.** Impossible, simply impossible is what you are promised! **37.** There is nothing beyond our worldly life. We die, others are born, and none will be resurrected. **38.** He is no more than a man who has fabricated a lie about God, and we will never believe in him."

The Blast

39. The messenger prayed, "My Lord! Help me, because they have denied ˹me˺." **40.** God responded, "Soon they will be truly regretful." **41.** Then the ˹mighty˺ blast overtook them with justice, and We reduced them to rubble. So away with the wrongdoing people!

More Prophets

42. Then We raised other generations after them. **43.** No people can advance their doom, nor can they delay it. **44.** Then We sent Our messengers in succession: whenever a messenger came to his people, they denied him. So We destroyed them, one after the other, reducing them to ˹cautionary˺ tales. So away with the people who refuse to believe!

Prophet Moses and Prophet Aaron

45. Then We sent Moses and his brother Aaron with Our signs[678] and compelling proof **46.** to Pharaoh and his chiefs, but they behaved arrogantly and were a tyrannical people. **47.** They argued, "Will we believe in two humans, like ourselves, whose people are slaves to us?" **48.** So they rejected them both, and ˹so˺ were among those destroyed. **49.** And We certainly gave Moses the Scripture, so perhaps his people would be ˹rightly˺ guided.

Prophet Jesus and His Mother

50. And We made the son of Mary and his mother a sign, and gave them refuge on high ground—a ˹suitable˺ place for rest with flowing water.

---

675 Noah was given a signal that once the water gushes out of a particular oven then the Flood is about to begin. It can also be translated as: "The fountains of the earth gushed forth."

676 lit., signs.

677 Some scholars believe this passage refers to Prophet Ṣâliḥ.

678 The nine signs are: the staff, the hand (both mentioned in 20:17-22), famine, shortage of crops, floods, locusts, lice, frogs, and blood (all mentioned in 7:130-133).

One Way

51. O messengers! Eat from what is good and lawful, and act righteously. Indeed, I fully know what you do. **52.** Surely this religion of yours is ˹only˺ one, and I am your Lord, so fear Me ˹alone˺. **53.** Yet the people have divided it into different sects, each rejoicing in what they have. **54.** So leave them ˹O Prophet˺ in their heedlessness for a while. **55.** Do they think, since We provide them with wealth and children, **56.** that We hasten to ˹honour˺ them ˹with˺ all kinds of good? No! They are not aware.

The True Believers

57. Surely those who tremble in awe of their Lord, **58.** and who believe in the revelations of their Lord, **59.** and who associate none with their Lord, **60.** and who do whatever ˹good˺ they do with their hearts fearful, ˹knowing˺ that they will return to their Lord[679]— **61.** it is they who race to do good deeds, always taking the lead. **62.** We never require of any soul more than what it can afford. And with Us is a record which speaks the truth. None will be wronged.

The Disbelievers

63. But the hearts of those ˹who disbelieve˺ are oblivious to ˹all of˺ this,[680] and they have other ˹evil˺ deeds, opposite to this, in which they are engrossed. **64.** But as soon as We seize their elite with torment, they start to cry for help. **65.** ˹They will be told,˺ "Do not cry for help today. Surely you will never be saved from Us. **66.** Indeed, My revelations were recited to you, but you used to back away ˹in disgust˺, **67.** boasting of the Sacred House, and babbling ˹nonsense about the Quran˺ by night."

Why the Denial?

68. Is it because they have never contemplated the Word ˹of God˺? Or ˹because˺ there has come to them something that did not come to their forefathers? **69.** Or ˹because˺ they failed to recognize their Messenger, and so they denied him? **70.** Or ˹because˺ they say, "He is insane?" In fact, he has come to them with the truth, but most of them are resentful of the truth. **71.** Had the truth followed their desires,[681] the heavens, the earth, and all those in them would have certainly been corrupted. In fact, We have brought them ˹the means to˺ their glory, but they turn away from it. **72.** Or ˹is it because˺ you ˹O Prophet˺ are asking them for tribute? But the reward of your Lord is best, for He is the Best Provider. **73.** And surely you are calling them to the Straight Path, **74.** but those who disbelieve in the Hereafter are certainly deviating from that Path.

Those Persisting in Denial

75. ˹Even˺ if We had mercy on them and removed their affliction,[682] they would still persist in their transgression, wandering blindly. **76.** And We have already seized them with torment, but they never humbled themselves to their Lord, nor did they ˹submissively˺ appeal ˹to Him˺. **77.** But as soon as We open for them a gate of severe punishment, they will be utterly desperate.

Ingratitude to the Almighty

78. He is the One Who created for you hearing, sight, and intellect. ˹Yet˺ you hardly give any thanks. **79.** And He is the One Who has dispersed you ˹all˺ over the earth, and to Him you will ˹all˺ be gathered. **80.** And He is the One Who gives life and causes death, and to Him belongs the

---

679 It is reported in an authentic narration collected by At-Tirmiẓi that 'Âishah, the Prophet's wife, asked him if this verse refers to those who steal or drink ˹alcohol˺. The Prophet answered, "No, it refers to those who pray, fast, and donate, but are afraid that their deeds are rejected because they are not good enough." Then he recited the last part of the verse: "It is they who race to do good deeds, always taking the lead."
680 This refers to the believers' good deeds mentioned in 23:57-62.
681 Their desire that the universe has more than one God. See 21:22.
682 This refers to famine which affected the pagans of Mecca.

alternation of the day and night. Will you not then understand? **81.** But they ʾjustʾ say what their predecessors said. **82.** They said, "Once we are dead and reduced to dust and bones, will we really be resurrected? **83.** We have already been promised this, as well as our forefathers earlier. This is nothing but ancient fables!"

Almighty God

84. Ask ʾthem, O Prophetʾ, "To whom belong the earth and all those on it, if you ʾreallyʾ know?" **85.** They will reply, "To God!" Say, "Why are you not then mindful?" **86.** ʾAndʾ ask ʾthemʾ, "Who is the Lord of the seven heavens and the Lord of the Mighty Throne?" **87.** They will reply, "God." Say, "Will you not then fear ʾHimʾ?" **88.** Ask ʾthem also,ʾ "In Whose Hands is the authority over all things, protecting ʾallʾ while none can protect against Him, if you ʾreallyʾ know?" **89.** They will reply, "God." Say, "How are you then so deluded?" **90.** In fact, We have brought them the truth, and they are certainly liars.

One True God

91. God has never had ʾanyʾ offspring, nor is there any god besides Him. Otherwise, each god would have taken away what he created, and they would have tried to dominate one another. Glorified is God above what they claim! **92.** ʾHe is theʾ Knower of the seen and unseen. Exalted is He above what they associate ʾwith Himʾ.

Advice to the Prophet

93. Say, ʾO Prophet,ʾ "My Lord! Should You show me what they[683] are threatened with, **94.** then, my Lord, do not count me among the wrongdoing people." **95.** We

are indeed able to show you what We have threatened them with. **96.** Respond to evil with what is best. We know well what they claim.[684] **97.** And say, "My Lord! I seek refuge in You from the temptations of the devils. **98.** And I seek refuge in You, my Lord, that they ʾevenʾ come near me."

Too Late for the Wicked

99. When death approaches any of them, they cry, "My Lord! Let me go back, **100.** so I may do good in what I left behind." Never! It is only a ʾuselessʾ appeal they make. And there is a barrier behind them until the Day they are resurrected.[685]

Judgment Day

101. Then, when the Trumpet will be blown,[686] there will be no kinship between them on that Day, nor will they ʾeven careʾ toʾ ask about one another.[687]

The Successful Ones

102. As for those whose scale is heavy ʾwith good deedsʾ, it is they who will be successful.

The Losers

103. But those whose scale is light, they will have doomed themselves, staying in Hell forever. **104.** The Fire will burn their faces, leaving them deformed. **105.** ʾIt will be said,ʾ "Were My revelations not recited to you, but you used to deny them?" **106.** They will cry, "Our Lord! Our ill-fate took hold of us, so we became a misguided people. **107.** Our Lord! Take us out of this ʾFireʾ. Then if we ever return ʾto denialʾ, we will truly be wrongdoers." **108.** God will respond, "Be despised in there! Do not ʾeverʾ plead with Me ʾagainʾ! **109.** Indeed, there

---

683 The Meccan pagans.
684 Their claims that there are many gods, and that the Prophet is a liar, a poet, etc.
685 Meaning, once they are dead, they will never return to the world.
686 On the Day of Judgment, the Trumpet will be blown by an angel—causing all to die. When it is blown a second time, everyone will be raised from the dead for judgment (*see* 39:68).
687 Everyone will be busy with their own situation.

was a group of My servants who used to pray, 'Our Lord! We have believed, so forgive us and have mercy on us, for You are the best of those who show mercy,' 110. but you were 'so busy' making fun of them that it made you forget My remembrance. And you used to laugh at them. 111. Today I have indeed rewarded them for their perseverance: they are certainly the triumphant."

Fleeting World

112. He will ask 'them', "How many years did you remain on earth?" 113. They will reply, "We remained 'only' a day or part of a day.[688] But ask those who kept count." 114. He will say, "You only remained for a little while, if only you knew. 115. Did you then think that We had created you without purpose, and that you would never be returned to Us?"

One God Only

116. Exalted is God, the True King! There is no god 'worthy of worship' except Him, the Lord of the Honourable Throne. 117. Whoever invokes, besides God, another god— for which they can have no proof—they will surely find their penalty with their Lord. Indeed, the disbelievers will never succeed.

Advice to the Prophet

118. Say, 'O Prophet,' "My Lord! Forgive and have mercy, for You are the best of those who show mercy."

24. The Light *(An-Nûr)*

This Medinian chapter takes its name from the divine light mentioned in verses 35-36. A large portion of this chapter deals with the issue of sexual misconduct hinted at in the previous chapter (23:7). The chapter also offers some guidelines to the believers on how they should have reacted to false rumours against 'Âishah, the Prophet's wife. Other issues are discussed, including modesty, entering people's homes, forced prostitution, hypocrisy, and false accusations of adultery. God's power, compliance with His judgment, and obedience to the Prophet are highly emphasized.

In the Name of God—the Most Compassionate, Most Merciful

The Introduction

1. 'This is' a chapter which We have revealed and made 'its rulings' obligatory, and revealed in it clear commandments so that you may be mindful.

Punishment for Fornication

2. As for female and male fornicators, give each of them one hundred lashes,[689] and do not let pity for them make you lenient in 'enforcing' the law of God, if you 'truly' believe in God and the Last Day. And let a number of believers witness their punishment.

---

688   Compared to the length and misery of their stay in the grave and Hell, their worldly life will seem very short to them.

689   The address here is to legal authorities. Adultery has to be proven either by confession or by the testimony of four reliable witnesses.

Like for Like

3. A male fornicator would only marry a female fornicator or idolatress. And a female fornicator would only be married to a fornicator or idolater. This is ˹all˺ forbidden to the believers.[690]

Unsupported Accusations

4. Those who accuse chaste women ˹of adultery˺ and fail to produce four witnesses, give them eighty lashes ˹each˺. And do not ever accept any testimony from them—for they are indeed the rebellious— 5. except those who repent afterwards and mend their ways, then surely God is All-Forgiving, Most Merciful.

Accusation to One's Wife

6. And those who accuse their wives ˹of adultery˺ but have no witness except themselves, the accuser must testify,[691] swearing four times by God that he is telling the truth, 7. and a fifth oath that God may condemn him if he is lying. 8. For her to be spared the punishment, she must swear four times by God that he is telling a lie, 9. and a fifth oath that God may be displeased with her if he is telling the truth.[692] 10. ˹You would have suffered,˺ had it not been for God's grace and mercy upon you, and had God not been Accepting of Repentance, All-Wise.

Those Who Slandered the Prophet's Wife[693]

11. Indeed, those who came up with that ˹outrageous˺ slander are a group of you. Do not think this is bad for you. Rather, it is good for you.[694] They will be punished, each according to their share of the sin. As for their mastermind,[695] he will suffer a tremendous punishment.

How the Believers Should Have Reacted

12. If only the believing men and women had thought well of one another, when you heard this ˹rumour˺, and said, "This is clearly ˹an outrageous˺ slander!" 13. Why did they not produce four witnesses? Now, since they have failed to produce witnesses, they are ˹truly˺ liars in the sight of God. 14. Had it not been for God's grace and mercy upon you in this world and the Hereafter, you would have certainly been touched with a tremendous punishment for what you plunged into— 15. when you passed it from one tongue to the other, and said with your mouths what you had no knowledge of, taking it lightly while it is ˹extremely˺ serious in the sight of God. 16. If only you had said upon hearing it, "How can we speak about such a thing! Glory be to You ˹O Lord˺! This is a heinous slander!" 17. God forbids you from ever doing something like this again, if you are ˹true˺ believers. 18. And God makes ˹His˺ commandments clear to you, for God is All-Knowing, All-Wise.

---

690 It is reported in a *hadîth* collected by At-Tirmiẓi that Marthad ibn Abi Marthad, a companion of the Prophet, asked if he could marry 'Anâq, a pagan prostitute he befriended in Mecca before he accepted Islam. So this verse was revealed. However, if someone committed a sin then later repented genuinely, they will be accepted by God and the rest of the believers.

691 In order to be spared the punishment for false accusation.

692 This ruling is called *li'ân* in Islamic legal system. Once the husband and the wife swear each five times, as specified in 24:6-9, the marriage is terminated forever—which means that they can never be remarried.

693 This is referring to an incident where the Prophet's wife, 'Âishah, was accused of adultery. She was part of a caravan, and when she lost her necklace and went looking for it, the caravan moved on without her. She waited until a man named Ṣafwân ibn Al-Mu'aṭṭal found her and escorted her to the caravan. When they returned, the hypocrites began accusing her of adultery. The rumour spread, and 'Âishah defended her innocence, saying "If I told you how I had not done this, you would not believe me. And if I told you that I had done it, you would believe me. I now say what Jacob had once said. He said (12:18): "I can only endure with˺ beautiful patience! It is God's help that I seek to bear your claims.'" Right after she said this, these verses were revealed to the Prophet, proclaiming her innocence.

694 Because now you can tell who is a true believer and who is a hypocrite.

695 This refers to 'Abdullâh ibn Ubai, the leader of the hypocrites in Medina.

24. The Light (An-Nûr)

Warning to Slanderers

19. Indeed, those who love to see indecency spread among the believers will suffer a painful punishment in this life and the Hereafter. God knows and you do not know. **20.** ʿYou would have suffered,ʾ had it not been for God's grace and mercy upon you, and had God not been Ever Gracious, Most Merciful.

Warning Against Satan

21. O believers! Do not follow the footsteps of Satan. Whoever follows Satan's footsteps, then ʿlet them know thatʾ he surely bids ʿallʾ to immorality and wickedness. Had it not been for God's grace and mercy upon you, none of you would have ever been purified. But God purifies whoever He wills. And God is All-Hearing, All-Knowing.

Uninterrupted Kindness

22. Do not let the people of virtue and affluence among you swear to suspend donations to their relatives, the needy, and the emigrants in the cause of God. Let them pardon and forgive. Do you not love to be forgiven by God? And God is All-Forgiving, Most Merciful.[696]

Punishment of the Slanderers

23. Surely those who accuse chaste, unsuspecting,[697] believing women are cursed in this life and the Hereafter. And they will suffer a tremendous punishment **24.** on the Day their tongues, hands, and feet will testify against them for what they used to do. **25.** On that Day, God will give them their just penalty in full, and they will ʿcome toʾ know that God ʿaloneʾ is the Ultimate Truth.

Birds of a Feather ...

26. Wicked women are for wicked men, and wicked men are for wicked women. And virtuous women are for virtuous men, and virtuous men are for virtuous women. The virtuous are innocent of what the wicked say. They will have forgiveness and an honourable provision.[698]

Entering People's Homes

27. O believers! Do not enter any house other than your own until you have asked for permission and greeted its occupants. This is best for you, so perhaps you will be mindful. **28.** If you find no one at home, do not enter it until you have been given permission. And if you are asked to leave, then leave. That is purer for you. And God has ʿperfectʾ knowledge of what you do.

Entering Public Places

29. There is no blame on you if you enter public places[699] where there is something of benefit for you. And God knows what you reveal and what you conceal.

Advice to Muslim Men

30. ʿO Prophet!ʾ Tell the believing men to lower their gaze and guard their chastity. That is purer for them. Surely God is All-Aware of what they do.

Advice to Muslim Women

31. And tell the believing women to lower their gaze and guard their chastity, and not to reveal their adornments[700] except what normally appears.[701] Let them draw their veils over their chests, and not reveal their ʿhiddenʾ adornments[702] except to their husbands,

---

696 This verse was revealed when Abu Bakr Aṣ-Ṣiddîq, ʾÂishah's father, swore to end his financial assistance to his poor cousin, Misṭaḥ ibn Athathah, for taking part in the rumours against ʾÂishah. Once the verse was revealed, Abu Bakr resumed his assistance to Misṭaḥ.
697 Immoral thoughts never cross the minds of these chaste women and, therefore, they never expect slander.
698 This passage declares the innocence of ʾÂishah, the Prophet's wife.
699 lit., non-residential buildings.
700 i.e., hair, body shape, and underclothes.
701 i.e., the face, hands, outer clothes, rings, kohl, and henna.
702 i.e., hair, arms, and legs.

their fathers, their fathers-in-law, their sons, their stepsons, their brothers, their brothers' sons or sisters' sons, their fellow women, those ˹bondwomen˺ in their possession, male attendants with no desire, or children who are still unaware of women's nakedness. Let them not stomp their feet, drawing attention to their hidden adornments. Turn to God in repentance all together, O believers, so that you may be successful.

Advice to Guardians

32. Marry off the ˹free˺ singles among you, as well as the righteous of your bondmen and bondwomen. If they are poor, God will enrich them out of His bounty. For God is All-Bountiful, All-Knowing. 33. And let those who do not have the means to marry keep themselves chaste until God enriches them out of His bounty. And if any of those ˹bondspeople˺ in your possession desires a contract ˹to buy their own freedom˺, make it possible for them, if you find goodness in them. And give them some of God's wealth which He has granted you. Do not force your ˹slave˺ girls into prostitution for your own worldly gains while they wish to remain chaste. And if someone coerces them, then after such a coercion God is certainly All-Forgiving, Most Merciful ˹to them˺.

Examples and Lessons[703]

34. Indeed, We have sent down to you clear revelations, along with examples of those who had gone before you, and a lesson to the God-fearing.

Parable for the Believer's Heart

35. God is the Light of the heavens and the earth. His light[704] is like a niche in which there is a lamp, the lamp is in a crystal, the crystal is like a shining star, lit from ˹the oil of˺ a blessed olive tree, ˹located˺ neither to the east nor the west,[705] whose oil would almost glow, even without being touched by fire. Light upon light! God guides whoever He wills to His light. And God sets forth parables for humanity. For God has ˹perfect˺ knowledge of all things.

True Believers

36. ˹That light shines˺ through houses ˹of worship˺ which God has ordered to be raised, and where His Name is mentioned. He is glorified there morning and evening 37. by men[706] who are not distracted—either by buying or selling—from God's remembrance, or performing prayer, or paying alms-tax. They fear a Day when hearts and eyes will tremble, 38. ˹hoping˺ that God may reward them according to the best of their deeds, and increase them out of His grace. And God provides for whoever He wills without limit.

Parable for the Disbelievers

39. As for the disbelievers, their deeds are like a mirage in a desert, which the thirsty perceive as water, but when they approach it, they find it to be nothing. Instead, they find God there ˹in the Hereafter, ready˺ to settle their account. And God is swift in reckoning.

Another Parable

40. Or ˹their deeds are˺ like the darkness in a deep sea, covered by waves upon waves,[707] topped by ˹dark˺ clouds. Darkness upon darkness! If one stretches out their hand, they can hardly see it. And whoever God does not bless with light will have no light!

---

703 Before 'Âishah, Mary and Prophet Joseph had each been falsely accused of fornication, but Almighty God declared their innocence.
704 This is a metaphor for the light of guidance in the heart of the believer.
705 Meaning, the olive tree is wholesome because it is located in a central place, so it is hit by sunrays all day-long, and, therefore, the oil is of a premium quality.
706 See footnote for 7:46.
707 This is another scientific fact mentioned in the Quran: the existence of underwater waves, like layers.

Submission to God

41. Do you not see that God is glorified by all those in the heavens and the earth, even the birds as they soar? Each 'instinctively' knows their manner of prayer and glorification. And God has 'perfect' knowledge of all they do. **42.** To God 'alone' belongs the kingdom of the heavens and the earth. And to God is the final return.

The Miracle of Rain

43. Do you not see that God gently drives the clouds, then joins them together, piling them up into masses, from which you see raindrops come forth? And He sends down from the sky mountains 'of clouds' loaded with hail, pouring it on whoever He wills and averting it from whoever He wills. The flash of the clouds' lightning nearly takes away eyesight. **44.** God alternates the day and night. Surely in this is a lesson for people of insight.

The Miracle of Creation

45. And God has created from water every living creature. Some of them crawl on their bellies, some walk on two legs, and some walk on four. God creates whatever He wills. Surely God is Most Capable of everything.

The Hypocrites and Judgment

46. We have indeed sent down revelations clarifying 'the truth'. But God 'only' guides whoever He wills to the Straight Path. **47.** And the hypocrites say, "We believe in God and the Messenger, and we obey." Then a group of them turns away soon after that. These are not 'true' believers. **48.** And as soon as they are called to God and His Messenger so he may judge between them, a group of them[708] turns away. **49.** But if the truth is in their favour, they come to him, ful-

ly submitting. **50.** Is there a sickness in their hearts? Or are they in doubt? Or do they fear that God and His Messenger will be unjust to them? In fact, it is they who are the 'true' wrongdoers.

The Believers and Judgment

51. The only response of the 'true' believers, when they are called to God and His Messenger so he may judge between them, is to say, "We hear and obey." It is they who will 'truly' succeed. **52.** For whoever obeys God and His Messenger, and fears God and is mindful of Him, then it is they who will 'truly' triumph.

Hypocrites' Lip Service

53. They swear by God their most solemn oaths that if you 'O Prophet' were to command them, they would certainly march forth 'in God's cause'. Say, "'You' do not 'have to' swear; your obedience is well known!"[709] Surely God is All-Aware of what you do." **54.** Say, "Obey God and obey the Messenger. But if you turn away, then he is only responsible for his duty[710] and you are responsible for yours.[711] And if you obey him, you will be 'rightly' guided. The Messenger's duty is only to deliver 'the message' clearly."

God's Promise to the Believers

55. God has promised those of you who believe and do good that He will certainly make them successors in the land, as He did with those before them; and will surely establish for them their faith which He has chosen for them; and will indeed change their fear into security—'provided that' they worship Me, associating nothing with Me. But whoever disbelieves after this 'promise', it is they who will be the rebellious. **56.** Moreover, establish prayer, pay alms-tax, and obey the Messenger, so you may be

---

708 Those at fault.
709 This is used in a sarcastic way. It means, "Save your oaths! Everyone knows you are only bluffing. It is actions that matter, not words."
710 The Prophet's only duty is to deliver the message.
711 Their only duty is to obey the Prophet by submitting to God.

shown mercy. **57.** Do not think ˹O Prophet˺ that the disbelievers can escape in the land. The Fire will be their home. Indeed, what an evil destination!

Permission at Three Times

58. O believers! Let those ˹bondspeople˺ in your possession and those of you who are still under age ask for your permission ˹to come in˺ at three times: before dawn prayer, when you take off your ˹outer˺ clothes at noon, and after the late evening prayer. ˹These are˺ three times of privacy for you. Other than these times, there is no blame on you or them to move freely, attending to one another. This is how God makes the revelations clear to you, for God is All-Knowing, All-Wise.

Permission at All Times

59. And when your children reach the age of puberty, let them seek permission ˹to come in˺, as their seniors do. This is how God makes His revelations clear to you, for God is All-Knowing, All-Wise.

Modesty for Elderly Women

60. As for elderly women past the age of marriage, there is no blame on them if they take off their ˹outer˺ garments, without revealing their adornments. But it is better for them if they avoid this ˹altogether˺. And God is All-Hearing, All-Knowing.

No Restrictions

61. There is no restriction on the blind, or the disabled, or the sick.[712] Nor on yourselves if you eat from your homes,[713] or the homes of your fathers, or your mothers, or your broth-ers, or your sisters, or your paternal uncles, or your paternal aunts, or your maternal uncles, or your maternal aunts, or from the homes in your trust, or ˹the homes of˺ your friends. There is no blame on you eating together or separately. However, when you enter houses, greet one another with a greeting ˹of peace˺ from God, blessed and good.[714] This is how God makes His revelations clear to you, so perhaps you will understand.

Sticking with the Prophet

62. The ˹true˺ believers are only those who believe in God and His Messenger, and when they are with him on a public matter, they do not leave without his permission. Indeed, those who ask your permission ˹O Prophet˺ are the ones who ˹truly˺ believe in God and His Messenger. So when they ask your permission for a private matter, grant permission to whoever you wish and ask God's forgiveness for them. Surely God is All-Forgiving, Most Merciful. **63.** Do not treat the Messenger's summons to you ˹as lightly˺ as your summons to one another.[715] God certainly knows those of you who slip away, hiding behind others.[716] So let those who disobey his orders beware, for an affliction may befall them, or a painful torment may overtake them.

God Knows Everything

64. Surely to God belongs whatever is in the heavens and the earth. He knows well what you stand for. And ˹on˺ the Day all will be returned to Him, He will inform them of what they did. For God has ˹perfect˺ knowledge of all things.

---

712 There is no blame on any of the three if they do not march forth in God's cause. Moreover, some Muslims would give the keys of their homes to one of those who could not march forth (namely the blind, the disabled, or the sick) or their own relatives and ask them to enter their houses and eat at will but these people were shy to do that.

713 i.e., the home of your spouse or children.

714 If someone is in the house, greet them by saying, 'As-salâmu 'alaikum' (peace be upon you)." But if there is no one there, you greet yourselves by saying, 'Asalâmu 'alaina wa 'ala 'ibâd-illâhi aṣ-ṣâliḥîn' (peace be upon us and all righteous servants of God)."

715 There is also a different interpretation: "Do not call the Messenger ˹by his name˺ as you call one another." In other words, Do not say, 'O Muḥammad.' Rather, say, 'O Prophet.'

716 Some hypocrites used to sneak out while the Prophet was talking.

25. The Decisive Authority (Al-Furqân)

This Meccan chapter takes its name from verses 1-6, which refute the pagan claims that the Quran was fabricated and plagiarized from earlier scriptures. Other passages condemn polytheism, denial of resurrection, and mocking the Prophet. God's power, manifested in the marvels of creation and rain, is emphasized in this chapter and the previous one. The qualities of the righteous servants of God are beautifully laid out in verses 63-76.

In the Name of God—the Most Compassionate, Most Merciful

Kingdom of Almighty God

1. Blessed is the One Who sent down the Decisive Authority[717] to His servant,[718] so that he may be a warner to the whole world.[719] 2. ʿGod isʾ the One to Whom belongs the kingdom of the heavens and the earth, Who has never had ʿanyʾ offspring, nor does He have a partner in ʿgoverningʾ the kingdom. He has created everything, ordaining it precisely.

The Polytheists

3. Yet they have taken besides Him gods who cannot create anything but are themselves created. Nor can they protect or benefit themselves. Nor can they control life, death, or resurrection.

Denying the Quran

4. The disbelievers say, "This ʿQuranʾ is nothing but a fabrication which he[720] made up with the help of others." Their claim is totally unjustified and untrue! 5. And they say, "ʾThese revelations are onlyʾ ancient fables which he has had written down, and they are rehearsed to him morning and evening."[721] 6. Say, ʿO Prophet,ʾ "This ʿQuranʾ

has been revealed by the One Who knows the secrets of the heavens and the earth. Surely He is All-Forgiving, Most Merciful."[722]

Denying the Prophet

7. And they say ʿmockinglyʾ, "What kind of messenger is this who eats food and goes about in market-places ʿfor a livingʾ? If only an angel had been sent down with him to be his co-warner, 8. or a treasure had been cast down to him, or he had had a garden from which he may eat!" And the wrongdoers say ʾto the believersʾ, "You are only following a bewitched man." 9. See ʿO Prophetʾ how they call you names![723] So they have gone so ʾfarʾ astray that they cannot find the ʿRightʾ Way. 10. Blessed is the One Who—if He wills—can give you far better than ʿallʾ that: gardens under which rivers flow, and palaces as well.

Torment for the Deniers

11. In fact, they deny the Hour.[724] And for the deniers of the Hour, We have prepared a blazing Fire. 12. Once it sees them from a distance, they will hear it fuming and growling. 13. And when they are tossed into a narrow place inside ʿHellʾ, chained together,

---

717 Al-Furqân, which is one of names of the Quran, means "the standard to distinguish between right and wrong."
718 Prophet Muḥammad.
719 For both humans and jinn.
720 The Prophet.
721 Some Arab pagans claimed that the Prophet had been taught the Bible by some non-Arab Christians. The Quran itself (16:103) refutes this claim by arguing that a non-Arab could not come up with an eloquent Arabic scripture like the Quran when eloquent Arabs failed to produce something like it. For more details, *see* the Introduction.
722 He forgives those who repent, and gives a grace period to those who do not.
723 i.e., a magician, a poet, a fabricator, and a mad man.
724 What they have said about you are only excuses to justify their denial of the Hereafter.

then and there they will cry out for ˈinstantˈ destruction. **14.** ˈThey will be told,ˈ "Do not cry only once for destruction Today, but cry many times over!"

Reward of the Righteous

15. Say, ˈO Prophet,ˈ "Is this better or the Garden of Eternity which the righteous have been promised, as a reward and ˈan ultimateˈ destination? **16.** There they will have whatever they wish for, forever. That is a promise ˈto be sought afterˈ, binding on your Lord."

The Disavowal

17. ˈWatch forˈ the Day He will gather them along with what they used to worship besides God, and ask ˈthe objects of worshipˈ,[725] "Was it you who misled these servants of Mine, or did they stray from the Way ˈon their ownˈ?" **18.** They will say, "Glory be to You! It was not right for ˈothers likeˈ us to take any lords besides You,[726] but You allowed enjoyment for them and their forefathers ˈfor so longˈ that they forgot ˈYourˈ remembrance and became a doomed people." **19.** ˈThe doomed will be toldˈ, "Your gods have clearly denied your claims. So now you can neither ward off ˈthe punishmentˈ nor get any help." And whoever of you does wrong, We will make them taste a horrible punishment.

Messengers Are Human

20. We never sent any messenger before you ˈO Prophetˈ, who did not eat food and go about in market-places. We have made some of you a trial for others. Will you ˈnot thenˈ be patient? And your Lord is All-Seeing.

Desperate to Meet the Angels

21. Those who do not expect to meet Us say, "If only the angels were sent down to us, or we could see our Lord!" They have certainly been carried away by their arrogance and have entirely exceeded all limits. **22.** ˈButˈ on the Day they will see the angels, there will be no good news for the wicked, who will cry, "Keep away! Away ˈfrom usˈ!"[727] **23.** Then We will turn to whatever ˈgoodˈ deeds they did, reducing them to scattered dust.[728] **24.** ˈButˈ on that Day the residents of Paradise will have the best settlement and the finest place to rest.

Judgment Day

25. ˈWatch forˈ the Day the heavens will burst with clouds, and the angels will be sent down in successive ranks. **26.** True authority on that Day will belong ˈonlyˈ to the Most Compassionate.[729] And it will be a hard day for the disbelievers.

Useless Remorse[730]

27. And ˈbeware ofˈ the Day the wrongdoer will bite his nails ˈin regretˈ and say, "Oh! I wish I had followed the Way along with the Messenger! **28.** Woe to me! I wish I had never taken so-and-so as a close friend. **29.** It was he who truly made me stray from the Reminder after it had reached me." And Satan has always betrayed humanity.

Pagans' Neglect of the Quran

30. The Messenger has cried, "O my Lord! My people have indeed received this Quran with neglect." **31.** Similarly, We made enemies for every prophet from among the wicked, but sufficient is your Lord as a

---

725 e.g., Jesus and the angels.

726 Another possible translation: "They will say, 'Glory be to You! We would not dare to take other lords besides You ˈso how can we claim to be lords?'ˈ"

727 Another possible translation: "And the angels will say, 'All good is forbidden to you!'"

728 The good deeds of the disbelievers (like charity) will have no weight on Judgment Day.

729 Some people (like kings and rulers) have some sort of authority in this world. But on Judgment Day God will be the sole authority.

730 This passage refers to 'Oqbah ibn Abi-Mu'aiṭ who had initially become Muslim, but later left Islam only to please his close friend, Ubai ibn Khalaf.

Guide and Helper. **32.** The disbelievers say, "If only the Quran had been sent down to him all at once!" ˹We have sent it˺ as such ˹in stages˺ so We may reassure your heart with it. And We have revealed it at a deliberate pace. **33.** Whenever they bring you an argument, We come to you with the right refutation and the best explanation. **34.** Those who will be dragged into Hell on their faces will be in the worst place, and are ˹now˺ farthest from the ˹Right˺ Way.

Destruction of Pharaoh's People

35. We certainly gave Moses the Book and appointed his brother Aaron as his helper. **36.** We had ordered ˹them˺, "Go to the people who would deny Our signs." Then We annihilated the deniers entirely.

Destruction of Noah's People

37. And when the people of Noah rejected the messengers,[731] We drowned them, making them an example to humanity. And We have prepared a painful punishment for the wrongdoers.

Destruction of Other Peoples

38. Also ˹We destroyed˺ 'Âd, Thamûd, and the people of the Water-pit,[732] as well as many peoples in between. **39.** For each We set forth ˹various˺ lessons, and We ultimately destroyed each.

Warning to Meccan Pagans

40. They have certainly passed by the city ˹of Sodom˺, which had been showered with a dreadful rain ˹of stones˺. Have they not seen its ruins? But they do not expect to be resurrected. **41.** When they see you ˹O Prophet˺, they only make fun of you, ˹saying,˺ "Is this the one that God has sent as a messenger? **42.** He would have almost tricked us away from our gods, had we not been so devoted to them." ˹But˺ soon they will know, when they face the punishment, who is far astray from the ˹Right˺ Way. **43.** Have you seen ˹O Prophet˺ the one who has taken their own desires as their god? Will you then be a keeper over them? **44.** Or do you think that most of them listen or understand?[733] They are only like cattle—no, more than that, they are astray from the ˹Right˺ Way![734]

God's Power: 1) The Sun and Shade

45. Have you not seen how your Lord extends the shade—He could have simply made it ˹remain˺ still if He so willed—then We make the sun its guide, **46.** causing the shade to retreat gradually?[735]

2) The Day and Night

47. He is the One Who has made the night for you as a cover, and ˹made˺ sleep for resting, and the day for rising.

3) The Rain

48. And He is the One Who sends the winds ushering in His mercy, and We send down pure rain from the sky, **49.** giving life to a lifeless land, and providing water for countless animals and humans of Our Own creation. **50.** We certainly disperse it among them so they may be mindful, but most people persist in ungratefulness.

---

731 Because denying Noah was equal to denying all of God's messengers.

732 *Ar-Rass* means "well" or "water-pit". This refers to a pagan people, along with Midian, to whom God sent Prophet Shu'aib.

733 They neither pay attention, nor think for themselves. They only follow others blindly.

734 Generally, animals are obedient and loyal to their masters who care for them and they seem to know their way, whereas Meccan pagans are disobedient and ungrateful to their Lord and Sustainer, choosing to stray from the right path.

735 This means that one of the great miracles of God is that He allows the sun to rise in the morning, causing darkness to retreat. He could have stopped the sun and the earth from rotating, so half of the world would be engulfed in complete darkness, leading to an imbalance in the earth's eco-systems and endangering life on the planet.

One Universal Messenger

51. Had We willed, We could have easily sent a warner to every society. **52.** So do not yield to the disbelievers, but strive diligently against them with this ˹Quran˺.

4) Fresh and Salt Water

53. And He is the One Who merges the two bodies of water: one fresh and palatable and the other salty and bitter, placing between them a barrier they cannot cross.[736]

5) Creation of Humans

54. And He is the One Who creates human beings from a ˹humble˺ liquid,[737] then establishes for them bonds of kinship and marriage. For your Lord is Most Capable.

Powerless Gods

55. Yet they worship besides God what can neither benefit nor harm them. And the disbeliever always collaborates against their Lord.

Advice to the Prophet: Trust in God

56. And We have sent you ˹O Prophet˺ only as a deliverer of good news and a warner. **57.** Say, "I do not ask you for any reward for this ˹message˺, but whoever wishes, let them pursue the Way to their Lord." **58.** Put your trust in the Ever-Living, Who never dies, and glorify His praises. Sufficient is He as All-Aware of the sins of His servants. **59.** ˹He is˺ the One Who created the heavens and the earth and everything in between in six Days,[738] then established Himself above the Throne. ˹He is˺ the Most Compassionate! Ask ˹none other than˺ the All-Knowledgeable about Himself.

Denying God

60. When it is said to them, "Prostrate to the Most Compassionate," they ask ˹in disgust˺, "What is 'the Most Compassionate'? Will we prostrate to whatever you order us to?" And it only drives them farther away.

God Almighty

61. Blessed is the One Who has placed constellations in the sky, as well as a ˹radiant˺ lamp[739] and a luminous moon. **62.** And He is the One Who causes the day and the night to alternate, ˹as a sign˺ for whoever desires to be mindful or to be grateful.

Qualities of the Righteous: 1) Humility

63. The ˹true˺ servants of the Most Compassionate are those who walk on the earth humbly, and when the foolish address them ˹improperly˺, they only respond with peace.

2) Sincere Devotion

64. ˹They are˺ those who spend ˹a good portion of˺ the night, prostrating themselves and standing before their Lord.

3) ˹Hope and˺ Fear

65. ˹They are˺ those who pray, "Our Lord! Keep the punishment of Hell away from us, for its punishment is indeed unrelenting. **66.** It is certainly an evil place to settle and reside."

4) Moderate Spending

67. ˹They are˺ those who spend neither wastefully nor stingily, but moderately in between.

5) Avoiding Major Sins

68. ˹They are˺ those who do not invoke any other god besides God, nor take a ˹hu-

---

736 This refers to estuaries where salt and fresh waters meet forming brackish water. Although both waters mix together, each still keeps its distinctive qualities.
737 The mixture of sperm and egg.
738 See footnote for 7:54.
739 The sun.

man' life—made sacred by God—except with 'legal' right,[740] nor commit fornication. And whoever does 'any of' this will face the penalty. 69. Their punishment will be multiplied on the Day of Judgment, and they will remain in it forever, in disgrace. 70. As for those who repent, believe, and do good deeds, they are the ones whose evil deeds God will change into good deeds. For God is All-Forgiving, Most Merciful. 71. And whoever repents and does good has truly turned to God properly.

6) Avoiding Falsehood

72. 'They are' those who do not bear false witness, and when they come across falsehood, they pass 'it' by with dignity.

7) Full Submission

73. 'They are' those who, when reminded of the revelation of their Lord, do not turn a blind eye or a deaf ear to it.

8) Righteous Company

74. 'They are' those who pray, "Our Lord! Bless us with 'pious' spouses and offspring who will be the joy of our hearts, and make us models for the righteous."

Reward of the Righteous

75. It is they who will be rewarded with 'elevated' mansions 'in Paradise' for their perseverance, and will be received with salutations and 'greetings of' peace, 76. staying there forever. What an excellent place to settle and reside!

Call to Humanity

77. Say, 'O Prophet,' "You 'all' would not 'even' matter to my Lord were it not for your faith 'in Him'. But now you 'disbelievers' have denied 'the truth', so the torment is bound to come."

26. The Poets *(Ash-Shu'arâ')*

This Meccan chapter takes its name from the reference to poets in verses 224-226. Since the previous chapter ends with a warning to the deniers of the truth, this chapter recounts several cautionary tales of destroyed deniers such as Pharaoh and the peoples of Noah, Shu'aib, Lot, and Ṣâliḥ. The divine origin of the Quran is emphasized at both ends of the chapter. The qualities of the believers mentioned in the last verse (227) are elaborated upon at the beginning of the next chapter.

In the Name of God—the Most Compassionate, Most Merciful

Warning to the Disbelievers

1. *Ṭâ-Sîn-Mîm.* 2. These are the verses of the clear Book. 3. Perhaps you 'O Prophet' will grieve yourself to death over their disbelief. 4. If We willed, We could send down upon them a 'compelling' sign from the heavens, leaving their necks bent in 'utter' submission to it. 5. Whatever new reminder comes to them from the Most Compassionate, they always turn away from it. 6. They have certainly denied 'the truth', so they will soon face the consequences of their ridicule. 7. Have they failed to look at the earth, 'to see' how many types

---

740   For example, in retaliation for intentional killing through legal channels.

of fine plants We have caused to grow in it? **8.** Surely in this is a sign. Yet most of them would not believe. **9.** And your Lord is certainly the Almighty, Most Merciful.

Prophet Moses

10. ˹Remember˺ when your Lord called out to Moses, "Go to the wrongdoing people— **11.** the people of Pharaoh. Will they not fear ˹God˺?" **12.** He replied, "My Lord! I fear that they will reject me. **13.** And ˹so˺ my heart will be broken and my tongue will be tied. So send Aaron along ˹as a messenger˺. **14.** Also, they have a charge against me,[741] so I fear they may kill me." **15.** God responded, "Certainly not! So go, both of you, with Our signs. We will be with you, listening. **16.** Go to Pharaoh and say, 'We are messengers from the Lord of all worlds, **17.** ˹commanded to say:˺ 'Let the Children of Israel go with us.'''"

Moses vs. Pharaoh

18. Pharaoh protested, "Did we not raise you among us as a child, and you stayed several years of your life in our care? **19.** Then you did what you did,[742] being ˹utterly˺ ungrateful!" **20.** Moses replied, "I did it then, lacking guidance. **21.** So I fled from you when I feared you. Then my Lord granted me wisdom and made me one of the messengers. **22.** How can that be a 'favour,' of which you remind me, when ˹it was only because˺ you ˹have˺ enslaved the Children of Israel?" **23.** Pharaoh asked, "And what is 'the Lord of all worlds'?" **24.** Moses replied, "˹He is˺ the Lord of the heavens and the earth and everything in between, if only you had sure faith." **25.** Pharaoh said to those around him, "Did you hear ˹what he said˺?" **26.** Moses added, "˹He is˺ your Lord and the Lord of your forefathers." **27.** Pharaoh said ˹mockingly˺, "Your messenger, who has been sent to you, must be insane." **28.** Moses responded: "˹He is˺ the

Lord of the east and west, and everything in between, if only you had any sense."

The Challenge

29. Pharaoh threatened, "If you take any other god besides me, I will certainly have you imprisoned." **30.** Moses responded, "Even if I bring you a clear proof?" **31.** Pharaoh demanded, "Bring it then, if what you say is true." **32.** So he threw down his staff and— behold!—it became a real snake. **33.** Then he drew his hand ˹out of his collar˺ and it was ˹shining˺ white for all to see. **34.** Pharaoh said to the chiefs around him, "He is indeed a skilled magician, **35.** who seeks to drive you from your land by his magic. So what do you propose?" **36.** They replied, "Let him and his brother wait and dispatch mobilizers to all cities **37.** to bring you every skilled magician." **38.** So the magicians were assembled at the set time on the appointed day. **39.** And the people were asked, "Will you join the gathering, **40.** so that we may follow the magicians if they prevail?"

Moses and the Magicians Face off

41. When the magicians came, they asked Pharaoh, "Shall we have a ˹suitable˺ reward if we prevail?" **42.** He replied, "Yes, and you will then certainly be among those closest to me." **43.** Moses said to them, "Cast whatever you wish to cast." **44.** So they cast down their ropes and staffs, saying, "By Pharaoh's might, it is we who will surely prevail." **45.** Then Moses threw down his staff, and— behold!—it devoured the objects of their illusion!

Magicians Become Believers

46. So the magicians fell down, prostrating. **47.** They declared, "We ˹now˺ believe in the Lord of all worlds— **48.** the Lord of Moses and Aaron." **49.** Pharaoh threatened, "How dare you believe in him before I give you permission? He must be your master

---

741 For killing an Egyptian by mistake before prophethood. See 28:15-17.
742 *See* previous footnote.

who taught you magic, but soon you will see. I will certainly cut off your hands and feet on opposite sides, then crucify you all." **50.** They responded, "'That would be' no harm! Surely to our Lord we will 'all' return. **51.** We really hope that our Lord will forgive our sins, as we are the first to believe."

Pharaoh Chases the Israelites

52. And We inspired Moses, 'saying,' "Leave with My servants at night, for you will surely be pursued." **53.** Then Pharaoh sent mobilizers to all cities, **54.** 'and said,' "These 'outcasts' are just a handful of people, **55.** who have really enraged us, **56.** but we are all on the alert." **57.** So We lured the tyrants[743] out of 'their' gardens, springs, **58.** treasures, and splendid residences. **59.** So it was. And We awarded it 'all' to the Children of Israel.

The End of Pharaoh

60. And so they pursued them at sunrise. **61.** When the two groups came face to face, the companions of Moses cried out, "We are overtaken for sure." **62.** Moses reassured 'them', "Absolutely not! My Lord is certainly with me—He will guide me." **63.** So We inspired Moses: "Strike the sea with your staff," and the sea was split, each part was like a huge mountain. **64.** We drew the pursuers to that place, **65.** and delivered Moses and those with him all together. **66.** Then We drowned the others. **67.** Surely in this is a sign. Yet most of them would not believe. **68.** And your Lord is certainly the Almighty, Most Merciful.

Prophet Abraham

69. Relate to them 'O Prophet' the story of Abraham, **70.** when he questioned his father and his people, "What is that you worship 'besides God'?" **71.** They replied, "We worship idols, to which we are fully devoted." **72.** Abraham asked, "Can they hear you when you call upon them? **73.** Or can they benefit or harm you?" **74.** They replied, "No! But we found our forefathers doing the same." **75.** Abraham responded, "Have you 'really' considered what you have been worshipping— **76.** you and your ancestors? **77.** They are 'all' enemies to me, except the Lord of all worlds. **78.** 'He is' the One Who created me, and He 'alone' guides me. **79.** 'He is' the One Who provides me with food and drink. **80.** And He 'alone' heals me when I am sick. **81.** And He 'is the One Who' will cause me to die, and then bring me back to life. **82.** And He is 'the One' Who, I hope, will forgive my flaws[744] on Judgment Day."

Abraham's Prayer

83. "My Lord! Grant me wisdom, and join me with the righteous. **84.** Bless me with honourable mention among later generations.[745] **85.** Make me one of those awarded the Garden of Bliss. **86.** Forgive my father, for he is certainly one of the misguided. **87.** And do not disgrace me on the Day all will be resurrected— **88.** the Day when neither wealth nor children will be of any benefit. **89.** Only those who come before God with a pure heart 'will be saved'."[746]

Judgment Day

90. 'On that Day' Paradise will be brought near to the God-fearing, **91.** and the Hell-

743 Pharaoh and his soldiers.
744 It is reported in an authentic narration collected by At-Tirmiẓi that Prophet Muḥammad said that Abraham did not tell the full truth only on three different occasions: when he justified his absence from the pagan festival by saying 'I am really sick' (see 37:89), and when he destroyed the idols and blamed it on the biggest one (see 21:63), and when he said that Sarah was his sister to save her from a tyrant ruler.
745 On a daily basis, Muslims invoke God's blessings upon Prophet Muḥammad and his family and Prophet Abraham and his family, in both obligatory and optional prayers.
746 A pure and sound heart is that of the believer, compared to that of the disbeliever and the hypocrite.

fire will be displayed to the deviant. 92. And it will be said to them, "Where are those you used to worship 93. besides God? Can they help you or even help themselves?" 94. Then the idols will be hurled headlong into Hell, along with the deviant 95. and the soldiers of *Iblîs*,[747] all together. 96. There the deviant will cry while disputing with their idols, 97. "By God! We were clearly mistaken, 98. when we made you equal to the Lord of all worlds. 99. And none led us astray other than the wicked. 100. Now we have none to intercede for us, 101. nor a close friend. 102. If only we could have a second chance, then we would be believers." 103. Surely in this is a sign. Yet most of them would not believe. 104. And your Lord is certainly the Almighty, Most Merciful.

Prophet Noah

105. The people of Noah rejected the messengers[748] 106. when their brother Noah said to them, "Will you not fear ˹God˺? 107. I am truly a trustworthy messenger to you. 108. So fear God, and obey me. 109. I do not ask you for any reward for this ˹message˺. My reward is only from the Lord of all worlds. 110. So fear God, and obey me." 111. They argued, "How can we believe in you, when you are followed ˹only˺ by the lowest of the low?"[749] 112. He responded, "And what knowledge do I have of what they do? 113. Their judgment is with my Lord, if you had any sense! 114. I am not going to expel the believers. 115. I am only sent with a clear warning."

Noah's People Destroyed

116. They threatened, "If you do not desist, O Noah, you will surely be stoned ˹to death˺." 117. Noah prayed, "My Lord! My people have truly rejected me. 118. So judge between me and them decisively, and save me and the believers with me." 119. So We saved him and those with him in the fully loaded Ark. 120. Then afterwards We drowned the rest. 121. Surely in this is a sign. Yet most of them would not believe. 122. And your Lord is certainly the Almighty, Most Merciful.

Prophet Hûd

123. The people of ʾÂd rejected the messengers 124. when their brother Hûd said to them, "Will you not fear ˹God˺? 125. I am truly a trustworthy messenger to you. 126. So fear God, and obey me. 127. I do not ask you for any reward for this ˹message˺. My reward is only from the Lord of all worlds. 128. ˹Why˺ do you build a landmark on every high place in vanity, 129. and construct castles, as if you are going to live forever, 130. and act so viciously when you attack ˹others˺? 131. So fear God, and obey me. 132. Fear the One Who has provided you with ˹the good˺ things you know: 133. He provided you with cattle, and children, 134. and gardens, and springs. 135. I truly fear for you the torment of a tremendous day."

Hûd's People Destroyed

136. They responded, "It is all the same to us whether you warn ˹us˺ or not. 137. This is simply the tradition of our predecessors. 138. And we will never be punished." 139. So they rejected him, and ˹so˺ We destroyed them. Surely in this is a sign. Yet most of them would not believe. 140. And your Lord is certainly the Almighty, Most Merciful.

Prophet Ṣâliḥ

141. The people of Thamûd rejected the messengers 142. when their brother Ṣâliḥ said to them, "Will you not fear ˹God˺? 143. I am truly a trustworthy messenger to you. 144. So

---

747 *Iblîs* was the name of Satan before his fall from grace. *See* footnote for 2:34.
748 lit., messengers, because denying Noah was equal to denying all of God's messengers.
749 The pagans were accusing the impoverished believers of following Noah only for personal gain, not out of sincere faith.

fear God, and obey me. **145.** I do not ask you for any reward for this 'message'. My reward is only from the Lord of all worlds. **146.** Do you think you will be 'forever' left secure in what you have here: **147.** amid gardens and springs, **148.** and 'various' crops, and palm trees 'loaded' with tender fruit; **149.** to carve homes in the mountains with great skill? **150.** So fear God, and obey me. **151.** And do not follow the command of the transgressors, **152.** who spread corruption throughout the land, never setting things right."

Ṣâliḥ's People Destroyed

153. They replied, "You are simply bewitched! **154.** You are only a human being like us, so bring forth a sign if what you say is true." **155.** Ṣâliḥ said, "Here is a camel. She will have her turn to drink as you have yours, each on an appointed day. **156.** And do not ever touch her with harm, or you will be overtaken by the torment of a tremendous day." **157.** But they killed her, becoming regretful. **158.** So the punishment overtook them. Surely in this is a sign. Yet most of them would not believe. **159.** And your Lord is certainly the Almighty, Most Merciful.

Prophet Lot

160. The people of Lot rejected the messengers **161.** when their brother Lot said to them, "Will you not fear 'God'? **162.** I am truly a trustworthy messenger to you. **163.** So fear God, and obey me. **164.** I do not ask you for any reward for this 'message'. My reward is only from the Lord of all worlds. **165.** Why do you 'men' lust after fellow men,[750] **166.** leaving the wives that your Lord has created for you? In fact, you are a transgressing people."

Lot's People Destroyed

167. They threatened, "If you do not desist, O Lot, you will surely be expelled." **168.** Lot responded, "I am truly one of those who despise your 'shameful' practice. **169.** My Lord! Save me and my family from 'the consequences of' what they do." **170.** So We saved him and all of his family, **171.** except an old woman,[751] who was one of the doomed. **172.** Then We utterly destroyed the rest, **173.** pouring upon them a rain 'of brimstone'. How evil was the rain of those who had been warned! **174.** Surely in this is a sign. Yet most of them would not believe. **175.** And your Lord is certainly the Almighty, Most Merciful.

Prophet Shu'aib

176. The residents of the Forest rejected the messengers **177.** when Shu'aib said to them,[752] "Will you not fear 'God'? **178.** I am truly a trustworthy messenger to you. **179.** So fear God, and obey me. **180.** I do not ask you for any reward for this 'message'. My reward is only from the Lord of all worlds. **181.** Give full measure, and cause no loss 'to others'. **182.** Weigh with an even balance, **183.** and do not defraud people of their property. Nor go about spreading corruption in the land. **184.** And fear the One Who created you and 'all' earlier peoples."

Shu'aib's People Destroyed

185. They replied, "You are simply bewitched! **186.** Also, you are only a human being like us, and we think you are indeed a liar. **187.** So cause 'deadly' pieces of the sky to fall upon us, if what you say is true." **188.** Shu'aib responded, "My Lord knows best whatever you do." **189.** So they rejected him, and 'so' were overtaken by the

---

750   lit., men of the world.
751   Lot's wife, who betrayed her husband.
752   Unlike other prophets in this chapter who are identified as the brothers of fellow tribesmen, Shu'aib is not identified as the brother of the people of the *Aykah* (which is the name of the forest where they used to worship a particular tree) because they are identified by faith, rather than a tribal connection.

torment of the day of the ˹deadly˺ cloud.[753] That was really a torment of a tremendous day. 190. Surely in this is a sign. Yet most of them would not believe. 191. And your Lord is certainly the Almighty, Most Merciful.

The Quran

192. This is certainly a revelation from the Lord of all worlds, 193. which the trustworthy spirit ˹Gabriel˺ brought down 194. into your heart ˹O Prophet˺—so that you may be one of the warners— 195. in a clear Arabic tongue. 196. And it has indeed been ˹foretold˺ in the Scriptures of those before. 197. Was it not sufficient proof for the deniers that it has been recognized by the knowledgeable among the Children of Israel?[754] 198. Had We revealed it to a non-Arab, 199. who would then recite it to the deniers ˹in fluent Arabic˺, still they would not have believed in it! 200. This is how We allow denial ˹to creep˺ into the hearts of the wicked. 201. They will not believe in it until they see the painful punishment, 202. which will take them by surprise when they least expect ˹it˺. 203. Then they will cry, "Can we be allowed more time?"

Warning to the Meccan Pagans

204. Do they ˹really˺ seek to hasten Our torment? 205. Imagine ˹O Prophet˺ if We allowed them enjoyment for years, 206. then there came to them what they had been threatened with: 207. would that enjoyment be of any benefit to them ˹at all˺? 208. We have never destroyed a society without warners 209. to remind ˹them˺, for We would never wrong ˹anyone˺.

The Quran Is God's Word

210. It was not the devils who brought this ˹Quran˺ down: 211. it is not for them ˹to do so˺, nor can they, 212. for they are strictly barred from ˹even˺ overhearing ˹it˺.[755]

Advice to the Prophet

213. So do not ever call upon any other god besides God, or you will be one of the punished. 214. And warn ˹all, starting with˺ your closest relatives, 215. and be gracious to the believers who follow you. 216. But if they disobey you, say, "I am certainly free of what you do." 217. Put your trust in the Almighty, Most Merciful, 218. Who sees you when you rise ˹for prayer at night˺, 219. as well as your movements ˹in prayer˺ along with ˹fellow˺ worshippers. 220. He ˹alone˺ is indeed the All-Hearing, All-Knowing.

The Devils

221. Shall I inform you of whom the devils ˹actually˺ descend upon? 222. They descend upon every sinful liar, 223. who gives an ˹attentive˺ ear ˹to half-truths˺, mostly passing on sheer lies.[756]

The Poets

224. As for poets, they are followed ˹merely˺ by deviants. 225. Do you not see how they rant in every field,[757] 226. only saying what they never do? 227. Except those who believe, do good, remember God often, and ˹poetically˺ avenge ˹the believers˺ after being wrongfully slandered. The wrongdoers will come to know what ˹evil˺ end they will meet.

---

753 They were targeted by scorching heat, so they did not know where to go. Finally, a soothing cloud appeared in the sky, so they rushed to it for shade, then the cloud rained torment upon them, as they had requested.

754 i.e., 'Abdullâh ibn Salâm, a Jewish authority, who accepted Islam during the time of the Prophet.

755 The devils can no longer eavesdrop on heaven. *See* 72:8-10.

756 This refers to fortune-tellers who listen to Satanic whispers, adding more lies as they pass on the information to people.

757 lit., roam aimlessly in every valley.

27. The Ants (An-Naml)

This Meccan chapter narrates the encounters of Solomon with ants (hence the chapter's name), a hoopoe, and the Queen of Sheba—which do not appear in any other chapter. God's power to create and provide is contrasted with the powerlessness of the idols. Some deterring examples are given to the pagans, along with a warning of the horrors of the apocalypse. The Prophet is reassured of the truth of the Quran and told that his duty is only to deliver the message. Judgment rests with God alone.

In the Name of God—the Most Compassionate, Most Merciful

Qualities of the Believers

1. *Ṭâ-Sĩn.* These are the verses of the Quran; the clear Book. 2. ˹It is˺ a guide and good news for the believers: 3. ˹those˺ who establish prayer, pay alms-tax, and have sure faith in the Hereafter.

Qualities of the Disbelievers

4. As for those who do not believe in the Hereafter, We have certainly made their ˹evil˺ deeds appealing to them, so they wander blindly. 5. It is they who will suffer a dreadful torment, and in the Hereafter they will ˹truly˺ be the greatest losers. 6. And indeed, you ˹O Prophet˺ are receiving the Quran from the One ˹Who is˺ All-Wise, All-Knowing.

Moses and the Nine Signs

7. ˹Remember˺ when Moses said to his family, "I have spotted a fire. I will either bring you some directions[758] from there, or a burning torch so you may warm yourselves." 8. But when he came to it, he was called ˹by God˺, "Blessed is the one at the fire, and whoever is around it![759] Glory be to God, the Lord of all worlds. 9. O Moses! It is truly I. I am God—the Almighty, All-Wise. 10. Now, throw down your staff!" But when he saw it slithering like a snake, he ran away without looking back. ˹God reassured him,˺ "O Mo-ses! Do not be afraid! Messengers should have no fear in My presence. 11. ˹Fear is˺ only for those who do wrong. But if they later mend ˹their˺ evil ˹ways˺ with good, then I am certainly All-Forgiving, Most Merciful. 12. Now put your hand through ˹the opening of˺ your collar, it will come out ˹shining˺ white, unblemished.[760] ˹These are two˺ of nine signs for Pharaoh and his people.[761] They have truly been a rebellious people." 13. But when Our enlightening signs came to them, they said, "This is pure magic." 14. And, although their hearts were convinced the signs were true, they still denied them wrongfully and arrogantly. See then what was the end of the corruptors!

David and Solomon

15. Indeed, We granted knowledge to David and Solomon. And they said ˹in acknowledgment˺, "All praise is for God Who has privileged us over many of His faithful servants."[762] 16. And David was succeeded by Solomon, who said, "O people! We have been taught the language of birds, and been given everything ˹we need˺. This is indeed a great privilege."

Solomon and the Ant

17. Solomon's forces of jinn, humans, and birds were rallied for him, perfectly orga-

---

758 lit., information. Moses and his family lost their way in the dark while they were travelling from Midian to Egypt.
759 This refers to the angels who were present around the light.
760 See footnote for 20:22.
761 See footnote for 23:45.
762 The privilege was their ability to communicate with members of the animal kingdom, control the wind, utilize the jinn for their service, etc.

nized. **18.** And when they came across a valley of ants, an ant warned, "O ants! Go quickly into your homes so Solomon and his armies do not crush you, unknowingly." **19.** So Solomon smiled in amusement at her words, and prayed, "My Lord! Inspire me to ˹always˺ be thankful for Your favours which You have blessed me and my parents with, and to do good deeds that please you. Admit me, by Your mercy, into ˹the company of˺ Your righteous servants."

Solomon and the Hoopoe

20. ˹One day˺ he inspected the birds, and wondered, "Why is it that I cannot see the hoopoe? Or could he be absent? **21.** I will surely subject him to a severe punishment, or ˹even˺ slaughter him, unless he brings me a compelling excuse." **22.** It was not long before the bird came and said, "I have found out something you do not know. I have just come to you from Sheba with sure news. **23.** Indeed, I found a woman ruling over them,[763] who has been given everything ˹she needs˺, and who has a magnificent throne. **24.** I found her and her people prostrating to the sun instead of God. For Satan has made their deeds appealing to them—hindering them from the ˹Right˺ Way and leaving them unguided— **25.** so they do not prostrate to God, Who brings forth what is hidden in the heavens and the earth, and knows what you ˹all˺ conceal and what you reveal. **26.** ˹He is˺ God! There is no god ˹worthy of worship˺ except Him, the Lord of the Mighty Throne."

Solomon's Letter

27. Solomon said, "We will see whether you are telling the truth or lying. **28.** Go with this letter of mine and deliver it to them, then stand aside and see how they will respond." **29.** The Queen ˹later˺ announced, "O chiefs! Indeed, a noble letter has been delivered to me. **30.** It is from Solomon, and it reads: 'In the Name of God—the Most Compassionate, Most Merciful. **31.** Do not be arrogant with me, but come to me, fully submitting ˹to God˺.'"

The Queen's Response

32. She said, "O chiefs! Advise me in this matter of mine, for I would never make any decision without you." **33.** They responded, "We are a people of strength and great ˹military˺ might, but the decision is yours, so decide what you will command." **34.** She reasoned, "Indeed, when kings invade a land, they ruin it and debase its nobles. They really do so! **35.** But I will certainly send him a gift, and see what ˹response˺ my envoys will return with."[764]

Solomon's Response

36. When the chief-envoy came to him, Solomon said, "Do you offer me wealth? What God has granted me is far greater than what He has granted you. No! It is you who rejoice in ˹receiving˺ gifts. **37.** Go back to them, for we will certainly mobilize against them forces which they can never resist, and we will drive them out from there in disgrace, fully humbled."[765]

The Queen's Throne

38. Solomon asked, "O chiefs! Which of you can bring me her throne before they come to me in ˹full˺ submission?"[766] **39.** One mighty jinn responded, "I can bring it to you before you rise from this council of yours. And I am quite strong and trustworthy for this ˹task˺." **40.** But the one who had knowledge of the

Scripture said,[767] "I can bring it to you in the blink of an eye." So when Solomon saw it placed before him, he exclaimed, "This is by the grace of my Lord to test me whether I am grateful or ungrateful. And whoever is grateful, it is only for their own good. But whoever is ungrateful, surely my Lord is Self-Sufficient, Most Generous." 41. ˹Then˺ Solomon said, "Disguise her throne for her so we may see whether she will recognize ˹it˺ or she will not be able to." 42. So when she arrived, it was said ˹to her˺, "Is your throne like this?" She replied, "It looks to be the same. We have ˹already˺ received knowledge ˹of Solomon's prophethood˺[768] before this ˹miracle˺,[769] and have submitted ˹to God˺." 43. But she had been hindered by what she used to worship instead of God, for she was indeed from a disbelieving people.

Solomon's Palace

44. Then she was told, "Enter the palace." But when she saw the hall, she thought it was a body of water, so she bared her legs. Solomon said. "It is just a palace paved with crystal." ˹At last˺ she declared, "My Lord! I have certainly wronged my soul. Now I ˹fully˺ submit myself along with Solomon to God, the Lord of all worlds."

Prophet Ṣâliḥ and His People

45. And We certainly sent to the people of Thamûd their brother Ṣâliḥ, proclaiming, "Worship God," but they suddenly split into two opposing groups.[770] 46. He urged ˹the disbelieving group˺, "O my people! Why do you ˹seek to˺ hasten the torment[771] rather than grace?[772] If only you sought God's forgiveness so you may be shown mercy!" 47. They replied, "You and your followers are a bad omen for us."[773] He respond-

ed, "Your omens are destined by God. In fact, you are ˹only˺ a people being tested."

An Attempt on Ṣâliḥ's Life

48. And there were in the city nine ˹elite˺ men who spread corruption in the land, never doing what is right. 49. They vowed, "Let us swear by God that we will take him and his family down by night. Then we will certainly say to his ˹closest˺ heirs, 'We did not witness the murder of his family. We are definitely telling the truth.'" 50. And ˹so˺ they made a plan, but We too made a plan, while they were unaware. 51. See then what the consequences of their plan were: We ˹utterly˺ destroyed them and their people all together. 52. So their homes are there, ˹but completely˺ ruined because of their wrongdoing. Surely in this is a lesson for people of knowledge. 53. And We delivered those who were faithful and were mindful ˹of God˺.

Prophet Lot and His People

54. And ˹remember˺ Lot, when he rebuked ˹the men of˺ his people, "Do you commit that shameful deed while you can see ˹one another˺? 55. Do you really lust after men instead of women? In fact, you are ˹only˺ a people acting ignorantly." 56. But his people's only response was to say, "Expel Lot's followers from your land! They are a people who wish to remain chaste!" 57. So We delivered him and his family, except his wife. We had destined her to be one of the doomed. 58. And We poured upon them a rain ˹of brimstone˺. How evil was the rain of those who had been warned!

---

767 This refers to 'Aṣif ibn Barkhiya, a knowledgeable and righteous assistant of Solomon.
768 Because he had refused her tribute.
769 Bringing her well-guarded, mighty throne all the way from Sheba, Yemen.
770 i.e., believers and disbelievers.
771 lit. evil
772 lit. good
773 They were struck with famine, which they blamed on Ṣâliḥ and his followers.

27. The Ants (An-Naml)

Questions to the Pagans:
1) Who Is the Creator?

59. Say, ˹O Prophet,˺ "Praise be to God, and peace be upon the servants He has chosen." ˹Ask the disbelievers,˺ "Which is better: God or whatever ˹gods˺ they associate ˹with Him˺?" 60. Or ˹ask them,˺ "Who created the heavens and the earth, and sends down rain for you from the sky, by which We cause delightful gardens to grow? You could never cause their trees to grow. Was it another god besides God? Absolutely not!" But they are a people who set up equals ˹to God˺! 61. Or ˹ask them,˺ "Who made the earth a place of settlement, caused rivers to flow through it, placed firm mountains upon it, and set a barrier between ˹fresh and salt˺ bodies of water?[774] Was it another god besides God? Absolutely not!" But most of them do not know.

2) Who Is the Most Gracious?

62. Or ˹ask them,˺ "Who responds to the distressed when they cry to Him, relieving ˹their˺ affliction, and ˹Who˺ makes you successors in the earth? Is it another god besides God? Yet you are hardly mindful!" 63. Or ˹ask them,˺ "Who guides you in the darkness of the land and sea,[775] and sends the winds ushering in His mercy?[776] Is it another god besides God? Exalted is God above what they associate ˹with Him˺! 64. Or ˹ask them,˺ "Who originates the creation then resurrects it, and gives you provisions from the heavens and the earth? Is it another god besides God?" Say, ˹O Prophet,˺ "Show ˹me˺ your proof, if what you say is true."

Only God Knows the Unseen[777]

65. Say, ˹O Prophet,˺ "None in the heavens and the earth has knowledge of the unseen except God. Nor do they know when they will be resurrected." 66. No! Their knowledge of the Hereafter amounts to ignorance. In fact, they are in doubt about it. In truth, they are ˹totally˺ blind to it.

Denying Resurrection

67. The disbelievers ask, "When we and our fathers are reduced to dust, will we really be brought forth ˹alive˺? 68. We have already been promised this, as well as our forefathers earlier. This is nothing but ancient fables!" 69. Say, ˹O Prophet,˺ "Travel throughout the land and see the fate of the wicked." 70. Do not grieve for them, nor be distressed by their schemes.

Ridiculing Punishment

71. They ask ˹the believers˺, "When will this threat come to pass, if what you say is true?" 72. Say, ˹O Prophet,˺ "Perhaps some of what you seek to hasten is close at hand." 73. Surely your Lord is ever Bountiful to humanity,[778] but most of them are ungrateful. 74. And surely your Lord knows what their hearts conceal and what they reveal.[779] 75. For there is nothing hidden in the heavens or the earth without being ˹written˺ in a perfect Record.[780]

Advice to the Prophet

76. Indeed, this Quran clarifies for the Children of Israel most of what they differ over. 77. And it is truly a guide and mercy for the believers. 78. Your Lord will certainly judge between them by His justice, for He is the Almighty, All-Knowing. 79. So put your trust in God, for you are surely upon the ˹Path of˺ clear truth. 80. You certainly cannot make the dead hear ˹the truth˺. Nor can you make the deaf hear the call when they

---

774 *See* footnote for 25:53.
775 Via the stars and constellations.
776 In the form of rain.
777 This passage was revealed when the polytheists asked the Prophet about the time of the Final Hour.
778 By delaying their punishment and allowing them time to repent.
779 Through their tongues or actions.
780 The Record refers to the Preserved Tablet (*Al-Lawḥ Al-Maḥfûz*) in which God has written the destiny of His entire creation.

203

turn their backs and walk away. **81.** Nor can you lead the blind out of their misguidance. You can make none hear ˹the truth˼ except those who believe in Our revelations, ˹fully˼ submitting ˹to God˼.

The Apocalypse

82. And when the decree ˹of the Hour˼ comes to pass against them, We will bring forth for them a beast from the earth,[781] telling them that the people had no sure faith in Our revelations. **83.** ˹Watch for˼ the Day We will gather from every faith-community a group of those who denied Our revelations, and they will be driven in ranks. **84.** When they ˹finally˼ come before their Lord, He will ask ˹them˼, "Did you deny My revelations without ˹even˼ comprehending them? Or what ˹exactly˼ did you do?" **85.** And the decree ˹of torment˼ will be justified against them for their wrongdoing, leaving them speechless.

God's Power 1)   The Day and Night

86. Do they not see that We made the night for them to rest in and the day bright?[782] Surely in this are signs for those who believe.

The Apocalypse

87. And ˹beware of˼ the Day the Trumpet will be blown, and all those in the heavens and all those on the earth will be horrified ˹to the point of death˼,[783] except those God wills ˹to spare˼. And all will come before Him, fully humbled.

God's Power 2)   Earth's Rotation

88. Now you see the mountains, thinking they are firmly fixed, but they are travelling ˹just˼ like clouds. ˹That is˼ the design of God, Who has perfected everything. Surely He is All-Aware of what you do.

Judgment Day

89. Whoever comes with a good deed will be rewarded with what is better, and they will be secure from the horror on that Day. **90.** And whoever comes with an evil deed will be hurled face-first into the Fire. Are you rewarded except for what you used to do?

Advice to the Prophet

91. Say, ˹O Prophet,˼ "I have only been commanded to worship the Lord of this city ˹of Mecca˼, Who has made it sacred, and to Him belongs everything. And I am commanded to be one of those who ˹fully˼ submit ˹to Him˼, **92.** and to recite the Quran." Then whoever chooses to be guided, it is only for their own good. But whoever chooses to stray, say, ˹O Prophet,˼ "I am only a warner." **93.** And say, "All praise is for God! He will show you His signs, and you will recognize them. And your Lord is never unaware of what you do."

---

781 The beast is believed to be one of the major signs of the Day of Judgment. No further details are given in reliable resources about this beast.

782 To demonstrate His ability to bring people back to life, God usually refers to some wonders of His creation, such as the planets, the alternation of the day and night, the mountains, and the development of the human embryo.

783 The Trumpet will be blown at two different occasions, signalling the beginning of Judgment Day. The first blow will cause all creation to die, except whoever God spares, and the second one will cause them to be raised from the dead.

28. The Whole Story *(Al-Qaṣaṣ)*

In 26:18-19, Pharaoh reminds Moses of his up-bringing in the care of Pharaoh and how Moses killed an Egyptian (accidentally). Unlike the previous chapter, this Meccan chapter focuses on these two aspects of Moses' life in Egypt, along with his escape to Midian where he met his future wife. Another aspect is the story of Korah, one of the people of Moses, who behaved arrogantly, leading to his own destruction. Just like the previous chapter, it reaffirms God's power and the authenticity of the Quran. Again, the Prophet is reminded that his duty is not to convert, but to convey. After criticizing the polytheists (verses 45-75), the chapter concludes by bidding the Prophet to be steadfast. The next chapter starts off by talking about steadfastness.

In the Name of God—the Most Compassionate, Most Merciful

Pharaoh's Tyranny

1. *Ṭâ-Sîn-Mîm.* 2. These are the verses of the clear Book. 3. We narrate to you ʿO Prophetʾ part of the story of Moses and Pharaoh in truth for people who believe. 4. Indeed, Pharaoh ʿarrogantlyʾ elevated himself in the land and divided its people into ʿsubservientʾ groups, one of which he persecuted, slaughtering their sons and keeping their women. He was truly one of the corruptors. 5. But it was Our Will to favour those who were oppressed in the land, making them models ʿof faithʾ as well as successors; 6. and to establish them in the land; and through them show Pharaoh, Hamân,[784] and their soldiers ʿthe fulfilment ofʾ what they feared.[785]

Baby Moses in the Nile

7. We inspired the mother of Moses: "Nurse him, but when you fear for him, put him then into the river, and do not fear or grieve. We will certainly return him to you, and make him one of the messengers." 8. And ʿit so happened thatʾ Pharaoh's people picked him up, only to become their enemy and source of grief. Surely Pharaoh, Hamân, and their soldiers were sinful.

Moses in the Palace

9. Pharaoh's wife said ʿto him', "ʿThis baby is' a source of joy for me and you. Do not kill him. Perhaps he may be useful to us or we may adopt him as a son." They were unaware ʿof what was to come'. 10. And the heart of Moses' mother ached so much that she almost gave away his identity, had We not reassured her heart in order for her to have faith ʿin God's promise'. 11. And she said to his sister, "Keep track of him!" So she watched him from a distance, while they were unaware. 12. And We had caused him to refuse all wet-nurses at first, so his sister suggested, "Shall I direct you to a family who will bring him up for you and take good care of him?" 13. This is how We returned him to his mother so that her heart would be put at ease, and not grieve, and that she would know that God's promise is ʿalways' true. But most people do not know. 14. And when he reached full strength and maturity, We gave him wisdom and knowledge. This is how We reward the good-doers.

---

784   It is commonly believed that Hamân was in charge of architecture during the reign of Pharaoh at the time of Moses.
785   The fulfilment of the Pharaoh's old dream that his reign would come to an end at the hands of a boy from the Children of Israel.

Unintentional Killing

15. ʿOne dayʾ he entered the city unnoticed by its people.[786] There he found two men fighting: one of his own people, and the other of his enemies. The man from his people called to him for help against his foe. So Moses punched him, causing his death. Moses cried, "This is from Satan's handiwork. He is certainly a sworn, misleading enemy." **16.** He pleaded, "My Lord! I have definitely wronged my soul, so forgive me." So He forgave him, ʿforʾ He is indeed the All-Forgiving, Most Merciful. **17.** Moses pledged, "My Lord! For all Your favours upon me, I will never side with the wicked."

The Incident Comes to Light

18. And so Moses became fearful, watching out in the city, when suddenly the one who sought his help the day before cried out to him again for help. Moses rebuked him, "Indeed, you are clearly a trouble-maker." **19.** Then when Moses was about to lay his hands on their foe,[787] the enemy said, "O Moses! Do you intend to kill me as you killed a man yesterday? You only want to be a tyrant in the land. You do not intend to make peace!"

Moses Escapes to Midian

20. And there came a man, rushing from the farthest end of the city. He said, "O Moses! The chiefs are actually conspiring against you to put you to death, so leave ʿthe cityʾ. I really advise you ʿto do soʾ." **21.** So Moses left the city in a state of fear and caution, praying, "My Lord! Deliver me from the wrongdoing people." **22.** And as he made his way towards Midian, he said, "I trust my Lord will guide me to the right way."

Moses Helps Two Women

23. When he arrived at the well of Midian, he found a group of people watering ʿtheir herdsʾ. Apart from them, he noticed two women holding back ʿtheir herdʾ. He asked ʿthemʾ, "What is the matter?" They replied, "We cannot water ʿour animalsʾ until the ʿotherʾ shepherds are done, for our father is a very old man." **24.** So he watered ʿtheir herdʾ for them, then withdrew to the shade and prayed, "My Lord! I am truly in ʿdesperateʾ need of whatever provision You may have in store for me."[788]

Moses Gets Married

25. Then one of the two women came to him, walking bashfully. She said, "My father is inviting you so he may reward you for watering ʿour animalsʾ for us." When Moses came to him and told him his whole story, the old man said, "Have no fear! You are ʿnowʾ safe from the wrongdoing people." **26.** One of the two daughters suggested, "O my dear father! Hire him. A strong, trustworthy person is definitely the best to hire." **27.** The old man proposed, "I wish to marry one of these two daughters of mine to you, provided that you stay in my service for eight years. If you complete ten, it will be ʿa favourʾ from you, but I do not wish to make it difficult for you. God willing, you will find me an agreeable man." **28.** Moses responded, "ʿThenʾ it is ʿsettledʾ between you and I. Whichever term I fulfill, there will be no ʿfurtherʾ obligation on me. And God is a Witness to what we say."

The Fateful Encounter

29. When Moses had completed the term and was travelling with his family, he spotted a fire on the side of Mount Ṭûr. He said to his family, "Stay here, ʿforʾ I have spotted a fire. Perhaps from there I can bring you some di-

---

786 In his adulthood, Moses and Pharaoh's people were not on good terms because he started to question their evil practices.
787 The man assumed that Moses was going to hit him.
788 Moses left Egypt with no food, money, or even shoes. He was completely worn out by the time he arrived in Midian. After he prayed for help, God gave him a wife, a job, and a home on the same day.

rections[789] or a torch from the fire so you may warm yourselves." 30. But when he came to it, he was called from the bush in the sacred ground to the right side of the valley: "O Moses! It is truly I. I am God—the Lord of all worlds. 31. Now, throw down your staff!" But when he saw it slithering like a snake, he ran away without looking back. ʿGod reassured him,ʾ "O Moses! Draw near, and have no fear. You are perfectly secure. 32. Now put your hand through ʿthe opening ofʾ your collar, it will come out ʿshiningʾ white, unblemished.[790] And cross your arms tightly to calm your fears.[791] These are two proofs from your Lord to Pharaoh and his chiefs. They have truly been a rebellious people."

Moses Asks God for Help

33. Moses appealed, "My Lord! I have indeed killed a man from them, so I fear they may kill me. 34. And my brother Aaron is more eloquent than I, so send him with me as a helper to support what I say, for I truly fear they may reject me." 35. God responded, "We will assist you with your brother and grant you both authority, so they cannot harm you. With Our signs, you and those who follow you will ʿcertainlyʾ prevail."

Pharaoh's Response

36. But when Moses came to them with Our clear signs, they said ʿarrogantlyʾ, "This is nothing but conjured magic ʿtricksʾ. We have never heard of this in ʿthe history ofʾ our forefathers." 37. Moses responded, "My Lord knows best who has come with ʿtrueʾ guidance from Him and will fare best in the end. Indeed, the wrongdoers will never succeed." 38. Pharaoh declared, "O chiefs! I know of no other god for you but myself. So

bake bricks out of clay for me, O Hamân, and build a high tower so I may look at the God of Moses, although I am sure he is a liar."

End of Pharaoh

39. And so he and his soldiers behaved arrogantly in the land with no right, thinking they would never be returned to Us. 40. So We seized him and his soldiers, casting them into the sea. See then what was the end of the wrongdoers! 41. We made them leaders inviting ʿothersʾ to the Fire. And on the Day of Judgment they will not be helped. 42. We caused a curse to follow them in this world. And on the Day of Judgment they will be among the outcasts.

Excellence of the Torah

43. Indeed, We gave Moses the Scripture—after destroying earlier nations—as an insight for the people, a guide, and mercy so perhaps they would be mindful.

Revealed Stories

44. You were not there ʿO Prophetʾ on the western side of the mountain when We entrusted the Commandments to Moses, nor were you present ʿin his timeʾ.[792] 45. But We ʿlaterʾ raised ʿseveralʾ generations, and the ages took their toll on them.[793] Nor were you living among the people of Midian, rehearsing Our revelations with them. But it is We Who have sent ʿthisʾ revelation to youʾ. 46. And you were not at the side of Mount Ṭûr when We called out ʿto Mosesʾ. But ʿyou have been sentʾ as a mercy from your Lord to warn a people to whom no warner has come before you, so perhaps they may be mindful. 47. Also so they would not say, if struck by an affliction for what their hands

---

789   lit., information. Moses and his family lost their way in the dark while they were travelling from Midian to Egypt.
790   See footnote for 20:22.
791   When Moses put his arm through the opening in his collar again, his hand returned to its original colour.
792   The pagans are reminded repeatedly in the Quran that the Prophet did not witness any of these events that happened centuries before he was born. For example, the conspiracies that were made against Joseph (12:102), the dispute on who should be the guardian of young Mary (3:44), and the drowning of Noah's son in the Flood (11:49). These details were not known to Arabs before the revelation of the Quran. So the only logical way that the Prophet knew about these stories is through divine revelation.
793   So they neglected the Commandments over time.

have done: "Our Lord! If only You had sent us a messenger, we would have followed Your revelations and become believers."

Pagan Response to the Quran

48. But when the truth came to them from Us, they said, "If only he was given the like of what Moses had been given."[794] Did they not deny what had been given to Moses earlier? They claimed, "Both ˹Scriptures˺ are works of magic, supporting each other!"[795] Adding, "We truly deny both." **49.** Say, ˹O Prophet,˺ "Bring then a scripture from God which is a better guide than these two so I may follow it, if your claim is true." **50.** So if they fail to respond to you, then know that they only follow their desires. And who could be more astray than those who follow their desires with no guidance from God? Surely God does not guide the wrongdoing people.

The Doubly Rewarded

51. Indeed, We have steadily delivered the Word ˹of God˺ to the people so they may be mindful. **52.** ˹As for˺ those ˹faithful˺ to whom We had given the Scripture before this ˹Quran˺, they do believe in it. **53.** When it is recited to them, they declare, "We believe in it. This is definitely the truth from our Lord. We had already submitted[796] ˹even˺ before this." **54.** These ˹believers˺ will be given a double reward for their perseverance, responding to evil with good, and for donating from what We have provided for them. **55.** When they hear slanderous talk, they turn away from it, saying, "We are accountable for our deeds and you for yours. Peace ˹is our only response˺ to you! We want nothing to do with those who act ignorantly."

Guidance Is from God Alone

56. You surely cannot guide whoever you like ˹O Prophet˺, but it is God Who guides whoever He wills, and He knows best who are ˹fit to be˺ guided.

Pagan Excuses

57. They say ˹to the Prophet˺, "If we were to follow ˹true˺ guidance with you, we would certainly be snatched away from our land." Have We not established for them a safe haven ˹in Mecca˺ to which fruits of all kinds are brought as a provision from Us? But most of them do not know ˹this favour˺. **58.** ˹Imagine˺ how many societies We have destroyed that had been spoiled by their ˹comfortable˺ living! Those are their residences, never inhabited after them except passingly.[797] And We ˹alone˺ were the Successor. **59.** Your Lord would never destroy a society until He had sent to its capital a messenger, reciting Our revelations to them. Nor would We ever destroy a society unless its people persisted in wrongdoing.

This World or the Hereafter?

60. Whatever ˹pleasure˺ you have been given is no more than ˹a fleeting˺ enjoyment and adornment of this worldly life. But what is with God is far better and more lasting. Will you not then understand? **61.** Can those to whom We have made a fine promise—which they will see fulfilled—be like those who We have allowed to enjoy the pleasures of this worldly life, but on the Day of Judgment will be brought ˹for punishment˺?

The Misleaders and the Misled

62. ˹Watch for˺ the Day He will call to them, "Where are those you claimed were My associate-gods?" **63.** Those ˹mislead-

---

794 The pagans of Mecca demanded that the Quran should have been revealed all at once like the Torah, and the Prophet should have had some tangible signs like the staff of Moses.
795 Some Meccan pagans approached some Jewish authorities to inquire about the Prophet's message and they were told that there are references of him in the Torah. So the pagans immediately rejected both the Torah and the Quran as two works of magic.
796 lit., 'We had already been Muslims.'
797 By travellers such as the Meccan pagans.

ers' against whom the decree 'of torment' is justified will cry, "Our Lord! These 'followers' are the ones we caused to deviate. We led them into deviance, for we ourselves were deviant. We disassociate ourselves 'from them' before You. It was not us that they used to worship." **64.** It will be said 'to the disbelievers', "Call upon your associate-gods 'for help'." So they will call them, but will receive no response. And they will face the punishment, wishing they had been 'rightly' guided!

A Question to the Disbelievers

65. And 'watch for' the Day He will call to them, asking, "What response did you give to the messengers?" **66.** They will be too dumbstruck on that Day to ask one another 'for answers'.

The True Believers

67. As for those who repent, believe, and do good 'in this world', it is right to hope that they will be among the successful.

God Almighty

68. Your Lord creates and chooses whatever He wills—the choice is not theirs. Glorified and Exalted is God above what they associate 'with Him'! **69.** And your Lord knows what their hearts conceal and what they reveal. **70.** He is God. There is no god 'worthy of worship' except Him. All praise belongs to Him in this life and the next. All authority is His. And to Him you will 'all' be returned.

God's Might and Grace

71. Ask 'them, O Prophet', "Imagine if God were to make the night perpetual for you until the Day of Judgment, which god other than God could bring you sunlight? Will you

not then listen?" **72.** Ask 'them also', "Imagine if God were to make the day perpetual for you until the Day of Judgment, which god other than God could bring you night to rest in? Will you not then see?" **73.** It is out of His mercy that He has made for you the day and night so that you may rest 'in the latter' and seek His bounty 'in the former', and perhaps you will be grateful.

Polytheists Rebuked Again

74. And 'watch for' the Day He will call to them, "Where are those you claimed were My associate-gods?" **75.** And We will bring forth a witness[798] from every faith-community and ask 'the polytheists', "Show 'Us' your proof." Then they will 'come to' know that the truth is with God 'alone'. And whatever 'gods' they fabricated will fail them.

Korah's Arrogance

76. Indeed, Korah[799] was from the people of Moses, but he behaved arrogantly towards them. We had granted him such treasures that even their keys would burden a group of strong men. 'Some of' his people advised him, "Do not be prideful! Surely God does not like the prideful. **77.** Rather, seek the 'reward' of the Hereafter by means of what God has granted you, without forgetting your share of this world. And be good 'to others' as God has been good to you. Do not seek to spread corruption in the land, for God certainly does not like the corruptors."

Korah's Response

78. He replied, "I have been granted all this because of some knowledge I have."[800] Did he not know that God had already destroyed some from the generations before him who were far superior to him in power and greater in accumulating 'wealth'? There will be no

---

798 A prophet.

799 Korah was the cousin of Moses. Because of Korah's close association with Pharaoh, he became very rich and started to behave arrogantly towards his own people. When he was asked repeatedly by Moses to pay his alms-tax to help poor Israelites, Korah refused and eventually conspired with a prostitute to damage the reputation of Moses, but Moses was cleared of any wrongdoing.

800 Or: "I have been granted all this because I know that God knows I deserve it."

need for the wicked to be asked about their sins.[801]

Debate on Korah

79. Then he came out before his people in all his glamour. Those who desired the life of this world wished, "If only we could have something like what Korah has been given. He is truly a man of great fortune!" **80.** But those gifted with knowledge said, "Shame on you! God's reward is far better for those who believe and do good. But none will attain this except the steadfast."

Korah's End

81. Then We caused the earth to swallow him up, along with his home. There was no one to help him against God, nor could he even help himself. **82.** And those who had craved his position the previous day began to say, "Ah! It is certainly God Who gives abundant or limited provisions to whoever He wills of His servants. Had it not been for the grace of God, He could have surely caused the earth to swallow us up! Oh, indeed! The disbelievers will never succeed."

Pay Day

83. That ˹eternal˺ Home in the Hereafter We reserve ˹only˺ for those who seek nei-ther tyranny nor corruption on the earth. The ultimate outcome belongs ˹only˺ to the righteous. **84.** Whoever comes with a good deed will be rewarded with what is better. And whoever comes with an evil deed, then the evildoers will only be rewarded for what they used to do.

Advice to the Prophet

85. Most certainly, the One Who has ordained the Quran for you will ˹ultimately˺ bring you back home ˹to Mecca˺.[802] Say, "My Lord knows best who has come with ˹true˺ guidance and who is clearly astray." **86.** You never expected this Book to be revealed to you, but ˹it came˺ only ˹as˺ a mercy from your Lord. So never side with the disbelievers ˹in their disbelief˺. **87.** Do not let them turn you away from the revelations of God after they have been sent down to you. Rather, invite ˹all˺ to ˹the Way of˺ your Lord, and never be one of the polytheists. **88.** And do not invoke any other god with God. There is no god ˹worthy of worship˺ except Him. Everything is bound to perish except He Alone.[803] All authority belongs to Him. And to Him you will ˹all˺ be returned.

29. The Spider *(Al-'Ankabût)*

This Meccan chapter takes its name from the parable of the spider in verse 41. The beginning of the chapter emphasizes the role of trials and tribulations in revealing those who are truly steadfast and those who are not. Noah, Abraham, Lot, and Shu'aib are noted for their perseverance. References are made to various peoples and the different ways they were destroyed for their denial of the truth (verse 40). The pagan arguments against the Prophet and the Quran are thoroughly refuted. The chapter concludes by commending those who put their trust in God and strive in His cause. This conclusion paves the way for the opening of the next chapter.

---

801   Since their sins are already known to God and written in perfect records, they will only be interrogated as a form of punishment.

802   This verse was revealed while the Prophet was on the way to Medina, emigrating from Mecca after years of persecution. Eventually the Prophet returned to Mecca and the majority of its people accepted Islam.

803   lit., except His Face. We believe that God has a Face, but not like ours. *See* the Introduction for details.

In the Name of God—the Most Compassionate, Most Merciful

The Test

1. *Alif-Lãm-Mĩm.* 2. Do people think once they say, "We believe," that they will be left without being put to the test? 3. We certainly tested those before them. And 'in this way' God will clearly distinguish between those who are truthful and those who are liars. 4. Or do the evildoers 'simply' think that they will escape Us? How wrong is their judgment!

The True Believers

5. Whoever hopes for the meeting with God, 'let them know that' God's appointed time is sure to come. He is the All-Hearing, All-Knowing. 6. And whoever strives 'in God's cause', only does so for their own good. Surely God is not in need of 'any of' His creation. 7. As for those who believe and do good, We will certainly absolve them of their sins, and reward them according to the best of what they used to do. 8. We have commanded people to honour their parents. But if they urge you to associate with Me what you have no knowledge of,[804] then do not obey them. To Me you will 'all' return, and then I will inform you of what you used to do. 9. Those who believe and do good will surely be admitted by Us into 'the company of' the righteous.

The Hypocrites

10. There are some who say, "We believe in God," but when they suffer in the cause of God, they mistake 'this' persecution at the hands of people for the punishment of God. But when victory comes from your Lord, they surely say 'to the believers', "We have always been with you." Does God not know best what is in the hearts of all beings? 11. God will certainly distinguish between those who have 'sure' faith and the hypocrites.

False Promise

12. The disbelievers say to the believers, "'Just' follow our way, and we will bear 'the burden of' your sins." But they would never 'want to' bear any of the believers' sins. They are simply lying. 13. Yet they will certainly 'be made to' carry their own burdens, as well as other burdens along with their own.[805] And they will surely be questioned on Judgment Day about what they used to fabricate.

Noah's People Destroyed

14. Indeed, We sent Noah to his people, and he remained among them for a thousand years, less fifty. Then the Flood overtook them, while they persisted in wrongdoing. 15. But We delivered him and those in the Ark, making it a sign for all people.

The People of Abraham

16. And 'remember' when Abraham said to his people, "Worship God, and fear Him. This is better for you, if only you knew. 17. You worship besides God nothing but idols, simply creating lies 'about them'. Those you worship besides God certainly cannot give you any provision. So seek provision from God 'alone', worship Him, and be grateful to Him. To Him you will 'all' be returned."

Warning to Meccan Pagans

18. If you persist in denial, so did 'many' communities before you. The Messenger's duty is only to deliver 'the message' clearly. 19. Have they not seen how God originates the creation then resurrects it? That is certainly easy for God. 20. Say, 'O Prophet,' "Travel throughout the land and see how He originated the creation, then God will bring it into being one more time. Surely God is Most Capable of ev-

804 Other gods.
805 The burdens of those they misled.

erything. **21.** He punishes whoever He wills, and shows mercy to whoever He wills. And you will ʿall˅ be returned to Him. **22.** And you cannot escape Him on earth or in heaven. Nor have you any protector or helper besides God." **23.** As for those who disbelieve in God's signs and the meeting with Him, it is they who will have no hope in His mercy.[806] And it is they who will suffer a painful punishment.

Abraham Prevails

24. But the only response of Abraham's people was to say: "Kill him or burn him!" But God saved him from the fire.[807] Surely in this are signs for people who believe. **25.** He said ʿto his peopleˀ, "You have taken idols ʿfor worshipˀ instead of God, only to keep ʿthe bond ofˀ harmony among yourselves in this worldly life. But on the Day of Judgment you will disown and curse one another. Your home will be the Fire, and you will have no helper!" **26.** So Lot believed in him. And Abraham said, "I am emigrating ʿin obedienceˀ to my Lord. He ʿaloneˀ is indeed the Almighty, All-Wise." **27.** We blessed him with Isaac and ʿlaterˀ Jacob, and reserved prophethood and revelation for his descendants. We gave him his reward in this life,[808] and in the Hereafter he will certainly be among the righteous.

The People of Lot

28. And ʿrememberˀ when Lot rebuked ʿtheˀ men ofˀ his people: "You certainly commit a shameful deed that no man has ever done before you. **29.** Do you really lust after ʿotherˀ men, abuse the travellers, and practice immorality ʿopenlyˀ in your gatherings?" His people's only response was to say ʿmockinglyˀ: "Bring God's punishment upon us, if what you say is true." **30.** Lot prayed, "My Lord! Help me against the people of corruption."

Abraham Visited by Angels

31. When Our messenger-angels came to Abraham with the good news ʿof the birth of Isaacˀ, they said, "We are going to destroy the people of this city ʿof Sodomˀ, for its people have persisted in wrongdoing." **32.** He said, "But Lot is there!" They responded, "We know best who is there. We will certainly save him and his family—except his wife, who is one of the doomed."

The People of Lot Destroyed

33. And when Our messenger-angels came to Lot, he was distressed and worried by their arrival.[809] They reassured ʿhimˀ, "Do not fear, nor grieve. We will surely deliver you and your family—except your wife, who is one of the doomed. **34.** We are certainly bringing down a punishment from the sky upon the people of this city for their rebelliousness." **35.** And We did leave ʿsome ofˀ its ruins as a clear lesson for people of understanding.

Shu'aib's People Destroyed

36. And to the people of Midian ʿWe sentˀ their brother Shu'aib. He said, "O my people! Worship God, and hope for ʿthe rewardˀ ofˀ the Last Day. And do not go about spreading corruption in the land." **37.** But they rejected him, so an ʿoverwhelmingˀ earthquake struck them and they fell lifeless in their homes.

Previously Destroyed Nations

38. And the people of 'Âd and Thamûd ʿmet a similar fateˀ, which must be clear to you ʿMeccansˀ from their ruins.[810] Satan made their ʿevilˀ deeds appealing to them, hindering them from the ʿRightˀ Way, although they were capable of reasoning. **39.** ʿWeˀ also ʿdestroyedˀ Korah, Pharaoh,

---

806 lit., My mercy.
807 The idolaters tried to burn Abraham because he smashed their idols. *See* 21:51-71 for the full story.
808 Through honourable mention, righteous family, etc.
809 Since the angels came in the form of handsome men, Lot was worried for the dignity and safety of his guests among his people—not knowing that they were angels.
810 Meccan caravans always passed by these ruins on the way to Yemen and Syria for business.

and Hamân. Indeed, Moses had come to them with clear proofs, but they behaved arrogantly in the land. Yet they could not escape 'Us'. 40. So We seized each 'people' for their sin: against some of them We sent a storm of stones, some were overtaken by a 'mighty' blast, some We caused the earth to swallow, and some We drowned. God would not have wronged them, but it was they who wronged themselves.

God Is the Mighty Protector

41. The parable of those who take protectors other than God is that of a spider spinning a shelter. And the flimsiest of all shelters is certainly that of a spider, if only they knew. 42. God surely knows that whatever 'gods' they invoke besides Him are 'simply' nothing. For He is the Almighty, All-Wise. 43. These are the parables We set forth for humanity, but none will understand them except the people of knowledge. 44. God created the heavens and the earth for a purpose. Surely in this is a sign for the people of faith.

Advice to the Prophet

45. Recite what has been revealed to you of the Book and establish prayer. Indeed, 'genuine' prayer should deter 'one' from indecency and wickedness. The remembrance of God is 'an' even greater 'deterrent'. And God 'fully' knows what you 'all' do.

Arguing with the People of the Book

46. Do not argue with the People of the Book unless gracefully, except with those of them who act wrongfully. And say, "We believe in what has been revealed to us and what was revealed to you. Our God and your God is 'only' One. And to Him we 'fully' submit."

One Last Revelation

47. Similarly 'to earlier messengers', We have revealed to you a Book 'O Prophet'. 'The faithful of' those to whom We gave the Scriptures believe in it, as do some of these 'pagan Arabs'. And none denies Our revelations except the 'stubborn' disbelievers. 48. You 'O Prophet' could not read any writing 'even' before this 'revelation', nor could you write at all. Otherwise, the people of falsehood would have been suspicious. 49. But this 'Quran' is 'a set of' clear revelations 'preserved' in the hearts of those gifted with knowledge. And none denies Our revelations except the 'stubborn' wrongdoers.

The Pagans Demand Signs[811]

50. They say, "If only 'some' signs had been sent down to him from his Lord!" Say, 'O Prophet,' "Signs are only with God. And I am only sent with a clear warning." 51. Is it not enough for them that We have sent down to you the Book, 'which is' recited to them. Surely in this 'Quran' is a mercy and reminder for people who believe. 52. Say, 'O Prophet,' "Sufficient is God as a Witness between me and you. He 'fully' knows whatever is in the heavens and the earth. And those who believe in falsehood and disbelieve in God, it is they who are the 'true' losers."

Hastening the Punishment

53. They challenge you 'O Prophet' to hasten the punishment. Had it not been for a time already set, the punishment would have certainly come to them 'at once'. But it will definitely take them by surprise when they least expect it. 54. They urge you to hasten the punishment. And Hell will certainly encompass the disbelievers 55. on the Day the punishment will overwhelm them from above them and from below their feet. And it will be said, "Reap what you sowed."

---

811 They were not convinced of the Quran's literary miracle and, therefore, asked for tangible signs similar to the staff of Moses.

Advice to Persecuted Believers[812]

56. O My believing servants! My earth is truly spacious, so worship Me ˹alone˺. **57.** Every soul will taste death, then to Us you will ˹all˺ be returned. **58.** ˹As for˺ those who believe and do good, We will certainly house them in ˹elevated˺ mansions in Paradise, under which rivers flow, to stay there forever. How excellent is the reward for those who work ˹righteousness!˺— **59.** those who patiently endure, and put their trust in their Lord! **60.** How many are the creatures that cannot secure their provisions! ˹It is˺ God ˹Who˺ provides for them and you ˹as well˺. He is indeed the All-Hearing, All-Knowing.

Questions to the Polytheists

61. If you ask them ˹O Prophet˺ who created the heavens and the earth and subjected the sun and the moon ˹for your benefit˺, they will certainly say, "God!" How can they then be deluded ˹from the truth˺? **62.** God gives abundant or limited provisions to whoever He wills of His servants. Surely God has ˹full˺ knowledge of everything. **63.** And if you ask them who sends down rain from the sky, giving life to the earth after its death, they will surely say, "God!" Say, "Praise be to God!" In fact, most of them do not understand. **64.** This worldly life is no more than play and amusement. But the Hereafter is indeed the real life, if only they knew.

The Disbelievers' Ingratitude

65. If they happen to be aboard a ship ˹caught in a storm˺, they cry out to God ˹alone˺ in sincere devotion. But as soon as He delivers them ˹safely˺ to shore, they associate ˹others with Him once again˺. **66.** So let them be ungrateful for all We have given them, and ˹let them˺ enjoy themselves ˹for now˺! For they will soon know.

Warning to Meccan Pagans

67. Have they not seen how We have made ˹Mecca˺ a safe haven, whereas people ˹all˺ around them are snatched away?[813] How can they then believe in falsehood[814] and deny God's favours? **68.** And who does more wrong than those who fabricate lies against God or reject the truth after it has reached them? Is Hell not a ˹fitting˺ home for the disbelievers?

The Faithful Reassured

69. As for those who struggle in Our cause, We will surely guide them along Our Way. And God is certainly with the good-doers.

30. The Romans *(Ar-Rûm)*

This Meccan chapter takes its name from the reference to the Romans in verse 2. The world's superpowers in the early 7ᵗʰ century were the Roman Byzantine and Persian Empires. When they went to war in 614 C.E., the Romans suffered a devastating defeat. The Meccan pagans rejoiced at the defeat of the Roman Christians at the hands of the Persian pagans. Soon verses 30:1-5 were revealed, stating that the Romans would be

---

812 This passage addresses poor Muslims who were subject to persecution in Mecca and had to move elsewhere. Some of them were worried that they would not find provisions if they moved to a new place.

813 Mecca was considered as a sanctuary. Therefore, fighting was not allowed there, and whoever entered Mecca (especially in the neighbourhood of the Ka'bah) was safe—a privilege that other cities in Arabia did not have.

814 i.e., the false gods and idols.

victorious in three to nine years. Eight years later, the Romans won a decisive battle against the Persians, reportedly on the same day the Muslims vanquished the Meccan army at the Battle of Badr. As the chapter progresses, several blessings and natural signs are cited to prove God's infinite mercy and power, coupled with condemnations to the pagans for their ingratitude and for associating powerless idols with God in worship. The chapter closes by bidding the Prophet not to be disheartened by what the deniers say.

In the Name of God—the Most Compassionate, Most Merciful

From Defeat to Victory

1. *Alif-Lãm-Mĩm.* 2. The Romans have been defeated 3. in a nearby land. Yet following their defeat, they will triumph 4. within three to nine years. The ˹whole˺ matter rests with God before and after ˹victory˺. And on that day the believers will rejoice 5. at the victory willed by God. He gives victory to whoever He wills. For He is the Almighty, Most Merciful. 6. ˹This is˺ the promise of God. ˹And˺ God never fails in His promise. But most people do not know. 7. They ˹only˺ know the worldly affairs of this life, but are ˹totally˺ oblivious to the Hereafter.

Wake-up Call to the Disbelievers

8. Have they not reflected upon their own being? God only created the heavens and the earth and everything in between for a purpose and an appointed term. Yet most people are truly in denial of the meeting with their Lord! 9. Have they not travelled throughout the land to see what was the end of those ˹destroyed˺ before them? They were far superior in might; they cultivated the land and developed it more than these ˹Meccans˺ ever have. Their messengers came to them with clear proofs. God would have never wronged them, but it was they who wronged themselves. 10. Then most evil was the end of the evildoers for denying and mocking the signs of God.

The Wicked on Judgment Day

11. It is God Who originates the creation, and will resurrect it. And then to Him you will ˹all˺ be returned. 12. On the Day the Hour will arrive, the wicked will be dumbstruck. 13. There will be no intercessors for them from among their associate-gods, and they will ˹totally˺ deny their associate-gods.

The Blessed and the Doomed

14. And on the Day the Hour will arrive, the people will then be split ˹into two groups˺. 15. As for those who believed and did good, they will be rejoicing in a Garden. 16. And as for those who disbelieved, and denied Our signs and the meeting ˹with God˺ in the Hereafter, they will be confined in punishment.

Keeping up Prayers

17. So glorify God in the evening and in the morning— 18. all praise is for Him in the heavens and the earth—as well as in the afternoon, and at noon.[815]

God's Power over Life and Death

19. He brings forth the living from the dead and the dead from the living. And He gives life to the earth after its death. And so will you be brought forth ˹from the grave˺.

---

815 This verse outlines the times of the five daily prayers. The evening refers to *Maghrib* and *'Ishã'* prayers, the morning refers to *Fajr*, the afternoon refers to *'Aṣr*, and noon refers to *Ẓuhr*.

God's Signs 1) Creation of Humankind

20. One of His signs is that He created you from dust, then—behold!—you are human beings spreading over 'the earth'.

God's Signs 2) Spouses

21. And one of His signs is that He created for you spouses from among yourselves so that you may find comfort in them. And He has placed between you compassion and mercy. Surely in this are signs for people who reflect.

God's Signs 3) Diversity

22. And one of His signs is the creation of the heavens and the earth, and the diversity of your languages and colours. Surely in this are signs for those of 'sound' knowledge.

God's Signs 4) Sleep and Work

23. And one of His signs is your sleep by night and by day 'for rest' as well as your seeking His bounty 'in both'. Surely in this are signs for people who listen.

God's Signs 5) Lightning

24. And one of His signs is that He shows you lightning, inspiring 'you with' hope and fear.[816] And He sends down rain from the sky, reviving the earth after its death. Surely in this are signs for people who understand.

God's Signs 6) The Universe

25. And one of His signs is that the heavens and the earth persist by His command. Then when He calls you out of the earth just once, you will instantly come forth. **26.** And to Him belong all those in the heavens and the earth—all are subject to His Will.[817] **27.** And He is the One Who originates the creation then will resurrect it—which is even easier for Him.[818] To Him belong the finest attributes in the heavens and the earth. And He is the Almighty, All-Wise.

An Example for the Polytheists

28. He sets forth for you an example 'drawn' from your own lives: would you allow some of those 'bondspeople' in your possession to be your equal partners in whatever 'wealth' We have provided you, keeping them in mind as you are mindful of your peers?[819] This is how We make the signs clear for people who understand. **29.** In fact, the wrongdoers merely follow their desires with no knowledge. Who then can guide those God has left to stray? They will have no helpers.

Hold Firmly to Faith

30. So be steadfast in faith in all uprightness 'O Prophet'—the natural Way of God which He has instilled in 'all' people. Let there be no change in this creation of God. That is the Straight Way, but most people do not know. **31.** 'O believers!' Always turn to Him 'in repentance', be mindful of Him, and establish prayers. And do not be polytheists— **32.** 'like' those who have divided their faith and split into sects, each rejoicing in what they have.

Human Ingratitude

33. When people are touched with hardship, they cry out to their Lord, turning to Him 'alone'. But as soon as He gives them a taste of His mercy, a group of them associates 'others' with their Lord 'in worship', **34.** becoming ungrateful for whatever 'favours' We have given them. So enjoy yourselves, for soon you will know. **35.** Or have We sent down to them an authority which attests to what they associate 'with Him'?

---

816 Hope of rain and fear of torment.
817 lit., to Him.
818 This is from a human perspective. Otherwise, both the creation of the universe and the resurrection of humans are easy for God.
819 The passage says that since humans would not allow those who are inferior to them to become their partners in wealth, how can they set up helpless partners with God in His kingdom?

Human Impatience

36. When We give people a taste of mercy, they become prideful ʿbecauseʾ of it. But if they are afflicted with an evil for what their hands have done, they instantly fall into despair.

Interest vs. Charity

37. Have they not seen that God gives abundant or limited provisions to whoever He wills? Surely in this are signs for people who believe. **38.** So give your close relatives their due, as well as the poor and the ʿneedyʾ traveller. That is best for those who seek the pleasure of God,[820] and it is they who will be successful. **39.** Whatever loans you give, ʿonlyʾ seeking interest at the expense of people's wealth[821] will not increase with God. But whatever charity you give, ʿonlyʾ seeking the pleasure of God— it is they whose reward will be multiplied.

God's Might

40. It is God Who created you, then gives you provisions, then will cause you to die, and then will bring you back to life. Can any of your associate-gods do any of this? Glorified and Exalted is He above what they associate with Him ʿin worshipʾ!

The Spread of Corruption

41. Corruption has spread on land and sea as a result of what people's hands have done, so that God may cause them to taste ʿthe consequences ofʾ some of their deeds and perhaps they might return ʿto the Right Pathʾ. **42.** Say, ʿO Prophet,ʾ "Travel throughout the land and see what was the end of those ʿdestroyedʾ before ʿyouʾ—most of them were polytheists."

The Successful and the Losers

43. So be steadfast in the Upright Faith ʿO Prophetʾ, before the coming of a Day from God that cannot be averted. On that Day the people will be divided: **44.** those who disbelieved will bear ʿthe burden ofʾ their own disbelief; and those who did good will have prepared for themselves ʿeternal homesʾ, **45.** so that He may ʿgenerouslyʾ reward those who believe and do good, out of His grace. He truly does not like the disbelievers.

God's Signs 7) The Wind

46. And one of His signs is that He sends the winds, ushering in good news ʿof rainʾ so that He may give you a taste of His mercy, and that ships may sail by His command, and that you may seek His bounty, and perhaps you will be grateful.

Warning to the Disbelievers

47. Indeed, We sent before you ʿO Prophetʾ messengers, each to their own people, and they came to them with clear proofs. Then We inflicted punishment upon those who persisted in wickedness. For it is Our duty to help the believers.

God's Signs 8) Rain

48. It is God Who sends the winds, which then stir up ʿvapour, formingʾ clouds, which He then spreads out in the sky or piles up into masses as He wills, from which you see rain come forth. Then as soon as He causes it to fall on whoever He wills of His servants, they rejoice, **49.** although they had utterly lost hope just before it was sent down to them. **50.** See then the impact of God's mercy: how He gives life to the earth after its death! Surely That ʿsame Godʾ can raise the dead. For He is Most Capable of everything. **51.** Then if We send a ʿharshʾ wind which they see withering ʿtheirʾ crops, they will definitely deny ʿold favoursʾ right after.

---

820 lit., seek the Face of God.
821 Another meaning is the gift given to someone with the intention of getting a more expensive gift in return—a common ancient practice.

The Dead, Deaf, and Blind

52. So you ˹O Prophet˺ certainly cannot make the dead hear ˹the truth˺. Nor can you make the deaf hear the call when they turn their backs and walk away. **53.** Nor can you lead the blind out of their misguidance. You can make none hear ˹the truth˺ except those who believe in Our revelations, ˹fully˺ submitting ˹to God˺.

God's Power of Creation

54. It is God Who created you in a state of weakness, then developed ˹your˺ weakness into strength, then developed ˹your˺ strength into weakness and old age.[822] He creates whatever He wills. For He is the All-Knowing, Most Capable.

Fleeting Life

55. And on the Day the Hour will arrive, the wicked will swear that they did not stay ˹in this world˺ more than an hour. In this way they were always deluded ˹in the world˺. **56.** But those gifted with knowledge and faith will say ˹to them˺, "You did actually stay—as destined by God—until the Day of Resurrection. So here is the Day of Resurrection ˹which you denied˺! But you did not know ˹it was true˺." **57.** So on that Day the wrongdoers' excuses will not benefit them, nor will they be allowed to appease ˹their Lord˺.

Advice to the Prophet

58. We have certainly set forth every ˹kind of˺ lesson for people in this Quran. And no matter what sign you bring to them ˹O Prophet˺, the disbelievers will definitely say ˹to the believers˺, "You are only a people of falsehood." **59.** This is how God seals the hearts of those unwilling to know ˹the truth˺. **60.** So be patient, for the promise of God certainly is true. And do not be disturbed by those who have no sure faith.

31. Luqmân *(Luqmân)*

This Meccan chapter is named after Luqmân, a wise African man who is quoted giving pieces of advice to his son (verses 12–19) on one's relationship with God and the people. While the believers are praised, the pagans are condemned for their ingratitude, distracting others from the Way of God, and for setting up idols as His equals. Similar to the previous chapter, references are made to God's natural marvels, challenging the deniers to point out anything their gods have created. The chapter concludes by warning humanity of the Day of Judgment, ushering in the next chapter.

In the Name of God—the Most Compassionate, Most Merciful

---

822 lit., grey hair.

Qualities of True Believers

1. *Alif-Lãm-Mĩm.* **2.** These are the verses of the Book, rich in wisdom. **3.** ˹It is˺ a guide and mercy for the good-doers— **4.** those who establish prayer, pay alms-tax, and have sure faith in the Hereafter. **5.** It is they who are ˹truly˺ guided by their Lord, and it is they who will be successful.

Distracting People from the Truth

6. But there are some who employ theatrics,[823] only to lead others away from God's Way—without any knowledge—and to make a mockery of it. They will suffer a humiliating punishment. **7.** Whenever Our revelations are recited to them, they turn away in arrogance as if they did not hear them, as if there is deafness in their ears. So give them good news ˹O Prophet˺ of a painful punishment.

Reward of the Believers

8. Surely those who believe and do good will have the Gardens of Bliss, **9.** staying there forever. God's promise is true. And He is the Almighty, All-Wise.

God's Creation

10. He created the heavens without pillars—as you can see—and placed firm mountains upon the earth so it does not shake with you, and scattered throughout it all types of creatures. And We send down rain from the sky, causing every type of fine plant to grow on earth. **11.** This is God's creation. Now show Me what those ˹gods˺ other than Him have created. In fact, the wrongdoers are clearly astray.

Luqmân's Advice: 1) Worship God Alone

12. Indeed, We blessed Luqmân with wisdom, ˹saying˺, "Be grateful to God, for whoever is grateful, it is only for their own good. And whoever is ungrateful, then surely God is Self-Sufficient, Praiseworthy."[824] **13.** And ˹remember˺ when Luqmân said to his son, while advising him, "O my dear son! Never associate ˹anything˺ with God ˹in worship˺, for associating ˹others with Him˺ is truly the worst of all wrongs."

2) Honour Your Parents[825]

14. And We have commanded people to ˹honour˺ their parents. Their mothers bore them through hardship upon hardship, and their weaning takes two years. So be grateful to Me and your parents. To Me is the final return. **15.** But if they pressure you to associate with Me what you have no knowledge of,[826] do not obey them. Still keep their company in this world courteously, and follow the way of those who turn to Me ˹in devotion˺. Then to Me you will ˹all˺ return, and then I will inform you of what you used to do.

3) Know That God Will Judge All Deeds

16. ˹Luqmân added,˺ "O my dear son! ˹Even˺ if a deed were the weight of a mustard seed—be it ˹hidden˺ in a rock or in the heavens or the earth—God will bring it forth. Surely God is Most Subtle, All-Aware.

4) Fulfil Your Duty to God

17. "O my dear son! Establish prayer, encourage what is good and forbid what is evil, and endure patiently whatever befalls you. Surely this is a resolve to aspire to.

---

823 Some pagan Arabs used to utilize singing, dancing, chanting, etc. to distract people's attention from listening to the recitation of the Quran.

824 Luqmân is believed to have been a righteous, wise man who lived around the time of Prophet David.

825 The Quran usually combines the command to worship God with the order to honour one's parents (*see* 6:151 and 17:23). This is why this passage interjects Luqmân's advice to his son. In some instances, the Quran follows the order to be kind to parents with emphasizing the role of the mother. This is because some of the mother's sacrifices take place before the child is born and when they are too young. So the Quran brings these sacrifices to the children's attention.

826 Other gods.

5) Be Humble

18. "And do not turn your nose up to people, nor walk pridefully upon the earth. Surely God does not like whoever is arrogant, boastful. **19.** Be moderate in your pace. And lower your voice, for the ugliest of all voices is certainly the braying of donkeys."

God's Favours

20. Have you not seen that God has subjected for you whatever is in the heavens and whatever is on the earth, and has lavished His favours upon you, both seen and unseen? ʿStillʾ there are some who dispute about God without knowledge, or guidance, or an enlightening scripture. **21.** When it is said to them, "Follow what God has revealed," they reply, "No! We ʿonlyʾ follow what we found our forefathers practicing." ʿWould they still do soʾ even if Satan is inviting them to the torment of the Blaze?

The Believers and the Disbelievers

22. Whoever fully submits themselves to God and is a good-doer, they have certainly grasped the firmest hand-hold. And with God rests the outcome of ʿallʾ affairs. **23.** But whoever disbelieves, do not let their disbelief grieve you ʿO Prophetʾ. To Us is their return, and We will inform them of all they did. Surely God knows best what is ʿhiddenʾ in the heart. **24.** We allow them enjoyment for a little while, then ʿin timeʾ We will force them into a harsh torment. **25.** And if you ask them who created the heavens and the earth, they will definitely say, "God!" Say, "Praise be to God!" In fact, most of them do not know.

God's Infinite Knowledge

26. To God belongs whatever is in the heavens and the earth. God is truly the Self-Sufficient, Praiseworthy. **27.** If all the trees on earth were pens and the ocean ʿwere inkʾ,

refilled by seven other oceans, the Words of God would not be exhausted. Surely God is Almighty, All-Wise.

God's Infinite Power

28. The creation and resurrection of you ʿallʾ is as simple ʿfor Himʾ as that of a single soul. Surely God is All-Hearing, All-Seeing. **29.** Do you not see that God causes the night to merge into the day and the day into the night, and has subjected the sun and the moon, each orbiting for an appointed term, and that God is All-Aware of what you do? **30.** That is because God ʿaloneʾ is the Truth and what they invoke besides Him is falsehood, and ʿbecauseʾ God ʿaloneʾ is the Most High, All-Great.

Human Ingratitude

31. Do you not see that the ships sail ʿsmoothlyʾ through the sea by the grace of God so that He may show you some of His signs? Surely in this are signs for whoever is steadfast, grateful. **32.** And as soon as they are overwhelmed by waves like mountains, they cry out to God ʿaloneʾ in sincere devotion. But when He delivers them ʿsafelyʾ to shore, only some become relatively grateful. And none rejects Our signs except whoever is deceitful, ungrateful.

Warning of Judgment Day

33. O humanity! Be mindful of your Lord, and beware of a Day when no parent will be of any benefit to their child, nor will a child be of any benefit to their parent. Surely God's promise is true. So do not let the life of this world deceive you, nor let the Chief Deceiver[827] deceive you about God.

---

827   Satan.

The Five Keys of the Unseen[828]

34. Indeed, God 'alone' has the knowledge of the Hour. He sends down the rain,[829] and knows what is in the wombs.[830] No soul knows what it will earn for tomorrow, and no soul knows in what land it will die. Surely God is All-Knowing, All-Aware.

32. The Prostration *(As-Sajdah)*

This Meccan chapter, which takes its name from the prostrations of the believers in worship mentioned in verse 15, makes it clear that the Quran is a divine revelation and that Almighty God is the sole Creator, most capable of resurrection. Similar to the previous chapter, a reference is made to the qualities of the believers and the disbelievers and the reward awaiting each. Both the end of this chapter and the beginning of the next urge the Prophet to turn away from the deniers and not yield to them.

In the Name of God—the Most Compassionate, Most Merciful

Reassuring the Prophet

1. *Alif-Lãm-Mĩm.* **2.** The revelation of this Book is—beyond doubt—from the Lord of all worlds. **3.** Or do they say, "He has fabricated it!"? No! It is the truth from your Lord in order for you to warn a people to whom no warner has come before you, so they may be 'rightly' guided.

God's Power of Creation

4. It is God Who has created the heavens and the earth and everything in between in six Days,[831] then established Himself above the Throne. You have no protector or intercessor besides Him. Will you not then be mindful? **5.** He conducts every affair from the heavens to the earth, then it all ascends to Him on a Day whose length is a thousand years by your counting. **6.** That is the Knower of the seen and unseen—the Almighty, Most Merciful, **7.** Who has perfected everything He created. And He originated the creation of humankind from clay.[832] **8.** Then He made his descendants from an extract of a humble fluid, **9.** then He fashioned them and had a spirit of His Own 'creation' breathed into them. And He gave you hearing, sight, and intellect. 'Yet' you hardly give any thanks.

The Deniers of Resurrection

10. 'Still' they ask 'mockingly', "When we are disintegrated into the earth, will we really be raised as a new creation?" In fact, they are in denial of the meeting with their

---

828 *See* footnote for 6:59.
829 He knows precisely when, where, and how much rain falls, and whether it is going to be drunk by people and animals or used for irrigation, or absorbed by the earth, etc.
830 The Prophet was reported in a *ḥadīth* collected by Bukhâri and Muslim to have said, "Indeed, the creation of each one of you is brought together in the womb of one's mother as a drop of 'male and female' discharges for forty days, then one becomes a clinging clot for a similar period, then a lump of flesh for a similar period. Then an angel is sent to blow the breath of life into the embryo. The angel is then commanded to write four things: one's destined provisions, lifespan, actions, and whether one will be happy or miserable 'in the Hereafter'."
831 *See* footnote for 7:54.
832 Adam.

Lord. **11.** Say, ˹O Prophet,˺ "Your soul will be taken by the Angel of Death, who is in charge of you. Then to your Lord you will ˹all˺ be returned." **12.** If only you could see the wicked hanging their heads ˹in shame˺ before their Lord, ˹crying:˺ "Our Lord! We have now seen and heard, so send us back and we will do good. We truly have sure faith ˹now˺!" **13.** Had We willed, We could have easily imposed guidance on every soul. But My Word will come to pass: I will surely fill up Hell with jinn and humans all together. **14.** So taste ˹the punishment˺ for neglecting the meeting of this Day of yours. We ˹too˺ will certainly neglect you. And taste the torment of eternity for what you used to do!

Qualities of the Believers

15. The only ˹true˺ believers in Our revelation are those who—when it is recited to them—fall into prostration and glorify the praises of their Lord and are not too proud. **16.** They abandon their beds, invoking their Lord with hope and fear, and donate from what We have provided for them. **17.** No soul can imagine what delights are kept in store for them as a reward for what they used to do.

The Faithful and the Rebellious

18. Is the one who is a believer equal ˹before God˺ to the one who is rebellious? They are not equal! **19.** As for those who believe and do good, they will have the Gardens of ˹Eternal˺ Residence—as an accommodation for what they used to do. **20.** But as for those who are rebellious, the Fire will be their home. Whenever they try to escape from it, they will be forced back into it, and will be told, "Taste the Fire's torment, which you used to deny." **21.** We will certainly make them taste some of the minor torment ˹in this life˺ before the major torment ˹of the Hereafter˺, so perhaps

they will return ˹to the Right Path˺. **22.** And who does more wrong than the one who is reminded of God's revelations then turns away from them? We will surely inflict punishment upon the wicked.

Divine Revelations

23. Indeed, We gave the Scripture to Moses—so let there be no doubt ˹O Prophet˺ that you ˹too˺ are receiving revelations—[833]and We made it a guide for the Children of Israel. **24.** We raised from among them leaders,[834] guiding by Our command, when they patiently endured and firmly believed in Our signs. **25.** Indeed, your Lord will decide between them on the Day of Judgment regarding their differences.

Warning to the Disbelievers

26. Is it not yet clear to them how many peoples We destroyed before them, whose ruins they still pass by? Surely in this are signs. Will they not then listen? **27.** Do they not see how We drive rain to parched land, producing ˹various˺ crops from which they and their cattle eat? Will they not then see?

The Deniers of Judgment

28. They ask ˹mockingly˺, "When is this ˹Day of final˺ Decision, if what you say is true?" **29.** Say, ˹O Prophet,˺ "On the Day of Decision it will not benefit the disbelievers to believe then, nor will they be delayed ˹from punishment˺." **30.** So turn away from them, and wait! They too are waiting.

---

833 Other possible translations: 1. "Do not be in doubt that Moses received it." 2. "Do not be in doubt of your meeting with Moses."
834 i.e., prophets.

33. The Enemy Alliance *(Al-Aḥzâb)*

This Medinian chapter takes its name from the enemy alliance (mentioned in verses 9–27) which laid a siege around Medina during the Battle of the Trench in 5 A.H./627 C.E. While the believers are reminded of God's aid against the enemy alliance, the hypocrites are condemned repeatedly. The chapter provides social guidelines regarding adoption, divorce, modesty, and the etiquette of dealing with the Prophet and his wives. In view of God's favours to the believers (including His forgiveness and generous reward at the end of the chapter), the next chapter starts off with praises to God.

In the Name of God—the Most Compassionate, Most Merciful

Orders to the Prophet

1. O Prophet! ˹Always˺ be mindful of God, and do not yield to the disbelievers and the hypocrites. Indeed, God is All-Knowing, All-Wise. 2. Follow what is revealed to you from your Lord. Surely God is All-Aware of what you ˹all˺ do. 3. And put your trust in God, for God is sufficient as a Trustee of Affairs.

Rules on Divorce and Adoption[835]

4. God does not place two hearts in any person's chest. Nor does He regard your wives as ˹unlawful for you like˺ your real mothers, ˹even˺ if you say they are.[836] Nor does He regard your adopted children as your real children.[837] These are only your baseless assertions. But God declares the truth, and He ˹alone˺ guides to the ˹Right˺ Way. 5. Let your adopted children keep their family names. That is more just in the sight of God. But if

you do not know their fathers, then they are ˹simply˺ your fellow believers and close associates. There is no blame on you for what you do by mistake, but ˹only˺ for what you do intentionally. And God is All-Forgiving, Most Merciful.

Guidelines for the Believers

6. The Prophet has a stronger affinity to the believers than they do themselves. And his wives are their mothers. As ordained by God, blood relatives are more entitled ˹to inheritance˺ than ˹other˺ believers and immigrants, unless you ˹want to˺ show kindness to your ˹close˺ associates ˹through bequest˺.[838] This is decreed in the Record.[839]

Covenant to Deliver the Truth

7. And ˹remember˺ when We took a covenant from the prophets, as well as from you ˹O

---

835 The passage says that as a person cannot have two hearts, similarly, a man cannot have two real mothers, nor can a child have two real fathers.

836 This divorce (called *ẓihâr*) was commonly practiced in Arabia before the Prophet. If a man declared his wife as unlawful for him as the *ẓahr* (back) of his mother, his wife would be divorced. Islam abolished this type of divorce (*see* 58:3-4).

837 The following distinction should be made:
Sponsorship (which is permissible): a person can sponsor a child or host them in their home and care for them as they care for their own children, except for legal matters. For example, adopted children keep their last names, are allowed to marry the children of their adopted parent, adopted and biological children of the opposite sex should dress modestly in front of each other, and do not have a share in the estate of their adopted parents, but can get a share of inheritance (up to one-third of the estate) through bequest (*waṣiyah*).
Adoption: a person is not allowed to take an orphan and give them his/her last name, give them a share of inheritance similar to their own children, etc.

838 This verse confirms a ruling mentioned in 8:75 which ended a previous ruling that allowed inheritance between Muslims from Mecca (*Al-Muhâjirûn*, the Emigrants) and Muslims from Medina (*Al-Anṣâr*, the Helpers). Now, only relatives can inherit from one another, whereas non-heirs can receive a share through bequest, up to one third of the estate. *See* 4:7, 11-13, 32-33, and 176.

839 The Record refers to the Preserved Tablet (*Al-Lawḥ Al-Maḥfûz*) in which God has written the destiny of His entire creation.

Prophet', and from Noah, Abraham, Moses, and Jesus, son of Mary. We did take a solemn covenant from 'all of' them **8.** so that He may question these men of truth about their 'delivery of the' truth. And He has prepared a painful punishment for the disbelievers.

The Battle of the Trench

9. O believers! Remember God's favour upon you when 'enemy' forces came to 'besiege' you 'in Medina',[840] so We sent against them a 'bitter' wind and forces you could not see.[841] And God is All-Seeing of what you do. **10.** 'Remember' when they came at you from east and west,[842] when your eyes grew wild 'in horror' and your hearts jumped into your throats, and you entertained 'conflicting' thoughts about God.[843] **11.** Then and there the believers were put to the test, and were violently shaken.

Stance of the Hypocrites

12. And 'remember' when the hypocrites and those with sickness in their hearts said, "God and His Messenger have promised us nothing but delusion!" **13.** And 'remember' when a group of them said, "O people of Yathrib![844] There is no point in you staying 'here', so retreat!" Another group of them asked the Prophet's permission 'to leave', saying, "Our homes are vulnerable," while 'in fact' they were not vulnerable. They only wished to flee. **14.** Had their city been sacked from all sides and they had been asked to abandon faith, they would have done so with little hesitation.

Warning to the Hypocrites

15. They had already pledged to God earlier never to turn their backs 'in retreat'.

And a pledge to God must be answered for. **16.** Say, 'O Prophet,' "Fleeing will not benefit you if you 'try to' escape a natural or violent death. 'If it is not your time,' you will only be allowed enjoyment for a little while."[845] **17.** Ask 'them, O Prophet', "Who can put you out of God's reach if He intends to harm you or show you mercy?" They can never find any protector or helper besides God.

Hypocritical Tactics

18. God knows well those among you who discourage 'others from fighting', saying 'secretly' to their brothers, "Stay with us," and who themselves hardly take part in fighting. **19.** 'They are' totally unwilling to assist you. When danger comes, you see them staring at you with their eyes rolling like someone in the throes of death. But once the danger is over, they slash you with razor-sharp tongues, ravenous for 'worldly' gains. Such people have not 'truly' believed, so God has rendered their deeds void. And that is easy for God.

Hypocrites Paranoid

20. They 'still' think that the enemy alliance has not 'yet' withdrawn. And if the allies were to come 'again', the hypocrites would wish to be away in the desert among nomadic Arabs, 'only' asking for news about you 'believers'. And if the hypocrites were in your midst, they would hardly take part in the fight.

The Prophet as a Role Model

21. Indeed, in the Messenger of God you have an excellent example for whoever has

---

840 In 5 A.H./627 C.E., the Meccan pagans along with some Arab and Jewish tribes (totalling around 10 000 soldiers) laid a siege around Medina, where the Prophet was positioned with 3000 soldiers. The Prophet had anticipated the offence and, upon an advice from one of his companions, dug a trench around the city to protect it from invaders. After several unsuccessful attempts to cross the trench, the allied enemies quickly lost morale, and were forced to end the siege due to severe weather conditions. This encounter is commonly known as the Battle of the Trench or the Enemy Alliance.
841 The angels.
842 lit., from above and below you.
843 The believers were reassured while the doubts of the hypocrites grew more fierce.
844 Yathrib was the name of Medina before the arrival of the Prophet and Muslim emigrants.
845 Until the end of your short life on earth.

hope in God and the Last Day, and remembers God often.

Stance of the Believers

22. When the believers saw the enemy alliance, they said, "This is what God and His Messenger had promised us. The promise of God and His Messenger has come true." And this only increased them in faith and submission. **23.** Among the believers are men who have proven true to what they pledged to God.[846] Some of them have fulfilled their pledge 'with their lives', others are waiting 'their turn'. They have never changed 'their commitment' in the least. **24.** 'It all happened' so God may reward the faithful for their faithfulness, and punish the hypocrites if He wills or turn to them 'in mercy'. Surely God is All-Forgiving, Most Merciful.

Defeat of the Enemy Alliance

25. And God drove back the disbelievers in their rage, totally empty-handed. And God spared the believers from fighting. For God is All-Powerful, Almighty. **26.** And He brought down those from the People of the Book[847] who supported the enemy alliance from their own strongholds, and cast horror into their hearts. You 'believers' killed some, and took others captive. **27.** He has also caused you to take over their lands, homes, and wealth, as well as lands you have not yet set foot on. And God is Most Capable of everything.

Advice to the Prophet's Wives: Your Choice

28. O Prophet! Say to your wives, "If you desire the life of this world and its luxury, then come, I will give you a 'suitable' compensation 'for divorce' and let you go graciously.

29. But if you desire God and His Messenger and the 'everlasting' Home of the Hereafter, then surely God has prepared a great reward for those of you who do good."

More Advice: Your Reward

30. O wives of the Prophet! If any of you were to commit a blatant misconduct, the punishment would be doubled for her. And that is easy for God. **31.** And whoever of you devoutly obeys God and His Messenger and does good, We will grant her double the reward, and We have prepared for her an honourable provision.

More Advice: Your Modesty

32. O wives of the Prophet! You are not like any other women: if you are mindful 'of God', then do not be overly effeminate in speech 'with men' or those with sickness in their hearts may be tempted, but speak in a moderate tone. **33.** Settle in your homes, and do not display yourselves as women did in the days of 'pre-Islamic' ignorance. Establish prayer, pay alms-tax, and obey God and His Messenger. God only intends to keep 'the causes of' evil away from you and purify you completely, O members of the 'Prophet's' family! **34.** 'Always' remember what is recited in your homes of God's revelations and 'prophetic' wisdom.[848] Surely God is Most Subtle, All-Aware.

Reward of the Righteous

35. Surely 'for' Muslim men and women, believing men and women,[849] devout men and women, truthful men and women, patient men and women, humble men and women, charitable men and women, fasting men and women, men and women who guard their

---

846   See footnote for 7:46.
847   The Jews of Banu Quraiẓah who had violated their treaty with the Muslims and sided with the enemy alliance. The Prophet asked how they wished to be judged, and they chose to be judged by their book, the Torah—in which the penalty for treason is death.
848   God's revelations refers to verses of the Quran whereas prophetic wisdom refers to the sayings and teachings of the Prophet, known collectively as ḥadîth.
849   Though Islam and Îmân are sometimes used interchangeably in the Quran, Îmân is a higher state of Islam. A Muslim is someone who observes the five pillars of Islam, but a believer is someone with strong faith, who does everything purely for the sake of God, and is mindful of God in everything they say or do. Every Mu'min (believer/faithful) is a Muslim, but not every Muslim is a Mu'min. See 49:14.

chastity, and men and women who remember God often—for ˹all of˺ them God has prepared forgiveness and a great reward.

Unconditional Obedience

36. It is not for a believing man or woman—when God and His Messenger decree a matter—to have any other choice in that matter.[850] Indeed, whoever disobeys God and His Messenger has clearly gone ˹far˺ astray.

The Case of Zaid

37. And ˹remember, O Prophet,˺ when you said to the one[851] for whom God has done a favour and you ˹too˺ have done a favour,[852] "Keep your wife and fear God," while concealing within yourself what God was going to reveal. And ˹so˺ you were considering the people, whereas God was more worthy of your consideration. So when Zaid totally lost interest in ˹keeping˺ his wife, We gave her to you in marriage, so that there would be no blame on the believers for marrying the ex-wives of their adopted sons after their divorce. And God's command is totally binding. **38.** There is no blame on the Prophet for doing what God has ordained for him. That has been the way of God with those ˹prophets˺ who had gone before. And God's command has been firmly decreed. **39.** ˹That is His way with˺ those ˹prophets˺ who deliver the messages of God, and consider Him and none but God. And sufficient is God as a ˹vigilant˺ Reckoner. **40.** Muḥammad is not the father of any of your men,[853] but is the Messenger of God and the seal of the prophets. And God has ˹perfect˺ knowledge of all things.

Reward of the Believers

41. O believers! Always remember God often, **42.** and glorify Him morning and evening. **43.** He is the One Who showers His blessings upon you—and His angels pray for you—so that He may bring you out of darkness and into light. For He is ever Merciful to the believers. **44.** Their greeting on the Day they meet Him will be, "Peace!" And He has prepared for them an honourable reward.

Excellence of the Prophet

45. O Prophet! We have sent you as a witness, and a deliverer of good news, and a warner, **46.** and a caller to ˹the Way of˺ God by His command, and a beacon of light. **47.** Give good news to the believers that they will have a great bounty from God. **48.** Do not yield to the disbelievers and the hypocrites. Overlook their annoyances, and put your trust in God. For God is sufficient as a Trustee of Affairs.

Divorce Before Consummation

49. O believers! If you marry believing women and then divorce them before you touch them,[854] they will have no waiting period for you to count,[855] so give them a ˹suitable˺ compensation, and let them go graciously.

Women Lawful to the Prophet

50. O Prophet! We have made lawful for you your wives to whom you have paid their ˹full˺ dowries as well as those ˹bondwomen˺ in your possession, whom God has granted you.[856] And ˹you are allowed to marry˺ the

---

850 Meaning, if God makes a ruling in the Quran or the Prophet makes a ruling, then a Muslim is not allowed to seek judgment from anyone else, nor follow their own desires.

851 This refers to Zaid ibn Ḥârithah, the Prophet's adopted son before adoption was made unlawful. His wife, Zainab bint Jaḥsh was from a prestigious family. Because Zaid and Zainab came from two different social classes, the marriage was not successful. Eventually, Zaid insisted on divorcing his wife, despite several appeals from the Prophet. Since one's adopted son was no longer considered to be one's own son, the Prophet was later allowed to marry Zainab.

852 God's favour to Zaid was to guide him to Islam, and the Prophet's favour was to free him from slavery.

853 He is not the father of Zaid (mentioned in 33:37) or any other man. The Prophet had three biological sons, who all died in childhood.

854 Before the marriage is consummated.

855 If divorce is pronounced after the consummation of marriage, a waiting period of three months is observed to give the couple a chance to get back together and to see if the wife is pregnant (see 65:4). But if the divorce happens before the marriage is consummated, then there is no waiting period.

856 See footnote for 4:3.

daughters of your paternal uncles and aunts, and the daughters of your maternal uncles and aunts, who have emigrated like you. Also ˹allowed for marriage is˺ a believing woman who offers herself to the Prophet ˹without dowry˺ if he is interested in marrying her—˹this is˺ exclusively for you, not for the rest of the believers.[857] We know well what ˹rulings˺ We have ordained for the believers in relation to their wives and those ˹bondwomen˺ in their possession. As such, there would be no blame on you. And God is All-Forgiving, Most Merciful.

Prophet's Visitation to His Wives

51. It is up to you ˹O Prophet˺ to delay or receive whoever you please of your wives. There is no blame on you if you call back any of those you have set aside.[858] That is more likely that they will be content, not grieved, and satisfied with what you offer them all. God ˹fully˺ knows what is in your hearts. And God is All-Knowing, Most Forbearing.

No Future Marriages

52. It is not lawful for you ˹O Prophet˺ to marry more women after this, nor can you replace any of your present wives with another, even if her beauty may attract you—except those ˹bondwomen˺ in your possession. And God is ever Watchful over all things.

On Visiting the Prophet

53. O believers! Do not enter the homes of the Prophet without permission ˹and if invited˺ for a meal, do not ˹come too early and˺ linger until the meal is ready. But if you are invited, then enter ˹on time˺. Once you have eaten, then go on your way, and do not stay for casual talk. Such behaviour is truly annoying to the Prophet, yet he is too shy to ask you to leave. But God is never shy of the truth. And when you ˹believers˺ ask his wives for something, ask them from behind a barrier. This is purer for your hearts and theirs. And it is not right for you to annoy the Messenger of God, nor ever marry his wives after him. This would certainly be a major offence in the sight of God. **54.** Whether you reveal something or conceal it, surely God has ˹perfect˺ knowledge of all things. **55.** There is no blame on the Prophet's wives ˹if they appear unveiled˺ before their fathers,[859] their sons, their brothers, their brothers' sons, their sisters' sons, their fellow ˹Muslim˺ women, and those ˹bondspeople˺ in their possession. And be mindful of God ˹O wives of the Prophet!˺ Surely God is a Witness over all things.

Blessings on the Prophet

56. Indeed, God showers His blessings upon the Prophet, and His angels pray for him. O believers! Invoke God's blessings upon him, and salute him with worthy greetings of peace.

Offending God, His Messenger, and the Believers

57. Surely those who offend God[860] and His Messenger[861] are condemned by God in this world and the Hereafter. And He has prepared for them a humiliating punishment. **58.** As for those who abuse believing men and women[862] unjustifiably, they will defi-

---

857 This ruling was exclusively for the Prophet (which he never took advantage of), but Muslims have to pay a dowry to their wives. Some women did offer themselves to the Prophet in marriage, but he declined.
858 The Prophet's married life can be classified as follows:
Until the age of 25: he was single.
Age 25–50: he was married only to Khadîjah.
Age 50–52: he was single after Khadîjah's death.
Age 53–his death at the age of 63: he had a total of ten wives. Many of these marriages were to widows (who had been left with their children without a provider) and in some cases to foster stronger ties with some of his companions and neighbouring tribes. Of all the women he married, ʿÂishah was the only virgin.
859 Paternal and maternal uncles are similar to the fathers.
860 By attributing children to Him or associating gods with Him in worship.
861 By calling him a liar or speaking ill of him and his family.
862 By harming them physically or accusing them falsely.

nitely bear the guilt of slander and blatant sin.

The Veil

59. O Prophet! Ask your wives, daughters, and believing women to draw their cloaks over their bodies. In this way it is more likely that they will be recognized ˹as virtuous˺ and not be harassed. And God is All-Forgiving, Most Merciful.[863]

Reward of the Wicked

60. If the hypocrites, and those with sickness in their hearts, and rumour-mongers in Medina do not desist, We will certainly incite you ˹O Prophet˺ against them, and then they will not be your neighbours there any longer. **61.** ˹They deserve to be˺ condemned. ˹If they were to persist,˺ they would get themselves seized and killed relentlessly wherever they are found![864] **62.** That was God's way with those ˹hypocrites˺ who have gone before. And you will find no change in God's way.

When Is the Hour?

63. People ask you ˹O Prophet˺ about the Hour. Say, "That knowledge is only with God. You never know, perhaps the Hour is near."

The Doomed

64. Surely God condemns the disbelievers, and has prepared for them a blazing Fire, **65.** to stay there for ever and ever—never will they find any protector or helper. **66.** On the Day their faces are ˹constantly˺ flipped in the Fire, they will cry, "Oh! If only we had obeyed God and obeyed the Messenger!" **67.** And they will say, "Our Lord! We obeyed our leaders and elite, but they led us astray from the ˹Right˺ Way. **68.** Our Lord! Give them double ˹our˺ punishment, and condemn them tremendously."

Advice to the Believers

69. O believers! Do not be like those who slandered Moses, but God cleared him of what they said. And he was honourable in the sight of God.[865] **70.** O believers! Be mindful of God, and say what is right. **71.** He will bless your deeds for you, and forgive your sins. And whoever obeys God and His Messenger, has truly achieved a great triumph.

The Trust[866]

72. Indeed, We offered the trust to the heavens and the earth and the mountains, but they ˹all˺ declined to bear it, being fearful of it. But humanity assumed it, ˹for˺ they are truly wrongful ˹to themselves˺ and ignorant ˹of the consequences˺, **73.** so that God will punish hypocrite men and women and polytheistic men and women, and God will turn in mercy to believing men and women. For God is All-Forgiving, Most Merciful.[867]

---

863 He has forgiven what Muslim women did in the past because they were not obligated to cover up.

864 This verse is intended to deter the hypocrites. The Prophet never killed any hypocrite as long as they did not join the enemy to attack and kill Muslims.

865 The Quran does not specify how Moses was slandered by some of his people. Some narrations suggest that he was either falsely accused of adultery (*see* footnote for 28:76), killing his brother Aaron (who died a natural death), or having a skin disease since he, unlike others, used to bathe with his clothes on.

866 This refers to free choice in shouldering religious commandments. The great majority of God's creation (like angels and animals) do not have free will. Therefore, they are inherently submissive to God. As for humans, they rely on their intelligence, and are free to choose between guidance and misguidance, and either to adhere to divine obligations and prohibitions or not.

867 This is a guarantee from God that if the hypocrites and polytheists ever turn to Him in repentance, He is always willing to forgive them.

34. Sheba *(Saba')*

This Meccan chapter takes its name from the reference to the people of Sheba (verses 15-20) who were punished for meeting God's favours with ingratitude. Both David and Solomon are cited as grateful servants of God. The Meccan pagans are reminded that only faith can bring them closer to God, not their wealth. They are criticized for calling the Prophet 'insane' and are warned of punishment in this life and the next. Both the last part of this chapter (verses 40-41) and the beginning of the next (verse 1) reaffirm the angels as God's faithful servants.

In the Name of God—the Most Compassionate, Most Merciful

Praises to the Almighty

1. All praise is for God, to Whom belongs whatever is in the heavens and whatever is on the earth. And praise be to Him in the Hereafter. He is the All-Wise, All-Aware. 2. He knows whatever goes into the earth and whatever comes out of it, and whatever descends from the sky and whatever ascends into it. And He is the Most Merciful, All-Forgiving.

Denying the Hour

3. The disbelievers say, "The Hour will never come to us." Say, ˹O Prophet,˺ "Yes—by my Lord, the Knower of the unseen—it will certainly come to you!" Not ˹even˺ an atom's weight is hidden from Him in the heavens or the earth; nor anything smaller or larger than that, but is ˹written˺ in a perfect Record.[868] 4. So He may reward those who believe and do good. It is they who will have forgiveness and an honourable provision. 5. As for those who strive to discredit Our revelations, it is they who will suffer the ˹worst˺ torment of agonizing pain. 6. Those gifted with knowledge ˹clearly˺ see that what has been revealed to you from your Lord ˹O Prophet˺ is the truth, and that it guides to the Path of the Almighty, the Praiseworthy.

Warning to the Deniers

7. The disbelievers say ˹mockingly to one another˺, "Shall we show you a man who

claims that when you have been utterly disintegrated you will be raised as a new creation? 8. Has he fabricated a lie against God or is he insane?" In fact, those who do not believe in the Hereafter are bound for torment and have strayed farthest ˹from the truth˺. 9. Have they not then seen all that surrounds them of the heavens and the earth? If We willed, We could cause the earth to swallow them up, or cause ˹deadly˺ pieces of the sky to fall upon them. Surely in this is a sign for every servant who turns ˹to God˺.

God's Favours to David

10. Indeed, We granted David a ˹great˺ privilege from Us, ˹commanding:˺ "O mountains! Echo his hymns! And the birds as well." We made iron mouldable for him, 11. instructing: "Make full-length armour, ˹perfectly˺ balancing the links. And work righteousness ˹O family of David!˺. Indeed, I am All-Seeing of what you do."

God's Favours to Solomon

12. And to Solomon ˹We subjected˺ the wind: its morning stride was a month's journey and so was its evening stride. And We caused a stream of molten copper to flow for him, and ˹We subjected˺ some of the jinn to work under him by his Lord's Will. And whoever of them deviated from Our command, We made them taste the torment of the blaze. 13. They made for

---

him whatever he desired of sanctuaries, statues,[869] basins as large as reservoirs, and cooking pots fixed ʿinto the groundʾ. ʿWe ordered:ʾ "Work gratefully, O family of David!" ʿOnlyʾ a few of My servants are ʿtrulyʾ grateful. **14.** When We decreed Solomon's death, nothing indicated to the ʿsubjectedʾ jinn that he was dead except the termites eating away his staff.[870] So when he collapsed, the jinn realized that if they had ʿreallyʾ known the unseen, they would not have remained in ʿsuchʾ humiliating servitude.

God's Favours to Sheba 1) Provision

15. Indeed, there was a sign for ʿthe tribe ofʾ Sheba in their homeland: two orchards—one to the right and the other to the left. ʿTheyʾ were told:ʾ "Eat from the provision of your Lord, and be grateful to Him. ʿYours isʾ a good land and a forgiving Lord." **16.** But they turned away. So We sent against them a devastating flood, and replaced their orchards with two others producing bitter fruit, fruitless bushes,[871] and a few ʿsparseʾ thorny trees.[872] **17.** This is how We rewarded them for their ingratitude. Would We ever punish ʿanyone in such a wayʾ except the ungrateful?

God's Favours to Sheba 2) Safe Travel

18. We had also placed between them and the cities[873] We showered with blessings ʿmany smallʾ towns within sight of one another. And We set moderate travel distances in between, ʿsaying,ʾ "Travel between them by day and night safely." **19.** But they said, "Our Lord! Make ʿthe distances ofʾ our journeys longer," wronging themselves.[874] So We reduced them

to ʿcautionaryʾ tales, and scattered them utterly. Surely in this are lessons for whoever is steadfast, grateful.

Satan's Vow Regarding Humans

20. Indeed, *Iblîs'* assumption about them has come true,[875] so they ʿallʾ follow him, except a group of ʿtrueʾ believers. **21.** He does not have any authority over them, but ʿOur Will isʾ only to distinguish those who believe in the Hereafter from those who are in doubt about it. And your Lord is a ʿvigilantʾ Keeper over all things.

Helpless Idols

22. Say, ʿO Prophet,ʾ "Call upon those you claim ʿto be divineʾ besides God. They do not possess ʿevenʾ an atom's weight either in the heavens or the earth, nor do they have any share in ʿgoverningʾ them. Nor is any of them a helper to Him." **23.** No intercession will be of any benefit with Him, except by those granted permission by Him. ʿAt last,ʾ when the dread ʿof Judgment Dayʾ is relieved from their hearts ʿbecause they are permitted to intercedeʾ, they will ʿexcitedlyʾ ask ʿthe angelsʾ, "What has your Lord ʿjustʾ said?" The angels will reply, "The truth! And He is the Most High, All-Great."

Message to the Polytheists

24. Ask ʿthem, O Prophetʾ, "Who provides for you from the heavens and the earth?" Say, "God! Now, certainly one of our two groups[876] is ʿrightlyʾ guided; the other is clearly astray." **25.** Say, "You will not be accountable for our misdeeds, nor will we be accountable for your deeds." **26.** Say, "Our

---

869 Which was permissible at the time of Solomon.
870 Which he died while leaning on.
871 lit., tamarisks.
872 lit., lote trees.
873 i.e., Mecca and Jerusalem.
874 They became bored of living comfortably and traveling easily. A similar example can be found in 2:61, where the Children of Israel became bored with the manna and quails and wanted to eat other things such as onions and garlic.
875 *Iblîs* was the name of Satan before his fall from grace (*see* footnote for 2:33). His assumption (or vow) was that he could easily mislead the majority of people (*see* 7:16-17, 15:39-40, and 38:82-83).
876 The believers and polytheists.

Lord will gather us together, then He will judge between us with the truth. For He is the All-Knowing Judge." 27. Say, "Show me those ˹idols˺ you have joined with Him as partners. No! In fact, He ˹alone˺ is God—the Almighty, All-Wise."

Warning of the Hour

28. We have sent you ˹O Prophet˺ only as a deliverer of good news and a warner to all of humanity, but most people do not know. 29. And they ask ˹the believers˺, "When will this threat come to pass, if what you say is true?" 30. Say, ˹O Prophet,˺ "A Day has ˹already˺ been appointed for you, which you can neither delay nor advance by a ˹single˺ moment."

The Misleaders and the Misled

31. The disbelievers vow, "We will never believe in this Quran, nor in those ˹Scriptures˺ before it." If only you could see when the wrongdoers will be detained before their Lord, throwing blame at each other! The lowly ˹followers˺ will say to the arrogant ˹leaders˺, "Had it not been for you, we would certainly have been believers." 32. The arrogant will respond to the lowly, "Did we ever hinder you from guidance after it came to you? In fact, you were wicked ˹on your own˺." 33. The lowly will say to the arrogant, "No! It was your plotting by day and night—when you ordered us to disbelieve in God and to set up equals with Him." They will ˹all˺ hide ˹their˺ remorse when they see the torment. And We will put shackles around the necks of the disbelievers. Will they be rewarded except for what they used to do?

Spoiled Elite

34. Whenever We sent a warner to a society, its elite would say, "We truly reject what you have been sent with." 35. Adding, "We are far superior ˹to the believers˺ in wealth and children, and we will never be punished." 36. Say, ˹O Prophet,˺ "Surely ˹it is˺ my Lord ˹Who˺ gives abundant or limited provisions to whoever He wills. But most people do not know." 37. It is not your wealth or children that bring you closer to Us. But those who believe and do good—it is they who will have a multiplied reward for what they did, and they will be secure in ˹elevated˺ mansions. 38. As for those who strive to discredit Our revelations, it is they who will be confined in punishment. 39. Say, ˹O Prophet,˺ "Surely ˹it is˺ my Lord ˹Who˺ gives abundant or limited provisions to whoever He wills of His servants. And whatever you spend in charity, He will compensate ˹you˺ for it. For He is the Best Provider."

The Worshippers and the Worshipped

40. And ˹consider˺ the Day He will gather them all together, and then ask the angels, "Was it you that these ˹polytheists˺ used to worship?" 41. They will say, "Glory be to You! Our loyalty is to You, not them. In fact, they ˹only˺ followed the ˹temptations of evil˺ jinn,[877] in whom most of them had faith." 42. So Today neither of you can benefit or protect each other. And We will say to the wrongdoers, "Taste the torment of the Fire, which you used to deny."

Response of the Polytheists

43. When Our clear revelations are recited to them, they say, "This is only a man who wishes to hinder you from what your forefathers used to worship." They also say, "This ˹Quran˺ is no more than a fabricated lie." And the disbelievers say of the truth when it has come to them, "This is nothing but pure magic." 44. ˹They say so even though˺ We had never given them any scriptures to study, nor did We ever send them a warner before you ˹O Prophet˺. 45. Those ˹destroyed˺ before them denied as well—and these ˹Meccans˺ have not attained even one-tenth of

---

877   i.e., the devils.

what We had given their predecessors.[878] Yet ʿwhenʾ they denied My messengers, how severe was My response!

Advice to Meccan Pagans

46. Say, ʿO Prophet,ʾ "I advise you to do ʿonlyʾ one thing: stand up for ʿthe sake ofʾ God—individually or in pairs—then reflect. Your fellow man[879] is not insane. He is only a warner to you before ʿthe coming ofʾ a severe punishment." **47.** Say, "If I had ever asked you for a reward, you could keep it. My reward is only from God. And He is a Witness over all things." **48.** Say, "Surely my Lord hurls the truth ʿagainst falsehoodʾ. ʿHe isʾ the Knower of all unseen." **49.** Say, "The truth has come, and falsehood will vanish, never to return." **50.** Say, "If I am astray, the loss is only mine. And if I am guided, it is ʿonlyʾ because of what my Lord reveals to me. He is indeed All-Hearing, Ever Near."

Too Late for the Deniers

51. If only you could see when they will be horrified with no escape ʿon Judgment Dayʾ! And they will be seized from a nearby place.[880] **52.** They will ʿthenʾ cry, "We do ʿnowʾ believe in it ʿallʾ." But how could they ʿpossiblyʾ attain faith from a place so far-off ʿfrom the worldʾ,[881] **53.** while they had already rejected it before, guessing blindly from a place ʿequallyʾ far-away ʿfrom the Hereafterʾ? **54.** They will be sealed off from whatever they desire, as was done to their counterparts before. Indeed, they were ʿallʾ in alarming doubt.

35. The Originator *(Fâṭir)*

This Meccan chapter demonstrates God's infinite power through the marvels of His creation, in contrast with the powerlessness of the pagan idols. The Prophet is consoled by the fact that many prophets were denied before him. The believers are promised of a great reward in Paradise (verses 31-35), while the disbelievers are warned of a scathing punishment in Hell (verses 36-39). All these themes are echoed in the next chapter.

In the Name of God—the Most Compassionate, Most Merciful

God's Power 1) Creation and Mercy

1. All praise is for God, the Originator of the heavens and the earth, Who made angels ʿasʾ His messengers with wings—two, three, or four. He increases in creation whatever He wills. Surely God is Most Capable of everything. **2.** Whatever mercy God opens up for people, none can withhold it. And whatever He withholds, none but Him can release it. For He is the Almighty, All-Wise.

One God Only

3. O humanity! Remember God's favours upon you. Is there any creator other than God who provides for you from the heavens and the earth? There is no god ʿworthy of

---

878 Like the people of Pharaoh, ʿÂd, and Thamûd.
879 i.e., Muḥammad.
880 From the place of Judgment to Hell.
881 When it is already too late.

worship' except Him. How can you then be deluded 'from the truth'?

Reassuring the Prophet

4. If you are rejected by them, so too were messengers before you. And to God 'all' matters will be returned 'for judgment'.

Warning Against Satan

5. O humanity! Indeed, God's promise is true. So do not let the life of this world deceive you, nor let the Chief Deceiver[882] deceive you about God. **6.** Surely Satan is an enemy to you, so take him as an enemy. He only invites his followers to become inmates of the Blaze.

The Evildoers and the Good-Doers

7. Those who disbelieve will have a severe punishment. But those who believe and do good will have forgiveness and a great reward. **8.** Are those whose evil-doing is made so appealing to them that they deem it good 'like those who are rightly guided'? 'It is' certainly God 'Who' leaves to stray whoever He wills, and guides whoever He wills. So do not grieve yourself to death over them 'O Prophet'. Surely God is All-Knowing of what they do.

God's Power 2)   The Wind

9. And it is God Who sends the winds, which then stir up 'vapour, forming' clouds, and then We drive them to a lifeless land, giving life to the earth after its death. Similar is the Resurrection.

All Honour and Power Belongs to God

10. Whoever seeks honour and power, then 'let them know that' all honour and power belongs to God. To Him 'alone' good words ascend, and righteous deeds are raised up by Him. As for those who

plot evil, they will suffer a severe punishment. And the plotting of such 'people' is doomed 'to fail'.

God's Power 3)   Creation of Humans

11. And 'it is' God 'Who' created you from dust,[883] then 'developed you' from a sperm-drop, then made you into pairs.[884] No female ever conceives or delivers without His knowledge. And no one's life is made long or cut short but is 'written' in a Record.[885] That is certainly easy for God.

God's Power 4)   Fresh and Salt Water

12. The two bodies of water are not alike: one is fresh, palatable, and pleasant to drink and the other is salty and bitter. Yet from them both you eat tender seafood and extract ornaments to wear. And you see the ships ploughing their way through both, so you may seek His bounty and give thanks 'to Him'.

God's Power 5)   Alternation of Day and Night

13. He merges the night into the day and the day into the night, and has subjected the sun and the moon, each orbiting for an appointed term. That is God—your Lord! All authority belongs to Him. But those 'idols' you invoke besides Him do not possess even the skin of a date stone. **14.** If you call upon them, they cannot hear your calls. And if they were to hear, they could not respond to you. On the Day of Judgment they will disown your worship 'of them'. And no one can inform you 'O Prophet' like the All-Knowledgeable.

God's Power 6)   Sustenance

15. O humanity! It is you who stand in need of God, but God 'alone' is the Self-Sufficient, Praiseworthy. **16.** If He willed, He

---

882   Satan.
883   Created your father, Adam, from dust.
884   Males and females.
885   *See* footnote for 33:6.

could eliminate you and produce a new creation. **17.** And that is not difficult for God ˈat allˈ.

Everyone Is Accountable for Themselves

18. No soul burdened with sin will bear the burden of another. And if a sin-burdened soul cries for help with its burden, none of it will be carried—even by a close relative. You ˈO Prophetˈ can only warn those who stand in awe of their Lord without seeing Him[886] and establish prayer. Whoever purifies themselves, they only do so for their own good. And to God is the final return.

Guidance vs. Misguidance

19. Those blind ˈto the truthˈ and those who can see are not equal, **20.** nor are the darkness and the light, **21.** nor the ˈscorchingˈ heat and the ˈcoolˈ shade.[887] **22.** Nor are the dead and the living equal. Indeed, God ˈaloneˈ makes whoever He wills hear, but you ˈO Prophetˈ can never make those in the graves hear ˈyour callˈ.

Reassuring the Prophet

23. You are only a warner. **24.** We have surely sent you with the truth as a deliverer of good news and a warner. There is no community that has not had a warner.[888] **25.** If they deny you, so did those before them. Their messengers came to them with clear proofs, divine Books, and enlightening Scriptures.[889] **26.** Then I seized those who persisted in disbelief. How severe was My response!

God's Power 7) Diversity

27. Do you not see that God sends down rain from the sky with which We bring forth fruits of different colours? And in the mountains are streaks of varying shades of white, red, and raven black; **28.** just as people, living beings, and cattle are of various colours as well. Of all of God's servants, only the knowledgeable ˈof His mightˈ are ˈtrulyˈ in awe of Him. God is indeed Almighty, All-Forgiving.

The Everlasting Reward

29. Surely those who recite the Book of God, establish prayer, and donate from what We have provided for them—secretly and openly—ˈcanˈ hope for an exchange that will never fail, **30.** so that He will reward them in full and increase them out of His grace. He is truly All-Forgiving, Most Appreciative.

Three Types of Believers

31. The Book We have revealed to you ˈO Prophetˈ is the truth, confirming what came before it.[890] Surely God is All-Aware, All-Seeing of His servants. **32.** Then We granted the Book to those We have chosen from Our servants. Some of them wrong themselves, some follow a middle course, and some are foremost in good deeds by God's Will. That is ˈtrulyˈ the greatest bounty.

Reward of the Believers

33. They will enter the Gardens of Eternity, where they will be adorned with bracelets of gold and pearls, and their clothing will be silk. **34.** And they will say, "Praise be to God, Who has kept away from us all ˈcauses ofˈ sorrow. Our Lord is indeed All-Forgiving, Most Appreciative. **35.** ˈHe is the Oneˈ Who—out of His grace—has settled us in the Home of Everlasting Stay, where we

---

886   This can also mean that they are in awe of their Lord as much in private as they are in public.

887   This implies Hell and Paradise.

888   According to a Prophetic narration collected by Ibn Ḥibbân, the total number of prophets sent around the world, from Adam to Muḥammad, is 124 000—of which only twenty-five are mentioned in the Quran.

889   i.e., the Torah, the Gospel, and Psalms.

890   *See* previous footnote.

will be touched by neither fatigue nor weariness."

Punishment of the Disbelievers

36. As for the disbelievers, they will have the Fire of Hell, where they will not be ˹allowed to be˺ finished by death, nor will its torment be lightened for them. This is how We reward every ˹stubborn˺ disbeliever. **37.** There they will be ˹fervently˺ screaming, "Our Lord! Take us out ˹and send us back˺. We will do good, unlike what we used to do." ˹They will be told,˺ "Did We not give you lives long enough so that whoever wanted to be mindful could have done so? And the warner came to you. So taste ˹the punishment˺, for the wrongdoers have no helper."

Denying the Almighty

38. Indeed, God is the Knower of the unseen of the heavens and the earth. He surely knows best what is ˹hidden˺ in the heart. **39.** He is the One Who has placed you as successors on earth. So whoever disbelieves will bear ˹the burden of˺ their own disbelief. The disbelievers' denial only increases them in contempt in the sight of their Lord, and it will only contribute to their loss.

Useless Idols

40. Ask ˹them, O Prophet˺, "Have you considered your associate-gods which you invoke besides God? Show me what they have created on earth! Or do they have a share in ˹the creation of˺ the heavens? Or have We given the polytheists a Book, which serves as a clear proof for them? In fact, the wrongdoers promise each other nothing but delusion."

God's Power 8) Maintaining the Universe

41. Indeed, God ˹alone˺ keeps the heavens and the earth from falling apart. If they were to fall apart, none but Him could hold them up. He is truly Most Forbearing, All-Forgiving.

Warning to the Disbelievers

42. They swore by God their most solemn oaths that if a warner were to come to them, they would certainly be better guided than any other community. Yet when a warner did come to them, it only drove them farther away— **43.** behaving arrogantly in the land and plotting evil. But evil plotting only backfires on those who plot. Are they awaiting anything but the fate of those ˹destroyed˺ before? You will find no change in the way of God, nor will you find it diverted ˹to someone else˺. **44.** Have they not travelled throughout the land to see what was the end of those ˹destroyed˺ before them? They were far superior in might. But there is nothing that can escape God in the heavens or the earth. He is certainly All-Knowing, Most Capable.

Allowing Time for Repentance

45. If God were to punish people ˹immediately˺ for what they have committed, He would not have left a single living being on earth. But He delays them for an appointed term. And when their time arrives, then surely God is All-Seeing of His servants.

36. Yâ-Sîn *(Yâ-Sîn)*

This Meccan chapter emphasizes the divine nature and purpose of the Quran. The Arab pagans are reminded of the fate of earlier disbelievers and condemned for following Satan, denying the Resurrection, discrediting the Quran, and rejecting the Prophet as 'a poet.' Similar to the next chapter, some examples of God's wonders of creation are cited to prove His ability to bring the dead back to life.

In the Name of God—the Most Compassionate, Most Merciful

Wake-up Call

1. *Yâ-Sîn.* 2. By the Quran, rich in wisdom! 3. You ʼO Prophetʼ are truly one of the messengers 4. upon the Straight Path. 5. ʼThis isʼ a revelation from the Almighty, Most Merciful, 6. so that you may warn a people whose forefathers were not warned, and so are heedless. 7. The decree ʼof tormentʼ has already been justified against most of them, for they will never believe. 8. ʼIt is as ifʼ We have put shackles around their necks up to their chins, so their heads are forced up, 9. and have placed a barrier before them and a barrier behind them and covered them ʼallʼ up, so they fail to see ʼthe truthʼ.

Who Benefits from Reminders

10. It is the same whether you warn them or not—they will never believe. 11. You can only warn those who follow the Reminder[891] and are in awe of the Most Compassionate without seeing Him.[892] So give them good news of forgiveness and an honourable reward. 12. It is certainly We Who resurrect the dead, and write what they send forth and what they leave behind. Everything is listed by Us in a perfect Record.[893]

The Three Messengers

13. Give them an example ʼO Prophetʼ of the residents of a town, when the messengers came to them. 14. We sent them two messengers, but they rejected both. So We reinforced ʼthe twoʼ with a third, and they de-clared, "We have indeed been sent to you ʼas messengersʼ." 15. The people replied, "You are only humans like us, and the Most Compassionate has not revealed anything. You are simply lying!" 16. The messengers responded, "Our Lord knows that we have truly been sent to you. 17. And our duty is only to deliver ʼthe messageʼ clearly." 18. The people replied, "We definitely see you as a bad omen for us. If you do not desist, we will certainly stone you ʼto deathʼ and you will be touched with a painful punishment from us." 19. The messengers said, "Your bad omen lies within yourselves. Are you saying this because you are reminded ʼof the truthʼ? In fact, you are a transgressing people."

An Advocate of the Truth

20. Then from the farthest end of the city a man came, rushing. He advised, "O my people! Follow the messengers. 21. Follow those who ask no reward of you, and are ʼrightlyʼ guided. 22. And why should I not worship the One Who has originated me, and to Whom you will be returned. 23. How could I take besides Him other gods whose intercession would not be of any benefit to me, nor could they save me if the Most Compassionate intended to harm me? 24. Indeed, I would then be clearly astray. 25. I do believe in your Lord, so listen to me." 26. ʼBut they killed him, thenʼ he was told ʼby the angelsʼ, "Enter Paradise!" He said, "If only my people knew 27. of how my Lord has forgiven me, and made me one of the honourable."

---

891   The Reminder is another name for the Quran.
892   See footnote for 35:18.
893   *See* footnote for 35:11.

The Wicked Destroyed

28. We did not send any soldiers from the heavens against his people after his death, nor did We need to. **29.** All it took was one ˹mighty˺ blast, and they were extinguished at once. **30.** Oh pity, such beings! No messenger ever came to them without being mocked. **31.** Have the deniers not considered how many peoples We destroyed before them who never came back to life again? **32.** Yet they will all be brought before Us.

God's Signs 1) the Earth

33. There is a sign for them in the dead earth: We give it life, producing grain from it for them to eat. **34.** And We have placed in it gardens of palm trees and grapevines, and caused springs to gush forth in it, **35.** so that they may eat from its fruit, which they had no hand in making. Will they not then give thanks? **36.** Glory be to the One Who created all ˹things in˺ pairs—˹be it˺ what the earth produces, their genders, or what they do not know!

God's Signs 2) Night

37. There is also a sign for them in the night: We strip from it daylight, then—behold!—they are in darkness.

God's Signs 3) the Sun and the Moon

38. The sun travels for its fixed term. That is the design of the Almighty, All-Knowing. **39.** As for the moon, We have ordained ˹precise˺ phases for it, until it ends up ˹looking˺ like an old, curved palm stalk. **40.** It is not for the sun to catch up with the moon,[894] nor does the night outrun the day. Each is travelling in an orbit of their own.

God's Signs 4) Mercy at Sea

41. Another sign for them is that We carried their ancestors ˹with Noah˺ in the fully loaded Ark, **42.** and created for them similar things to ride in. **43.** If We willed, We could drown them: then no one would respond to their cries, nor would they be rescued— **44.** except by mercy from Us, allowing them enjoyment for a ˹little˺ while.

Stance of the Polytheists

45. ˹Still they turn away˺ when it is said to them, "Beware of what is ahead of you ˹in the Hereafter˺ and what is behind you ˹of destroyed nations˺ so you may be shown mercy." **46.** Whenever a sign comes to them from their Lord, they turn away from it. **47.** And when it is said to them, "Donate from what God has provided for you," the disbelievers say to the believers, "Why should we feed those whom God could have fed if He wanted to? You are clearly astray!"

Too Late for the Deniers

48. And they ask ˹the believers˺, "When will this threat come to pass, if what you say is true?" **49.** They must be awaiting a single Blast,[895] which will seize them while they are ˹entrenched˺ in ˹worldly˺ disputes. **50.** Then they will not be able to make a ˹last˺ will, nor can they return to their own people. **51.** The Trumpet will be blown ˹a second time˺, then—behold!—they will rush from the graves to their Lord. **52.** They will cry, "Woe to us! Who has raised us up from our place of rest? This must be what the Most Compassionate warned us of; the messengers told the truth!" **53.** It will only take one Blast, then at once they will all be brought before Us. **54.** On that Day no soul will be wronged in the least, nor will you be rewarded except for what you used to do.

Reward of the Believers

55. Indeed, on that Day the residents of Paradise will be busy enjoying themselves. **56.** They and their spouses will be in ˹cool˺

---

894 The moon completes a cycle every month (waxing and waning), while the sun takes a whole year to complete its cycle (resulting in the spring, summer, fall, and winter seasons).

895 On the Day of Judgment, the Trumpet will be blown by an angel—causing all to die. When it is blown a second time, everyone will be raised from the dead for judgment (*see* 39:68).

shade, reclining on ʿcanopiedʾ couches.
57. There they will have fruits and whatever they desire. **58.** And "Peace!" will be ʿtheirʾ greeting from the Merciful Lord.

Reward of the Disbelievers

59. ʿThen the disbelievers will be told,ʾ "Step away ʿfrom the believersʾ this Day, O wicked ones! **60.** Did I not command you, O Children of Adam, not to follow Satan, for he is truly your sworn enemy, **61.** but to worship Me ʿaloneʾ? This is the Straight Path. **62.** Yet he already misled great multitudes of you. Did you not have any sense? **63.** This is the Hell you were warned of. **64.** Burn in it Today for your disbelief." **65.** On this Day We will seal their mouths, their hands will speak to Us, and their feet will testify to what they used to commit.

God's Power over the Deniers

66. Had We willed, We could have easily blinded their eyes, so they would struggle to find their way. How then could they see? **67.** And had We willed, We could have transfigured them on the spot,[896] so they could neither progress forward nor turn back. **68.** And whoever We grant a long life, We reverse them in development.[897] Will they not then understand?

The Prophet Is Not a Poet

69. We have not taught him poetry, nor is it fitting for him. This ʿBookʾ is only a Reminder and a clear Quran **70.** to warn whoever is ʿtrulyʾ alive and fulfil the decree ʿof tormentʾ against the disbelievers.

God's Signs 5) Domesticated Animals

71. Do they not see that We singlehandedly[898] created for them, among other things, cattle which are under their control? **72.** And We have subjected these ʿanimalsʾ to them, so they may ride some and eat others. **73.** And they derive from them other benefits and drinks. Will they not then give thanks?

Ingratitude of the Deniers

74. Still they have taken other gods besides God, hoping to be helped ʿby themʾ. **75.** They cannot help the pagans, even though they serve the idols as dedicated guards.[899] **76.** So do not let their words grieve you ʿO Prophetʾ. Indeed, We ʿfullyʾ know what they conceal and what they reveal.

God's Power to Resurrect

77. Do people not see that We have created them from a sperm-drop, then—behold!—they openly challenge ʿUsʾ? **78.** And they argue with Us—forgetting they were created—saying, "Who will give life to decayed bones?" **79.** Say, ʿO Prophet,ʾ "They will be revived by the One Who produced them the first time, for He has ʿperfectʾ knowledge of every created being. **80.** ʿHe is the Oneʾ Who gives you fire from green trees, and—behold!—you kindle ʿfireʾ from them.[900] **81.** Can the One Who created the heavens and the earth not ʿeasilyʾ resurrect these ʿdeniersʾ?" Yes ʿHe canʾ! For He is the Master Creator, All-Knowing. **82.** All it takes, when He wills something ʿto beʾ, is simply to say to it: "Be!" And it is! **83.** So glory be to the One in Whose Hands is the authority over all things, and to Whom ʿaloneʾ you will ʿallʾ be returned.

---

896   Meaning, We have the ability to turn them into stone or any other inanimate object.
897   Human beings are born weak, then they reach their prime, then they grow weak after a certain age. *See* 30:54.
898   lit., 'what Our Own Hands have created.' God has hands, but not like ours.
899   Another meaning is that those idols will be assembled to witness the torment of their worshippers on Judgment Day.
900   The verse refers to two types of Arabian trees, *markh* and *'afâr*, which produce fire when their green branches are rubbed together.

37. Those ⸢Angels⸣ Lined up in Ranks *(Aṣ-Ṣâffât)*

For the most part, this Meccan chapter explains verse 31 from the previous chapter: "Have the deniers not considered how many peoples We destroyed before them ...?". Hence, several examples of destroyed disbelievers are cited here, including the peoples of Noah, Lot, and Elias. Some basic truths are emphasized, including the oneness of God, the Resurrection, and the prophethood of Muḥammad. The pagans are criticized for calling the Prophet 'a mad poet' and for claiming that the angels are God's daughters. This chapter provides more details on the punishment of the disbelievers and the reward of the believers in the Hereafter (verses 19-68). In conclusion, the Prophet is reassured that God's messengers always prevail.

In the Name of God—the Most Compassionate, Most Merciful

One God Only

1. By those ⸢angels⸣ lined up in ranks, 2. and those who diligently drive ⸢the clouds⸣, 3. and those who recite the Reminder! 4. Surely your God is One! 5. ⸢He is⸣ the Lord of the heavens and the earth and everything in between, and the Lord of all points of sunrise.

The Heavens Decorated and Protected

6. Indeed, We have adorned the lowest heaven with the stars for decoration 7. and ⸢for⸣ protection from every rebellious devil. 8. They cannot listen to the highest assembly ⸢of angels⸣ for they are pelted from every side, 9. ⸢fiercely⸣ driven away. And they will suffer an everlasting torment. 10. But whoever manages to stealthily eavesdrop is ⸢instantly⸣ pursued by a piercing flare.

A Question to Resurrection Deniers

11. So ask them ⸢O Prophet⸣, which is harder to create: them or other marvels of Our creation?[901] Indeed, We created them from a sticky clay.[902] 12. In fact, you are astonished ⸢by their denial⸣, while they ridicule ⸢you⸣. 13. When they are reminded, they are never mindful. 14. And whenever they see a sign, they make fun of it, 15. saying, "This is nothing but pure magic. 16. When we are dead and reduced to dust and bones, will we really be resurrected? 17. And our forefathers as well?" 18. Say, "Yes! And you will be fully humbled."

The Deniers After Resurrection

19. It will only take one Blast,[903] then at once they will see ⸢it all⸣. 20. They will cry, "Oh, woe to us! This is the Day of Judgment!" 21. ⸢They will be told,⸣ "This is the Day of ⸢Final⸣ Decision which you used to deny." 22. ⸢God will say to the angels,⸣ "Gather ⸢all⸣ the wrongdoers along with their peers, and whatever they used to worship 23. instead of God, then lead them ⸢all⸣ to the path of Hell. 24. And detain them, for they must be questioned." 25. ⸢Then they will be asked,⸣ "What is the matter with you that you can no longer help each other?" 26. In fact, on that Day they will be ⸢fully⸣ submissive.

The Misleaders vs. the Misled

27. They will turn on each other, throwing blame. 28. The misled will say, "It was you who deluded us away from what is right."[904]

---

901   i.e., the angels, the sun, the moon, the stars, and the mountains.
902   Their father Adam.
903   This is when the Trumpet will be blown the second time.
904   Other possible translations: 1. "It was you who used to pressure us." 2. "It was you who tricked us in the name of the truth." 3. "It was you who dissuaded us from doing good." 4. "It was you who deceived us with false oaths."

29. The misleaders will reply, "No! You disbelieved on your own. **30.** We had no authority over you. In fact, you yourselves were a transgressing people. **31.** The decree of our Lord has come to pass against us ʿallʾ: we will certainly taste ʿthe punishmentʾ. **32.** We caused you to deviate, for we ourselves were deviant." **33.** Surely on that Day they will ʿallʾ share in the punishment.

Warning to Arab Pagans

34. That is certainly how We deal with the wicked. **35.** For whenever it was said to them ʿin the worldʾ, "There is no god ʿworthy of worshipʾ except God," they acted arrogantly **36.** and argued, "Should we really abandon our gods for a mad poet?" **37.** In fact, he came with the truth, confirming ʿearlierʾ messengers. **38.** You will certainly taste the painful torment, **39.** and will only be rewarded for what you used to do.

Reward of the Devout

40. But not the chosen servants of God. **41.** They will have a known provision: **42.** fruits ʿof every typeʾ.[905] And they will be honoured **43.** in the Gardens of Bliss, **44.** facing each other on thrones.[906] **45.** A drink ʿof pure wineʾ will be passed around to them from a flowing stream: **46.** crystal-white, delicious to drink. **47.** It will neither harm ʿthemʾ, nor will they be intoxicated by it. **48.** And with them will be maidens of modest gaze and gorgeous eyes, **49.** as if they were pristine pearls.[907]

The People of Paradise Chatting

50. Then they will turn to one another inquisitively.[908] **51.** One of them will say, "I once had a companion ʿin the worldʾ **52.** who used to ask ʿmeʾ, 'Do you actually believe ʿin resurrectionʾ? **53.** When we are dead and reduced to dust and bones, will we really be brought to judgment?'" **54.** He will ʿthenʾ ask, "Would you care to see ʿhis fateʾ?" **55.** Then he ʿand the othersʾ will look and spot him in the midst of the Hellfire. **56.** He will ʿthenʾ say, "By God! You nearly ruined me. **57.** Had it not been for the grace of my Lord, I ʿtooʾ would have certainly been among those brought ʿto Hellʾ." **58.** ʿThen he will ask his fellow believers,ʾ "Can you imagine that we will never die, **59.** except our first death, nor be punished ʿlike the othersʾ? **60.** This is truly the ultimate triumph. **61.** For such ʿhonourʾ all should strive.

Hospitality for the People of Hell

62. Is this ʿblissʾ a better accommodation or the tree of *Zaqqûm*?[909] **63.** We have surely made it a test for the wrongdoers. **64.** Indeed, it is a tree that grows in the depths of Hell, **65.** bearing fruit like devils' heads. **66.** The evildoers will certainly ʿbe left toʾ eat from it, filling up their bellies with it. **67.** Then on top of that they will be given a blend of boiling drink. **68.** Then they will ultimately return to ʿtheir place inʾ Hell.

Blind Following

69. Indeed, they found their forefathers astray, **70.** so they rushed in their footsteps! **71.** And surely most of the earlier generations had strayed before them, **72.** although We had certainly sent warners among them. **73.** See then what was the end of those who had been warned. **74.** But not the chosen servants of God.

Prophet Noah

75. Indeed, Noah cried out to Us, and how excellent are We in responding! **76.** We

---

905 This implies all sorts of delicacies, not just fruits.
906 Facing each other implies that no one will have anything in their hearts against others.
907 *Baiḍun maknûn* can also mean spotless eggs.
908 It is assumed that they will ask each other about their lives in the world and what led them to Paradise.
909 The pagans of Mecca used to make fun of the Prophet when he warned them of this tree. They asked, "How can a tree grow in Hell?" So God revealed this verse in response.

delivered him and his family[910] from the great distress, **77.** and made his descendants the sole survivors.[911] **78.** And We blessed him ʿwith honourable mentionʾ among later generations: **79.** "Peace be upon Noah among all peoples." **80.** Indeed, this is how We reward the good-doers. **81.** ʿForʾ he was truly one of Our faithful servants. **82.** Then We drowned the others.

Prophet Abraham

83. And indeed, one of those who followed his way was Abraham. **84.** ʿRememberʾ when he came to his Lord with a pure heart, **85.** and said to his father and his people, "What are you worshipping? **86.** Is it false gods that you desire instead of God? **87.** What then do you expect from the Lord of all worlds?" **88.** He later looked up to the stars ʿin contemplationʾ,[912] **89.** then said, "I am really sick."[913] **90.** So they turned their backs on him and went away. **91.** Then he ʿstealthilyʾ advanced towards their gods, and said ʿmockinglyʾ, "Will you not eat ʿyour offeringsʾ? **92.** What is wrong with you that you cannot speak?" **93.** Then he swiftly turned on them, striking ʿthemʾ with his right hand. **94.** Later, his people came rushing towards him ʿfuriouslyʾ. **95.** He argued, "How can you worship what you carve ʿwith your own handsʾ, **96.** when it is God Who created you and whatever you do?" **97.** They said ʿto one anotherʾ, "Build him a furnace and cast him into the blazing fire." **98.** And so they sought to harm him, but We made them inferior.

Abraham, Ishmael and the Sacrifice

99. He later said, "I am leaving ʿin obedienceʾ to my Lord. He will guide me. **100.** My Lord! Bless me with righteous offspring." **101.** So We gave him good news of a forbearing son. **102.** Then when the boy reached the age to work with him, Abraham said, "O my dear son! I have seen in a dream that I ʿmustʾ sacrifice you. So tell me what you think." He replied, "O my dear father! Do as you are commanded. God willing, you will find me steadfast." **103.** Then when they submitted ʿto God's Willʾ, and Abraham laid him on the side of his forehead ʿfor sacrificeʾ, **104.** We called out to him, "O Abraham! **105.** You have already fulfilled the vision." Indeed, this is how We reward the good-doers. **106.** That was truly a revealing test. **107.** And We ransomed his son with a great sacrifice,[914] **108.** and blessed Abraham ʿwith honourable mentionʾ among later generations: **109.** "Peace be upon Abraham." **110.** This is how We reward the good-doers. **111.** He was truly one of Our faithful servants. **112.** We ʿlaterʾ gave him good news of Isaac—a prophet, and one of the righteous.[915] **113.** We blessed him[916] and Isaac as well. Some of their descendants did good, while others clearly wronged themselves.

Prophet Moses and Prophet Aaron

114. And We certainly showed favour to Moses and Aaron, **115.** and delivered them and their people from the great distress. **116.** We helped them so it was they who prevailed. **117.** We gave them the clear Scripture, **118.** and guided them to the Straight Path. **119.** And We blessed them ʿwith honourable mentionʾ among later generations:

---

910 i.e., the believers in his family.
911 Noah's sons: Shem, Ham, and Japheth.
912 His people reportedly made decisions based on constellations, so Abraham pretended to do the same to convince them he was not able to join them at their pagan feast.
913 *See* footnote for 26:82.
914 God sent a ram to be sacrificed in place of Ishmael.
915 The birth of Isaac is announced after the story of sacrifice. So this is a proof that the son who was going to be sacrificed was Ishmael, not Isaac. This is also supported by 11:71, where Sarah is told that she would give birth to Isaac, who would (reach adulthood and) have a son by the name of Jacob.
916 Abraham or Ishmael.

120. "Peace be upon Moses and Aaron." **121.** Indeed, this is how We reward the good-doers. **122.** They were truly 'two' of Our faithful servants.

Prophet Elias

123. And Elias was indeed one of the messengers. **124.** 'Remember' when he said to his people, "Will you not fear 'God'? **125.** Do you call upon 'the idol of' Ba'l and abandon the Best of Creators— **126.** God, your Lord and the Lord of your forefathers?" **127.** But they rejected him, so they will certainly be brought 'for punishment'. **128.** But not the chosen servants of God. **129.** We blessed him 'with honourable mention' among later generations: **130.** "Peace be upon Elias." **131.** Indeed, this is how We reward the good-doers. **132.** He was truly one of Our faithful servants.

Prophet Lot

133. And Lot was indeed one of the messengers. **134.** 'Remember' when We delivered him and all of his family, **135.** except an old woman,[917] who was one of the doomed. **136.** Then We 'utterly' destroyed the rest. **137.** You 'Meccans' certainly pass by their ruins day **138.** and night. Will you not then understand?

Prophet Jonah

139. And Jonah was indeed one of the messengers. **140.** 'Remember' when he fled to the overloaded ship. **141.** Then 'to save it from sinking,' he drew straws 'with other passengers'. He lost 'and was thrown overboard'. **142.** Then the whale engulfed him while he was blameworthy.[918] **143.** Had he

not 'constantly' glorified 'God',[919] **144.** he would have certainly remained in its belly until the Day of Resurrection.[920] **145.** But We cast him onto the open 'shore', 'totally' worn out, **146.** and caused a squash plant to grow over him.[921] **147.** We 'later' sent him 'back' to 'his city of' at least one hundred thousand people, **148.** who then believed 'in him', so We allowed them enjoyment for a while.

Questions to Arab Pagans

149. Ask them 'O Prophet' if your Lord has daughters,[922] while the pagans 'prefer to' have sons. **150.** Or 'ask them' if We created the angels as females right before their eyes. **151.** Indeed, it is one of their 'outrageous' fabrications to say, **152.** "God has children." They are simply liars. **153.** Has He chosen daughters over sons?[923] **154.** What is the matter with you? How do you judge? **155.** Will you not then be mindful? **156.** Or do you have 'any' compelling proof? **157.** Then bring 'us' your scripture, if what you say is true! **158.** They have also established a 'marital' relationship between Him and the jinn. Yet the jinn 'themselves' know well that such people will certainly be brought 'for punishment'.[924] **159.** Glorified is God far above what they claim! **160.** But not the chosen servants of God. **161.** Surely you 'pagans' and whatever 'idols' you worship **162.** can never lure 'anyone' away from Him **163.** except those 'destined' to burn in Hell.

Angels' Response

164. 'The angels respond,' "There is not one of us without an assigned station 'of

---

917 Lot's wife.
918 For abandoning his city without God's permission.
919 Before being swallowed and while inside the whale (*see* 21:87). The lesson is: good deeds are of great help during difficult times.
920 The belly of the whale would have become his grave.
921 The squash plant provided Jonah with shade and repelled harmful insects.
922 Some pagan Arabs believed that the angels were God's daughters. Some of them were ashamed to have daughters and took pride in their own sons.
923 Both sexes are equal before God, so the verse questions pagan chauvinism.
924 Or "Yet the jinn know well that they themselves will be brought 'for judgment'." This is based on the claim of some pagan Arabs that the angels are God's daughters through female jinn.

worship'. **165.** We are indeed the ones lined up in ranks ʼfor God'. **166.** And we are indeed the ones ʼconstantly' glorifying ʼHis praise'."

The Pagans Before the Quran

167. They certainly used to say, **168.** "If only we had a Reminder like ʼthose of' earlier peoples,[925] **169.** we would have truly been God's devoted servants." **170.** But ʼnow' they reject it, so they will soon know.

Reassuring the Prophet

171. Our Word has already gone forth to Our servants, the messengers, **172.** that they would surely be helped, **173.** and that Our forces will certainly prevail. **174.** So turn away from the deniers for a while ʼO Prophet'. **175.** You will see ʼwhat will happen to'

them, and they too will see! **176.** Do they ʼreally' wish to hasten Our punishment? **177.** Yet when it descends upon them:[926] how evil will that morning be for those who had been warned! **178.** And turn away from them for a while. **179.** You will see, and they too will see!

The Conclusion

180. Glorified is your Lord—the Lord of Honour and Power—above what they claim! **181.** Peace be upon the messengers. **182.** And praise be to God—Lord of all worlds.

38. Ṣād *(Ṣād)*

This chapter is perceived as a continuation of the previous chapter since it mentions some prophets that are not mentioned there—such as David, Solomon, and Job. Again, the pagans are condemned for denying the oneness of God, rejecting the Prophet as 'a magician, a total liar,' and for claiming that the world was created without purpose. Reference is made to the creation of Adam and the enmity Satan has for him and his descendants (verses 71-85), and the punishment awaiting the misleaders and their followers (verses 55-64), contrasted with the bliss in store for the righteous (verses 49-54). The end of this chapter emphasizes the universality of the Quran whereas the beginning of the next speaks of its divine nature.

In the Name of God—the Most Compassionate, Most Merciful

Arab Deniers

1. *Ṣād.* By the Quran, full of reminders! **2.** ʼThis is the truth,' yet the disbelievers are ʼentrenched' in arrogance and opposition. **3.** ʼImagine' how many peoples We destroyed before them, and they cried out

when it was too late to escape. **4.** Now, the pagans are astonished that a warner has come to them from among themselves.[927] And the disbelievers say, "This is a magician, a total liar! **5.** Has he reduced ʼall' the gods to One God? Indeed, this is something totally astonishing."

---

925 The "Reminder" mentioned here refers to Scriptures such as the Torah and the Gospel. It is commonly used in the Quran as another name for Islam's holy book.
926 lit., when it lands in their courtyards.
927 The pagans demanded an angel to deliver the message, not a human being like themselves.

Chief Deniers

6. The chiefs among them went forth saying, "Carry on, and stand firm in devotion to your gods. Certainly this is just a scheme ˹for power˺.⁹²⁸ **7.** We have never heard of this in the previous faith.⁹²⁹ This is nothing but a fabrication. **8.** Has the Reminder been revealed ˹only˺ to him out of ˹all of˺ us?" In fact, they are ˹only˺ in doubt of My ˹revealed˺ Reminder.⁹³⁰ In fact, ˹they do so because˺ they have not yet tasted My punishment. **9.** Or ˹is it because˺ they possess the treasuries of the mercy of your Lord—the Almighty, the Giver ˹of all bounties˺. **10.** Or ˹is it because˺ the kingdom of the heavens and the earth and everything in between belongs to them? Let them then climb their way ˹to heaven, if their claim is true˺.

Warning to the Deniers

11. This is just another ˹enemy˺ force bound for defeat out there.⁹³¹ **12.** Before them, the people of Noah denied ˹the truth˺, as did ʾĀd, Pharaoh of the mighty structures,⁹³² **13.** Thamūd, the people of Lot, and the residents of the Forest.⁹³³ These were ˹all˺ enemy forces. **14.** Each rejected their messenger, so My punishment was justified. **15.** These ˹pagans˺ are awaiting nothing but a single Blast that cannot be stopped. **16.** They say ˹mockingly˺, "Our Lord! Hasten for us our share ˹of the punishment˺ before the Day of Reckoning."

Prophet David

17. Be patient ˹O Prophet˺ with what they say. And remember Our servant, David, the man of strength. Indeed, he ˹constantly˺ turned ˹to God˺. **18.** We truly subjected the mountains to hymn ˹Our praises˺ along with him in the evening and after sunrise. **19.** And ˹We subjected˺ the birds, flocking together. All turned to him ˹echoing his hymns˺. **20.** We strengthened his kingship, and gave him wisdom and sound judgment.

David and the Disputing Partners

21. Has the story of the two plaintiffs, who scaled the ˹wall of David's˺ sanctuary, reached you ˹O Prophet˺? **22.** When they came into David's presence, he was startled by them. They said, "Have no fear. ˹We are merely˺ two in a dispute: one of us has wronged the other. So judge between us with truth—do not go beyond ˹it˺—and guide us to the right way. **23.** This is my brother.⁹³⁴ He has ninety-nine sheep while I have ˹only˺ one. ˹Still˺ he asked me to give it up to him, overwhelming me with ˹his˺ argument." **24.** David ˹eventually˺ ruled, "He has definitely wronged you in demanding ˹to add˺ your sheep to his. And certainly many partners wrong each other, except those who believe and do good—but how few are they!" Then David realized that We had tested him so he asked for his Lord's forgiveness, fell down in prostration, and turned ˹to Him in repentance˺. **25.** So We forgave that for him. And he will indeed have ˹a status of˺ closeness to Us and an honourable destination! **26.** ˹We instructed him:˺ "O David! We have surely made you an authority in the land, so judge between people with truth. And do not follow ˹your˺ desires or they will lead you astray from God's Way. Surely those who go astray from God's Way will suffer a severe punishment for neglecting the Day of Reckoning."

---

928   They meant that the Prophet is not concerned with their guidance, and that he only wants to gain dominance over them.
929   This refers either to the concept of the Trinity in Christianity or Arab polytheistic beliefs.
930   In other words, they do not question the honesty of the Prophet, but question the Quran itself. This verse is similar to 6:33.
931   This verse alludes to the defeat of the Meccan pagans later at Badr.
932   i.e., pyramids and obelisks.
933   i.e., the people of Shuʿaib.
934   Brother in faith or business partner.

38. Ṣād (Ṣād)

God Is Just

27. We have not created the heavens and earth and everything in between without purpose—as the disbelievers think. So woe to the disbelievers because of the Fire! **28.** Or should We treat those who believe and do good like those who make mischief throughout the land? Or should We treat the righteous like the wicked?

The Purpose of the Quran

29. ˹This is˺ a blessed Book which We have revealed to you ˹O Prophet˺ so that they may contemplate its verses, and people of reason may be mindful.

Solomon's Love for Fine Horses

30. And We blessed David with Solomon—what an excellent servant ˹he was˺! Indeed, he ˹constantly˺ turned ˹to God˺. **31.** ˹Remember˺ when the well-trained, swift horses were paraded before him in the evening. **32.** He then proclaimed, "I am truly in love with ˹these˺ fine things out of remembrance for my Lord," until they went out of sight. **33.** ˹He ordered,˺ "Bring them back to me!" Then he began to rub down their legs and necks.[935]

Solomon's Authority

34. And indeed, We tested Solomon, placing a ˹deformed˺ body on his throne,[936] then he turned ˹to God in repentance˺. **35.** He prayed, "My Lord! Forgive me, and grant me an authority that will never be matched by anyone after me. You are indeed the Giver ˹of all bounties˺." **36.** So We subjected to him the wind, blowing gently at his command to wherever he pleased. **37.** And ˹We subjected to him˺ every builder and diver[937] of the jinn, **38.** and others bound together in chains. **39.** ˹God said,˺ "This is Our gift, so give or withhold ˹as you wish˺, never to be called to account." **40.** And he will indeed have ˹a status of˺ closeness to Us and an honourable destination!

Prophet Job

41. And remember Our servant Job, when he cried out to his Lord, "Satan has afflicted me with distress and suffering." **42.** ˹We responded,˺ "Stomp your foot: ˹now˺ here is a cool ˹and refreshing˺ spring for washing and drinking." **43.** And We gave him back his family, twice as many, as a mercy from Us and a lesson for people of reason. **44.** ˹And We said to him,˺ "Take in your hand a bundle of grass, and strike ˹your wife˺ with it, and do not break your oath."[938] We truly found him patient. What an excellent servant ˹he was˺! Indeed, he ˹constantly˺ turned ˹to God˺.

Other Mighty Prophets

45. And remember Our servants: Abraham, Isaac, and Jacob—the men of strength and insight. **46.** We truly chose them for the honour of proclaiming the Hereafter. **47.** And in Our sight they are truly among the chosen and the finest. **48.** Also remember Ishmael, Elisha, and Ẓul-Kifl.[939] All are among the best.

---

935 Some commentators have a different interpretation, which is not supported by reliable sources. They maintain that Solomon kept watching these fine horses until the sun set, then he realized that he had missed the noon prayer because of his love for horses, so he killed them, striking at their legs and necks.

936 It is reported in a ḥadīth collected by Bukhâri that one night Solomon said that each of his wives would conceive a boy who would struggle in God's cause. He forgot to say 'God willing,' so only one of them gave birth to a deformed, dead baby. So Solomon prayed to God for forgiveness.

937 The jinn dived to bring him pearls.

938 Job was afflicted with losing his children, community, and with a long illness. Only his wife stayed with him. He once became angry with his wife and vowed to give her one hundred lashes if he recovered. When Job's affliction was lifted, he became remorseful at what he had said. To help Job fulfil his vow without harming his wife, God ordered him to strike her with a bundle of one hundred blades of grass.

939 Scholars are in disagreement as to whether Ẓul-Kifl was a prophet or just a righteous man. Those who maintain that he was a prophet identify him with various Biblical prophets such as Ezekiel, Isaiah, and Obadiah.

Reward of the Righteous

49. This is ˹all˺ a reminder. And the righteous will certainly have an honourable destination: **50.** the Gardens of Eternity, whose gates will be open for them. **51.** There they will recline, calling for abundant fruit and drink. **52.** And with them will be maidens of modest gaze and equal age. **53.** This is what you are promised for the Day of Reckoning. **54.** This is indeed Our provision that will never end.

Reward of the Wicked

55. That is that. And the transgressors will certainly have the worst destination: **56.** Hell, where they will burn. What an evil place to rest! **57.** Let them then taste this: boiling water and ˹oozing˺ pus, **58.** and other torments of the same sort!

Disputes of the Wicked

59. ˹The misleaders will say to one another,˺ "Here is a crowd ˹of followers˺ being thrown in with us. They are not welcome, ˹for˺ they ˹too˺ will burn in the Fire."⁹⁴⁰ **60.** The followers will respond, "No! You are not welcome! You brought this upon us. What an evil place for settlement!" **61.** Adding, "Our Lord! Whoever brought this upon us, double their punishment in the Fire." **62.** The tyrants will ask ˹one another˺, "But why do we not see those we considered to be lowly? **63.** Were we wrong in mocking them ˹in the world˺?⁹⁴¹ Or do our eyes ˹just˺ fail to see them ˹in the Fire˺?" **64.** This dispute between the residents of the Fire will certainly come to pass.

The Messenger and His Message

65. Say, ˹O Prophet,˺ "I am only a warner. And there is no god ˹worthy of worship˺ except God—the One, the Supreme. **66.** ˹He is the˺ Lord of the heavens and the earth and everything in between—the Almighty, Most Forgiving." **67.** Say, "This ˹Quran˺ is momentous news, **68.** from which you ˹pagans˺ are turning away." **69.** ˹And say,˺ "I had no knowledge of the highest assembly ˹in heaven˺ when they differed ˹concerning Adam˺.⁹⁴² **70.** What is revealed to me is that I am only sent with a clear warning."

Satan's Arrogance

71. ˹Remember, O Prophet˺ when your Lord said to the angels, "I am going to create a human being from clay. **72.** So when I have fashioned him and had a spirit of My Own ˹creation˺ breathed into him, fall down in prostration to him." **73.** So the angels prostrated all together— **74.** but not *Iblîs*⁹⁴³ who acted arrogantly,⁹⁴⁴ becoming unfaithful. **75.** God asked, "O *Iblîs*! What prevented you from prostrating to what I created with My Own Hands? Did you ˹just˺ become proud? Or have you always been arrogant?" **76.** He replied, "I am better than he is: You created me from fire and him from clay." **77.** God commanded, "Then get out of Paradise, for you are truly cursed. **78.** And surely upon you is My condemnation until the Day of Judgment." **79.** Satan appealed, "My Lord! Then delay my end until the Day of their resurrection." **80.** God said, "You will be delayed **81.** until the appointed Day." **82.** Satan said, "By Your Glory! I will certainly mislead them all, **83.** except Your chosen servants among them." **84.** God concluded, "The truth is—and I ˹only˺ say the truth—: **85.** I will surely fill up Hell with you and whoever follows you from among them, all together."

---

940 Meaning, they are not welcome since their presence in Hell with us will not benefit us in anyway.
941 In other words, did we underestimate them?
942 When the angels obeyed God's orders to prostrate before Adam, whereas Satan refused to comply.
943 See footnote for 2:34.
944 The command to bow down was a test of obedience. Satan arrogantly refused to comply because he believed he was superior to Adam.

Message to the Deniers

86. Say, 'O Prophet,' "I do not ask you for any reward for this 'Quran', nor do I pretend to be someone I am not. **87.** It is only a reminder to the whole world. **88.** And you will certainly know its truth before long."

❦

39. The 'Successive' Groups *(Az-Zumar)*

This Meccan chapter builds on the story of the creation of Adam in the previous chapter by referring to the creation of Adam's spouse, and how their descendants were created in the womb, developing in successive stages. Some of those descendants choose to be faithful and grateful to their Creator, while others choose not to. Eventually, following a fair judgment, the former will be led to their places in Paradise and the latter to their places in Hell—each in successive groups (hence the chapter's name). God's willingness to forgive sins is highly emphasized in the last part of this chapter and the beginning of the next.

In the Name of God—the Most Compassionate, Most Merciful

Worship God Alone

1. The revelation of this Book is from God—the Almighty, All-Wise. **2.** Indeed, We have sent down the Book to you 'O Prophet' in truth, so worship God 'alone', being sincerely devoted to Him. **3.** Indeed, sincere devotion is due 'only' to God. As for those who take other lords besides Him, 'saying,' "We worship them only so they may bring us closer to God," surely God will judge between all[945] regarding what they differed about. God certainly does not guide whoever persists in lying and disbelief.

God's Power of Creation

4. Had it been God's Will to have offspring, He could have chosen whatever He willed of His creation. Glory be to Him! He is God—the One, the Supreme. **5.** He created the heavens and the earth for a purpose. He wraps the night around the day, and wraps the day around the night. And He has subjected the sun and the moon, each orbiting for an appointed term. He is truly the Almighty, Most Forgiving. **6.** He created you 'all' from a single soul,[946] then from it He made its mate.[947] And He produced for you four pairs of cattle.[948] He creates you in the wombs of your mothers 'in stages', one development after another, in three layers of darkness.[949] That is God—your Lord! All authority belongs to Him. There is no god 'worthy of worship' except Him. How can you then be turned away?

Belief and Disbelief

7. If you disbelieve, then 'know that' God is truly not in need of you, nor does He ap-

---

945 Those who are devoted to God alone and those who associate other gods with Him.
946 i.e., Adam.
947 i.e., Eve.
948 The four pairs (males and females), as listed in 6:143-144, are: a pair of sheep, a pair of goats, a pair of camels, and a pair of oxen.
949 The three layers of darkness are: the belly, the womb, and the amniotic sac.

prove of disbelief from His servants. But if you become grateful ʿthrough faithʾ, He will appreciate that from you. No soul burdened with sin will bear the burden of another. Then to your Lord is your return, and He will inform you of what you used to do. He certainly knows best what is ʿhiddenʾ in the heart.

Disbelievers' Ingratitude

8. When one is touched with hardship, they cry out to their Lord, turning to Him ʿaloneʾ. But as soon as He showers them with blessings from Him, they ʿtotallyʾ forget the One they had cried to earlier, and set up equals to God to mislead ʿothersʾ from His Way. Say, ʿO Prophet,ʾ "Enjoy your disbelief for a little while! You will certainly be one of the inmates of the Fire." 9. ʿAre they betterʾ or those who worship ʿtheir Lordʾ devoutly in the hours of the night, prostrating and standing, fearing the Hereafter and hoping for the mercy of their Lord? Say, ʿO Prophet,ʾ "Are those who know equal to those who do not know?" None will be mindful ʿof thisʾ except people of reason.

Orders to the Prophet

10. Say ʿO Prophet, that God saysʾ, "O My servants who believe! Be mindful of your Lord. Those who do good in this world will have a good reward. And God's earth is spacious. Only those who endure patiently will be given their reward without limit." 11. Say, "I am commanded to worship God, being sincerely devoted to Him ʿaloneʾ. 12. And I am commanded to be the first of those who submit ʿto His Willʾ." 13. Say, "I truly fear—if I were to disobey my Lord—the torment of a tremendous Day." 14. Say, "It is ʿonlyʾ God that I worship, being sincere in my devotion to Him. 15. Worship then whatever ʿgodsʾ you want instead of Him." Say, "The ʿtrueʾ losers are those who will lose themselves and their families on Judgment Day. That is

indeed the clearest loss." 16. They will have layers of fire above and below them. That is what God warns His servants with. So fear Me, O My servants!

The Faithful and the Unfaithful

17. And those who shun the worship of false gods, turning to God ʿaloneʾ, will have good news. So give good news to My servants ʿO Prophetʾ— 18. those who listen to what is said and follow the best of it.[950] These are the ones ʿrightlyʾ guided by God, and these are ʿtrulyʾ the people of reason. 19. What about those against whom the decree of torment has been justified? Is it you ʿO Prophetʾ who will then save those bound for the Fire? 20. But those mindful of their Lord will have ʿelevatedʾ mansions, built one above the other, under which rivers flow. ʿThat isʾ the promise of God. ʿAndʾ God never fails in ʿHisʾ promise.

Parable for This Fleeting Life

21. Do you not see that God sends down rain from the sky—channelling it through streams in the earth—then produces with it crops of various colours, then they dry up and you see them wither, and then He reduces them to chaff? Surely in this is a reminder for people of reason.

The Believers and the Disbelievers

22. Can ʿthe misguided be likeʾ those whose hearts God has opened to Islam, so they are enlightened by their Lord? So woe to those whose hearts are hardened at the remembrance of God! It is they who are clearly astray.

Excellence of the Quran

23. ʿIt isʾ God ʿWhoʾ has sent down the best message—a Book of perfect consistency and repeated lessons—which causes the skin ʿand heartsʾ of those who fear their

---

950 This verse can apply to anything that a person listens to, and it can also apply specifically to the Quran—meaning, for example, those who read verses about retaliation and other verses about forgiveness, then they opt for forgiveness.

Lord to tremble, then their skin and hearts soften at the mention of ʿthe mercy ofʾ God. That is the guidance of God, through which He guides whoever He wills. But whoever God leaves to stray will be left with no guide. **24.** Are those who will only have their ʿbareʾ faces to shield themselves from the awful torment on Judgment Day ʿbetter than those in Paradiseʾ? It will ʿthenʾ be said to the wrongdoers: "Reap what you sowed!"

Rejection Leads to Punishment

25. Those before them ʿalsoʾ rejected ʿthe truthʾ, then the torment came upon them from where they least expected. **26.** So God made them taste humiliation in this worldly life, but far worse is the punishment of the Hereafter, if only they knew.

Perfection of the Quran

27. We have certainly set forth every ʿkind ofʾ lesson for people in this Quran, so perhaps they will be mindful. **28.** ʿIt isʾ a Quran ʿrevealedʾ in Arabic without any crookedness, so perhaps they will be conscious ʿof Godʾ.

Parable for a Polytheist and a Monotheist

29. God sets forth the parable of a slave owned by several quarrelsome masters, and a slave owned by only one master. Are they equal in condition?[951] Praise be to God! In fact, most of them do not know.

All Will Die

30. You ʿO Prophetʾ will certainly die, and they will die too. **31.** Then on the Day of Judgment you will ʿall settle yourʾ dispute before your Lord.

Reward of the Believers and Disbelievers

32. Who then does more wrong than those who lie about God and reject the truth after it has reached them? Is Hell not a ʿfittingʾ home for the disbelievers? **33.** And the one who has brought the truth and those who embrace it—it is they who are the righteous. **34.** They will have whatever they desire with their Lord. That is the reward of the good-doers. **35.** As such, God will absolve them of ʿevenʾ the worst of what they did and reward them according to the best of what they used to do.

God Protects His Messenger

36. Is God not sufficient for His servant? Yet they threaten you with other ʿpowerlessʾ gods besides Him! Whoever God leaves to stray will be left with no guide. **37.** And whoever God guides, none can lead astray. Is God not Almighty, capable of punishment?

Almighty God or Powerless Gods

38. If you ask them ʿO Prophetʾ who created the heavens and the earth, they will certainly say, "God!" Ask ʿthemʾ, "Consider then whatever ʿidolsʾ you invoke besides God: if it was God's Will to harm me, could they undo that harm? Or if He willed ʿsomeʾ mercy for me, could they withhold His mercy?" Say, "God is sufficient for me. In Him ʿaloneʾ the faithful put their trust."

Warning to the Pagans

39. Say, ʿO Prophet,ʾ "O my people! Persist in your ways, for I ʿtooʾ will persist in mine. You will soon come to know **40.** who will be visited by a humiliating torment ʿin this lifeʾ and overwhelmed by an everlasting punishment ʿin the nextʾ."

---

951 The slave owned by several quarrelsome masters will always be confused because their masters will always give them conflicting orders—similarly, one who worships multiple gods will never find peace between them. This parable is a logical argument against the existence of multiple gods, since each god would try to covet what it created. *See* 23:91 for a similar argument.

Free Choice

41. Surely We have revealed to you the Book ʿO Prophetʾ with the truth for humanity. So whoever chooses to be guided, it is for their own good. And whoever chooses to stray, it is only to their own loss. You are not a keeper over them.

Sleep: The Twin Brother of Death

42. ʿIt isʾ God ʿWhoʾ calls back the souls ʿof peopleʾ upon their death as well as ʿthe soulsʾ of the living during their sleep. Then He keeps those for whom He has ordained death, and releases the others until ʿtheirʾ appointed time. Surely in this are signs for people who reflect.

God or the Idols

43. Or have they taken others besides God as intercessors? Say, ʿO Prophet,ʾ "ʿWould they do so,ʾ even though those ʿidolsʾ have neither authority nor intelligence?" **44.** Say, "All intercession belongs to God ʿaloneʾ. To Him belongs the kingdom of the heavens and the earth. Then to Him you will ʿallʾ be returned." **45.** Yet when God alone is mentioned, the hearts of those who disbelieve in the Hereafter are filled with disgust. But as soon as those ʿgodsʾ other than Him are mentioned, they are filled with joy.

God Is the Judge

46. Say, ʿO Prophet,ʾ "O God—Originator of the heavens and the earth, Knower of the seen and unseen! You will judge between Your servants regarding their differences." **47.** Even if the wrongdoers were to possess everything in the world twice over, they would certainly offer it to ransom themselves from the horrible punishment on Judgment Day, for they will see from God what they had never expected. **48.** And the evil ʿconsequencesʾ of their deeds will unfold before them, and they will be overwhelmed by what they used to ridicule.

Human Ingratitude

49. When one is touched with hardship, they cry out to Us ʿaloneʾ. Then when We shower Our blessings upon them, they say, "I have been granted all this only because of ʿmyʾ knowledge." Not at all! It is ʿno more thanʾ a test. But most of them do not know. **50.** The same had already been said by those ʿdestroyedʾ before them,[952] but their ʿworldlyʾ gains were of no benefit to them. **51.** So the evil ʿconsequencesʾ of their deeds overtook them. And the wrongdoers among these ʿpagansʾ will be overtaken by the evil ʿconsequencesʾ of their deeds. And they will have no escape. **52.** Do they not know that God gives abundant or limited provisions to whoever He wills? Surely in this are signs for people who believe.

God Forgives All Sins

53. Say, ʿO Prophet, that God says,ʾ "O My servants who have exceeded the limits against their souls! Do not lose hope in God's mercy, for God certainly forgives all sins.[953] He is indeed the All-Forgiving, Most Merciful. **54.** Turn to your Lord ʿin repentanceʾ, and ʿfullyʾ submit to Him before the punishment reaches you, ʿforʾ then you will not be helped. **55.** Follow ʿthe Quran,ʾ the best of what has been revealed to you from your Lord, before the punishment takes you by surprise while you are unaware, **56.** so that no ʿsinfulʾ soul will say ʿon Judgment Dayʾ, 'Woe to me for neglecting ʿmy duties towardsʾ God, while

---

952 Like Korah (see 28:76-81).

953 No matter how big someone's sins are, they cannot be bigger than God's mercy. Based on 4:48, the only unforgivable sin in Islam is if someone dies while disbelieving in God or associating others with Him in worship. In an authentic narration collected by At-Tirmizi, the Prophet reports that Almighty God says, "O children of Adam! As long as you call upon Me, putting your hope in Me, I will forgive you for what you have done, and I will not mind. O children of Adam! If your sins were to reach the clouds of the sky and then you sought My forgiveness, I would ʿstillʾ forgive you. O children of Adam! If you were to come to Me with sins filling the whole world and then you came to Me without associating other gods with Me, I would certainly match your sins with forgiveness."

ridiculing 'the truth'.' **57.** Or 'a soul will' say, 'If only God had guided me, I would have certainly been one of the righteous.' **58.** Or say, upon seeing the torment, 'If only I had a second chance, I would have been one of the good-doers.' **59.** Not at all! My revelations had already come to you, but you rejected them, acted arrogantly, and were one of the disbelievers."

Judgment Day

60. On the Day of Judgment you will see those who lied about God with their faces gloomy. Is Hell not a 'fitting' home for the arrogant? **61.** And God will deliver those who were mindful 'of Him' to their place of 'ultimate' triumph. No evil will touch them, nor will they grieve. **62.** God is the Creator of all things, and He is the Maintainer of everything. **63.** To Him belong the keys 'of the treasuries' of the heavens and the earth. As for those who rejected the signs of God, it is they who will be the 'true' losers.

One God Alone

64. Say, 'O Prophet,' "Are you urging me to worship 'anyone' other than God, O ignorant ones?" **65.** It has already been revealed to you—and to those 'prophets' before you—that if you associate others 'with God', your deeds will certainly be void and you will truly be one of the losers. **66.** Rather, worship God 'alone' and be one of the grateful.

Beginning of the End

67. They have not shown God His proper reverence—when on the Day of Judgment the 'whole' earth will be in His Grip, and the heavens will be rolled up in His Right Hand. Glorified and Exalted is He above

what they associate 'with Him'! **68.** The Trumpet will be blown and all those in the heavens and all those on the earth will fall dead, except those God wills 'to spare'. Then it will be blown again and they will rise up at once, looking on 'in anticipation'.

Divine Justice

69. The earth[954] will shine with the light of its Lord, the record 'of deeds' will be laid 'open', the prophets and the witnesses will be brought forward—and judgment will be passed on all with fairness. None will be wronged. **70.** Every soul will be paid in full for its deeds, for God knows best what they have done.

Reward of the Wicked

71. Those who disbelieved will be driven to Hell in 'successive' groups. When they arrive there, its gates will be opened and its keepers will ask them: "Did messengers not come to you from among yourselves, reciting to you the revelations of your Lord and warning you of the coming of this Day of yours?" The disbelievers will cry, "Yes 'indeed'! But the decree of torment has come to pass against the disbelievers." **72.** It will be said to them, "Enter the gates of Hell, to stay there forever." What an evil home for the arrogant!

Reward of the Righteous

73. And those who were mindful of their Lord will be led to Paradise in 'successive' groups. When they arrive at its 'already' open gates, its keepers will say, "Peace be upon you! You have done well, so come in, to stay forever." **74.** The righteous will say, "Praise be to God Who has fulfilled His promise to us, and made us inherit the

---

954 This refers to the place where the judgment will be held. The Prophet is reported in a ḥadîth collected by Aṭ-Ṭabarâni to have said, "The Judgment will be passed on an earth where neither blood has been shed nor any sin committed."

'everlasting' land[955] to settle in Paradise wherever we please." How excellent is the reward of those who work 'righteousness'!

Praising God's Grace and Justice

75. You will see the angels all around the Throne, glorifying the praises of their Lord,

for judgment will have been passed on all with fairness. And it will be said,[956] "Praise be to God—Lord of all worlds!"

40. The Forgiver *(Ghâfir)*

In essence, this Meccan chapter emphasizes the main concepts highlighted both in the previous and following chapters—namely God being infinite in mercy and severe in punishment, and humanity being either grateful or ungrateful to their Lord along with the reward that ensues. All this is embodied in the story of Moses (verses 23-54)—with Pharaoh as the ungrateful disbeliever and an unidentified man from Pharaoh's people as the grateful believer. The Prophet is repeatedly advised to be patient, keeping in mind that God never lets His prophets down (verses 51 and 77).

In the Name of God—the Most Compassionate, Most Merciful

The Quran Is from the Almighty

1. *Ḥâ-Mīm.* **2.** The revelation of this Book is from God—the Almighty, All-Knowing, **3.** the Forgiver of sin and Accepter of repentance, the Severe in punishment, and Infinite in bounty. There is no god 'worthy of worship' except Him. To Him 'alone' is the final return.

Warning to the Disbelievers

4. None disputes the signs of God except the disbelievers, so do not be deceived by their prosperity throughout the land. **5.** Before them, the people of Noah denied 'the truth', as did 'other' enemy forces afterwards. Every community plotted against its prophet to seize him, and argued in falsehood, 'hop-ing' to discredit the truth with it. So I seized them. And how 'horrible' was My punishment! **6.** And so your Lord's decree has been proven true against the disbelievers—that they will be the inmates of the Fire.

Angels Pray for the Believers

7. Those 'angels' who carry the Throne and those around it glorify the praises of their Lord, have faith in Him, and seek forgiveness for the believers, 'praying:' "Our Lord! You encompass everything in 'Your' mercy and knowledge. So forgive those who repent and follow Your Way, and protect them from the torment of the Hellfire. **8.** Our Lord! Admit them into the Gardens of Eternity which You have promised them, along with the

---

955 This is emphasized in 21:105. The meaning is that God will award Paradise to the believers to be its residents forever. Some commentators say that the word "inherit" is used because of the understanding that when God created Paradise and Hell, He made places for all of humanity in both. Those who will go to Paradise will inherit the spots of the disbelievers who chose misguidance (which leads to Hell), and those who will go to Hell will inherit the spots of those who chose guidance (which leads to Paradise).

956 The believers will praise Him for His grace, and the disbelievers will praise Him for His justice.

righteous among their parents, spouses, and descendants. You ˹alone˺ are truly the Almighty, All-Wise. **9.** And protect them from ˹the consequences of their˺ evil deeds. For whoever You protect from the evil of their deeds on that Day will have been shown Your mercy. That is ˹truly˺ the ultimate triumph."

The Inmates of Hell

10. Indeed, it will be announced to the disbelievers, "God's contempt for you—as you disbelieved when invited to belief—was far worse than your contempt for one another ˹Today˺." **11.** They will plead, "Our Lord! You made us lifeless twice, and gave us life twice.[957] Now we confess our sins. So is there any way out?" **12.** ˹They will be told,˺ "˹No!˺ This is because when God alone was invoked, you ˹staunchly˺ disbelieved. But when others were associated with Him ˹in worship˺, you ˹readily˺ believed. So ˹Today˺ judgment belongs to God ˹alone˺—the Most High, All-Great."

God's Might in Both Worlds

13. He is the One Who shows you His signs and sends down ˹rain as˺ a provision for you from the sky. ˹But˺ none will be mindful except those who turn ˹to Him˺. **14.** So call upon God with sincere devotion, even to the dismay of the disbelievers. **15.** ˹He is˺ Highly Exalted in rank, Lord of the Throne. He sends down the revelation by His command to whoever He wills of His servants to warn ˹all˺ of the Day of Meeting— **16.** the Day all will appear ˹before God˺. Nothing about them will be hidden from Him. ˹He will ask,˺ "Who does all authority belong to this Day? To God—the One, the Supreme![958] **17.** Today every soul will be rewarded for what it has done.

No injustice Today! Surely God is swift in reckoning."

Horrors of Judgment Day

18. Warn them ˹O Prophet˺ of the approaching Day when the hearts will jump into the throats, suppressing distress. The wrongdoers will have neither a close friend nor intercessor to be heard. **19.** God ˹even˺ knows the sly glances of the eyes and whatever the hearts conceal. **20.** And God judges with the truth, while those ˹idols˺ they invoke besides Him cannot judge at all. Indeed, God ˹alone˺ is the All-Hearing, All-Seeing.

Fate of the Deniers

21. Have they not travelled throughout the land to see what was the end of those ˹destroyed˺ before them? They were far superior in might and ˹richer in˺ monuments throughout the land. But God seized them for their sins, and they had no protector from God. **22.** That was because their messengers used to come to them with clear proofs, but they persisted in disbelief. So God seized them. Surely He is All-Powerful, severe in punishment.

Moses Denied in Egypt

23. Indeed, We sent Moses with Our signs and compelling proof **24.** to Pharaoh, Hamân, and Korah. But they responded: "Magician! Total liar!" **25.** Then, when he came to them with the truth from Us, they said, "Kill the sons of those who believe with him and keep their women." But the plotting of the disbelievers was only in vain. **26.** And Pharaoh said, "Let me kill Moses, and let him call upon his Lord! I truly fear that he may change your traditions or cause mischief in the land." **27.** Moses replied, "I seek refuge in my Lord and

---

957 You created us from nothing, then gave us life in the wombs of our mothers, then caused us to die at the end of our worldly lives, and finally resurrected us after our death (*see* 2:28).

958 It is reported in a *ḥadîth* collected by Imâm Muslim that everyone and everything that has ever existed will die on that Day, except for God—the Eternal. He will then ask, "Who does all authority belong to this Day? Where are the kings of the world? I am the King." Since no one will be there to answer, God will answer Himself, "˹All authority belongs˺ to God—the One, the Supreme!"

your Lord from every arrogant person who does not believe in the Day of Reckoning."

The Believer's Advice:
1) Do Not Persecute for Belief

28. A believing man from Pharaoh's people, who was hiding his faith, argued, "Will you kill a man[959] 'only' for saying: 'My Lord is God,' while he has in fact come to you with clear proofs from your Lord? If he is a liar, it will be to his own loss. But if he is truthful, then you will be afflicted with some of what he is threatening you with. Surely God does not guide whoever is a transgressor, a total liar. **29.** O my people! Authority belongs to you today, reigning supreme in the land. But who would help us against the torment of God, if it were to befall us?" Pharaoh assured 'his people', "I am telling you only what I believe, and I am leading you only to the way of guidance."

Advice 2) Learn from History

30. And the man who believed cautioned, "O my people! I truly fear for you the doom of 'earlier' enemy forces— **31.** like the fate of the people of Noah, 'Âd, Thamûd, and those after them. For God would never will to wrong 'His' servants. **32.** O my people! I truly fear for you the Day all will be crying out 'to each other'— **33.** the Day you will 'try in vain to' turn your backs and run away, with no one to protect you from God. And whoever God leaves to stray will be left with no guide. **34.** Joseph already came to you[960] earlier with clear proofs, yet you never ceased to doubt what he came to you with. When he died you said, 'God will never send a messenger after him.' This is how God leaves every transgressor and doubter to stray— **35.** those who dispute God's signs with no proof given to them. How despicable is that for God and the be-

lievers! This is how God seals the heart of every arrogant tyrant."

Pharaoh's Response

36. Pharaoh ordered, "O Hamân! Build me a high tower so I may reach the pathways **37.** leading up to the heavens and look for the God of Moses, although I am sure he is a liar."[961] And so Pharaoh's evil deeds were made so appealing to him that he was hindered from the 'Right' Way. But the plotting of Pharaoh was only in vain.

Advice 3) Mend Your Ways

38. And the man who believed urged, "O my people! Follow me, 'and' I will lead you to the Way of Guidance. **39.** O my people! This worldly life is only 'a fleeting' enjoyment, whereas the Hereafter is truly the home of settlement. **40.** Whoever does an evil deed will only be paid back with its equivalent. And whoever does good, whether male or female, and is a believer, they will enter Paradise, where they will be provided for without limit. **41.** O my people! How is it that I invite you to salvation, while you invite me to the Fire! **42.** You invite me to disbelieve in God and associate with Him what I have no knowledge of, while I invite you to the Almighty, Most Forgiving. **43.** There is no doubt that whatever 'idols' you invite me to 'worship' are not worthy to be invoked either in this world or the Hereafter.[962] 'Undoubtedly,' our return is to God, and the transgressors will be the inmates of the Fire. **44.** You will remember what I say to you, and I entrust my affairs to God. Surely God is All-Seeing of all 'His' servants."

God's Response

45. So God protected him from the evil of their schemes. And Pharaoh's people

---

959   i.e., Moses.
960   Meaning, your ancestors, because Joseph died over 400 hundred years before Moses.
961   *See* 28:38.
962   Another possible translation: "Without a doubt, whatever 'gods' you are calling me to 'worship' have no claim 'to divinity' in this world or the Hereafter."

were overwhelmed by an evil punishment: **46.** they are exposed to the Fire ʾin theirʾ graves' morning and evening. And on the Day the Hour will be established ʾit will be said', "Admit Pharaoh's people into the harshest punishment ʾof Hell'."

Disputes Among Hell's Inmates

47. ʾConsider the Dayʾ when they will dispute in the Fire, and the lowly ʾfollowers' will appeal to the arrogant ʾleaders', "We were your ʾdedicated' followers, will you then shield us from a portion of the Fire?" **48.** The arrogant will say, "We are all in it! ʾFor' God has already passed judgment over ʾHis' servants."

Appeals from Hell

49. And those in the Fire will cry out to the keepers of Hell,⁹⁶³ "Pray to your Lord to lighten the torment for us ʾeven' for one day!" **50.** The keepers will reply, "Did your messengers not ʾconstantly' come to you with clear proofs?" They will say, "Yes ʾthey did'." The keepers will say, "Then pray! Though the prayer of the disbelievers is only in vain."

God's Help for the Believers

51. We certainly help Our messengers and the believers, ʾboth' in this worldly life and on the Day the witnesses will stand forth ʾfor testimony'— **52.** the Day the wrongdoers' excuses will be of no benefit to them. They will be condemned, and will have the worst outcome.⁹⁶⁴

Reassuring the Prophet

53. And indeed, We gave Moses ʾtrue' guidance, and made the Children of Isra-el inherit the Scripture— **54.** a guide and a reminder to people of reason. **55.** So be patient ʾO Prophet', ʾfor' God's promise is certainly true. Seek forgiveness for your shortcomings.⁹⁶⁵ And glorify the praises of your Lord morning and evening. **56.** Surely those who dispute God's signs—with no proof given to them—have nothing in their hearts but greed for dominance, which they will never attain. So seek refuge in God. Indeed, He alone is the All-Hearing, All-Seeing.

Greater Creation

57. The creation of the heavens and the earth is certainly greater than the re-creation of humankind, but most people do not know.

Parable of Belief and Disbelief

58. Those blind ʾto the truth' and those who can see are not equal, nor are those who believe and do good ʾequal' to those who do evil. Yet you are hardly mindful. **59.** The Hour is certainly coming, there is no doubt about it. But most people do not believe.

God Answers Prayers

60. Your Lord has proclaimed, "Call upon Me, I will respond to you. Surely those who are too proud to worship Me will enter Hell, fully humbled."

God Is Merciful to His Creation

61. It is God Who has made the night for you to rest in and the day bright. Surely God is ever Bountiful to humanity, but most people are ungrateful. **62.** That is God, your Lord, the Creator of all things.

---

963 The verse does not say "Those in the Fire will cry out to its keepers," simply because there are levels in the Fire: those in higher levels will plead to the keepers of the depths of Hell to appeal to God to lighten the punishment even for one day, since they think they are better than those at the bottom.

964 i.e., the Hellfire.

965 Like other prophets, Muḥammad was infallible of sin. The verse here refers to misjudgments, such as the Prophet's response to the blind man (80:1-10), Jonah's departure from his city without God's permission (21:87-88), and David's suspicions of the two men who scaled the wall of his sanctuary (38:21-25). If the Prophet himself is urged to seek forgiveness, then the believers are even more in need of praying for God's forgiveness.

There is no god 'worthy of worship' except Him. How can you then be deluded 'from the truth'? **63.** This is how those who used to reject God's signs were 'also' deluded.

God Provides for All

64. It is God Who made the earth a place of settlement for you and the sky a canopy. He shaped you 'in the womb', perfecting your form. And He has provided you with what is good and lawful. That is God—your Lord. So Blessed is God, Lord of all worlds. **65.** He is the Ever-Living. There is no god 'worthy of worship' except Him. So call upon Him with sincere devotion, 'saying,' "All praise is for God—Lord of all worlds."

God Has Power over Life and Death

66. Say, 'O Prophet,' "I have been forbidden to worship those 'idols' you worship besides God, since clear proofs have come to me from my Lord. And I have been commanded to 'fully' submit to the Lord of all worlds." **67.** He is the One Who created you[966] from dust, then from a sperm-drop,[967] then 'developed you into' a clinging clot,[968] then He brings you forth as infants, so that you may reach your prime, and become old—though some of you 'may' die sooner—reaching an appointed time, so perhaps you may understand 'God's power'. **68.** He is the One Who gives life and causes death. When He decrees a matter, He simply tells it, "Be!" And it is!

Punishment of the Deniers

69. Have you not seen how those who dispute God's signs are turned away? **70.** 'They are' the ones who reject this Book and all 'scriptures' We sent Our messengers with. So they will know 'the consequences' **71.** when shackles will be around their necks and chains 'on their legs'. They will be dragged **72.** through boiling water, then burned in the Fire 'as fuel'. **73.** Then they will be asked, "Where are those 'idols' you used to associate **74.** with God?" They will cry, "They have 'all' failed us. In fact, we did not invoke anything 'real' before." This is how God leaves the disbelievers to stray. **75.** 'They will be told,' "This 'punishment' is for being prideful on earth unjustly and for acting arrogantly. **76.** Enter the gates of Hell, to stay there forever. What an evil home for the arrogant!"

Advice to the Prophet

77. So be patient 'O Prophet'. Surely God's promise is true. Whether We show you some of what We threaten them with, or cause you to die 'before that', to Us they will 'all' be returned. **78.** We already sent messengers before you. We have told you the stories of some of them, while others We have not. It was not for any messenger to bring a sign without God's permission. But when God's decree comes, judgment will be passed with fairness, and the people of falsehood will then be in 'total' loss.

Some of God's Favours

79. It is God Who made cattle for you so that you may ride some and eat others. **80.** Also, you find in them 'other' benefits.[969] And by means of them you may reach destinations you desire. And you are carried upon 'some of' them and upon ships. **81.** And He shows you His signs. Now which of God's signs will you deny?

More Warning to the Deniers

82. Have they not travelled throughout the land to see what was the end of those

---

966 Your father, Adam.
967 *Nutfah* refers to the union of male and female gametes (sperm and egg) which results in the zygote after fertilization.
968 *'Alaqah*, meaning the embryo resembles a leech.
969 i.e., milk, wool, and hide.

who were ˹destroyed˺ before them? They were far superior in number and might and ˹richer in˺ monuments throughout the land, but their ˹worldly˺ gains were of no benefit to them. **83.** When their messengers came to them with clear proofs, they were prideful in whatever ˹worldly˺ knowledge they had,[970] and were ˹ultimately˺ overwhelmed by what they used to ridicule. **84.** When they saw Our punishment, they cried, "˹Now˺ we believe in God alone and reject what we had been associating with Him!" **85.** But their faith was of no benefit to them when they saw Our torment. This has ˹always˺ been God's way ˹of dealing˺ with His ˹wicked˺ servants. Then and there the disbelievers were in ˹total˺ loss.

41. 'Verses' Perfectly Explained *(Fuṣṣilat)*

This Meccan chapter, which takes its name from the description of the Quran in verse 3, rebukes the pagans for turning away from the truth; abusing the Quran; and for denying God, the sole Creator of the heavens and the earth. The deniers are warned that their own bodily organs will testify against them on Judgment Day, landing them in Hell forever. Reference to the destruction of the arrogant, ungrateful peoples of 'Âd and Thamûd is made because the pagan Arabs used to pass by their ruins on their journeys to Syria and Yemen, respectively. A profound description of the righteous is given in verses 30-36. The truth of the Quran is emphasized at the end of this chapter and the beginning of the next.

In the Name of God—the Most Compassionate, Most Merciful

The Deniers of the Truth

1. Ḥâ-Mîm. **2.** ˹This is˺ a revelation from the Most Compassionate, Most Merciful. **3.** ˹It is˺ a Book whose verses are perfectly explained—a Quran in Arabic for people who know, **4.** delivering good news and warning. Yet most of them turn away, so they do not hear. **5.** They say, "Our hearts are veiled against what you are calling us to, there is deafness in our ears, and there is a barrier between us and you. So do ˹whatever you want˺ and so shall we!"

A Message to the Deniers

6. Say, ˹O Prophet,˺ "I am only a man like you, ˹but˺ it has been revealed to me that your God is only One God. So take the Straight Way towards Him, and seek His forgiveness. And woe to the polytheists— **7.** those who do not pay alms-tax and are in denial of the Hereafter. **8.** ˹But˺ those who believe and do good will certainly have a never-ending reward.

A Question to the Deniers

9. Ask ˹them, O Prophet˺, "How can you disbelieve in the One Who created the earth in two Days? And how can you set up equals with Him? That is the Lord of all worlds. **10.** He placed on the earth firm mountains, standing high, showered His blessings upon it, and ordained ˹all˺ its means of suste-

---

970   And ridiculed the divine knowledge brought to them by their messengers.

nance—totaling four Days exactly[971]—for all who ask. 11. Then He turned towards the heaven when it was ʿstill likeʾ smoke, saying to it and to the earth, 'Submit, willingly or unwillingly.' They both responded, 'We submit willingly.' 12. So He formed the heaven into seven heavens in two Days, assigning to each its mandate. And We adorned the lowest heaven with ʿstars likeʾ lamps ʿfor beautyʾ and for protection. That is the design of the Almighty, All-Knowing."[972]

The Fate of ʾĀd and Thamûd

13. If they turn away, then say, ʿO Prophet,ʾ "I warn you of a ʿmightyʾ blast, like the one that befell ʾĀd and Thamûd." 14. The messengers had come to them from all angles, ʿproclaiming,ʾ "Worship none but God." They responded, "Had our Lord willed, He could have easily sent down angels ʿinstead . So we totally reject what you have been sent with." 15. As for ʾĀd, they acted arrogantly throughout the land with no right, boasting, "Who is superior to us in might?" Did they not see that God ʿHimselfʾ, Who created them, was far superior to them in might? Still they persisted in denying Our signs. 16. So We sent against them a furious wind,[973] for ʿseveralʾ miserable days, to make them taste a humiliating punishment in this worldly life. But far more humiliating will be the punishment of the Hereafter. And they will not be helped. 17. As for Thamûd, We showed them guidance, but they preferred blindness over guidance. So the blast of a disgracing punishment overtook them for what they used to commit. 18. And We delivered those who were faithful and were mindful ʿof Godʾ.

Testimony of Organs

19. ʿConsiderʾ the Day ʿwhenʾ the enemies of God will be gathered for the Fire, all driven in ranks. 20. When they reach it, their ears, eyes, and skin will testify against what they used to do.[974] 21. They will ask their skin ʿfuriouslyʾ, "Why have you testified against us?" It will say, "We have been made to speak by God, Who causes all things to speak. He ʿis the One Whoʾ created you the first time, and to Him you were bound to return. 22. You did not ʿbother toʾ hide yourselves from your ears, eyes, and skin to prevent them from testifying against you. Rather, you assumed that God did not know much of what you used to do. 23. It was that ʿfalseʾ assumption you entertained about your Lord that has brought about your doom, so you have become losers." 24. Even if they endure patiently, the Fire will ʿalwaysʾ be their home. And if they ʿbeg toʾ appease ʿtheir Lordʾ, they will never be allowed to.

What Caused That Fate

25. We placed at their disposal ʿevilʾ associates who made their past and future ʿmisdeedsʾ appealing to them.[975] ʿSoʾ the fate of earlier communities of jinn and humans has been justified against them ʿas wellʾ, ʿforʾ they were truly losers. 26. The disbelievers advised ʿone anotherʾ, "Do not listen to this Quran but drown it out so that you may prevail." 27. So We will certainly make the disbelievers taste a severe punishment, and We will surely repay them according to the worst of their deeds. 28. That is the reward of God's enemies: the Fire, which will be their eternal home—a ʿfittingʾ reward for their denial of Our revelations. 29. The disbelievers will ʿthenʾ cry, "Our Lord! Show us those jinn and humans who led us astray:

---

971   These four Days include the first two, so the total period of creation is six heavenly Days.

972   See footnote for 7:54.

973   lit., a bitter and screaming wind.

974   It is reported in Ibn Kathîr's commentary that, on the Day of Judgment, the wicked will deny the evil deeds in their records—as a desperate attempt to escape the horrible punishment in Hell. They will be asked if they accept God, the angels, or even their own families and neighbours as witnesses, but they will refuse. So God will make their organs testify against them.

975   i.e., associating others with God in worship and denying the Hereafter. See 43:36-37.

we will put them under our feet so that they will be among the lowest 'in Hell'."

Reward of the Devout

30. Surely those who say, "Our Lord is God," and then remain steadfast, the angels descend upon them,[976] 'saying,' "Do not fear, nor grieve. Rather, rejoice in the good news of Paradise, which you have been promised. **31.** We are your supporters in this worldly life and in the Hereafter. There you will have whatever your souls desire, and there you will have whatever you ask for: **32.** an accommodation from the All-Forgiving, Most Merciful 'Lord'."

Qualities of True Believers

33. And whose words are better than someone who calls 'others' to God, does good, and says, "I am truly one of those who submit."?[977] **34.** Good and evil cannot be equal. Respond 'to evil' with what is best, then the one you are in a feud with will be like a close friend. **35.** But this cannot be attained except by those who are patient and who are truly fortunate. **36.** And if you are tempted by Satan, then seek refuge with God. Indeed, He 'alone' is the All-Hearing, All-Knowing.

Worship the Creator, Marvel at Creation

37. Among His signs are the day and the night, the sun and the moon. Do not prostrate to the sun or the moon, but prostrate to God, Who created them 'all', if you 'truly' worship Him 'alone'. **38.** But if the pagans are too proud, then 'let them know that' those 'angels' nearest to your Lord glorify Him day and night, and never grow weary. **39.** And among His signs is that you see the earth devoid of life, but as soon as We send down rain upon it, it begins to stir 'to life'

and swell. Indeed, the One Who revives it can easily revive the dead. He is certainly Most Capable of everything.

Warning to the Quran Deniers

40. Indeed, those who abuse Our revelations[978] are not hidden from Us. Who is better: the one who will be cast into the Fire or the one who will be secure on Judgment Day? Do whatever you want. He is certainly All-Seeing of what you do. **41.** Indeed, those who deny the Reminder[979] after it has come to them 'are doomed', for it is truly a mighty Book. **42.** It cannot be proven false from any angle. 'It is' a revelation from the 'One Who is' All-Wise, Praiseworthy. **43.** 'O Prophet!' Nothing is said to you 'by the deniers' except what was already said to the messengers before you. Surely your Lord is 'the Lord' of forgiveness and painful punishment.

Response to Demanding Non-Arabic Quran

44. Had We revealed it as a non-Arabic Quran, they would have certainly argued, "If only its verses were made clear 'in our language'. What! A non-Arabic revelation for an Arab audience!" Say, 'O Prophet,' "It is a guide and a healing to the believers. As for those who disbelieve, there is deafness in their ears and blindness to it 'in their hearts'. It is as if they are being called from a faraway place."[980]

Moses Was Denied Too

45. Indeed, We had given Moses the Scripture, but differences arose regarding it. Had it not been for a prior decree from your Lord,[981] their differences would have been settled 'at once'. They are truly in alarming doubt about it.

---

976 Especially at the time of their death.
977 lit., Muslims.
978 This refers to the noise the disbelievers used to make when the Quran was recited (*see* 41:26), or those who twist the meaning of Quranic passages and take them out of context.
979 The Reminder is one of the names of the Quran.
980 So they neither hear nor understand the call.
981 That He will delay their judgment until the Hereafter.

The Good and the Wicked

46. Whoever does good, it is to their own benefit. And whoever does evil, it is to their own loss. Your Lord is never unjust to ˹His˺ creation.

God's Infinite Knowledge

47. With Him ˹alone˺ is the knowledge of the Hour. No fruit comes out of its husk, nor does a female conceive or deliver without His knowledge. And ˹consider˺ the Day He will call to them, "Where are My ˹so-called˺ associate-gods?" They will cry, "We declare before you that none of us testifies to that ˹any longer˺." **48.** Whatever ˹idols˺ they used to invoke besides God will fail them. And they will realize that they will have no escape.

Ingratitude of the Deniers

49. One never tires of praying for good. And if touched with evil, they become desperate and hopeless. **50.** And if We let them taste a mercy from Us after being touched with adversity, they will certainly say, "This is what I deserve. I do not think the Hour will ˹ever˺ come. And if in fact I am returned to my Lord, the finest reward with Him will definitely be mine." But We will surely inform the disbelievers of what they used to do. And We will certainly make them taste a harsh torment. **51.** When We show favour to someone, they turn away, acting arrogantly. And when touched with evil, they make endless prayers ˹for good˺.

Denying God's Revelation

52. Ask ˹them, O Prophet˺, "Imagine if this ˹Quran˺ is ˹truly˺ from God and you deny it: who can be more astray than those who have gone too far in opposition ˹to the truth˺?"

Creation Testifies to the Truth

53. We will show them Our signs in the universe and within themselves until it becomes clear to them that this ˹Quran˺ is the truth. Is it not enough that your Lord is a Witness over all things? **54.** They are truly in doubt of the meeting with their Lord! ˹But˺ He is indeed Fully Aware of everything.

❧

42. Consultation *(Ash-Shûra)*

This Meccan chapter takes its name from verse 38 which talks about conducting affairs by mutual consultation as one of the qualities of the true believers. The chapter emphasizes that God has decreed for Muslims the same religion ordained for all the previous prophets. The believers are commanded to resort to God's judgment if disagreement arises. God's oneness, power, and wisdom are emphasized as the pagans' faith in powerless idols is condemned. Both the end of this chapter and the beginning of the next stress the fact that the Quran has been revealed by God.

In the Name of God—the Most Compassionate, Most Merciful

God Almighty

1. Ḥâ-Mîm. **2.** 'Aȋn-Sȋn-Qâf. **3.** And so you ˹O Prophet˺ are sent revelation, just like those before you, by God—the Almighty, All-Wise. **4.** To Him belongs whatever is in the heavens and whatever is on the earth. And He is the Most High, the Greatest. **5.** The heavens nearly burst, one above the other, ˹in awe of Him˺. And the angels glorify the praises of their Lord, and seek forgiveness for those on earth. Surely God alone is the All-Forgiving, Most Merciful.

God Is the Protector

6. As for those who take other protectors besides Him, God is Watchful over them. And you ˹O Prophet˺ are not a keeper over them. **7.** And so We have revealed to you a Quran in Arabic, so you may warn the Mother of Cities[982] and everyone around it, and warn of the Day of Gathering—about which there is no doubt—˹when˺ a group will be in Paradise and another in the Blaze. **8.** Had God willed, He could have easily made all ˹humanity˺ into a single community ˹of believers˺. But He admits into His mercy whoever He wills. And the wrongdoers will have no protector or helper. **9.** How can they take protectors besides Him? God alone is the Protector. He ˹alone˺ gives life to the dead. And He ˹alone˺ is Most Capable of everything.

Advice to the Believers

10. ˹Say to the believers, O Prophet,˺ "Whatever you may differ about, its judgment rests with God. That is God—my Lord. In Him I put my trust, and to Him I ˹always˺ turn."

God Is the Creator and Provider

11. ˹He is˺ the Originator of the heavens and the earth. He has made for you spouses from among yourselves, and ˹made˺ mates for cattle ˹as well˺—multiplying you ˹both˺. There is nothing like Him, for He ˹alone˺ is the All-Hearing, All-Seeing. **12.** To Him belong the keys ˹of the treasuries˺ of the heavens and the earth. He gives abundant or limited provisions to whoever He wills. Indeed, He has ˹perfect˺ knowledge of all things.

One Message, Different Laws[983]

13. He has ordained for you ˹believers˺ the Way which He decreed for Noah, and what We have revealed to you ˹O Prophet˺ and what We decreed for Abraham, Moses, and Jesus,[984] ˹commanding:˺ "Uphold the faith, and make no divisions in it." What you call the polytheists to is unbearable for them. God chooses for Himself whoever He wills, and guides to Himself whoever turns ˹to Him˺. **14.** They did not split ˹into sects˺ out of mutual envy until knowledge came to them.[985] Had it not been for a prior decree from your Lord for an appointed term,[986] the matter would have certainly been settled between them ˹at once˺. And surely those who were made to inherit the Scripture[987] after them are truly in alarming doubt about this ˹Quran˺.

Call to the People of the Book

15. Because of that, you ˹O Prophet˺ will invite ˹all˺. Be steadfast as you are commanded, and do not follow their desires. And say, "I believe in every Scripture God has revealed. And I am commanded to judge fairly among you. God is our Lord and your Lord. We will be accountable for our deeds and you for yours. There is no ˹need for˺ contention between us. God will gather us together ˹for judgment˺. And to Him is the final return." **16.** As for those who dispute about God after He is ˹already˺ acknowledged ˹by many˺, their argument is futile in the sight of their Lord. Upon them is wrath, and they will suffer a severe punishment.

A Reminder of the Hour

17. It is God Who has revealed the Book with the truth and the balance ˹of justice˺. You never know, perhaps the Hour is near.

---

982 "The Mother of Cities" is an honorary title given to the City of Mecca because of its great religious significance as the home of God's first house of worship ever built on earth, and perhaps because of its central location as well.
983 All prophets came with the same message: have faith in one God and do good. But each faith-community had their own law.
984 Like 33:7, this verse names the five greatest prophets of Islam: Noah, Abraham, Moses, Jesus, and Muḥammad.
985 No community split into believers and disbelievers until they received the knowledge given by their prophet.
986 That He will delay their judgment until the Hereafter.
987 i.e., the Jews and Christians.

18. Those who disbelieve in it ˈask toˈ hasten it ˈmockinglyˈ. But the believers are fearful of it, knowing that it is the truth. Surely those who dispute about the Hour have gone far astray.

God's Graciousness

19. God is Ever Kind to His servants. He provides ˈabundantlyˈ to whoever He wills. And He is the All-Powerful, Almighty.

Worldly Gains and Heavenly Rewards

20. Whoever desires the harvest of the Hereafter, We will increase their harvest. And whoever desires ˈonlyˈ the harvest of this world, We will give them some of it, but they will have no share in the Hereafter.

Reward of the Believers and Polytheists

21. Or do they have associate-gods who have ordained for them some ˈpolytheisticˈ beliefs, which God has not authorized? Had it not been for ˈpriorˈ decree on Judgment, the matter would have certainly been settled between them ˈat onceˈ. And surely the wrongdoers will suffer a painful punishment. **22.** You will see the wrongdoers fearful ˈof the punishmentˈ for what they committed but it will be inevitable for them, whereas those who believe and do good will be in the lush Gardens of Paradise. They will have whatever they desire from their Lord. That is ˈtrulyˈ the greatest bounty. **23.** That ˈrewardˈ is the good news which God gives to His servants who believe and do good. Say, ˈO Prophet,ˈ "I do not ask you for a reward for this ˈmessageˈ—only honour for ˈourˈ kinship."[988] Whoever earns a good deed, We will increase it in goodness for them. Surely God is All-Forgiving, Most Appreciative.

The Quran Fabricated?

24. Or do they say, "He has fabricated a lie about God!"? ˈIf you had,ˈ God would have

sealed your heart, if He willed. And God wipes out falsehood and establishes the truth by His Words. He certainly knows best what is ˈhiddenˈ in the heart.

God's Grace and Might

25. He is the One Who accepts repentance from His servants and pardons ˈtheirˈ sins. And He knows whatever you do. **26.** He responds to those who believe and do good, and increases their reward out of His grace. As for the disbelievers, they will suffer a severe punishment.

God's Mercy: Provisions and Rain

27. Had God given abundant provisions to ˈallˈ His servants, they would have certainly transgressed throughout the land. But He sends down whatever He wills in perfect measure. He is truly All-Aware, All-Seeing of His servants. **28.** He is the One Who sends down rain after people have given up hope, spreading out His mercy. He is the Guardian, the Praiseworthy.

God's Mercy: The Universe

29. And among His signs is the creation of the heavens and the earth, and all living beings He dispersed throughout both. And He is Most Capable of bringing all together whenever He wills. **30.** Whatever affliction befalls you is because of what your own hands have committed. And He pardons much. **31.** You can never escape ˈHimˈ on earth, nor do you have any protector or helper besides God.

God's Mercy: Sailing Ships

32. And among His signs are the ships like mountains ˈsailingˈ in the sea. **33.** If He wills, He can calm the wind, leaving the ships motionless on the water. Surely in this are signs for whoever is steadfast, grateful. **34.** Or He can wreck the ships for what the people have committed—though He

---

988   This could also be a call to all believers to love and respect the immediate family of the Prophet.

forgives much— **35.** so those who dispute about Our signs may know that they have no refuge.

Qualities of the Devout

36. Whatever ˹pleasure˺ you have been given is ˹no more than a fleeting˺ enjoyment of this worldly life. But what is with God is far better and more lasting for those who believe and put their trust in their Lord; **37.** who avoid major sins and shameful deeds, and forgive when angered; **38.** who respond to their Lord, establish prayer, conduct their affairs by mutual consultation, and donate from what We have provided for them; **39.** and who enforce justice when wronged. **40.** The reward of an evil deed is its equivalent. But whoever pardons and seeks reconciliation, then their reward is with God. He certainly does not like the wrongdoers. **41.** There is no blame on those who enforce justice after being wronged. **42.** Blame is only on those who wrong people and transgress in the land unjustly. It is they who will suffer a painful punishment. **43.** And whoever endures patiently and forgives— surely this is a resolve to aspire to.

The Wicked on Judgment Day

44. And whoever God leaves to stray will have no guide after Him. You will see the wrongdoers, when they face the torment, pleading, "Is there any way back ˹to the world˺?" **45.** And you will see them exposed to the Fire, fully humbled out of disgrace, stealing glances ˹at it˺. And the believers will say, "The ˹true˺ losers are those who have lost themselves and their families on Judgment Day." The wrongdoers will certainly be in everlasting torment. **46.** They will have no protectors to help them against God. And whoever God leaves to stray, for them there is no way.

Warning to Ungrateful Disbelievers

47. Respond to your Lord before the coming of a Day from God that cannot be averted. There will be no refuge for you then, nor ˹grounds for˺ denial ˹of sins˺.[989] **48.** But if they turn away, We have not sent you ˹O Prophet˺ as a keeper over them. Your duty is only to deliver ˹the message˺. And indeed, when We let someone taste a mercy from Us, they become prideful ˹because˺ of it. But when afflicted with evil because of what their hands have done, then one becomes totally ungrateful.[990]

God's Gift of Children

49. To God ˹alone˺ belongs the kingdom of the heavens and the earth. He creates whatever He wills. He blesses whoever He wills with daughters, and blesses whoever He wills with sons, **50.** or grants both, sons and daughters, ˹to whoever He wills˺, and leaves whoever He wills infertile. He is indeed All-Knowing, Most Capable.

Forms of Divine Communication

51. It is not ˹possible˺ for a human being to have God communicate with them, except through inspiration, or from behind a veil, or by sending a messenger-angel to reveal whatever He wills by His permission. He is surely Most High, All-Wise.

The Light of the Quran

52. And so We have sent to you ˹O Prophet˺ a revelation by Our command. You did not know of ˹this˺ Book and faith ˹before˺. But We have made it a light, by which We guide whoever We will of Our servants. And you are truly leading ˹all˺ to the Straight Path— **53.** the Path of God, to Whom belongs whatever is in the heavens and whatever is on the earth. Surely to God all matters will return ˹for judgment˺.

---

989 Other possible translations: 1. "You will have no refuge then, nor will you have an advocate ˹against punishment˺." 2. "You will have no refuge then, nor ˹grounds˺ to protest ˹the torment˺."
990 They totally deny previous favours.

43. Ornaments (Az-Zukhruf)

This Meccan chapter takes its name from the ornaments mentioned in verse 35. The pagans are scorned for following their forefathers blindly, labelling the angels as God's daughters, claiming that Muḥammad is not worthy to receive revelations because he is not rich, and for associating idols with God in worship, although they admit that He is the sole Creator of the heavens and the earth. Similar to the next chapter, the pagans are warned of a horrifying punishment in Hell and the believers are promised a great reward in Paradise.

In the Name of God—the Most Compassionate, Most Merciful

Excellence of the Quran

1. Ḥâ-Mîm. 2. By the clear Book! 3. Certainly, We have made it a Quran in Arabic so perhaps you will understand. 4. And indeed, it is—in the Master Record[991] with Us—highly esteemed, rich in wisdom.

Warning to the Deniers

5. Should We then turn the ˹Quranic˺ Reminder away from you ˹simply˺ because you have been a transgressing people? 6. ˹Imagine˺ how many prophets We sent to those ˹destroyed˺ before! 7. But no prophet ever came to them without being mocked. 8. So We destroyed those who were far mightier than these ˹Meccans˺. The examples of ˹their˺ predecessors have ˹already˺ been related.[992]

God Is the Creator

9. If you ask them ˹O Prophet˺ who created the heavens and the earth, they will certainly say, "The Almighty, All-Knowing did." 10. ˹He is the One˺ Who has laid out the earth for you, and set in it pathways for you so that you may find your way. 11. And ˹He is the One˺ Who sends down rain from the sky in perfect measure, with which We give life to a lifeless land. And so will you be brought forth ˹from the grave˺. 12. And ˹He is the One˺ Who created all ˹things in˺ pairs,[993] and made for you ships and animals to ride 13. so that you may sit firmly on their backs, and remember your Lord's blessings once you are settled on them, saying, "Glory be to the One Who has subjected these for us, for we could have never done so ˹on our own˺. 14. And surely to our Lord we will ˹all˺ return."

God's Daughters?

15. Still the pagans have made some of His creation out to be a part of Him.[994] Indeed, humankind is clearly ungrateful. 16. Has He taken ˹angels as His˺ daughters from what He created, and favoured you ˹O pagans˺ with sons? 17. Whenever one of them is given the good news of what they attribute to the Most Compassionate,[995] his face grows gloomy, as he suppresses his rage. 18. ˹Do they attribute to Him˺ those who are brought up in fineries and are not commanding in disputes? 19. Still they have labelled the angels, who are servants of the Most Compassionate, as female. Did they witness their creation? Their statement will be recorded, and they will be questioned!

---

991   This refers to the Preserved Tablet, *Al-Lawḥ Al-Maḥfûz*, in which God has written the destiny of His entire creation.
992   For example, in the stories of the people of Noah, Lot, Shu'aib and other nations that were destroyed, found throughout the Quran.
993   For example, male and female, sweet and bitter, day and night, plains and mountains, heat and cold, light and darkness.
994   See footnote for 37:149.
995   i.e., the birth of a baby girl.

43. Ornaments (Az-Zukhruf)

Blind Following

20. And they argue, "Had the Most Compassionate willed, we would have never worshipped them." They have no knowledge ˹in support˺ of this ˹claim˺. They do nothing but lie. **21.** Or have We given them a Book ˹for proof˺, before this ˹Quran˺, to which they are holding firm? **22.** In fact, they say, "We found our forefathers following a ˹particular˺ way, and we are following in their footsteps." **23.** Similarly, whenever We sent a warner to a society before you ˹O Prophet˺, its ˹spoiled˺ elite would say, "We found our forefathers following a ˹particular˺ way, and we are walking in their footsteps." **24.** Each ˹warner˺ asked, "Even if what I brought you is better guidance than what you found your forefathers practicing?" They replied, "We totally reject whatever you have been sent with." **25.** So We inflicted punishment upon them. See then what was the fate of the deniers!

The Case of Abraham's People

26. ˹Remember, O Prophet˺ when Abraham declared to his father and his people, "I am totally free of whatever ˹gods˺ you worship, **27.** except the One Who originated me, and He will surely guide me." **28.** And he left this enduring declaration among his descendants, so they may ˹always˺ turn back ˹to God˺.[996]

The Case of Meccan Pagans

29. In fact, I had allowed enjoyment for these ˹Meccans˺ and their forefathers, until the truth came to them along with a messenger making things clear. **30.** ˹But˺ when the truth came to them, they said, "This is magic, and we totally reject it." **31.** And they exclaimed, "If only this Quran was revealed to a great man from ˹one of˺ the two cities!"[997] **32.** Is it they who distribute your Lord's mercy? We ˹alone˺ have distributed their ˹very˺ livelihood among them in this worldly life and raised some of them in rank above others so that some may employ others in service. ˹But˺ your Lord's mercy is far better than whatever ˹wealth˺ they amass.

Worthlessness of Material Wealth

33. Were it not that people might ˹be tempted to˺ become one community ˹of disbelievers˺, We would have supplied the homes of ˹only˺ those who disbelieve in the Most Compassionate with silver roofs and ˹silver˺ stairways to ascend, **34.** as well as ˹silver˺ gates and thrones to recline on, **35.** and ornaments ˹of gold˺. Yet all this is no more than a ˹fleeting˺ enjoyment in this worldly life. ˹But˺ the Hereafter with your Lord is ˹only˺ for those mindful ˹of Him˺.

Devilish Associates

36. And whoever turns a blind eye to the Reminder of the Most Compassionate, We place at the disposal of each a devilish one as their close associate, **37.** who will certainly hinder them from the ˹Right˺ Way while they think they are ˹rightly˺ guided. **38.** But when such a person comes to Us, one will say ˹to their associate˺, "I wish you were as distant from me as the east is from the west! What an evil associate ˹you were˺!" **39.** ˹It will be said to both,˺ "Since you all did wrong, sharing in the punishment will be of no benefit to you this Day."[998]

Advice to the Prophet

40. Can you make the deaf hear, or guide the blind or those clearly astray? **41.** Even if We take you away ˹from this world˺, We will surely inflict punishment upon them. **42.** Or if We show you what We threaten them with, We certainly have full power over them. **43.** So hold firmly to what has been revealed to you ˹O Prophet˺. You are

---

996 *See* 2:130-132.

997 This refers to Mecca and Ṭâif, two cities in Arabia, around 100 km apart

998 From a worldly perspective, many people are comforted when they hear of others who went through similar trials as them. But this will not be the case on Judgment Day. Everyone will be desperate to save themselves from the punishment, regardless of others.

truly on the Straight Path. **44.** Surely this 'Quran' is a glory for you and your people. And you will 'all' be questioned 'about it'. **45.** Ask 'the followers of' the messengers that We already sent before you if We 'ever' appointed 'other' gods to be worshipped besides the Most Compassionate.

The Case of Pharaoh's People

46. Indeed, We sent Moses with Our signs to Pharaoh and his chiefs, and he said: "I am a messenger of the Lord of all worlds." **47.** But as soon as he came to them with Our signs, they laughed at them, **48.** although every sign We showed them was greater than the one before.[999] Ultimately, We seized them with torments so that they might return 'to the Right Path'.[1000] **49.** 'Then' they pleaded, "O 'mighty' magician! Pray to your Lord on our behalf, by virtue of the covenant He made with you.[1001] We will certainly accept guidance." **50.** But as soon as We removed the torments from them, they broke their promise.

Pharaoh's Arrogance

51. And Pharaoh called out to his people, boasting, "O my people! Am I not sovereign over Egypt as well as 'all' these streams[1002] flowing at my feet? Can you not see? **52.** Am I not better than this nobody who can hardly express himself?[1003] **53.** Why then have no golden bracelets 'of kingship' been granted to him or angels come with him as escorts!" **54.** And so he fooled his people, and they obeyed him. They were truly a rebellious people. **55.** So when they enraged Us, We inflicted punishment upon them, drowning

them all. **56.** And We made them an example and a lesson for those after them.

All Objects of Worship in Hell?

57. When the son of Mary was cited as an example 'in argument', your people 'O Prophet' broke into 'joyful' applause.[1004] **58.** They exclaimed, "Which is better: our gods or Jesus?" They cite him only to argue. In fact, they are a people prone to dispute. **59.** He was only a servant We showed favour to, and made as an example for the Children of Israel. **60.** Had We willed, We could have easily replaced you 'all' with angels,[1005] succeeding one another on earth. **61.** And his 'second' coming is truly a sign for the Hour. So have no doubt about it, and follow me. This is the Straight Path. **62.** And do not let Satan hinder you, 'for' he is certainly your sworn enemy.

The Truth About Jesus

63. When Jesus came with clear proofs, he declared, "I have come to you with wisdom, and to clarify to you some of what you differ about. So fear God, and obey me. **64.** Surely God 'alone' is my Lord and your Lord, so worship Him 'alone'. This is the Straight Path." **65.** Yet their 'various' groups have differed among themselves 'about him', so woe to the wrongdoers when they face the torment of a painful Day! **66.** Are they waiting for the Hour to take them by surprise when they least expect 'it'?

Reward of the Righteous

67. Close friends will be enemies to one another on that Day, except the righteous,

---

999 i.e., the hand and the staff (*see* 20:17-22).
1000 The torments were: famine, shortage of crops, floods, locusts, lice, frogs, and blood (*see* 7:130-133).
1001 *See* 7:134.
1002 Branches of the Nile.
1003 Moses used to have a speech impediment. But when he became a prophet he prayed to God to help him speak clearly, and his prayer was answered (*see* 20:25-36).
1004 When 21:98 was revealed, warning the polytheists that all false gods will be in Hell, 'Abdullâh ibn Az-Ziba'ra, a poet who always attacked Islam, argued with the Prophet that if what the verse says is true, then Jesus will be in Hell as well! The polytheists, who were present, laughed in agreement with this argument. The Prophet replied that the verse was talking exclusively about idols, adding that Jesus himself did not ask anyone to worship him. Verse 21:101 was later revealed in support of the Prophet's argument. Eventually, 'Abdullâh accepted Islam.
1005 Or "We could have easily produced angels from you …"

68. 'who will be told,' "O My servants! There is no fear for you Today, nor will you grieve— **69.** 'those' who believed in Our signs and 'fully' submitted 'to Us'. **70.** Enter Paradise, you and your spouses, rejoicing." **71.** Golden trays and cups will be passed around to them. There will be whatever the souls desire and the eyes delight in. And you will be there forever. **72.** That is the Paradise which you will be awarded for what you used to do. **73.** There you will have abundant fruit[1006] to eat from.

Reward of the Wicked

74. Indeed, the wicked will be in the torment of Hell forever. **75.** It will never be lightened for them, and there they will be overwhelmed with despair. **76.** We did not wrong them, but it was they who were the wrongdoers. **77.** They will cry, "O Mâlik![1007] Let your Lord finish us off." He will answer, "You are definitely here to stay." **78.** We certainly brought the truth to you, but most of you were resentful of the truth.

Warning to the Polytheists

79. Or have they mastered some 'evil' plan? Then We 'too' are surely planning. **80.** Or do they think that We do not hear their 'evil' thoughts and secret talks? Yes 'We do'! And Our messenger-angels are in their presence, recording 'it all'. **81.** Say, 'O Prophet,' "If the Most Compassionate 'really' had offspring, I would be the first worshipper." **82.** Glorified is the Lord of the heavens and the earth, the Lord of the Throne, far above what they claim. **83.** So let them indulge 'in falsehood' and amuse 'themselves' until they face their Day, which they have been warned of.

The Only God Worthy of Worship

84. He Alone is 'the only True' God in the heavens and 'the only True' God on earth. For He is the All-Wise, All-Knowing. **85.** And Blessed is the One to Whom belongs the kingdom of the heavens and the earth and everything in between! With Him 'alone' is the knowledge of the Hour. And to Him you will 'all' be returned.

Call to the Worshippers of False Gods

86. 'But' those 'objects of worship' they invoke besides Him have no right to intercede, except those who testify to the truth knowingly.[1008] **87.** If you ask them 'O Prophet' who created them, they will certainly say, "God!" How can they then be deluded 'from the truth'? **88.** 'God is Aware of' the Prophet's cry: "O my Lord! Indeed, these are a people who persist in disbelief." **89.** So bear with them and respond with peace. They will soon come to know.

1006 Fruit also implies delicacies.
1007 Angel Mâlik is the chief keeper of Hell.
1008 i.e., Jesus, Ezra, and the angels.

44. The Haze *(Ad-Dukhân)*

This Meccan chapter takes its name from the haze (caused by drought), which is mentioned in verse 10. Similar to the previous chapter, the Meccan pagans are equated with Pharaoh's people for going back on their promise of full submission to God once the plague is removed from them. The Quran is said to have been revealed on a blessed night for the guidance of humanity. Those who embrace its guidance will be honoured in Paradise and those who reject it will be debased in Hell. This fate is the underlying theme in the next chapter.

In the Name of God—the Most Compassionate, Most Merciful

The Quran as a Mercy

1. Ḥâ-Mîm. 2. By the clear Book! 3. Indeed, We sent it down on a blessed night,[1009] for We always warn ˹against evil˺. 4. On that night every matter of wisdom is ordained 5. by a command from Us, for We have always sent ˹messengers˺ 6. as a mercy from your Lord. He ˹alone˺ is truly the All-Hearing, All-Knowing— 7. the Lord of the heavens and the earth and everything in between, if only you had sure faith. 8. There is no god ˹worthy of worship˺ except Him. He ˹alone˺ gives life and causes death. ˹He is˺ your Lord, and the Lord of your forefathers.

Meccans Warned of Famine[1010]

9. In fact, they are in doubt, amusing themselves. 10. Wait then ˹O Prophet˺ for the day ˹when˺ the sky will be veiled in haze,[1011] clearly visible, 11. overwhelming the people. ˹They will cry,˺ "This is a painful torment. 12. Our Lord! Remove ˹this˺ torment from us, ˹and˺ we will certainly believe." 13. How can they be reminded when a messenger has already come to them, making things clear, 14. then they turned away from him, saying, "A madman, taught by others!"? 15. Indeed,

We will remove ˹that˺ torment for a while, and you ˹Meccans˺ will return ˹to disbelief˺. 16. ˹Then˺ on the Day We will deal ˹you˺ the fiercest blow, We will surely inflict punishment.

Moses and Pharaoh's People

17. Indeed, before them We tested Pharaoh's people: a noble messenger came to them, 18. ˹proclaiming,˺ "Hand over the servants of God to me.[1012] I am truly a trustworthy messenger to you. 19. And do not be arrogant with God. I have certainly come to you with a compelling proof. 20. And indeed, I seek refuge with my Lord and your Lord so you do not stone me ˹to death˺. 21. ˹But˺ if you do not believe me, then let me be." 22. Ultimately, he cried out to his Lord, "These are a wicked people!"

Tyrants Destroyed

23. ˹God responded,˺ "Leave with My servants at night, for you will surely be pursued. 24. And leave the sea parted, for they are certainly an army bound to drown." 25. ˹Imagine˺ how many gardens and springs the tyrants[1013] left behind, 26. as well as ˹var-

---

1009 The revelation of the Quran started on the 27ᵗʰ night of Ramaḍân—the 9ᵗʰ month of the Islamic calendar (*see* 97:1 and 2:185)

1010 According to Al-Qurṭubi, this passage either refers to the overwhelming Smoke, which is one of the major signs of Judgment Day, or a severe haze caused by drought. Verse 15 supports the 2ⁿᵈ opinion, because if it was the Smoke it would not have been removed from the Meccans.

1011 This refers to the drought that affected the Meccan pagans so badly that they came to the Prophet, begging him to pray to God to remove the affliction from them.

1012 Meaning, let my people go.

1013 i.e., Pharaoh and his soldiers.

ious' crops and splendid residences, **27.** and luxuries which they fully enjoyed. **28.** So it was. And We awarded it 'all' to another people. **29.** Neither heaven nor earth wept over them, nor was their fate delayed. **30.** And We certainly delivered the Children of Israel from the humiliating torment **31.** of Pharaoh. He was truly a tyrant, a transgressor. **32.** And indeed, We chose the Israelites knowingly above the others. **33.** And We showed them signs in which there was a clear test.

Warning to Deniers of Resurrection

34. Indeed, these 'Meccans' say, **35.** "There is nothing beyond our first death, and we will never be resurrected. **36.** Bring 'back' our forefathers, if what you say is true." **37.** Are they superior to the people of Tubba'[1014] and those before them? We destroyed them 'all', 'for' they were truly wicked. **38.** We did not create the heavens and the earth and everything in between for sport. **39.** We only created them for a purpose, but most of these 'pagans' do not know. **40.** Surely the Day of 'Final' Decision is the time appointed for all— **41.** the Day no kith or kin will be of benefit to another whatsoever, nor will they be helped, **42.** except those shown mercy by God. He is truly the Almighty, Most Merciful.

The Tree of Hell

43. Surely 'the fruit of' the tree of *Zaqqûm*[1015] **44.** will be the food of the evildoer. **45.** Like molten metal, it will boil in the bellies **46.** like the boiling of hot water. **47.** 'It will be said,' "Seize them and drag them into the depths of the Hellfire. **48.** Then pour over their heads the torment of boiling water." **49.** 'The wicked will be told,' "Taste this. You mighty, noble one![1016] **50.** This is truly what you 'all' used to doubt."

The Pleasures of Paradise

51. Indeed, the righteous will be in a secure place, **52.** amid Gardens and springs, **53.** dressed in fine silk and rich brocade, facing one another. **54.** So it will be. And We will pair them to maidens with gorgeous eyes. **55.** There they will call for every fruit in serenity. **56.** There they will never taste death, beyond the first death. And He will protect them from the punishment of the Hellfire— **57.** as 'an act of' grace from your Lord. That is 'truly' the ultimate triumph.

The Quran Is Easy

58. Indeed, We have made this 'Quran' easy in your own language 'O Prophet' so perhaps they will be mindful. **59.** Wait then! They too are certainly waiting.

1014 Tubba' Al-Ḥimiari was an ancient righteous Yemeni king whose people persisted in disbelief and were destroyed, although they were superior to Meccans in strength and manpower.
1015 *Zaqqûm* is a tree that grows in the depths of Hell as mentioned in 37:62-65. The pagans of Mecca used to make fun of the Prophet and say, "How can a tree grow in Hell?"
1016 Abu Jahl, a Meccan pagan leader, met the warning of punishment in the Hereafter by exclaiming, "How can I be punished when I am the mighty, noble one!"

45. The Kneeling *(Al-Jâthiyah)*

This Meccan chapter, which takes its name from the kneeling of every faith-community on Judgment Day mentioned in verse 28, is critical of those who turn away from God's revelations, deny the Resurrection, ridicule the truth, and fail to appreciate God's count-less favours and marvels of creation. The dreadful judgment of these deniers is featured in the last part of the chapter. All these themes are emphasized in the next chapter as well.

In the Name of God—the Most Compassionate, Most Merciful

God's Signs

1. *Ḥâ-Mîm.* 2. The revelation of this Book is from God—the Almighty, All-Wise. 3. Surely in ʿthe creation ofʾ the heavens and the earth are signs for the believers. 4. And in your own creation, and whatever living beings He dispersed, are signs for people of sure faith. 5. And ʿinʾ the alternation of the day and the night, the provision[1017] sent down from the skies by God—reviving the earth after its death—and the shifting of the winds, are signs for people of understanding. 6. These are God's revelations which We recite to you ʿO Prophetʾ in truth. So what message will they believe in after ʿdenyingʾ God and His revelations?

Warning to the Deniers

7. Woe to every sinful liar. 8. They hear God's revelations recited to them, then persist ʿin denialʾ arrogantly as if they did not hear them. So give them good news of a painful punishment. 9. And whenever they learn anything of Our revelations, they make a mockery of it. It is they who will suffer a humiliating punishment. 10. Awaiting them is Hell. Their ʿworldlyʾ gains will not be of any benefit to them whatsoever, nor will those protectors they have taken besides God. And they will suffer a tremendous punishment. 11. This ʿQuranʾ is ʿtrueʾ guidance. And those who deny their Lord's revelations will suffer the ʿworstʾ torment of agonizing pain.

God's Favours to Humanity

12. God is the One Who has subjected the sea for you so that ships may sail upon it by His command, and that you may seek His bounty, and that perhaps you will be grateful. 13. He ʿalsoʾ subjected for you whatever is in the heavens and whatever is on the earth—all by His grace. Surely in this are signs for people who reflect.

Advice to the Believers

14. ʿO Prophet!ʾ Tell the believers to forgive those who do not fear God's days ʿof tormentʾ, so that He will reward each group for what they used to commit. 15. Whoever does good, it is to their own benefit. And whoever does evil, it is to their own loss. Then to your Lord you will ʿallʾ be returned.

Differences Among the Israelites

16. Indeed, We gave the Children of Israel the Scripture, wisdom, and prophethood; granted them good, lawful provisions; and favoured them above the others.[1018] 17. We ʿalsoʾ gave them clear commandments regarding ʿtheirʾ faith. But it was not until knowledge came to them that they differed out of mutual envy.[1019] Surely your Lord will judge between them on the Day of Judgment regarding their differences.

Advice to the Prophet

18. Now We have set you ʿO Prophetʾ on the ʿclearʾ Way of faith. So follow it, and

---

1017 i.e., rain.
1018 By sending many prophets, and showing them unique miracles such as the splitting of the sea.
1019 No community split into believers and disbelievers until they received the knowledge given by their prophet.

do not follow the desires of those who do not know ˈthe truthˈ. **19.** They certainly can be of no benefit to you against God whatsoever. Surely the wrongdoers are patrons of each other, whereas God is the Patron of the righteous. **20.** This ˈQuranˈ is an insight for humanity—a guide and mercy for people of sure faith.

Good and Evil Are Not Equal

21. Or do those who commit evil deeds ˈsimplyˈ think that We will make them equal—in their life and after their death—to those who believe and do good? How wrong is their judgment! **22.** For God created the heavens and the earth for a purpose, so that every soul may be paid back for what it has committed. And none will be wronged.

Those Led by Desire

23. Have you seen ˈO Prophetˈ those who have taken their own desires as their god? ˈAnd soˈ God left them to stray knowingly, sealed their hearing and hearts, and placed a cover on their sight. Who then can guide them after God? Will you ˈallˈ not then be mindful?

Arguments of the Deniers of Resurrection

24. And they argue, "There is nothing beyond our worldly life. We die; others are born. And nothing destroys us but ˈthe passage ofˈ time." Yet they have no knowledge ˈin supportˈ of this ˈclaimˈ. They only speculate. **25.** And whenever Our clear revelations are recited to them, their only argument is to say: "Bring our forefathers back, if what you say is true!" **26.** Say, ˈO Prophet,ˈ "ˈIt isˈ God ˈWhoˈ gives you life, then causes you to die, then will gather you ˈallˈ on the Day of Judgment, about which there is no doubt. But most people do not know."

The Judgment

27. To God ˈaloneˈ belongs the kingdom of the heavens and the earth. On the Day the Hour will be established, the people of false-

hood will then be in ˈtotalˈ loss. **28.** And you will see every faith-community on its knees. Every community will be summoned to its record ˈof deedsˈ. ˈThey all will be told,ˈ "This Day you will be rewarded for what you used to do. **29.** This record of Ours speaks the truth about you. Indeed, We always had your deeds recorded ˈby the angelsˈ."

Reward of the Believers

30. As for those who believed and did good, their Lord will admit them into His mercy. That is ˈtrulyˈ the absolute triumph.

Punishment of the Disbelievers

31. And as for those who disbelieved, ˈthey will be told,ˈ "Were My revelations not recited to you, yet you acted arrogantly and were a wicked people? **32.** And whenever it was said ˈto youˈ, 'Surely God's promise ˈof judgmentˈ is true and there is no doubt about the Hour,' you said ˈmockinglyˈ, 'We do not know what the Hour is! We think it is no more than speculation, and we are not convinced ˈthat it will ever comeˈ.'" **33.** And the evil ˈconsequencesˈ of their deeds will unfold before them, and they will be overwhelmed by what they used to ridicule. **34.** It will be said, "This Day We will neglect you as you neglected the meeting of this Day of yours! Your home will be the Fire, and you will have no helpers. **35.** This is because you made a mockery of God's revelations, and were deluded by ˈyourˈ worldly life." So ˈfromˈ that Day ˈonˈ they will not be taken out of the Fire, nor will they be allowed to appease ˈtheir Lordˈ.

Praises to the Almighty

36. So all praise is for God—Lord of the heavens and Lord of the earth, Lord of all worlds. **37.** To Him belongs ˈallˈ Majesty in the heavens and the earth. And He is the Almighty, All-Wise.

46. The Sand-Hills *(Al-Aḥqâf)*

This Meccan chapter takes its name from the sand-hills mentioned in verse 21 in the story of the people of Hûd who were destroyed for their disbelief, even though they were far superior to the Arab pagans (verses 21-28). Again, God's infinite power is contrasted with the powerlessness of the idols. The pagan arguments against the Quran and the Resurrection are refuted, and reference is made to a group of jinn who readily embraced the truth once they heard the Prophet's recitation of the Quran. The Prophet is urged to be patient, and reminded of the fate awaiting those who challenge the truth at the end of this chapter and the beginning of the next.

In the Name of God—the Most Compassionate, Most Merciful

A Message to Idolaters

1. Ḥâ-Mîm. **2.** The revelation of this Book is from God—the Almighty, All-Wise. **3.** We only created the heavens and the earth and everything in between for a purpose and an appointed term. Yet the disbelievers are turning away from what they have been warned about. **4.** Ask ˹them, O Prophet˺, "Have you considered whatever ˹idols˺ you invoke besides God? Show me what they have created on earth! Or do they have a share in ˹the creation of˺ the heavens? Bring me a scripture ˹revealed˺ before this ˹Quran˺ or a shred of knowledge, if what you say is true." **5.** And who could be more astray than those who call upon others besides God—˹others˺ that cannot respond to them until the Day of Judgment, and are ˹even˺ unaware of their calls? **6.** And when ˹such˺ people will be gathered together, those ˹gods˺ will be their enemies and will disown their worship.

Pagan Denial of the Quran

7. Whenever Our clear revelations are recited to them, the disbelievers say of the truth when it has come to them, "This is pure magic." **8.** Or do they say, "He[1020] has fabricated this ˹Quran˺!"? Say, ˹O Prophet,˺ "If I have done so, then there is nothing whatsoever you can do to save me from God. He knows best what ˹slurs˺ you indulge about it. Sufficient is He as a Witness between you and me. And He is the All-Forgiving, Most Merciful." **9.** Say, "I am not the first messenger ever sent, nor do I know what will happen to me or you. I only follow what is revealed to me. And I am only sent with a clear warning."

Pagan Arrogance Towards God

10. Ask ˹them, O Prophet˺, "Consider if this ˹Quran˺ is ˹truly˺ from God and you deny it, and a witness from the Children of Israel attests to it and then believes,[1021] whereas you act arrogantly. Surely God does not guide the wrongdoing people."

Belittling the Quran

11. The disbelievers say of the believers, "Had it been ˹something˺ good, they[1022] would not have beaten us to it." Now since they reject its guidance, they will say, "˹This is˺ an ancient fabrication!" **12.** And before this ˹Quran˺ the Book of Moses was ˹revealed as˺ a guide and mercy. And this Book is a confirmation, in the Arabic tongue, to warn those who do wrong, and as good news to those who do good.

Reward of the Devout

13. Surely those who say, "Our Lord is God," and then remain steadfast—there

---

1020 Muḥammad.
1021 This refers to 'Abdullâh ibn Salâm, a Jewish scholar, who embraced Islam when the Prophet emigrated to Medina.
1022 Poor and powerless Muslims.

46. The Sand-Hills (Al-Aḥqâf)

will be no fear for them, nor will they grieve. **14.** It is they who will be the residents of Paradise, staying there forever, as a reward for what they used to do.

Stance of the Faithful

15. We have commanded people to honour their parents. Their mothers bore them in hardship and delivered them in hardship. Their ˹period of˺ bearing and weaning is thirty months. In time, when the child reaches their prime at the age of forty, they pray, "My Lord! Inspire me to ˹always˺ be thankful for Your favours which You blessed me and my parents with, and to do good deeds that please You. And instil righteousness in my offspring. I truly repent to You, and I truly submit ˹to Your Will˺." **16.** It is from these ˹people˺ that We will accept the good they did, and overlook their misdeeds—along with the residents of Paradise, ˹in fulfilment of˺ the true promise they have been given.

Stance of the Deniers

17. But some scold their parents, "Enough with you! Are you warning me that I will be brought forth ˹from the grave˺, while many generations had already perished before me ˹for good˺?" The parents cry to God for help, ˹and warn their child,˺ "Pity you. Have faith! Surely God's promise is true." But the deniers insist, "This is nothing but ancient fables." **18.** These are the ones against whom the fate of earlier communities of jinn and humans has been justified, ˹for˺ they were truly losers.

Reward of the Faithful and the Deniers

19. Each ˹of the two groups˺ will be ranked according to what they have done so He may fully reward all. And none will be wronged. **20.** ˹Watch for˺ the Day ˹when˺ the disbelievers will be exposed to the Fire. ˹They will be told,˺ "You ˹already˺ exhausted your ˹share of˺ pleasures during your worldly life, and ˹fully˺ enjoyed them. So Today you will be rewarded with the torment of disgrace for your arrogance throughout the land with no right, and for your rebelliousness."

Prophet Hûd

21. And remember the brother of ˹Âd, when he warned his people, who inhabited the sand-hills[1023]—there were certainly warners before and after him—˹saying,˺ "Worship none but God. I truly fear for you the torment of a tremendous day." **22.** They argued, "Have you come to turn us away from our gods? Bring us then whatever you threaten us with, if what you say is true." **23.** He responded, "The knowledge ˹of its time˺ is only with God. I only convey to you what I have been sent with. But I can see that you are a people acting ignorantly." **24.** Then when they saw the torment as a ˹dense˺ cloud approaching their valleys, they said ˹happily˺, "This is a cloud bringing us rain." ˹But Hûd replied,˺ "No, it is what you sought to hasten: a ˹fierce˺ wind carrying a painful punishment!" **25.** It destroyed everything by the command of its Lord, leaving nothing visible except their ruins. This is how We reward the wicked people.

Warning to Meccan Pagans

26. Indeed, We had established them[1024] in a way We have not established you ˹Meccans˺. And We gave them hearing, sight, and intellect. But neither their hearing, sight, nor intellect were of any benefit to them whatsoever, since they persisted in denying God's signs. And ˹so˺ they were overwhelmed by what they used to ridicule. **27.** We certainly destroyed the societies around you after having varied the signs so perhaps they would return ˹to the Right Path˺. **28.** Why then did those ˹idols˺ they took as gods besides God—hoping to get closer ˹to Him˺—not come to their aid? Instead, they failed them.

1023 The people of ˹Âd were the residents of the hills in the southern part of the Arabian Peninsula.
1024 The people of Hûd.

273

That is ˹the result of˺ their lies and their fabrications.

The Jinn Listen to the Quran

29. ˹Remember, O Prophet,˺ when We sent a group of jinn your way to listen to the Quran. Then, upon hearing it, they said ˹to one another˺, "Listen quietly!" Then when it was over, they returned to their fellow jinn as warners. **30.** They declared, "O our fellow jinn! We have truly heard a scripture revealed after Moses, confirming what came before it. It guides to the truth and the Straight Way. **31.** O our fellow jinn! Respond to the caller of God and believe in him, He will forgive your sins and protect you from a painful punishment. **32.** And whoever does not respond to the caller of God will have no escape on earth, nor will they have any protectors against Him. It is they who are clearly astray."

Warning to Deniers of Resurrection

33. Do they not realize that God, Who created the heavens and the earth and did not tire in creating them,[1025] is able to give life to the dead? Yes ˹indeed˺! He is certainly Most Capable of everything. **34.** And on the Day the disbelievers will be exposed to the Fire, ˹they will be asked,˺ "Is this ˹Hereafter˺ not the truth?" They will cry, "Absolutely, by our Lord!" It will be said, "Then taste the punishment for your disbelief."

Advice to the Prophet

35. So endure patiently, as did the Messengers of Firm Resolve.[1026] And do not ˹seek to˺ hasten ˹the torment˺ for the deniers. On the Day they see what they have been threatened with, it will be as if they had only stayed ˹in this world˺ for an hour of a day.[1027] ˹This is˺ a ˹sufficient˺ warning! Then, will anyone be destroyed except the rebellious people?

47. Muḥammad *(Muḥammad)*

This Medinian chapter, which takes its title from the Prophet's name in verse 2, discusses the etiquette of fighting in the battlefield. The faithful believers are promised different types of rivers and delicacies in Paradise, whereas the disbelievers and the hypocrites are warned of an evil fate. To preserve the reward of their good deeds, the believers are urged to strive in the Way of God and donate in His cause, culminating in the clear triumph in the next chapter.

In the Name of God—the Most Compassionate, Most Merciful

Reward of the Believers and Disbelievers

1. Those who disbelieve and hinder ˹others˺ from the Way of God, He will render their deeds void. **2.** As for those who believe, do good, and have faith in what has been revealed to Muḥammad—which is the truth from their Lord—He will absolve them of their sins and improve their con-

---

1025 Or never failed in creating them.
1026 Noah, Abraham, Moses, Jesus, and Muḥammad are called the Messengers of Firm Resolve.
1027 i.e., only for a very short period of time.

dition. **3.** This is because the disbelievers follow falsehood, while the believers follow the truth from their Lord. This is how God shows people their true state ʿof faithʾ.

Rules of Engagement[1028]

4. So when you meet the disbelievers ʿin battleʾ, strike ʿtheirʾ necks until you have thoroughly subdued them, then bind them firmly. Later ʿfree them either asʾ an act of grace or by ransom until the war comes to an end. So will it be. Had God willed, He ʿHimselfʾ could have inflicted punishment on them. But He does ʿthis only toʾ test some of you by means of others. And those who are martyred in the cause of God,[1029] He will never render their deeds void. **5.** He will guide them ʿto their rewardʾ, improve their condition, **6.** and admit them into Paradise, having made it known to them.[1030]

Warning to the Deniers

7. O believers! If you stand up for God, He will help you and make your steps firm. **8.** As for the disbelievers, may they be doomed and may He render their deeds void. **9.** That is because they detest what God has revealed, so He has rendered their deeds void. **10.** Have they not travelled throughout the land to see what was the end of those before them? God annihilated them, and a similar fate awaits the disbelievers. **11.** This is because God is the Patron of the believers while the disbelievers have no patron.

The Final Destination

12. Surely God will admit those who believe and do good into Gardens under which rivers flow. As for the disbelievers,

they enjoy themselves and feed like cattle.[1031] But the Fire will be their home.

Evil Fate

13. ʿImagine, O Prophet,ʾ how many societies We destroyed that were far superior in might than your society—which drove you out—and there was none to help them! **14.** Can those ʿbelieversʾ who stand on clear proof from their Lord be like those whose evil deeds are made appealing to them and ʿonlyʾ follow their desires?

Delights of Paradise

15. The description of the Paradise promised to the righteous is that in it are rivers of fresh water, rivers of milk that never changes in taste, rivers of wine delicious to drink, and rivers of pure honey. There they will ʿalsoʾ have all kinds of fruit, and forgiveness from their Lord. ʿCan they beʾ like those who will stay in the Fire forever, left to drink boiling water that will tear apart their insides?

Qualities of the Hypocrites 1) Mockery

16. There are some of them who listen to you ʿO Prophetʾ, but when they depart from you, they say ʿmockinglyʾ to those ʿbelieversʾ gifted with knowledge, "What did he just say?" These are the ones whose hearts God has sealed and who ʿonlyʾ follow their desires. **17.** As for those who are ʿrightlyʾ guided, He increases them in guidance and blesses them with righteousness. **18.** Are they only waiting for the Hour to take them by surprise? Yet ʿsome ofʾ its signs have already come.[1032] Once it actually befalls them, will it not be too late to be mindful?

1028 This passage discusses armed combat in the battlefield only.
1029 Another possible interpretation: "And those who fight in the cause of God."
1030 Once in Paradise, the believers will recognize their mansions just like they recognized their homes in the world.
1031 Meaning, the disbelievers enjoy their life to the fullest while they are heedless of what will happen to them in the Hereafter, just like the cattle that graze in the pasture are unaware that they will probably end up in the slaughter house.
1032 The coming of Muḥammad is one of the signs of the Hour.

Advice to the Prophet

19. So, know ˹well, O Prophet,˺ that there is no god ˹worthy of worship˺ except God. And seek forgiveness for your shortcomings[1033] and for ˹the sins of˺ the believing men and women. For God ˹fully˺ knows your movements and places of rest ˹O people˺.

Qualities of the Hypocrites 2) Cowardice

20. And the believers say, "If only a chapter was revealed ˹allowing self-defence˺!" Yet when a precise chapter is revealed, in which fighting is ˹explicitly˺ mentioned, you see those with sickness in their hearts staring at you like someone in the throes of death. It would have been better for them **21.** to obey and speak rightly. Then when fighting was ordained, it surely would have been better for them if they were true to God. **22.** Now if you ˹hypocrites˺ turn away, perhaps you would then spread corruption throughout the land and sever your ˹ties of˺ kinship![1034] **23.** These are the ones who God has condemned, deafening them and blinding their eyes. **24.** Do they not then reflect on the Quran? Or are there locks upon their hearts?

Warning to Hypocrites

25. Indeed, those who relapse ˹into disbelief˺ after ˹true˺ guidance has become clear to them, ˹it is˺ Satan ˹that˺ has tempted them, luring them with false hopes. **26.** That is because they said ˹privately˺ to those who ˹also˺ detest what God has revealed, "We will obey you in some matters."[1035] But God ˹fully˺ knows what they are hiding. **27.** Then how ˹horrible˺ will it be when the angels take their souls, beating their faces and backs! **28.** This is because they follow whatever displeases God and hate whatever pleases Him, so He has rendered their deeds void.

Another Warning to Hypocrites

29. Or do those with sickness in their hearts think that God will not ˹be able to˺ expose their malice? **30.** Had We willed, We could have truly shown them to you ˹O Prophet˺, and you would have certainly recognized them by their appearance. But you will surely recognize them by their tone of speech. And God ˹fully˺ knows your doings ˹O people˺.

Wisdom Behind the Test

31. We will certainly test you ˹believers˺ until We prove those of you who ˹truly˺ struggle ˹in God's cause˺ and remain steadfast, and reveal how you conduct yourselves.

Reward of the Disbelievers

32. Indeed, those who disbelieve, hinder ˹others˺ from the Way of God, and defy the Messenger after ˹true˺ guidance has become clear to them; they will not harm God in the least, but He will render their deeds void.

Advice to the Believers

33. O believers! Obey God and obey the Messenger, and do not let your deeds be in vain. **34.** Surely those who disbelieve, hinder ˹others˺ from the Way of God, and then die as disbelievers; God will never forgive them. **35.** So do not falter or cry for peace, for you will have the upper hand and God is with you. And He will never let your deeds go to waste.

Test of Faith

36. This worldly life is no more than play and amusement. But if you are faithful and mindful ˹of God˺, He will grant you your ˹full˺ reward, and will not ask you ˹to donate all˺ your wealth. **37.** If He were to do so and pressure you, you would withhold and He

---

1033 Like other prophets, Muḥammad was infallible of sin. The verse here refers to misjudgments, such as the example given in 80:1-10. If the Prophet himself is urged to seek forgiveness, then the believers are even more in need of praying for God's forgiveness.
1034 As you did before Islam.
1035 i.e., your opposition to the Prophet.

would bring out your resentment. **38.** Here you are, being invited to donate ˹a little˺ in the cause of God. Still some of you withhold. And whoever does so, it is only to their own loss. For God is the Self-Sufficient, whereas you stand in need ˹of Him˺. If you ˹still˺ turn away, He will replace you with another people. And they will not be like you.

48. The Triumph *(Al-Fath)*

This Medinian chapter takes its name from the clear triumph (i.e., Treaty of Ḥudaibiyah) in verse 1. The Prophet and 1400 of his companions travelled to Mecca to perform the minor pilgrimage ('umrah) in 6 A.H./628 C.E. He sent 'Uthmân ibn 'Affân to let the Meccans know that the Muslims had come in peace, only to visit the Sacred House. When the Meccans delayed 'Uthmân, the Prophet thought they might have killed his envoy. So he called upon the faithful to pledge allegiance to him under a tree at Ḥudaibiyah in the outskirts of Mecca. Shortly after, 'Uthmân returned safely and a peace agreement was signed by the Muslims and Meccan pagans, stating in part that the Muslims would have to return to Medina and come back next year for 'umrah. The Treaty of Ḥudaibiyah is described as a clear triumph since it established peace, temporarily diffused the tension between the Muslims and the Meccan pagans, and gave the Muslims plenty of time to spread awareness and understanding of their faith. Thousands from different tribes accepted Islam during that truce. The chapter commends the believers for proving true to God and His Messenger, criticizes the hypocrites for not marching forth with the Prophet, and condemns the pagans for denying the believers access to the Sacred House. The description of the true believers both in the Torah and the Gospel is given at the end of the chapter, followed by instructions on proper conduct with the Prophet and other believers in the next chapter.

In the Name of God—the Most Compassionate, Most Merciful

Treaty of Ḥudaibiyah

1. Indeed, We have granted you a clear triumph ˹O Prophet˺ **2.** so that God may forgive you for your past and future shortcomings,[1036] perfect His favour upon you, guide you along the Straight Path, **3.** and so that God will help you tremendously. **4.** He is the One Who sent down serenity upon the hearts of the believers so that they may increase even more in their faith. To God ˹alone˺ belong the forces of the heavens and the earth. And God is All-Knowing, All-Wise. **5.** So He may admit believing men and women into Gardens under which rivers flow—to stay there forever—and absolve them of their sins. And that is a supreme achievement in the sight of God. **6.** Also ˹so that˺ He may punish hypocrite men and women and polytheistic men and women, who harbour evil thoughts of God.[1037] May ill-fate befall

---

1036 See footnote for 47:19.
1037 i.e., that God will not support His Prophet and that misfortune will befall the believers.

them! God is displeased with them. He has condemned them and prepared for them Hell. What an evil destination! **7.** To God ˹alone˺ belong the forces of the heavens and the earth. And God is Almighty, All-Wise.

The Prophet's Duty

8. Indeed, ˹O Prophet,˺ We have sent you as a witness, a deliverer of good news, and a warner, **9.** so that you ˹believers˺ may have faith in God and His Messenger, support and honour him, and glorify God morning and evening.[1038]

Allegiance Under the Tree[1039]

10. Surely those who pledge allegiance to you ˹O Prophet˺ are actually pledging allegiance to God. God's Hand is over theirs. Whoever breaks their pledge, it will only be to their own loss. And whoever fulfils their pledge to God, He will grant them a great reward.

Fake Excuses for Not Travelling to Mecca

11. The nomadic Arabs, who stayed behind, will say to you ˹O Prophet˺, "We were preoccupied with our wealth and families, so ask for forgiveness for us." They say with their tongues what is not in their hearts. Say, "Who then can stand between you and God in any way, if He intends harm or benefit for you? In fact, God is All-Aware of what you do. **12.** The truth is: you thought that the Messenger and the believers would never return to their families again. And that was made appealing in your hearts. You harboured evil thoughts ˹about God˺, and ˹so˺ became a doomed people." **13.** And whoever does not believe in God and His Messenger, then We surely have prepared for the disbelievers a blazing Fire. **14.** To God

˹alone˺ belongs the kingdom of the heavens and the earth. He forgives whoever He wills, and punishes whoever He wills. And God is All-Forgiving, Most Merciful.

Shares in the Spoils of War

15. Those who stayed behind will say, when you ˹believers˺ set out to take the spoils of war, "Let us accompany you." They wish to change God's promise.[1040] Say, ˹O Prophet,˺ "You will not accompany us. This is what God has said before." They will then say, "In fact, you are driven by jealousy against us!"[1041] The truth is: they can hardly comprehend.

A Second Chance

16. Say to nomadic Arabs, who stayed behind, "You will be called ˹to fight˺ against a people of great might,[1042] who you will fight unless they submit. If you then obey, God will grant you a fine reward. But if you turn away as you did before, He will inflict upon you a painful punishment."

Those Exempted from Fighting

17. There is no blame on the blind, or the disabled, or the sick ˹for staying behind˺. And whoever obeys God and His Messenger will be admitted by Him into Gardens under which rivers flow. But whoever turns away will be subjected by Him to a painful punishment.

Allegiance of the Faithful

18. Indeed, God was pleased with the believers when they pledged allegiance to you ˹O Prophet˺ under the tree. He knew what was in their hearts, so He sent down serenity upon them and rewarded them with a vic-

---

1038 Another possible translation: "... so that you ˹all˺ may believe in God and His Messenger, support ˹His cause˺, revere, and glorify Him morning and evening."
1039 *See* the introduction of this chapter.
1040 Those who pledged allegiance at Ḥudaibiyah were promised by God that the spoils of war obtained from the Tribe of Khaibar would be exclusively theirs.
1041 Meaning, you only say so to deprive us of our share.
1042 This refers to Hawâzin and Thaqîf, two pagan Arab tribes.

tory at hand,[1043] **19.** and many spoils of war they will gain. For God is Almighty, All-Wise. **20.** God has promised you ʿbelieversʾ abundant spoils, which you will gain, so He hastened this ʿtruceʾ[1044] for you. And He has held people's hands back from ʿharmingʾ you, so it may be a sign for the believers, and so He may guide you along the Straight Path. **21.** And ʿthere areʾ other gains which are beyond your reach that God is keeping in store ʿfor youʾ. For God is Most Capable of everything.

The Believers Will Prevail

22. If the disbelievers were to fight you, they would certainly flee.[1045] Then they would never find any protector or helper. **23.** ʿThis isʾ God's way, already long established ʿin the pastʾ. And you will find no change in God's way.

Wisdom Behind the Truce

24. He is the One Who held back their hands from you and your hands from them in the valley of ʿHudaibiyah, nearʾ Mecca, after giving you the upper hand over ʿa group ofʾ them.[1046] And God is All-Seeing of what you do. **25.** They are the ones who persisted in disbelief and hindered you from the Sacred Mosque, preventing the sacrificial animals from reaching their destination.[1047] ʿWe would have let you march through Mecca,ʾ had there not been believing men and women, unknown to you. You might have trampled them underfoot, incurring guilt for ʿwhat you did toʾ them unknowingly. That was so God may admit into His mercy whoever He wills.[1048] Had those ʿunknownʾ believers stood apart, We would have certainly inflicted a painful punishment on the disbelievers.

Meccan Arrogance

26. ʿRememberʾ when the disbelievers had filled their hearts with pride—the pride of ʿpre-Islamicʾ ignorance[1049]—then God sent down His serenity upon His Messenger and the believers, inspiring them to uphold the declaration of faith,[1050] for they were better entitled and more worthy of it. And God has ʿperfectʾ knowledge of all things.

The Prophet's Vision[1051]

27. Indeed, God will fulfil His Messenger's vision in all truth: God willing, you will surely enter the Sacred Mosque, in security—ʿsome withʾ heads shaved and ʿothers withʾ hair shortened—without fear.[1052] He knew what you did not know, so He first granted you the triumph at hand.[1053] **28.** He is the One Who has sent His Messenger with ʿrightʾ guidance and the religion of truth, making it prevail over all others. And sufficient is God as a Witness.

Believers' Description in the Torah and the Gospel

29. Muḥammad is the Messenger of God. And those with him are firm with the dis-

---

1043 The conquest of Khaibar in 7 A.H./628 C.E.
1044 Or the spoils of Khaibar.
1045 lit., turn their backs.
1046 A group of Meccans wanted to attack the Muslims on their way to Mecca, but were taken captive by the Muslims, then were released.
1047 The animals that Muslims had brought along to be sacrificed after completing the rituals of the minor pilgrimage (ʿumrah).
1048 By doing so, the Meccan Muslims who were unknown to their fellow believers were safe, along with the pagans who later accepted Islam.
1049 This is when the pagans prevented the Prophet and the believers from entering the Sacred House for ʿumrah and the arrogance they showed when drafting the peace agreement.
1050 The declaration of faith that there is only one God to be worshipped and that Muḥammad is His Messenger.
1051 The Prophet had a dream that he and his companions were going to enter the Sacred Mosque in peace.
1052 Pilgrims are required to shave or trim their hair upon successfully completing the rituals of pilgrimage.
1053 This refers to the Treaty of Ḥudaibiyah and/or the gains of Khaibar before the fulfilment of the Prophet's vision to enter Mecca for ʿumrah.

believers[1054] and compassionate with one another. You see them bowing and prostrating[1055] ʿin prayerʾ, seeking God's bounty and pleasure. The sign ʿof brightness can be seenʾ on their faces from the trace of prostrating ʿin prayerʾ. This is their description in the Torah.[1056] And their parable in the Gospel is that of a seed that sprouts its ʿtinyʾ branches, making it strong. Then it becomes thick, standing firmly on its stem, to the delight of the planters[1057]—in this way God makes the believers a source of dismay for the disbelievers.[1058] To those of them who believe and do good, God has promised forgiveness and a great reward.

⌘⌘⌘

49. The Private Quarters *(Al-Ḥujurât)*

This Medinian chapter, which takes its name from the reference to the Prophet's private quarters in verse 4, instructs the believers on the proper conduct towards the Prophet (verses 1-5) and the social etiquette of dealing with other believers (verses 6-12) and the rest of humanity (verse 13). At the end of the chapter, the nomadic Arabs are taught that true faith is proven by action not only words.

In the Name of God—the Most Compassionate, Most Merciful

Manners with the Prophet 1)
Respect Authority

1. O believers! Do not proceed ʿin any matterʾ before ʿa decree fromʾ God and His Messenger. And fear God. Surely God is All-Hearing, All-Knowing.

Manners with the Prophet 2)
Watch Your Tongue

2. O believers! Do not raise your voices above the voice of the Prophet, nor speak loudly to him as you do to one another,[1059] or your deeds will become void while you are unaware. **3.** Indeed, those who lower their voices in the presence of God's Messenger are the ones whose hearts God has refined for righteousness. They will have forgiveness and a great reward.

Manners with the Prophet 3)
Respect Privacy

4. Indeed, most of those who call out to you ʿO Prophetʾ from outside ʿyourʾ private quarters have no understanding ʿof

---

1054 This passage and the next should be understood in their historical context. The Muslims were urged to be firm with the Arab pagans and their allies who were at war with the Muslims at that time. Otherwise, Islam encourages Muslims to treat peaceful non-Muslims with kindness and fairness. *See* 60:8-9.

1055 Prostration means lying down on one's face (i.e., touching the ground with the forehead and nose while resting on knees and flat palms of both hands) as an act of prayer and submission to God.

1056 In Deuteronomy 33:1-3, ʿMoses proclaimed:ʾ "The Lord came from Sinai. Rising from Seir upon us, he shone forth from Mount Paran, accompanied by a myriad of his holy ones, with flaming fire from his right hand for them. Indeed, lover of people, all of his holy ones are in your control. They gather at your feet to do as you have instructed. [*sic*]" Paran is a mountain in Mecca.

1057 In Matthew 13:3-9, "ʿJesusʾ spoke many things to them in parables, saying, "Behold, the sower went out to sow. ... ʿA seedʾ fell on the good soil and yielded a crop, some a hundredfold, some sixty, and some thirty. "He who has ears, let him hear."ʾ Or the parable of the growing seed in Mark 4:26-28.

1058 *See* the first footnote for 48:29.

1059 There is also a different interpretation: "... nor call him ʿby his nameʾ as you call one another." In other words, Do not say, ʿO Muḥammad.ʾ Rather, say, ʿO Prophet.ʾ

manners".[1060] **5.** Had they been patient until you could come out to them, it would have certainly been better for them. And God is All-Forgiving, Most Merciful.

Social Etiquette 1) Verifying News

6. O believers, if an evildoer brings you any news, verify ʿit' so you do not harm people unknowingly, becoming regretful for what you have done.[1061] **7.** And keep in mind that God's Messenger is ʿstill' in your midst. If he were to yield to you in many matters, you would surely suffer ʿthe consequences'.[1062] But God has endeared faith to you, making it appealing in your hearts. And He has made disbelief, rebelliousness, and disobedience detestable to you. Those are the ones rightly guided. **8.** ʿThis is' a bounty and a blessing from God. And God is All-Knowing, All-Wise.

Social Etiquette 2) Sense of Brotherhood

9. And if two groups of believers fight each other, then make peace between them. But if one of them transgresses against the other, then fight against the transgressing group until they ʿare willing to' submit to the rule of God. If they do so, then make peace between both ʿgroups' in all fairness and act justly. Surely God loves those who uphold justice. **10.** The believers are but one brotherhood, so make peace between your brothers. And be mindful of God so you may be shown mercy.

Social Etiquette 3) Respect for All

11. O believers! Do not let some ʿmen' ridicule others, they may be better than them, nor let ʿsome' women ridicule other women, they may be better than them. Do not defame one another, nor call each other by offensive nicknames. How evil it is to act rebelliously after having faith! And whoever does not repent, it is they who are the ʿtrue' wrongdoers. **12.** O believers! Avoid many suspicions, ʿfor' indeed, some suspicions are sinful. And do not spy, nor backbite one another. Would any of you like to eat the flesh of their dead brother? You would despise that![1063] And fear God. Surely God is ʿthe' Accepter of Repentance, Most Merciful.

Social Etiquette 4) Equality

13. O humanity! Indeed, We created you from a male and a female, and made you into peoples and tribes so that you may ʿget to' know one another. Surely the most noble of you in the sight of God is the most righteous among you. God is truly All-Knowing, All-Aware.[1064]

Actions Speak Louder than Words

14. ʿSome of' the nomadic Arabs say, "We believe." Say, ʿO Prophet,' "You have not believed. But say, 'We have submitted,' for faith has not yet entered your hearts.[1065] But if you obey God and His Messenger ʿwholeheartedly', He will not discount anything from ʿthe reward of' your deeds. God is truly All-Forgiving, Most Merciful." **15.** The

---

1060 A group from the tribe of Bani Tamîm came to see the Prophet while he was taking a nap in the afternoon. They stood outside the homes of his wives and started calling him out loud.

1061 Al-Walîd ibn 'Uqbah ibn Abi Mu'aiṭ was sent by the Prophet to collect alms-tax from Bani Al-Muṣṭaliq. They went out to receive Al-Walîd but he assumed they wanted to harm him. Therefore, he quickly returned to the Prophet with the bad news so he would punish them. Shortly after, a delegation from Bani Al-Muṣṭaliq came to clarify the misunderstanding.

1062 Or things would have been difficult for you.

1063 Backbiting people is likened to eating their dead bodies. So if eating someone's flesh is detestable, then backbiting them is no different.

1064 The Prophet is reported in a ḥadîth collected by Imâm Aḥmed to have said, "O humanity! Your Lord is one, and your ancestry is one. No Arab is superior to a non-Arab, nor is any non-Arab superior to any Arab. No white is superior to any black, nor is any black superior to any white except on account of their righteousness."

1065 The verse makes a distinction between Islam (the declaration of accepting the faith, then performing Islamic duties such as prayers and fasting) and Îmân (a higher state of Islam, which means to embrace the faith wholeheartedly). This distinction is very clear in a famous narration from the Prophet, commonly known as the Ḥadîth of Gabriel.

'true' believers are only those who believe in God and His Messenger—never doubting—and strive with their wealth and their lives in the cause of God. They are the ones true in faith. **16.** Say, "Do you inform God of your faith, when God 'already' knows whatever is in the heavens and whatever is on the earth? And God has 'perfect' knowledge of all things." **17.** they regard their acceptance

of Islam as a favour to you. Tell 'them, O Prophet', "Do not regard your Islam as a favour to me. Rather, it is God Who has done you a favour by guiding you to the faith, if 'indeed' you are faithful. **18.** Surely God knows the unseen of the heavens and earth. And God is All-Seeing of what you do."

50. Qāf *(Qāf)*

Since the previous chapter primarily addresses the believers, this chapter mainly talks about the disbelievers—particularly the deniers of resurrection. References are made to earlier destroyed deniers and God's infinite power to prove His ability to create and resurrect. The deniers of resurrection are told what to expect after death and judgment. The Prophet is urged to be steadfast. The certainty of the Hereafter is emphasized both at the end of this chapter and the beginning of the next.

In the Name of God—the Most Compassionate, Most Merciful

Pagan Denial of Resurrection

1. *Qāf.* By the glorious Quran! **2.** 'All will be resurrected,' yet the deniers are astonished that a warner has come to them from among themselves 'warning of resurrection'. So the disbelievers say, "This is an astonishing thing! **3.** 'Will we be returned to life,' when we are dead and reduced to dust? Such a return is impossible." **4.** We certainly know what the earth consumes of them 'after their death', and with us is a well-preserved Record.[1066] **5.** In fact, they reject the truth when it has come to them, so they are in a confused state.[1067]

God's Power to Create

6. Have they not then looked at the sky above them: how We built it and adorned

it 'with stars', leaving it flawless? **7.** As for the earth, We spread it out and placed upon it firm mountains, and produced in it every type of pleasant plant— **8.** 'all as' an insight and a reminder to every servant who turns 'to God'. **9.** And We send down blessed rain from the sky, bringing forth gardens and grains for harvest, **10.** and towering palm trees 'loaded' with clustered fruit, **11.** 'as' a provision for 'Our' servants. And with this 'rain' We revive a lifeless land. Similar is the emergence 'from the graves'.

Deniers Before Arab Pagans

12. Before them, the people of Noah denied 'the truth,' as did the people of the Water-pit,[1068] Thamûd, **13.** 'Âd, Pharaoh, the kinfolk of Lot, **14.** the residents of the

---

1066 Or a Record preserving 'everything'.

1067 Meaning, they are confused about the Prophet: some say he is a poet, some say he is a fabricator, while others say he is insane. They also rejected the Quran as poetry, magic, or ancient fables.

1068 *Ar-Rass* means "well" or "water-pit". This refers to a pagan people, along with Midian, to whom God sent Prophet Shu'aib.

Forest,[1069] and the people of Tubba'.[1070] Each rejected 'their' messenger, so My warning was fulfilled.

God's Power to Resurrect and Know All

15. Were We incapable of creating 'them' the first time? In fact, they are in doubt about 'their' re-creation. 16. Indeed, 'it is' We 'Who' created humankind and 'fully' know what their souls whisper to them, and We are closer to them than 'their' jugular vein. 17. As the two recording-angels—'one' sitting to the right, and 'the other to' the left—note 'everything', 18. not a word does a person utter without having a 'vigilant' observer ready 'to write it down'.[1071]

Bad News for the Deniers

19. 'Ultimately,' with the throes of death will come the truth.[1072] This is what you were trying to escape! 20. And the Trumpet will be blown.[1073] This is the Day 'you were' warned of. 21. Each soul will come forth with an angel to drive it and another to testify. 22. 'It will be said to the denier,' "You were totally heedless of this. Now We have lifted this veil of yours, so Today your sight is sharp!" 23. And one's accompanying-angel will say, "Here is the record ready with me." 24. 'It will be said to both angels,' "Throw into Hell every stubborn disbeliever, 25. withholder of good, transgressor, and doubter, 26. who set up another god with God. So cast them into the severe punishment."

The Misleaders and the Misled

27. One's 'devilish' associate will say, "Our Lord! I did not make them transgress. Rather, they were far astray 'on their own'." 28. God will respond, "Do not dispute in My presence, since I had already given you a warning. 29. My Word cannot be changed,[1074] nor am I unjust to 'My' creation." 30. 'Beware of' the Day We will ask Hell, "Are you full 'yet'?" And it will respond, "Are there any more?"

Good News for the Righteous

31. And Paradise will be brought near to the righteous, not far off. 32. 'And it will be said to them,' "This is what you were promised, for whoever 'constantly' turned 'to God' and kept up 'His commandments'— 33. who were in awe of the Most Compassionate without seeing 'Him',[1075] and have come with a heart turning 'only to Him'. 34. Enter it in peace. This is the Day of eternal life!" 35. There they will have whatever they desire, and with Us is 'even' more.[1076]

Warning to Meccan Pagans

36. 'Imagine' how many peoples We destroyed before them, who were far mightier than them. Then 'when the torment came,' they 'desperately' sought refuge in the land. 'But' was there any escape? 37. Surely in this is a reminder for whoever has a 'mindful' heart and lends an attentive ear.

Did God Get Tired?

38. Indeed, We created the heavens and the earth and everything in between in six

---

1069 The people of Shu'aib.
1070 Tubba' Al-Ḥimiari was an ancient righteous Yemeni king whose people persisted in disbelief and were destroyed, although they were superior to the Meccans in strength and manpower.
1071 The angel to the right records the good deeds of each person, while the one to the left records every evil deed. They always accompany the person at all times, except when one uses the toilet or is intimate with their spouse.
1072 When a denier dies, they will realize that resurrection, judgment, Paradise, and Hell are all true.
1073 This is the second blow which will cause all to come back to life for judgment.
1074 Meaning, the decree to punish wicked humans and jinn (see 11:119 and 32:13).
1075 This can also mean that they are in awe of their Lord as much in private as they are in public.
1076 i.e., looking at the Face of the Almighty (see 10:26 and 75:22-23).

Days,[1077] and We were not ʿevenʾ touched with fatigue.[1078] **39.** So be patient ʿO Prophetʾ with what they say. And glorify the praises of your Lord before sunrise and before sunset. **40.** And glorify Him during part of the night[1079] and after the prayers.

Reassuring the Prophet

41. And listen! On the Day the caller will call out from a near place, **42.** the Day all will hear the ʿmightyʾ Blast in ʿallʾ truth,[1080]

that will be the Day of emergence ʿfrom the gravesʾ. **43.** It is certainly We Who give life and cause death. And to Us is the final return. **44.** ʿBeware ofʾ the Day the earth will split open, letting them rush forth. That will be an easy gathering for Us. **45.** We know best what they say. And you ʿO Prophetʾ are not ʿthereʾ to compel them ʿto believeʾ. So remind with the Quran ʿonlyʾ those who fear My warning.

51. Scattering Winds *(Aẓ-Ẓâriyât)*

Like the previous chapter, this Meccan chapter makes the case for the Resurrection, citing some of God's natural signs in the universe to prove His ability to bring the dead back life. Several examples are given of the deniers of judgment who were destroyed, which contrast with the reward of the believers. The Prophet is urged to carry on reminding. Both the end of this chapter and the beginning of the next pose a warning of the Day of Judgment.

In the Name of God—the Most Compassionate, Most Merciful

Judgment Is Inevitable

1. By the winds scattering ʿdustʾ, **2.** and ʿthe cloudsʾ loaded with rain, **3.** and ʿthe ships'ʾ gliding with ease, **4.** and ʿthe angels'ʾ administering affairs by ʿGod'sʾ command! **5.** Indeed, what you are promised is true. **6.** And the Judgment will certainly come to pass.

Warning to the Deniers

7. ʿAndʾ by the heavens in their marvellous design![1081] **8.** Surely you are ʿlostʾ in conflicting views ʿregarding the truthʾ.[1082]

9. Only those ʿdestined to beʾ deluded are turned away from it.[1083] **10.** Condemned are the liars— **11.** those who are ʿsteepedʾ in ignorance, totally heedless. **12.** They ask ʿmockinglyʾ, "When is this Day of Judgment?" **13.** ʿIt isʾ the Day they will be tormented over the Fire. **14.** ʿThey will be told,ʾ "Taste your torment! This is what you sought to hasten."

Good News for the Devout

15. Indeed, the righteous will be amid Gardens and springs, **16.** ʿjoyfullyʾ receiving

---

1077 See footnote for 7:54.
1078 Some scholars believe this verse comes in response to Exodus 31:17, which says, "The Lord made the heavens and the earth in six days, but on the seventh day He rested and was refreshed."
1079 This verse refers to the times of the five daily prayers.
1080 See footnote for 50:20.
1081 Or "By the heavens with their marvellous orbits."
1082 See footnote for 50:5.
1083 Other possible translations: 1. "... by which the deluded are turned away." 2. "Whoever is turned away from it is ʿtrulyʾ deluded."

what their Lord will grant them. Before this ˹reward˺ they were truly good-doers ˹in the world˺: 17. they used to sleep only little in the night, 18. and pray for forgiveness before dawn.[1084] 19. And in their wealth there was a rightful share ˹fulfilled˺ for the beggar and the poor.

God's Signs in Creation

20. There are ˹countless˺ signs on earth for those with sure faith, 21. as there are within yourselves. Can you not see? 22. In heaven is your sustenance and whatever you are promised. 23. Then by the Lord of heaven and earth! ˹All˺ this is certainly as true as ˹the fact that˺ you can speak!

Abraham Visited by Angels

24. Has the story of Abraham's honoured guests reached you ˹O Prophet˺? 25. ˹Remember˺ when they entered his presence and greeted ˹him with˺, "Peace!" He replied, "Peace ˹be upon you˺!" ˹Then he said to himself,˺ ˹"These people must be strangers!" 26. Then he slipped off to his family and brought a fat ˹roasted˺ calf,[1085] 27. and placed it before them, asking, "Will you not eat?" 28. ˹They did not eat,˺ so he grew fearful of them.[1086] They reassured ˹him˺, "Do not be afraid," and gave him good news of a knowledgeable son.[1087] 29. Then his wife came forward with a cry, clasping her forehead ˹in astonishment˺, exclaiming, ˹"A baby from˺ a barren, old woman!" 30. They replied, "Such has your Lord decreed. He is truly the All-Wise, All-Knowing."

Destruction of the People of Lot

31. ˹Later,˺ Abraham asked, "What is your mission, O messenger-angels?" 32. They

replied, "We have actually been sent to a wicked people, 33. to send upon them stones of ˹baked˺ clay, 34. marked by your Lord for the transgressors." 35. Then ˹before the torment˺ We evacuated the believers from the city. 36. But We only found one family that had submitted ˹to God˺.[1088] 37. And We have left a sign there[1089] ˹as a lesson˺ for those who fear the painful punishment.

Destruction of Pharaoh's People

38. And in ˹the story of˺ Moses ˹was another lesson,˺ when We sent him to Pharaoh with compelling proof, 39. but Pharaoh was carried away by his power, saying ˹of Moses˺, "A magician or a madman!" 40. So We seized him and his soldiers, casting them into the sea while he was blameworthy.[1090]

Destruction of the People of Hûd

41. And in ˹the story of˺ 'Âd ˹was another lesson,˺ when We sent against them the devastating wind.[1091] 42. There was nothing it came upon that it did not reduce to ashes.

Destruction of the People of Ṣâliḥ

43. And in ˹the story of˺ Thamûd ˹was another lesson,˺ when they were told, "Enjoy yourselves ˹only˺ for a ˹short˺ while."[1092] 44. Still they persisted in defying the commands of their Lord, so they were overtaken by a ˹mighty˺ blast while they were looking on. 45. Then they were not able to rise up, nor were they helped.

Destruction of the People of Noah

46. And the people of Noah ˹had also been destroyed˺ earlier. They were truly a rebellious people.

1084 Optional prayers before dawn are recommended, and are more likely to be accepted.

1085 Abraham did not want his guests to know that he was going to prepare a meal for them so they would not ask him not to.

1086 As mentioned in 11:69-70, the angels came to Abraham in the form of men and when he offered them food, they did not eat. In ancient Middle Eastern culture, if a guest refused to eat the food provided by their host, it was a sign of ill-will.

1087 Prophet Isaac.

1088 Lot and his two daughters.

1089 The ruins of Sodom.

1090 Because of his arrogance and disbelief.

1091 lit., 'a barren wind,' since the wind was not productive—it did not carry rain or fertilize trees.

1092 Meaning, you have only three days to live. See 11:65.

God's Power of Creation

47. We built the universe with ˹great˺ might, and We are certainly expanding ˹it˺. **48.** As for the earth, We spread it out. How superbly did We smooth it out![1093] **49.** And We created pairs of all things[1094] so perhaps you would be mindful.

Wake-up Call to the Deniers

50. So ˹proclaim, O Prophet˺: "Flee to God! I am truly sent by Him with a clear warning to you. **51.** And do not set up another god with God. I am truly sent by Him with a clear warning to you."

Earlier Deniers

52. Similarly, no messenger came to those before them without being told: "A magician or a madman!" **53.** Have they passed this ˹cliché˺ down to one another? In fact, they have ˹all˺ been a transgressing people. **54.** So ˹now˺ turn away from them ˹O

Prophet˺, for you will not be blamed.[1095] **55.** But ˹continue to˺ remind. For certainly reminders benefit the believers.

The Purpose of Life

56. I did not create jinn and humans except to worship Me. **57.** I seek no provision from them, nor do I need them to feed Me. **58.** Indeed, God ˹alone˺ is the Supreme Provider—Lord of all Power, Ever Mighty.

Warning to the Deniers

59. The wrongdoers will certainly have a share ˹of the torment˺ like that of their predecessors. So do not let them ask Me to hasten ˹it˺. **60.** Woe then to the disbelievers when they face their Day which they are warned of!

༄

52. Mount Ṭûr *(Aṭ-Ṭûr)*

This Meccan chapter takes its name from verse 1, where God swears by Mount Ṭûr, among other things, that the Day of Judgment is inevitable. The punishment of those skeptical of judgment is described, followed by a detailed description of the reward of the believers along with their offspring (verses17-28). Atheism is also rejected (verses 35-36). The Prophet is reassured of God's support, while the pagan beliefs and arguments are refuted both in this chapter and the next.

In the Name of God—the Most Compassionate, Most Merciful

Judgment Is the Truth

1. By Mount Ṭûr![1096] **2.** And by the Book written **3.** on open pages ˹for all to read˺![1097] **4.** And by the ˹Sacred˺ House frequently visited![1098] **5.** And by the canopy raised ˹high˺! **6.** And by the seas set on fire![1099] **7.** Indeed,

---

1093 The globe was spread out to accommodate God's creation. The spherical shape of the earth is expressed in 39:5.
1094 For example, male and female, sweet and bitter, day and night, plains and mountains, heat and cold, light and darkness.
1095 Since you have already delivered the message clearly.
1096 Where Moses communicated with God.
1097 i.e., the Quran.
1098 This is either the Sacred House in Mecca, which is frequented by pilgrims, or a sanctuary in Heaven, which is frequented by angels.
1099 The seas and oceans will be on fire on Judgment Day.

the punishment of your Lord will come to pass— 8. none will avert it— 9. on the Day the heavens will be shaken violently, 10. and the mountains will be blown away entirely.

Horrors Awaiting the Deniers

11. Then woe on that Day to the deniers— 12. those who amuse themselves with falsehood! 13. ʿIt isʾ the Day they will be fiercely shoved into the Fire of Hell. 14. ʿThey will be told,ʾ "This is the Fire which you used to deny. 15. Is this magic, or do you not see? 16. Burn in it! It is the same whether you endure ʿitʾ patiently or not.[1100] You are only rewarded for what you used to do."

Pleasures Awaiting the Faithful

17. Indeed, the righteous will be in Gardens and bliss, 18. enjoying whatever their Lord will have granted them. And their Lord will have protected them from the torment of the Hellfire. 19. ʿThey will be told,ʾ "Eat and drink happily for what you used to do." 20. They will be reclining on thrones, ʿneatlyʾ lined up ʿfacing each otherʾ. And We will pair them to maidens with gorgeous eyes. 21. As for those who believe and whose descendants follow them in faith, We will elevate their descendants to their rank, never discounting anything ʿof the rewardʾ of their deeds. Every person will reap only what they sowed.[1101] 22. And We will ʿcontinuallyʾ provide them with whatever fruit or meat they desire. 23. They will pass around to each other a drink ʿof pure wine,ʾ which leads to no idle talk or sinfulness. 24. And they will be waited on by their youthful servants like spotless pearls.

Remembering Past Lives in Paradise

25. They will turn to one another inquisitively.[1102] 26. They will say, "Before ʿthis rewardʾ we used to be in awe ʿof Godʾ in the midst of our people. 27. So God has graced us and protected us from the torment of ʿHell'sʾ scorching heat. 28. Indeed, we used to call upon Him ʿaloneʾ before. He is truly the Most Kind, Most Merciful."

Why Do Meccans Deny the Truth?

29. So ʿcontinue toʾ remind ʿall, O Prophetʾ. For you, by the grace of your Lord, are not a fortune-teller or a madman. 30. Or do they say, "ʿHe isʾ a poet, for whom we ʿeagerlyʾ await an ill-fate!"? 31. Say, "Keep waiting! I too am waiting with you." 32. Or do their ʿintelligentʾ minds prompt them to this ʿparadoxʾ?[1103] Or are they ʿjustʾ a transgressing people? 33. Or do they say, "He made this ʿQuranʾ up!"? In fact, they have no faith. 34. Let them then produce something like it, if what they say is true![1104] 35. Or were they created by nothing, or are they ʿtheir ownʾ creators? 36. Or did they create the heavens and the earth? In fact, they have no certainty. 37. Or do they possess the treasuries of your Lord, or are they in control ʿof everythingʾ? 38. Or do they have a stairway, by which they eavesdrop ʿon the heavensʾ? Then let those who do so bring a compelling proof. 39. Or does He have daughters ʿas you claimʾ, while you ʿprefer toʾ have sons?[1105] 40. Or are you ʿO Prophetʾ asking them for a reward ʿfor the messageʾ so that they are overburdened by debt? 41. Or do they have access to ʿthe Record inʾ the unseen, so they copy it ʿfor all to seeʾ? 42. Or do they intend to scheme ʿagainst the Prophetʾ? Then

---

1100 One gets the reward for being patient in difficult times in this world. As for the Hereafter, those who suffer patiently in Hell will not be rewarded for their patience.
1101 Meaning, no one will carry the burden of another's sins.
1102 It is assumed that they will ask each other about their lives in the world and what led them to Paradise.
1103 The pagan leaders claimed to be Mecca's most intelligent minds. So this verse questions their intelligence, arguing that the Prophet cannot be a madman and a poet at the same time.
1104 Arab pagans were challenged in the Quran to produce its equivalent (52:34), or ten chapters (11:13), or at least one chapter (2:23), but the challenge has never been met.
1105 See footnote for 37:149.

it is the disbelievers who will fall victim to ˹their˺ schemes. **43.** Or do they have a god other than God? Glorified is God far above what they associate ˹with Him˺!

Reassuring the Prophet

44. If they were to see a ˹deadly˺ piece of the sky fall down ˹upon them˺, still they would say, "˹This is just˺ a pile of clouds." **45.** So leave them until they face their Day in which they will be struck dead— **46.** the Day their scheming will be of no benefit to them whatsoever, nor will they be helped.

47. Also, the wrongdoers will certainly have another torment before that ˹Day˺, but most of them do not know.[1106] **48.** So be patient with your Lord's decree, for you are truly under Our ˹watchful˺ Eyes. And glorify the praises of your Lord when you rise. **49.** And glorify Him during part of the night and at the fading of the stars.

---

53. The Stars *(An-Najm)*

This Meccan chapter takes its name from the reference to the fading of the stars in the first verse (as well as the last verse of the previous chapter). The divine source of the Prophet's message is emphasized, followed by reference to his ascension to heaven during the Night Journey (see the introduction to Chapter 17). The pagans are condemned for associating idols with God in worship and for claiming that the angels are God's daughters. Manifestations of God's infinite power are cited to prove His ability to resurrect. Both the end of this chapter and the beginning of the next stress the imminence of the Hour.

In the Name of God—the Most Compassionate, Most Merciful

The Prophet's Encounter with Gabriel

1. By the stars when they fade away! **2.** Your fellow man[1107] is neither misguided nor astray. **3.** Nor does he speak of his own whims. **4.** It is only a revelation sent down ˹to him˺. **5.** He has been taught by one ˹angel˺ of mighty power[1108] **6.** and great perfection, who once rose to ˹his˺ true form[1109] **7.** while on the highest point above the horizon, **8.** then he approached ˹the Prophet˺, coming so close **9.** that he was only two arms-lengths away or even less.[1110] **10.** Then God revealed to His servant what He revealed ˹through Gabriel˺. **11.** The ˹Prophet's˺ heart did not doubt what he saw. **12.** How can you ˹O pagans˺ then dispute with him regarding what he saw? **13.** And he certainly saw that ˹angel descend˺ a second time **14.** at the Lote Tree of

---

1106 i.e., famine, droughts, or the defeat at the Battle of Badr (*see* 32:21). The Battle of Badr took place in the 15th year of the Prophet's mission. The previous passage poses fifteen questions to the Meccan pagans before warning them in this passage.
1107 Muḥammad.
1108 The angel Gabriel.
1109 Gabriel used to come to the Prophet in a human form. But he appeared to him twice in his angelic form: once at the beginning of the Prophet's mission (when the angel manifested himself, filling the horizon, the Prophet lost his consciousness), and another time during the Prophet's Night Journey to the seventh heaven to receive the order to pray directly from God (*see* 17:1).
1110 lit., he was only two bow-draws away.

the most extreme limit 'in the seventh heaven'— **15.** near which is the Garden of 'Eternal' Residence— **16.** while the Lote Tree was overwhelmed with 'heavenly' splendours! **17.** The 'Prophet's' sight never wandered, nor did it overreach. **18.** He certainly saw some of his Lord's greatest signs.[1111]

Wake-up Call to Pagans

19. Now, have you considered 'the idols of' *Lât* and *'Uzza,* **20.** and the third one, *Manât,* as well? **21.** Do you 'prefer to' have sons while 'you attribute' to Him daughters?[1112] **22.** Then this is 'truly' a biased distribution! **23.** These 'idols' are mere names that you and your forefathers have made up[1113]—a practice God has never authorized. They follow nothing but 'inherited' assumptions and whatever 'their' souls desire, although 'true' guidance has already come to them from their Lord. **24.** Or should every person 'simply' have whatever 'intercessors' they desire?[1114] **25.** In fact, to God 'alone' belongs this world and the next. **26.** 'Imagine' how many 'noble' angels are in the heavens! 'Even' their intercession would be of no benefit whatsoever, until God gives permission to whoever He wills and 'only for the people He' approves.

Are Angels God's Daughters?

27. Indeed, those who do not believe in the Hereafter label angels as female, **28.** although they have no knowledge 'in support' of this. They follow nothing but 'inherited' assumptions. And surely assumptions can in no way replace the truth. **29.** So turn away 'O Prophet' from whoever has shunned Our Reminder,[1115] only seeking the 'fleeting' life of this world.

30. This is the extent of their knowledge. Surely your Lord knows best who has strayed from His Way and who is 'rightly' guided.

God Knows Who Is Righteous

31. To God 'alone' belongs whatever is in the heavens and whatever is on the earth so that He may reward the evildoers according to what they did, and reward the good-doers with the finest reward[1116]— **32.** those who avoid major sins and shameful deeds, despite 'stumbling on' minor sins. Surely your Lord is infinite in forgiveness. He knew well what would become of you as He created you from the earth[1117] and while you were 'still' fetuses in the wombs of your mothers.[1118] So do not 'falsely' elevate yourselves. He knows best who is 'truly' righteous.

The One Who Returned to Disbelief[1119]

33. Have you seen the one who turned away 'from Islam,' **34.** and 'initially' paid a little 'for his salvation', and then stopped? **35.** Does he have the knowledge of the unseen so that he sees 'the Hereafter'? **36.** Or has he not been informed of what is in the Scripture of Moses, **37.** and 'that of' Abraham, who 'perfectly' fulfilled 'his covenant'? **38.** 'They state' that no soul burdened with sin will bear the burden of another, **39.** and that each person will only have what they endeavoured towards, **40.** and that 'the outcome of' their endeavours will be seen 'in their record', **41.** then they will be fully rewarded, **42.** and that to your Lord 'alone' is the ultimate return 'of all things'.

It Is All in God's Hands

43. Moreover, He is the One Who brings about joy and sadness.[1120] **44.** And He is

---

1111 The Prophet was taken to heaven to see some of God's magnificent signs. He only saw what he was told to see.
1112 *See* footnote for 52:39.
1113 Meaning, "You call them gods while in fact they are not gods."
1114 Arab pagans took these idols as intermediaries to intercede for them on the Day of Judgment (*see* 39:3)
1115 i.e., the Quran.
1116 i.e., Paradise.
1117 i.e., your father, Adam.
1118 *See* footnote for 31:34.
1119 This passage refers to Al-Walîd ibn Al-Mughîrah who initially accepted Islam, and then a man persuaded him to leave Islam, promising to be punished in his place in the Hereafter for a small fee in this world. Initially, Al-Walîd paid him some of the amount they had agreed upon then refused to pay the rest.
1120 lit., laughter and weeping.

the One Who gives life and causes death. **45.** And He created the pairs—males and females— **46.** from a sperm-drop when it is emitted. **47.** And it is upon Him to bring about re-creation. **48.** And He is the One Who enriches and impoverishes. **49.** And He alone is the Lord of Sirius.[1121] **50.** And He destroyed the first ˹people of˺ 'Âd, **51.** and ˹then˺ Thamûd,[1122] sparing no one. **52.** And before ˹that He destroyed˺ the people of Noah, who were truly far worse in wrongdoing and transgression. **53.** And ˹it was˺ He ˹Who˺ turned the cities ˹of Sodom and Gomorrah˺ upside down. **54.** How overwhelming was what covered ˹them˺!![1123] **55.** Now, which of your Lord's favours will you dispute?

Warning to Arab Pagans

56. This ˹Prophet˺ is a warner like earlier ones. **57.** The approaching ˹Hour˺ has drawn near. **58.** None but God can disclose it. **59.** Do you find this revelation astonishing, **60.** laughing ˹at it˺ and not weeping ˹in awe˺, **61.** while persisting in heedlessness? **62.** Instead, prostrate to God and worship ˹Him alone˺!

54. The Moon *(Al-Qamar)*

This Meccan chapter, which takes its name from the splitting of the moon mentioned in verse 1, criticizes the disbelievers for rejecting warnings of the fast-approaching Hour. The pagans are warned of a dreadful fate similar to that of earlier disbelievers, who were mentioned passingly in the previous chapter (53:50-54). The chapter concludes by announcing that the righteous will be honoured in the presence of the Almighty, which is the highlight of the next chapter.

In the Name of God—the Most Compassionate, Most Merciful

Warning to Meccan Deniers

1. The Hour has drawn near and the moon was split ˹in two˺.[1124] **2.** Yet, whenever they see a sign, they turn away,[1125] saying, "Same old magic!" **3.** They rejected ˹the truth˺ and followed their own desires— and every matter will be settled— **4.** even though the stories ˹of destroyed nations˺ that have already come to them are a sufficient deterrent. **5.** ˹This Quran is˺ profound ˹in˺ wisdom, but warnings are of no benefit ˹to them˺. **6.** So turn away from them ˹O

1124 The Meccan pagans challenged the Prophet to perform a miracle if he wanted them to believe in him. So, he split the moon for them as reported by several eyewitnesses, but still the pagans refused to believe, calling this miracle "sheer magic."

1125 A miracle (usually referred to as a 'sign' in the Quran) can be defined as an extraordinary event manifesting divine intervention in human affairs. Every prophet was given miracles to prove he was commissioned by God. Moses was given the miracle of the staff and many others. Jesus gave life to the dead and healed the blind and the leper. And Muḥammad received the Quran, a literary miracle, to challenge the masters of Arabic eloquence. The Prophet performed some other miracles such as splitting the moon, multiplying food and water, and healing some of his companions.

1121 A star worshipped by some ancient pagans.

1122 Also known as the second 'Âd.

1123 The stones of baked clay that were rained upon them (*see* 11:82-83).

54. The Moon (Al-Qamar)

Prophet'. 'And wait for' the Day 'when' the caller[1126] will summon 'them' for something horrifying.[1127] 7. With eyes downcast, they will come forth from the graves as if they were swarming locusts, 8. rushing towards the caller. The disbelievers will cry, "This is a difficult Day!"

The People of Noah

9. Before them, the people of Noah denied 'the truth' and rejected Our servant, calling 'him' insane. And he was intimidated. 10. So he cried out to his Lord, "I am helpless, so help 'me'!" 11. So We opened the gates of the sky with pouring rain, 12. and caused the earth to burst with springs, so the waters met for a fate already set. 13. We carried him on that 'Ark made' of planks and nails, 14. sailing under Our 'watchful' Eyes—a 'fair' punishment on behalf of the one 'they' denied. 15. We certainly left this[1128] as a sign. So is there anyone who will be mindful? 16. Then how 'dreadful' were My punishment and warnings! 17. And We have certainly made the Quran easy to remember. So is there anyone who will be mindful?

The People of Hûd

18. 'Âd 'also' rejected 'the truth'. Then how 'dreadful' were My punishment and warnings! 19. Indeed, We sent against them a furious wind,[1129] on a day of unrelenting misery, 20. that snatched people up, leaving them like trunks of uprooted palm trees. 21. Then how 'dreadful' were My punishment and warnings! 22. And We have certainly made the Quran easy to remember. So is there anyone who will be mindful?

The People of Şâliḥ

23. Thamûd rejected the warnings 'as well', 24. arguing, "How can we follow one 'av-

erage' human being from among us? We would then truly be misguided and insane. 25. Has the revelation been sent down 'only' to him out of 'all of' us? In fact, he is a boastful liar." 26. 'It was revealed to Şâliḥ,' "They will soon know who the boastful liar is. 27. We are sending the she-camel as a test for them. So watch them 'closely', and have patience. 28. And tell them that the 'drinking' water must be divided between them 'and her', each taking a turn to drink 'every other day'." 29. But they roused a companion of theirs, so he dared to kill 'her'. 30. Then how 'dreadful' were My punishment and warnings! 31. Indeed, We sent against them 'only' one 'mighty' blast, leaving them like the twigs of fence-builders. 32. And We have certainly made the Quran easy to remember. So is there anyone who will be mindful?

The People of Lot

33. The people of Lot 'also' rejected the warnings. 34. We unleashed upon them a storm of stones. As for 'the believers of' Lot's family, We delivered them before dawn 35. as a blessing from Us. This is how We reward whoever gives thanks. 36. He had already warned them of Our 'crushing' blow but they disputed the warnings. 37. And they even demanded his angel-guests from him,[1130] so We blinded their eyes. 'And they were told,' "Taste then My punishment and warnings!" 38. And indeed, by the early morning they were overwhelmed by an unrelenting torment. 39. 'Again they were told,' "Taste now My punishment and warnings!" 40. And We have certainly made the Quran easy to remember. So is there anyone who will be mindful?

The People of Pharaoh

41. And indeed, the warnings 'also' came to the people of Pharaoh. 42. 'But' they re-

---

1126 Angel Isrâfîl will blow the Trumpet, causing all to be raised from the dead for judgment.
1127 i.e., the Judgment.
1128 The Flood or the Ark.
1129 lit., a bitter and screaming wind.
1130 Who came in the form of handsome men.

jected all of Our signs, so We seized them with the ˹crushing˺ grip of the Almighty, Most Powerful.

Warning to Pagan Deniers

43. Now, are you ˹Meccan˺ disbelievers superior to those ˹destroyed peoples˺? Or have you ˹been granted˺ immunity ˹from punishment˺ in divine Books? **44.** Or do they say, "We are all ˹a˺ united ˹front˺, bound to prevail."? **45.** ˹Soon˺ their united front will be defeated and ˹forced to˺ flee.[1131] **46.** Better yet, the Hour is their appointed time—and the Hour will be most catastrophic and most bitter. **47.** Indeed, the wicked are ˹entrenched˺ in misguidance, and ˹are bound for˺ blazes. **48.** On the Day they will be dragged into the Fire on their faces, ˹they will be told,˺ "Taste the touch of Hell!"[1132] **49.** Indeed, We have created everything, perfectly preordained. **50.** Our command[1133] is but a single word,[1134] done in the blink of an eye. **51.** We have already destroyed the likes of you. So will any ˹of you˺ be mindful? **52.** Everything they have done is ˹listed˺ in ˹their˺ records. **53.** Every matter, small and large, is written ˹precisely˺.

Reward of the Righteous

54. Indeed, the righteous will be amid Gardens and rivers,[1135] **55.** at the Seat of Honour in the presence of the Most Powerful Sovereign.

55. The Most Compassionate *(Ar-Raḥmân)*

This Meccan chapter is a call to humans and jinn to acknowledge God's infinite blessings, hence the recurring question: "Then which of your Lord's favours will you both deny?" which is repeated thirty-one times. Life on earth will come to an end, ushering in the Day of Judgment, where people will be classified into three groups based on their deeds and consequent rewards: the disbelievers (verses 31-45), the best of the believers (verses 46-61), and the average believers (verses 62-78).

In the Name of God—the Most Compassionate, Most Merciful

God's Favours: 1) Speech

1. The Most Compassionate **2.** taught the Quran, **3.** created humanity, **4.** ˹and˺ taught them speech.

Favour 2) The Universe

5. The sun and the moon ˹travel˺ with precision. **6.** The stars and the trees bow down ˹in submission˺.[1136] **7.** As for the sky, He raised it ˹high˺, and set the balance ˹of justice˺ **8.** so that you do not defraud the scales. **9.** Weigh with justice, and do not give short measure.

Favour 3) Provisions

10. He laid out the earth for all beings. **11.** In it are fruit, palm trees with date

---

1132 *Saqar* is one of the names of Hell.
1133 To bring anything into being.
1134 "Be!" And it is!
1135 Rivers of water, milk, honey, and wine. *See* 47:15.
1136 lit., prostrate.

stalks, **12.** and grain with husks, and aromatic plants. **13.** Then which of your Lord's favours will you ˹humans and jinn˺ both deny?[1137]

Favour 4) Humans and Jinn

14. He created humankind from ˹sounding˺ clay like pottery, **15.** and created jinn from a ˹smokeless˺ flame of fire. **16.** Then which of your Lord's favours will you both deny?

Favour 5) Natural Marvels

17. ˹He is˺ Lord of the two easts and the two wests.[1138] **18.** Then which of your Lord's favours will you both deny? **19.** He merges the two bodies of ˹fresh and salt˺ water, **20.** yet between them is a barrier they never cross.[1139] **21.** Then which of your Lord's favours will you both deny? **22.** Out of both ˹waters˺ come forth pearls and coral. **23.** Then which of your Lord's favours will you both deny? **24.** To Him belong the ships with raised sails, sailing through the seas like mountains. **25.** Then which of your Lord's favours will you both deny?

Only God Is Eternal

26. Every being on earth is bound to perish. **27.** Only your Lord Himself,[1140] full of Majesty and Honour, will remain ˹for-

ever˺.[1141] **28.** Then which of your Lord's favours will you both deny?

All Stand In Need of God

29. All those in the heavens and the earth are dependent on Him. Day in and day out He has something to bring about.[1142] **30.** Then which of your Lord's favours will you both deny?

Punishment of the People of the Left[1143]

31. We will soon attend to you ˹for judgment˺, O two multitudes ˹of jinn and humans˺! **32.** Then which of your Lord's favours will you both deny? **33.** O assembly of jinn and humans! If you can penetrate beyond the realms of the heavens and the earth, then do so. ˹But˺ you cannot do that without ˹Our˺ authority. **34.** Then which of your Lord's favours will you both deny? **35.** Flames of fire and ˹molten˺ copper will be sent against you, and you will not be able to defend one another. **36.** Then which of your Lord's favours will you both deny? **37.** ˹How horrible will it be˺ when the heavens will split apart, becoming rose-red like ˹burnt˺ oil! **38.** Then which of your Lord's favours will you both deny? **39.** On that Day there will be no need for any human or jinn to be asked about their sins.[1144] **40.** Then which of your Lord's favours will you both deny? **41.** The

---

1137 This question is repeated thirty-one times in this chapter: eight times after reminders of God's favours, seven times in the passage talking about the punishment of the deniers of judgment (which is the number of the gates of Hell), and eight times in each of the two following passages talking about Paradise, which has eight gates.
1138 The two points of sunrise and sunset in the summer and the winter.
1139 *See* footnote for 25:53.
1140 lit., your Lord's Face. We believe that God has a Face, but not like ours. *See* the Introduction for details.
1141 Death is listed as one of God's favours since it puts an end to tyrants, ends the suffering of the oppressed, makes all people equal, ushers in judgment and the enforcement of justice, and leads the believers to eternal joy and peace in Paradise.
1142 Giving life and causing death, making some rich and others poor, elevating some and debasing others, etc.
1143 According to the next three passages (as well as the next chapter), people will be divided into three groups on Judgment Day; the foremost, the righteous who are always ahead of others in faith and goodness; the people of the right, the average believers who will receive their records of deeds with their right hands; and the people of the left, the disbelievers who will receive their records with their left hands.
1144 Since their sins are already known to God and written in perfect records, they will only be interrogated as a form of punishment.

wicked will be recognized by their appearance, then will be seized by 'their' forelocks and feet. **42.** Then which of your Lord's favours will you both deny? **43.** 'They will be told,' "This is the Hell which the wicked denied." **44.** They will alternate between its flames and scalding water. **45.** Then which of your Lord's favours will you both deny? [1145]

Reward of the Foremost Believers

46. And whoever is in awe of standing before their Lord will have two Gardens. **47.** Then which of your Lord's favours will you both deny? **48.** 'Both will be' with lush branches. **49.** Then which of your Lord's favours will you both deny? **50.** In each 'Garden' will be two flowing springs. **51.** Then which of your Lord's favours will you both deny? **52.** In each will be two types of every fruit. **53.** Then which of your Lord's favours will you both deny? **54.** Those 'believers' will recline on furnishings lined with rich brocade. And the fruit of both Gardens will hang within reach. **55.** Then which of your Lord's favours will you both deny? **56.** In both 'Gardens' will be maidens of modest gaze, who no human or jinn has ever touched before. **57.** Then which of your Lord's favours will you both deny? **58.** Those 'maidens' will be 'as elegant' as rubies and coral. **59.** Then which of your Lord's favours will you both deny?

60. Is there any reward for goodness except goodness? **61.** Then which of your Lord's favours will you both deny?

Reward of the People of the Right

62. And below these two 'Gardens' will be two others. **63.** Then which of your Lord's favours will you both deny? **64.** Both will be dark green. **65.** Then which of your Lord's favours will you both deny? **66.** In each will be two gushing springs. **67.** Then which of your Lord's favours will you both deny? **68.** In both will be fruit, palm trees, and pomegranates. **69.** Then which of your Lord's favours will you both deny? **70.** In all Gardens will be noble, pleasant mates. **71.** Then which of your Lord's favours will you both deny? **72.** 'They will be' maidens with gorgeous eyes, reserved in pavilions. **73.** Then which of your Lord's favours will you both deny? **74.** No human or jinn has ever touched these 'maidens' before.[1146] **75.** Then which of your Lord's favours will you both deny? **76.** All 'believers' will be reclining on green cushions and splendid carpets. **77.** Then which of your Lord's favours will you both deny? **78.** Blessed is the Name of your Lord, full of Majesty and Honour.

⚜

56. The Inevitable Event *(Al-Wâqi'ah)*

This Meccan chapter is identical to the previous one in classifying people into three groups on Judgment Day and discussing how God's blessings are taken for granted. These blessings should be seen as a proof of His ability to raise the dead for judgment.

1145 Warning of the punishment in Hell is listed as a favour just like the promise of the reward in Paradise. Think of this as a road sign: the latter is like a sign about food, gas, etc., and the former is like a cautionary sign about an accident ahead or something hazardous. Both signs benefit people.

1146 Before these righteous servants in Paradise.

56. The Inevitable Event (Al-Wâqi'ah)

Moreover, references are made to the creation of the human race, the divine nature of the Quran, and the horrors of the apocalypse. God is glorified in the last verse of this chapter and the first verse of the next chapter.

In the Name of God—the Most Compassionate, Most Merciful

The Three Groups on Judgment Day[1147]

1. When the Inevitable Event takes place, 2. then no one can deny it has come. 3. It will debase ˹some˺ and elevate ˹others˺.[1148] 4. When the earth will be violently shaken, 5. and the mountains will be crushed to pieces, 6. becoming scattered ˹particles of˺ dust, 7. you will ˹all˺ be ˹divided into˺ three groups: 8. the people of the right, how ˹blessed˺ will they be; 9. the people of the left, how ˹miserable˺ will they be; 10. and the foremost ˹in faith˺ will be the foremost ˹in Paradise˺.

1) The Foremost

11. They are the ones nearest ˹to God˺, 12. in the Gardens of Bliss. 13. ˹They will be˺ a multitude from earlier generations 14. and a few from later generations. 15. ˹All will be˺ on jewelled thrones, 16. reclining face to face. 17. They will be waited on by eternal youths 18. with cups, pitchers, and a drink ˹of pure wine˺ from a flowing stream, 19. that will cause them neither headache nor intoxication. 20. ˹They will also be served˺ any fruit they choose 21. and meat from any bird they desire. 22. And ˹they will have˺ maidens with gorgeous eyes, 23. like pristine pearls, 24. ˹all˺ as a reward for what they used to do. 25. There they will never hear any idle or sinful talk— 26. only good and virtuous speech.[1149]

2) People of the Right

27. And the people of the right—how ˹blessed˺ will they be! 28. ˹They will be˺ amid thornless lote trees, 29. clusters of bananas, 30. extended shade, 31. flowing water, 32. abundant fruit— 33. never out of season nor forbidden— 34. and elevated furnishings. 35. Indeed, We will have perfectly created their mates, 36. making them virgins, 37. loving and of equal age, 38. for the people of the right, 39. ˹who will be˺ a multitude from earlier generations 40. and a multitude from later generations.

3) People of the Left

41. And the people of the left—how ˹miserable˺ will they be! 42. ˹They will be˺ in scorching heat and boiling water, 43. in the shade of black smoke, 44. neither cool nor refreshing. 45. Indeed, before this ˹torment˺ they were spoiled by luxury, 46. and persisted in the worst of sin.[1150] 47. They used to ask ˹mockingly˺, "When we are dead and reduced to dust and bones, will we really be resurrected? 48. And our forefathers as well?" 49. Say, ˹O Prophet,˺ "Most certainly, earlier and later generations 50. will surely be gathered ˹together˺ for the appointed Day. 51. Then you, O misguided deniers, 52. will certainly eat from ˹the fruit of˺ the trees of *Zaqqûm*,[1151] 53. filling up ˹your˺ bellies with it. 54. Then on top of that you will drink boiling water— 55. and you will drink ˹it˺ like

1147 *See* footnote for verses 31-45 in the previous chapter.
1148 Unlike this world of sheer injustice, the Hereafter will put everyone in their right place. The righteous will be elevated in Paradise, while the wicked will be humiliated in Hell.
1149 Another possible translation: "only exchanging greetings of peace."
1150 i.e., associating others with God in worship and denying the resurrection and judgment.
1151 See footnote for 44:43.

thirsty camels do." **56.** This will be their accommodation on the Day of Judgment.

God's Power: 1) Creating Humans

57. It is We Who created you. Will you not then believe ʿin resurrectionʾ? **58.** Have you considered what you ejaculate? **59.** Is it you who create ʿa child out ofʾ it, or is it We Who do so? **60.** We have ordained death for ʿall ofʾ you, and We cannot be prevented **61.** from transforming and recreating you in forms unknown to you. **62.** You already know how you were first created. Will you not then be mindful?

2) Causing Plants to Grow

63. Have you considered what you sow? **64.** Is it you who cause it to grow, or is it We Who do so? **65.** If We willed, We could simply reduce this ʿharvestʾ to chaff, leaving you to lament, **66.** "We have truly suffered a ʿgreatʾ loss. **67.** In fact, we have been deprived ʿof our livelihoodʾ."

3) Bringing Rain down

68. Have you considered the water you drink? **69.** Is it you who bring it down from the clouds, or is it We Who do so? **70.** If We willed, We could make it salty. Will you not then give thanks?

4) Producing Fire from Trees

71. Have you considered the fire you kindle?[1152] **72.** Is it you who produce its trees, or is it We Who do so? **73.** We have made it ʿasʾ a reminder ʿof the Hellfireʾ and a provision for the travellers. **74.** So glorify the Name of your Lord, the Greatest.

Message to Quran Deniers

75. So I do swear by the positions of the stars— **76.** and this, if only you knew, is indeed a great oath— **77.** that this is truly a noble Quran, **78.** in a well-preserved Record,[1153] **79.** touched by none except the purified ʿangelsʾ.[1154] **80.** ʿIt isʾ a revelation from the Lord of all worlds. **81.** How can you then take this message lightly, **82.** and repay ʿGod forʾ your provisions with denial?[1155]

A Challenge to Deniers of the Hereafter

83. Why then ʿare you helplessʾ when the soul ʿof a dying personʾ reaches ʿtheirʾ throat, **84.** while you are looking on? **85.** And We are nearer to such a person than you, but you cannot see. **86.** Now, if you are not subject to Our Will ʿas you claimʾ, **87.** bring that soul back, if what you say is true.

Which of the Three Will You Be?

88. So, if the deceased is one of those brought near ʿto Usʾ, **89.** then ʿsuch a person will haveʾ serenity, fragrance,[1156] and a Garden of Bliss. **90.** And if the deceased is one of the people of the right, **91.** then ʿthey will be told,ʾ "Greetings to you from the people of the right." **92.** But if such person is one of the misguided deniers, **93.** then their accommodation will be boiling water ʿto drinkʾ **94.** and burning in Hellfire. **95.** Indeed, this is the absolute truth. **96.** So glorify the Name of your Lord, the Greatest.

1152 This verse refers to two types of Arabian trees, *markh* and *'afâr*, which produce fire when their green branches are rubbed together.
1153 See 43:4.
1154 This verse refutes the pagan claim that the Quran was sent down by devils (see 26:210-212). Based on this verse, many jurists maintain that a Muslim should perform ablutions before reading the Quran.
1155 Some pagans believed that rain was caused by some stars.
1156 lit., fragrant basil. Throughout the Quran, Paradise is described as being pleasant to the eye, the heart, and the ear. This verse emphasizes the scent as well.

57. Iron *(Al-Ḥadîd)*

This Medinian chapter, which takes its name from the reference to iron in verse 25, is an invitation to strive in God's cause and spend in His Way. Similar to the next chapter, a strong emphasis is placed on God's knowledge and power. It is made clear that God is able to revive faith in the hearts of the believers just as He can revive the earth after its death. The believers are advised regarding destiny and the life of this world, while the hypocrites are warned of the evil fate awaiting them. Some prophets are mentioned passingly before making a final invitation to the People of the Book to believe in God and His Prophet.

In the Name of God—the Most Compassionate, Most Merciful

God's Knowledge and Might

1. Whatever is in the heavens and the earth glorifies God, for He is the Almighty, All-Wise. 2. To Him belongs the kingdom of the heavens and the earth. He gives life and causes death. And He is Most Capable of everything. 3. He is the First and the Last, the Most High and Most Near,[1157] and He has ˹perfect˺ knowledge of all things. 4. He is the One Who created the heavens and the earth in six Days,[1158] then established Himself above the Throne. He knows whatever goes into the earth and whatever comes out of it, and whatever descends from the sky and whatever ascends into it. And He is with you wherever you are.[1159] For God is All-Seeing of what you do. 5. To Him belongs the kingdom of the heavens and the earth. And to God all matters are returned. 6. He merges the night into day and the day into night. And He knows best what is ˹hidden˺ in the heart.

Believe and Support God's Cause

7. Believe in God and His Messenger, and donate from what He has entrusted you with. So those of you who believe and donate will have a mighty reward.

Why Do You Not Believe?

8. Why do you not believe in God while the Messenger is inviting you to have faith in your Lord, although He has already taken your covenant,[1160] if you will ever believe. 9. He is the One Who sends down clear revelations to His servant to bring you out of darkness and into light. For indeed God is Ever Gracious and Most Merciful to you.

Why Do You Not Donate?

10. And why should you not spend in the cause of God, while God is the ˹sole˺ inheritor of the heavens and the earth? Those of you who donated and fought before the victory ˹over Mecca˺ are unparalleled. They are far greater in rank than those who donated and fought afterwards.[1161] Yet God has promised each a fine reward. And God is All-Aware of what you do.

1157 Another possible translation: "the Manifest ˹through His signs˺ and the Hidden ˹from His creation˺."
1158 *See* footnote for 7:54.
1159 By His knowledge.
1160 See 7:172.
1161 Prior to the victory over Mecca, Muslims were outnumbered and perceived as weak. Once Mecca surrendered to the Muslims, many tribes either accepted Islam or made peace agreements with the Muslim victors. Therefore, the believers who donated and strived at the time of hardship and weakness deserve more rewards than those who did so at the time of ease and prominence.

57. Iron (Al-Ḥadîd)

A Generous Reward for the Generous

11. Who is it that will lend to God a good loan which God will multiply ʿmany times overʾ for them, and they will have an honourable reward?[1162] **12.** On that Day you will see believing men and women with their light shining ahead of them and on their right. ʿThey will be told,ʾ "Today you have good news of Gardens, under which rivers flow, ʿfor youʾ to stay in forever. This is ʿtrulyʾ the ultimate triumph."

The Hypocrites Entrenched in Darkness

13. On that Day hypocrite men and women will beg the believers, "Wait for us so that we may have some of your light." It will be said ʿmockinglyʾ, "Go back ʿto the worldʾ and seek a light ʿthereʾ!" Then a ʿseparatingʾ wall with a gate will be erected between them. On the near side will be grace and on the far side will be torment.[1163] **14.** The tormented will cry out to those graced, "Were we not with you?" They will reply, "Yes ʿyou wereʾ. But you chose to be tempted ʿby hypocrisyʾ, ʿeagerlyʾ awaited ʿour demiseʾ, doubted ʿthe truthʾ, and were deluded by false hopes until God's decree ʿof your deathʾ came to pass. And ʿsoʾ the Chief Deceiver[1164] deceived you about God. **15.** So Today no ransom will be accepted from you ʿhypocritesʾ, nor from the disbelievers. Your home is the Fire—it is the ʿonlyʾ fitting place for you. What an evil destination!"

Hardened Hearts

16. Has the time not yet come for believers' hearts to be humbled at the remembrance of God and what has been revealed of the truth, and not be like those given the Scripture before—ʿthoseʾ who were spoiled for so long that their hearts became hardened. And many of them are ʿstillʾ rebellious.

17. Know that God revives the earth after its death.[1165] We have certainly made the signs clear for you so perhaps you will understand.

Reward of the Faithful

18. Indeed, those men and women who give in charity and lend to God a good loan will have it multiplied for them, and they will have an honourable reward.[1166] **19.** ʿAs forʾ those who believe in God and His messengers, it is they who are ʿtrulyʾ the people of truth. And the martyrs, with their Lord, will have their reward and their light. But ʿas forʾ those who disbelieve and reject Our signs, it is they who will be the residents of the Hellfire.

Fleeting Life vs. Eternal Life

20. Know that this worldly life is no more than play, amusement, luxury, mutual boasting, and competition in wealth and children. This is like rain that causes plants to grow, to the delight of the planters. But later the plants dry up and you see them wither, then they are reduced to chaff. And in the Hereafter there will be either severe punishment or forgiveness and pleasure of God, whereas the life of this world is no more than the delusion of enjoyment. **21.** ʿSoʾ compete with one another for forgiveness from your Lord and a Paradise as vast as the heavens and the earth, prepared for those who believe in God and His messengers. This is the favour of God. He grants it to whoever He wills. And God is the Lord of infinite bounty.

Everything Is Destined

22. No calamity ʿor blessingʾ occurs on earth or in yourselves without being ʿwrittenʾ in a Record before We bring it into being. This is certainly easy for God. **23.** ʿWe let you know thisʾ so that you neither grieve over what you have missed nor boast over what

---

1162 i.e., Paradise.
1163 This wall is said to be the barrier of *Al-A'râf* (or the heights) between Paradise and Hell. *See* 7:46-49.
1164 Satan.
1165 So it is easy for Him to soften your hearts as well.
1166 i.e., Paradise.

298

He has granted you. For God does not like whoever is arrogant, boastful— **24.** those who are stingy and promote stinginess among people. And whoever turns away ʿshould know thatˋ God ʿaloneˋ is truly the Self-Sufficient, Praiseworthy.

Prophets and Justice

25. Indeed, We sent Our messengers with clear proofs, and with them We sent down the Scripture and the balance ʿof justiceˋ so that people may administer justice. And We sent down iron with its great might, benefits for humanity, and means for God to prove who ʿis willing toˋ stand up for Him and His messengers without seeing Him. Surely God is All-Powerful, Almighty.

Noah and Abraham

26. And indeed, We sent Noah and Abraham and reserved prophethood and revelation for their descendants. Some of them are ʿrightlyˋ guided, while most are rebellious.

Jesus and His Followers

27. Then in the footsteps of these ʿprophetsˋ, We sent Our messengers, and ʿafter themˋ We sent Jesus, son of Mary, and granted him the Gospel, and instilled compassion and mercy into the hearts of his followers. As for monasticism, they made it up—We never ordained it for them—only seeking to please God, yet they did not ʿevenˋ observe it strictly. So We rewarded those of them who were faithful. But most of them are rebellious.

An Appeal to Jews and Christians

28. O people of faith! Fear God and believe in His Messenger. ʿAndˋ He will grant you a double share of His mercy, provide you with a light to walk in ʿon Judgment Dayˋ, and forgive you. For God is All-Forgiving, Most Merciful. **29.** ʿThis is soˋ that the People of the Book ʿwho deny the Prophetˋ may know that they do not have any control over God's grace, and that all grace is in God's Hands. He grants it to whoever He wills. For God is the Lord of infinite bounty.

58. The Pleading Woman *(Al-Mujâdilah)*

A companion named Khawlah bint Thaʿlabah had a disagreement with her husband, Aws ibn Aṣ-Ṣâmit, who then told her that she was as unlawful for him as the ẓahr (back) of his mother. This statement had been considered to be a form of divorce (known as ẓihâr) in Arabia. Khawlah came to the Prophet to ask for his opinion. He told her that he had not received any revelation in this regard, and that, based on tradition, she was divorced. She argued that she and her husband had children together who would suffer if their parents were separated. Then she started to plead to God as the Prophet repeated the same answer. Eventually, this Medinian chapter was revealed in response to her pleas, thereby abolishing this ancient practice. The chapter emphasizes God's infinite knowledge and overwhelming power, and makes it clear that those who ally themselves with God and comply with His orders are bound to prevail, whereas those who challenge Him and ally themselves with His enemies will be debased and vanquished. This concept is elaborated upon in the next chapter (verses 59:1-4 and 11-17).

those gifted with knowledge in rank. And God is All-Aware of what you do.

Charity Before Consulting the Prophet[1169]

12. O believers! When you consult the Messenger privately, give something in charity before your consultation. That is better and purer for you. But if you lack the means, then God is truly All-Forgiving, Most Merciful. 13. Are you afraid of spending in charity before your private consultations ˹with him˺? Since you are unable to do so, and God has turned to you in mercy, then ˹continue to˺ establish prayer, pay alms-tax, and obey God and His Messenger. And God is All-Aware of what you do.

Satan's Party

14. Have you not seen those ˹hypocrites˺ who ally themselves with a people with whom God is displeased? They are neither with you nor with them. And they swear to lies knowingly. 15. God has prepared for them a severe punishment. Evil indeed is what they do. 16. They have made their ˹false˺ oaths as a shield, hindering ˹others˺ from the cause of God. So they will suffer a humiliating punishment. 17. Neither their wealth nor children will be of any help to them against God whatsoever. It is they who will be the residents of the Fire. They will be there forever. 18. On the Day God resurrects them all, they will ˹falsely˺ swear to Him as they swear to you, thinking they have something to stand on. Indeed, it is they who are the ˹total˺ liars. 19. Satan has taken hold of them, causing them to forget the remembrance of God. They are the party of Satan. Surely Satan's party is bound to lose.

God's Party

20. ˹As for˺ those who defy God and His Messenger, they will definately be among the most debased. 21. God has decreed, "I and My messengers will certainly prevail." Surely God is All-Powerful, Almighty. 22. You will never find a people who ˹truly˺ believe in God and the Last Day loyal to those who defy God and His Messenger, even if they were their parents, children, siblings, or extended family. For those ˹believers˺, God has instilled faith in their hearts and strengthened them with a spirit from Him.[1170] He will admit them into Gardens under which rivers flow, to stay there forever. God is pleased with them and they are pleased with Him. They are the party of God. Indeed, God's party is bound to succeed.

༺◈༻

59. The Banishment *(Al-Ḥashr)*

This Medinian chapter takes its name from verse 2, which refers to the exile of the Jewish tribe of Banu An-Naḍîr from Medina for conspiring with the Meccan pagans to violate peace agreements with the Muslims. The hypocrites are condemned for their secret alliance with Banu An-Naḍîr. Some instructions are given regarding the distribution of the spoils of war. The chapter closes by stressing unwavering obedience to Almighty God, which is further emphasized at the beginning of the next chapter.

1169 Some companions used to ask the Prophet unnecessary and sometimes meaningless questions. For example: who their fathers were, where their lost animals were, and what they had in their pockets. Some would ask for new rulings that would probably make things difficult for some Muslims or even themselves. So this verse was revealed to cut down such practice. Eventually, the ruling was lifted in order not to make it difficult for people with good questions, who could not afford to give a charity.

1170 Spirit here can mean revelation, light, or help.

59. The Banishment (Al-Ḥashr)

In the Name of God—the Most Compassionate, Most Merciful

Banu An-Naḍîr Exiled

1. Whatever is in the heavens and whatever is on the earth glorifies God. For He is the Almighty, All-Wise. **2.** He is the One Who expelled the disbelievers of the People of the Book from their homes for ˈtheirˈ first banishment ˈeverˈ. You never thought they would go. And they thought their strongholds would put them out of God's reach. But ˈthe decree ofˈ God came upon them from where they never expected. And He cast horror into their hearts so they destroyed their houses with their own hands and the hands of the believers.[1171] So take a lesson ˈfrom thisˈ, O people of insight! **3.** Had God not decreed exile for them, He would have certainly punished them in this world. And in the Hereafter they will suffer the punishment of the Fire. **4.** This is because they defied God and His Messenger. And whoever defies God, then God is truly severe in punishment.

Ruling on Palm Trees and Gains

5. Whatever palm trees you ˈbelieversˈ cut down or left standing intact, it was ˈallˈ by God's Will, so that He might disgrace the rebellious.[1172] **6.** As for the gains God has turned over to His Messenger from them—you did not ˈevenˈ spur on any horse or camel for such gains. But God gives authority to His messengers over whoever He wills. For God is Most Capable of everything.

Distribution of Future Gains[1173]

7. As for gains granted by God to His Messenger from the people of ˈotherˈ lands, they are for God and the Messenger, his close relatives, orphans, the poor, and ˈneedyˈ travellers so that wealth may not merely circulate among your rich. Whatever the Messenger gives you, take it. And whatever he forbids you from, leave it. And fear God. Surely God is severe in punishment. **8.** ˈSome of the gains will beˈ for poor emigrants who were driven out of their homes and wealth, seeking God's bounty and pleasure, and standing up for God and His Messenger. They are the ones true in faith.

Excellence of the People of Medina[1174]

9. As for those who had settled in the city and ˈembracedˈ the faith before ˈthe arrival ofˈ the emigrants, they love whoever immigrates to them, never having a desire in their hearts for whatever ˈof the gainsˈ is given to the emigrants. They give ˈthe emigrantsˈ preference over themselves even though they may be in need. And whoever is saved from the selfishness of their own souls, it is they who are ˈtrulyˈ successful.

Later Believers

10. And those who come after them will pray, "Our Lord! Forgive us and our fellow believers who preceded us in faith, and do not allow bitterness into our hearts towards those who believe. Our Lord! Indeed, You are Ever Gracious, Most Merciful."

The Hypocrites and Banu An-Naḍîr

11. Have you ˈO Prophetˈ not seen the hypocrites who say to their fellow disbelievers from the People of the Book,[1175] "If you are expelled, we will certainly leave with you, and We will never obey anyone against

---

1171 The Prophet allowed Banu An-Naḍîr to carry whatever they could on their camels, so they removed the wooden pillars of their homes, causing them to collapse.

1172 The Prophet had instructed the Muslim army not to cut down trees, but some soldiers had to remove some palm trees to be able to enter the fort, to the dismay of Banu An-Naḍîr. When Muslims disagreed on that act, this verse was revealed.

1173 The verses here talk about the distribution of gains acquired without fighting. These gains are mostly distributed among the poor and the needy. As for the spoils of war, four-fifths of the spoils are distributed among the fighters. See 8:41.

1174 Commonly known as Al-Anṣâr (or the Helpers).

1175 Meaning, Banu An-Naḍîr.

you. And if you are fought against, we will surely help you."? But God bears witness that they are truly liars. **12.** Indeed, if they are expelled, the hypocrites will never leave with them. And if they are fought against, the hypocrites will never help them. And even if the hypocrites did so, they would certainly flee, then the disbelievers would be left with no help.

Cowardice of Both Groups

13. Indeed, there is more fear in their hearts for you ˹believers˺ than for God. That is because they are a people who do not comprehend. **14.** Even united, they would not ˹dare˺ fight against you except ˹from˺ within fortified strongholds or from behind walls. Their malice for each other is intense: you think they are united, yet their hearts are divided. That is because they are a people with no ˹real˺ understanding. **15.** They are ˹both just˺ like those who recently went down before them:[1176] they tasted the evil consequences of their doings. And they will suffer a painful punishment.

The Hypocrites Luring the Disbelievers

16. ˹They are˺ like Satan when he lures someone to disbelieve. Then after they have done so, he will say ˹on Judgment Day˺, "I have absolutely nothing to do with you. I truly fear God—the Lord of all worlds."[1177] **17.** So they will both end up in the Fire, staying there forever. That is the reward of the wrongdoers.

Judge Yourselves Before Judgment Day

18. O believers! Be mindful of God and let every soul look to what ˹deeds˺ it has sent forth for tomorrow.[1178] And fear God, ˹for˺ certainly God is All-Aware of what you do. **19.** And do not be like those who

forgot God, so He made them forget themselves. It is they who are ˹truly˺ rebellious. **20.** The residents of the Fire cannot be equal to the residents of Paradise. ˹Only˺ the residents of Paradise will be successful.

Impact of the Quran

21. Had We sent down this Quran upon a mountain, you would have certainly seen it humbled and torn apart in awe of God. We set forth such comparisons for people, ˹so˺ perhaps they may reflect.[1179]

God's Beautiful Names

22. He is God—there is no god ˹worthy of worship˺ except Him: Knower of the seen and unseen. He is the Most Compassionate, Most Merciful. **23.** He is God—there is no god except Him: the King, the Most Holy, the All-Perfect, the Source of Serenity, the Watcher ˹of all˺, the Almighty, the Supreme in Might,[1180] the Majestic. Glorified is God far above what they associate with Him ˹in worship˺! **24.** He is God: the Creator, the Inventor, the Shaper. He ˹alone˺ has the Most Beautiful Names. Whatever is in the heavens and the earth ˹constantly˺ glorifies Him. And He is the Almighty, All-Wise.

1176 This refers to the pagans of Mecca and the Jews of Banu Qainuqā' who were defeated a few months earlier at the Battle of Badr.
1177 *See* 14:22.
1178 i.e., the Hereafter.
1179 Meaning, that the hearts of the disbelievers are harder than the mountains concerning the Quran.
1180 *Jabbâr* comes from the root word *ja-ba-ra* which means to impose, support, or console. For example, *Jabîrah* means the cast that supports a broken bone. Hence, God is the One Whose Will cannot be resisted, and Who comforts those who are broken or oppressed.

60. The Test of Faith *(Al-Mumtaḥanah)*

This Medinian chapter was revealed prior to the Prophet's conquest of Mecca following the pagans' violation of the peace treaty they had signed with the Muslims at Ḥudaibiyah. Despite the Prophet's orders to keep this plan secret, a companion by the name of Ḥâṭib ibn Abi Balta'ah sent a warning letter to the Meccans, hoping that in turn they would protect his family—who were still in Mecca—in case the Muslims failed to enter the city. Soon the Prophet received a revelation about what Ḥâṭib did. The letter was intercepted, and Ḥâṭib was later forgiven. Mecca surrendered peacefully to the Muslims, and its residents were pardoned by the Prophet. Muslims are instructed to be loyal to God and fellow believers, following the example of Prophet Abraham (verses 4-6). The believers are not forbidden from courtesy to non-Muslims as long as they are not persecuting Muslims (verses 8-9). This chapter takes its name from testing the faith of women fleeing Mecca by asking them, for example, if they have emigrated for Islam or only to be separated from their pagan husbands (verse 10). Other instructions to the believers are given at the end of this chapter and the beginning of the next chapter.

In the Name of God—the Most Compassionate, Most Merciful

Allying with the Enemy

1. O believers! Do not take My enemies and yours as trusted allies, showing them affection even though they deny what has come to you of the truth. They drove the Messenger and yourselves out ˹of Mecca˺, simply for your belief in God, your Lord. If you ˹truly˺ emigrated[1181] to struggle in My cause and seek My pleasure, ˹then do not take them as allies,˺ disclosing secrets ˹of the believers˺ to the pagans out of affection for them, when I know best whatever you conceal and whatever you reveal. And whoever of you does this has truly strayed from the Right Way. **2.** If they gain the upper hand over you, they would be your ˹open˺ enemies, unleashing their hands and tongues to harm you, and wishing that you would abandon faith. **3.** Neither your relatives nor children will benefit you on Judgment Day—He will decide between you ˹all˺. For God is All-Seeing of what you do.

The Example of Abraham and His Followers

4. You already have an excellent example in Abraham and those with him, when they said to their people, "We totally dissociate ourselves from you and ˹shun˺ whatever ˹idols˺ you worship besides God. We reject you. The enmity and hatred that has arisen between us and you will last until you believe in God alone." The only exception is when Abraham said to his father, "I will seek forgiveness for you,'" adding, "but˺ I cannot protect you from God at all." ˹The believers prayed,˺ "Our Lord! In You we trust. And to You we ˹always˺ turn. And to You is the final return. **5.** Our Lord! Do not subject us to the persecution of the disbelievers. Forgive us, our Lord! You ˹alone˺ are truly the Almighty, All-Wise." **6.** You certainly have an excellent example in them for whoever has hope in God and the Last Day. But whoever turns away, then surely God ˹alone˺ is the Self-Sufficient, Praiseworthy.

1181 lit., come out ˹of Mecca˺.

Yesterday's Enemies, Tomorrow's Friends

7. 'In time,' God may bring about goodwill between you and those of them you 'now' hold as enemies. For God is Most Capable. And God is All-Forgiving, Most Merciful.

Kindness to Non-Muslims

8. God does not forbid you from dealing kindly and fairly with those who have neither fought nor driven you out of your homes. Surely God loves those who are fair. **9.** God only forbids you from befriending those who have fought you for 'your' faith, driven you out of your homes, or supported 'others' in doing so. And whoever takes them as friends, then it is they who are the 'true' wrongdoers.

Marriage of Female Emigrants

10. O believers! When the believing women come to you as emigrants,[1182] test their intentions—their faith is best known to God—and if you find them to be believers, then do not send them back to the disbelievers. These 'women' are not lawful 'wives' for the disbelievers, nor are the disbelievers lawful 'husbands' for them. 'But' repay the disbelievers whatever 'dowries' they had paid. And there is no blame on you if you marry these 'women' as long as you pay them their dowries. And do not hold on to marriage with poly-

theistic women.[1183] 'But' demand 'repayment of' whatever 'dowries' you had paid, and let the disbelievers do the same. That is the judgment of God—He judges between you. And God is All-Knowing, All-Wise.

When Dowry Is Not Repaid to Muslims

11. And if any of your wives desert you to the disbelievers, and later you take spoils from them, then pay those whose wives have gone, the equivalent of whatever 'dowry' they had paid. And be mindful of God, in Whom you believe.

Women Pledge Allegiance

12. O Prophet! When the believing women come to you, pledging to you that they will neither associate anything with God 'in worship', nor steal, nor fornicate, nor kill their children, nor falsely attribute 'illegitimate' children to their husbands,[1184] nor disobey you in what is right, then accept their pledge, and ask God to forgive them. Surely God is All-Forgiving, Most Merciful.

Do Not Ally with the Enemy

13. O believers! Do not ally yourselves with a people God is displeased with. They already have no hope for the Hereafter, just like the disbelievers lying in 'their' graves.

61. The 'Solid' Ranks *(Aṣ-Ṣaff)*

The believers are instructed to strive in God's cause in solid battle formations (verse 4), hence the name of this Medinian chapter. The disciples of Jesus, who stood up for God, are cited as an example for the believers to emulate. The believers are reassured that the truth will prevail despite the disbelievers' unrelenting plots against it. Those who stand up for God are promised great rewards in both worlds. The next chapter provides more instructions to the believers.

1182 According to the Treaty of Ḥudaibiyah (*see* footnote for 48:1-3), Muslims who chose to move to Mecca would not be returned to Muslims in Medina, and Meccan pagans who accepted Islam and chose to move to Medina would be returned to Mecca (except for women).
1183 Those who moved to Mecca to marry pagans.
1184 lit., nor come up with a falsehood they have forged between their own hands and legs.

61. The 'Solid' Ranks (Aṣ-Ṣaff)

In the Name of God—the Most Compassionate, Most Merciful

God Is Glorified by All

1. Whatever is in the heavens and whatever is on the earth glorifies God. For He 'alone' is the Almighty, All-Wise.

Do What You Say[1185]

2. O believers! Why do you say what you do not do? **3.** How despicable it is in the sight of God that you say what you do not do! **4.** Surely God loves those who fight in His cause in 'solid' ranks as if they were one concrete structure.

Moses and His People

5. 'Remember, O Prophet,' when Moses said to his people, "O my people! Why do you hurt me when you already know I am God's messenger to you?" So when they 'persistently' deviated, God caused their hearts to deviate. For God does not guide the rebellious people.

Jesus and the Israelites

6. And 'remember' when Jesus, son of Mary, said, "O children of Israel! I am truly God's messenger to you, confirming the Torah which came before me, and giving good news of a messenger after me whose name will be Aḥmad."[1186] Yet when the Prophet came to them with clear proofs, they said, "This is pure magic."

Rejecting Islam

7. Who does more wrong than the one who fabricates lies about God when invited to submit 'to Him'?[1187] For God does not guide the wrongdoing people. **8.** They wish to extinguish God's light with their mouths, but God will 'certainly' perfect His light, even to the dismay of the disbelievers. **9.** He is the One Who has sent His Messenger with 'true' guidance and the religion of truth, making it prevail over all others, even to the dismay of the polytheists.

A Profitable Bargain

10. O believers! Shall I guide you to an exchange that will save you from a painful punishment? **11.** 'It is to' have faith in God and His Messenger, and strive in the cause of God with your wealth and your lives. That is best for you, if only you knew. **12.** He will forgive your sins, and admit you into Gardens under which rivers flow, and 'house you in' splendid homes in the Gardens of Eternity. That is the ultimate triumph. **13.** 'He will also give you' another favour that you long for: help from God and an imminent victory. 'So' give good news 'O Prophet' to the believers.

Jesus and the Disciples

14. O believers! Stand up for God, as Jesus, son of Mary, asked the disciples, "Who will stand up with me for God?" The disciples replied, "We will stand up for God." Then a group from the Children of Israel believed while another disbelieved. We then supported the believers against their enemies, so they prevailed.

1185 Some companions desperately asked the Prophet about the best deeds. When he told them that one of the best deeds is to fight in self-defence, they pledged to do so. But when the order came to fight the Meccan pagans, some either did not comply or fled in battles like Uḥud.

1186 Aḥmad is another name for Prophet Muḥammad. Both are derived from *ḥa-ma-da* which means 'praise.' Some Muslim scholars believe this verse refers to John 14:16, where Jesus says: "And I will ask the Father, and he will give you another *periklytos*, to be with you forever." *Periklytos* is a Greek word that means 'the praised one.' The name of Prophet Muḥammad appears several times in the Gospel of Barnabas, which is deemed apocryphal by Christian authorities.

1187 Submission to God means 'Islam' in Arabic.

62. Friday Congregation *(Al-Jumu'ah)*

This chapter and the previous one have much in common. Both start by praising God. Those among the Jews who harmed Moses, according to the previous chapter (61:5), are criticized here for not upholding the Torah (verse 5). Since the disciples of Jesus are commended in the previous chapter (61:14), the companions of Muḥammad are honoured in this chapter (verses 2-4). The Prophet is foretold by Jesus in the previous chapter (61:6) and is presented in this chapter as God's favour to the believers. Similar to the previous chapter, some instructions are given to the believers—this time, regarding the Friday congregation (verse 9), which gives this Medinian chapter its name.

In the Name of God—the Most Compassionate, Most Merciful

God's Favour to the Believers

1. Whatever is in the heavens and whatever is on the earth ˹constantly˺ glorifies God—the King, the Most Holy, the Almighty, the All-Wise. 2. He is the One Who raised for the illiterate ˹people˺ a messenger from among themselves—reciting to them His revelations, purifying them, and teaching them the Book and wisdom, for indeed they had previously been clearly astray— 3. along with others of them who have not yet joined them ˹in faith˺. For He is the Almighty, All-Wise. 4. This is the favour of God. He grants it to whoever He wills. And God is the Lord of infinite bounty.

Unutilized Knowledge[1188]

5. The example of those who were entrusted with ˹observing˺ the Torah but failed to do so, is that of a donkey carrying books.[1189] How evil is the example of those who reject God's signs! For God does not guide the wrongdoing people.

Challenge to the Israelites

6. Say, ˹O Prophet,˺ "O Jews! If you claim to be God's chosen ˹people˺ out of all humanity, then wish for death, if what you say is true." 7. But they will never wish for that because of what their hands have done.[1190] And God has ˹perfect˺ knowledge of the wrongdoers. 8. Say, "The death you are running away from will inevitably come to you. Then you will be returned to the Knower of the seen and unseen, and He will inform you of what you used to do."

Attending Friday Congregation

9. O believers! When the call to prayer is made on Friday, then proceed ˹diligently˺ to the remembrance of God and leave off ˹your˺ business. That is best for you, if only you knew. 10. Once the prayer is over, disperse throughout the land and seek the bounty of God. And remember God often so you may be successful.

1188 Some Jews used to boast that they were God's most beloved and that they had been favoured with the Torah and the Sabbath, so the three following passages came in response:
What is the benefit of the Torah if it is not followed properly (62:5)?
If you are truly God's favourite servants then you should wish to meet Him (62:-6-8).
Muslims have been blessed with Friday, equivalent to the Sabbath (62:9-10).
1189 Meaning, they can carry the physical burden of the books, but not understand a word of them.
1190 i.e., disobeying God, killing some of the prophets (including Zachariah and John the Baptist), claiming to have killed Jesus, accusing Mary of adultery, and dealing with usury. See 4:153-158.

Leaving the Sermon

11. When they saw the fanfare along with the caravan, they ˹almost all˺ flocked to it, leaving you ˹O Prophet˺ standing ˹on the pulpit˺. Say, "What is with God is far better than amusement and merchandise. And God is the Best Provider."[1191]

63. The Hypocrites *(Al-Munâfiqûn)*

Similar to the two previous chapters, this Medinian chapter closes by offering more advice to the believers. The hypocrites are rebuked for hindering others from the path of God and discouraging people from donating in His cause. In contrast, the believers are advised to donate before they are overtaken by death—a reality that can come at any time.

In the Name of God—the Most Compassionate, Most Merciful

The Hypocrites Have No Faith

1. When the hypocrites come to you ˹O Prophet˺, they say, "We bear witness that you are certainly the Messenger of God"—and surely God knows that you are His Messenger—but God bears witness that the hypocrites are truly liars. **2.** They have made their ˹false˺ oaths as a shield, hindering ˹others˺ from the Way of God. Evil indeed is what they do! **3.** This is because they believed and then abandoned faith. Therefore, their hearts have been sealed, so they do not comprehend.

All That Glitters Is Not Gold

4. When you see them, their appearance impresses you. And when they speak, you listen to their ˹impressive˺ speech. But they are ˹just˺ like ˹worthless˺ planks of wood leaned ˹against a wall˺. They think every cry is against them. They are the enemy, so beware of them. May God condemn them! How can they be deluded ˹from the truth˺?

Hypocrites' Unwillingness to Repent[1192]

5. When it is said to them, "Come! The Messenger of God will pray for you to be forgiven," they turn their heads ˹in disgust˺, and you see them ˹O Prophet˺ turn away in arrogance. **6.** It is the same whether you pray for their forgiveness or not, God will not forgive them. Surely God does not guide the rebellious people.

Hypocrites' Contempt for the Believers

7. They are the ones who say ˹to one another˺, "Do not spend ˹anything˺ on those ˹emigrants˺ with the Messenger of God so that they will break away ˹from him˺." But to God ˹alone˺ belong the treasuries of the heavens and the earth, yet the hypocrites do not comprehend. **8.** They say, "If we return to Medina, the honourable will definitely expel the inferior." But all honour and power belongs to God, His Messenger, and the believers, yet the hypocrites do not know.

1191 Initially, the Friday congregational prayer was performed first, followed by the sermon. On one occasion, a caravan of food arrived in Medina during a time of hardship while the Prophet was on the pulpit. Following ancient traditions, the caravan was received with drum-beats. Most congregants rushed to receive the caravan, leaving the Prophet in the middle of the sermon. Henceforth, the sermon was given first so everyone would stay for the prayer.

1192 This passage and the next refer to 'Abdullâh ibn Ubai, the chief hypocrite in Medina.

Be Faithful and Charitable

9. O believers! Do not let your wealth or your children divert you from the remembrance of God. For whoever does so, it is they who are the 'true' losers. **10.** And donate from what We have provided for you before death comes to one of you, and you cry, "My Lord! If only You delayed me for a short while, I would give in charity and be one of the righteous." **11.** But God never delays a soul when its appointed time comes. And God is All-Aware of what you do.

෴

64. Mutual Loss and Gain *(At-Taghâbun)*

This Medinian chapter takes its name from the reference to the Day of Judgment in verse 9, where people are divided into winners and losers. Since the last chapter closes by urging the believers to donate before they are overtaken by death, this chapter opens by emphasizing God's power to create and His ability to bring the dead back to life for judgment. The chapter concludes by bidding the believers to spend in the cause of God, and not be discouraged by concerns for their spouses and children. The rights of spouses and children after divorce are laid out in the next chapter.

In the Name of God—the Most Compassionate, Most Merciful

God's Infinite Power and Knowledge

1. Whatever is in the heavens and whatever is on the earth 'constantly' glorifies God. The kingdom is His, and all praise is for Him. For He is Most Capable of everything. **2.** He is the One Who created you, yet some of you are disbelievers while some are believers. And God is All-Seeing of what you do. **3.** He created the heavens and the earth for a purpose. He shaped you 'in the womb', perfecting your form. And to Him is the final return. **4.** He knows whatever is in the heavens and the earth. And He knows whatever you conceal and whatever you reveal. For God knows best what is 'hidden' in the heart.

Earlier Deniers

5. Have the stories of those who disbelieved before not reached you 'pagans'? They tasted the evil consequences of their doings, and they will suffer a painful punishment. **6.** That was because their messengers used to come to them with clear proofs, but they said 'mockingly', "How can humans be our guides?" So they disbelieved and turned away. And God was not in need 'of their faith'. For God is Self-Sufficient, Praiseworthy.

A Message to Present Deniers

7. The disbelievers claim they will not be resurrected. Say, 'O Prophet,' "Yes, by my Lord, you will surely be resurrected, then you will certainly be informed of what you have done. And that is easy for God." **8.** So believe in God and His Messenger and in the Light[1193] We have revealed. And God is All-Aware of what you do. 9. ˹Consider˺ the Day He will gather you ˹all˺ for the Day of Gathering—that will be the Day of mutual loss and gain. So whoever believes in God and does good, He will absolve them of their sins and admit them into Gardens under which rivers flow, to stay there for ever and ever. That is the ultimate triumph. 10. As for those who disbelieve and reject Our signs, they will be the residents of the Fire, staying there forever. What an evil destination!

Reassuring the Believers

11. No calamity befalls ˹anyone˺ except by God's Will. And whoever has faith in God, He will ˹rightly˺ guide their hearts ˹through adversity˺. And God has ˹perfect˺ knowledge of all things. 12. Obey God and obey the Messenger! But if you turn away, then Our Messenger's duty is only to deliver ˹the message˺ clearly. 13. God—there is

no god ˹worthy of worship˺ except Him. So in God let the believers put their trust.

The Test of Family and Wealth

14. O believers! Indeed, some of your spouses and children are enemies to you,[1194] so beware of them. But if you pardon, overlook, and forgive ˹their faults˺, then God is truly All-Forgiving, Most Merciful. 15. Your wealth and children are only a test, but God ˹alone˺ has a great reward. 16. So be mindful of God to the best of your ability, hear and obey, and spend in charity—that will be best for you. And whoever is saved from the selfishness of their own souls, it is they who are ˹truly˺ successful. 17. If you lend to God a good loan, He will multiply it for you and forgive you. For God is Most Appreciative, Most Forbearing. 18. ˹He is the˺ Knower of the seen and unseen—the Almighty, All-Wise.

65. Divorce *(Aṭ-Ṭalâq)*

This Medinian chapter outlines the manner of divorce and accommodation of divorced women and their young children (verses 1-7). Those who comply with God's commands are promised a great reward, whereas those who defy Him are warned of the fate of those who were destroyed before. Complying with God's orders is elaborated upon in the next chapter.

In the Name of God—the Most Compassionate, Most Merciful

Proper Divorce

1. O Prophet! ˹Instruct the believers:˺ When you ˹intend to˺ divorce women, then divorce them with concern for their waiting period,[1195] and count it accurately. And fear God,

1193 i.e., the Quran.
1194 This verse was revealed when some early Muslims were prevented from emigrating to Medina by their own spouses and children, so they could not join the Prophet and the rest of the believers to practice their faith freely.
1195 Meaning, when a husband intends to divorce his wife—after the consummation of marriage—he should divorce her outside her monthly cycle, provided that he has not touched her after her period. This makes it easy for the wife to observe her *'iddah* (waiting period for around three months, *see* 65:4). Otherwise, things will be complicated for her. For example, if divorce happens after sexual intercourse, she might get pregnant, which delays the end of *'iddah* until the end of her pregnancy. If divorce happens during a monthly cycle, scholars are in disagreement as to whether the divorce counts or not. If it does not, she has to wait until her menstruation is over to see if her husband still wants to divorce her.

your Lord. Do not force them out of their homes, nor should they leave—unless they commit a blatant misconduct. These are the limits set by God. And whoever transgresses God's limits has truly wronged his own soul. You never know, perhaps God will bring about a change ʿof heartʾ later.[1196]

Divorced Women After the Waiting Period

2. Then when they have ʿalmostʾ reached the end of their waiting period, either retain them honourably or separate from them honourably.[1197] And call two of your reliable men to witness ʿeither wayʾ—and ʿlet the witnessesʾ bear true testimony for ʿthe sake ofʾ God. This is enjoined on whoever has faith in God and the Last Day. And whoever is mindful of God, He will make a way out for them, 3. and provide for them from sources they could never imagine. And whoever puts their trust in God, then He ʿaloneʾ is sufficient for them. Certainly God achieves His Will. God has already set a destiny for everything.

Waiting Periods for Divorced Women

4. As for your women past the age of menstruation, in case you do not know, their waiting period is three months, and those who have not menstruated as well. As for those who are pregnant, their waiting period ends with delivery.[1198] And whoever is mindful of God, He will make their matters easy for them. 5. This is the commandment of God, which He has revealed to you. And whoever is mindful of God, He will absolve them of their sins and reward them immensely.

Housing for Divorced Women

6. Let them live where you live ʿduring their waiting periodʾ, according to your means. And do not harass them to make their stay unbearable. If they are pregnant, then maintain them until they deliver. And if they nurse your child,[1199] compensate them, and consult together courteously. But if you fail to reach an agreement, then another woman will nurse ʿthe childʾ for the father. 7. Let the man of wealth provide according to his means. As for the one with limited resources, let him provide according to whatever God has given him. God does not require of any soul beyond what He has given it. After hardship, God will bring about ease.

An Invitation to True Faith

8. ʿImagineʾ how many societies rebelled against the commandments of their Lord and His messengers, so We called each ʿsocietyʾ to a severe account and subjected them to a horrible punishment. 9. So they tasted the evil consequences of their doings, and the outcome of their doings was ʿtotalʾ loss. 10. God has ʿalsoʾ prepared for them a severe punishment. So fear God, O people of reason and faith. God has indeed revealed to you a Reminder,[1200] 11. ʿand sentʾ a messenger reciting to you God's revelations, making things clear so that He may bring those who believe and do good out of darkness and into light. And whoever believes in God and does good will be admitted by Him into Gardens under which rivers flow, to stay there for ever and ever. God will have indeed granted them an excellent provision.

1196 Perhaps the husband who has divorced his wife may change his mind and restore the marriage before the end of her waiting period (after the first or second count of divorce).
1197 A husband may separate from his wife after each of the first two counts of divorce or at the end of her waiting period with dignity. If he chooses to stay with her after the first two counts of divorce then divorces her a third time, the marriage is terminated at the end of her third waiting period. The wife will have to marry and divorce another man before she can be remarried to her ex-husband (see 2:230). However, a woman marrying someone with the intention of getting divorced, in order to return to her first husband, is forbidden.
1198 This applies to pregnant women who are divorced or widowed.
1199 After the divorce is finalized.
1200 This is one of the names of the Quran.

God's Infinite Power and Knowledge

12. God is the One Who created seven heavens 'in layers', and likewise for the earth. The 'divine' command descends between them so you may know that God is Most Capable of everything and that God certainly encompasses all things in 'His' knowledge.

⚜️

66. The Prohibition *(At-Taḥrîm)*

This Medinian chapter deals with an incident that happened within the Prophet's household. The Prophet used to visit all of his wives in the evening. It so happened that he stayed longer than usual at the home of Zainab bint Jaḥsh, where he was offered honey—something he liked very much. Out of jealousy, two other wives (Ḥafṣah and 'Âishah) agreed between themselves to tell the Prophet, when he visited each of them, that his mouth gave off a bad smell, knowing that he did not like bad smells. Eventually, the Prophet made an oath that he would never eat honey again, and told Ḥafṣah not to tell anyone about this. But she told 'Âishah that their plan worked. Both wives are subtly advised to learn from the example of the two believing women mentioned at the end of the chapter—Mary and Âsiyah, the wife of Pharaoh—and take a lesson from the fate of the wives of Noah and Lot, who were both destroyed despite being wives of prophets. The believers are urged in this chapter to mend their ways and genuinely repent to God in order to win His eternal reward, whereas the disbelievers are warned of a horrible fate. The fate of the disbelievers is elaborated upon in the next chapter.

In the Name of God—the Most Compassionate, Most Merciful

A Lesson to the Prophet's Wives

1. O Prophet! Why do you prohibit 'yourself' from what God has made lawful to you, seeking to please your wives? And God is All-Forgiving, Most Merciful. **2.** God has already ordained for you 'believers' the way to absolve yourselves from your oaths.[1201] For God is your Guardian. And He is the All-Knowing, All-Wise. **3.** 'Remember' when the Prophet had 'once' confided something to one of his wives, then when she disclosed it 'to another wife' and God made it known to him, he presented 'to her' part of what was disclosed and overlooked a part. So when he informed her of it, she exclaimed, "Who told you this?" He replied, "I was informed by the All-Knowing, All-Aware." **4.** 'It will be better' if you 'wives' both turn to God in repentance, for your hearts have certainly faltered. But if you 'continue to' collaborate against him, then 'know that' God Himself is his Guardian. And Gabriel, the righteous believers, and the angels are 'all' his supporters as well. **5.** Perhaps, if he were to divorce you 'all', his Lord would replace you with better wives who are submissive 'to God', faithful 'to Him', devout, repentant, dedicated to worship and fasting—previously married or virgins.

Warning of Judgment Day

6. O believers! Protect yourselves and your families from a Fire whose fuel is people and stones, overseen by formidable and severe angels, who never disobey whatever God or-

---

1201 *See* 5:89.

ders—always doing as commanded. 7. ˹The deniers will then be told,˺ "O disbelievers! Make no excuses this Day! You are only rewarded for what you used to do."

Reward of Sincere Repentance

8. O believers! Turn to God in sincere repentance, so your Lord may absolve you of your sins and admit you into Gardens, under which rivers flow, on the Day God will not disgrace the Prophet or the believers with him. Their light will shine ahead of them and on their right, ˹and˺ they will say, "Our Lord! Perfect our light for us, and forgive us. ˹For˺ You are truly Most Capable of everything."

Responding to Evildoers

9. O Prophet! Struggle against the disbelievers and the hypocrites, and be firm with them. Hell will be their home. What an evil destination!

Two Examples for the Disbelievers

10. God sets forth an example for the disbelievers: the wife of Noah and the wife of Lot. Each was married to one of Our righteous servants, yet betrayed them.[1202] So their husbands were of no benefit to them against God whatsoever. Both were told, "Enter the Fire, along with the others!"

Two Examples for the Believers

11. And God sets forth an example for the believers: the wife of Pharaoh, who prayed, "My Lord! Build me a house in Paradise near You, deliver me from Pharaoh and his ˹evil˺ doing, and save me from the wrongdoing people." 12. ˹There is˺ also ˹the example of˺ Mary, the daughter of 'Imrân, who guarded her chastity, so We breathed into her ˹womb˺ through Our angel ˹Gabriel˺.[1203] She testified to the words of her Lord and His Scriptures, and was one of the ˹sincerely˺ devout.

67. All Authority *(Al-Mulk)*

This Meccan chapter stresses that God's infinite power is manifested through His perfect creation. Those who disbelieve in God and deny the Resurrection will be regretful in Hell, whereas those in awe of their Lord will be richly rewarded in Paradise. God's absolute authority is contrasted with the powerlessness of false gods. The fact that there is no protection from God's torment is emphasized in this chapter (verses 20, 21, and 30) and the next (68:17-33).

In the Name of God—the Most Compassionate, Most Merciful

Life Is a Test

1. Blessed is the One in Whose Hands rests all authority. And He is Most Capable of everything. 2. ˹He is the One˺ Who created death and life in order to test which of you is best in deeds. And He is the Almighty, All-Forgiving.

God's Perfect Creation

3. ˹He is the One˺ Who created seven heavens, one above the other. You will

---

1202 Both wives were disbelievers. Noah's wife used to give away the identity of the new believers so the disbelievers could persecute them. And Lot's wife used to tell the men about her husband's handsome male visitors so they could approach them.
1203 Gabriel breathed into the sleeves of Mary's garment so she conceived Jesus.

never see any imperfection in the creation of the Most Compassionate.[1204] So look again: do you see any flaws? **4.** Then look again and again—your sight will return frustrated and weary. **5.** And indeed, We adorned the lowest heaven with ˹stars like˺ lamps, and made them ˹as missiles˺ for stoning ˹eavesdropping˺ devils, for whom We have also prepared the torment of the Blaze.[1205]

Reward of the Disbelievers

6. Those who disbelieve in their Lord will suffer the punishment of Hell. What an evil destination! **7.** When they are tossed into it, they will hear its roaring as it boils over, **8.** almost bursting in fury. Every time a group is cast into it, its keepers will ask them, "Did a warner not come to you?" **9.** They will reply, "Yes, a warner did come to us, but we denied and said, 'God has revealed nothing. You are extremely astray.'" **10.** And they will lament, "If only we had listened and reasoned, we would not be among the residents of the Blaze!" **11.** And so they will confess their sins. So away with the residents of the Blaze!

Reward of the Believers

12. Indeed, those in awe of their Lord without seeing Him[1206] will have forgiveness and a mighty reward.

Question 1)
Does God Not Know His Creation?

13. Whether you speak secretly or openly—He surely knows best what is ˹hidden˺ in the heart. **14.** How could He not know His Own creation? For He ˹alone˺ is the Most Subtle, All-Aware. **15.** He is the One Who smoothed out the earth for you, so move about in its regions and eat

from His provisions. And to Him is the resurrection ˹of all˺.

Question 2) Are You out of God's Reach?

16. Do you feel secure that the One above the heavens will not cause the earth to swallow you up as it quakes violently? **17.** Or do you feel secure that the One above the heavens will not unleash upon you a storm of stones. Only then would you know how ˹serious˺ My warning was! **18.** And certainly those before them denied ˹as well˺, then how severe was My response!

Question 3) Do You Not See God's Power?

19. Have they not seen the birds above them, spreading and folding their wings? None holds them up except the Most Compassionate. Indeed, He is All-Seeing of everything. **20.** Also, which ˹powerless˺ force will come to your help instead of the Most Compassionate? Indeed, the disbelievers are only ˹lost˺ in delusion. **21.** Or who is it that will provide for you if He withholds His provision? In fact, they persist in arrogance and aversion ˹to the truth˺.

Question 4)
Are Believers and Disbelievers Equal?

22. Who is ˹rightly˺ guided: the one who crawls facedown or the one who walks upright on the Straight Path?

Question 5) Who Created You?

23. Say, ˹O Prophet,˺ "He is the One Who brought you into being and gave you hearing, sight, and intellect. ˹Yet˺ you hardly give any thanks." **24.** ˹Also˺ say, "He is the One Who has dispersed you ˹all˺ over the earth, and to Him you will ˹all˺ be gathered."

1204 Some may point to birth defects, genetic mutations, etc. and say these are flaws. This verse means that, in the grand scheme of creation, everything created has its place, form, and purpose, and that it does exactly what God ordained for it.
1205 *See* 72:8-10.
1206 This can also mean that they are in awe of their Lord as much in private as they are in public.

Question 6) Do You Still Deny the Hour?

25. ˹Still˺ they ask ˹the believers˺, "When will this threat come to pass, if what you say is true?" **26.** Say, ˹O Prophet,˺ "That knowledge is with God alone, and I am only sent with a clear warning." **27.** Then when they see the torment drawing near, the faces of the disbelievers will become gloomy, and it will be said ˹to them˺, "This is what you claimed would never come."[1207]

Question 7) Who Else Can Aid You?

28. Say, ˹O Prophet,˺ "Consider this: whether God causes me and those with me to die or shows us mercy, who will save the disbelievers from a painful punishment?"[1208] **29.** Say, "He is the Most Compassionate—in Him ˹alone˺ we believe, and in Him ˹alone˺ we trust. You will soon know who is clearly astray." **30.** Say, "Consider this: if your water were to sink ˹into the earth˺, then who ˹else˺ could bring you flowing water?"

68. The Pen *(Al-Qalam)*

In this Meccan chapter, the Prophet's heart is reassured and his character is highly praised. He is advised to be steadfast and not to yield to the pagans who reject his message and call him insane. The pagans are warned of an evil fate in this world and the Hereafter. To deter the pagans, the fate of some earlier disbelievers is cited in the next chapter.

In the Name of God—the Most Compassionate, Most Merciful

Excellence of the Prophet

1. *Nūn.* By the pen and what everyone writes! **2.** By the grace of your Lord, you ˹O Prophet˺ are not insane. **3.** You will certainly have a never-ending reward. **4.** And you are truly ˹a man˺ of outstanding character. **5.** Soon you and the pagans will see, **6.** which of you is mad. **7.** Surely your Lord ˹alone˺ knows best who has strayed from His Way and who is ˹rightly˺ guided.

Warning the Prophet About the Deniers

8. So do not give in to the deniers. **9.** They wish you would compromise so they would yield ˹to you˺. **10.** And do not obey the despicable, vain oath-taker, **11.** slanderer, gossip-monger, **12.** withholder of good, transgressor, evildoer, **13.** brute, and—on top of all that—an illegitimate child. **14.** Now, ˹simply˺ because he has been blessed with ˹abundant˺ wealth and children, **15.** whenever Our revelations are recited to him, he says, "Ancient fables!" **16.** We will soon mark his snout.[1209]

1207 Another possible translation: "This is what you were calling for."
1208 Meaning, whether God takes our lives (as you wish) or grants us a long life, it is all good for us. But who will protect you from God if you disbelieve in Him.
1209 Like 53:33-35 and 74:11-26, these verses refer to Al-Walîd ibn Al-Mughîrah, a leader of the Meccan opposition against Islam. He rejected the Prophet as a madman, so the Quran responded by listing ten of his qualities—two of which were unknown to him: the fact that he was born out of wedlock and that his nose would be chopped off several years later at the Battle of Badr. At least three of his ten sons accepted Islam—including Khâlid ibn Al-Walîd.

The Test of the Garden Owners[1210]

17. Indeed, We have tested those ˹Meccans˺ as We tested the owners of the garden—when they swore they would surely harvest ˹all˺ its fruit in the early morning, **18.** leaving no thought for God's Will.[1211] **19.** Then it was struck by a torment from your Lord while they slept, **20.** so it was reduced to ashes. **21.** Then by daybreak they called out to each other, **22.** ˹saying,˺ "Go early to your harvest, if you want to pick ˹all˺ the fruit." **23.** So they went off, whispering to one another, **24.** "Do not let any poor person enter your garden today." **25.** And they proceeded early, totally fixated on their purpose. **26.** But when they saw it ˹devastated˺, they cried, "We must have lost ˹our˺ way! **27.** In fact, we have been deprived ˹of our livelihood˺." **28.** The most sensible of them said, "Did I not urge you to say, 'God willing.'?" **29.** They replied, "Glory be to our Lord! We have truly been wrongdoers." **30.** Then they turned on each other, throwing blame. **31.** They said, "Woe to us! We have certainly been transgressors. **32.** We trust our Lord will give us a better garden than this, ˹for˺ we are indeed turning to our Lord with hope."[1212] **33.** That is the ˹way of Our˺ punishment ˹in this world˺. But the punishment of the Hereafter is certainly far worse, if only they knew.[1213]

Questions to the Pagans

34. Indeed, the righteous will have the Gardens of Bliss with their Lord. **35.** Should We then treat those who have submitted like the wicked? **36.** What is the matter with you? How do you judge? **37.** Or do you have a scripture, in which you read **38.** that you will have whatever you choose? **39.** Or do you have oaths binding on Us until the Day of Judgment that you will have whatever you decide? **40.** Ask them ˹O Prophet˺ which of them can guarantee all that. **41.** Or do they have associate-gods ˹supporting this claim˺? Then let them bring forth their associate-gods, if what they say is true.

Warning of Judgment Day

42. ˹Beware of˺ the Day the Shin will be bared,[1214] and all will be asked to prostrate, but the wicked will not be able to do so, **43.** with eyes downcast, totally covered with disgrace. For they were ˹always˺ called to prostrate ˹in the world˺ when they were fully capable ˹but they chose not to˺. **44.** So leave to Me ˹O Prophet˺ those who reject this message. We will gradually draw them to destruction in ways they cannot comprehend. **45.** I ˹only˺ delay their end for a while, but My planning is flawless. **46.** Or are you asking them for a reward ˹for the message˺ so that they are overburdened by debt? **47.** Or do they have access to ˹the Record in˺ the unseen, so they copy it ˹for all to see˺?

A Lesson to the Prophet

48. So be patient with your Lord's decree, and do not be like ˹Jonah,˺ the Man of the Whale, who cried out ˹to God˺, in total distress.[1215] **49.** Had he not been shown grace by his Lord, he would have certainly been cast onto the open ˹shore˺, still blameworthy. **50.** Then his Lord chose him, making

---

1210 This is the story of a righteous man who owned a garden and used to give a share of the harvest to the poor. Following his death, his children decided to keep all the produce for themselves and give nothing to the poor.
1211 Another possible translation: "without leaving some for the poor."
1212 It is believed that God accepted their repentance and replaced their garden with a better one.
1213 i.e., if only the Meccan pagans knew.
1214 Like the Face and the Hands, the Shin is believed by many to be one of the qualities of God, in a way befitting His Majesty and Honour. The fact that God has a Shin is supported by an authentic ḥadîth narrated by Bukhâri and Muslim. According to Ibn Kathîr and Aṭ-Ṭabari, since baring the shin in the Arab culture is associated with the heat of battle, some interpret the verse metaphorically, so the meaning would be: "˹Beware of˺ the Day when horror sets in."
1215 While inside the whale. See 21:87 and 37:139-148.

him one of the righteous. **51.** The disbeliev-ers would almost cut you down with their eyes when they hear ˹you recite˺ the Re-minder,[1216] and say, "He is certainly a

madman." **52.** But it is simply a reminder to the whole world.

69. The Inevitable Hour *(Al-Ḥâqqah)*

This Meccan chapter refers to the destruction of the peoples of 'Âd, Thamûd, Pharaoh, and Lot for denying the Hereafter. A reference is made to the apocalypse, followed by a touching description of the reward of the believers and the punishment of the disbe-lievers (verses 18-37). The pagan arguments against the Prophet and the Quran are thoroughly refuted (verses 38-52). The horrors of the apocalypse are further described in the next chapter.

In the Name of God—the Most Compassionate, Most Merciful

The Final Hour

1. The Inevitable Hour! **2.** What is the In-evitable Hour? **3.** And what will make you realize what the Inevitable Hour is?

Examples of Destroyed Peoples

4. ˹Both˺ Thamûd and 'Âd denied the Strik-ing Disaster.[1217] **5.** As for Thamûd, they were destroyed by an overwhelming blast. **6.** And as for 'Âd, they were destroyed by a furious, bitter wind **7.** which God unleashed on them non-stop for seven nights and eight days, so that you would have seen its peo-ple lying dead like trunks of uprooted palm trees. **8.** Do you see any of them left alive? **9.** Also, Pharaoh and those before him, and ˹the people of˺ the overturned cities ˹of Lot˺ indulged in sin, **10.** each disobeying their Lord's messenger, so He seized them with a crushing grip. **11.** Indeed, when the flood-water had overflowed, We carried you[1218] in the floating Ark ˹with Noah˺, **12.** so that We may make this a reminder to you, and that attentive ears may grasp it.

Horrors of Judgment Day

13. At last, when the Trumpet will be blown with one blast, **14.** and the earth and moun-tains will be lifted up and crushed with one blow, **15.** on that Day the Inevitable Event will have come to pass. **16.** The sky will then be so torn that it will be frail, **17.** with the angels on its sides. On that Day eight ˹mighty angels˺ will bear the Throne of your Lord above them. **18.** You will then be pre-sented ˹ before Him for judgment˺, and none of your secrets will stay hidden.

The Winners

19. As for those given their records in their right hand, they will cry ˹happily˺, "Here ˹everyone˺! Read my record! **20.** I surely knew I would face my reckoning." **21.** They will be in a life of bliss, **22.** in an elevated Garden, **23.** whose fruit will hang with-in reach. **24.** ˹They will be told,˺ "Eat and drink joyfully for what you did in the days gone by."

1216 This is one of the names of the Quran.
1217 The Striking Disaster is another name for the Day of Judgment.
1218 i.e., your ancestors.

The Losers

25. And as for those given their record in their left hand, they will cry ꞌbitterlyꞌ, "I wish I had not been given my record, **26.** nor known anything of my reckoning! **27.** I wish death was the end! **28.** My wealth has not benefited me! **29.** My authority has been stripped from me." **30.** ꞌIt will be said,ꞌ "Seize and shackle them, **31.** then burn them in Hell, **32.** then tie them up with chains seventy arms long. **33.** For they never had faith in God, the Greatest, **34.** nor encouraged the feeding of the poor. **35.** So this Day they will have no close friend here, **36.** nor any food except ꞌoozingꞌ pus, **37.** which none will eat except the evildoers."

The Quran Is God's Word

38. Now, I do swear by whatever you see, **39.** and whatever you cannot see! **40.** Indeed, this ꞌQuranꞌ is the recitation of a noble Messenger. **41.** It is not the prose of a poet ꞌas you claimꞌ, ꞌyetꞌ you hardly have any faith. **42.** Nor is it the mumbling of a fortune-teller, ꞌyetꞌ you are hardly mindful. **43.** ꞌIt isꞌ a revelation from the Lord of all worlds.

The Quran Is Not a Fabrication

44. Had the Messenger made up something in Our Name, **45.** We would have certainly seized him by his right hand, **46.** then severed his aorta, **47.** and none of you could have shielded him ꞌfrom Usꞌ!

The Quran Is the Absolute Truth

48. Indeed, this ꞌQuranꞌ is a reminder to those mindful ꞌof Godꞌ. **49.** And We certainly know that some of you will persist in denial, **50.** and it will surely be a source of regret for the disbelievers. **51.** And indeed, this ꞌQuranꞌ is the absolute truth. **52.** So glorify the Name of your Lord, the Greatest.

✦

70. Pathways of ꞌHeavenlyꞌ Ascent *(Al-Maꞌârij)*

This Meccan chapter, which takes its name from verse 3, condemns the pagans for ridiculing the Day of Judgment (verses 1-2) and the Prophet (verses 36-37). The truth of the Hour is reaffirmed, along with the horrors that will ensue. The qualities of the people of Hell and the people of Paradise are described (verses 16-35). The Prophet is reassured, while the pagans are warned—both themes are embedded in the story of Noah in the next chapter.

In the Name of God—the Most Compassionate, Most Merciful

A Mocker Asks for Judgment Day

1. A challenger[1219] has demanded a punishment bound to come **2.** for the disbelievers— to be averted by none— **3.** from God, Lord of pathways of ꞌheavenlyꞌ ascent, **4.** ꞌthrough whichꞌ the angels and the ꞌholyꞌ spirit[1220] will ascend to Him on a Day fifty thousand

---

1219 According to 8:32, An-Naḍr ibn Al-Ḥârith challenged God, saying, "If this is indeed the truth from You, then rain down stones upon us from the sky or overcome us with a painful punishment."
1220 The holy spirit is the angel Gabriel.

years in length.[1221] 5. So endure ⸢this denial, O Prophet,⸣ with beautiful patience. 6. They truly see this ⸢Day⸣ as impossible, 7. but We see it as inevitable.

Horrors of Judgment Day

8. On that Day the sky will be like molten brass 9. and the mountains like ⸢tufts of⸣ wool. 10. And no close friend will ask ⸢about⸣ their friends, 11. ⸢although⸣ they will be made to see each other. The wicked will wish to ransom themselves from the punishment of that Day by their children, 12. their spouses, their siblings, 13. their clan that sheltered them, 14. and everyone on earth altogether, just to save themselves. 15. But no! There will certainly be a raging Flame 16. ripping off scalps. 17. It will summon whoever turned their backs ⸢on God⸣ and turned away ⸢from the truth⸣, 18. and gathered and hoarded ⸢wealth⸣.

Excellence of the Faithful

19. Indeed, humankind was created impatient: 20. distressed when touched with evil, 21. and withholding when touched with good— 22. except those who pray, 23. consistently performing their prayers; 24. and who give the rightful share of their wealth 25. to the beggar and the poor; 26. and who ⸢firmly⸣ believe in the Day of Judgment; 27. and those who fear the punishment of their Lord— 28. ⸢knowing that⸣ none should feel secure from their Lord's punishment— 29. and those who guard their chastity[1222] 30. except with their wives or those ⸢bondwomen⸣ in their possession,[1223] for then they are free from blame, 31. but whoever seeks beyond that are the transgressors. 32. ⸢The faithful are⸣ also those who are true to their trusts and covenants; 33. and who are honest in their testimony; 34. and who are ⸢properly⸣ observant of their prayers. 35. These will be in Gardens, held in honour.

Warning to the Mockers

36. So what is the matter with the disbelievers that they rush ⸢head-long⸣ towards you ⸢O Prophet⸣, 37. from the right and the left, in groups ⸢to mock you⸣?[1224] 38. Does every one of them expect to be admitted into a Garden of Bliss? 39. But no! Indeed, they ⸢already⸣ know what We created them from.[1225] 40. So, I do swear by the Lord of ⸢all⸣ the points of sunrise and sunset[1226] that We are truly capable 41. of replacing them with ⸢others⸣ better than them, and We cannot be prevented ⸢from doing so⸣. 42. So let them indulge ⸢in falsehood⸣ and amuse ⸢themselves⸣ until they face their Day, which they have been threatened with— 43. the Day they will come forth from the graves swiftly, as if racing to an idol ⸢for a blessing⸣,[1227] 44. with eyes downcast, utterly covered with disgrace. That is the Day they have ⸢always⸣ been warned of.

꒰꒱꒰꒱

1221 Judgment Day will seem like 50 000 years for a disbeliever, but it will seem like a very short period for a believer. The Prophet is reported in a *ḥadîth* collected by Imâm Aḥmed to have said that, for the believer, this long period will be like the time they took to perform a single prayer in the world.

1222 lit., private parts.

1223 *See* footnote for 4:3.

1224 Some Meccan pagans used to gather around the Prophet to mock him and the believers, saying that if there is in fact a Hereafter, they are better entitled to Paradise than poor believers.

1225 i.e., from a humble fluid. *See* 32:8.

1226 The daily points of sunrise and sunset, caused by the earth's rotation around its own axis.

1227 Or "as if rushing towards a target."

71. Noah *(Nûḥ)*

This Meccan chapter describes how Noah strived to deliver the message to his people for 950 years (corresponding to the total number of Arabic letters in this chapter). He called them to the truth secretly and publically, using logical arguments to prove the mercy and oneness of God. But his people persisted in denial, only to perish in the Flood. The stubbornness of the Arab pagans in the previous chapter and the long denial of the people of Noah in this chapter are contrasted with how some jinn instantly believed once they heard the truth in the next chapter.

In the Name of God—the Most Compassionate, Most Merciful

Noah's Appeal to His People

1. Indeed, We sent Noah to his people ʿsaying to himʾ, "Warn your people before a painful punishment comes to them." 2. Noah proclaimed, "O my people! I am truly sent to you with a clear warning: 3. worship God ʿaloneʾ, fear Him, and obey me. 4. He will forgive your sins, and delay your end until the appointed time.[1228] Indeed, when the time set by God comes, it cannot be delayed, if only you knew!"

950 Years of Preaching

5. He cried, "My Lord! I have surely called my people day and night, 6. but my calls only made them run farther away. 7. And whenever I invite them to be forgiven by You, they press their fingers into their ears, cover themselves with their clothes, persist ʿin denialʾ, and act very arrogantly. 8. Then I certainly called them openly, 9. then I surely preached to them publicly and privately, 10. saying, 'Seek your Lord's forgiveness, ʿforʾ He is truly Most Forgiving. 11. He will shower you with abundant rain, 12. supply you with wealth and children, and give you gardens as well as rivers. 13. What is the matter with you that you are not in awe of the Majesty of God, 14. when He truly created you in stages ʿof developmentʾ?[1229] 15. Do you not see how God created seven heavens, one above the other, 16. placing the moon within them as a ʿreflectedʾ light, and the sun as a ʿradiantʾ lamp? 17. God ʿaloneʾ caused you[1230] to grow from the earth like a plant. 18. Then He will return you to it, and then simply bring you forth ʿagainʾ. 19. And God ʿaloneʾ spread out the earth for you 20. to walk along its spacious pathways.'"

The Flood

21. ʿEventually,ʾ Noah cried, "My Lord! They have certainly persisted in disobeying me, and followed ʿinsteadʾ those ʿeliteʾ whose ʿabundantʾ wealth and children only increase them in loss, 22. and who have devised a tremendous plot, 23. urging ʿtheir followersʾ, 'Do not abandon your idols—especially *Wadd*, *Suwâ'*, *Yaghûth*, *Ya'ûq*, and *Nasr*.'[1231] 24. Those ʿeliteʾ have already led many astray. So ʿO Lordʾ, only allow the wrongdoers to stray farther away." 25. So because of their sins, they were drowned, then admitted into the Fire. And they found none to help them against God.

1228 Meaning, it is out of God's mercy that He does not hasten your punishment but delays your death until your destined time.

1229 *See* 22:5 and 23:12-14.

1230 i.e., your father Adam, who was created from clay.

1231 These are the names of their main idols. Initially, these idols had been erected to commemorate some righteous people before the time of Noah. After many generations, however, the idols were taken as objects of worship.

Noah's Prayer Before the Flood[1232]

26. Noah had prayed, "My Lord! Do not leave a single disbeliever on earth. **27.** For if You spare ʿany ofʾ them, they will certainly mislead Your servants, and give birth only to ʿwickedʾ sinners, staunch disbelievers. **28.** My Lord! Forgive me, my parents, and whoever enters my house in faith, and ʿallʾ believing men and women. And increase the wrongdoers only in destruction."

72. The Jinn *(Al-Jinn)*

This Meccan chapter gives an account of a group of jinn who fully submitted to the One True God as soon as they heard the Prophet's recitation of the Quran. In comparison, the Arab pagans are criticized for their polytheistic beliefs. The pagans are told that the Prophet's duty is only to deliver the message. Bringing about the punishment, which the pagans demanded, is only within the power of God. The next chapter provides more warning to the pagans and reassurance to the Prophet.

In the Name of God—the Most Compassionate, Most Merciful

Some Jinn Embrace Islam

1. Say, ʿO Prophet,ʾ "It has been revealed to me that a group of jinn listened ʿto the Quran,ʾ and said ʿto their fellow jinnʾ: ʿIndeed, we have heard a wondrous recitation. **2.** It leads to Right Guidance so we believed in it, and we will never associate anyone with our Lord ʿin worshipʾ. **3.** ʿNow, we believe thatʾ our Lord—Exalted is His Majesty—has neither taken a mate nor offspring, **4.** and that the foolish of us used to utter ʿoutrageousʾ falsehoods about God.[1233] **5.** We certainly thought that humans and jinn would never speak lies about God. **6.** And some men used to seek refuge with some jinn—so they increased each other in wickedness.[1234] **7.** And those ʿhumansʾ thought, just like you ʿjinnʾ, that God would not resurrect anyone ʿfor judgmentʾ.

No More Eavesdropping on Heaven

8. ʿEarlierʾ we tried to reach the sky ʿfor newsʾ, only to find it filled with stern guards and shooting stars.[1235] **9.** We used to take up positions there for eavesdropping, but whoever dares eavesdrop now will find a flare lying in wait for them. **10.** Now, we have no clue whether evil is intended for those on earth, or their Lord intends for them what is right.

Righteous and Deviant Jinn

11. Among us are those who are righteous and those who are less so. We have been of different factions. **12.** ʿNow,ʾ we truly know that we cannot frustrate God on earth, nor can we escape from Him ʿinto heavenʾ.

1232 Noah prayed for his people's destruction after God revealed to him that no one else was going to believe. *See* 11:36.
1233 Meaning, evil jinn tempted some pagan Arabs to believe that the angels are God's daughters through female jinn.
1234 *See* footnote for 6:128.
1235 Some jinn used to eavesdrop on the heaven, then pass on what they heard to fortune-tellers. But this practice came to an end once Muḥammad was sent as a messenger with the Quran.

13. When we heard the guidance ˹of the Quran˺, we ˹readily˺ believed in it. For whoever believes in their Lord will have no fear of being denied ˹a reward˺ or wronged. **14.** And among us are those who have submitted ˹to God˺ and those who are deviant. So ˹as for˺ those who submitted, it is they who have attained Right Guidance. **15.** And as for the deviant, they will be fuel for Hell.'"

A Message to the Deniers

16. Had the deniers followed the Right Way, We would have certainly granted them abundant rain to drink— **17.** as a test for them.[1236] And whoever turns away from the remembrance of their Lord will be admitted by Him into an overwhelming punishment.

Worship God Alone

18. The places of worship are ˹only˺ for God, so do not invoke anyone besides Him. **19.** Yet when the servant of God[1237] stood up calling upon Him, the pagans almost swarmed over him. **20.** Say, ˹O Prophet,˺ "I call only upon my Lord, associating none with Him ˹in worship˺." **21.** Say, "It is not in my power to harm

or benefit you." **22.** Say, "No one can protect me from God ˹if I were to disobey Him˺, nor can I find any refuge other than Him. **23.** ˹My duty is˺ only to convey ˹the truth˺ from God and ˹deliver˺ His messages." And whoever disobeys God and His Messenger will certainly be in the Fire of Hell, to stay there for ever and ever.

Warning to Pagan Deniers

24. Only when they see what they have been threatened with will they know who is weaker in helpers and inferior in manpower. **25.** Say, "I do not know if what you are promised is near or my Lord has set a distant time for it. **26.** ˹He is the˺ Knower of the unseen, disclosing none of it to anyone, **27.** except messengers of His choice. Then He appoints angel-guards before and behind them **28.** to ensure that the messengers fully deliver the messages of their Lord— though He ˹already˺ knows all about them, and keeps account of everything."

73. The Wrapped One *(Al-Muzzammil)*

This early Meccan chapter prepares the Prophet for the commandments yet to be revealed and the challenges ahead. The Prophet is advised, both in this chapter and the next, to seek comfort in patience and prayer, whereas the arrogant disbelievers are warned of a horrible punishment in Hell.

In the Name of God—the Most Compassionate, Most Merciful

Empowering the Prophet Through Prayer

1. O you wrapped ˹in your clothes˺! **2.** Stand all night ˹in prayer˺ except a little— **3.** ˹pray˺ half the night, or a little less, **4.** or a little more—and recite the Quran ˹properly˺ in a measured way. **5.** ˹For˺ We will soon send upon you a weighty revelation. **6.** Indeed, worship in the night is more impactful and suitable for recitation. **7.** For during the day you are over-occupied ˹with

---

1236 Meaning, to see if they will be grateful to God for rain and other provisions.
1237 i.e., Muḥammad.

worldly duties'. **8.** 'Always' remember the Name of your Lord, and devote yourself to Him wholeheartedly. **9.** 'He is the' Lord of the east and the west. There is no god 'worthy of worship' except Him, so take Him 'alone' as a Trustee of Affairs.

Reassuring the Prophet

10. Be patient 'O Prophet' with what they say, and depart from them courteously. **11.** And leave to Me the deniers—the people of luxury—and bear with them for a little while. **12.** 'For' We certainly have shackles, a 'raging' Fire, **13.** choking food, and a painful punishment 'in store for them' **14.** on the Day the earth and mountains will shake 'violently', and mountains will be 'reduced to' dunes of shifting sand.

A Warning to the Polytheists

15. Indeed, We have sent to you a messenger as a witness over you, just as We sent a messenger to Pharaoh. **16.** But Pharaoh disobeyed the messenger, so We seized him with a stern grip. **17.** If you 'pagans' persist in disbelief, then how will you guard yourselves against 'the horrors of' a Day which will turn children's hair grey? **18.** It will 'even' cause the sky to split apart. His promise 'of judgment' must be fulfilled. **19.** Surely this is a reminder. So let whoever wills take the 'Right' Way to their Lord.

Night Prayers Eased

20. Surely your Lord knows that you 'O Prophet' stand 'in prayer' for nearly two-thirds of the night, or 'sometimes' half of it, or a third, as do some of those with you. God 'alone' keeps a 'precise' measure of the day and night. He knows that you 'believers' are unable to endure this, and has turned to you in mercy.[1238] So recite 'in prayer' whatever you can from the Quran. He knows that some of you will be sick, some will be travelling throughout the land seeking God's bounty, and some fighting in the cause of God. So recite whatever you can from it. And 'continue to' perform 'regular' prayers, pay alms-tax, and lend to God a good loan.[1239] Whatever good you send forth for yourselves, you will find it with God far better and more rewarding.[1240] And seek God's forgiveness. Surely God is All-Forgiving, Most Merciful.

74. The One Covered up *(Al-Muddaththir)*

Following his first encounter with the angel Gabriel at a cave in the outskirts of Mecca, the Prophet rushed to his house in total shock, asking his wife to cover him up with his cloak. Later, this Meccan chapter was revealed, urging him to shoulder the responsibility of delivering the message. God promises to deal with the pagan tyrants who oppose the truth, defame the Quran, and ridicule warnings of Hell. The pagan denial of the Hereafter is dealt with in the next chapter.

In the Name of God—the Most Compassionate, Most Merciful

1238 This passage lightens the ruling mentioned in 73:2-4. So from now on, the believers do not have to stick to any of the portions specified at the beginning of this chapter. Rather, they can pray whatever they can at night.
1239 i.e., giving for charity and good causes.
1240 The reward for your charity will be far better than what you left behind or what you have given in charity because it will be rewarded ten-fold, or even 700-fold, and God gives more to whoever He wills. *See* 2:261.

A Message to the Prophet

1. O you covered up 'in your clothes'! 2. Arise and warn 'all'. 3. Revere your Lord 'alone'. 4. Purify your garments. 5. 'Continue to' shun idols. 6. Do not do a favour expecting more 'in return'.[1241] 7. And persevere for 'the sake of' your Lord. 8. 'For' when the Trumpet will be sounded,[1242] 9. that will 'truly' be a difficult Day— 10. far from easy for the disbelievers.

The Fate of a Denier[1243]

11. And leave to me 'O Prophet' the one I created all by Myself, 12. and granted him abundant wealth, 13. and children always by his side, 14. and made life very easy for him. 15. Yet he is hungry for more. 16. But no! 'For' he has been truly stubborn with Our revelations. 17. I will make his fate unbearable, 18. for he contemplated and determined 'a degrading label for the Quran'. 19. May he be condemned! How evil was what he determined! 20. May he be condemned even more! How evil was what he determined! 21. Then he re-contemplated 'in frustration', 22. then frowned and scowled, 23. then turned his back 'on the truth' and acted arrogantly, 24. saying, "This 'Quran' is nothing but magic from the ancients. 25. This is no more than the word of a man." 26. Soon I will burn him in Hell! 27. And what will make you realize what Hell is? 28. It does not let anyone live or die,[1244] 29. scorching the skin. 30. It is overseen by nineteen 'keepers'.

The Nineteen Keepers of Hell

31. We have appointed only 'stern' angels as wardens of the Fire. And We have made their number only as a test for the disbelievers,[1245] so that the People of the Book will be certain, and the believers will increase in faith, and neither the People of the Book nor the believers will have any doubts, and so that those 'hypocrites' with sickness in their hearts and the disbelievers will argue, "What does God mean by such a number?" In this way God leaves whoever He wills to stray and guides whoever He wills. And none knows the forces of your Lord except He. And this 'description of Hell' is only a reminder to humanity.

Warning of Hell

32. But no! By the moon, 33. and the night as it retreats, 34. and the day as it breaks! 35. Surely Hell is one of the mightiest catastrophes— 36. a warning to humankind, 37. to whichever of you chooses to take the lead or lag behind.

What Leads the Wicked to Hell

38. Every soul will be detained for what it has done, 39. except the people of the right, 40. who will be in Gardens, asking one another 41. about the wicked 'who will then be asked': 42. "What has landed you in Hell?" 43. They will reply, "We were not of those who prayed, 44. nor did we feed the poor. 45. We used to indulge 'in falsehood' along with others, 46. and deny the Day of Judgment, 47. until the inevitable came to us." 48. So the pleas of intercessors will be of no benefit to them.

1241 It was a common practice to give someone a gift, hoping to receive a more valuable gift in return. This practice is disliked in Islam.

1242 This is when the Trumpet will be blown for the second time, causing everyone to rise from the dead for judgment. See 39:68.

1243 This refers to Al-Walîd ibn Al-Mughîrah, a leader of Meccan opposition against Islam. See footnote for 64:10-16.

1244 Another possible translation: "It spares none and leaves nothing."

1245 Some pagans made fun of the Prophet when they were told that the keepers of Hell are nineteen angels. One of them said mockingly to other pagans, "You take care of two angels and I will vanquish the rest all by myself."

Warning to Pagan Deniers

49. Now, what is the matter with them that they are turning away from the reminder, **50.** as if they were spooked zebras **51.** fleeing from a lion? **52.** In fact, each one of them wishes to be given a 'personal' letter 'from God' for all 'to read'.[1246] **53.** But no! In fact,

they do not fear the Hereafter. **54.** Enough! Surely this 'Quran' is a reminder. **55.** So let whoever wills be mindful of it. **56.** But they cannot do so unless God wills. He 'alone' is worthy to be feared and entitled to forgive.

❧

75. The 'Rising for' Judgment *(Al-Qiyamah)*

This Meccan chapter refutes the pagan denial of resurrection and judgment. The chapter makes it clear that death and judgment are inescapable. The fact that God created humans from humble fluids and is able to bring all to account is detailed in the next chapter.

In the Name of God—the Most Compassionate, Most Merciful

Warning to Deniers of Resurrection

1. I do swear by the Day of Judgment! **2.** And I do swear by the self-reproaching soul! **3.** Do people think We cannot reassemble their bones? **4.** Yes 'indeed'! We are 'most' capable of restoring 'even' their very fingertips.[1247] **5.** Still people want to deny what is yet to come, **6.** asking 'mockingly', "When is this Day of Judgment?" **7.** But when the sight is stunned, **8.** and the moon is dimmed, **9.** and the sun and the moon are brought together,[1248] **10.** on that Day one will cry, "Where is the escape?" **11.** But no! There will be no refuge. **12.** On that Day all will end up before your Lord. **13.** All will then be informed of what they have sent forth and left behind. **14.** In fact, people will testify against their own souls,[1249] **15.** despite the excuses they come up with.

The Prophet's Rush to Memorize the Quran

16. Do not rush your tongue trying to memorize 'a revelation of' the Quran. **17.** It is

certainly upon Us to 'make you' memorize and recite it. **18.** So once We have recited a revelation 'through Gabriel', follow its recitation 'closely'. **19.** Then it is surely upon Us to make it clear 'to you'.

Another Warning to the Deniers

20. But no! In fact, you love this fleeting world, **21.** and neglect the Hereafter. **22.** On that Day 'some' faces will be bright, **23.** looking at their Lord. **24.** And 'other' faces will be gloomy, **25.** anticipating something devastating to befall them.

Death of a Denier

26. But no! 'Beware of the day' when the soul reaches the collar bone 'as it leaves', **27.** and it will be said, "Is there any healer 'who can save this life'?" **28.** And the dying person realizes it is 'their' time to depart, **29.** and 'then' their feet are tied together 'in a shroud'. **30.** On that day they will be driven to your Lord 'alone'. **31.** This denier neither

---

1246 Another possible translation: "In fact, each of them wishes to be given a scripture open 'for all to read'." See 6:124.
1247 This refers to the fact that every human has a unique set of fingerprints.
1248 They both will rise from the west and lose their light.
1249 Their organs will testify against them. See 41:19-24.

believed nor prayed, **32.** but persisted in denial and turned away, **33.** then went to their own people, walking boastfully. **34.** Woe to you, and more woe! **35.** Again, woe to you, and even more woe!

God's Ability to Create and Resurrect

36. Do people think they will be left without purpose? **37.** Were they not ˹once˺ a sperm-drop emitted? **38.** Then they became a clinging clot,[1250] then He developed and perfected their form, **39.** producing from it both sexes, male and female. **40.** Is such ˹a Creator˺ unable to bring the dead back to life?

76. Humans *(Al-Insân)*

This Meccan chapter reminds the human beings of how God created them, equipped them with different faculties, showed them the Way, and gave them free choice. The reward of those who choose to believe is mentioned at length in this chapter but passingly in the next chapter (77:41-44), whereas the reward of those who choose to disbelieve is mentioned passingly in this chapter (verse 4) but in great detail in the next. The Prophet is advised to be steadfast and not yield to the deniers of Judgment Day.

In the Name of God—the Most Compassionate, Most Merciful

Free Choice

1. Is there not a period of time when each human is nothing yet worth mentioning?[1251] **2.** ˹For˺ indeed, We ˹alone˺ created humans from a drop of mixed fluids,[1252] ˹in order˺ to test them, so We made them hear and see. **3.** We already showed them the Way, whether they ˹choose to˺ be grateful or ungrateful.

Reward of the Ungrateful

4. Indeed, We have prepared for the disbelievers chains, shackles, and a blazing Fire.

Reward of the Grateful

5. Indeed, the virtuous will have a drink ˹of pure wine˺—flavoured with camphor— **6.** ˹from˺ a spring where God's servants will drink, flowing at their will. **7.** They ˹are those who˺ fulfil ˹their˺ vows and fear a Day of sweeping horror, **8.** and give food—despite their desire for it—to the poor, the orphan, and the captive, **9.** ˹saying to themselves,˺ "We feed you only for the sake of God, seeking neither reward nor thanks from you. **10.** We fear from our Lord a horribly distressful Day." **11.** So God will deliver them from the horror of that Day, and grant them radiance and joy, **12.** and reward them for their perseverance with a Garden ˹in Paradise˺ and ˹garments of˺ silk.

Pleasures in Paradise

13. There they will be reclining on ˹canopied˺ couches, never seeing scorching heat or bitter cold.[1253] **14.** The Garden's shade will be right above them, and its fruit will be made very easy to reach. **15.** They will be

---

1250 *'Alaqah*, meaning the embryo resembles a leech.
1251 This is the time before a human comes into being and as an embryo.
1252 The mixture of male and female gametes (sperm and egg) which form the zygote after fertilization.
1253 There will be no day or night, sun or moon, winter or summer in Paradise. It will always be bright and temperate.

waited on with vessels and cups of crystal— 16. crystalline silver, filled precisely as desired. 17. And they will be given a drink 'of pure wine' flavoured with ginger 18. from a spring there, called *Salsabîl*. 19. They will be waited on by eternal youths. If you saw them, you would think they were scattered pearls. 20. And if you looked around, you would see 'indescribable' bliss and a vast kingdom. 21. The virtuous will be 'dressed' in garments of fine green silk and rich brocade, and adorned with bracelets of silver, and their Lord will give them a purifying drink.[1254] 22. 'And they will be told,' "All this is surely a reward for you. Your striving has been appreciated."

Reassuring the Prophet

23. Indeed, it is We Who have revealed the Quran to you 'O Prophet' in stages. 24. So be patient with your Lord's decree, and do not yield to any evildoer or 'staunch' disbeliever from among them. 25. 'Always' remember the Name of your Lord morning and evening, 26. and prostrate before Him during part of the night,[1255] and glorify Him long at night.[1256]

A Message to the Deniers

27. Surely those 'pagans' love this fleeting world, 'totally' neglecting a weighty Day ahead of them. 28. It is We Who created them and perfected their 'physical' form. But if We will, We can easily replace them with others. 29. Surely this is a reminder. So let whoever wills take the 'Right' Way to their Lord. 30. But you cannot will 'to do so' unless God wills. God is truly All-Knowing, All-Wise. 31. He admits whoever He wills into His mercy. As for the wrongdoers, He has prepared for them a painful punishment.

✦

77. Those 'Winds' Sent Forth *(Al-Mursalât)*

Like the two previous chapters and the next two chapters, this Meccan chapter makes it clear that God's power to create should be taken as a proof of His ability to bring the dead back to life for judgment. The horrors of the Hour and the punishment of the wicked are stated in strong terms.

In the Name of God—the Most Compassionate, Most Merciful

Judgment Day Is Inevitable

1. By those 'winds' sent forth successively, 2. and those blowing violently, 3. and those scattering 'rainclouds' widely! 4. And 'by' those 'angels' fully distinguishing 'truth from falsehood', 5. and those delivering revelation, 6. ending excuses and giving warnings. 7. Surely, what you are promised will come to pass.

Horrors of Judgment Day

8. So when the stars are put out, 9. and the sky is torn apart, 10. and the mountains are blown away, 11. and the messengers' time

---

1254 The word *ṭahûr* implies that once the believers take that pure drink, there will be no bad feelings in their hearts or ailments in their bodies.

1255 This verse refers to the five daily prayers: the dawn prayer, then noon and afternoon prayers, then sunset and late evening prayers, respectively.

1256 Extra prayers offered at night. *See* 73:20.

'to testify' comes up—12. for which Day has all this been set? 13. For the Day of 'Final' Decision! 14. And what will make you realize what the Day of Decision is? 15. Woe on that Day to the deniers!

God's Infinite Power

16. Did We not destroy earlier disbelievers? 17. And We will make the later disbelievers follow them. 18. This is how We deal with the wicked. 19. Woe on that Day to the deniers! 20. Did We not create you from a humble fluid, 21. placing it in a secure place 22. until an appointed time?[1257] 23. We 'perfectly' ordained 'its development'. How excellent are We in doing so! 24. Woe on that Day to the deniers! 25. Have We not made the earth a lodging 26. for the living and the dead, 27. and placed upon it towering, firm mountains, and given you fresh water to drink? 28. Woe on that Day to the deniers!

Bad News to the Deniers of Hell

29. 'The disbelievers will be told,' "Proceed into that 'Fire' which you used to deny! 30. Proceed into the shade 'of smoke' which rises in three columns, 31. providing neither coolness nor shelter from the flames. 32. Indeed, it hurls sparks 'as big' as huge castles, 33. and 'as dark'

as black camels."[1258] 34. Woe on that Day to the deniers! 35. On that Day they will not 'be in a position to' speak, 36. nor will they be permitted to offer excuses. 37. Woe on that Day to the deniers! 38. 'They will be told by God,' "This is the Day of 'Final' Decision: We have gathered you along with earlier disbelievers 'for punishment'. 39. So if you have a scheme 'to save yourselves', then use it against Me." 40. Woe on that Day to the deniers!

Good News for the Believers

41. Indeed, the righteous will be amid 'cool' shade and springs 42. and any fruit they desire. 43. 'They will be told,' "Eat and drink happily for what you used to do." 44. Surely this is how We reward the good-doers. 45. 'But' woe on that Day to the deniers!

Warning to the Deniers

46. "Eat and enjoy yourselves for a little while, 'for' you are truly wicked." 47. Woe on that Day to the deniers! 48. When it is said to them, "Bow down 'before God,'" they do not bow. 49. Woe on that Day to the deniers! 50. So what message after this 'Quran' would they believe in?

78. The Momentous News *(An-Naba')*

This Meccan chapter thoroughly refutes the arguments of those who deny the Hereafter by citing some of the marvels of God's creation to prove His ability to raise the dead to life and reward everyone according to their deeds.

1257 *See* 23:12-14 and 22:5.
1258 lit., yellow camels. Black camels' hair glistens yellow in sunlight.

78. The Momentous News (An-Naba')

In the Name of God—the Most Compassionate, Most Merciful

Pagans Mock the Truth

1. What are they asking one another about? 2. About the momentous news, 3. over which they disagree.[1259] 4. But no! They will come to know. 5. Again, no! They will come to know.

Miracle of God's Creation

6. Have We not smoothed out the earth 'like a bed', 7. and 'made' the mountains as 'its' pegs,[1260] 8. and created you in pairs, 9. and made your sleep for rest, 10. and made the night as a cover, 11. and made the day for livelihood, 12. and built above you seven mighty 'heavens', 13. and placed in them a shining lamp, 14. and sent down from rainclouds pouring water, 15. producing by it grain and 'various' plants, 16. and dense orchards?

Horrors of Judgment Day

17. Indeed, the Day of 'Final' Decision is an appointed time— 18. 'it is' the Day the Trumpet will be blown, and you will 'all' come forth in crowds. 19. The sky will be 'split' open, becoming 'many' gates, 20. and the mountains will be blown away, becoming 'like' a mirage.

Punishment of the Disbelievers

21. Indeed, Hell is lying in ambush 22. as a home for the transgressors, 23. where they will remain for 'endless' ages. 24. There they will not taste any coolness or drink, 25. except boiling water and 'oozing' pus— 26. a fitting reward. 27. For they never expected any reckoning, 28. and totally rejected Our signs. 29. And We have everything recorded precisely. 30. 'So the deniers will be told,' "Taste 'the punishment', for all you will get from Us is more torment."

Reward of the Believers

31. Indeed, the righteous will have salvation— 32. Gardens, vineyards, 33. and full-bosomed maidens of equal age, 34. and full cups 'of pure wine', 35. never to hear any idle talk or lying therein—36. a 'fitting' reward as a generous gift from your Lord, 37. the Lord of the heavens and the earth and everything in between, the Most Compassionate. No one will dare speak to Him 38. on the Day the 'holy' spirit[1261] and the angels will stand in ranks. None will talk, except those granted permission by the Most Compassionate and whose words are true. 39. That Day is the 'ultimate' truth. So let whoever wills take the path leading back to their Lord.

Wake-up Call to Humanity

40. Indeed, We have warned you of an imminent punishment—the Day every person will see 'the consequences of' what their hands have done, and the disbelievers will cry, "I wish I were dust."

1259 The pagans used to mock the teachings of the Quran (e.g., resurrection and judgment). They disagreed whether the Quran was magic, poetry, or fortune-telling.
1260 Just like tent pegs and icebergs, mountains go deep below the surface, slowing tectonic movement.
1261 i.e., the angel Gabriel.

79. Those ⌐Angels⌐ Stripping out ⌐Souls⌐ *(An-Nâzi'ât)*

This Meccan chapter emphasizes that the Day of Judgment is inevitable and its time is known only to God. The destruction of Pharaoh is cited as a deterrent to the disbelievers.

In the Name of God—the Most Compassionate, Most Merciful

The Hereafter Is Inevitable

1. By those ⌐angels⌐ stripping out ⌐evil souls⌐ harshly, 2. and those pulling out ⌐good souls⌐ gently, 3. and those gliding ⌐through heavens⌐ swiftly, 4. and those taking the lead vigorously, 5. and those conducting affairs ⌐obediently⌐! 6. ⌐Consider⌐ the Day ⌐when⌐ the quaking Blast will come to pass,[1262] 7. followed by a second Blast. 8. ⌐The deniers'⌐ hearts on that Day will be trembling ⌐in horror⌐, 9. with their eyes downcast. 10. ⌐But now⌐ they ask ⌐mockingly⌐, "Will we really be restored to our former state, 11. even after we have been reduced to decayed bones?" 12. They add, "Then such a return would be a ⌐total⌐ loss ⌐for us⌐!" 13. But indeed, it will take only one ⌐mighty⌐ Blast, 14. and at once they will be above ground.

Pharaoh Destroyed for Denial

15. Has the story of Moses reached you ⌐O Prophet⌐? 16. His Lord called him in the sacred valley of Ṭuwa, 17. ⌐commanding⌐, "Go to Pharaoh, for he has truly transgressed ⌐all bounds⌐. 18. And say, 'Would you ⌐be willing to⌐ purify yourself, 19. and let me guide you to your Lord so that you will be in awe ⌐of Him⌐?'" 20. Then Moses showed him the great sign,[1263] 21. but he denied and disobeyed ⌐God⌐, 22. then turned his back, striving ⌐against the truth⌐. 23. Then he summoned ⌐his people⌐ and called out, 24. saying, "I am your lord, the most high!" 25. So God overtook him, making him an example in this life and the next. 26. Surely in this is a lesson for whoever stands in awe of ⌐God⌐.

Resurrection Is Easier than Creation

27. Which is harder to create: you or the sky?[1264] He built it, 28. raising it high and forming it flawlessly. 29. He dimmed its night, and brought forth its daylight. 30. As for the earth, He spread it out as well,[1265] 31. bringing forth its water and pastures 32. and setting the mountains firmly ⌐upon it⌐— 33. all as ⌐a means of⌐ sustenance for you and your animals.

Horrors of Judgment Day

34. But, when the Supreme Disaster[1266] comes to pass— 35. the Day every person will remember all ⌐their⌐ striving, 36. and the Hellfire will be displayed for all to see— 37. then as for those who transgressed 38. and preferred the ⌐fleeting⌐ life of this world, 39. the Hellfire will certainly be ⌐their⌐ home. 40. And as for those who were in awe of standing before their Lord

---

1262 The first Blast will cause everyone to die except those spared by God. Then the second one will cause the dead to come to life for judgment. See 39:68.

1263 The staff turning into a snake. *See* 20:17-23.

1264 This is from a human perspective. Otherwise, both the creation of the universe and the resurrection of humans are easy for God.

1265 The Arabic verb *daḥa* also suggests that the earth is egg-shaped. The noun form *diḥya* is still used in some Arab dialects to mean an egg. Based on 2:29, 41:9-12, and 79:27-33, God ordained both realms, then formed the earth and created its provisions, then formed the heaven into seven heavens—all in six ⌐heavenly⌐ Days. *See* footnote for 7:54.

1266 This is the second Blast which will cause the dead to come to life for judgment. See 39:68.

and restrained themselves from 'evil' desires, 41. Paradise will certainly be 'their' home.

The Deniers' Mocking Question

42. They ask you 'O Prophet' regarding the Hour, "When will it be?" 43. But it is not for you to tell its time.[1267] 44. That knowledge rests with your Lord 'alone'. 45. Your duty is only to warn whoever is in awe of it. 46. On the Day they see it, it will be as if they had stayed 'in the world' no more than one evening or its morning.

෴

80. He Frowned *('Abasa)*

In a ḥadîth collected by At-Tirmiẓi, a blind man by the name of 'Abdullâh ibn um Maktûm, an early Muslim, came to the Prophet seeking to learn more about the faith, while the Prophet was in the middle of a discussion with an elite Meccan pagan, trying to convince him to abandon his idols and believe in the One True God. 'Abdullâh was so impatient that he interrupted the discussion several times. The Prophet frowned and turned all his attention to the man he was already talking to. This Meccan chapter was later revealed, telling the Prophet that he should have tended to the faithful man who was eager to learn. After this chapter was revealed, the Prophet would honour 'Abdullâh, calling him 'the man for whom my Lord rebuked me.' He (ﷺ) even appointed him several times as a deputy to lead prayers in his absence. The chapter calls upon the ungrateful disbelievers to reflect on how God produces plants out of the earth to realize how He can bring the dead out of their graves. The description of the horrors of the apocalypse is carried over to the next chapter.

In the Name of God—the Most Compassionate, Most Merciful

A Lesson to the Prophet[1268]

1. He frowned and turned 'his attention' away, 2. 'simply' because the blind man came to him 'interrupting'. 3. You never know 'O Prophet', perhaps he may be purified, 4. or he may be mindful, benefitting from the reminder. 5. As for the one who was indifferent, 6. you gave him your 'undivided' attention, 7. even though you are not to blame if he would not be purified. 8. But as for the one who came to you, eager 'to learn', 9. being in awe 'of God', 10. you were inattentive to him. 11. But no! This 'revelation' is truly a reminder. 12. So let whoever wills be mindful of it. 13. It is 'written' on pages held in honour— 14. highly esteemed, purified— 15. by the hands of angel-scribes, 16. honourable and virtuous.

A Reminder to Resurrection Deniers

17. Condemned are 'disbelieving' humans! How ungrateful they are 'to God'!

1267 Another possible translation: "What is this question? You 'O Prophet' are one of its signs." It is believed—based on authentic narrations from the Prophet—that he is one of the signs of the Day of Judgment.

1268 This passage, along with others that are critical of some things the Prophet did (such as 66:1), proves that the Prophet delivered the revelations in all honesty.

18. From what substance did He create them? **19.** He created them from a sperm-drop, and ordained their development. **20.** Then He makes the way easy for them,[1269] **21.** then causes them to die and be buried.[1270] **22.** Then when He wills, He will resurrect them. **23.** But no! They have failed to comply with what He ordered. **24.** Let people then consider their food: **25.** how We pour down rain in abundance **26.** and meticulously split the earth open ⌈for sprouts⌉, **27.** causing grain to grow in it, **28.** as well as grapes and greens, **29.** and olives and palm trees, **30.** and dense orchards, **31.** and fruit and fodder— **32.** all as ⌈a means of⌉ sustenance for you and your animals.

The Overwhelming Day

33. Then, when the Deafening Blast[1271] comes to pass— **34.** on that Day every person will flee from their own siblings, **35.** and ⌈even⌉ their mother and father, **36.** and ⌈even⌉ their spouse and children. **37.** For then everyone will have enough concern of their own. **38.** On that Day ⌈some⌉ faces will be bright, **39.** laughing and rejoicing, **40.** while ⌈other⌉ faces will be dusty, **41.** cast in gloom— **42.** those are the disbelievers, the ⌈wicked⌉ sinners.

81. Putting out ⌈the Sun⌉ *(At-Takwîr)*

This Meccan chapter describes some of the apocalyptic events leading up to the Day of Judgment, stating that everyone will meet the consequences of their deeds. The chapter closes by emphasizing that the Quran is God's revealed Word and that the Prophet is not insane, as the pagans claim.

In the Name of God—the Most Compassionate, Most Merciful

Horrors of the Apocalypse

1. When the sun is put out, **2.** and when the stars fall down, **3.** and when the mountains are blown away, **4.** and when pregnant camels are left untended,[1272] **5.** and when wild beasts are gathered together,[1273] **6.** and when the seas are set on fire,[1274] **7.** and when the souls ⌈and their bodies⌉ are paired ⌈once more⌉, **8.** and when baby girls, buried alive, are asked **9.** for what crime they were put to death,[1275] **10.** and when the records ⌈of deeds⌉ are laid open, **11.** and when the sky is stripped away, **12.** and when the Hellfire is fiercely flared up, **13.** and when Paradise is brought near— **14.** ⌈on that Day⌉ each soul will know what ⌈deeds⌉ it has brought along.

1269 The way to true guidance or the way out of their mothers' wombs.
1270 Burial is perceived as a way of honouring human beings after their death.
1271 This is the second Blast which will cause the dead to come to life for judgment. *See* 39:68.
1272 Ten-month pregnant camels were the most precious thing for nomadic Arabs, who cared for and treasured them.
1273 All animals will be brought together for judgment and then they will be reduced to dust.
1274 On the Day of Judgment the oceans and seas will be on fire.
1275 Some pagan Arabs used to bury their infant daughters alive for fear of shame or poverty. This practice was condemned and abolished by Islam. *See* 16:58-59.

A Message to the Deniers

15. I do swear by the receding stars 16. which travel and hide,[1276] 17. and the night as it falls 18. and the day as it breaks![1277] 19. Indeed, this 'Quran' is the Word of 'God delivered by Gabriel,' a noble messenger-angel, 20. full of power, held in honour by the Lord of the Throne, 21. obeyed there 'in heaven', and trustworthy. 22. And your fellow man[1278] is not insane. 23. And he did see that 'angel' on the clear horizon,[1279] 24. and he does not withhold 'what is revealed to him of' the unseen. 25. And this 'Quran' is not the word of an outcast devil.[1280] 26. So what 'other' path would you take? 27. Surely this 'Quran' is only a reminder to the whole world— 28. to whoever of you wills to take the Straight Way. 29. But you cannot will 'to do so', except by the Will of God, the Lord of all worlds.

❦

82. The 'Sky' Splitting Open *(Al-Infiṭâr)*

Like the previous chapter, this Meccan chapter describes some of the horrors of the Day of Judgment. The disbelievers are criticized for being ungrateful to their Creator. Everyone—including the cheaters mentioned in the next chapter—will be held accountable for their deeds, which are perfectly recorded by vigilant angels.

In the Name of God—the Most Compassionate, Most Merciful

Horrors of the Final Hour

1. When the sky splits open, 2. and when the stars fall away, 3. and when the seas burst forth, 4. and when the graves spill out, 5. 'then' each soul will know what it has sent forth or left behind.

Human Ingratitude

6. O humanity! What has emboldened you against your Lord, the Most Generous, 7. Who created you, fashioned you, and perfected your design, 8. moulding you in whatever form He willed? 9. But no! In fact, you deny the 'final' Judgment, 10. while you are certainly observed by vigilant, 11. honour-able angels, recording 'everything'. 12. They know whatever you do.

Warning of Judgment Day

13. Indeed, the virtuous will be in bliss, 14. and the wicked will be in Hell, 15. burning in it on Judgment Day, 16. and they will have no escape from it. 17. What will make you realize what Judgment Day is? 18. Again, what will make you realize what Judgment Day is? 19. 'It is' the Day no soul will be of 'any' benefit to another whatsoever, for all authority on that Day belongs to God 'entirely'.

❦

1276 This probably refers to black holes. *Kanasa* means to sweep or hide. *Miknasah* is derived from this, and is the standard word for a vacuum cleaner.
1277 lit., the day as it takes its first breath.
1278 i.e., Muḥammad.
1279 This is first time the Prophet saw Gabriel in his angelic form. He saw him a second time in heaven during the Night Journey. *See* 53:5-15.
1280 See 26:210-212.

83. Defrauders *(Al-Muṭaffifîn)*

This Meccan chapter begins with a warning to those who defraud scales about the horrible Day ahead, where the wicked will be severely punished and the virtuous will be richly rewarded. The chapter closes by stating that the disbelievers will be paid back for making fun of the believers.

In the Name of God—the Most Compassionate, Most Merciful

Warning to Those Who Cheat Others

1. Woe to the defrauders! 2. Those who take full measure ˹when they buy˺ from people, 3. but give less when they measure or weigh for buyers. 4. Do such people not think that they will be resurrected 5. for a tremendous Day— 6. the Day ˹all˺ people will stand before the Lord of all worlds?

Fate of the Wicked

7. But no! The wicked are certainly bound for *Sijjîn*[1281] ˹in the depths of Hell˺— 8. and what will make you realize what *Sijjîn* is?— 9. a fate ˹already˺ sealed.[1282] 10. Woe on that Day to the deniers— 11. those who deny Judgment Day! 12. None would deny it except every evildoing transgressor. 13. Whenever Our revelations are recited to them, they say, "Ancient fables!" 14. But no! In fact, their hearts have been stained by all ˹the evil˺ they used to commit! 15. Undoubtedly, they will be sealed off from their Lord on that Day. 16. Moreover, they will surely burn in Hell, 17. and then be told, "This is what you used to deny."

Fate of the Virtuous

18. But no! The virtuous are certainly bound for *'Illiyûn*[1283] ˹in elevated Gardens˺— 19. and what will make you realize what *'Illiyûn* is?— 20. a fate ˹already˺ sealed, 21. witnessed by those nearest ˹to God˺. 22. Surely the virtuous will be in bliss, 23. ˹seated˺ on ˹canopied˺ couches, gazing around. 24. You will recognize on their faces the glow of delight. 25. They will be given a drink of sealed, pure wine, 26. whose last sip will smell like musk. So let whoever aspires to this strive ˹diligently˺. 27. And this drink's flavour will come from *Tasnîm*— 28. a spring from which those nearest ˹to God˺ will drink.

The Last Laugh

29. Indeed, the wicked used to laugh at the believers, 30. wink to one another whenever they passed by, 31. and muse ˹over these exploits˺ upon returning to their own people. 32. And when they saw the faithful, they would say, "These ˹people˺ are truly astray," 33. even though they were not sent as keepers over the believers. 34. But on that Day the believers will be laughing at the disbelievers, 35. as they sit on ˹canopied˺ couches, looking on. 36. ˹The believers will be asked,˺ "Have the disbelievers ˹not˺ been paid back for what they used to do?"

⚜

1281 *Sijjîn* is the name of place (such as a confinement) in the depths of Hell.
1282 This is based on the commentary of Ibn Kathîr.
1283 *'Illiyûn* is an elevated place in Paradise.

84. The ᴦSkyᴧ Bursting Open *(Al-Inshiqâq)*

As a follow-up to the previous chapters, this Meccan chapter elaborates upon what to expect on Judgment Day. The believers will receive their records of deeds in their right hands and rejoice after an easy judgment, whereas the disbelievers will receive their records in their left hands and cry for instant destruction. The disbelievers are criticized for failing to submit to God, contrasted with the full submission of the sky and the earth in verses 1-5. More warnings to the evildoers appear in the next chapter.

In the Name of God—the Most Compassionate, Most Merciful

Horrors of Judgment Day

1. When the sky bursts open, 2. obeying its Lord as it must, 3. and when the earth is flattened out, 4. and ejects ᴦallᴧ its contents[1284] and becomes empty, 5. obeying its Lord as it must, ᴦsurely you will all be judgedᴧ.

Fate of the Faithful and the Wicked

6. O humanity! Indeed, you are labouring restlessly towards your Lord, and will ᴦeventuallyᴧ meet the consequences. 7. As for those who are given their record in their right hand, 8. they will have an easy reckoning, 9. and will return to their people joyfully. 10. And as for those who are given their record ᴦin their left handᴧ from behind their backs, 11. they will cry for ᴦinstantᴧ destruction, 12. and will burn in the blazing Fire. 13. For they used to be prideful among their people, 14. thinking they would never return ᴦto Godᴧ. 15. Yes ᴦthey wouldᴧ! Surely their Lord has always been All-Seeing of them.

Invitation to Believe

16. So, I do swear by the twilight! 17. And by the night and whatever it envelops! 18. And by the moon when it waxes full! 19. You will certainly pass from one state to another.[1285] 20. So what is the matter with them that they do not believe, 21. and when the Quran is recited to them, they do not bow down ᴦin submissionᴧ?[1286] 22. In fact, the disbelievers persist in denial. 23. But God knows best whatever they hide. 24. So give them good news of a painful punishment. 25. But those who believe and do good will have a never-ending reward.

❧

85. Constellations *(Al-Burûj)*

The beginning of this Meccan chapter condemns the persecution of the Christians of Najrân (a city on the border of Yemen and Saudi Arabia) at the hands of the pagans around 524 C.E. The tyrants are warned of the torment of burning, whereas the believers are promised a great reward in Paradise. Both this chapter and the next swear by the towering sky, emphasize God's infinite power, pose a warning to the evildoers, and stress the divinity of the Quran.

1284 i.e., treasures and dead bodies.
1285 You will pass from life to death and from death to resurrection, from well-being to sickness and from sickness to well-being, from poverty to richness and from richness to poverty, etc.
1286 lit., they do not prostrate.

In the Name of God—the Most Compassionate, Most Merciful

The People of the Fire Pit

1. By the sky full of constellations, 2. and the promised Day 'of Judgment', 3. and the witness and what is witnessed![1287] 4. Condemned are the makers of the ditch— 5. the fire 'pit', filled with fuel— 6. when they sat around it, 7. watching what they had 'ordered to be' done to the believers, 8. who they resented for no reason other than belief in God—the Almighty, the Praiseworthy— 9. 'the One' to Whom belongs the kingdom of the heavens and earth. And God is a Witness over all things. 10. Those who persecute the believing men and women and then do not repent will certainly suffer the punishment of Hell and the torment of burning. 11. Surely those who believe and do good will have Gardens under which rivers flow. That is the greatest triumph.

Warning to Arab Pagans

12. Indeed, the 'crushing' grip of your Lord is severe. 13. 'For' He is certainly the One Who originates and resurrects 'all'. 14. And He is the All-Forgiving, All-Loving— 15. Lord of the Throne, the All-Glorious, 16. Doer of whatever He wills. 17. Has the story of the 'destroyed' forces reached you 'O Prophet'— 18. 'the forces of' Pharaoh and Thamûd? 19. Yet the disbelievers 'still' persist in denial. 20. But God encompasses them from all sides. 21. In fact, this is a glorious Quran, 22. 'recorded' in a Preserved Tablet.

◈

86. The Nightly Star *(Aṭ-Ṭâriq)*

In this Meccan sûrah, an oath is made that whatever a person does is recorded by vigilant angels and that the Resurrection is as easy for Allah as the first creation. Another oath is made that the Quran is a decisive message, and a warning is given to those who plot against Allah.

In the Name of God—the Most Compassionate, Most Merciful

God's Power to Create and Resurrect

1. By the sky and the nightly star! 2. And what will make you realize what the nightly star is? 3. 'It is' the star of piercing brightness. 4. There is no soul without a vigilant angel 'recording everything'. 5. Let people then consider what they were created from! 6. 'They were' created from a spurting fluid, 7. stemming from between the backbone and the ribcage.[1288] 8. Surely He is fully capable

---

1287 The witness can be God, the angels, or the prophets, and the witnessed can be the people standing for judgment or the overwhelming events of Judgment Day.

1288 Testes and ovaries are formed in the abdomen of the fetus during the first weeks of pregnancy, before descending to their permanent place in the pelvis. Both are sustained by arteries originating between the backbone and the ribcage.

of bringing them back 'to life'— 9. on the Day all secrets will be disclosed. 10. Then one will have neither power nor 'any' helper.

Warning to Arab Pagans

11. By the sky with its recurring cycles, 12. and the earth with its sprouting plants! 13. Surely this 'Quran' is a decisive word,

14. and is not to be taken lightly. 15. They are certainly devising 'evil' plans, 16. but I too am planning. 17. So bear with the disbelievers 'O Prophet'. Let them be for 'just' a little while.

87. The Most High (Al-A'la)

Unlike the wicked who plot against God (according to the end of the previous chapter), the Prophet is ordered at the beginning of this Meccan chapter to glorify his Lord. This fleeting world is compared to the short life of plants (verses 4-5). The Prophet is reassured of God's support, and the wicked are warned of burning in Hell. This warning is emphasized in the next chapter.

In the Name of God—the Most Compassionate, Most Merciful

The Master Creator

1. Glorify the Name of your Lord, the Most High, 2. Who created and 'perfectly' fashioned 'all', 3. and Who ordained precisely and inspired accordingly, 4. and Who brings forth 'green' pasture, 5. then reduces it to withered chaff.

The Quran and the Way of Ease

6. We will have you recite 'the Quran, O Prophet,' so you will not forget 'any of it', 7. unless God wills otherwise.[1289] He surely knows what is open and what is hidden. 8. We will facilitate for you the Way of Ease.[1290] 9. So 'always' remind 'with the Quran'—'even' if the reminder is beneficial 'only to some'. 10. Those in awe 'of God' will be mindful 'of it'. 11. But it will be shunned by the most wretched, 12. who will

burn in the greatest Fire, 13. where they will not 'be able to' live or die.

The Way to Success

14. Successful indeed are those who purify themselves, 15. remember the Name of their Lord, and pray. 16. But you 'deniers only' prefer the life of this world, 17. even though the Hereafter is far better and more lasting. 18. This is certainly 'mentioned' in the earlier Scriptures— 19. the Scriptures of Abraham and Moses.

1289 Meaning, We will have you memorize the revelations and apply the rulings contained in them, unless one ruling is replaced by another.
1290 The Islamic way of life which brings about ease in this life and salvation in the next.

88. The Overwhelming Event *(Al-Ghâshiyah)*

This Meccan chapter compares the fate of the evildoers in the Hereafter to that of the good-doers. Those who disbelieve in God's might are criticized for failing to reflect on the wonders of His creation, and are warned of the fate of some destroyed disbelievers mentioned at the beginning of the next chapter.

In the Name of God—the Most Compassionate, Most Merciful

The People of Hell

1. Has the news of the Overwhelming Event reached you ˹O Prophet˺? 2. On that Day ˹some˺ faces will be downcast, 3. ˹totally˺ overburdened, exhausted, 4. burning in a scorching Fire, 5. left to drink from a scalding spring. 6. They will have no food except a foul, thorny shrub, 7. neither nourishing nor satisfying hunger.

The People of Paradise

8. On that Day ˹other˺ faces will be glowing with bliss, 9. ˹fully˺ pleased with their striving, 10. in an elevated Garden, 11. where no idle talk will be heard. 12. In it will be a running spring, 13. along with thrones raised high, 14. and cups set at hand, 15. and ˹fine˺ cushions lined up, 16. and ˹splendid˺ carpets spread out.

A Message to the Deniers

17. Do they not ever reflect on camels—how they were ˹masterfully˺ created;[1291] 18. and the sky—how it was raised ˹high˺; 19. and the mountains—how they were firmly set up; 20. and the earth—how it was levelled out? 21. So, ˹continue to˺ remind ˹them, O Prophet˺, for your duty is only to remind. 22. You are not ˹there˺ to compel them ˹to believe˺. 23. But whoever turns away, persisting in disbelief, 24. then God will inflict upon them the major punishment.[1292] 25. Surely to Us is their return, 26. then surely with Us is their reckoning.

෴

89. Dawn *(Al-Fajr)*

The Prophet is reassured in this Meccan chapter that the Arab pagans are not immune to the torments that befell 'Âd, Thamûd, and Pharaoh. A reference is made to the wicked who fail to be grateful in prosperity and patient in adversity. The evildoers will be regretful on Judgment Day, whereas the righteous will be honoured. Those who withhold God's bounties are criticized in this chapter (verses 17-20) and the next (90:11-16).

In the Name of God—the Most Compassionate, Most Merciful

1291 Another possible translation: "Do they not ever reflect on rainclouds—how they are formed?"
1292 The Hellfire is the major punishment. The minor punishment includes disasters in this life as well as torments in the grave. *See* 32:21.

Fate of the Deniers

1. By the dawn,[1293] 2. and the ten nights,[1294] 3. and the even and the odd, 4. and the night when it passes! 5. Is all this 'not' a sufficient oath for those who have sense? 6. Did you not see how your Lord dealt with 'Âd— 7. 'the people' of Iram—with 'their' great stature, 8. unmatched in any other land; 9. and Thamûd who carved 'their homes into' the rocks in the 'Stone' Valley; 10. and the Pharaoh of mighty structures?[1295] 11. They all transgressed throughout the land, 12. spreading much corruption there. 13. So your Lord unleashed on them a scourge of punishment.[1296] 14. 'For' your Lord is truly vigilant.

Bad News for the Deniers

15. Now, whenever a human being is tested by their Lord through 'His' generosity and blessings, they boast, "My Lord has 'deservedly' honoured me!" 16. But when He tests them by limiting their provision, they protest, "My Lord has 'undeservedly' humiliated me!" 17. Absolutely not! In fact, you are not 'even' gracious to the orphan, 18. nor do you urge one another to feed the poor. 19. And you devour 'others'' inheritance greedily,[1297] 20. and love wealth fervently. 21. Enough! When the earth is entirely crushed over and over, 22. and your Lord comes 'to judge' with angels, rank upon rank, 23. and Hell is brought forth on that Day—this is when every 'disbelieving' person will remember 'their own sins'. But what is the use of remembering then? 24. They will cry, "I wish I had sent forth 'something good' for my 'true' life." 25. On that Day He will punish 'them' severely, like no other, 26. and bind 'them' tightly, like no other.[1298]

Good News for the Faithful

27. 'God will say to the righteous,' "O tranquil soul! 28. Return to your Lord, well pleased 'with Him' and well pleasing 'to Him'. 29. So join My servants, 30. and enter My Paradise."

❦

90. The City *(Al-Balad)*

The underlying theme of this Meccan chapter is that human beings are equipped with the necessary faculties to choose between right and wrong. The good-doers are promised Paradise and the evildoers are promised Hell. This theme is emphasized in the next chapter.

In the Name of God—the Most Compassionate, Most Merciful

1293 Like many chapters, this one begins with an oath from God. He has the right to swear by any object of His creation (i.e., the sun, the moon, the stars, the dawn, or the angels). As for us, we are only allowed to swear by God alone.
1294 This refers to the first ten days of the month of Ẓul-Ḥijjah, in which the rituals of pilgrimage are performed.
1295 i.e., pyramids and obelisks.
1296 lit., so your Lord poured on them a whip of punishment.
1297 They take over the inheritance of orphans and women.
1298 Another possible translation: "None has ever punished the way He will punish on that Day, nor has anyone bound the way He will bind."

Ungrateful Disbelievers

1. I do swear by this city ʾof Meccaʾ— **2.** even though you ʾO Prophetʾ are subject to abuse in this city— **3.** and by every parent and ʾtheirʾ child! **4.** Indeed, We have created humankind in ʾconstantʾ struggle. **5.** Do they think that no one has power over them, **6.** boasting, "I have wasted enormous wealth!"? **7.** Do they think that no one sees them? **8.** Have We not given them two eyes, **9.** a tongue, and two lips; **10.** and shown them the two ways ʾof right and wrongʾ?

The Challenging Path of Good

11. If only they had attempted the challenging path ʾof goodness insteadʾ! **12.** And what will make you realize what ʾattemptingʾ the challenging path is? **13.** It is to free a slave; **14.** or to give food in times of famine **15.** to an orphaned relative **16.** or to a poor person in distress; **17.** and—above all—to be one of those who have faith and urge each other to perseverance and urge each other to compassion. **18.** These are the people of the right. **19.** As for those who deny Our signs, they are the people of the left.[1299] **20.** The Fire will be sealed over them.

91. The Sun *(Ash-Shams)*

This Meccan chapter states that people have free choice to purify or corrupt their souls. Those who choose purity will be successful, and those who choose corruption will be destroyed like the people of Thamûd. Free choice is the highlight of the next chapter as well.

In the Name of God—the Most Compassionate, Most Merciful

Purifying and Corrupting the Soul

1. By the sun and its brightness, **2.** and the moon as it follows it,[1300] **3.** and the day as it unveils it, **4.** and the night as it conceals it! **5.** And by heaven and ʾthe Oneʾ Who built it, **6.** and the earth and ʾthe Oneʾ Who spread it! **7.** And by the soul and ʾthe Oneʾ Who fashioned it, **8.** then with ʾthe knowledge ofʾ right and wrong inspired it. **9.** Successful indeed is the one who purifies their soul, **10.** and doomed is the one who corrupts it!

Destruction of the People of Ṣâliḥ

11. Thamûd rejected ʾthe truthʾ out of arrogance, **12.** when the most wicked of them was roused ʾto kill the she-camelʾ. **13.** But the messenger of God warned them, "ʾDo not disturbʾ God's camel and her ʾturn toʾ drink!" **14.** Still they defied him and slaughtered her. So their Lord crushed them for their crime, levelling all to the ground.[1301] **15.** He has no fear of consequences.

1299 Other chapters describing the people of the right and the people of the left include 56 and 69.

1300 Or "when it reflects the sun's light."

1301 It is true that while Qudâr ibn Sâlif was the individual who killed the camel, the rest of the people were supportive of what he did, so they were all punished collectively.

92. The Night *(Al-Layl)*

This Meccan chapter emphasizes God's power to create and show the Way, the people's ability to choose between good and evil, and the consequences of each route. The fact that the believers will be rewarded to their satisfaction is highlighted in this chapter (verse 21) and the next (93:5).

In the Name of God—the Most Compassionate, Most Merciful

The Faithful and the Faithless

1. By the night when it covers, 2. and the day when it shines! 3. And by ˹the One˺ Who created male and female! 4. Surely the ends you strive for are diverse. 5. As for the one who is charitable, mindful ˹of God˺, 6. and ˹firmly˺ believes in the finest reward, 7. We will facilitate for them the Way of Ease. 8. And as for the one who is stingy, indifferent ˹to God˺, 9. and ˹staunchly˺ denies the finest reward, 10. We will facilitate for them the path of hardship. 11. And their wealth will be of no benefit to them when they tumble ˹into Hell˺.

Reward of the Righteous and the Wicked

12. It is certainly upon Us ˹alone˺ to show ˹the way to˺ guidance. 13. And surely to Us ˹alone˺ belong this life and the next. 14. And so I have warned you of a raging Fire, 15. in which none will burn except the most wretched— 16. who deny and turn away. 17. But the righteous will be spared from it— 18. who donate ˹some of˺ their wealth only to purify themselves, 19. not in return for someone's favours, 20. but seeking the pleasure of their Lord, the Most High. 21. They will certainly be pleased.

93. The Morning Sunlight *(Aḍ-Ḍuḥa)*

It is reported that the revelation stopped for a while after the initial chapters of the Quran, so some Meccan pagans started to mock the Prophet, saying that God has become neglectful and hateful of him. Therefore, this Meccan chapter was revealed to refute their false allegations and remind the Prophet of some of God's favours.

In the Name of God—the Most Compassionate, Most Merciful

Reassuring the Prophet

1. By the morning sunlight, 2. and the night when it falls still! 3. Your Lord ˹O Prophet˺ has not abandoned you, nor has He become hateful ˹of you˺. 4. And the next life is certainly far better for you than this one. 5. And ˹surely˺ your Lord will give so much to you that you will be pleased. 6. Did He not find you as an orphan then sheltered you? 7. Did He not find you unguided then guided you? 8. And did He not find you needy then satisfied your needs? 9. So do not oppress the orphan, 10. nor repulse the beggar.[1302] 11. And proclaim the blessings of your Lord.

1302 And, by extension, anyone asking for help.

94. Uplifting the Heart *(Ash-Sharḥ)*

Like the previous chapter, this chapter reminds the Prophet of more blessings to reassure him of God's continued support in the city of Mecca, which is mentioned in the next chapter.

In the Name of God—the Most Compassionate, Most Merciful

More Reassurance to the Prophet

1. Have We not uplifted your heart for you 'O Prophet', 2. relieved you of the burden 3. which weighed so heavily on your back, 4. and elevated your renown for you?[1303] 5. So, surely with hardship comes ease. 6. Surely with 'that' hardship comes 'more' ease.[1304] 7. So once you have fulfilled 'your duty', strive 'in devotion', 8. turning to your Lord 'alone' with hope.

95. The Fig *(At-Tîn)*

This Meccan chapter emphasizes that God honours humans but many of them debase themselves by denying the meeting with Him in the Hereafter. Abu Jahl, one of the most notorious deniers is referred to in the next chapter.

In the Name of God—the Most Compassionate, Most Merciful

Reward of Ungrateful Deniers

1. By the fig and the olive 'of Jerusalem', 2. and Mount Sinai, 3. and this secure city 'of Mecca'![1305] 4. Indeed, We created humans in the best form. 5. But We will reduce them to the lowest of the low 'in Hell', 6. except those who believe and do good—they will have a never-ending reward. 7. Now, what makes you deny the 'final' Judgment? 8. Is God not the most just of all judges?

1303 The Prophet's name is always mentioned in the call to prayer, along with God's Name. Close to the end of each of the five daily prayers, worshippers invoke God's blessings upon the Prophet and his family. When someone reverts to Islam, they testify that God is their Lord and Muḥammad is His Messenger. Muslims, even those who are not practicing, love the Prophet and many name their children after him.

1304 If a definite noun is repeated in Arabic, it means that we are referring to the same thing. For example, "I met the man and I gave the man some money." But if an indefinite noun is repeated, it means we are referring to two different things. For example, "I met a man and I gave a man some money." With this in mind, we realize that 94:5-6 refers to one hardship (a definite noun) and two different eases (an indefinite noun). Hence, the Arabic saying: "Two eases cannot be overcome by one hardship."

1305 This passage refers to the land of figs and olives where Jesus lived, Mount Sinai where Moses communicated with God, and the City of Mecca where the Prophet started his mission. A similar reference can be found in Deuteronomy 33:1, 'Moses proclaimed:' "The Lord came from Sinai. Rising from Seir upon us, he [sic] shone forth from Mount Paran." Seir is a mountain near Jerusalem, and Paran is a mountain near Mecca.

96. The Clinging Clot *(Al-'Alaq)*

Verses 1-5 are known to be the first ever revealed of the Quran. The Prophet was re-treating at a cave in the outskirts of Mecca when the angel Gabriel appeared to him, squeezing him tightly and ordering him to read. Since the Prophet was unlettered, he re-sponded, "I cannot read." Ultimately, Gabriel taught him: "Read in the Name of your Lord ..." Some scholars believe that this encounter is the fulfilment of Isaiah 29:12, which states, "Then the book will be given to the one who is illiterate, saying, 'Read this.' And he will say, 'I cannot read.'" (The New American Standard Bible). The rest of the chapter was later revealed to deter Abu Jahl, a Meccan pagan elite, from abusing the Prophet.

In the Name of God—the Most Compassionate, Most Merciful

The First Revelation

1. Read, ʿO Prophet,ʾ in the Name of your Lord Who created— 2. created humans from a clinging clot.[1306] 3. Read! And your Lord is the Most Generous, 4. Who taught by the pen— 5. taught humanity what they knew not.

The Man Who Abused the Prophet

6. Most certainly, one exceeds all bounds 7. once they think they are self-sufficient. 8. ʿButʾ surely to your Lord is the return ʿof allʾ. 9. Have you seen the man who prevents 10. a servant ʿof Oursʾ from pray-ing?[1307] 11. What if this ʿservantʾ is ʿrightlyʾ guided, 12. or encourages righteousness? 13. What if that ʿmanʾ persists in denial and turns away? 14. Does he not know that God sees ʿallʾ? 15. But no! If he does not desist, We will certainly drag him by the forelock— 16. a lying, sinful forelock.[1308] 17. So let him call his associates. 18. We will call the wardens of Hell. 19. Again, no! Never obey him ʿO Prophetʾ! Rather, ʿcon-tinue toʾ prostrate and draw near ʿto Godʾ.

❧

97. The Night of Glory *(Al-Qadr)*

Since the previous chapter commemorates the first revelation, this Meccan chapter cel-ebrates the glorious night the Quran was revealed, which is believed to be the night of Ramaḍân 27, 610 C.E. The reason why the Prophet was sent with the Quran is spelled out in the next chapter.

In the Name of God—the Most Compassionate, Most Merciful

1306 *'Alaq*, meaning the embryo resembles a leech.
1307 Abu Jahl was a staunch leader of the Meccan opposition to Islam. There are many authentic stories of his abuse of the Prophet.
1308 This refers to the frontal lobe of the brain, where reasoning is processed.

1. Indeed, ʿit isʾ We ʿWhoʾ sent this ʿQuranʾ down on the Night of Glory.[1309] 2. And what will make you realize what the Night of Glory is? 3. The Night of Glory is better than a thousand months. 4. That night the angels and the ʿholyʾ spirit[1310] descend, by the permission of their Lord, for every ʿdecreedʾ matter. 5. It is all peace until the break of dawn.

98. The Clear Proof *(Al-Bayyinah)*

According to this Medinian chapter, the Prophet was sent so the disbelievers may change their ways and devote their worship to God alone. Those who believe are promised a great reward, whereas those who persist in disbelief are warned of a horrible punishment. The judgment of the believers and disbelievers is the highlight of the next chapter.

In the Name of God—the Most Compassionate, Most Merciful

The Prophet Is the Clear Proof

1. The disbelievers from the People of the Book and the polytheists were not going to desist ʿfrom disbeliefʾ until the clear proof came to them: 2. a messenger from God, reciting scrolls of ʿutmostʾ purity, 3. containing upright commandments. 4. It was not until this clear proof came to the People of the Book that they became divided ʿabout his prophethoodʾ— 5. even though they were only commanded to worship God ʿaloneʾ with sincere devotion to Him in all uprightness, establish prayer, and pay alms-tax. That is the upright Way.

Fate of the Deniers

6. Indeed, those who disbelieve from the People of the Book and the polytheists will be in the Fire of Hell, to stay there forever. They are the worst of ʿallʾ beings.

Fate of the Believers

7. Indeed, those who believe and do good—they are the best of ʿallʾ beings. 8. Their reward with their Lord will be Gardens of Eternity, under which rivers flow, to stay there for ever and ever. God is pleased with them and they are pleased with Him. This is ʿonlyʾ for those in awe of their Lord.

99. The ʿUltimateʾ Quake *(Az-Zalzalah)*

This Medinian chapter states that all deeds will be brought to light and accounted for on Judgment Day, which is also emphasized in the next chapter.

In the Name of God—the Most Compassionate, Most Merciful

1309 It is also believed that the angels descend with all decreed matters for the whole year during that night (*al-qadr* also means ordainment or destiny).
1310 i.e., the angel Gabriel.

Horrors of Judgment Day

1. When the earth is shaken 'in' its ultimate quaking, 2. and when the earth throws out 'all' its contents,[1311] 3. and humanity cries, "What is wrong with it?"— 4. on that Day the earth will recount everything, 5. having been inspired by your Lord 'to do so'. 6. On that Day people will proceed in separate groups[1312] to be shown 'the consequences of' their deeds. 7. So whoever does an atom's weight of good will see it. 8. And whoever does an atom's weight of evil will see it.

100. The Galloping 'Horses' *(Al-'Âdiyât)*

This Meccan chapter stresses the fact that people will be accountable on Judgment Day for their ingratitude to their Lord. The scene of the people emerging from their graves (verse 9) is elaborated upon in the next chapter.

In the Name of God—the Most Compassionate, Most Merciful

Human Ingratitude

1. By the galloping, panting horses, 2. striking sparks of fire 'with their hoofs', 3. launching raids at dawn, 4. stirring up 'clouds of' dust, 5. and penetrating into the heart of enemy lines! 6. Surely humankind is ungrateful to their Lord— 7. and they certainly attest to this— 8. and they are truly extreme in their love of 'worldly' gains. 9. Do they not know that when the contents of the graves will be spilled out, 10. and the secrets of the hearts will be laid bare— 11. surely their Lord is All-Aware of them on that Day.

101. The Striking Disaster *(Al-Qâri'ah)*

This Meccan chapter describes the Resurrection and the weighing of deeds in the Hereafter, followed by the final destination to either Paradise or Hell. The reason why many people will end up in the Fire is given in the next chapter.

In the Name of God—the Most Compassionate, Most Merciful

Fate of the Righteous and the Wicked

1. The Striking Disaster! 2. What is the Striking Disaster? 3. And what will make you realize what the Striking Disaster is? 4. 'It is' the Day people will be like scattered moths, 5. and the mountains will be like carded wool. 6. So as for those whose scale is heavy 'with good deeds', 7. they will be in a life of bliss. 8. And as for those whose scale is light, 9. their home will be the abyss. 10. And what will make you realize what that is? 11. 'It is' a scorching Fire.

1311 lit., burdens (i.e., treasures and dead bodies).
1312 The believers will head to Paradise and the disbelievers will head to Hell.

102. Competition for More ⌈Gains⌉ *(At-Takâthur)*

In this Meccan chapter and the next, the disbelievers are criticized for wasting their lives doing things that do not matter in the Hereafter, most importantly hoarding wealth.

In the Name of God—the Most Compassionate, Most Merciful

Wasted Lives

1. Competition for more ⌈gains⌉ diverts you ⌈from God⌉, 2. until you end up in ⌈your⌉ graves. 3. But no! You will soon come to know. 4. Again, no! You will soon come to know. 5. Indeed, if you were to know ⌈your fate⌉ with certainty, ⌈you would have⌉ acted differently⌉. 6. ⌈But⌉ you will surely see the Hellfire. 7. Again, you will surely see it with the eye of certainty. 8. Then, on that Day, you will definitely be questioned about ⌈your worldly⌉ pleasures.

---

103. The ⌈Passage of⌉ Time *(Al-'Aṣr)*

This Meccan chapter emphasizes that, unlike the evildoers mentioned in the next chapter, only those who take advantage of this fleeting life by doing good will be successful in the eternal life to come.

In the Name of God—the Most Compassionate, Most Merciful

Wake-up Call to Humanity

1. By the ⌈passage of⌉ time! 2. Surely humanity is in ⌈grave⌉ loss, 3. except those who have faith, do good, and urge each other to the truth, and urge each other to perseverance.

---

104. The Backbiters *(Al-Humazah)*

This Meccan chapter is critical of those who slander others and withhold God's bounties. It is made clear that their punishment in Hell is as easy for God as the destruction of the evil force mentioned in the next chapter.

In the Name of God—the Most Compassionate, Most Merciful

Warning to Defamers

1. Woe to every backbiter, slanderer, 2. who amasses wealth ⌈greedily⌉ and counts it ⌈repeatedly⌉, 3. thinking that their wealth will make them immortal! 4. Not at all! Such a person will certainly be tossed into the Crusher. 5. And what will make you realize what the Crusher is? 6. ⌈It is⌉ God's kindled Fire, 7. which rages over the hearts. 8. It will be sealed over them, 9. ⌈tightly secured⌉ with long braces.[1313]

1313 Other possible translations: 1. "The Fire will be in towering columns." 2. "They will be tied to long pillars."

105. The Elephant *(Al-Fîl)*

This Meccan chapter recounts the story of Abraha Al-Ḥabashi (lit., the Abyssinian), who led a large army of men and elephants to demolish the Ka'bah in 570 C.E. so pilgrims would visit the cathedral he had built in Yemen instead. However, the army was destroyed before reaching Mecca. It is commonly believed that the Prophet was born the same year.

In the Name of God—the Most Compassionate, Most Merciful

God's Protection of the Ka'bah

1. Have you not seen 'O Prophet' how your Lord dealt with the Army of the Elephant? 2. Did He not frustrate their scheme? 3. For He sent against them flocks of birds, 4. that pelted them with stones of baked clay, 5. leaving them like chewed up straw.[1314]

❧

106. 'The People of' Quraysh *(Quraysh)*

This Meccan chapter is viewed as a continuation of the previous one. The general idea is that the Meccan pagans must be grateful and devoted to God alone for saving the Ka'bah from the Army of the Elephant. Those who are unfaithful to God and unkind to the helpless are criticized in the next chapter.

In the Name of God—the Most Compassionate, Most Merciful

God's Major Favour to the Meccans[1315]

1. 'At least' for 'the favour of' making Quraysh habitually secure— 2. secure in their trading caravan 'to Yemen' in the winter and 'Syria' in the summer— 3. let them worship the Lord of this 'Sacred' House, 4. Who has fed them against hunger and made them secure against fear.[1316]

❧

107. 'Simplest' Aid *(Al-Mâ'ûn)*

This Meccan chapter, which takes its name from verse 7, condemns the deniers of the Hereafter for their lack of devotion to God and lack of compassion towards the needy. In the next chapter, the Prophet is ordered to be devoted to God alone and share the meat of his sacrificial animals with those in need.

1314 Or worm-eaten leaves.
1315 Quraysh is another name for the people of Mecca.
1316 Blessing the people of Quraysh with provision and security is probably the answer to Abraham's prayer in 14:35-37.

In the Name of God—the Most Compassionate, Most Merciful

Qualities of Judgment Deniers

1. Have you seen the one who denies the ˹final˺ Judgment? 2. That is the one who repulses the orphan, 3. and does not encourage the feeding of the poor. 4. So woe to those ˹hypocrites˺ who pray 5. yet are unmindful of their prayers; 6. those who ˹only˺ show off, 7. and refuse to give ˹even the simplest˺ aid.[1317]

---

108. Abundant Goodness (Al-Kawthar)

This Meccan chapter was revealed to reassure the Prophet. Since the Prophet's sons died in childhood, Al-ʾÂṣ ibn Wâ'il, an infamous Meccan pagan, used to say that Muḥammad would be forgotten because he had no son to carry his name. Today, 'Muḥammad' is the most common name in the world, whereas the name of Al-ʾÂṣ is barely mentioned. The Prophet is ordered to be devoted to God alone, which is the underlying theme of the next chapter.

In the Name of God—the Most Compassionate, Most Merciful

Good News to the Prophet

1. Indeed, We have granted you ˹O Prophet˺ abundant goodness.[1318] 2. So pray and sacrifice to your Lord ˹alone˺. 3. Only the one who hates you is truly cut off ˹from any goodness˺.

---

109. The Disbelievers (Al-Kâfirûn)

It is reported that the pagans offered to worship God alone for one year, provided that the Prophet worshipped their multiple gods for a year. So this Meccan chapter was revealed, telling them that he will be dedicated only to the worship of God until the last breath of his life, which is the highlight of the next chapter.

In the Name of God—the Most Compassionate, Most Merciful

No Compromise in Worshipping God

1. Say, ˹O Prophet,˺ "O you disbelievers! 2. I do not worship what you worship, 3. nor do you worship what I worship. 4. I will never worship what you worship, 5. nor will you ever worship what I worship. 6. You have your way, and I have my Way."

1317 They refuse to help others with small things like salt or water, let alone alms-tax.
1318 This includes a heavenly river as well other favours in both worlds.

110. The 'Ultimate' Help *(An-Naṣr)*

This Medinian chapter was revealed close to the end of the Prophet's life, instructing him that once his mission is complete and his message is embraced by many, he should be ready to meet his Creator. A deterring example of those who rejected his message is given in the next chapter.

In the Name of God—the Most Compassionate, Most Merciful

Nearing the Journey's End

1. When God's help comes and the victory ʿover Mecca is achievedʾ, 2. and you ʿO Prophetʾ see the people embracing God's Way in crowds, 3. then glorify the praises of your Lord and seek His forgiveness, for certainly He is ever Accepting of Repentance.

111. The Palm-Fibre Rope *(Al-Masad)*

This Meccan chapter is a warning to Abu Lahab (lit., the Father of Flames), who was an uncle of the Prophet. Both Abu Lahab and his wife Um Jamîl used to abuse the Prophet and deny the One True God, Who is described in the next chapter.

In the Name of God—the Most Compassionate, Most Merciful

The Fate of an Evil Couple

1. May the hands of Abu Lahab perish, and he ʿhimselfʾ perish! 2. Neither his wealth nor ʿworldlyʾ gains will benefit him. 3. He will burn in a flaming Fire, 4. and ʿso willʾ his wife, the carrier of ʿthornyʾ kindling,[1319] 5. around her neck will be a rope of palm-fibre.[1320]

112. Purity of Faith *(Al-Ikhlâṣ)*

This Meccan chapter refutes the Trinity, idolatry, atheism, and polytheism and calls for full devotion to the only God, Who is worthy to be worshipped and Whose protection is to be sought, according to the next two chapters.

In the Name of God—the Most Compassionate, Most Merciful

1319 Since she used to carry thorny branches and throw them in the way of the Prophet, she will be carrying firewood in Hell.

1320 This was one of the earliest chapters revealed of the Quran. Paradoxically, for Abu Lahab to disprove the Quran, all he had to do was accept Islam because this verse condemns him to Hell.

God's Absolute Oneness

1. Say, 'O Prophet,' "He is God—the Unique One;[1321] 2. God—the Sustainer 'needed by all'. 3. He has never had off-spring, nor was He born. 4. And there is none comparable to Him."[1322]

113. The Daybreak *(Al-Falaq)*

This Medinian chapter is recited as a supplication to the Almighty against any kind of evil, especially external ones. The next chapter deals with internal evil caused by whispers.

In the Name of God—the Most Compassionate, Most Merciful

Seeking Protection Against All Evil

1. Say, 'O Prophet,' "I seek refuge in the Lord of the daybreak 2. from the evil of whatever He has created, 3. and from the evil of the night when it grows dark, 4. and from the evil of those 'witches casting spells by' blowing onto knots, 5. and from the evil of an envier when they envy."

114. Humankind *(An-Nâs)*

Like the previous chapter, this Medinian chapter is a supplication against the evil of humans and jinn. This final chapter emphasizes the fact that God is the Lord and Master of all and that He is the only One to be called upon for help, which connects full circle with the central theme of the first chapter of the Quran.

In the Name of God—the Most Compassionate, Most Merciful

Seeking Protection Against Evil Whispers

1. Say, 'O Prophet,' "I seek refuge in the Lord of humankind, 2. the Master of humankind, 3. the God of humankind, 4. from the evil of the lurking whisperer— 5. who whispers into the hearts of humankind— 6. from among jinn and humankind."

1321 He cannot be divided into a father, a son, and a holy spirit as many Christians claim.
1322 As mentioned in the Introduction, the Quran has three main themes: 1. Stories, 2. Muslim teachings, 3. And belief in the unseen. Since Chapter 112 covers the third theme, the Prophet says in a *hadîth* collected by Bukhâri and Muslim that reading this chapter equals reading one third of the Quran.

Thematic Index

☪

DOCTRINE

Basic tenets: Faith perfected 5:3; only Way accepted by God 3:19, 3:85; no compulsion in accepting Islam 2:256; one religion with different faiths and codes of law 5:48, 22:67-70, 42:13-14; prophets of Islam 2:135-136, 3:84, 4:163-165; commandments (have faith in God and do good) 4:36, 6:151-154, 17:23-39, 18:107-108; five objectives of *Sharia*: protecting faith 5:54; protecting life 5:32, 6:151; protecting wealth 5:38; protecting honour 5:5, 24:4; protecting one's ability to think 5:90.

1. RELATIONSHIP WITH GOD
A. **The Five Pillars of Islam**
1) **Belief in God and the Prophet**

Divine qualities of God: Beautiful Names 57:1-6, 59:22-24, 85:13-16, 112:1-4; only god worthy of worship 1:1-4, 2:285, 6:3, 43:84; all authority belongs to Him 3:26; His Throne (*'Arsh*) 7:54, 11:7; His Seat (*Kursi*) 2:255; countless favours upon humanity 14:32-34, 2:164, 16:2-93, 31:20, 55:1-25; gives life and causes death 44:8, 53:44, 57:2, 67:2; brings about joy and sadness 53:43; gives abundant or limited provisions 13:26, 17:30, 29:62; Best of all judges 95:8; Most Merciful of the merciful 12:92; All-Loving 85:14; Full of Forgiveness and severe in punishment 13:6, 40:3; the First and Last 57:3; all honour and power belongs to Him 35:10; knows the unknown and sees the unseen 6:59, 6:73, 9:94, 9:105, 13:8-10, 31:34, 32:6, 34:48, 35:38, 39:46, 49:18, 59:22, 62:8, 64:18, 72:26, 74:31, 87:7; knows best what is hidden in the heart 5:7, 11:5, 31:23; knows what happened and what yet to come 2:255; wrote everything in the Record (or the Preserved Tablet) 6:38, 13:39, 36:12; able to do anything 2:117, 3:189, 8:41, 9:116, 11:4, 16:40, 40:68, 41:39, 42:49, 57:2; His infinite power 3:26-27, 24:45, 31:28-30; created the heavens and earth in six Days and never got tired 46:33, 50:38; creates with the word 'Be!' 36:81-83; never unjust to His creation 3:108, 4:40, 17:71, 21:47, 22:10, 26:209, 40:31, 41:46, 45:22, 50:29, 64:11, 78:6-16; everything submits to His Will 3:83, 22:18, 30:26; all stand in need of Him 11:6, 35:15, 55:29; trust in Him 10:84-85, 12:67, 25:58; forms of divine communication 42:51; worthy to be mindful of 2:21, 3:102, 4:1, 33:70-71, 59:18; wisdom is a gift from Him 2:269; He is not in need of any one 3:97, 6:133, 112:2; not one in a Trinity 4:171; has no mate 6:101; has no children 10:68, 19:35, 43:81, 72:3, 112:3; has no partners or associate-gods 6:94, 7:191-195, 46:4-5; nothing like Him 42:11, 112:4.

Order to reflect on the marvels of His creation 3:190, 6:99, 10:5-6, 13:3-4, 16:10-16, 88:17-20.

Signs in creation 2:164, 6:95-99, 7:57-58, 10:5-6, 13:2-4, 16:10-13, 16:65-69, 16:79, 23:27-30, 27:60-65, 30:19-25, 50:6-11; created everything for a purpose 10:5-6, 15:85, 16:3, 23:115, 29:44, 30:8, 38:27, 44:38-39, 75:36; universe perfected 67:3-4; merges day into night 3:27; diversity 30:22, 35:27-28; honey 16:68-69; milk 16:66; gift of children 42:49-50; planets and orbits 21:33, 36:38-44; constellations 25:61, 85:1; stars 37:6-7, 67:5; clouds 7:57, 30:48; earthquake 7:78, 7:155; landslide 28:81, 29:40; storm 10:22; drizzle, hail, and rain 2:265, 6:99, 24:43, 50:9-11; thunder and lightning 13:12-13.

Scientific references: humans created from male and female gametes 76:2; formation and developmental phases of an embryo 22:5, 23:12-14; fetus in three layers of darkness 39:6; earth's rotation 27:88; constant expansion of the universe 51:47-48; spherical shape of the earth 39:5, 79:30; the Big Bang 21:30; black holes 81:15-16; brackish water 25:53-54, 35:12, 55:19-20; wind pollination 15:22; fingerprints 75:3-4; air pressure 6:125; mountains as pegs 78:7; iron sent down 57:25; pain receptors 4:56; the sun as a radiant source and the moon as a reflected light 10:5; moon splitting 54:1; sky as a well-protected canopy 21:32; all beings created from water 21:30, 24:45; ants communicate 27:17-19; internal waves 24: 40; preservation of Pharaoh's body 10:90-92.

Living beings: angels 39:75; humans (an authority on earth) 2:30, 6:165, 16:4; jinn 72:1-15; animals belong to communities like humans 6:38 (calf 11:69, camel 7:40, dog 18:22, elephant 105:1, horses, mules, and donkeys 16:8, lion and zebras 74:50-51, monkeys 2:65, pigs 2:173, she-camel 7:73, sheep and goats 6:143, wolf 12:17); amphibians (frogs 7:133, snake 7:107); birds 24:41 (crow 5:31, hoopoe 27:20, quails 2:57); sea animals (fish 18:61, whale 37:142); insects (ants 27:18, bees 16:68, mosquito 2:26, fly 22:73, lice and locusts 7:133, spider 29:41); others unknown to us 16:8.

Plants and fruits: 6:99, 13:4, 16:11, 36:33-35 bananas 56:29, dates 19:25, herbs, cucumbers, garlic, lentils, and onions 2:61, grapes 80:28, olives 6:99, fig 95:1, pomegranates 55:68, squash 37:146.

- Belief in Muḥammad 3:144, 33:40, 47:2, 48:29.

Qualities of the Prophet: only a prophet 3:144, 6:50, 7:188, 18:110; to deliver the truth 2:119, 35:24, 42:48; seal of prophets 33:40; noble character 3:159, 68:4; a role model 33:21; as a favour to the believers 3:164; a mercy to the whole world 21:107; a universal messenger 4:170, 7:157-158, 34:28; leads to the Straight Path 42:52-53; cares about people 9:129; as a witness on Judgment Day 4:42, 16:89; unlettered prophet 7:157-158, 29:48, 62:2; prophesied in the Torah and Gospel 7:157; foretold by Jesus 61:6.

Challenges faced by the Prophet: pagans' meaningless demands 8:32, 15:7, 17:89-93, 25: 7-8; false accusations 10:2, 11:13, 21:5, 24:11-26, 25:4-6, 37:36, 38:4, 52:29-30; attempts on his life 8:30, 9:74; warning to those who harm or oppose him 4:115, 8:13, 9:61, 15:95, 33:57, 47:32, 96:9-19; ordered to respond to denial with patience 20:130, 30:60, 46:35, 70:5; ordered to seek comfort in prayer 15:97-99; reassured by God 5:67, 93:1-11, 94:1-8.

Lessons from the Prophet: from his emigration (*hijrah*) to Medina 9:40; Battle of Badr 3:121-129, 8:42-44, 8:65-71; Battle of Uḥud 3:151-180; Battle of the Trench 33:9-27; Battle of Ḥunain 9:25-27; Tabûk 9:38-123; Banu An-Naḍîr 59:2-6; Ḥamrâ' Al-Asad 3:172-175; Truce of Ḥudaibiyah 48:1-7, 48:10-29.

Honours bestowed on the Prophet: God and His angels bless him 33:56; night journey from Mecca to Jerusalem 17:1; journey to the heavens 53:1-18; honoured in this life and the next 17:79, 66:8, 108:1; obedience to him is obedience to God 4:80; reward of obedience to God and His Messenger 4:69; his family purified 33:33-34; sees Gabriel in his true form 53:1-18; believers ordered to obey him 59:7; etiquette of speaking to him 49:1-5; etiquette of visiting him 33:53; etiquette of dealing with his wives 33:53; God is pleased with him and his companions 9:100, 9:117; excellence of his faith-community 2:143, 3:110.

2)   **Prayer** (*ṣalâh*)
Importance of Prayer: 2:45, 9:103, 51:18, 70:22-23, 75:31, 96:10, 108:2; Friday congregation 62:9; direction of prayer (*qiblah*) 2:144, 2:149-150; should deter one from evil deeds 29:45; times 11:114, 17:78, 17:79, 20:130, 24:36, 24:58, 30:17-18, 32:16, 38:18, 50:39-40, 51:17, 52:48-49, 73:2-4, 76:25-26; while in danger or on a journey 2:239, 4:101-102; warning to those who neglect prayers 19:59, 74:38-47, 107:5-7; hypocrites' prayers 4:142, 9:54.

Purification: ablution (*wuḍû'*) 5:6; full bath (*ghusl*) 2:222, 4:43; dry ablution (*tayammum*) 4:43, 5:6.

Supplications (*du'â'*): of Abraham 2:126-129, 14:35-41, 26:83-89; Adam and Eve 7:23; Jesus 5:114; Job 21:83; Jonah 21:87; Joseph 12:33, 12:101; Moses 10:88-89, 20:25-35; Muḥammad 17:80, 20:114; Noah 23:26, 26:117-118, 54:9-10, 71:26, 71:28; Solomon 38:35; Shu'aib 7:89; Zachariah 3:38, 19:2-6, 21:89-90; angels 40:8-9; Mary's mother 3:35-36; Pharaoh's wife 66:11; Pharaoh's magicians 7:126; King Saul and the believers with him 2:250; the believers of the Children of Israel 10:85-86; the people of the cave 18:10; the righteous 2:285-286, 3:8-9, 3:16, 3:147, 3:191-194, 25:74, 59:10; the oppressed 4:75.

Prostration verses (*sajadât*, pl. of *sajdah*) 7:206, 13:15, 16:49, 17:109, 19:58, 22:18, 22:77, 25:60, 27:26, 32:15, 38:24, 41:37, 53:62, 84:21, 96:19.

3)   **Alms-tax** (*zakâh*)
Importance of alms-tax: as an obligation 2:110, 2:177, 2:277, 6:141; one of the qualities of the believers 22:41, 23:4, 51:19; recipients 9:60.

Charity (*ṣadaqah*) 2:177, 2:261-263, 2:267-274, 3:92, 63:10.

Warning to those who withhold 3:180, 9:34, 47:38.

4)   **Fasting** (*ṣawm*)
Importance of Fasting: in Ramaḍân 2:183-185; hours of fasting 2:187; exemptions 2:184-185; intimate relations during the night preceding the fast 2:187; fasting during pilgrimage 2:196.

5)   **Pilgrimage** (*ḥajj*)
Importance of pilgrimage: an obligation one those who can afford it 3:97; rituals and rulings 2:158, 2:189, 2:196-203, 5:2, 22:26-37; sacrificial offerings 2:196, 22:36-37; prohibition of hunting on land while on pilgrimage 5:1, 5:94-95; permissibility of hunting at sea 5:96.

Minor pilgrimage (*'umrah*) 2:158, 2:196.

B.   **The Six Articles of Faith**
1)   **Devotion to the One True God,** *see* God under DOCTRINE
Faith-communities: Muslims 2:132-136, 3:64, 3:84, 5:111, 22:77-78, 33:35, 41:33, 43:67-70, 72:14-15; guardians of one another 3:28, 9:71; Christians 2:62, 2:111-140,

4:171-172, 5:14-19, 5:82-86, 5:116-120, 9:30-31, 22:17; Jews 2:62, 2:111-140, 5:44-45, 6:146, 22:17, 62:6-8; Children of Israel 2:40-103, 2:122-123, 2:246-251, 3:49, 3:93-94, 5:12-13, 5:20-26, 5:32, 5:70-71, 5:78-81, 7:137-141, 7:148-153, 7:159-171, 10:83-93, 14:5-8, 17:2-8, 17:104, 20:80-98, 26:52-67, 26:197, 27:76, 44:23-33, 45:16-17, 46:10, 61:5-6; People of the Book (mainly Jews and Christians) 2:109, 3:64-115, 3:199, 4:123-172, 5:15-77, 6:20-21, 13:36, 28:52-55, 29:46-47, 57:16, 57:28-29, 74:31, 98:1-5; Muslims can eat from animals sacrificed by them and marry their women 5:5; foods forbidden to Jews 6:146; Sabians 2:62, 22:17; Magi 22:17; polytheists (pagans, idol worshippers) 3:186, 6:148, 9:6, 9:17, 10:28, 16:86, 22:17, 53:19-30; pagan superstitious practices 2:189, 5:103; 6:138-144; atheists 52:35-36.

Pagan practices abolished: burying daughters alive 16:58-59, 81:8-9; killing children for fear of poverty 6:137, 6:151, 17:31; whistling and clapping around the Ka'bah 8:35; dedicating camels to idols 5:103, 6:136; sacrificing in the name of idols 6:121; *zihâr*-divorce 33:4, 58:2-4; *ilâ'* (for more than four months) 2:226-227; drawing lots for decisions 5:3; circling the Ka'bah while naked 7:26-28; entering homes from backdoors after pilgrimage 2:189.

Objects of worship: angels (among some pagan Arabs) 34:40; *Al-Aykah* (among the people of Shu'aib) 26:176; Ba'l (among the people of Elias) 37:125; Jesus (in Christianity) 5:17; idols (among the people of Abraham) 21:52-53; the idols of *Lât, 'Uzza,* and *Manât* (among Arab pagans) 53:19-20; the idols of *Wadd, Suwâ', Yaghûth, Ya'ûq,* and *Nasr* (among the people of Noah) 71:23; the sun (the people of Sheba) 27:24; Sirius (among some pagan Arabs) 53:49; Pharaoh (in ancient Egypt) 26:29, 28:38, 79:24; desires 25:43-44, 45:23; belief in multiple gods refuted 17:42-43, 21:21-24, 25:3.

Places of worship: mosques 9:18; churches, synagogues, and monasteries 22:40; sanctuary 3:39, 38:21; temple 17:7.

Religious titles, priests, monks, and rabbis 5:44, 5:63, 5:82, 9:31-34.

2)   Angels
Inquire about the creation of Adam 2:30-34, never disobey God 21:26-27, 66:6; are not the daughters of God 21:26, 43:16-19; guarding angels 13:11; two recording angels 50:16-18, 82:10-12; eight carrying God's Throne on Judgment Day 69:17; nineteen keepers of Hell 74:26-31; Angels of Death 6:93, 16:28, 32:11; Gabriel 2:97, 66:4, 26:192-195, 53:1-14; Michael 2:98; Mâlik 43:77.

3)   Messengers (*see* Prophets under Stories),
From among angels and humans 22:75; Messengers of Firm Resolve (Abraham, Noah, Moses, Jesus, and Muḥammad) 33:7, 42:13, 46:35.

4)   Scriptures
Quran: a revelation from God 12:2-3, 20:2-4, 26:192-195, 32:2-3; a reminder to the whole world 68:51-52; guides to the most upright way of life 17:9; revelation started in the month of Ramaḍân 2:185; on a blessed night 44:3, 97:1-5; revealed in stages 17:105-106; made easy to remember 54:17; confirms the truth in previous revelations 3:3-4; a supreme authority on earlier scriptures 5:48; no doubt in it 2:2, 10:37; no contradictions 4:82; not fabricated 10:37-39; not copied from the Bible 25:4-6; not revealed by dev-

ils 26:210-212; no one can produce something like it 17:88, 2:23-24,10:13-14, 11:13; protected from corruption 15:9; protected in the Preserved Tablet 56:75-80; cannot be proven false 41:42; foretells future events 30:1-7, 48:27; moves the believers to tears 5:83, 17:107-109; touches hearts 39:23; brilliant light 4:174, 42:52; healing and mercy for the believers 17:82.

Torah 3:3, 3:93, 5:46, 5:66-68, 5:110, 7:157, 9:111, 48:29, 61:6, 62:5.

Gospel 3:3, 3:48, 5:46-47, 5:66-68, 5:77, 5:110, 7:157, 9:111, 48:29, 57:27.

Psalms 4:163, 17:55.

Scrolls of Abraham 53:36-44, 87:14-19.

5)   Fate and destiny
3:145, 9:51, 10:107, 11:6, 54:49, 67:30; free choice 6:148-150, 11:118-119, 16:93, 33:72-73, 39:41, 76:1-3, 91:1-10.

6)   Day of Judgment
No injustice 2:281, 18:49, 40:17; horrors of the apocalypse 22:1-2, 27:82-84, 27:87, 40:18, 52:11-16, 69:13-18, 70:8-18, 73:17-18, 75:7-15, 77:8-15, 78:17-20, 79:34-36, 80:33-42, 81:1-14, 82:1-5, 84:1-5, 87:17-40, 99:1-8, 101:1-11; the righteous and the wicked on that Day 11:105-108, 16:27-33, 16:84-89, 18:52-53, 20:100-111, 25:24-29, 30:12-16, 33:63-68, 39:68-75, 50:20-35, 55:37-41, 83:4-36; intercession (*shafâ'ah*) 2:48, 2:255, 6:51, 6:70, 10:3, 21:28, 32:4, 36:23, 39:43-44, 43:86, 53:26, 74:48.

Records of deeds: 17:13, 18:49; believers receive their record with their right hand 69:19-24, 84:7-9; disbelievers receive their record with their left hand 69:25-37, 84:10-15; nothing will be hidden from God 21:47, 40:16; weighing of deeds 7:8, 23:102-104, 101:1-11; testimony of bodily organs 41:19-24, 24:24; reward for good and evil deeds 6:160, 27:89-90, 28:84.

Types of people: believers 18:107-108; disbelievers 4:167-169; hypocrites 4:145, 57:13-15; residents of Paradise (foremost believers 55:46-61, 56:10-26; people of the right 55:62-78, 56:27-40); residents of Hell (people of the left 55:31-45, 56:41-56); people on the heights 7:46-49.

2.   RELATIONSHIP WITH PEOPLE
A.   Financial
Business guidelines 2:188, 2:275, 2:282-283, 4:29, 4:58, 6:152, 17:34-35, 24:36-37, 26:182, 30:39, 55:7-9, 62:9.

Bequests: optional bequests to non-heirs 2:180-183, 4:11-12; before death while on a journey 5:106-108.

Bribery 2:188.

Debts: kindness in collecting debts 2:280; writing and witnessing a debt contract 2:282; taking collateral 2:283.

Inheritance: guidelines 4:7, 4:32-33, 8:75; shares of offspring and parents 4:11; spouses and maternal siblings 4:12; full siblings 4:176; warning to those who don't comply 4:13-14.

Interest: prohibition and warning 2:275-281, 3:130-132; rendered profitless 30:39.

B. Legal
Anti-terrorism law (*hirâbah*) 5:33-34.

Justice: standing up for justice 4:135, 5:8, 16:90-91; standing up for the rights of orphans and women 4:127; justice to a Jew 4:105-112; justice to a pagan 4:58; fairness with non-Muslims 60:8-9.

Retaliation through legal channels (with the option to forgive), 2:178-179, 5:45, 16:126, 17:33, 42:37-43.

Separation between husband and wife: *khul'* 2:229; *li'ân* 24:6-10.

C. Political
Conducting affairs by consultation (*shûra*), 3:159, 42:38.

Fighting in self-defence (*jihad*): etiquette 2:190-192, 2:216, 22:38-40; not to attack indiscriminately 4:94; fighting for oppressed men, women, and children 4:75; protecting places of worship 22:37; reward of martyrs 2:154, 3:169-171, 9:111, 57:19; military might deters potential enemies 8:60; opting for peace 2:192, 8:61.

Making peace between parties, 49:9-10.

Prisoners of war, treatment 8:70, 47:4, 76:8.

D. Social
Adoption 33:4-5.

Caring for orphans 2:220, 4:2-10, 4:127, 6: 152, 17:34.

Decency: 7:26, 16:81; the veil 24:31; lowering the gaze 24:30-31.

Divorce: arbitration and reconciliation 4:35, 4:128; etiquette of divorce 2:229-231, 65:1-2; dowry and waiting period 2:226-241, 4:19-21, 33:49, 65:1-7; husband not to take back anything of the dowry 4:20; wife not be harassed 65:6; wife to be supported financially during pregnancy 65:6; during her waiting period 65:6; if she nurses ex-husband's child, 65:6; no parent should suffer because of their child 2:233; opting for wet-nurse 65:6.

Encouraging good and forbidding evil 3:104, 3:110, 7:157, 9:71-72, 31:17.

Equality of human beings: 49:13; equality between men and women before God and the law, 3:195, 4:124, 5:38, 16:97, 24:2, 40:40; men have a degree of responsibility above women 2:228.

Feeding the poor, orphans, and captives 76:8-9.

Forgiveness and anger control 3:134, 42:40.

Freeing slaves and helping them 4:92, 5:89, 9:60, 24:33, 58:3, 90:13.

Honouring one's own **parents** 4:36, 17:23-25, 31:14-15.

Humility 17:37, 31:18-19.

Interpretation of dreams: of Abraham 37:102; Joseph 12:4, 12:36, 12:43; Muḥammad 8:43, 48:27.

Kindness to non-Muslims 60:8.

Marriage: 4:3, 4:129, 16:72, 30:21; lawful and unlawful women to marry 4:22-24; etiquette of intimacy 2:222-223; pregnancy and nursing 2:233, 31:4, 46:15, 65:6; remarrying one's own ex-wife 2:230; helping singles to marry 24:32; subtly showing interest during the waiting period 2:235.

Oaths: 2:224-225, 16:91-92, 16:94; making up for a broken oath 5:89.

Patience in difficult times 2:45, 2:153-157, 3:186, 12:18, 12:83, 16:127-128, 70:5.

Permission: to enter 24:58-60; entering people's homes 24:27-28; entering public places 24:29.

Social etiquette: verifying news 4:83, 49:6; respect for all 49:11-12; etiquette of gatherings 58:11; private talks 4:114, 58:9.

Vows 2:270, 9:75-77, 22:29, 76:7.

Wasting and stinginess 7:31, 17:29, 25:67.

⏳

STORIES

1.   **Prophets** (twenty-five mentioned by name)

Aaron, with his brother Moses as messengers to Pharaoh and his people 7:122-172, 10:75, 20:30-92, 21:48, 23:45, 25:35, 26:12-48, 28:34, 37:114-120.

Abraham, raises the foundations of the Ka'bah 2:124-129; calls his people to the worship of the One True God 2:130-132, 26:69-89, 29:16, 29:24-27; debates arrogant king 2:258, inquires about resurrection 2:260; neither Jew nor Christian 3:65-68; refutes celestial worship 6:74-87; receives news of the birth of Isaac 11:69-76, 51:24-30; his prayer at the Ka'bah 14:35-41; visited by angels 15:51-56; a role model 16:123; calls his father to the truth 19:41-50; destroys idols and is saved from the fire 21:51-73, 37:83-113; calls all to the pilgrimage 22:26.

Adam, honoured by God, tempted by Satan 2:30-38, 7:11-25, 17:61-65, 18:50, 20:115-123, 38:71-85; forgiven by God 2:37, 20:122.

David, kills Goliath 2:251; passes a judgment 21:78-79; mountains and birds join him in praising God 34:10, 38:17-20; judges between two people 38:21-26; succeeded by his son Solomon 27:15-16.

Elias, with his people 37:123-130.

Elisha, (mentioned passingly) 6:86, 38:48.

Enoch, (mentioned passingly) 19:56-57.

Hûd, with his people 7:65-72, 11:50-60, 26:124-140, 46:21-25.

Isaac, birth and prophethood 2:136, 3:84, 4:163, 6:84, 11:71, 12:6, 37:112-113.

Ishmael, raises foundations of the Ka'bah with his father 2:125-140; story of the sacrifice 37:100-113.

Jacob (Israel), as a prophet 3:84, 3:93, 4:163, 6:84; in the story of his son Joseph 12:4-100.

Jesus, his virgin birth, message, and miracles 3:45-51, 19:16-38; reminded of God's favours 5:110-115; no more than a messenger 4:171-172, 5:75, 19:30; created by a word from God like Adam 3:59; honoured in this world and the Hereafter 3:45-46; his mother chosen over all women of the world 3:42; denies being divine 5:116-120; Christians asked not to deify him 4:171; neither killed nor crucified 4:157; his second coming 43:61; his disciples stand up for God 3:52, 61:14; compassion and grace in the hearts of his followers 5:82, 57:27.

Job, tested then rewarded 21:83, 38:41-44.

John the Baptist, birth and prophethood 3:38-41, 19:7-15, 21:90.

Jonah, swallowed by whale then saved 10:98, 21:87, 37:139-148, 68:48-50.

Joseph, best of stories 12:1-3; young Yusuf's dream 12:4-6; conspiracy by his brothers 12:7-18; sold into slavery 12:19-20; raised in Egypt's Chief Minister's house 12:21-22; Chief Minster's wife tries to seduce him 12:23-29; banquet incident 12:30-32; goes to jail 12:33-35; the two inmates 12:36-42; King's dream 12:43-53; becomes Chief Minister 12:54-57; brothers come to him for supplies 12:58-68; takes his brother Benjamin 12:69-82; his father's renewed grief 12:83-87; reveals his true identity 12:88-98; old dream comes true 12:99-100; concluding prayer 12:101.

Lot, with his people 7:80-84, 11:77-83, 15:61-74, 21:71-75, 26:160-175, 29:28-35, 37:133-138, 54:33-39.

Moses, childhood 20:38-40; 28:7-13; fateful encounter at the burning bush 20:9-36, 27:7-14; 28:29-35; story with Pharaoh 7:103-137, 10:75-92, 11:96-99, 26:10-68; nine signs for Pharaoh and his people 7:130-133, 20:17-22, 17:101; defeats Pharaoh's magicians 20:70-73, 26:46-52; kills an Egyptian by mistake 28:14-21; escape to Midian and marriage 28:22-28; receives the Tablets 7:142-154, asks to see God on the Mount 7:142-145; honoured by God 33:69; God's favours to Israelites 2:47-61; rebukes his people for calf-worship 7:148-156, 20:83-99; Israelites refuse to enter Jerusalem 5:20-26.

Muḥammad, *see* DOCTRINE

Noah, mocked 11:38; the Ark and the Flood 7:59-64, 11:25-48, 23:23-31, 26:105-122, 71:1-28; his son drowned 11:42-48.

Sâliḥ, with his people 7:73-79, 11:61-68, 26:142-158, 27:45-53, 91:11-15.

Shu'aib, with his people 7:85-93, 11:84-95, 26:176-191.

Solomon, helps his father David reach a fairer judgment 21:78-82; story with the ant 27:15-19; story with the hoopoe 27:20-28; story with the Queen of Sheba 27:22-44; God's favours upon him 34:12-14, 38:34-40; his love for fine horses 38:30-33.

Zachariah, praying for a child 3:37-41, 19:2-12, 21:89-90.

Ẓul-Kifl, (mentioned passingly) 21:85, 38:48.

2. **Other stories**

Abel and Cain 5:27-31; Al-Khaḍir and Moses 18:60-82; Army of the Elephant 105:1-4; the believer from Pharaoh's people 40:28-46; birth of Mary 3:35-36; Cow of the Children of Israel 2:67-74; Ezra 2:259; garden owners 68:17-32; Hârût and Mârût 2:102; Korah 28:76:82; Luqmân's advice to his son 31:12-19; owner of the two gardens 18:32-44; people of Sheba 34:15-19; people of the cave 18:9-26; people of the trench 85:1-8; Sabbath-breakers 7:163-165; Sâmiri and the Golden Calf 20:83-97; Saul and Samuel 2:247-251; Ẓul-Qarnain 18:83-98.

3. **Parables**

Accepted charity 2:265; God vs. false gods 13:14, 16:76; associating others with God in worship 22:31; believers and disbelievers 6:122, 7:58, 11:24, 40:58; believer's heart 24:35; believers' example in the Torah and Gospel 48:29; charity and grain 2:261; deeds of the disbelievers 3:117, 14:18, 24:39; evil word 14:26; good word 14:24-25; fleeting world 10:24, 18:45, 39:21, 57:20; hardened hearts 57:16-17; hypocrites 2:17-20; misguided scholar 7:175-176; monotheist vs. polytheist 39:29; resurrection 7:57, 22:5; 41:39; shepherd and sheep 2:171; spider 29:41; truth vs. falsehood 13:17; unbeneficial knowledge 62:5; wasted charity 2:264, 2:266; wasting the reward of good deeds 16:91-92.

☼

THE UNSEEN

God, *see* DOCTRINE

Angels, *see* DOCTRINE

Jinn, created from fire 15:25, 55:15; believing and disbelieving jinn 72:1-15; some believed in the message of the Quran 46:29-32; humans and jinn created for a purpose 51:56-58. **Satan** (*Iblîs*), arrogance 2:34, 7:11-27, 15:26-43, 17:61-65, 38:73-85; a jinn 18:50-51; Adam's temptation and fall 7:20-23, 20:116-121; has no authority over the believers 16:98-100; his goal 35:6-8; a sworn enemy to humanity 12:5, 17:53; his party

359

53:14-19; his handiwork 5:90-91; discourages good deeds 2:268; believers seek refuge in God from him 7:200-202; his schemes are weak 4:76; lets his followers down 8:48; talk to his followers in Hell 14:22. **Devils** 2:102, 6:71, 6:112, 6:121, 7:27, 7:30, 17:27, 19:68, 19:83, 22:3-4, 23:97-98, 26:210, 37:7-10, 38:37-38, 67:5; devilish humans and jinn 6:112, 114:6; heaven protected against devils 15:16-18.

Death 3:185, 4:78, 6:61, 6:93, 21:35, 23:99-108, 31:34, 32:11, 44:56, 47:27, 50:19-20, 56:60-62, 56:83-96, 75:26-35; cannot be stopped or delayed 63:10-11; twin brother of sleep 6:60, 39:42; believers and disbelievers at the time of death 8:50, 16:27-32, 41:30; punishment in the grave 40:46.

Final Hour, signs 21:96, 27:82, 43:61, 47:18, 54:1-2; names 1:3, 2:4, 3:55, 19:39, 30:56, 37:21, 40:15, 41:47, 42:7, 50:20, 56:1, 64:9, 69:1, 79:34, 80:33, 88:1, 101:1-3; time known only to God 7:187, 31:34, 33:63, 79:42-46; fast approaching 54:1; will take people by surprise 6:31, 7:187; Trumpet will be blown 6:73, 23:101, 39:68.

Resurrection 2:28, 16:38, 22:5-7, 23:16, 31:28, 41:39, 64:7; example in the story of Ezra 2:259, Abraham 2:260, people of the cave 18:9-26; warning to resurrection deniers 17:49-52, 17:97-100, 19:66-72, 37:11-27, 50:1-15, 80:17-42.

Day of Judgment, *see* DOCTRINE

Paradise, as vast as the heavens and the earth 3:133, 57:21; running water, cool shade, delicacies, and pure mates 2:25, 4:57, 36:55-58, 37:40-49, 38:50-54, 44:51-57, 52:17-24, 69:19-24; 76:5-22; reward of the believers 55:46-78, 56:10-40; rivers of honey, milk, water, and wine 47:15; prayers and greetings 10:9-10, 39:73-74; saluted with greetings of peace 13:23-24, 14:32; everlasting stay in Bliss 11:108; never asked to leave 15:45-48; light shining ahead of them and on their right 57:12; no heat or cold 76:13; all wishes granted 16:30-32, 41:31-32; bracelets of gold and clothes of fine silk 18:30-31, 22:23-24, 44:51-53; trays of golden cups 43:67-73; silver vessels and fruits hanging within reach 76:14-16; reclining on thrones 15:47, 37:44, 52:20; believers will see their Lord 75:22-23.

Hell, burning and boiling water 22:19-22, 23:103-104; pus 14:14-17, 38:55-58, 69:35-37; tree of *Zaqqûm* 37:62-70, 44:43-50, 56:41-56; residents' inability to live or die 87:13; blame throwing 26:91-101, 34:31-33; calls for instant destruction 25:13-14, 43:74-78; fervent cries 35:36-37; Fire growling and roaring 25:11-12, 67:6-11; roasted skins replaced with new ones 4:56; shackles and clothes of tar 14:48-50; maces of iron 22:19-22; chains 13:5; keepers of Hell 39:71, 40:49-50, 43:77, 66:6, 67:8, 74:30-31, 96:18; no ransom accepted 5:36-37; intercession denied 6:94, 26:100, 30:13, 74:48.

Regrets, not following the Prophet 25:27; not obeying God and His Messenger 4:41-42, 33:64-68; taking evil friends 25:28-29, 26:96-102, 43:36-39; denying God's signs 6:27-30; not working for the Hereafter 89:23-24.

Desperate pleas, begging for return to the world 2:167, 6:27-28, 32:12-14, 42:44; for a second chance 35:36-37; to be removed from the Fire 40:10-12; for food and water 7:51-52; for intercessors 7:52-53; to be leveled to dust 4:41-42, 78:40; for death 43:74-78.

Road to the Hereafter:

Qualities of the righteous, observing the rights of the Creator and His creation 3:133-136, 4:36, 4:69-70, 6:151-154, 8:2-4, 13:19-24, 17:23-39, 18:107-108, 23:1-11, 25:63-76, 42:36-43.

Qualities of the wicked, ungrateful 14:34; stingy 17:100; hasty 21:37; remember God only in difficult times 10:12, 41:51; impatient 70:19; argumentative 18:54.

Major Sins, associating others with God in worship (*shirk*) 4:48, 4:116, 5:72, 6:19, 31:13; abusing one's own parents 4:36, 6:151, 17:23; neglecting obligatory prayers 19:59-60; not paying alms-tax 41:6-7; murder 6:151, 17:33; killing a believer intentionally 4:93; theft 5:38; fraud 7:85, 11:85, 26:182-183, 83:1-6; lying 2:10, 9:77, 39:60; lying about God 6:93, 29:68, 61:7; prohibited sexual relations 2:222, 17:32, 24:2, 25:68, 29:28-30; false accusations of adultery 24:4-5; apostasy 2:217, 5:54; eating swine and other forbidden foods (carrion, blood, etc.) 5:3, 6:145; alcohol and gambling 5:90-91; backbiting 49:11; false testimony 22:30; magic 2:102, 10:77, 20:69.

Doors to forgiveness wide open 4:110, 5:74, 39:53; evil deeds changed into good deeds 25:68-71.

⟡

For references, visit:
www.theclearquran.org/about-the-translation

What They Said About the Prophet Muḥammad

"In all things Muḥammad was profoundly practical. When his beloved son Ibrahim died, an eclipse occurred, and rumours of God's personal condolence quickly arose. Whereupon Muḥammad announced, 'An eclipse is a phenomenon of nature. It is foolish to attribute such things to the death or birth of a human being.'"

James A. Michener, "Islam: The Misunderstood Religion," in *Reader's Digest*, May 1955.

"My choice of Muḥammad to lead the list of the world's most influential persons may surprise some readers and may be questioned by others, but he was the only man in history who was supremely successful on both the religious and secular levels."

Michael H. Hart, *The 100: A Ranking of the Most Influential Persons in History*, New York, 1978, p. 33.

"I have studied Muḥammad–the wonderful man, and in my opinion, he must be called the Savior of Humanity. I believe that if a man like him were to assume the leadership of the modern world, he would succeed in solving its problems in a way that would bring it much needed peace and happiness."

George Bernard Shaw, *The Genuine Islam*, Singapore, Vol. 1, No. 8, 1936.

"I became more than ever convinced that it was not the sword that won a place for Islam in those days in the scheme of life. It was the rigid simplicity, the utter self-effacement of the Prophet, the scrupulous regard for pledges, his intense devotion to his friends and followers, his intrepidity, his fearlessness, his absolute trust in God and in his own mission. These and not the sword carried everything before them and surmounted every obstacle."

Mahatma Gandhi, *Young India*, 1924.

❋❋❋

About the Translator

Dr. Mustafa Khattab is an authority on interpreting the Quran. He was a member of the first team that translated the Ramadan night prayers (*Tarawîḥ*) live from the Sacred Mosque in Mecca and the Prophet's Mosque in Medina (2002-2005). He memorized the entire Quran at a young age, and later obtained a professional *ijâzah* in the Ḥafṣ style of recitation with a chain of narrators going all the way to Prophet Muḥammad ﷺ. Dr. Khattab received his Ph.D., M.A., and B.A. in Islamic Studies in English with Honors from Al-Azhar University's Faculty of Languages & Translation. He lectured on Islam at Clemson University (OLLI Program, 2009-2010), held the position of Lecturer at Al-Azhar University for over a decade starting in 2003, and served as the Muslim Chaplain at Brock University (2014-2016). He is a member of the Canadian Council of Imams and a Fulbright Interfaith Scholar. He has served as an Imam in the U.S.A. and Canada since 2007 and is the author of *The Nation of Islam* (2011), *Outfoxing Fox News* (2017), *The Clear Quran® Tafsir for Kids,* 4 volumes (2019-2023), *Shukran* (an illustrated story for kids, 2020), and *The Clear Quran® Dictionary* (2020), *The Clear Quran Made Easy: Story-based Tafsir* (2023), *The Clear Sirah for Kids: 365 Days with the Prophet* ﷺ (2024), and contributor to the *Encyclopedia of Muslim American History* (2010).

❖❖❖